How Do I Teach Reading?

How Do I Teach Reading?

Robert C. Aukerman
University of Rhode Island

Louise R. Aukerman

John Wiley & Sons
NEW YORK   CHICHESTER   BRISBANE   TORONTO

Photo Research by Teri Leigh Stratford.

Library of Congress Cataloging in Publication Data:

Aukerman, Robert C   1910-
   How do I teach reading?

   Includes index.
   1. Reading (Elementary) I. Aukerman,
Louise R., joint author. II. Title.
LB1573.A88   372.4044   80-23380
ISBN 0-471-03687-0

Printed in the United States of America

10 9 8 7 6 5 4 3 2 1

Preface

This book has been more than ten years in the making. During these years of the book's gestation, of writing and rewriting, we deferred its completion and publication because we felt uneasy about the unsettled state of the reading profession as it attempted to respond to an increasing number of challenges. Now, however, we see some stability on the horizon.

For example, the controversy about phonics seems to have subsided, with the consensus now being that, although not a panacea, phonics is one of the specific reading skills needed for "mastery learning" and diagnostic prescriptive teaching. For example, an eclectic approach to method again seems to have replaced an earlier notion that individualized reading would fully supplant basal readers as *the* medium of reading instruction. In addition, writers and publishers of major basal reader series have now had time to respond to criticisms of earlier series and have greatly improved the literary and visual quality and the skills-development and management components of their offerings.

Contemporary research and experience indicate what most of us suspected all along: that reading has components that can be isolated and identified, taught, learned, and practiced, and that mastery of these components can be tested. Hence, we believe, now is the time for a truly comprehensive and contemporary how-to-do-it book on the teaching of reading. Hence, too, the title of this book: *How Do I Teach Reading?*

We make absolutely no apologies that this is indeed a how-to-do-it text. We firmly believe that now, perhaps more than ever before, such a book is needed. Far too many students go through a college or university course in the teaching of reading and emerge knowing very little, if anything, about how to apply what they have learned to the day-to-day classroom situation. That is what this book is all about. It is, basically, a practical guidebook to the day-to-day teaching of reading.

We have limited the coverage in this book to those facets of reading that are most pertinent to you, the classroom teacher in the elementary school, touching only when necessary upon more advanced subjects such as remedial reading, diagnostic testing, psycholinguistics, children's literature, and supervision.

In Chapter 1, we review and discuss modern principles of learning as they apply to the learning and teaching of reading. The chapter includes a discussion of psychological variables in reading and the application of learning theories to reading. It also includes a psychological learning model applied to learning a single word.

Chapter 2 discusses readiness for reading and training for reading readiness. A strong readiness program, we believe, is an essential foundation of successful reading instruction.

Chapter 3 details methods and materials for first steps in the learning and teaching of reading. A sequence of practical teaching strategies is presented, supported by research and sound psychological principles of learning.

In Chapter 4, we deal with word-recognition skills, that is, with how children actually begin to learn to identify printed words. Special attention is given to the acquisition of a whole-word vocabulary, words in context, and word segments that are learned long before most children become familiar with phonics.

In Chapter 5, we discuss phonics and offer strategies for teaching phonics skills.

In Chapter 6, we consider vocabulary development. Our approach here is grounded on the sound psychological principle of commencing with the known. Areas of everday living form the basis of vocabulary lists and teaching methods presented in this chapter, a feature unique to this text.

In Chapter 7, we present methods and materials for teaching comprehension. In this chapter, instead of traditional "levels" of comprehension, we employ the concept of "modes" of comprehending, a concept that we believe is more logically suited to instruction for comprehension. This chapter also includes more than 250 sample comprehension questions.

Chapter 8 is concerned with the acquisition of reading-study skills. Concrete suggestions are offered for instruction in library and reference-work use and for development of specific study skills.

Chapter 9 presents a detailed discussion of one of the two major general methods of teaching reading: the individualized reading program.

Chapter 10 presents a discussion of the other major general method: the basal reader program.

In Chapter 11, the final chapter, we discuss ways and means of teaching reading to children who have special needs—intellectual, cultural, linguistic, emotional, physical, and educational.

We have not attempted to make this a "scholarly" work, in the usual meaning of the word. The book has been written not for scholars (or for our colleagues) but for you, the classroom teacher. It is to your problems and to your potential that we have addressed ourselves. This is not to say that we have dispensed with the works of reading experts and scholars in writing this book. On the contrary, the procedures and practices presented are based on sound research and scholarship, as evident in the extensive bibliographies presented at the conclusion of each chapter.

Basically, however, this is an "experiential" book. In it we are sharing with you our experiences, our successes, and, yes, our failures in a lifetime of teaching reading. In presenting this book to you, we would like to think we are taking you for a visit to the many classrooms in which we have taught and to the scores of classrooms we have visited here and in many other parts of the English-speaking world. We would like to think that, with us, you are watching teachers teach, watching them use methods and materials, routines, and devices that you, yourself, can and will use.

We would like to think, also, that when you are finished with your methods course, you will not be finished with this book. We have designed it to be a companion for you throughout your teaching of reading in the elementary school, a companion always at hand to help you in your search for day-to-day classroom answers to the question, "How Do I Teach Reading?"

We subscribe to the principle of learning-by-doing, yet we know it is not feasible in most instances for you to be out teaching reading while taking a methods course. Consequently, we have provided for some vicarious experiences in teaching reading and in learning more about the process and product of reading through pre-service, competency-based modules in a separate "Professor's Resource Manual."

ACKNOWLEDGMENTS

Our special thanks to Mrs. Esther Bourziel, Coordinator of Elementary Education, Fremont, Michigan; Dr. Robert Byrne, Director of the Reading Center, Eastern Kentucky State University; Mrs. Lucille Dardiri, Reading Consultant, Southold, Long Island, Schools; Dr. Lawrence Carillo, Professor of Reading, San Francisco State University; Dr. Lawrence Kasdon, Director of the Graduate Reading Program, Yeshiva University; Mrs. Virginia Murphy, 1977 "Teacher of the Year," St. Charles, Missouri, Schools; Dr. Joy Pitterman; Dr. Paul C. Burns, University of Tennessee; Professor Johanna DeStefano, Ohio State University; Dr. Marian M. Gray, Canisius College; Dr. Christine LaConte, University of Connecticut; Mrs. Rose Merenda, Rhode Island College; Professor Stanley I. Mour, University of Louisville.

Each contributed many hours of thoughtful criticism, resulting in valuable suggestions that have been woven into this book. Because of their dedication, this is a much better book than we could have produced on our own.

Meet the Authors

This textbook is an extension of the personalities of its authors. It is, in a sense, a conversation with them, whereby they discuss many facets of reading, answer those questions that are frequently asked, and describe scores of techniques that they have found to be highly successful.

Because of their experiences in classrooms, the authors hold a positive point of view toward children and reading. This is bound to be evident as they share experiences with you, the reader. Throughout the book, they state in effect that "this is the position we hold" and they buttress their position with logical and practical reasons.

Throughout the book they are talking to you, suggesting that you try this and/or think about a point of view. They have tried to make this book on *How Do I Teach Reading?* just as practical and down-to-earth as its title suggests. They have written this book with the hope that it will be your guide to becoming an outstandingly successful and happy teacher of reading.

Dr. Robert C. Aukerman received his A.B. and A.M. degrees at Wayne State University and his Ph.D. at the University of Michigan, where he specialized in studying the application of psychological principles of learning to the field of reading. After a career as a classroom teacher for fifteen years in the Detroit Public Schools, he became the Dean of Instruction at Northeast Missouri State Teachers College, after which he joined the faculty at the University of Rhode Island as Professor of Education. He established the Annual Conference on Reading and the Graduate Center for the Study of Reading; he founded and edited for seven years the New England Reading Association *Journal*, lectured at more than a score of universities in this country and abroad and authored three previous books on reading. He is also a member of the American Psychological Association.

Louise R. Aukerman, his wife, has been a companion in all his writing projects, although this is the first on which she has permitted her name to appear. She received her A.A. degree from Highland Park Michigan Junior College; and, after helping raise their three sons, received her B.Sc. in Early

Childhood Education "With Highest Honors" from the University of Rhode Island. She taught kindergarten for thirteen years, during which time she received many honors and acclaim. She has attended reading conferences and courses in reading at a number of colleges and universities, accumulating more than 60 semester hours in that field.

Contents

UNIT ONE

Reading is both a process and a product. As a product, it is a learned skill or set of skills. As both process and product, it involves *things, ideas,* and the mental function we call *human learning.*

Reading involves specific things such as letters, words, phrases, and sentences; these language characteristics are learned by most children in spoken communication long before they see them represented on a printed page.

Reading also involves ideas based on prior experiences and stored in the memory. Situations depicted in words on a page stimulate memory of these experiences and bring meaning to reading. Thus, prior sensory experiences provide the basis for comprehending what is read.

Above all, reading is a process and product of human learning. As such, foundations for the teaching of reading to children must be built upon modern learning theory, including knowledge and principles of child development and individual differences, buttressed by relevant linguistic principles and a wide acquaintance with the body of literature for children.

In this single chapter of unit one of our text, we invoke modern psychology of learning to lay our basic foundation for the teaching of reading.

FOUNDATIONS

CHAPTER ONE

Reading: A Complicated Psychological Process

Psychological Variables in Reading
Perceptual Learning (Perceptual Discrimination)
  Sensory Modalities
  Discrimination of Distinctive Features
  Heightened Attending to Distinctive Features
  Multifaceted Stimuli
  Set (or Mind Set)
  Consistent Invariants in Reading
  Mediation
  Preferred Learning Modalities
  Transfer of Learning
  Associative Learning
  Paired Associates
  Cognitive Learning
  Utilization of Past Experience
  Gestalt Theory and Reading
  Restructuring
  Forward Scanning
  Affective Learning
  Identification
    A Psychological Learning Model Applied to Learning a Single Word
  Self and Individual Differences
  Constellations of Associated Ideas

Reading is the common denominator of most classroom learning. Thus, learning and reading are inextricably interwoven skills. An understanding of the psychological process of learning is therefore basic to an understanding of how children read and how we teach them to read. Hence in this chapter, we present modern research in the psychology of learning as it relates to the process of learning to read.

The chapter is divided into two parts: (1) a discussion of psychological variables in reading and the application of learning theories to reading, and (2) a psychological learning model applied to learning a single word.

Throughout this chapter and all those that follow, we place strong emphasis on individual differences, one of the major realities that underlie all teaching—especially reading.

PSYCHOLOGICAL VARIABLES IN READING

Some individuals hold the naive notion that reading is merely pronouncing words and that, if one can learn phonics, then words can be decoded and pronounced, and *presto,* one can read. There is far more to learning to read than that—for learning to read is, indeed, a very complicated psychological process. To help simplify this process, let us arbitrarily divide it into four major categories:

1. *Perceptual* learning (or perceptual discrimination).
2. *Associative* learning (or stimulus-response association).
3. *Cognitive* learning
4. *Affective* learning.

PERCEPTUAL LEARNING (PERCEPTUAL DISCRIMINATION)

When we realize that very young children can make progress in establishing perceptual discrimination, first of gross shapes, objects, people, places, etc., and, then of finer shapes such as letters and words, we are awed at the marvelous learning mechanism that makes this possible and that apparently marks a major distinction between humans and lower species. This facet of human achievement is, like all human traits and abilities, subject to a wide range of differences. However, in spite of the fact that some individuals have far greater capacity than others, there are a number of features of the perceptual process that are common to all learners. Those that relate to reading are discussed below.

SENSORY MODALITIES

At the origin of perception are sensory modalities, especially vision, hearing, touching, feeling, and, perhaps, echoing. It is through these modalities that we are able to perceive letters and words in print and to echo the sounds we hear associated with them.

DISCRIMINATION OF DISTINCTIVE FEATURES

At the center of perception is the ability to discriminate *distinctive features* a term psychologists use for those special parts of any stimulus (in the case of reading, the parts of letters, letter-strings, and words) that make it possible for an individual to distinguish one from another. For example, letter-strings (such as *-ing, pre-, -ante, -ologist*) have distinctive features that permit us to recognize them without concentration on each letter separately. Words, too, have characteristics by which we can make instant decisions as to what they represent without the need to resort to letter analysis or phonetic analysis.

Visual-Perceptual Discrimination of Distinctive Features

How does a child learn that these various symbols represent the *same* letter? Are they the same grapheme?

There are basically three visual elements in our alphabet letters: the circle, the straight line, and the slanted line. All letters (both capital and small) are composed of those three elements, separately or in combination. They account for letter contrasts.

Sometimes, however, the contrasts are so slight that fast and accurate identification is difficult. Slight contrast may frequently result in visual confusion that leads to reading errors. According to Gibson and Levin, the following pairs of capital letters are most often confused by children: M/W, N/M, Q/O, E/F, P/R, K/X.

Fortunately, even if letter contrast is slight, in the reading process letters are clustered together in words and these clusters help provide patterns that the reader recognizes as "wholes." This phenomenon is referred to by psychologists as the *relational aspect* of distinctive features.

The ability to discriminate distinctive features leads to an important strategy for the reading teacher—the employment of contrast in word learning. One study of visual discrimination training with 160 kindergartners indicated that

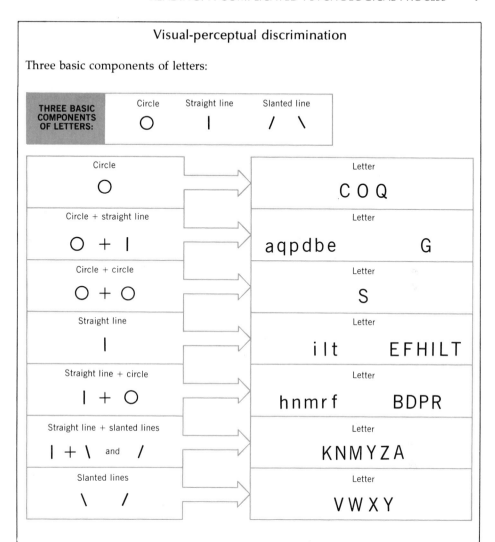

Visual-perceptual discrimination

Three basic components of letters:

THREE BASIC COMPONENTS OF LETTERS:	Circle $\bigcirc$	Straight line $\mid$	Slanted line $/$ $\backslash$

Circle $\bigcirc$	Letter C O Q
Circle + straight line $\bigcirc$ + $\mid$	Letter a q p d b e G
Circle + circle $\bigcirc$ + $\bigcirc$	Letter S
Straight line $\mid$	Letter i l t E F H I L T
Straight line + circle $\mid$ + $\bigcirc$	Letter h n m r f B D P R
Straight line + slanted lines $\mid$ + $\backslash$ and $/$	Letter K N M Y Z A
Slanted lines $\backslash$ $/$	Letter V W X Y

A child learns through the development of visual-perceptual discrimination to distinguish among these symbols, all of which contain only three basic graphemic elements. Most children also learn the names of the letters and learn, through *associative learning,* to match names to letter symbols, both small and capital. Later, children learn to associate one or several phonemes with specific letters and/or combinations of letters. The entire process involves visual-perceptual discrimination, audio-perceptual discrimination, pronounciation and associative learning. What may appear to be simple is, actually, a complicated psychological process.

Distinctive Features of Letters

O C G Q

b d   n m h

p q q   u ɯ ɥ

Children look for distinguishing features of letters that enable them to differentiate one letter from another. Some distinctive features are found in several letters. Some letters have actually *reversals* of other letters.

How does the young child learn or distinguish among these letters with distinctive features?

Distinctive Features of Words

Sears   **Mickey Mouse**

McDonald's ®    **Woolworth**

Monster   **Milk**

Many young children recognize these words long before they actually undertake formal instruction. Here are a few words and symbols that young children frequently can "read." What are the distinctive features that enable them to learn these as sight words?

---

dissimilar words were significantly easier to learn than similar words and a study of 165 fourth-, fifth-, and sixth-graders indicated that visual-form discrimination was closely related to reading ability.

Auditory discrimination has also been shown to be important as a determinant of learning to read. From a study of 448 first-graders, Dr. Helen Robinson concluded that subjects with well-developed visual and auditory modalities scored highest on tests of reading at the end of the first and third grades.

The perceptual learning ability to discriminate distinctive features might seem to support the idea of whole-word reading. However, whole-word reading depends on a child's ability to learn the distinctive features of thousands of words and to differentiate among them without confusion or error. The beginning reader—usually a child of five or six—will develop the power to discriminate specific details over a period of time.

Differentiation of Distinctive Features

Good Night

GOOD NIGHT

Gute Nacht

Boa Noite

Buona Notte

Bonne Nuit

Buenas Noches

Доброй Ночи

晚 安

ילה טוב

Obviously, a child is not born with the ability to read. The visual discrimination task of learning "Good Night" in one's own language is partially dependent upon the child's exposure to the spoken language. What other discrimination factors are involved? (Good Night symbols produced courtesy of the Hyatt Hotel Corporation.)

HEIGHTENED ATTENDING TO DISTINCTIVE FEATURES

Like all perceptual learners, the child who is learning to read is bombarded by countless stimuli, not only from the printed page but also from the immediate and larger environment. Thus, learning to read requires *heightened attending.* The child must purposefully ignore irrelevant stimuli that operate as distractions to attendance to distinctive features.

MULTIFACETED STIMULI

Psychological research suggests that information stimuli are usually multifaceted. This means that seldom, except in the laboratory, do we experience a simple stimulus in isolation.

Applying this concept to reading, we observe that most words that elementary school children encounter in their reading have multifaceted meanings because of the variety of experiences to which children have been exposed. The word *mother,* for example, may mean different things to a child from a normal nuclear home than it does to a child brought up by foster parents or to a child reared in an institution. In addition, context contributes to the multifaceted nature of words. For example, *mother* takes on different meanings in different settings—*mother church, mother tongue, motherlode, mother earth,* and so on.

SET (OR MIND SET)

Set and *mind set* are terms psychologists use to indicate the readiness of an individual for interpreting a stimulus. As we have indicated, stimuli are not simple. Even in the beginning stages of learning to read, children must be *set for diversity.* This is disturbing to them, for they respond best to regularity and to the concrete features of life that can be depended upon and that give them security. However, in learning to read, they must be able to deal with those "diverse" features of our language that are frequently called "exceptions." Researchers Levin and Watson suggested that a *set for diversity* be developed in which a child learns to try out various phonemic correspondences when faced with an unfamiliar word in print, and not just "give up" when the first try fails to result in a familiar and appropriate word.

CONSISTENT INVARIANTS IN READING

Behavioral psychologists have pointed to the consistent features of the universe that surrounds us as being those things that give our lives stability, predictability, and security. Without some consistency, living would be chaos. Similarly, with reading. Fortunately, there are many distinctive features of words that retain their distinctive characteristics regardless of their setting (at the beginning, middle, end, or wherever they appear in the word). Psychologists refer to them as *invariants* (they do not vary).

The consistent invariants provide some solid bases that help children. They are parts of words, such as roots, prefixes, and suffixes. For example, *-ing* is always *-ing; -ist* is always *-ist.* Invariants such as *-ent, pre-, an, am, at,* and so on remain consistent parts of words regardless of their position in them. For generations, teachers have employed invariants in the form of "word families" and "phonogram" practice. More recently, the so-called "linguistic" readers have based their story lines on this principle of consistency, for example, *Can Dan fan Sam and Ann?* even though such sentences make little or no sense.

SIMPLE-TO-COMPLEX

Psychologists have long recommended that all perceptual learning should progress from the simple to the complex. When applied to reading, this might seem to indicate that the shortest, easiest words should be learned first, then the more difficult words in progressively increasing order of difficulty of discrimination. However, this is seldom the way children learn to read, except in rigidly controlled programmed reading.

There is, in fact, plenty of evidence that children can just as easily learn *monster, dinosaur,* or *astronaut* as *man, dog,* or *ant.* This fact does not, however, entirely negate the principle of proceeding from the simple to the complex. When a child is dealing with *monster, dinosaur,* or *astronaut,* he or she may be handling the distinctive features of a whole entity that has prior meaning attached to it. If, on the other hand, we were to ask the child to identify the word *monsterous,* without prior training in the suffix *-ous,* we would be introducing a complex problem with which the child could probably not cope.

Another application of the psychological principle of simple-to-complex learning is to proceed from the known to the unknown. This process is described in some detail in further sections below.

MEDIATION

Regardless of how fast an individual responds to a stimulus, psychologists have demonstrated that there is a period of measurable time between stimulus and response during which *mediation* takes place. Simply put, *mediation* means that the individual is "thinking about" what to do in response to a stimulus. As one drives a car, the countless stimuli being sensed by visual and auditory receptors are rapidly mediated by the brain, with resultant proper responses. Similarly, in reading, a child is constantly "thinking about" the visual stimuli that are being received from words, word strings, and letters within words. Along comes a word that is new but has recognizable parts. During mediation, the child considers how those parts go together and considers alternative pronunciations. In mediation, the child may also consider the relationships of words within a phrase in order to arrive at the intended meaning. In the mediation period, each child draws from his or her reservoir of past experiences to endow words and phrases with reality and meanings.

PREFERRED LEARNING MODALITIES

Psychologists use the term *learning modalities* to refer to the senses (sight, hearing, etc.) through which learning occurs. Some reading specialists have suggested that a teacher should determine the "preferred learning mode" of each child and then employ that modality as the chief medium of instruction. The conclusions of a recent three-year study by Dr. Margaret Donovan and Dr. Mary C. Austin support the claim that when teachers use reading materials and strategies in keeping with the preferred modalities of children, reading achievement is significantly better than that attained by those children whose preferred modalities are ignored. This difference was shown to be significant on measures of vocabulary, comprehension, and general reading.

INCREASED ECONOMY OF PERCEPTION

When a child starts to learn to read, ability to perceive likenesses and differences is minimal. With maturation and learning, discrimination becomes more specific, more rapid, and more inclusive. This increase in perceptual ability is called "increased economy of perception."

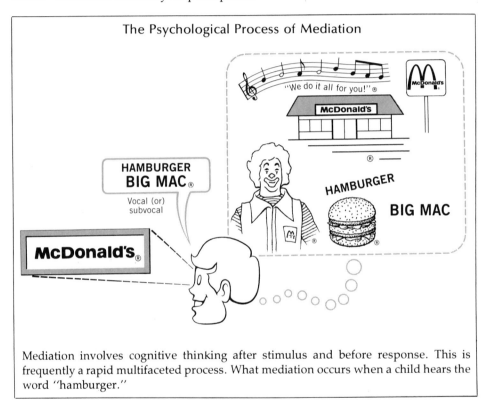

The Psychological Process of Mediation

Mediation involves cognitive thinking after stimulus and before response. This is frequently a rapid multifaceted process. What mediation occurs when a child hears the word "hamburger."

Most beginning readers from a standard English-speaking environment have already mastered sufficient basic grammatical forms of spoken language to permit some sequencing involving subject, verb, and object: "Me go your house," and so on. They have had three or more years practice with spoken patterns and have internalized great numbers of spoken phrases and sentences in countless forms (transformations) before seeing them in print. So they come to reading with a "language sense" and foundation on which to increase

The Multi-Sensory Components of Reading

	Sense	
seeing	vision	printed word or phrase
auding	hearing	spoken word or phrase
writing	kinesthetic tactile	printed word or phrase
tracing	kinesthetic tactile	tracing letters or word or phrase
visualizing . . .	visual and/or	imagining (visualizing) appearance
	auditory memory	and sound of word or phrase

The more learning modalities employed, the more mutual reinforcement each provides.

economy of perception even though the story lines are likely to be foreign to their normal speech patterns.

As language sense increases through the development of awareness (even if subconscious) of grammatical structural relationships, children usually acquire an increased economy of perception. This does not occur at any given moment in time, but is, rather, the result of a developmental process. Suffice it to say here that so-called "word chunks" provide clues that make it possible for a reader to select only those distinctive features that are necessary for meaning and to ignore all others. The mature reader does this. The beginner will gradually acquire this skill.

Increased economy of perception is also fostered by the child's developing perception of the contextual meanings of words, phrases, and clauses. Reading perception depends upon seeing thought units as wholes, not as separate letters and/or words.

CUE REDUCTION

In the beginning phases of learning to read, picture cues are frequently introduced and associated with printed word symbols. A picture of a dog may be shown on a flash card with the printed word, *dog*. Later the picture is omitted in hope that the child will be able to pronounce the word *dog* from the printed word as stimulus alone. This is known as *cue reduction*.

A good example of cue reduction is found in Houghton Mifflin's *Getting Ready to Read* program. In it, for example, when children are learning the intial consonant *b*, a card is first shown containing a picture of a baseball bat and ball. Going from the known to the unknown, the next card shows the baseball bat and ball superimposed on the letter *b*. In practice with both cards, children are becomming familiar with the sound of *b* as an initial consonant sound in *baseball bat* and *baseball* and *bat*. In the final card, the picture is dropped and only the grapheme *b* remains as the stimulus for the sound /b/. At this point, cue reduction is assumed to have occurred.

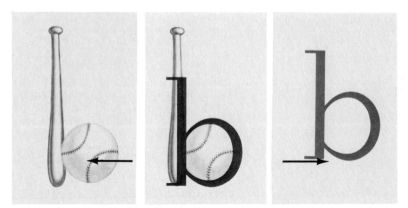

What is already known by the child that helps him/her recognize the letter *b* and the sound it represents?

FEEDBACK

Psychological feedback may help a child monitor the appropriateness or absurdity of words in context. Some form of the query "Does the word make sense?" is often used as a cue in the feedback process. If feedback indicates that the word (as understood by the child) is incongruous with the rest of the phrase or sentence, then the child knows that something is wrong and attempts to correct it. After the child learns the habit of continuous check on contextual meaning during reading, the process becomes what is known as a *self-monitoring* strategy.

REDUNDANCY

Repetition of grammatical patterns and thought units as well as specific words and letter strings is a learning device that psycholinguists call *redundancy*. It was once thought that repetition alone would insure that a child would memorize sight words, a misapprehension that led to the overuse of flashcards and rote memorization of words in isolation. It also led to excessive repetition of words in the story lines of the older basal readers.

Despite earlier overuse, redundancy remains a valid perceptual learning device. Today it is often used with grammatical structures and thought patterns such as *over the hill, in the park, ready for bed, when the sun comes up, see you at McDonalds*, and so on. Through repetition, such patterns of speaking and thought become internalized, resulting in "automatic information processing"—that is, the reader transfers the internalized invariants to a variety of reading situations.

TRANSFER OF LEARNING

Without what psychologists call *transfer of learning* we would have to begin every bit of learning with no previous knowledge to guide us. Fortunately, the human mind is able to transfer to new learning experiences applicable knowledge gained from previous experiences. As a child builds up a store of language patterns and basic elements, opportunities for transfer become more and more numerous.

Transfer of learning is not, however, entirely automatic. The learner must be taught to look for the subfactors of transfer: *similarity* of elements or *identical* elements. "Rules" for transfer may be helpful to the beginner, but at some time in the process of becoming a skillful reader, the child will develop an "unconscious" response to the similar and identical elements of language.

In addition to utilizing already-learned patterns of language and the meanings those patterns convey, the child who is learning to read perceives many repetitions in spelling and in grammar that become generalized into a system of subconscious "rules" and are then used in learning transfer. The child learns to put recurring letter-elements together and concludes that a particular letter—*d*, for example—always stands for the sound /d/. In other words, the young child tries to get through reading by handling as few exceptions as possible, concentrating on systematic generalization of the invariants of the language.

In many of these cases, children "find the little word in the big word," a practice that is not acceptable to reading specialists even though the word-segment, *man*, is clearly visible within the word. It should be obvious that the meanings of *man* vary from word to word. The conclusion is that we can expect

Some Examples of Transfer of Learning for the word "man"

Man *may transfer to*		
manned	manifold	manual
almanac	manage	showman
mango	mailman	mangled
mandate	mandatory	manners
bushman	command	commandment
sportsmanship	human	humanity
emancipate	mandarin	demand
dismantle	manifestation	German
manicure	mankind	manikin
manipulative	manipulate	mantis
manufacture	manuscript	superman
seaman	Roman	romanticism

children to recognize the word-segment, *man,* and to pronounce it in the only way it can be pronounced, leaving whole-word meaning to evolve from consideration of the total word of which it is a part.

ASSOCIATIVE LEARNING (OR STIMULUS/RESPONSE ASSOCIATION)

Learning alphabet letters is a stimulus-response (S-R) associative learning process—that is, a given stimulus calls forth a given response. Learning basic letter-sounds is also a S-R process, even though several sounds may be associated with one letter. In any case, sounds and letters do pattern together in predictable ways. Some approaches teach the various letter-sounds simultaneously, for example, the three sounds associated with the letter *a,* the other multiple vowel sounds, "hard" and "soft," *g, s, c,* and so on.

Rote learning of whole words in isolation is also S-R learning.

ASSOCIATION BY ROTE

For the better part of this century, psychologists have held that rote memorization results in minimal learning and rapid loss of what little is learned. More recently, reading theories have been uncovering evidence that this holds true for reading. Nevertheless, rote learning is a necessary part of the teaching-to-read process.

What is it that children need to memorize in the process of learning to read? There are a number of things—chiefly correspondences between words in print and spoken words; between single letter sounds and printed letters; the multisounds associated with those single printed letters; between phonemes and single or multiple letters; strings of words that constitute meaningful phrases; and many other features of spoken and written language. A large portion of the nitty-gritty of learning to read is rote memorization.

CONTIGUITY

One of the earliest associationists was the famous psychologist, Thorndike. His explanations of many features of learning by association remain valid today. E. R. Guthrie, expanding on Thorndike's notions, suggested a "Law of Contiguity" to explain the effects of "togetherness" in time and place: "Things that occur together in time and place tend to become associated together." There are countless examples of "go-togethers" in the field of reading: word families, similar and contrasting word elements, reversals, synonyms and antonyms, homonyms, homographs, and so on. In reading, one of the most common associative learning situations is the learning of "paired associates," sometimes referred to as "letter/sound correspondence."

New England Primer, 1727

Children in schools in Colonial America learned their ABCs by rote from hornbooks (see illustration on previous page) and from the *New England Primer* (see above). What additional facets of association with past experiences helped in such rote learning?

PAIRED ASSOCIATES

The most simple *paired associates* situation is the learning of alphabet letters. As the child learns to discriminate both printed letters and letter names, each letter and its associated name becomes paired.

Contrasting letter-pairs provide another means for associative learning. The letters in contrasting pairs are actually identical so far as line and curve are concerned. The contrast lies in the fact that each is the reverse of the other: M/W n/u s/z d/b p/q d/p d/q b/p b/q h/y. Other letters are so similar that they can also be learned as paired-associates: h/n i/l X/Y E/F i/j C/G O/Q P/R K/X K/Y m/n.

One thing soon becomes clear to the teacher of reading: there must be association between letters and sounds, spoken and printed words, and spoken and printed word strings. Reliance upon such association has been dubbed by many critics as the "look-say" method, implying that the child merely looks and then pronounces. However, years ago, psychologists Irving Anderson and Walter Dearborn, working at Harvard, suggested that it is more correctly a "look-while-you-think-and-say" method, involving *contiguity* in time of perception, mediation, and pronouncing. This is a more adequate view of what takes place through associative learning in the field of reading.

STIMULUS SUBSTITUTION

In the first section of this chapter, we spoke of cue reduction and the use of picture clues for learning letters. Classroom teachers also frequently make use of key pictures as cues for beginning sounds and for words themselves, substituting one stimulus for another.

For example, a child who has already learned to say "dog" sees a flashcard showing a picture of a dog. The association between the picture and the spoken word is the same as between the sight of the real animal and the spoken word, an association that has been established long before. The teacher now can utilize this previous learning by having the child associate the printed word *dog* with the picture (and simultaneously with the child's mental image of any kind of dog with which the child is already familiar). The visual stimulus consisting of the picture of the dog or the mental image of a dog is now replaced with the visual printed word, but the printed word and the spoken word still recall the image of a dog. Learning the word *dog* through association this way is not as difficult as learning the printed word in isolation.

TRANSFER OF LEARNING IN ASSOCIATIVE LEARNING

We discussed transfer of learning in the previous section. Let us now consider it again in connection with associative learning.

Continuing the example above, to promote transfer of learning the teacher introduces the notion that the word *dog* commences with the initial sound /d/. It is to be hoped that the child, after much associative practice, will establish this connection and will visualize the picture of a dog as the clue to the beginning sound /d/ for any word that begins with printed *d*. To establish this habit teachers frequently clue the child by saying, "The word begins like *dog*." The child is supposed to respond with the sound /d/, and *transfer* that knowledge to the beginning sound of any new word beginning with *d*.

VARIABLES IN ASSOCIATIVE LEARNING

Some associations are established immediately. These frequently are those of greatest "intensity." Thorndike promulgated one of his "principles" of associative learning on this basis: the strength of the "bond" is in proportion to the intensity of the stimulus. Sylvia Ashton-Warner noted the existence of "one-look" words that children in her New Zealand classroom were able to learn with one look. These were words of intense feeling to the children, words that the Maori children themselves suggested as evoking for them intense feelings of fear, hate, and love.

There are so many variables in associative learning, however, that it is impossible to predict precisely how much repetition, if any, each individual child will need to establish connections between a printed word and its spoken counterpart. Intelligence, past experience, motivation, physical alertness (vitality), experience with picture books, and so on are some of the many variables in the associative process of learning to read. Suffice it to say here that the child whose experiences are minimal will have little basis for development of associative learning in reading and that any other limiting variables will have a further retarding effect on the associative process as it applies to reading.

REWARDS

Conscious learning involves hard work for most of us. We need a reason to endure it. It is likewise with children who are learning to read—they need to feel they will be rewarded for their efforts. The reward may be intrinsic, such as satisfaction of a child's natural curiosity, the pleasing of someone who wants the child to learn to read, or satisfaction of a desire to imitate a cherished peer or

Flashcard routines can easily become tedious and boring. It appears, however, that this teacher has motivated her group. Do you think the children are motivated by intrinsic or by extrinsic rewards? What rewards would you use for flashcard practice?

sibling. The reward may also be extrinsic, such as a good grade or a prize. In any case, the reward serves as what Thorndike called a "satisfier."

Extrinsic satisfiers in the form of prizes, gold stars, candy, or money are called "tokens" (bribes) by psychologists. Occasionally (in planned experiments) actual tokens are given for reading achievement, and the tokens can be exchanged later for goods or entertainment. They are, in effect, the "Green Stamps" of such reading experiments! It has been wisely suggested, however, that "token reinforcement may result in only token learning." Internalized satisfaction appears to be more lasting than external gratification, perhaps because it is more closely related to the intrinsic needs of the learner.

Some children seem to need both extrinsic and intrinsic satisfiers when learning to read. Their needs should, of course, be met. Individual differences should always be considered in the matter of amount and kind of rewards offered to children learning to read.

MEMORY SYSTEMS

What is stored in our memory systems depends to a considerable degree on our senses of sight and hearing. But other senses also make their contributions. Consider for a moment the various memory systems activated by the following phrases: fresh donuts and cider on a cold autumn evening, the salt pond at low tide, soft and silky hair, the delicatessen on a hot summer afternoon, the starlit sky on a cold winter night.

Later in this chapter we illustrate how the "memory bank" serves as the central mediating mechanism in associative learning in the reading process. There is good evidence that there is no such thing as "forgetting" once something has been experienced and/or learned through our memory system. All of the experiences of one's lifetime are stored in memory cells to be reactivated and retrieved under just the right conditions. Much of what we call forgetting is, in reality, inability to recall. Inability to recall may be due to retroactive inhibition resulting from the learning of new skills or facts. The recently learned materials inhibit recall of previously learned skills or facts. Associative learning makes use of those previously established memory cells that, when activated, give meaning to what is read.

COGNITIVE LEARNING

As we have previously noted, reading is more than learning to pronounce words. It also involves understanding and recognizing meanings that have their wellsprings in one's past experiences. Reading specialists refer to this process as *comprehension*. Psychologists call it *cognition*. Cognitive learning is as essential to learning to read as are perceptual and associational learning.

UTILIZATION OF PAST EXPERIENCES

Cognition is the relating of new experiential stimuli to past experiences and to past learnings. This involves comparing, recognizing similarities and differences, evaluating, and interpreting meanings, values, and truths in keeping with reality. However, Piaget's (the famous Swiss philosopher) famous experiments concerning children's perceptions of conservation demonstrated that children interpret "reality" differently at different stages of development. His findings are significant to learning to read. In her doctoral dissertation on Piaget's work, Kathleen Roberts noted that "research in conservation theory has already indicated to us that instruction presented before a child has acquired the developmental competencies is useless. Once the child has the competencies, instruction of many varied types appears to be effective."

Inasmuch as the past experiences of each individual are different from those of all other individuals, all learning, and especially reading, is subject to an enormously wide range of individual differences. Consequently, some children easily understand what they are reading, whereas others do not. Much of this difference may be accounted for by breadth and depth of past experiences that are brought to the printed page.

A simplistic approach to reading has led some people to aver that reading is getting meaning *from* the printed page. Obviously, such a feat is impossible inasmuch as meaning springs from the past experiences of each individual.

GESTALT THEORY AND READING

Cognition means knowing. The *gestalt* school of psychology tells us that one learns to know by relating a concept to the field in which it is set. In reading, meanings are embellished by the setting in which the words are found, just as a stage setting adds mood, feeling, and "reality" to a play. Broadly speaking, the meanings of words are colored by the other words in the sentence patterns of which they are a part. Reading specialists refer to this aspect of *gestalt* as *context*. Gestalt theory indicates that word meanings are taught best in relationship to word strings. Gestalt psychology has consistenly demonstrated that the relationships of words in phrases and sentences determine the reader's response to them. Consequently, children who persist in reading word-by-word seldom become fluent readers. Word-by-word reading violates this basic principle of learning. Similarly, pronunciation of a letter frequently depends on its position in the word and the relationship to the other letters in the word. For example: the *a* in *hat* and in *hate*. Here the whole is greater than the sum of its parts because the parts, pronounced separately, do not result in the whole pronunciation. This is a basic principle of the psychology of cognition.

In reading, adjective and adverbial modifiers help establish gestalt for our

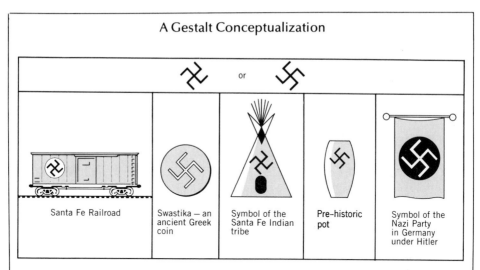

A Gestalt Conceptualization

| Santa Fe Railroad | Swastika — an ancient Greek coin | Symbol of the Santa Fe Indian tribe | Pre-historic pot | Symbol of the Nazi Party in Germany under Hitler |

A gestalt is a design or pattern. It frequently depends upon the field or background on which it is placed for conveying meaning. Note how the meaning of *swastika* changes with various backgrounds

Similarly, in reading, the meaning(s) of many words are changed by their contextual settings.

language. They give quality and quantity to the objects and actions to which they relate. In language we can build entire strings of modifiers, each of which adds to or describes the parameters of meaning of the word to which they are attached. For example, the meaning of *dog* can be embellished by modifiers to become a *little, nasty, wire-haired, snappy, yappy, vicious bundle of skin and bones.* Another word string might create an entirely different image: a *big, lovable, slobbery bundle of brown wool who is sure he is man's best friend.*

RESTRUCTURING

Psycholinguistic scholars, such as Kenneth Goodman and others, suggest that what are commonly thought of as reading mistakes (Goodman called them *miscues*) may not be errors at all, but the result of *restructuring*. Psycholinguists observe that some children can translate the surface structure of a phrase into "deep meanings" and then change it into their own normal speech patterns, which may be dialect. The fact that many children can and do this restructuring simultaneously while reading seems to be evidence of cognitive learning on their part.

FORWARD SCANNING

If by the third grade or so a child has become proficient in reading, we are likely to find that he or she has acquired the skill of *forward scanning* in which the reader is simultaneously looking ahead while mediating words that have already been perceived. This anticipatory information processing goes on as a continuum during reading. It allows the reader to anticipate "chunks" of meaning from strings of words that lie immediately ahead. The more efficient the reader, the larger the unit of reading material that can be processed through forward scanning.

Children can be taught to develop this skill, first, by discouraging their word-by-word reading and, second, by encouraging expectancy of what is to come.

Here is how the process works:

1. Phrases, punctuation, and meaning-markers are used as guides.
2. Syntactic materials are received and immediately compared with previously stored information and experiences (*mediation*). This includes identification, comparison, verification, and storage.
3. While the latter is taking place, the reader is visually scanning up-coming words and/or phrases (forward scanning) in anticipation of their relationship to material that is presently being processed.

AFFECTIVE LEARNING

As we have seen, learning to read involves perceptual, associative, and cognitive learning. It also involves another important mode: affective learning. Affective learning is triggered by the emotions. In reading, it takes place when the learner's emotions are aroused by the printed word. Joy, delight, excitement, and so on act as satisfiers to quicken and deepen the learning process. A poem, biography, novel, or even a single word may "affect" the reader and provide incentive for learning to read.

It follows, then, that learning to read should be made as interesting and pleasurable as possible. Obviously, this goal will not be achieved by mere repetition of words and rote drills. For example, most children love to be frightened, so long as they know that the "fright" is momentary and really make-believe. Consequently, they will respond with delight to a story about wicked witches, monsters, and danger narrowly avoided. (Mature readers may become mystery and horror-story enthusiasts for much the same reason.)

IDENTIFICATION

Learning to read should also be relevant to the child's experiences. For affective learning to occur, the child must be able to "identify" with the story characters

What facets of a story make it "just right" for each individual? These boys are engrossed in their books. What *affect* are the stories apparently having on these pupils? What features of a story are necessary for *identification* to occur?

and experiences met on the printed page. Such identification depends, of course, upon the learner's past experiences. What brings pleasure and delight to one child may draw a blank from another, or even arouse a negative reaction to learning.

Identification is at the heart of *affective* reading. Past experience, which is fundamental to identification and effective learning, is individualized. What brings pleasure, delight, and joy to one may "draw a blank" from another child. The more universal the theme, the more one is able to identify with it. This explains, we believe, the universality of some of the literary gems for children and some of the literary characters that continue to delight children regardless of time or place. It is in the realm of affective learning that psychological "emotions" hold sway. This is the ultimate objective of a great story and/or poem for children and is what makes learning to read a worthwhile effort.

SELF AND INDIVIDUAL DIFFERENCES

Self is at the center of one's private universe. How an individual perceives his/her own self determines thought and resultant action in behalf of self and toward others. Self-satisfaction is the intrinsic motivating factor of all learning, even though it may take the form of *avoidance* as well as positive endeavor.

In an invitational address before the American Psychological Association in Honolulu, September, 1972, Dr. Ulric Neisser had this to say about self:

> Much of our cognitive activity, when we are not processing stimulus information (and even when we are) consists of the manipulation and reorganization of representations, subsystems of stored information which represent entities in the world. Among the most important of these are our representations of ourselves and of other people, operating within a larger encompassing cognitive structure of social relations. Most of our actions in the social and interpersonal sphere are determined by these representations, which, in turn, are further shaped by our actions as we perceived them.

We cannot think of the teaching of reading or of learning to read as processes operating outside the self-concepts of the individual learners, and the effect others have on each learner.

There is nothing more individual than the individual. Even twins, triplets, quadruplets, or quintuplets are each different and each one a self-entity. Moreover, we can not assume that children are alike, even if they could be grouped according to the most rigid measures of homogeneity.

All throughout this book we emphasize the individuality of children as learners. Individual differences are the reality with which all teachers must cope. All through my years of teaching kindergarten, I have kept this motto displayed on the wall behind my desk:

> "Children are as alike as thumbs and as different as thumbprints!"

A PSYCHOLOGICAL LEARNING MODEL APPLIED TO LEARNING A SINGLE WORD

Reading is an accumulative skill involving most of the sensory modalities and most of one's memory faculties. The ability to read depends upon one's ability to learn to associate many sensory images and, after establishing those associations, to store them in one's memory bank and to retrieve them rapidly when the occasion demands. As C K. Staats noted, "Reading is a complex cognitive skill, many of whose components must be developed on the basis of already-learned, more basic skills . . . . a cumulative hierarchy."

Let us now proceed to illustrate the cumulative process of learning to read one particular word. We have developed a model in which memory cells are visualized, with each cell assumed to be a unit of one's entire memory complex and also a part of one's "memory bank." Each memory cell is conceived of as containing the cumulative product of a particular associative learning process. For purposes of illustration, the memory cell is shown as three-dimensional, consisting of the four types of learning discussed in the first half of this chapter: perceptual, associative, cognitive, and affective. The model in its progressive form attempts to conceptualize the development of the relationships between stimuli, cumulative product, and recall of stored impressions (retrieval).

The basic empty memory cell may be visualized:

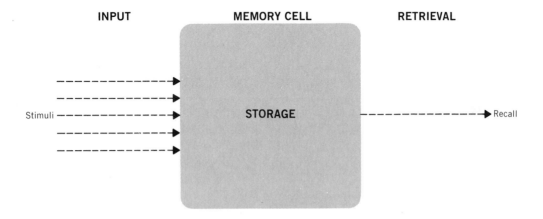

This simplified version of the empty memory cell can be elaborated.

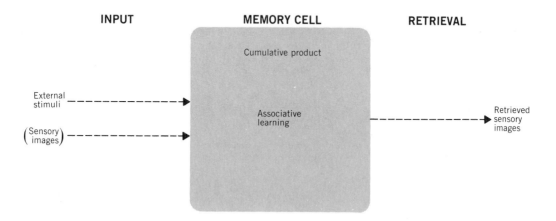

Reading provides the individual with a continuous flow of concepts, with the total meaning of what is read being dependent upon a mental construct consisting of a number of memory cells in the "memory bank." Each memory cell is capable of being expanded or developed by stimuli concomitant with various sequential and cumulative learning phases. The process is envisioned as follows:

External stimuli are received, associated, and stored in the memory cell to be recalled later. The accumulation of stimuli in the memory cell is a complex psychological process. Nevertheless, as the process of learning advances from phase to phase, the basic method of receiving, associating, storing, and retrieving is exactly the same for each.

To illustrate the total cumulative process, let us use the word *hamburger*, a common and popular word in our language. Here is how we envision the complicated learning process at work as the learner copes with the word *hamburger*:

Learning Phase 1

Someone says "hamburger." The learner hears the word for the first time. The learner receives an aural stimulus with no meaning. A "product," the word *hamburger*, is stored in the memory bank as a very weak auditory image. This is purely rote learning. With no associative learning, there will be little, if any, retrievable product.

The memory cell might now look like this:

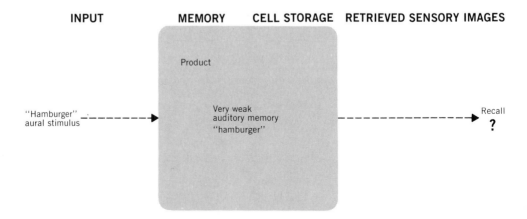

Learning Phase 2

Two stimuli, one immediately following the other, become associated.

Stimulis 1 (aural).   Someone says "hamburger."

Stimulus 2 (echoic).   Learner repeats (imitates) the sound "hamburger."

Cumulative product. Association of aural and echoic stimuli/product.

Recall. The learner can perhaps recall the sound "hamburger" and reproduce it again, but at this point in the learning process most words are stored only briefly.

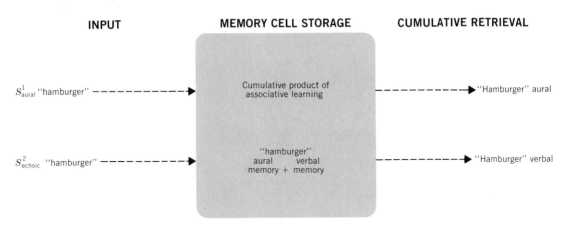

Learning Phase 3

In learning phase three, a symbolic stimulus is added. It is the photograph of a hamburger (visual stimulus).

Stimulus 1. Someone says "hamburger." (Aural stimulus)

Stimulus 2. The stimulus of the sound "hamburger" triggers the memory cell where the sound has been associated with the pronounciation of hamburger. The retrieved associated stimulus of verbalized *hamburger* now becomes associated with stimulus 3.

Stimulus 3. Mental image of *hamburger* (symbolic stimulus).

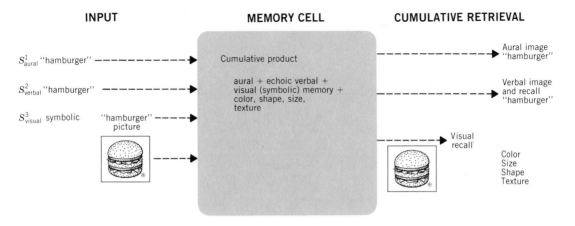

Learning Phase 4

Concrete experience is added in learning phase four. A real hamburger is "experienced" by the learner, producing additional sensory experiences in the following modalities: visual, olfactory, gustatory, tactile, thermal, kinesthetic, and muscular.

Stimulus 1. Someone says "hamburger" (aural stimulus).

Stimulus 2. Learner retrieves sound of word from the memory bank subvocally (echoic stimulus).

Stimulus 3. Visual symbol is retrieved from memory bank (symbolic stimulus). Visual memory photo of hamburger provides recognition and reinforcement. Concrete experience with a real hamburger provides the following stimuli:

Stimulus 4. Sight of hamburger (visual).

Stimulus 5. Smell of hamburger (olfactory).

Stimulus 6. Taste of hamburger (gustatory)

Stimulus 7. Textures of hamburger (tactile).

Stimulus 8. Temperature of hamburger (thermal).

Stimulus 9. Feel of hamburger in hands and feel of biting through it (kinesthetic).

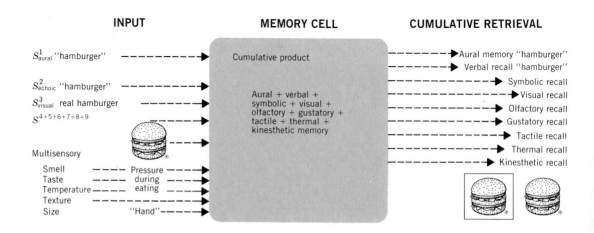

Stimulus 10. Muscular activities in mouth, throat, and other parts of the body while hamburger is being consumed (muscular).

Cumulative products. Ten associated stimuli stored in the memory cell: aural + verbal + visual-symbolic + visual + olfactory + gustatory + tactile + thermal + kinesthetic + muscular.

Learning phase 4 is the most important step in learning to read, for it provides the experiential background for cognitive learning. Experiencing results in permanent storage in the memory cell. Without concrete experience, we have merely rote learning and transient storage. A satisfying and pleasurable experience also triggers affective learning to reinforce the learning process.

Learning Phase 5

In learning phase five, the learner establishes an association between printed word and spoken word—in our example, association between the printed word *h a m b u r g e r* and the pronunciation of *hamburger*. (Flashcards are commonly used for this purpose.) When the establishment is accomplished, the association between aural stimulus (someone says *hamburger*) and symbolic visual stimulus (the printed word *h a m b u r g e r*) triggers all the other associated stimuli (visual, olfactory, gustatory, etc.) stored in the "hamburger" cell in the memory bank. All these stimuli are retrieved and rush to consciousness as the learner is pronouncing the word *hamburger* as a retrieval echoic memory.

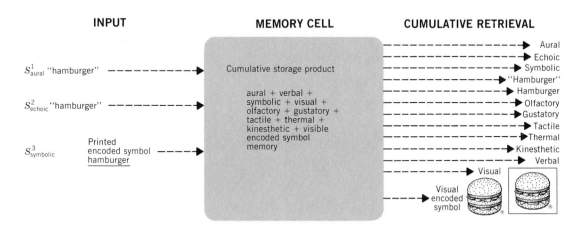

Learning Phase 6

In this learning phase a new and separate memory cell is developed. The word *hamburger* is printed (*h a m b u r g e r*) in manuscript by the learner at the same time that the word is spoken orally or subvocally. The mental input necessary in the process provides a stimulus that may be called *manucodic* and results in the establishment of a manucodic cell for the word *hamburger*. The manucodic cell then becomes associated with the previously developed "hamburger cell." The cumulative result looks like this:

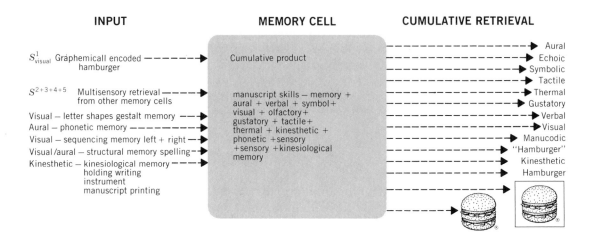

The manucodic cell itself develops through utilization of other previously established memory cells in the memory bank. Memory products retrieved from these cells are transferred to the new cell. The manucodic cell thus established contains learning transferred from memory cells that have stored the ability to hold a writing instrument, knowledge of left-to-right progression, letter shapes, and spelling, and, perhaps, phonetic information.

Learning Phase 7

In this phase, the learner adds cognitive refinement and extensions to the basic concept of hamburger, refinements such as raw ground beef, cooked ground beef, ground-beef quality and quantity, and so on. These cognitive aspects of the word are acquired through experience.

Learning Phase 8

In learning phase eight, a *substitute visual stimulus* triggers cumulative associated stimuli stored in the memory bank. Such a substitute stimulus may be the name "McDonald's®" or "Burger King," or "Bun 'n Burger," or a symbol such as McDonald's® arches. In the final learning phase, any such substitute stimuli might trigger all previously associated stimuli in the "hamburger cell."

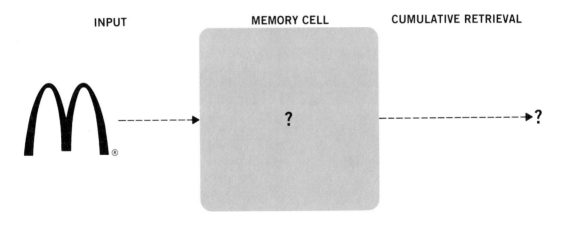

INPUT   MEMORY CELL   CUMULATIVE RETRIEVAL

? → ?

CONSTELLATIONS OF ASSOCIATED IDEAS

As the learner accumulates a meaningful whole-word vocabulary, those words are assembled into language sequences (syntactic constructs) that parallel aural and oral patterns the individual has internalized as a very young child. These syntactic constructs are influenced by the learner's environment and, therefore, may differ slightly from one language community to another. But the basic patterns of the English language are essentially universal. What construct differences do exist are likely to add color rather than confusion to the use of language. When the child begins to learn to read, he/she makes use of aural and oral constructs that have been internalized and stored in memory cells long before. The child is able to speak in such normalized syntactic constructs as "I want a hamburger," "Let's go to McDonald's®," "Oh, look! There's a Burger King!" "Let's go for hamburgers," "Let's get a 'burger and a coke."

How is it that a small child who is just beginning to read can apparently "read" an entire string of words associated with hamburger just as easily as the one word *hamburger*? The answer is probably to be found in the likelihood that word strings that have been heard as complete stimuli and stored together in one or in connected memory cells are retrieved together when the first stimulus or first few stimuli trigger recall of an entire string of connected ideas. We call this concept "the constellation of ideas" theory of input, storage, and retrieval. One word can trigger an entire constellation of ideas. Let us, for example, consider the constellation of ideas triggered by the word *hamburger*. Here is how the constellation might look in diagrammatical form.

We postulate that all of the associated concepts in the diagram are the result of past experiences, that each has been established within its own memory cell, and that, through experience, they have bcome associated with the printed word *hamburger*. The visual stimulus of the printed word *hamburger* triggers this

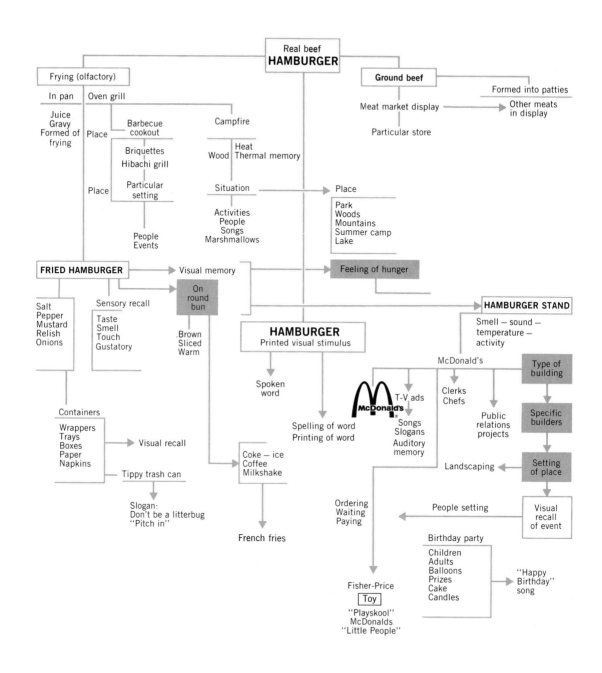

constellation of associated memory cells, bringing into conscious memory many or all of the sensory stimuli (visual, auditory, kinesthetic, gustatory, olfactory, tactile, muscular, thermal) stored there.

We may also postulate that more than just associative memory is involved in this process. We may postulate that the perceptual, cognitive, and affective memories are also involved. For example, the remembered pleasure of a child's birthday party at a McDonald's® may be re-experienced at the sight or sound of the word *hamburger*. Indeed, the constellation of ideas associated with *hamburger* may be triggered by associated words rather than the word itself—French fries, campfire, marshmallows, and so on.

Recall of a constellation of ideas is of tremendous significance for the learning of reading, for it underscores the importance of experiences in the learning-to-read process. Letters, words, phonics, syntax, and so forth, are but the mechanics of reading. Words—regardless of whether they are learned as sight words, by synthetic or analytic phonics, or by encoded manuscript printing—are merely words until sensory experiences make them meaningful to the learner. The breadth and depth of the reader's past learning experiences is all-important. The greater the constellation of associated sensory images that can be recalled from the memory cells, the deeper the understanding, the more lasting the memory, and the more instant the recall.

Throughout the remainder of this text, we cite the psychological foundations for the strategies we recommend. In this way, we not only provide insights into materials and methods that are successfully being used in our schools, but also the reasons *why* they are being used.

BIBLIOGRAPHY

Adams, M. J. "Perceptual Components in Attention and Language Apprehension Effect," *Studies in Attention and Learning*, Providence, RI: Walter S. Hunter Laboratory in Psychology, Brown University, 1976.

Anderson, Irving H., and Walter F. Dearborn, *Psychology of Teaching Reading*. New York: Ronald Press, 1952. One of the first "classics" that undertook to apply principles of learning to the teaching of reading.

Anderson, J. R., and G. H. Bower, *Human Associative Memory* Washington, DC: Winston, 1973.

Anderson, P. H., and S. Jay Samuels, "Visual Recognition Memory, Paired-Associated Learning, and Reading Achievement," paper presented to the Annual Convention of the American Education Research Association, Minneapolis.

Anderson, R. P., "Physiologic Considerations in Learning: The Tactual Mode," in *Learning Disorders*, Vol. III, J. Hellmuth, (Editor), Seattle: Special Child Publications, 1968, 41–58.

Appel, L. F., P. G. Cooper, N. McCarrell, J. Sims-Knight, S. R. Yussen, and J. H. Flavell, "The Development of the Distinction Between Perceiving and Memorizing," *Child Development*, **43** (1972), 1365–1381.

Armstrong, Robert J., and Robert F. Mooney, "The Slosson Intelligence Test: Implications for Reading Specialists," *Reading Teacher*, **24**:4 (1971), 336–340. This is a convincing report of the value of using the Slosson test. The test takes 17 minutes and can be administered by a classroom teacher. The Stanford-Binet takes 64 minutes and needs a specialist to administer it.

Ashton-Warner, Sylvia. *Teacher.* New York: Simon and Schuster, 1963.

Athey, Irene J., "Synthesis of Papers on Language Development and Reading," *Reading Research Quarterly*, **7**:1 (1971), 9–15. Athey warns that "no model, however sophisticated, makes provision for group or individual differences," and that "deviations from a model are frequently viewed as 'deficits' rather than differences."

Athey, Irene J., "Language Models and Learning," *Reading Research Quarterly*, **7**:1 (1971), 16–110. This gives a scholarly analysis of models originating from three main sources: developmental psychology, psycholinguistics, and information processing. (This presentation may be too technical for the beginner.)

Ausubel, David P., "The Use of Advance Organizers in the Learning and Retention of Meaningful Material," *Journal of Educational Psychology*, **51**:5 (1960), 267–272. Ausubel developed the strategy of introducing declarative statements (which he called "advance organizers") into the textual discourse prior to the appearance of new concepts. The "advance organizers" frequently consisted of 250 to 300 words preceeding a discourse of 2000 or more words. The method is explained in more detail in a subsequent publication by Ausubel and Fitzgerald (1962).

Ausubel, David P., and Donald Fitzgerald, "Organizer, General Background, and Antecedent Learning Variables, in Sequential Verbal Learning," *Journal of Educational Psychology*, **53** (1962), 243–249.

Bandura, Albert (Editor) *Psychological Modeling: Conflicting Theories*, Chicago: Aldine-Atherton, 1971. Especially Chapters 5 and 7 on "imitation."

Becker, C. A., "The Allocation of Attention During Visual Word Recognition," *Journal of Experimental Psychology: Human Perception and Performance* **2** (1976), 556–566.

Beilin, Harry, *Studies in Cognitive Bases of Language Development*, New York: Academic Press, 1975.

Belmont, J. M., and E. C. Butterfield, "The Relations of Short-term Memory to Development and Intelligence," *Advances in Child Development and Behavior*, G. H. Bower and J. T. Spence (Editors), Vol 4, New York: Academic Press, 1969.

Bernbach, H. A., "Stimulus Learning and Recognition in Paired-Associate Learning," *Journal of Experimental Psychology*, **75** (1967), 513–519.

Blank, M., "Cognitive Processes in Auditory Discrimination in Normal and Retarded Readers," *Child Development*, **39** (1968), 1091–1101.

Bloom, Benjamin S., *Human Characteristics and School Learning*. New York: McGraw-Hill, 1976.

Bloom, Richard D., "Learning to Read: An Operant Perspective," *Reading Research Quarterly*, **8**:2 (1973), 147–166.

Bower, Gordon H., "Mental Imagery and Associative Learning," in *Cognition in Learning and Memory*, Lee W. Gregg (Editor), New York: Wiley, 1972, 51–88.

Brekke, Beverly, "Conservation and Reading Readiness," *Journal of Genetic Psychology*, **123** (September, 1973), 133–138.

Broadbent, Donald E., "The Hidden Attentive Processes," *American Psychologist*, **32**:2 (1977), 109–118.

Brown, Eric, "The Bases of Reading Acquisition," *Reading Research Quarterly*, **6**:1 (1970), 49–74. Brown devised a "psycholinguistic" model of the reading process. In it, he emphasized the point that an oral rendering of a passage must be done preliminary to further cognitive processing. Much of his thinking was influenced by the theories of Chomsky.

Brown, G., and C. Desforges, "Piagetian Psychology and Education: Time for Revision," *British Journal of Educational Psychology*, **47**:1 (1977), 7–17.

Brown, Roger, *Psycholinguistics*. New York: The Free Press, 1970.

Brown, Roger, "Psychology and Reading," in *Basic Studies on Reading*, Harry Levin and Joanna P. Williams (Editors), New York: Basic Books, 1970, 164–187.

Briggs, Chari, and David Elkind, "Cognitive Development in Early Readers," *Developmental Psychology*, **9** (1973), 279–280.

Calfee, Robert C., "Assessment of Independent Reading Skills: Basic Research and Practical Applications," in *Toward a Psychology of Reading*, Arthur S. Reber and Don L. Scarborough (Editors), Hillsdale, NJ: Earlbaum, 1977, 289–323.

Calfee, Robert C., R. Chapman, and Richard Venezky, "How a Child Needs to Think to Learn to Read," in *Cognition in Learning and Memory*, L. W. Gregg (Editor), New York, Wiley, 1972.

Chafe, Wallace L., *Meaning and the Structure of Language*, Chicago: University of Chicago Press, 1970.

Chomsky, Carol S., *The Acquisition of Syntax in Children from 5 to 10.* Cambridge, MA: MIT Press, 1969. In this important volume, the author presents her position on the manner in which children acquire spoken language patterns, proceeding from the simple to the complex. Her's is a significant contribution to understanding this aspect of reading readiness.

Church, Marilyn, "Does Visual Perceptual Training Help Beginning Readers?" *Reading Teacher*, **27**:4 (1974), 361–364. Children with Frostig training did no better, and those in self-selected fun activities had fun, and still did as well.

Clark, A. D., and C. J. Richards, "Auditory Discrimination Among Economically-Disadvantaged Preschool Children," *Exceptional Children*, **33** (1966), 259–262.

Cognition: International Journal of Cognitive Psychology, Elsevier Sequoia SA, P.O. Box 851, Lausanne 1, Switzerland.

Cohn, Marvin, and George Strickler, "Inadequate Perception vs. Reversals," *Reading Teacher*, **30**:2 (1976), 162–167.

Cole, R. A., and B. Scott, "Toward a Theory of Speech Perception," *Psychological Review*, **81** (1974), 348–374.

Conkie, George W., "What the Study of Eye Movement Reveals About Reading," in *Theory and Practice of Reading.* Lauren B. Resnick and Phyllis A. Weaver (Editors), Hillsdale, N.J.: Erlbaum, 1980.

Cox, Mary B., "The Effect of Conservation Ability on Reading Competency," *Reading Teacher*, **30**:3 (1976), 251–258.

Crary, Helen L., and Robert W. Fidgway, "Relationships between Visual Form-Perception Abilities and Reading Achievement in the Intermediate Grades," *Journal of Experimental Education.* **40**:1 (1971), 16–22.

Crouse, J. H., "Retroactive Interference in Reading Prose Materials," *Journal of Educational Psychology*, **62** (1971), 39–44.

Daniel, P. N., and R. S. Tacker, "Preferred Modality of Stimulus Input and Memory for CVC Triagrams," *Journal of Educational Research.* **67** (1974), 255–258.

deHirsch, Katrina, Jeanette Lansky, and William S. Langford *Predicting Reading Failure*, New York: Harper and Row, 1966.

Dehn, Mechthild, "Children's Strategies in Learning to Read and Write: An Examination of the Learning Process," *The Reading Teacher*, 33:3 (1979), 270–277. Presents case studies of first-graders in German schools. This report indicates that children's individual learning is related to their own personalities and physiology regardless of method.

Donovan, Margaret A., and Mary C. Austin, "Does Modality Preference Make a Difference?" paper presented at the May 4, 1978 meeting of the International Reading Association, Houston, Texas.

Downing, John (Editor), *Comparative Reading: Cross-National Studies of Behavior and Processes in Reading and Writing*, New York: Macmillan, 1973.

Entwistle, Doris R., "Young Children's Expectations for Reading," in *Aspects of Reading Acquisition*, John T. Guthrie (Editor), Baltimore: Johns Hopkins University Press, 1976.

Fine, Benjamin, *The Stranglehold of the I.Q.*, Garden City, NY: Doubleday, 1975.

Fodor, Jerome, Thomas G. Bever, and Michael F. Garrett, *The Psychology of Language*, New York: McGraw-Hill, 1974.

Gagne, Robert M., "Observing the Effects of Learning," *Educational Psychologist*, **11**:3 (1975), 144–157.

Gagne, R. M. (Editor), *Learning and Individual Differences*, Columbus OH: Charles E. Merrill, 1977.

Gaspar, Radomir, and David Brown, *Perceptual Processes in Reading*, London: Hutchinson Educational, 1973.

Geyer, John J., "Comprehensive and Partial Models Related to the Reading Process," *Reading Research Quarterly*, **7**:4 (1972), 541–587. Geyer reviewed 48 models.

Gibson, Eleanor J., *Principles of Perceptual Learning and Development*, New York: Appleton-Century-Crofts, 1969.

Gibson, Eleanor J., "The Ontogeny of Reading," *American Psychologist*, **25**:2 (1970), 136–143.

Gibson, Eleanor J., and Harry Levin, *The Psychology of Reading*, Cambridge, MA: MIT Press, 1975.

Gilbert, L. C., "Speed of Processing Visual Stimuli and its Relation to Reading," *Journal of Educational Psychology*, **50** (1959), 8–14.

Goldschmid, M. L., "Different Types of Conservation and Non-Conservation and Their Relation to Age, Sex, I.Q., M. A., and Vocabulary," *Child Development*, **38** (1967), 1229–1246.

Gough, P. B., and M. J. Cosky, "One Second of Reading Again," in *Cognitive Theory*, Vol. 2, N. Castellan, Jr., D. Pisoni, and G. Potts (Editors), Hillsdale, NJ: Lawrence Erlbaum Associates, 1977.

Groff, Patrick, "Reading Ability and Auditory Discrimination: Are They Related?" *Reading Teacher*, **28**:8 (1975), 742–747.

Guilford, J. P., "Intelligence: 1965 Model," *American Psychologist*, **20** (1966), 20–26. Address to the American Psychological Association in which he expanded the "structure-of-intellect" model.

Guralnick, Michael J., "Alphabet Discrimination and Distinctive Features," *Journal of Learning Disabilities*, **5** (1972), 428–434.

Guthrie, E. R., "Conditioning: A Theory of Learning in Terms of Stimulus, Response, and Association," *Psychology of Learning*, Forty-first Yearbook, National Society for the Study of Education, Part II. Chicago: University of Chicago Press, 1942.

Guthrie, John T. (Editor), *Aspects of Reading Acquisition*. Proceedings of the Fifth Annual Hyman Blumberg Symposium on Research in Early Childhood Education. Baltimore: Johns Hopkins University Press, 1976.

Hafner, Lawrence E., Wendell Weaver, and Kathryn Powell, "Psychological and Perceptual Correlates of Reading Achievement Among Fourth Graders," *Journal of Reading Behavior*, **2**:4 (1970), 281–290. Reported that *word knowledge* is *the* most important factor in comprehension.

Hathaway, W. E., and Hathaway-Theunissen, A., "The Unique Contributions of Piagetian Measurement to Diagnosis, Prognosis, and Research of Children's Mental Development," *Proceedings of Fifth Annual UAP Conference*, **5** (1975), 229–329.

Hebb, Donald O., *A Textbook of Psychology*, Philadelphia: W. B. Saunders Co., 1958. One of the "classics" in associative learning, in which he proposed the "cell assembly" theory.

Herriot, Peter, *An Introduction to the Psychology of Language*. London: Methuen, 1970.

Hilgard, Ernest R., "Psychology's Influence on Educational Practices: A Puzzling History," *Education*, **97** :3 (1977), 203–219.

Hockberg, Julian, "Attention in Perception and Reading," in *Early Experience and Visual Information Processing in Perceptual and Reading Disorders*, F. A. Young and D. B. Lindsley (Editors), Washington DC: National Academy of Sciences, 1970, 219–224.

King, Ethel V., and Siegmar Muehl, "Effects of Visual Discrimination Training on Immediate and Delayed Word Recognition in Kindergarten Children," *Alberta Journal of Educational Research*, **17** (1971), 77—87.

Kintsch, Walter, "Notes on the Structure of Semantic Memory," in *Organization of Memory*, E. Tulving and W. Donaldson (Editors), New York: Academic Press, 1972.

Kinsbourne, Marcel, "Looking and Listening Strategies and Beginning Reading," in *Aspects of Reading Acquisition*, John T. Guthrie (Editor), Baltimore: Johns Hopkins University Press, 1976, 141—161.

LaBerge, D., and S. Jay Samuels, "Toward a Theory of Automatic Information Processing in Reading," *Cognitive Psychology*, **6** (1974), 292—323.

Levin, Harry, and Joanna P. Williams (Editors), *Basic Studies on Reading*, New York: Basic Books, 1970. This is one of the landmark contributions to reading in recent years.

Levine, Fredric M., and Geraldine Fasnacht, "Token Rewards May Lead to Token Learning," *American Psychologist*, **9** (1974), 816—820.

Lott, Deborah, and Frank Smith, "Knowledge of Intra-word Redundancy by Beginning Readers," *Psychonomic Science*, **19** (1970), 343—344. The authors reported that Grade I children showed a lower recognition threshold for three-letter words than for single letters and that Fourth-grade children had reached mature skill in using sequential probabilities for word recognition.

Mackworth, Jane F., "Some Models of the Reading Process: Learners and Skilled Readers," *Reading Research Quarterly*, **3**:4 (1972), 701—733. This is an excellent treatment (albeit quite technical) of three types of memory involved in the reading process. The author, having researched memory processes in reading for more than a decade, concludes that reading, as a cognitive process, involves most of the brain functions: sensory, motor, language, attending, expectancy, coding, categorization, comprehension, and selection. Of special significance to us is her statement that

"The child learning to read stores each word in his visual long-term stores, together with the auditory and articulatory programs concerned with saying the word. The result of storing visual words is that sequential probabilities for letters are built up. Each letter in the input will tend to activate other letters that are most often found in relation to it." p. 719.

Mackworth, Norman H., "Seven Cognitive Skills in Reading," *Reading Research Quarterly.*, **7**:4 (1972), 679—700. A highly technical summary of a proposed research study.

McCracken, Robert A., "A Comparative Study of Modalities in Beginning Reading Instruction," *Reading Teacher,* **28**:1 (1974), 6–9. A delightful spoof on the so-called "preference for learning through a specific modality." Required reading!

Manzo, Anthony V., Lyndell Grey, and Martha R. Haggard, "Psychological Approaches for the Reading Specialist: A Reclamation Project," *Reading World,* **16**:3 (1977), 188–195.

Martin, E., "Relation Between Stimulus Recognition and Paired-Associate Learning," *Journal of Experimental Psychology,* **74** (1967), 500–505.

Memory and Cognition Journal

Miller, George A., *The Psychology of Communication,* New York: Basic Books, 1967.

Norman, D. A., *Memory and Attention: An Introduction to Human Information Processing,* New York: Wiley, 1969.

Pearson, P. David, "The Effects of Grammatical Complexity on Children's Comprehension, Recall, and Conception of Certain Semantic Relations," *Reading Research Quarterly,* **10**:2 (1974–1975), 155–192. Pearson investigated three alternatives: readability, deep structure, and "chunk", as means of affecting comprehension.

Peters, Nathaniel A., "Application of Jensen's Bidimensional Model of Learning to the Reading Process," *Project on Individually-Guided Instruction in Elementary Reading.* Madison, WI: University of Wisconsin Research and Development Center for Cognitive Learning, 1972.

Pikulski, John J., "Assessing Information About Intelligence and Reading," *Reading Teacher.* **29**:2 (1975), 157–163.

Rachner, Jane, "Gestalten in Reading," *Reading Teacher,* **27**:4 (1974), 385–388.

Raven, Ronald J., and Richard T. Saltzer, "Piaget and Reading Instruction," *Reading Teacher,* **24**:7 (1971) 630–639. This is a very informational article delineating the applications of Piaget's stages and sequence of intellectual development and their significance in beginning reading.

Reber, Arthur S., and Don L. Scarborough (Editors), *Toward a Psychology of Reading,* (Proceedings of the 1974 CUNY Conference), Hillsdale, NJ: Erlbaum 1977.

Resnick, Lauren B., "Toward a Usable Psychology of Reading Instruction," in *Theory and Practice of Early Reading,* Lauren B. Resnick and Phyllis A. Weaver (Editors), Hillsdale, NJ: Erlbaum, 1980.

Rickards, John P., "Processing Effects of Advance Organizers Interspersed in Text," *Reading Research Quarterly* **11**:4 (1975–1976), 599–622. The results of this study indicate the advantage of interspersing advance organizers in the form of questions within the text rather than providing a lengthy prelude prior to reading of the textual concepts.

Ringler, L., and I Smith, "Learning Modality and Word Recognition of First-Grade Children," *Journal of Learning Disabilities,* **6** (1973), 307–312.

Robeck, Mildred C., and John A. R. Wilson, *Psychology of Reading,* New York: Wiley, 1974.

Roberts, Kathleen P., "Piaget's Theory of Conservation and Reading Readiness," *Reading Teacher,* **30**:3 (1976), 246–250.

Robinson, Helen M., "Visual and Auditory Modalities Related to Methods for Beginning Reading," *Reading Research Quarterly,* **8**:1 (1973), 7–39.

Roe, A., "A Psychologist Examines Sixty-Four Eminent Scientists," *Creativity,* P. E. Vernon (Editor) Baltimore: Penguin Books, 1970.

Rosner, Jerome, "Perceptual Skills—A Concern of the Classroom Teacher?" *Reading Teacher,* **24**:6 (1971), 543–549. Fifteen specific strategies for assisting visual-motor function and twenty specific strategies to assist auditory-motor function are clearly presented in this article.

Royer, James M., "Theories of the Transfer of Learning," *Educational Psychologist,* **14** (1979), 53–69.

Rozin, Paul, "The Evolution of Intelligence and Access to the Cognitive Unconscious," in *Progress in Psychobiology and Physiological Psychology,* J. Sprague and A. N. Epstein (Editors), New York: Academic Press, 1975.

Samuels, S. Jay, "The Effect of Distinctive Feature Training on Paired-Associate Learning," *Journal of Educational Psychology,* **64** (1972), 164–170.

Samuels, S. Jay, "Success and Failure in Learning to Read; a Critique of the Research," *Reading Research Quarterly* **8**:2 (1973), 200–239.

Samuels, S. Jay, and Roger B. Anderson, "Visual Recognition Memory, Paired Associative Learning, and Reading Achievement," *Journal of Educational Psychology,* **65** (1973), 160–167.

Sawyer, C. E., and B. J. Brown, "Laterality and Intelligence in Relationship to Reading Ability," *Education Review* (Birmingham, England) **29**:2 (1977), 81–86.

Schiffman, H. R., "Some Components of Sensation and Perception for the Reading Process," *Reading Research Quarterly,* **7**:4 (1972), 588–612. This is a highly technical report of research on the amount of stimulation provided by the peripheral retina in helping the learner determine pattern and form discrimination, and, perhaps, reading.

Schuell, T. J., and G. Keppel, "Learning Ability and Retention," *Journal of Educational Psychology,* **61** (1970), 59–65.

Schwebel M., and J. Rapha, *Piaget in the Classroom,* New York: Basic Books, 1973. 17.

Shavelson, Richard, Judith Hubner, and George Stanton, "Self-Concept Validation of Construct Interpretation," *Review of Educational Research,* **46** (1976), 409–411.

Shiffrin, R. M., and R. C. Atkinson, Storage and Retrieval Processes in Long-Term Memory," *Psychological Review,* **76** (1969), 179–193.

Silverston, R. A., and Deichmann, J. W., "Sense Modality Research and the Acquisition of Reading Skills," *Review of Educational Research,* 1975, **45,** 149–172.

Singer, Harry, "IQ Is and Is NOT Related to Reading," in *Intelligence and Reading,* Stanley Wanat (Editor) Newark, DE: International Reading Association, 1974.

Singer, Harry, and Robert B. Ruddell (Editors), *Theoretical Models and Processes of Reading* (Second Edition). Newark, DE: International Reading Association, 1976. This is the most exhaustive collection of articles on the structure of the reading process by theoreticians from several disciplines. They are categorized as theories of language, visual processing, perception, word recognition, cognition and reading, affective domain, information processing, psycholinguistic models.

Smith, Frank, *Understanding Reading: A Psycholinguistic Analysis of Reading and Learning to Read,* New York: Holt, Rinehart, and Winston, 1971.

Smith, Helen K. (Editor) *Perception and Reading,* Newark, DE: International Reading Association, 1967.

Smith, Henry P., and Emerald V. Dechant, *Psychology in Teaching Reading,* Englewood Cliffs, NJ, Prentice-Hall, 1961.

Solan, Harold A. (Editor), *The Psychology of Learning and Reading Difficulties,* New York: Simon and Schuster, 1973. A very worthwhile collection.

Staats, C. K., R. E. Schutz, and M. M. Wolf, "The Conditioning of Reading Responses Using 'Extrinsic' Reinforcers," *Journal of Experimental Analysis of Behavior,* **5** (1962), 33–40.

Staats, C. K., *Learning, Language, and Cognition,* New York: Holt, Rinehart, and Winston, 1968.

Terman, Louis M. *Genetic Studies of Genius, Vol. 1: Mental and Physical Traits of a Thousand Gifted Children.* Stanford: Stanford University Press, 1925.

Thorndike, Edward L., *Educational Psychology, Vol II, Psychology of Learning,* New York: Teachers College Press, 1913.

Thorndyke, P. W., and B. Hayes-Roth, "The Use of Schemata in the Acquisition and Transfer of Knowledge," *Cognitive Psychology,* **11** (1979), 82–106.

Tulving, E., and S. A. Madigan, "Memory and Verbal Learning," *Annual Review of Psychology,* **21** (1970), 437–484.

Underwood, B. J., and R. W. Schulz, *Meaningfulness and Verbal Learning,* New York: Lippincott, 1960.

U. S. Commissioner of Education and USOE, *Education of the Gifted and Talented,* Washington, DC: U. S. Government Printing Office, 1972.

Vandever, T. R., and D. D. Neville, "Modality Aptitude and Word Recognition," *Journal of Reading Behavior,* **6** (1974), 195–201.

Venezky, Richard L., and R. C. Calfee, "The Reading Competency Model," in *Theoretical Models and Processes in Reading.* Harry Singer (Editor), Newark, International Reading Association, 1970, 273–291.

Vernon, Philip E., and Margaret C. Mitchell, "Social-Class Differences in Associative Learning," *Journal of Special Education,* **8**:4 (1974), 294–311.

Wanat, Stanley F., "Language Acquisition: Basic Issues," *Reading Teacher,* **25**:2 (1972), 142–147. The author described three theoretical bases for language acquisition: (1) *behavioristic,* in which the child imitates the models of language that are heard and is reinforced; (2) *nativistic,* that holds that language is a developmental process paralleling other physical maturation and is biologically determined: and (3) *cognitive,* in which the child plays an active role through thinking and information processing.

Willerman, Lee, "Effects of Families on Intellectual Development," *American Psychologist,* **34**:10 (1979), 923–929.

Williams, Joanna, "From Basic Research on Reading to Educational Practice," in *Basic Studies on Reading,* Harry Levin and Joanna P. Williams (Editors), New York: Basic Books, 1970.

Williams, Joanna, "Learning to Read," in *The Literature of Research in Reading,* F. B. Davis (Editor), New Brunswick, Rutgers, 1971.

Williams, Joanna, "Learning to Read: A Review of Theories and Models," *Reading Research Quarterly,* **8**:2 (1973), 121–146. This is one of the most significant contributions to our knowledge of reading through "models."

Dr. Williams has done a scholarly work. One statement is of special significance here.

"The rejection of a simple associative learning model for orthography-sound correspondence learning reflects the acknowledgement that a great many tasks are more profitably evaluated as 'active' processes. Even in simple paired-associate and serial learning, the subject shows evidence that he has organized and coded the material." In this observation, she was emphasizing the new focus within the psychology of cognition.

Williams, Joanna, "Building Perceptual and Cognitive Strategies into a Reading Curriculum," in *Toward a Psychology of Reading,* Arthur S. Reber and Don L. Scarborough (Editors), Hillsdale, NJ: Earlbaum, 1977, 157–287.

Winkeljohann, Sister Rosemary, "Jean's Influence on Dick and Jane," *Elementary English,* **51,** (1974), 870–873.

Wolpert, Edward M., "Modality and Reading: A Perspective," *Reading Teacher,* **24**:7 (1971), 640–643.

Wohwill, Joachim, "The Place of Structured Experience in Early Cognitive Development," *Revisiting Early Childhood Education,* Joe L. Frost (Editor), New York: Holt, Rinehart and Winston, 1973. This is a practical application of some of the thinking skills that need to be developed through direct teaching of patterning, classification, comparison, prediction, and hypothesizing.

Zeaman, D., and B. J. House, "The Relation of I.Q. and Learning," in *Learning and Individual Differences,* R. M. Gagne (Editor), Columbus, OH: Charles E. Merrill, 1967, 192–217.

UNIT TWO

In contrast to talking, which is a natural, largely untaught, imitative, cumulative skill, reading is an unnatural, taught, largely structured skill that cannot be learned solely by imitation. Learning to talk is motivated by the need to establish and maintain one's place within the human environment. It is, in a sense, motivated by self-preservation. A child learns to talk because he or she must respond to and communicate with other human beings if the child's human needs are to be met. It is an act of becoming human, of joining the human race.

Learning to talk, then, is a "natural" process. It is not, however, an unconscious process. It involves effort and purpose. Observe the purposeful efforts of the very young child as it tries to respond to and imitate the sounds of an adult, its facial expression contorted by its efforts. Still, learning to talk is "natural" in the sense that most normal children acquire the skill with little more than a model to imitate.

Learning to read, on the other hand, requires much more than imitation. It requires a purposeful and structured sequence of instruction. It is, in a sense, "unnatural" in that its motivation is not innate. Motivation to read must be inculcated in the child. In Chapter 1, we touched upon some of the reasons a child decides to learn to read. Suffice it to say here that the decision is not likely to be a sudden one. It will have incubated in the child's mind for a considerable period before the realization or announcement that "I want to learn to read."

Learning to read begins with that wonderful moment of *readiness*. Here, too, begin our efforts to teach the skill of reading, to do all we can do to assist the beginner to learn to read. It is to these "beginnings" that the two chapters of this unit of our text are directed.

BEGINNINGS

CHAPTER TWO

Readiness for Reading
and Reading Readiness

It is useful to make a distinction between what we call readiness for reading and reading-readiness training. Readiness for reading is a state of being, the product of a child's maturational development, including physical and intellectual development. Reading readiness is the process of those educational activities and strategies designed to prepare children for formal reading instruction.

In this chapter we first discuss the concept of readiness as it applies to learning to read and then discuss in considerable detail instructional activities and practical strategies for promoting reading readiness.

READINESS FOR READING

Readiness for reading may be considered as a point along each individual's line of maturation, the point at which any particular child is at optimum readiness for learning to read. Any attempt to teach a child to read before that point of readiness will yield unsatisfactory or, frequently, negative results.

The optimum time for beginning to learn to read has been speculated upon by a number of researchers. The most satisfactory answer to the question, "When shall we begin to teach reading?" is to be found in the developmental approach to human learning. This approach to what we might call *"maturational readiness"* includes the following aspects of maturation: physical, mental, emotional, psychological, experiential, and social.

PHYSICAL FACTORS IN READINESS

Although successful readers may be tall or short, fat or thin, the teacher should be alert to atypical physical development in a child that may indicate health problems detrimental to learning. In general, however, the reading teacher will be concerned primarily with the child's speech, hearing, and visual-perception development.

Speech   Most educational psychologists and reading experts agree that a child should not be taught to read until he/she has developed "normal" speech patterns. Fortunately, most children have developed such patterns by the time they reach kindergarten—the *readiness year*. Unfortunately, it is not always easy to judge the disabling potential of minor or transient deviations in normal patterns, or even of extreme deviations.

For example, a pair of twins arrived at my kindergarten speaking what might be called gibberish. In their isolated togetherness, Penny and Patty had developed their own language and pattern of speech which they used to communicate between themselves but which even their parents could not understand. Their conversation went something like this:

"Aig wu fon dret?"
"Ih, yal fon."
"Zja, Patty, zja hig fee po."
"Zja."

At the end of the kindergarten year, the twins were diagnosed as not ready to learn to read, although they had acquired a minimal amount of normal words which, together with gestures ("silent language"), served to get them through most situations. Were Patty and Penny really not ready to learn to read? Might they have been made ready with special tutorial help? Perhaps. Perhaps not. The point is that we should not trust to judgment in dealing with deviations from the norms of maturational development.

Children whose parents have overindulged themselves in "baby talk" or some other special jargon are likely to bring unacceptable speech patterns to the classroom. Such deviations from the norm can usually be easily and quickly dealt with by the kindergarten teacher.

It is imperative, however, that the teacher does not confuse individual differences in pronunciation and speech patterns with lack of maturation. If, for example, an American Oriental child says *lice* for *rice*, does that mean the child is not ready to learn to read? Spanish-speaking children are apt to say *bet* for *pet*, *vrilliant* for *brilliant*, *hitted* for *heated*, and *estop* for *stop*. New Zealand children say *ny* for *no* and *yees* for *yes*. In Australia, many say *trine* for *train*, *myte* for *mate*, and *yarite, mate?* for *are you O.K., friend?* In Missouri, *cow* is apt to be pronounced *kyou*; in Detroit and some other places they say *eh?* for *isn't that so?*; in the south one often hears *"Y'all come back, heeah?*

Do these and countless other colloquial pronunciations mean that children who use them are not ready for reading? Of course not. According to most research, such phonological differences have little or no effect upon readiness for reading.

Auditory Discrimination   Many experts believe that auditory discrimination should have matured to the point where the child is able to discriminate the sounds of consonants and vowels before learning to read. It is generally agreed that the child who can distinguish differences among spoken initial consonants will be able to learn the visual symbols for them and will then be able to put these two factors together and discriminate between words that begin with the same sound. We must assume that reading success is related to the ability to discriminate language sounds and to differentiate phonemes.

Visual-Perceptual Discrimination   Small children with visual anomalies may have trouble discriminating parts of words and even gross shapes of words.

One of the problems in the kindergarten year is that vision problems may go undiscovered. The teacher should be on the alert for any indications that a child has vision problems and, if so, seek professional advice as to what the child should do to correct them. Inability to see well at far-point or near-point may, however, merely mean that the child has not yet developed sufficient visual accommodation power. Fortunately, most six-year-olds have developed sufficient accommodation power to read at near-point, where reading is normally done.

MENTAL FACTORS IN READINESS

It seems reasonable to suppose that a mental age of somewhere near six years is required for the readiness of first-grade children (who are six chronological years old) to learn to read. But "mental age" as a readiness factor is subject to important qualifications. A mental age of below six might well be sufficient for learning to read in a one-to-one laboratory situation, whereas a mental age of at least six would be required in a normal classroom of 20 or 30 children. It is not realistic to speak of "mental age" as a fixed factor of readiness existing independently of the teaching method employed in learning to read. Intelligence is, of course, a very significant factor in readiness for reading, but it cannot stand alone in determining readiness.

EMOTIONAL FACTORS IN READINESS

In any average classroom, personality differences are evident. Some children are shy, some are bold; some are gregarious, some prefer their privacy; some exhibit neatness, some seem to enjoy being messy, and so on. Such individual differences are normal and to be expected. But severe deviation from behavioral norms may indicate lack of the emotional maturity necessary for learning to read.

One obvious symptom of emotional immaturity is a persistent tendency to withdraw from the rigors of classroom activities. The child who exhibits strong feelings of insecurity, who consistently withdraws from participation in work and play, who is "psychologically absent" from show-and-tell time, or who is overly reluctant to attend school may be signaling that he/she is not yet emotionally mature enough to learn to read. Observation by the teacher over a reasonable period of time will help identify such children.

PSYCHOLOGICAL FACTORS IN READINESS

The child's psychological development is an important factor in readiness. Without a clear concept of self and of reality, without motivation as evidenced by goal setting and goal seeking, the child may exhibit many of the symptoms associated with emotional immaturity. These are largely the same components described in Chapter 1. Psychological maturation is closely related to reading readiness.

EXPERIENTIAL FACTORS IN READINESS

In the previous chapter, we have suggested that wide differences exist in the experiential backgrounds of children entering school. Some bring experiences gained from travel, from listening to stories read to them by parents, from relationships with siblings, grandparents, and others, from exposure to the arts and sciences, and so on. Some, on the other hand, bring little or no such experiences.

Many five-year-olds are already at home in the world of books, eager to be on their own in reading. To others, the printed page may be just another facet of social environment that is foreign to them.

Many experientially disadvantaged children will have difficulty in achieving readiness because of lack of experiences to relate to their reading. Fortunately, in most kindergartens and infant rooms the environment is designed to provide enrichment experiences. Here, exposure to music, art, poetry, stories, drama, to the wonders of science, to the joy of festivals, and holidays, and so on, can

BLOCKS, BEADS, PEG BOARDS — THEY'RE FILLING MY HEAD WITH STUFF I'LL NEVER USE!

Cartoon by Lepper. *Phi Delta Kappah*, November, 1976.

Readiness activities are predicated upon the notion that *transfer* will take place. What elements must be common to the readiness activity *and* to reading for transfer to occur? How about "blocks, beads, and peg boards"?

provide experiences conducive to readiness that may have been lacking in the learner's previous environment.

SOCIAL FACTORS IN READINESS

Although reading is an individual and personal act, it is ordinarily learned in a social setting—the school. Some degree of social maturation is, then, necessary for readiness in reading. Lack of social skills is evidence of lack of social maturity. If the lack is extreme, readiness may be severely inhibited. Fortunately, the social setting of the kindergarten or infant room itself is conducive to social maturation. Through their daily routines and learning experiences, the children are able to practice social skills that will later be necessary in a formal learning-to-read group.

Socially immature children may be taught to read through individualized, one-on-one teaching. Removing such children from the social setting helps eliminate the factor inhibiting achievement. But this method is impractical in most classroom situations and, of course, it will not eliminate the basic problem of social immaturity.

Our experience convinces us that the child who has not learned social skills is not yet a candidate for group instruction in reading.

ASSESSING READINESS FOR READING

Fortunate is the first-grade teacher who inherits a class which has had a good year of enrichment and readiness for reading activities. More than likely, the readiness year teacher can predict the problems each child is apt to have and will be able to pass on to the First Grade teacher a portfolio of valuable information on each child. Lacking such help, the first-grade teacher must face the problem (1) of *assessing* readiness for reading; (2) of grouping for reading-readiness activities for those who show that they need such help before they can commence formal reading instruction; and (3) of detecting those children who may not yet be ready even for reading-readiness activities.

To aid assessment, the teacher may seek the help of standardized reading-readiness tests. Such tests provide valuable *comparisons* of performance on a number of variables associated with reading readiness. When the results of the readiness tests are added to information obtained from *comparative* measures of intelligence, together they may be used to verify or modify the informal observations of readiness passed along from the kindergarten teacher to the first-grade teacher. Thus, the readiness test, the intelligence test, and teacher observation *together* provide the basis for an educated judgment of each child's *relative* maturity and readiness for formalized reading instruction.

WHAT DO READING-READINESS TESTS TELL US?

Reading-readiness tests provide information on a child's performance compared with the performance of thousands of other children who also took the same test at approximately the same age. The *comparative* nature of such tests should always be kept in mind. They do not measure absolutes.

Used as *comparative* measures, the tests make it possible to place a child in a percentile, a decile, a quartile, or a stanine, indicating where the child stands at that particular time in relationship to the whole group upon whom the test was standardized. Thus, if performance on the test places a child in the 99th percentile, it means that few children of the same age equal the child in performance of the factors measured by that test. If on the other hand, the individual's performance on the test places the child in the 8th percentile, we can be certain that 90% or more of the children of the same age are superior in the factors measured. Indeed, it means that the child is at the bottom of the heap.

In addition to providing a percentile ranking, reading-readiness tests provide subscores which indicate a child's relative performance on specific variables. Thus, reading-readiness tests can provide information as to a child's relative ability to perform certain tasks, including the ability to do the following:

1. Discriminate gross shapes and likenesses and/or differences.
2. Discriminate fine details and the finer likenesses and differences among them.
3. Identify pictures that match vocabulary dictated by the teacher.
4. Match word symbols that are alike.
5. Follow directions.
6. Follow from left-to-right across the page.
7. Recognize letters when dictated by teacher.
8. Recognize beginning sounds of words.
9. Discriminate endings and rhyming sounds.
10. Copy gestalts, letters, and/or words.
11. Select a picture that illustrates a concept or situation in a story paragraph read by the teacher.
12. Follow sequence of events in a story.

At the present time there is no one readiness test that includes subscores on all twelve measures, although they all undertake a sampling of those variables that the originators of each test believe to be most closely associated with readiness.

The *Metropolitan Readiness Test* is, without doubt, the most popular and most widely used, although it also assesses skills other than reading. Reliance upon the *Metropolitan* total score, in conjunction with teacher judgment and other measures, consistently results in an exceptionally high degree of accuracy in the proper placement of children on the readiness spectrum.

From time to time, researchers have undertaken to determine whether or not a combination of readiness tests will yield more precise measures than does

Obtain a copy of the *Metropolitan Readiness Test* and consider what elements make it a reliable predictor of a child's probable success in beginning reading.

the *Metropolitan* alone. The findings to date indicate that the additional increments added by other tests are not significant enough to be worth the additional time needed to administer and score them.

READING-READINESS TRAINING

Now that we have discussed the maturational concept of readiness for reading and assessment of readiness for reading, let us turn our attention to reading readiness—that is, to planned activities, in the home and in the classroom, designed to prepare the child for learning to read.

PLANNED EXPERIENCES

Many things about children are assumed that, in many cases, are not really so. One such erroneous assumption is that children have been places, have seen things, have had experiences that bring cognitive meaning and affective response to words. Some children have; some haven't. Can we assume that a child who lives in a large city has been to a department store, the zoo, the botanical garden, the airport, "downtown," a shopping mall, or the park? Can we assume that one who lives on an island has seen the sea, fished from a boat, or gone swimming? Can we assume that one who lives on a farm has been through a dairy plant, a cheese factory, a meat-freezing works, a slaughter house, a grannary, or has been to a cattle or produce auction?

The answer, obviously, is "No!" Moreover, the middle-class teacher who has traveled, seen places, things, and people frequently may have little conception of the experiential deficits of large percentages of children who come to the readiness year. The children, consequently suffer from what Dr. Harold Herber fittingly called "assumptive teaching."

Some five-year-olds need fewer planned readiness activities than do others. Indeed, some actually come to the readiness year able to perform some "look-say" reading. Many of the advantaged have elaborate vocabularies, highly structured speech patterns, and are the beneficiaries of wide and deep experiencing. They need advanced reading-readiness activities that soon merge into actual reading.

In general, the main segments of a total readiness program for the usual five-year-old may be visualized in the following illustration:

READING-READINESS ACTIVITES IN AND THROUGH THE HOME

It has been aptly said that reading readiness begins at home. More accurately, one might say that it *should* begin in the home. Unfortunately, it does not always do so. The kindergarten and first-grade teacher is likely to be faced with a number of children whose experiential development is so meager that they are

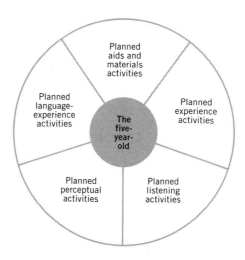

Planned Reading-Readiness Activities Surround the Five-Year-Old

severely handicapped in their efforts to learn to read. These children have experienced in the home little or no developmental learning. The deficit is cumulative, and some of them will carry the mask of this neglect throughout their school years and into adult life. They start behind their peers in the learning process and remain behind. In the droll expression of the old Pennsylvania Dutch, "The farther they go, the behinder they get."

Teachers are frequently asked by parents, "What can I do to help my child get ready for reading?" One answer might be, "Whatever it is, you should have started to do it long ago." Such a response would be entirely truthful—but, one might assume, it would also be unproductive, and something less than polite. In point of fact, there are many things the parent can do to provide experiences conducive to reading readiness.

1. Verbal Identification   First, of course, is the simple give and take of ordinary conversation between parent and child. Helping the child to apply the correct names to things in the household will help build spoken vocabulary. Explaining the parts of things and how things work will do likewise. Using accurate lan-

Siblings as well as parents usually enjoy playing "teacher" and helping a younger family member begin to learn the sounds of the language and vocabulary associated with common objects of the environment. In this case, who is probably learning the most?

guage correctly and speaking in normal speech patterns will elicit imitation of these attributes from the child, attributes that can later be transferred to the business of learning to read.

2. Excursions and Field Trips As often as possible, children in their formative years should accompany parents on trips outside the home. Trips around the block, to the store, supermarket, bakery, farmers' market, to "town," park, pet shop, toy store, shopping mall, playground, service station, post office, bank, printshop, bottling plant, dairy, sand-and-gravel (Metal) pit, waterworks, art museum, aquarium, zoo, botanical garden, cattle ranch, sheep station, fire station, train station, airport, forest, stream, marina, children's petting zoo, farm, skyscraper roof observatory, or a ride on a carousel (merry-go-round), shoot-the-shoots, ski-lift, funicular, gondola, camel, elephant, horse, mule, pony, train, airplane, canoe, rubber raft, outrigger, sailboat, catamaran, escalator,

We stress the point that readiness activities should be planned. There are times and situations, however, when the parent or teacher must be prepared for the unplanned moment or situation that is optimum for learning. When planning a field trip, how can a parent or teacher prepare for learning opportunities such as this?

elevator, moving walkway, ship. Such excursions can add immeasurably to the child's experiential development, especially if the parent converses intelligently with the child about the new sights and sounds to which the child is being exposed. The world is indeed "full of such wonderous things," and it is up to the parents to see that as many of these wonderous things as possible contribute to the child's experiential development.

3. Story, Poetry, and Song   In the home, the child should have access to as many books as possible. The market is replete with books specifically designed to appeal to preschool children. The child should be encouraged to handle such books, look at them, care for them, and cherish them.

At every opportunity, the child should be read to. Nursery rhymes and other poetry, holiday and Holyday stories, classical childhood stories, contemporary children's stories, all will be listened to avidly by the normal preschool child and will help build a foundation for reading experiences to come. Rhythm and rhyme of nursery rhymes soon gives way to more meaningful poetry. Yet, how often parents fail to carry on with poetry and, consequently, lose the momentum of this form of literature previously built up with the rhymes and jingles. The songs and poems of the seasons, holidays, and Holy Days bring the child closer to his/her cultural heritage. They help convert the child into a normal social creature. Moreover, the reading of poetry to children introduces them to one of our most enjoyable literary forms. It creates in them the motivation to want to read. And poetry, once heard, is easy to "read" through rote memorization. The rhythm and sense of the poem carries the flow of language along so that the child can supply the last few words of the rhyming line. This greatly enhances comprehension habits.

The fantasy contained in children's literature is never out of date. Little Red Riding Hood is still about to be gobbled up by "Grandma," and babes still get lost in the woods. Stories that commence with "Once upon a time . . ." are eye-openers to little ones today just as they have been for generations. The morals from Aesop's Fables are just as relevant today as they were in ancient Greece, primarily because human nature is the same.

A recent movement among "activists" has attempted to remove "scarey" stories from children. This is contrary to reality; children love to be frighted as long as they realize it is fantasy. Some time ago, when *Dark Shadows* was a popular late afternoon adult mystery series on TV, one little fellow assured me that it was his favorite "Because it scares Hell out of me!" What better recommendation; especially from a five-year-old?

We have all grown up with the excitement and mystery of witches, goblins, monsters, and sorcerers. In fact, the stories of childhood are society's way of helping its young to cope with reality, fantasy, good, and evil, and to learn how to safely escape to the world of fantasy. Through children's literature, all of the good and bad characteristics of mankind are paraded for the examination of the child. By reading to and with the child, parents convey a love of books and the concept of reading to the child.

4. Television Television, although often indicted as a detriment to reading, can provide meaningful learning experiences if the parents manage television viewing wisely and, especially, if they share such experiences with the child. Travelogues, children's theaters, and special educational programs for young children are representative of the types of programs that can be helpful. The child can, of course, watch such offerings alone, but parental involvement will reinforce the child's concept of the value and, indeed, the fun of such learning experiences.

In short, parents who wish to help their children learn to read should do all they can to establish a home environment in which books and learning are respected and cherished.

READING-READINESS ACTIVITIES IN SCHOOL AND COMMUNITY

The kindergarten or readiness year is, for the child, a transition from the home to a larger, more complex environment. Ideally, planned readiness activities should be a continuation of similar activities already commenced in the home. But, as we noted in the previous section, this is not always the case. Many children—too many, unfortunately—come to the school environment with few, if any, previous readiness experiences. Such children will need to learn readiness skills almost from the ground up.

In all cases, the teacher—especially the teacher of very young children—stands *in loco parentis*, the Latin term for "in place of the parent." It is the teacher's task to foster and develop the skills the child will need to learn to read. The teacher will accomplish this task through a program of planned readiness activities: experience activities, listening activities, language-experience activities, and perceptual-training activities. Let us now take a rather detailed look at what is involved in each of these elements of the reading readiness program.

Planned Experience Activities As we have repeatedly pointed out, experiences are the building blocks of learning to read, indeed of all learning. What can the teacher do to help supply these building blocks? Here are some of the more commonly used activities designed to provide the kindergarten child with experiences that will foster reading readiness.

Book Table Activities The classroom "book table" (or "library table") should contain as many interesting books and other readng materials as possible. Books and materials should be changed periodically, with obvious favorites being kept on the table longer than less favored works. Children should be encouraged to browse freely among the books and to select what they wish for private, indi-

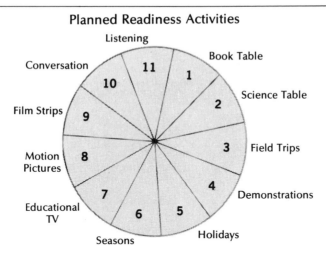

Planned Readiness Activities

Readiness activities can and should be planned for optimum results. Home, school, and community resources all provide enriching activities if prearranged as part of a total readiness program.

vidual perusal when feasible. Some children will have handled few if any books before coming to the classroom. For such youngsters the book table can become a setting for learning to use and care for books, thus providing a kind of psychological set that will ,prepare them to appreciate the value of books and, by extension, the fun and value of learning to read.

Science Table Activities Children in the reading readiness classroom should be given access to objects and books that will appeal to their normal curiosity about the wonders of science and nature. A so-called "science table" may be used to display such materials. Suitable objects for display might include plants and germinating seeds, rocks, bird nests and eggs, a glass-enclosed "ant farm", toy models of airplanes, machines, engines—the list is limited only by availability and the teacher's ingenuity.

The science table is a constantly changing array of seasonal objects and phenomena. The bugs and crawling things of spring; the birds' nests and bees' homes; the rocks and twigs; the weather, and the ways of nature through the changing seasons provide a spectacular and awe-inspiring panorama for learning.

Reading about the wonders of nature that are brought for display on the science table is a natural follow-up. Motivation for reading is inherent in the curiosity that is generated by the objects. Inevitable is the development of a vocabulary supported by experience and an understanding that is readiness for cognitive learning through reading.

The children should be encouraged to look closely at the objects, when feasible to handle them, and, of course, to discuss their properties and func-

What planning must you do to make science table activities most effective in the reading readiness program?

tions. In short, children should "experience" the objects. They will then be able to bring these experiences to the reading of stories about the objects and, through transfer of learning, to stories about related topics.

Field Trips Field trips to parks, museums, zoos, and so on provide reinforcement of science-table experiences and, of course, also provide many new reading-readiness experiences. In addition, well-monitored field trips can provide training in perceptual learning. Children can be taught what to look for, to "see" rather than merely to look. Such experiences will help build vocabulary and can contribute much to the experiential development so necessary to learning to read.

Demonstrations Children have to see how things work. Five-year-olds are not interested in abstractions. They live in the world of the concrete and are fascinated by "process." For children, words become meaningful only after what a word represents becomes concrete. For example the words *freeze* and *melt* are meaningful to children because youngsters have observed the process of water freezing and melting in nature—or perhaps in the refrigerator. Demonstrations of process in the classroom (or on field trips or television programs) will increase meaningful vocabulary and thus increase readiness. The word *churn,* for example, may become meaningful to a youngster only after seeing the churning process at work in a classroom demonstration of cream being turned into butter.

Holiday and Seasonal Activities Holidays and the changing seasons present many opportunities for experiential development and vocabulary building. In the hands of a skillful readiness teacher, anything from Easter bunnies to autumn leaves can provide developmental experiences for young children. Holiday and seasonal stories, poems, and songs can be used to reinforce such experiences and to build meaningful vocabulary.

Educational Television, Motion Pictures, and Film Strips Educational television, motion pictures, and film strips provide an abundanace of vicarious experiences relevant to readiness. In addition, most contain an element of entertainment which may serve to highlight the "fun" of learning to read. Furthermore they can easily be correlated with other learning activities. A film about Thanksgiving, for example, may be correlated with classroom stories about that holiday. Or the dramatization of a story about a lost pet, say, may be followed by the reading of a story or poem on the same general theme. Here, as with all experiential activities, careful planning is necessary if the optimum benefits for readiness are to be achieved.

Planned Listening Activities Development of good listening skills is an important prerequisite of readiness. Let us look at some of the classroom activities that can help children acquire these skills which, in turn, will help them acquire other skills necessary to the learning-to-read process.

Conversation Conversation is the basic vehicle through which the infant is exposed to the flow of language. Through conversation, he/she "gets the feel" of language and, somehow, comes to sense when language "sounds right" and "doesn't sound right." In short, it is by conversation that the child first begins to really "listen to" the language and first begins to develop listening skills.

Teacher-monitored conversation in the classroom can help further these skills. Normal, low-key conversation should be allowed as the children work together in the classroom. (Bedlam, however, must be avoided. If the noise level of a classroom becomes unbearable, you can be certain that "listening" is no longer occurring.)

In addition, time should be made for conversation between teacher and children so that children can ask and answer questions and discuss their work with the teacher. Listening to the teacher should provide the child with a model to emulate. This means that the teacher should enunciate clearly and speak grammatically in acceptable English syntax. It does not mean that the child's natural tendency to "play" with language and to experiment with it should be curbed. It does mean that the teacher should not regress to substandard speech in order to "communicate" with the child. The child, not the teacher, is to do the emulating.

Countless situations in the readiness year can provide topics for conversation to help perfect listening skills. Snack time might lead into a conversation about table manners. A snow storm could generate a discussion about walking in snow or the difference between snow and rain, or number of related topics.

The leaves are turning color; the birds are flying south; we saw our first Robin; and just a few of the almost endless possibilities.

Listening to Stories Listening to stories read by the teacher is a delight to all children—if they are read with enthusiasm and matching delight. The rapt attention paid to the story is an excellent indication that listening skills are being developed. If at all possible, a regular period of story-reading should be scheduled daily.

Five year olds particularly like so-called "picture books." Such books are published especially for very young children and contain simple-word captions of one or two lines beneath each picture. Many children are able to memorize these captions and thus, in a sense, "read" them. Other types of story books, of course, should also be used as appropriate.

You will sometimes hear the expression "trade book," a term that indicates that a book is sold and may be bought in a commercial bookstore. Such books are thus distinguished from books published strictly for school use such as textbooks and basal readers. There are literally thousands of trade books suitable for reading aloud to five-year-olds. Here are some of the features one should look for in selecting stories to be read to children.

1. The illustrations should be large enough for an entire group of children to see from a distance of 10 feet.
2. The illustrations must be sharp, clear, and colorful. It is best to avoid the grotesque or impressionistic.
3. The book should be so bound that facing double-page spreads can be held open without difficulty.
4. Story line must be in the language of five-year-olds, with only an occasional strange word. Avoid stories that have to be "translated" as they are being read unless you have prepared for this beforehand.
5. Illustrations should correlate with the story segments in which they appear.
6. The story should enable you to act out the parts with your voice and use gestures to generate excitement in the children as they listen.
7. The story should have characters who personify good or evil forces. Not *all* good children's stories do so, but it is characteristic of many of the best.
8. The story should be in a setting which children can imagine, even though they have never been there. "Once upon a time in a far away land . . ." is better than "A decade ago there lived in the town of Swarthmore. . . ." The first is universal; the second is puzzling.
9. The conversation in a story can be in dialect, but be sure you can pronounce the dialect adequately before reading it aloud to children. Remember to change from dialect to standard speech for all parts other than conversation. This may take a bit of doing!
10. First picture books should require no more than 5 minutes to complete. Book lengths may be increased as the readiness year progresses. A maximum of 15

minutes pushes the attention span of many children to the limit, even by the end of the school year.

11. The outcome of the story must be satisfying to little children, leaving them with a feeling of self-fulfillment. Satisfaction is frequently signalled by their applause at the end. You will know almost instantly when a story hits the mark. A few "duds" will help you sense the type of story to avoid.
12. The story should be one that children will like to hear over and over again—a "read-it-again" story. Experience will help you make this kind of judgment.
13. The story must be one that you feel comfortable in reading. You must like it, too, in order to do your part as actor and interpreter.
14. The story should appeal to both boys and girls and should be free of sexist connotations.
15. The story should permit a value judgment concerning the actions of the characters and the outcome.
16. The story should have plot and suspense, with eventual resolution of problems. Avoid open-ended narrative at this point, for children at this age are usually more comfortable with concrete endings.

Such rapt attention and involvment in a story do not "just happen." What planning would you have to do to duplicate the learning experience illustrated in this picture?

17. Don't overlook the "golden oldies." They are perennial favorites because they are universal in characterization, time, place and theme, not just because someone has labeled them "classics."

Listening to Sounds Sounds add reinforcement to experiential and cognitive learning. The simple sound of a dog's bark or a pig's squeal (whether the actual sound or its imitation) may reinforce the experiencing of "dog" and "pig" as prelude to learning the words *dog* and *pig*. On a somewhat higher developmental level, the sound of an angry sea crashing against the rocks may reinforce, and add to, a more complex experience and hence to the learning of more complex language relationships.

Today, fortunately, television and films provide the child with access to many sounds that might not otherwise become part of the child's experience. Through such media, for example, most children are aware of the sound of a crashing sea even though they may never have been near the sea.

But transfer of sound-experience to the reading process is not entirely automatic. The teacher should help the child to make this transfer, particularly through comparison and contrast. "In our story, the big storm blew down the house. Do you think the wind sounded like the crashing sea we saw on television (or read about) yesterday? The wind must have made a very loud noise. Was it like the loud noise of a fire engine's siren?"

As the child learns to discriminate sounds (pitch, intensity, etc.) and apply this discrimination to the learning process, he or she will likely begin to construct "sound" similes ("The refrigerator sounds like a cat purring," etc.). Construction of similes (and other figures of speech) is an important step on the road to reading readiness.

Listening to Words in Context Words are the building blocks of language, and five year olds, through listening and imitating, have long since learned to fit them together in language patterns. They have somehow learned to internalize basic language structure by listening to words in context. This capacity can be capitalized upon in the readiness program.

One very successful approach to this kind of listening activity in the classroom may be found in the "Getting Ready to Read" segment of the Houghton-Mifflin basal reader series. The authors use a kind of "What word makes sense?" technique in their suggested listening activity. The activity might also be called the "give-me-a-word" game. It is an instructional game that children love to play, for it is challenging and fun. The teaching strategy of the game goes like this:

1. "We all know lots of words, but sometimes we can't think of just the *right* word." If we practice thinking of 'just the right word,' maybe we will be able to do it better."
2. "I know a game that I think you will like. We can all play it. It is called "Give Me a Word." Here is how we play."

3. "I am going to say something and you will think of the word that makes sense out of what I say. You will give me that word so I can finish what I am saying. Let's try one."
4. "I opened the book and looked at the. . . . ."

The usual word that five year olds supply to this open-ended statement is *pictures.* But, depending on their past experiences, children might respond with "maps," "pages," "story," "title," "table-of-contents," "book to see if there were any pictures"—which are all endings that make sense.

A simple statement such as "I went wading in the . . ." may elicit responses such as "pool," "ocean," "surf," "bathtub," "stream," "creek," "river," "bay," "mud," "salt-pond," "pond," "lake," "canal," "water," and "lagoon."

This kind of listening activity alerts the child to two important aspects of reading: (a) that sentence context determines the word that finishes the idea and (b) that the particular word that finishes an idea makes a lot of difference in meaning.

Any word supplied by a child can be the nucleus of discussion. "Can we really wade in the bathrub?" "What does it mean, *to wade?*" "How can we wade in a pool?" "Yes, some people have 'wading pools' for children in their yards. Some parks have 'wading pools,' too." "Why do you think they have 'wading pools'?"

The "give me a word" technique can be refined a bit to further implement the readiness process. For example, the teacher might say "I am going to say something, and the word you give must begin with the same beginning sound as /d/ in dog" (or any other beginning sound. Children specially like to use the beginning sound of some child's name as the key sound).

"When I hear music, I feel like . . . . Give me a word that begins with /d/, as in dog."

Listening to words in this kind of refinement of the game requires each child to find a word that "makes sense" in context, and that also begins with the proper sound. The child is thus exposed to two essentials of learning to read: awareness of contextual clues and auditory discrimination of initial consonant sounds.

Whole-word awareness is another skill that may be developed through give-me-a-word techniques. As each child's word is accepted by the teacher, it is printed on the chalkboard or on a paper fastened to an easel. Nothing need be said about how the word looks. Just printing it is enough to demonstrate that the words being printed are the words the children are supplying. When the words that make sense are exhausted, each word is emphasized as a whole word by repeating it, along with the entire sentence, and pointing it out on the list: "I went wading in the pool" (point to *pool*). "I went wading in the ocean" (point to *ocean*). "I went wading in the river" (point to *river*).

As children become proficient in the give-me-a-word game, some of them will want to make up their own open-ended sentences. You should encourage them to do so. But the teacher must insist that the child have a real sentence to say *before* they raise their hands to be selected. Otherwise, much time will be wasted as the child struggles to compose one.

Language Experience Activities Throughout this text, we have emphasized the importance of experiences in learning to read. Let us look now at some classroom activities that allow children to apply their language experiences to the reading process in the readiness year.

Experience Stories One such activity is having the children tell a story based on actual experiences—a story about the children's pets, for example, or about the greening of nature in springtime, or a story based on a trip to the zoo or to the museum. While the child is telling the story, the teacher transcribes it on the chalkboard, or on a pad of large, lined sheets on an easel, called an "experience" or "story chart." Thus, the child sees his or her own words come into being as symbols printed by the teacher. The story remains on the chart over a period of days, where the child can see it over and over again and "read" it with the help of the teacher. The child knows what the words on the chart mean because they are the child's very own words, based upon the child's very own experiences.

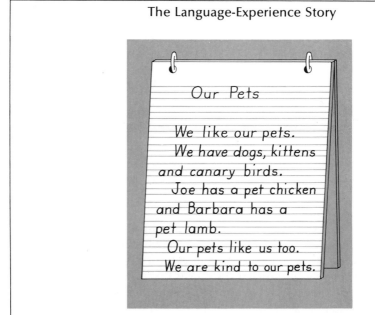

The Language-Experience Story

> Our Pets
>
> We like our pets.
> We have dogs, kittens
> and canary birds.
> Joe has a pet chicken
> and Barbara has a
> pet lamb.
> Our pets like us too.
> We are kind to our pets.

The children compose the elements of the story while the teacher prints it carefully on "story-chart" wide-spaced paper; using a felt-tipped pen. What elements of transfer are possible through this activity?

An Experience Chart is a "Natural" Follow-up to a Field Trip to the Zoo

Our Trip To The Zoo

We went to the zoo on the train. Some mothers went with us.
First we saw the birds.
We liked the white parrots best. Then we saw the snakes and lizzards.
The lions and bears are dangerous. They growled at us.
The monkeys were silly.
Giraffes have long necks.
We saw a mother kangaroo with little Joey in the pocket.
We had fun.

A classroom daily "newspaper" may serve a function similar to the experience charts. Here children dictate stories based on news occurrences

John's Cat is Lost

Louise Is Sick

Someone Broke Our Window Last Night

Antonio's Mother had a Baby Yesterday

which are transcribed by the teacher to a portion of the chalkboard representing the class newspaper. Thus some of the joy and pathos of everday living becomes part of the reading during the readiness year. There is always something to be noted, even though it is just the obvious. Whatever it is, can be written down and everyone can know what the words are and can "read" it.

Show-and-Tell Show-and-Tell time is another, and very popular, language-experience activity for readiness enhancement. It is indeed likely to be a "show," full of surprises and dramatic turns. There will be snakes and lizards pulled out of pockets. (The teacher can only pray that the things are harmless.) One little fellow of our acquaintance came to Show-and-Tell with a glass jar containing his recently removed tonsils! There will be show treasures lost on the way to school (which can lead to a lesson on caring for one's possessions). There will be personal matters and family secrets bared that shouldn't be bared anywhere, let alone in a kindergarten. (The alert teacher will quickly shift the subject in such instances.) Mind-boggling fancies will be presented as prosaic facts. (Separating fact and fancy will be up to the teacher.)

Fun and excitement notwithstanding, Show-and-Tell is a valuable readiness activity. Performers and audience alike get to practice language experiences to help increase comprehension and vocabulary. Most importantly, the children will be encouraged to turn to books and other materials about the subjects and objects met in Show-and-Tell time. The experienced teacher will learn to anticipate what objects are most likely to show up on Show-and-Tell sessions and can provide accordingly for correlated reading materials.

Obviously, Show-and-Tell activities call for careful planning and ground rules if they are not to deteriorate into something like a theater of the absurd. The ground rules should be relatively rigid and clearly explained to the children. Here are some suggested rules for Show-and-Tell time as the teacher might present them:

1. Each child will have a chance, but only a few will show-and-tell each day.
2. We will take turns. If you show-and-tell one day, you will be a listener while others show-and-tell. Do you know why?
3. We want to hear about really special things. Don't just bring any old thing. Bring something very special. (Give a few examples). Do you know why?
4. We will all listen while someone is showing and telling so we can learn a lot. Also, we want to be courteous. We want to show that we are glad that person brought such an interesting thing to tell us about.
5. If you are going to bring anything from home, be sure your mother or father says it is alright to bring it. We wouldn't want something that is very valuable to get lost.
6. Anything that is brought from home will be placed on the take-home table. It is *not* to be touched after Show-and-Tell time by anyone except the person who brought it. Do you know why?
7. Some days we will just "tell" about something, because we might not be able to bring it to school. Can anyone think of an example? ("A new baby has been born." "I went to see a circus." etc.)
8. Sometimes one of you may just sing a new song you have learned. That will be fun, too. Maybe we all can learn the song too.
9. We must never bring any dangerous thing to show. Do you know why? What might be a dangerous thing that we shouldn't bring?

10. If we want to bring a pet, we should talk it over with the teacher the day before. Do you know why? (There may be a problem of keeping the pet in school during the day. Most readiness rooms find it advisable to have a cage for "visiting pets."
11. We must know what we want to say before we get up to show-and-tell. Do you know why?

All this routine may sound very stilted, but it is necessary for five-year-olds. They will feel secure in having a part in discussing the "why?" for these operational rules. Children of this age are anxious to operate under regulations that provide fairness and reason, and they insist upon conformity from their peers and teacher. Without these strategies, Show-and-Tell can become a disaster.

Role Playing Role playing can also be used as a language-experience activity. The teacher can assign roles for the children or the roles may be chosen by the children themselves. Most commonly, the children will choose mother and father roles. The kindergarten should have a "housekeeping corner" (homemaker area or "home") equipped with scaled-down replicas of various home furnishings (appliances, dolls, etc.). Ideally, experiences and interests arising from role playing will not only enhance comprehension and vocabulary but will also lead to interest in relevant reading materials. (One sign of changing times may be seen in the fact that mother and father roles are no longer rigidly differentiated by the children. "Mothers" feel free to drive trucks and fire engines; "fathers" may do dishes and take care of the children.)

Dramatization and Puppetry Dramatization and puppet play can provide excellent language experiences. Both are, of course, types of role playing, and offer much the same readiness opportunities as that activity. In addition, acting out the parts of a story reinforces its impact and, by extension, reinforces interest in reading in general. Dramatization also gives the young child practice in following the story line, the "thread of the story." The ability to follow the story line is one indication of reading readiness.

Planned Perceptual Activities The readiness program usually includes a variety of planned activities designed to quicken and sharpen sensory awareness (perception). In Chapter 1, we noted that perception has its origin in our sensory modalities, vision, hearing, feeling, and so on, and that it is through these modalities that we learn to perceive letters and words. We also noted that perception is a multisensory process.

Perceptual readiness activities should also be multisensory, employing visual, auditory, kinesthetic, and tactile modalities—or, VAKT as they are sometimes referred to for short. VAKT perceptual training activities have been in use since the inception of the kindergarten movement in Europe more than a century ago. In fact many of the VAKT strategies employed by Pestalozzi (Swiss, 1746−1827), Rousseau (French, 1844−1910), and Montessori (Italian, 1870−1952) are, with some adaptations, being used today in many kindergartens.

Auditory-Perceptual Training In Chapter 1 we noted that researchers hold conflicting views on the value of auditory training as a factor in reading. In spite of such conflict, there seems to be considerable reason to believe that it is helpful for children to be *taught* to attend to significant auditory differences and similarities in words in isolation. As linguists have learned, a *phoneme* is the smallest distinctive unit of a language. For example, the phoneme /p/ is what distinguishes *pip* from *nip* and *tip,* and *rumble* from *rumple.* If it is true that phonemes signal differences, it seems logical to train children to attend to these differences. The usual routine is as follows:

"I am going to say two words that you know. Listen to them and see if you can tell whether or not the two words are the same or different: *pie/pig.*" This kind of activity leads to discrimination of "minimal pairs" and most reading specialists believe it to be a valid prereading strategy.

Later in the kindergarten year, it may be fruitful to have children listen to whole sentences that are similar or contrasting to train them for attending to meaning as well as phonemes. For example, the teacher might pair sentences such as "The boy went to the store," and "the boy sent for more" or "Sandra had a little cat" and "Andy has a baseball bat."

Visual-Perceptual Training Visual letter discrimination is another perceptual skill that can be practiced during the readiness year. It is not necessary that the learner be able to give the names of the letters. All the learner is required to do is indicate whether or not a letter is similar to the shape of another, or different. (Because of TV programs such as *Sesame Street* many young children arrive at kindergarten already able to name letters.)

Until recently, most visual-discrimination practice was done with shapes of objects, rather than with letter and/or word shapes. It was assumed that five year olds would be more successful if they were asked to "Find the ball that is the same as the one on the left," or "Mark the kitten that is different from the others." These were the usual tasks in the readiness workbooks of past decades. However, learning psychologists have discovered that children can just as easily learn to differentiate letter and word shapes as to differentiate bunnies with and without ears. This is no momentous discovery, but it does allow the teacher to conserve learning time and to make learning more directly related to the real tasks ahead. The psychological principal involved is "learn in the manner in which the learning will be used." Since readiness activities are meant to lead to the identification of letters and words, it is far more productive to spend activity time on letters and words than to spend it discriminating squares, triangles, circles, rabbits without ears, or whatever.

Directional Training In the readiness year, children learn the "look" of their own names, and of the names of their classmates. When they begin to print their names, some youngsters may exhibit directionality reversals: treboR for Robert, ennaoJ for Joanne.

Parents can easily become overanxious about this problem, and, consequently, they should, if necessary, be warned against considering it as an indication of dyslexia or "brain damage" calling for immediate, extensive (and expensive) professional help. Reversals are quite common in these early years and should not be cause for undue alarm. After all, directionality from left-to-right in our English language is a learned skill. Children must acquire it. They are not born with it any more than Israeli children are born with right-to-left directionality. Most children will have established left-to-right progression by about the age of six.

Materials such as the *Frostig Developmental Program in Visual Perception* have been used for directional training, but such tests may merely help the child obtain higher scores on the next such test. The old and simple teacher technique of moving the hand across the page or chalkboard from left to right and then asking the child to indicate which direction the hand moved may actually be more productive. Pointing, once taboo with teachers, is also an effective means of helping the child focus and move the eyes from left-to-right in sweeps. A card or ruler can also be used to help the child's eyes move more easily across a line of print.

AIDS AND MATERIALS FOR THE READINESS PROGRAM

Throughout this chapter we have, in passing, mentioned various teaching aids available to the readiness teacher. Almost any appropriate material, from chalkboard to housekeeping corner, can be a teaching aid in the hands of an imaginative teacher. There are, however, several more or less standardized aids and devices commonly used in the readiness classroom and with which you should be familiar:

The Montessori Circle, Square, and Triangle Practically all readiness training programs include visual perception exercises using the Montessori circle, square, and triangle. Some use additional shapes: star, crescent, diamond, and rectangle.

Most Montessori-type kindergartens have "form boards," a large board with cut-out sections into which are fitted corresponding shapes of circles, squares, and triangles usually in three sizes each.

The objective claimed for these exercises is that they aid the child in discriminating shapes and sizes. There may or may not be a direct transfer of this skill in reading. The inability to perform these tasks is, however, an indication that the child is not "ready" to learn to read. It also may be an indication of visual-motor disorganization, or of visual-motor immaturity.

Workbooks for Matching Shapes   In workbook matching, the child selects a cardboard shape and places it upon one of the same size and shape in the workbook. The workbook figures are usually printed in different colors as well as different sizes and shapes. The child must select the disc, for example, that is equal in size to the circle in the workbook and also is the same color.

It may be difficult to justify this activity as a reading-readiness exercise, but it is generally argued that letters are made of circles, vertical lines, and slanted lines, as are the workbook shapes. Dr. Renee Fuller and her associates trained several severely retarded individuals to read through the use of three basic shapes: circle, vertical line, and V-shape, labeled, "ball," "bat," and "bird." She reported that her subjects' success in learning to read may be largely credited to their ability in learning to discriminate the shapes.

Parquetry Blocks   Parquetry blocks may also be used for exercises involving the matching and positioning of shapes. The mosaics made from the blocks are usually entirely composed of triangular shapes, with contrasting colors accounting for the design.

Simple parquetry designs may be followed by more complicated patterns as the child becomes more proficient in this task. It is logical to assume that parquetry work helps develop visual concentration, which skill may be transferred to the task of visual discrimination of letters and words. However, we know that such transfer is not automatic. There must be training for transfer of skill as well as for attainment of the skill in the first place.

Mazes   We have already mentioned that directionality is one of the necessary skills in reading. Following a maze can help develop a child's awareness of direction. Although a maze pattern does not necessarily proceed from left to right, finding one's way through a maze has always been an intriguing pastime for children.

Rough-Surface Letters   Rough-surface letters have been used for decades as a learning device to help develop kinesthetic and tactile skills. Dr. Maria Montessori used them at the turn of the century with children from the slums of Rome. Later, Dr. Grace Fernald reported their successful use with remedial-reading students and incorporated them as part of the now-famous "Fernald Technique."

The child who traces over the rough surface of sandpaper or flocked letters utilizes kinesthetic and tactile learning modalities to reinforce auditory and visual pathways. The letters are easily obtainable and flocking can be applied by means of a flocking spray (Christmas "snow"). Sandpaper letters can be made by attaching letters to the back of the paper with rubber cement and then cutting them out. More-permanent sandpaper alphabets can be made with plywood backing. Sandpaper or flocked letters should be a part of every readiness program.

(In a related exercise, some teachers have reported success in using "sky writing." The child with eyes closed, traces a letter in the air after seeing the letter in print and watching the teacher trace its shape in the air. Others have reported that having one child trace a letter on the back of another child helps both the tracer and "tracee" to develop letter discrimination.)

Stencils   Like sandpaper letters, stencils help develop kinesthetic and tactile skills as a child traces around the inner periphery of letters. Stencils are familiar to many children by the time they reach kindergarten, having used them around the home to trace objects for fun. Cookie cutters at home have often provided hours of fun for tracing. But tracing around cookie shapes is not as effective for transfer of learning to the reading process as tracing the actual shapes of letters.

Cut Pictures   Cut picture exercises call for matching the parts of a picture that has been cut in two. Such exercises are, of course, exercises in visual-perceptual discrimination, but one is hard-pressed to identify their direct—or even indirect—contribution to reading readiness.

Consonant Picture Cards   Consonant-picture cards depict common animals and objects. The child sorts out the pictures to match them with the beginning consonant sounds of the name of the object or animal depicted. For example, pictures of *horse, hen, hand, head* would be matched with the letter *h* and/or the sound /h/. Before this "game" can be played, a child must know (in this instance) the /h/ sound and must be able to identify the beginning consonant sounds of words beginning with /h/. Consequently, it may be just a fun game that allows the child to practice skills the child has already developed. On the other hand children without these skills who play the game with a buddy who already knows the initial consonant sounds and letter correspondences may profit greatly from it.

Visual-Perceptual Worksheets   Visual-perceptual worksheets are spirit-master ditto sheets designed for concentrated practice in visual perception. Teachers have long used such commercially produced sheets (published by Continental Press). More recently, Frostig's *Developmental Program in Visual Perception,* is strikingly similar in many respects to the older worksheets that appeared on the market.

There is, however, little research evidence that visual-perceptual paperwork leads to significant improvement in reading readiness and none at all that such work can be directly transferred to discrimination of letters and words. On the other hand, some children are greatly in need of improvement in general visual perception. For such children, worksheets may help meet this need.

Picture Sequence   Story-line pictures consist of a series of three, four, or five pictures which the children arrange in sequence so that they tell a story. The pictures can consist of just two or three sequential events. For example:

1. chicken on nest;
2. chicken cackling over freshly laid egg;
3. egg being fried in pan.

Another sequence might be:

1. Father gives girl and boy each a large coin.
2. They examine it and talk over what they might purchase with it.
3. They run together to the ice cream peddler's cart on the street.
4. They both enjoy their ice cream cones.

The mounted pictures are placed in scrambled sequence on the chalk rail. The event portrayed in each picture is discussed separately, giving each child adequate time to relate his or her own experiences to the picture and to postulate on its meaning. The group then reaches a decision as to which event comes first, next, and so on. Each child is encouraged to support his or her decision with logical reasons.

After several training sessions of this sort, most children can take a set of pictures illustrating a sequence of events common to their environmental experiences and place them in sequence and then tell a story from them. The teacher can expect only minimal concepts at first, such as "First the dog saw the cat, then he chased the cat, then the cat ran up a tree," and so on. Later in the readiness year, children should be able to take a set of five or more sequence pictures and place them in proper order and then concoct a delightful story, replete with dialogue and dramatic narration. This development will not, however, happen of its own accord. (Picture sequences help foster creativity as well as reading readiness.)

Flannel Board   The flannel board is one of the most valuable pieces of equipment for group work. Generally it is about 80 × 100 cm, covered with flannel cloth, and placed on an easel low enough to be at the eye level of five year olds. Flocked letters, words, and phrases will adhere to the flannel surface. They can be repositioned at will in demonstrating letter and word relationships and constructing verbal concepts.

Attendance Name Cards   During the early part of the readiness year, an effort is usually made to help each child print his/her own name. To foster this skill, the teacher prints each child's name on a separate attendance card, large enough for the entire group to see. Attendance is taken by holding up the card and asking that the child raise his or her hand when the child's name is recognized. Other children soon begin to recognize names of their classmates, at which time a giant step has been taken toward whole-word recognition.

During this routine, many children will learn what sounds and/or letters their own names begin with. Capitalizing on this fact, while calling out a name, the teacher, should encourage the children to point out other people in the room whose names also begin with the same sound, and, at the same time, the teacher should remind the children that the names all begin with the same letter, too. (Children's names are also listed on the board in connection with certain classroom duties, which also aids in name recognition by kindergartners.)

What may seem to be incidental learning is actually planned readiness practice in visual and auditory perceptual discrimination of actual words.

Object Labels

Inasmuch as much beginning reading will be whole-word recognition, it is useful to place name labels on common objects in the kindergarten, such as *chair, table, desk, piano, radio, turtle, bird, books, guppies, window, clock,* and so on. These word symbols should be pointed out frequently and discussed so the kindergartners will get the concept of names in print and will begin to acquire the ability of identifying whole words. These words may not be the most useful in their sight vocabulary, but skills learned in this practice in visual discrimination of names of real things can be transferred to the learning of other sight words. We will discuss this process in more detail in another chapter. Suffice it to say here that children who have not been exposed to this prereading routine are in general slower in recognizing sight words when they commence reading.

BIBLIOGRAPHY

Allen, R. Van, and Clarice Allen, *Language Experiences in Reading*, Chicago: Encyclopaedia Britannica Educational Corporation, 1967

Barrett, Thomas C., "The Relationship between Measures of Prereading Visual Discrimination and First-Grade Reading Achievement: A Review of the Literature," *Reading Research Quarterly*, **1** (1965), 51–76.

Beck, Isabel, "A Longitudinal Study of the Reading Achievement Effects of Formal Reading Instruction in the Kindergarten," unpublished doctoral dissertation, University of Pittsburgh, 1973.

Bernetta, Sister M., "Visual Readiness and Developmental Visual Perception for Reading," *Journal of Developmental Reading,* **5** (1962), 82–86.

Bijou, Sidney W., "Development in the Preschool Years," *American Psychologist,* **10** (1975), 829–838.

Bogatz, Gerry Ann, and Samuel Ball, *A Survey of the Major Findings in the Second Year of Sesame Street,* Princeton: Educational Testing Services, 1971.

Bolig, J. R., and G. O. Fletcher, "The Metropolitan Readiness Test versus Ratings of Kindergarten Teachers as Predictors of Success in First Grade," *Educational Leadership,* **30** (1973), 637–639.

Brekke, Beverly, and John D. Williams, "Teachers' Prediction of Reading Readiness," *Perceptual and Motor Skills,* **37** (1973), 521–522.

Bremmer, N., "Do Readiness Tests Predict Success in Reading?", *Elementary School Journal,* **59**:4 (1959), 222–224.

Calfee, Robert C., "Diagnostic Evaluation of Visual, Auditory, and General Language Factors in Prereaders," paper presented to Annual Convention, American Psychological Association, Honolulu, September, 1972.

Chissom, Brad S., Jerry R. Thomas, and Delores G. Collins, "Relationships Among Perceptual-Motor Measures and their Correlations with Academic Readiness in Preschool Children)" *Perceptual and Motor Skills,* **39** (1974), 467–523.

Ching, Doris C., "The Teaching of Reading in Kindergarten," *California Journal of Educational Research,* **23** (1972), 156–162.

Church, Marilyn, "Does Visual Perceptual Training Help Beginning Readers?" *Reading Teacher,* **27**:4 (1974), 361–364. When the Frostig program was compared with the non-Frostig program, there were no significant differences between the two groups of kindergartners, in reading readiness.

Clay, Marie M., *Reading: The Patterning of Complex Behaviour,* Auckland: Heinemann Educational Books, 1972.

Clay, Marie M., *Test of Concepts in Print,* Auckland: Heinemann Educational Books, 1974.

Cochrane, Kathleen J., "Reading Readiness Tests: A Survey of Current Trends," *Exceptional Child,* **23**:2 (1976), 119–127.

Cullinan, Bernice E., "Changing Perspectives in Black English and Reading," *Reading Instruction Journal,* **18** (1975), 32.

deHirsch, Katrina, Jeannette J. Jansky, and William S. Langford, *Predicting Reading Failure,* New York: Harper & Row, 1966. A ten-test battery for determining kindergartner's overall readiness for formal learning experiences.

deHirsch, Katrina and Jeannette J. Jansky, "Early Prediction of Reading, Writing, and Spelling Ability," in *Corrective Reading in the Elementary Classroom*, Marjorie S. Johnson and Roy A. Kress (Editors), Newark, DE:International Reading Association, 1967.

Downing, John, and Sara Lundsteen, "Understanding New Perspectives of Early Childhood," in *Handbook for Administrators and Teachers; Reading in the Kindergarten*, Lloyd O. Ollila (Editor), Newark, DE: International Reading Association, 1980, 18–41.

Dunn-Rankin, P., "The Similarity of Lower-Case Letters of the English Alphabet," *Journal of Verbal Learning and Verbal Behavior*, **7** (1968), 990–995.

Durkin, Dolores, "A Language Arts Program for Pre-First-Grade Children: Two-Year Achievement Report," *Reading Research Quarterly*, **V**:4 (1970), 534–565.

Durkin, Dolores, "Reading Readiness," *Reading Teacher*, **23**:6 (1970), 528–534.

Durkin, Dolores, "A Six-Year Study of Children Who Learned to Read in School at the Age of Four," *Reading Research Quarterly*, **10**:1 (1974–1975), 9–61.

Durkin, Dolores, "Facts About Pre-First-Grade Reading," in *The Kindergarten Child and Reading*, Lloyd O. Ollila (Editor) Newark, DE: International Reading Association, 1977, 1–12.

Dykstra, Robert, "Auditory Discrimination Abilities and Beginning Reading Achievement," *Reading Research Quarterly*, **1** (1966), 5–34.

Eimas, P. "Linguistic Processing of Speech by Young Infants," in *Language Perspectives*, R. Schiefelbusch (Editor), Baltimore: University Park Press, 1974, 55–74.

Evans, James R., and Linda J. Smith, "Psycholinguistic Skills of Early Readers," *Reading Teacher*, **30**:1 (1976), 39–43.

Ferguson, Charles A., and Dan Isaac Slobin (Editors), *Studies of Child Language Development*, New York: Holt, Rinehart, and Winston, 1973.

Fredericksen, Carl H., "Discourse Comprehension and Early Reading," in *Theory and Practice of Early Reading*, Lauren B. Resnick and Phyllis A. Weaver (Editors), Hillsdale, NJ: Erlbaum, 1980.

Gates, Arthur, I., "The Necessary Mental Age for Beginning Reading," *Elementary School Journal*, **37** (1937), 498–508.

Goins, Jean T., "Visual Perceptual Abilities and Early Reading Progress,"

Supplementary Educational Monographs, No. 87, University of Chicago Press, 1958.

Goldin-Meadow, Susan, Martin E. P. Seligman, and Rochel Gelman, "Language in the Two-Year Old," *Cognition,* **4**:2 (1976), 189—201.

Goodman, Kenneth S., "Do You Have to Be Smart to Read? Do You Have to Read to Be Smart?" *Reading Teacher,* **28**:7 (1975), 625—632.

Gredler, Gilbert R., "Readiness for School: A Look at Some Critical Issues," in *Reading and Related Skills,* Margaret Clark and Alastair Milne (Editors), London: Ward Lock Educational, 1973, 37—45.

Hammon, S., "Sound Polluted Schools," *School Management,* **14** (1970), 14—15.

Herber, Harold H., *Teaching in the Content Areas,* Englewood Cliffs, NJ: Prentice-Hall, 1973.

Hoffman, Earl, "Pre-Kindergarten Experiences and Their Relationships to Reading Achievement," *Illinois School Research,* **8**:1 (1971), 6—12.

Hoffman, Stevie, and H. Thompson Fillmer, "Thought, Language, and Reading Readiness," *The Reading Teacher,* **33**:3 (1979), 290—294.

Hurley, Oliver L., Alfred Hirshoren, and Jacob T. Hunt, "The Development of Auditory Sequential Memory in Young Black and White Children," *Journal of Educational Research,* **70**:2 (1976), 83—86. "In every comparison, White children scored higher."

Karlin, Robert, "The Prediction of Reading Success and Reading Readiness Tests," *Elementary English,* **34** (1957), 320—322.

Kind, Ethel M., and Doris T. Friesen, "Children Who Read in Kindergarten," *Alberta Journal of Educational Research,* **18**:1 (1972), 147—161.

King, Ethel, and Siegmar Muehl, "Effects of Visual Discrimination Training on Immediate and Delayed Word Recognition in Kindergarten Children," *Alberta Journal of Educational Research,* **17** (1971), 77—87.

Lamoreaux, Lillian, and Doris M. Lee, *Learning to Read Through Experience,* New York: Appleton-Century-Crofts, 1943. Later, revised by Doris Lee and Roach Van Allen, 1963.

Lavine, Linda O., "Differentiation of Letterlike Forms in Prereading Children," *Developmental Psychology,* **13**:2 (1977), 89—94.

Leibert, Robert E., and John E. Sherk, "Three Frostig Visual Perception Sub-tests and Specific Reading Tasks for Kindergarten, First-, and Second-Grade Children," *Reading Teacher,* **24**:2 (1970), 130—137.

Lewis, M., and S. Goldberg, "The Acquisition and Violation of Expectancy: An Experimental Paradigm," *Journal of Experimental Child Psychology,* **7** (1969),

70–80. A study of abilities of young children in identifying shapes, objects, etc., from printed symbols.

Loban, Walter, *Language Development: Kindergarten Through Grade Twelve.* Urbana, IL: National Council of Teachers of English, 1976.

Lober, Linda W., "Auditory Discrimination and Classroom Noise," *Reading Teacher,* **27**:3 (1973), 288–291.

McCormick, J., "The Effect of Perceptual-Motor Training on Reading Achievement," *Academic Therapy Quarterly,* **4** (1969), 171–176.

McCormack, P. D., "Language as an Attribute of Memory," *Canadian Journal of Psychology,* **30**:4 (1976), 238–248.

MacGinitie, Walter H., "Evaluating Readiness for Learning to Read: A Critical Review and Evaluation of Research," *Reading Research Quarterly,* **4** (1969), 396–410.

Marsh, G., and M. Sherman, "Kindergarten Children's Discrimination and Production of Phonemes in Isolation and in Words," *Southwest Regional Laboratory Technical Memorandum* No. TM-2-71-07, 1971.

Mason, Jana M., "When Do Children Begin to Read: An Exploration of Four-Year-Old Children's Letter- and Word-Reading Competencies," *Reading Research Quarterly,* **XV**:2 (1980), 203–237.

Mitchell, Blythe C., "The Metropolitan Readiness Tests as Predictors of First Grade Achievement," *Educational and Psychological Measurement,* **22** (1962), 765–772.

Morphett, Mabel V., and Carelton Washburne, "When Should Children Begin to Read?", *Elementary School Journal,* **31** (1931), 496–503.

Mustico, Thomas W., "Some Implications from Paired Associate Learning on the Development of Reading Readiness," in *20th Yearbook, National Reading Conference,* 1971, Frank P. Greene (Editor), 283–291.

Nurss, Joanne R., "The Schedule: Organizing for Individual Instruction," in *The Kindergarten Child and Reading,* Lloyd O. Ollila (Editor), Newark, DE: International Reading Association, 1977, pp. 56–76.

Ollila, Lloyd O. (Editor) *The Kindergarten Child and Reading,* Newark, DE: International Reading Association, 1977.

Ollila, Lloyd O., Jean Dey, and Kathleen Ollila, "What Is the Function of Kindergarten Reading Materials?" in *The Kindergarten Child and Reading,* Lloyd O. Ollila, Editor, Newark, DE: International Reading Association, 1977, 68–80.

Ollila, Lloyd O., "What Have We Learned About Kindergarten Reading Programs?" in *Handbook for Administrators and Teachers; Reading in the Kindergarten*, Llloyd O. Ollila (Editor), Newark, DE: International Reading Association, 1980, 1–17.

Otto, Wayne, and Carole Pizillo, "Effect of Intralist Similarity on Kindergarten Pupils' Rate of Word Acquisition and Transfer," *Journal of Reading Behavior,* **3**:1 (1970–1971), 14–19.

Paradis, Edward E., "The Appropriateness of Visual Discrimination Exercises in Reading Readiness Materials," *Journal of Educational Research,* **67**(1974), 276–278.

Phillips, Mary, "Reading In English Infant Schools," *Minnesota Reading Quarterly,* **15**:2 (1970), 41–47.

Pryzwansky, Walter B., "Effects of Perceptual-Motor Training and Manuscript Writing on Reading Readiness Skills in Kindergarten," *Journal of Educational Psychology,* **63** (1972), 110–115.

Randel, Mildred A., Maurice A. Fry, and Elizabeth M. Ralls, "Two Readiness Measures as Predictors of First-Grade and Third-Grade Reading Achivement," *Psychology in the Schools* **14**:1 (1977), 37–40.

Read, Charles, "Preschool Children's Knowledge of English Phonology," *Harvard Educational Review,* **41** (1971), 1–34.

Resnick, Lauren B., "Theories and Prescriptions for Early Reading Instruction," in *Theory and Practice of Early Reading*, Lauren B. Resnick and Phyllis A. Weaver (Editors), Hillsdale, NJ: Erlbaum, 1980.

Robertson, Jean E., "Kindergarten Perception Training: Its Effect on First Grade Reading," in *Perception and Reading*, Helen K. Smith (Editor), International Reading Association *Proceedings,* **12**:4 (1968), 93–98.

Robinson, Helen M., "Visual and Auditory Modalities Related to Methods for Beginning Reading, *Reading Research Quarterly,* **VIII**:1 (1972), 7–39.

Robinson, Violet B., Dorothy S. Strickland, and Bernice Cullinan, "The Child: Ready or Not?" in *The Kindergarten Child and Reading*, Lloyd O. Ollila (Editor), Newark, DE: International Reading Association, 1977, 13–39.

Rosner, Jerome, "Auditory Analysis Training with Pre-Readers," *Reading Teacher,* **27** (1974), 379–384.

Roser, Nancy L. "Electric Company Critique: Can Great be Good Enough?" *Reading Teacher,* **27**:7 (1974), 680–684.

Royal, Mildred, "Performance Objectives and C-R Tests—We Wrote Our Own!" *Reading Teacher,* **27**:7 (1972), 701–703. This article presents 20 readiness objectives agreed upon by a group of kindergarten teachers.

Rubin, Rosalyn, "Sex Differences in Effects of Kindergarten Attendance on Development of School Readiness and Language Skills," *Elementary School Journal,* **72** (1972), 265–274.

Rubin, Rosalyn, A., "Preschool Application of the Metropolitan Readiness Tests," *Educational and Psychological Measurement,* **34** (1974), 417–422.

Rubin, Rosalyn, and Bruce Balow, "A Comparison of Pre-Kindergarten and Pre-First-Grade Boys and Girls on Measures of School Readiness and Language Development," Department of Special Education, University of Minnesota, August, 1968.

Rubin, Rosalyn A., and O. Lyle, "The Relationship of Speech Articulation to School Readiness, Reading Achivement, and Other Language Skills," Department of Psychoeducational Studies, University of Minnesota, September, 1974.

Sanders, D., "Noise Conditions in Normal School Classrooms," *Exceptional Children,* **32** (1965), 344–353.

Scherwitzky, Marjorie, "Reading in the Kindergarten: A Survey in Virginia, *Young Children,* **29** (1974), 161–169.

Scollon, Ronald, *Conversations With a One Year Old,* University of Hawaii Press, 1976.

Silberberg, N. E., M. D. Silberberg, and I. A. Iverson, "The Effects of Kindergarten Instruction in Alphabet and Numbers on First-grade Reading, *Journal of Learning Disabilities,* **5** (1972), 7–12.

Smith, Helen K., (Editor) *Perception and Reading,* Part 4, Vol 12. *Annual Proceedings, International Reading Association,* 1968. This entire volume contains many significant reports on the relationship of various aspects of perception and beginning reading.

Springle, Herbert J., "Who Wants to Live on Sesame Street?" *Young Children,* **28** (1972), 91–109.

Stanchfield, Jo M., "The Development of Pre-Reading Skills in an Experimental Kindergarten Program," *Elementary School Journal,* **71** (1971), 438–447.

Telegdy, G. A., "The Effectiveness of Four Readiness Tests as Predictors of First-Grade Academic Achievement," *Psychology in the Schools,* **12** (1975), 4–11.

Veatch, Jeannette, *Reading in the Elementary School.* New York: Wiley, 1978.

Vukelich, Carol, and Ian Beattie, "Teaching Reading in the Kindergarten: A Review of Recent Studies," *Childhood Education.* **48** (1972), 327–329.

Wallbrown, Jane D., Fred H. Wallbrown, and Ann W. Engin, "The Relative Importance of Mental Age and Selected Assessors of Auditory and Visual Perception in the Metropolitan Readiness Test," *Psychology in the Schools,* **11** (1974), 136–143.

Webster, J., "The Effects of Noise on Speech Intelligibility," in *Noise as a Public Health Hazard,* W. Ward and J. Fricke (Editors), Washington, DC: American Speech and Hearing Association, 1969, 40–48.

Willems, Arnold L., and Wanda L., "Please, Read Me a Book!" *Language Arts,* **52**:6 (1975), 831–835. Good bibliography of books for preschool children.

Williams, Joanna P., "Training Kindergarten Children to Discriminate Letter-Like Forms," *American Educational Research Journal,* **6** (1969), 501–514.

CHAPTER THREE

How Do I Teach
Beginning Reading?

For centuries, children have memorized the looks of words, and parents have been delighted when their young offspring have been able to perform well in pronouncing those memorized words. Although no knowledgeable person would accept such performances as being "reading," nevertheless, we must admit that it is a step toward reading. But pronounciation alone, is not enough.

For generations, children have memorized rules such as "*i* before *e*, except after *c* . . ."; "When an *e* is added to a 3-letter word (CVC+e), the *e* is silent and the preceding vowel is long." But rules alone cannot teach a child to read!

Here and abroad, choruses of young children have intoned vowel sounds and have spit and spluttered consonants and blends, the purpose being to "sound-out" words according to a sequencing of phonics sounds. But, a knowledge of phonics does not, by itself, produce a good reader.

Many young children are able to listen to a story being read and are able to memorize and repeat the story, "word-for-word." Those who possess such excellent verbal memory can fake the reading of a story up to a point, but are certain to be caught when turning a page too soon or too late. In one sense they are employing two of the elements of reading. They are moving through the story in sequence and are using the vocabulary with alterations. But we cannot concede that they are actually reading.

If these are *not* reading; yet are elements *of* reading, they cannot be mutually exclusive, but must be considered together. In so doing, we must struggle with the questions:

Does a child learn to read by memorizing whole words?

Is a knowledge of the ABCs part of reading?

Are there any rules that help an individual to learn to read?

Is a knowledge of phonics an essential element?

Does listening to stories promote the ability to read?

And finally, how does one put it all together?

There *are* some answers to these questions, and we present a number of them on the pages that follow.

In the previous chapter we emphasized the individual differences in the readiness of children. Some children will be ready to respond to almost any proper technique you may choose to use. Others may need enormous amounts of preparation and careful guidance before your chosen methods and materials will be truly effective. Other children are somehow able, without direct instruction, to excerpt the common elements of our printed language and to develop their own phonics and pronounciation schemes. Observation of such children in action indicates that they possess unusual drives to master the system of reading; that they have persistence to ask: "What is this word?" and "What is that word?"; and that they concentrate their efforts on materials that are meaningful and satisfying to them.

How you begin should not be *laissez faire,* haphazard, unstructured. In our many years of work with children who were beginning to learn to read, we have observed three things:

1. There are some strategies that, if omitted from beginning reading instruction (either purposefully or accidentally) will almost assuredly result in poor or even "disabled" readers.
2. There are some skills that are common to all successful beginning readers.
3. There are some fundamental skills that can be segmented into units, steps, components, kernels, modules, bits-and-pieces, or whatever one wishes to call them.

WHEN DO I BEGIN?

Several decades ago, a number of research studies attempted to determine the optimum *mental age* necessary for successful beginning reading. Two such studies were undertaken in 1931. They reported that "very little, if any, progress was made by those children with a mental age below 6½, and that the percentage of children making 'satisfactory' reading progress rose sharply at a mental age of six years-six months."

In the half-century since those results were published, there has been strong debate, considerable misinterpretation, and vastly different notions concerning the nature of intelligence. Although most reading specialists tend to ignore mental age *per se* as the prime factor among the many facets of readiness, there is little doubt that one's ability to function intellectually has a definite bearing on one's ability to learn

WHEN-TO-BEGIN SIGNALS

How does the child signal readiness? Or, as the professional educator might put it, "How does the child manifest 'entry skills' that indicate readiness to enter the reading process?"

SPOKEN LANGUAGE

The child does so in a variety of ways, particularly in the child's patterns of speech and reactions to printed symbols. The child's speaking vocabulary and language facility can be a signal of readiness (or nonreadiness). Is the vocabulary varied and appropriately used? Is the child able to speak in complex sentences? Or does the child rely solely on strings of simple sentences? Does the child use adjectives and adverbs to modify and embellish statements? Or does the child rarely do so? Does the child make a conscious effort to investigate the meanings of words so they can be made part of his or her expanding vocabulary? Signals that the child is doing this are questions such as "What does that word mean, Mommy?" "I don't know what such-and-such word means." "That's a funny word. Why do they say it that way?" and so on.

Many children come to the classroom having already learned to internalize a variety of graphic visual designs and symbols—Mickey Mouse, Smokey the Bear, McDonald's double arch, the hexagon shape of a stop sign. Some children, however, have developed little or no such awareness. More closely relevant to reading, some children will signal readiness by their already-acquired ability to discriminate and internalize certain letters and words common to their environment.

Does the child respond to the efforts of educational television programs such as *Sesame Street* and *The Electric Company* to inculcate awareness of letter names (alphabet) and word development? Is the child able to identify particular letters on a scrambled-letter chart? Does the child try to make words out of moveable letters on blocks, *Scrabble, Anagrams,* letter tabs, and so on? Does the child want to print letters? Does the child exhibit aptitude for identifying and remembering words in print? Can he or she "find" a particular word that appears several times in a story? Does the child show satisfaction and excitement in recognizing whole words ("I know *that* one! And *that* one!")?

ATTENTION SPAN

In general, an attention span of less than five minutes indicates nonreadiness. Our most successful sessions with beginning reading have been from ten to fifteen minutes. If within that span and on a one-to-one basis, the child's attention does not significantly waver during a variety of activities (naming letters, "sounding" some letters, printing a few letters and words, listening to a story or poem), readiness is being clearly signaled.

THE CHILD'S RELATIONSHIP TO BOOKS

The child may also signal readiness by reaction to books and other reading materials. These are signals to observe: Does the youngster seek out books? Ask to have them read? Does the book engross the child, or is one book quickly discarded for another? Does the child indicate awareness of story-line progression through the book? Does the child "study" illustrations and attempt to understand their relationship to the story line? Does the child memorize the story line and then pretend to "read" the book, turning pages at approximately the correct time? Positive responses to such questions represent positive signals of readiness.

TEACHER JUDGMENT AND READINESS TESTS

Proper reading of readiness signals and assessment of readiness in general depend, of course, on teacher judgment, and judgment is sharpened by experience. But even the most inexperienced teacher need not "fly blind." Such teachers should seek the help of more experienced practitioners, particularly that of the kindergarten or infant room teacher who has already spent an entire academic year observing each child's progress in readiness. As noted in Chapter 2, readiness tests are also useful, especially in determining the approximate "level of entry" for each child about to begin learning to read.

HOW DO I BEGIN?

CREATING A READING ENVIRONMENT

As any marketing expert can attest, environment can be a subtle or not-so-subtle persuader. If a department store's layout and displays are conducive to buying, sales go up. We come to browse and remain to buy. Exhibits and other environmental enticements of an Auto Show can make us yearn to get behind the wheel of a new car. The firmest of pledges to watch one's weight is likely to crumble when overwhelmed by the bakery's environment of delicious-looking pastries and appetizing odors.

As a teacher, you are in a sense "marketing" the joy of reading. How can you persuade your class to "buy" this marvelous "product"? The first step is to create a physical and intellectual environment conducive to "selling" it. Here are some ways you can set up such an environment.

Our Story Place Storytelling is older than history itself. Indeed, storytellers were the historians of civilizations long before the advent of the written word. "Stories themselves," as Sam L. Sebasta puts it, "hold the veins of continuity and the consciouness of all cultures, even the whole unified theme of civilization. Stories live on, even when history is forgotten." The child, of course, knows nothing about the story's lofty place in history and culture. But all normal children respond with anticipation and joy to the art of storytelling.

Storytelling, then, can be the child's introduction to the world of fact and imagination later to be met in the printed word—in short, it is the child's introduction to learning to read. As teachers, some of us are born storytellers and some of us need practice in the art. We have, in a previous chapter, already noted some of the do's and don'ts of successful storytelling (and story reading). Suffice it to say here that the good storyteller should know the story thoroughly but should not give the impression it has been memorized word-for-word, should use minimum props, should avoid distracting movements (violent arm moving, jumping about, etc.), should master the use of pause to arouse anticipation, and should vary tone and pitch from soft to crescendo.

The classroom environment for storytelling is perhaps as important as storytelling itself. Set up a special "story place" or story corner for storytelling activities—a special place to which the child comes for a special treat. One easy way to create "our story place" is to use an inexpensive rug to mark its boundaries. On the rug may be a few pillows, a few boy and girl dolls, some small chairs, and if it fits the style of the teacher, a rocker for the teacher. Clearly delineated boundaries for the story place help constrain the listening group (children who crawl off the rug, or out of the designated place are "out"). Time should be planned for calling the group together in "our story place" at least once a day to hear a good story or poem.

Library Corner   A "library corner" is essential to the learning-to-read environment. Low-standing bookshelves should be well-stocked with books from the school library, books on a two-week loan from the public library, and books on loan from the children themselves. P.T.A. projects and books bought for a pittance at garage, yard, and rummage sales are also sources for furnishing the library corner.

Picture Books   Although we usually associate picture books (books with little or no story lines) with three- and four-year-olds, it is wise to have a number of picture books on hand for children who are not quite ready for story-line books. These children will have the satisfaction of "reading" picture books while others are actually reading. This prevents failure before the child actually begins. In addition to "saving face," children can learn from the pictures in picture books, can spin yarns about the stories that they suggest, can admire the artwork, and can establish good habits with books. Picture books can be a bridge between near readiness and beginning reading.

Read-Along Material   Read-along books and stories are essential to the reading environment. Six or eight identical copies of such material should be available so that the children can "read along" as the teacher reads the story aloud. This is an excellent teaching technique and an activity most children enjoy.

If the classroom supply of read-along copies is sparse, the teacher can help make up the deficit with a bit of ingenuity. Multiple copies of old preprimers and primers from discarded basal reader series can often be found gathering dust in some school storage areas. Rescue them. (We have known of instances where they have been burned and/or carted to the dump.)

Have some strong individual rip off the hard covers (if any) and pull out the staples that bind the pages together. Now, separate the stories and restaple each story separately. You will have quite a collection of read-along stories.

A tape recorder and listening post make it possible for a small group to read along independently. The children, working in pairs as "buddies," monitor each other as they follow the story lines and turn pages as the story sequence progresses. What preparation would you have to give your pupils to make this a successful operation?

Another source of read-along books is the child's home collection. Many children have collections of small books in the "I Can Read" series, the "Elf Books," "Little Wonder Books," and "Little Golden Books." It is surprising how many duplicates one can garner merely for the asking. Most of these books are not suitable for a child to attempt to read alone in the beginning stages of learning. They are truly "read-along" books that necessitate the help of the adult, but the children can follow along in their own copies. Over a period of two or three years, the teacher can accumulate a collection of six or eight identical donated copies of several stories in this type.

Object Labels   Labels on objects around the room can be used to contribute to the environment of reading. Here are a few that we have used:
door, wall, clock, floor, ceiling, light, window, calendar, desk, chair, science table, sink, helpers, Today is . . .
Labels per se, however, soon become ignored. Specific reference to them should be made frequently.

Book Jackets   Most trade books for children come covered with book jackets. Children may be asked to contribute jackets from their own books or, with a little coaxing, jackets may be obtained from the school librarian. To be effective as motivators, jackets should be grouped and displayed appropriately and discussed with the children.

Posters   Posters announcing or illustrating holidays, seasons, special days, or special events can become effective parts of the environment for reading, especially when correlated with classroom reading projects.

Mobiles   Mobiles can provide an effective inducement to reading. Artists' sketches of story characters can be cut out and pasted on heavy cardboard or the names of the characters can be printed in manuscript, cut out, and hung from the arms of the mobile. (An annual Book Week mobile may be obtained from the American Library Association.)

Puppets and Other 3-D Characters   Storybook characters, molded in plaster-of-Paris or papier-mache help bring stories alive for beginning readers. They need not be perfect; in fact, children enjoy caricatures. If you cannot make them yourself, some interested parent or other creative adult may be encouraged to do the job.

Realia   Realia are objects used by the teacher to illustrate everyday living. The reading environment can be enhanced by display of objects relevant to the reading activity at hand. For example, an ear of Indian corn or bow-and-arrow could be effective realia for a story about Thanksgiving; a tray of germinating seeds could be used with a science story. Besides adding interest and reality to the story at hand, realia frequently spark related interests and thus provide motivation for further reading.

A WHOLE-WORD APPROACH

As we have previously noted, most children in their readiness years (and before) acquire a number of sight words—meaning-bearing units that trigger memories from the child's store of experiences. Words such as *go, stop, look, hamburger, shoe, dress, T.V., Coke, milk, dog,* and *kitten* have meaning for the child even when seen in isolation from other words. We know, then, that although meaning-through-context is essential to mature reading, learners begin with single-word comprehension. So let us begin at the beginning, with single, whole-word identification. Later, as one of the objectives of the total learning-to-read program, we can help children move from one-word reading to reading in word groups and phrases.

Whole-Word Identification   How do children learn to identify whole words in isolation? Research indicates that they do so through awareness of several identifying characteristics: beginning letters and sounds of words, letter groupings in words, length and gross shape of words, internal structure of words, and other clues. It is not likely that just one of these identifying characteristics is enough. It seems more certain that beginners use several or all to identify a word.

Beginning Letters and Sounds   "How does the word begin?" is commonly one of the first questions put to children learning to read. Answering the question is not difficult for most youngsters. Generally, beginning sounds of words are fairly consistent with spellings of beginning consonants and vowels (short and long). The child may, of course, in a few cases be faced with making a choice between hard and soft sounds, as with the letter *g* in *Gus* and *George,* or *c* in *came* and *cent.* Words that commence with digraphs (two letters representing a single speech sound) or blends of consonants are not ordinarily found in reading material for beginners.

Since many children recognize beginning consonants as identifying characteristics of whole words, should youngsters be taught all initial consonant sounds before beginning to read? Proponents of this procedure must assume that each sound has a letter associated with it and that each letter can be used as a clue to a sound. This assumption, however, does not correspond with the real features of spoken language. Phonemes may have to be represented in our spelling system by more than one letter, and, of course, one letter may represent several different sounds, depending upon the other letters with which it is related within a word. For example, the *s* in *strawberry* does not represent the same sound as the *s* in *shrimp.* In fact, the *s* in shrimp does not represent a phoneme at all, but requires the two letters, *sh* to identify the word as *shrimp* rather than *scimp.* Thus, it may not be productive to teach the child all the beginning consonant sounds prior to reading for letter-sound correspondences are not that simple.

It has been suggested that we should teach only those beginning sounds found in the restricted vocabulary of beginning reading books. This procedure may have worked well enough when children's first efforts at reading were exclusively in materials from the preprimers of the old basal reader series. Today, however, beginning-to-read materials go beyond the confines of stories with controlled vocabulary, and out-of-school experiences such as television viewing bring children in daily contact with nonschool reading matter.

Can rote memorization ever be useful in teaching initial letter/sound relationships? With some children, yes, although about 25 percent of youngsters cannot cope with memorization of such "nonsense" material. For direct instruction in letter/sound relationships and phoneme/letter(s) relationships, the child should be taught the sounds of *key words* (sometimes called "reference words" or "pilot words"). When the child meets a new word, he or she can then respond that "the word begins like . . ." (This is the strategy used by the readiness teacher who asks, "Who else in the room has a name that begins with the same sound??") Drill in key-word learning may utilize flash cards, wall charts, phonic games, workbooks, or other such aids. Key words must be common nouns. They should be current in the speaking vocabulary of the children, regardless of the child's socioeconomic level. Key words should represent objects that can readily be recalled from visual memory. Below is a sampling of useful and relevant key words which we have found to be most useful:

Key Words
The word begins like . . .

a	apple	g	giant	n	nail	u	umbrella
a	angel	g	gum	o	olive	u	United States
b	bubblegum	h	hat	o	oak	v	Valentine
c	cent	i	Indian	p	Pepsi	w	watch
c	Coke	i	ice cream	qu	queen	x	X-ray
d	dog	j	jet	r	ring	y	yo-yo
e	egg	k	key	s	saw	z	zipper
e	ear	l	ladder	t	telephone		
f	fish	m	milk	t	t-shirt		

As a visual aid to memorization of some key words, we suggest that the teacher and class build a series of three-dimensional key picture reference cards utilizing small objects obtained at the variety store. Children enjoy bringing objects in and have a vested interest in the reference cards when they have had a part in making them. Learning-by-doing enhances recall and is vastly more effective than detached rote memorization.

A few specific examples of objects should suffice to convey the nature of the project.

A small plastic apple.

An angel decoration from a Christmas tree.

A small plastic Coke charm from a key ring.

A stick of gum.

A small map of the USA.

A zipper.

Each is glued to a sheet of heavy cardboard. The name (key word) is carefully printed in lower case manuscript. We must caution, however, that beginnings of words are but one clue to word identification.

Interword Features   Some fifty years ago Dr. Guy T. Buswell's classic eye-movement films showed that beginning readers made interword fixations as they attempted to identify whole words, and at about the same time, Meek found that children selected one or two letters and/or a small group of letters as their word-identification clues. In 1961, Siegmar Muehl added further support to the probability that beginning readers "discriminate among similar-length words of different shape on the basis of specific letter differences." More recently, Dr. Henry G. Timko concluded that children who are beginning to learn to read pay more attention to the features of letters within the words than they do to total word shapes. Further research on this subject reveals that children do not rely upon shape, but actually do some visual scanning of the details *within* a word, and subsequently, hit upon certain features that help them identify the word. A study by Dr. Mary B. Hill concluded that children who are beginning to learn to read and who make many errors are children who rely primarily on the beginnings and ends of words. This would indicate that, had they paid additional attention to other features—especially some letter or letters *within* the word (even though they knew little, if any, phonics)—they would have avoided many of their errors and much of their difficulty in learning whole words. Shankweiler and Liberman also found that "children in the early stages of learning to read tend to get the initial segment correct and fail on subsequent ones. . . ."

Together, the results of such studies indicate that children who are beginning to learn to read by the whole-word method need more than "How does the word begin?" to guarantee success. They need to attend to some particular features within the word, even though they know little or no phonics or other word identification skills.

Letter Groupings in Words   Letter groupings provide cues for whole-word identification, for words are not strings of isolated letters but are formed by letter groupings, some of which have a fairly high degree of regularity. It is expedient, therefore, that the young child who is beginning to read be directly helped to internalize some of the more simple groupings of letters. Awareness of the recurrence of these simple groupings may, otherwise, escape large numbers of children.

Direct instruction in letter groups may be either *"inductive"* or *"deductive."* When a child is helped to discover relationships and generalizations through inductive reasoning, the child gains cognitive insights that are more lasting than those gained from rote memorization. Letter groupings and the patterns of the language can also be learned by deductive reasoning, wherein general rules (structural phonics and syllabication) are applied to specific cases. Both methods have advantages that can be capitalized upon in the learning process.

Here are a few simple letter groupings that are helpful in beginning reading:

-ad	-up	fa-	bu-
-am	bi-	ha-	cu-
-an	di-	ja-	hu-
-at	hi-	ma-	nu-
-en	li-	ra-	ru-
-in	pi-	ho-	-un
-is	ri-	lo-	-ub
-it	si-	mo-	-ug
-ob	ba-	po-	-ut
-od	ca-	ro-	co-

Several linguistically regular words can be made from each of these groupings. There are, however, at least eight similar patterns that should be avoided: be-, me-, do-, go-, to-, no-, he-. Their pronounciation represents whole words that are not in the "short" vowel pattern. We cannot go from patterns such as these to *bet, met, dog, got, top, not, net,* or *hen.* The grouping *fo-* should also be avoided because, although *fob* and *fog* can be derived from it, *for* creates a problem that we don't need at this point.

To help the child develop words from these letter groupings, consonant letters may be prominently displayed in a vertical column, preferably on a large flannel board. The particular pattern to be developed is then placed on the flannelboard to the far left as shown below.

The teacher pronounces bĭ with the *short-ĭ* and suggests that, "if we bring this other b over to meet it, we can say *bib.* This is an easy one to start with. With the next consonant sound, /k/ represented by *c,* the children have to decide whether or not *bic* is a word. Some knowledgeable ones may associate it with BIC pens. What do you do then? Of course you accept that perceptive contribution. The alert teacher who has done his/her "homework" will, in fact, have anticipated this possible response and will have a BIC pen on hand or, perhaps, an advertisement with the word *BIC* printed large enough for all to see. (By the same token, the teacher must anticipate and be willing to accept the fact that some street language may turn up as the completely natural responses of children to this kind of whole-word identification exercise.)

The consonant letters used in our sample letter groupings above are those most useful for forming three-letter words. Fortunately, our language is replete with enough three-letter words with high incidence of recurrence. Such words may be learned by rote as sight words, but those that can be "discovered" inductively through working with the patterns proposed will be recalled more easily. The words thus formed follow the CVC (consonant-vowel-consonant) pattern. Through inductive reasoning, children can internalize the notion that such words (there are only a few exceptions) contain short vowels within them. The child who knows the simple letter/sound relationships of the consonants and the short vowel sounds (ă, ĕ, ĭ, ŏ, ŭ) can process most of the three-letter words found in beginning reading materials.

Moreover, the child can be taught to observe that double consonants at the ends of many three-letter words convert them into four-letter words, yet do not change their short-vowel pronunciations. Children can thus add four-letter words to their vocabulary of sight words. For example:

sell	Bill	kiss	dull
fell	fill	miss	gull
jell	bill	boss	hull
tell	kill	loss	lull
well	mill	toss	lull
yell	pill	huff	fuss
	sill	puff	muss
	till		
	will		

Note that the short-ā usually cannot be used in this letter grouping because the addition of a double-*l*, a double-*s*, or a double-*f* to short-ā creates patterns that are not in keeping with others in this category. The words *bass, lass, mass,* and *pass* are about all we can use with the short-ā as the medial vowel.

Double-*e* at the end of a word is easy to teach, since it does not change the pronunciation from that of the single long-ê. There are four words in this pattern that are helpful to use in working with beginners:

bee,   tree,   see,   free

Studies of words of highest frequency in the reading materials for children reveal a few exceptions to the patterns we have been discussing and a few three-letter words that are not in the CVC pattern. Such words *should* be learned as sight words by rote just as soon as possible.

Sight Words to be Learned by Rote

the	and	you	was
she	for	her	out
one	see	are	now
ask	day	boy	any
how	put	too	way
old	saw	two	eat
who	may	buy	eye
say	cry	try	Mrs
our	why	all	new
yes	far	use	toy

Length and Shape According to some research studies, the length and shape of a word provide only minimal cues for word identification. In fact, they are the least-useful features of words. Nevertheless, they should not be ignored.

We do know that children can learn numerous long words by sight, and that they use the length as *one* of the features that helps them determine what the word is. But, to suggest to a child that "this is a *long* word that you know," merely encourages the child to respond with *any* long word as a guess. In fact, many children do not recognize the difference between long and short words when they hear them or when they speak them. They can, of course, see the difference when the words are in print, and we may surmise that length helps to some degree in word identification.

Shape, also, adds a slight increment to word identification, but, at the same time, can be misleading. Some approaches to beginning reading emphasize word shapes as *gestalts* (shapes; forms). In this technique, word shapes are illustrated thus:

Although we have no way of knowing exactly how five and six year olds process these visual cues, we can guess from what they tell us that they select certain top parts of *some* of the letters as aids to word identification. It is difficult, however, if not impossible, to directly teach specific shapes to children—for example: "Look at the tall letters in the word, *mother."* Certainly, it would be misleading to encourage them to generalize that the "tall letters" *th* will always signal that the word is *mother,* for it could be *father, another, bother,* or *nothing.* It is more probable that children use the *th* in this case together with the beginning letters of the word plus contextual setting to distinguish the word from all other words that contain those ascenders in the middle. (In Chapter 4, we will consider word shapes in more detail.)

Internal Structure of Words   Internal structure of words provides children with another clue to whole-word identification. Lists of high-frequency words (words appearing over and over again) contain a number of word parts that also seem to appear over and over again—for example, *th, -nd, ăn, ăt, ar, er, -ay, the, -ĕn, wh, -ther, -ter.* Such letter combinations are found repeatedly in the internal structure of words used in beginning reading. Once learned, they can be utilized as aids to whole-word identification. A few suggestions to the child as to how to put word segments together to form new words will help the beginner recognize them when they are part of a word's internal structure, for example, *wa + ter, wa + nd, wh + en, o + ther,* and *an + o + ther.*

Other Clues to Whole-Word Identification   Some children may find clues to word identification in roots and derivatives. In the beginning weeks of learning to read the child will encounter roots and derivatives such as *go*-ing; to-*day; her's; ask*-ed; *child*-ren, *farm*-er. One must be careful with the technique of asking the child to "look for the little word in the bigger word," for they could just as easily discover *arm* instead of *farm* in *farmer; was* instead of *wash* in *washer; he* instead of *hear* in *hearing,* and countless other inconsistencies that defeat the purpose of studying roots and derivatives.

Some children discover word identifying features that have relevance only for themselves. "Look! That word has part of my name in it!" or "I know that word. It is like the one on the sign near my house." The teacher should, of course, encourage the conjuring of such clues.

WORDS OF HIGHEST FREQUENCY

Common sense tells us that we should begin the teaching of reading with those words the child is most likely to encounter in reading materials specifically designed for children. All else being equal, the more often a child is exposed to a word, the more likely it is that the word will become part of the child's sight vocabulary. What, then, are the words the beginning reader is most likely to encounter? Researchers have compiled several lists of such words.

The most widely used list is the "Dolch 220-Word List," originally compiled over 40 years ago by the late Dr. Edward W. Dolch. Dr. Dolch selected his list from the words most frequently found on three other lists then in current use. Dolch considered the words on his list "basic," because the list included "the 'service words' that are used in all writing, no matter what subject." Dolch's list contains no nouns, since the nouns used in basal readers, individual books, and other materials for children are in some measure peculiar to the subject matter therein. Dolch did, however, compile a separate list of 95 nouns that appeared on all three of the frequency lists from which he had compiled his 220-word list. The "Dolch 220-Word List" and Dolch's high-frequency noun list are reproduced below.

A Basic Sight Vocabulary of 220 Words

a	buy	five	hot	may	pretty	take	walk
about	by	fly	how	me	pull	tell	want
after		for	hurt	much	put	ten	warm
again	call	found		must		thank	was
all	came	four	I	my	ran	that	wash
always	can	from	if	myself	read	the	we
am	carry	full	in		red	their	well
an	clean	funny	into	never	ride	them	went
and	cold		is	new	right	then	were
any	come	gave	it	no	round	there	what
are	could	get	its	not	run	these	when
around	cut	give		now		they	where
as		go	jump		said	think	which
ask	did	goes	just	of	saw	this	white
at	do	going		off	say	those	who
ate	does	good	keep	old	see	three	why
away	done	got	kind	on	seven	to	will
	don't	green	know	once	shall	today	wish
be	down	grow		one	she	together	with
because	draw		laugh	only	show	too	work
been	drink	had	let	open	sing	try	would
before		has	light	or	sit	two	write
best	eat	have	like	our	six		
bring	eight	he	little	out	sleep	under	yellow
big	every	help	live	over	small	up	yes
black		her	long	own	so	upon	you
blue	fall	here	look		some	us	your
both	far	him		pick	soon	use	
brings	fast	his	made	play	start		
brown	find	hold	make	please	stop	very	
but	first		many				

SOURCE: Dolch, Edward W., *Psychology and Teaching of Reading,* Champaign, IL: Garrard Press, 1951, 507–508. Reproduced through the courtesy of Garrard Press.

95 Nouns Common to the Three Word Lists

apple	children	flower	money	sister
baby	Christmas	game	morning	snow
back	coat	garden	mother	song
ball	corn	girl	name	squirrel
bear	cow	goodbye	nest	stick
bed	day	grass	night	street
bell	dog	ground	paper	sun
bird	doll	hand	party	table
birthday	door	head	picture	thing
boat	duck	hill	pig	time
box	egg	home	rabbit	top
boy	eye	horse	rain	toy
bread	farm	house	ring	tree
brother	farmer	kitty	robin	watch
cake	father	leg	Santa Clause	water
car	feet	litter	school	way
cat	fire	man	seed	wind
chair	fish	men	sheep	window
chicken	floor	milk	shoe	wood

To familiarize the child with so-called service words or, instead, with the words on any list of basic words calls for rote learning as the strategy for instruction. However, we cannot assume that repeated encounters with a word will in itself assure memorization. Direct instruction is required by means of simple stimulus-response through the use of flash cards which must be followed by learning through context.

Dolch, himself, prepared flash cards for use with his list. These cards are still available (through Garrard Press). It is probably better to use these commercially printed cards rather than hand-prepare one's own, for the consistent type face used in the commercial product is an aid to associative learning for the beginning reader who eventually must be able to identify words on the printed page.

Flash cards may also be used for learning through context. Cards for learning basic conjunctions should contain context such as the following:

It is as big as . . .   The dog and the cat . . .
I like it because . . .   Because we are afraid . . .
But I can do it.   I like it, but . . .
If she goes . . .   She can go if . . .
You go, or I will . . .   Eat or go to bed.

Other categories that feature prepositions, pronouns, adverbs, adjectives, and verbs that are common to the conversation of six year olds should be planned.

Memorization through context may also utilize worksheets with phrases containing a blank for the basic word, which is to be supplied by the child from two printed alternatives. For group work, a flannelboard may be used in place of individual worksheets.

Another aid to memorization is to have the child copy phrases containing the high-frequency words and read them back to the teacher. The phrases should be carefully designed to include as many basic words as possible. For example, a sentence such as

Put the black and green box *on the* table.

has only two "nonservice" words—*box* and *table.* This kind of sentence, loaded with basic words, provides a high-intensity learning experience.

In 1973, William K. Durr, using a computer, devised a list of 188 high-frequency words found in popular trade books published for children. There are some nouns on the list and a number of other words not found on the Dolch list. Durr's 188 words account for 64 percent of all the words used in samples from 80 selected trade books for children.

188 Words of Highest Frequency in Popular Trade Books for Children

(Listed in descending order of frequencies)

the	6277	so	375	got	187	say	120
to	3063	see	371	take	185	tree	119
and	2916	not	364	where	184	tell	119
he	2513	were	351	every	182	school	119
a	2451	get	346	dog	182	still	117
I	1664	them	340	way	181	much	117
you	1566	like	340	away	181	keep	116
it	1555	just	336	man	179	children	114
of	1504	this	326	old	178	give	113
in	1501	my	320	by	177	work	112
was	1429	would	319	their	176	king	112
said	1429	me	318	here	175	first	112
his	1066	will	315	saw	173	even	112
that	981	big	315	call	173	cry	112
she	820	mother	313	turn	172	try	111
for	752	went	310	after	172	new	111
on	750	are	305	well	170	must	111
they	723	come	296	think	169	grand	111
but	651	back	293	ran	168	start	107
had	631	if	280	let	165	soon	107
at	617	now	279	help	165	made	104
him	614	other	275	side	159	run	103
with	600	long	271	house	158	hand	103
up	577	no	266	home	155	began	103
all	568	came	263	thought	153	gave	102

188 Words of Highest Frequency in Popular Trade Books for Children

look	564	ask	257	make	149	friend	102
is	531	day	256	walk	148	next	100
her	528	very	253	water	145	open	98
there	506	boy	246	two	145	has	98
some	490	an	243	or	145	hard	98
out	488	over	240	head	141	enough	98
as	485	your	235	door	140	wait	97
be	483	time	234	before	139	Mrs.	97
have	468	from	232	more	137	morning	97
go	466	good	228	eat	133	find	97
we	455	any	225	oh	132	only	96
one	455	about	214	again	132	us	93
then	451	Mr.	213	play	131	three	93
little	429	father	208	who	129	our	93
down	424	around	208	been	129	found	93
do	402	want	206	may	129	why	92
can	392	don't	204	stop	128	girl	91
could	386	how	199	off	128	place	90
when	385	know	195	never	125	under	90
did	378	right	191	eye	122	while	89
what	377	put	191	took	121	told	89
thing	376	too	190	people	121	than	89

SOURCE Durr, William K., "A Computer Study of High-Frequency Words in Popular Trade Juveniles," *Reading Teacher*, **27** (1973), 14. Used by permission of the International Reading Association and Dr. Durr.

One reading program (of which Dr. Durr is one of the editors) utilizes 16 high-frequency words which the publishers claim "account for 28 % of everything we read." The words are *a, go, not, she, as, to, on, the, in, you, and, he, I, will, we,* and *it.*

Any serviceable list of high-frequency words for beginners should include (a) words most-frequently encountered in beginning reading materials, (b) words in current usage *(astronaut, car* instead of *automobile, plane* instead of *airplane, TV,* etc.), and (c) words common to the speech of five- and six-year-old children. A list suitable for more advanced learners should, of course, also contain words beyond the common vocabulary of six year olds.

A "revised" Dolch list published in 1976 appears to meet those criteria, even though it does not include up-to-date nouns. It is based upon several computer studies of word frequencies, children's spoken vocabulary, and the viability of words from first grade through adulthood. Thirty-one of the words on the original Dolch list have been deleted and 37 new words added, for a total of 226 words.

Revised Dolch List

a	don't	into	or	thought*
about	down	is	other*	three
across*	draw	it	our	through*
after	eat	its	out	to
again	enough*	just	over	today
all	even*	keep	own	together
always	every	kind	play	told*
am	far	know	put	too
an	fast	last*	ran	took*
and	find	leave*	read	toward*
another*	first	left*	red	try
any	five	let	right	turn*
are	for	light	round	two
around	found	like	run	under
as	four	little	said	up
ask	from	long	same*	upon
at	full	look	saw	us
away	gave	made	say	use
be	get	make	see	very
because	give	many	she	walk
been	go	may	short*	want
before	going	me	should*	warm
began*	gone*	mean*	show	was
best	good	might*	six	we
better	got	more*	small	well
big	green	most*	so	went
black	grow	much	some	were
blue	had	must	soon	what
both	hard*	my	start	when
bring	has	near*	still*	where
but	have	need*	stop	which
by	he	never	take	while*
call	heard*	next*	tell	white
came	help	new	ten	who
can	her	no	than*	why
close*	here	not	that	will
cold	high*	now	the	with
come	him	of	their	work
could	his	off	them	would
cut	hold	oh*	then	yes
did	hot	old	there	yet*
didn't*	how	on	these	you
do	I	once	they	your
does	I'm*	one	think	
done	if	only	this	
	in	open	those	

*Words added to the 189 word revision of the Dolch basic sight vocabulary done previously by Dr. Johns.

SOURCE Johns, Jerry L., "Updating the Dolch Basic Sight Vocabulary," *Reading Horizons,* **16**:2 (1976), 104–111. Reproduced by permission of the Reading Center and Clinic, Western Michigan University and Dr. Johns.

PERSONAL, EMOTIONAL WORDS

Words that are personally and emotionally meaningful to a child are most easily remembered, as demonstrated in Sylvia Ashton-Warner's book, *Teacher*, in which she described her experiences in teaching beginning reading to Maori children in New Zealand schools. Her students had a high degree of success in learning words they had themselves chosen to express "gut" feelings: words of "love," "fear," and "hate." She identified a common key vocabulary associated with the child's inner world: *Mommy, Daddy, kiss, frightened, ghost*. As each child suggested his or her own special word, the teacher printed it on a separate piece of tagboard. The child studied the word, and when it was learned kept that word card.

Fun games may be played with personal word cards. A small group of children assemble with their cards, which are mixed up in a pile on the floor. The children then scramble to claim their own cards, but must prove that they know each word that they claim as their own.

Here are a few questions that can help children suggest words that have personal emotional appeal.

What words would you use to show you are happy?

What words make you feel unhappy?

What words or names don't you really like?

What do you say when you see food you don't like?

What words would you use to tell about some person you don't like?

What words do you use to tell about things or people you do like?

There is some indication that words heavily loaded with personal emotion may be learned as sight words almost instantly (Ashton-Warner named them "instant words"). We believe, however, that they must be encountered in print and in context several times before they can be recognized with ease.

REPETITION IN CONTEXT

No sensible teacher would attempt to teach a list of sight words in isolation to beginners. New words should be put into meaningful phrases. For example, the sight word, *here*, may be given in context as:

Here is Mark.	Susan is here.
Mark is here.	Mark is here.
Here is Susan.	Susan is here.

Here is another way you can entice children to use *personal* words. Note, too, that even in the beginning stage of written language usage, children can achieve rhyming. Shouldn't this encourage us to use more poetry as part of the daily reading menu?

Stacy
I want corn on the cob
and an ice cream job
Thats what I want for
supper.

cream job
ice cream job
corn
me

Will Hall — Will
I want mashed potatoes
with Butter but not in
a gutter
thats what I want
for supper.

Tammitt
I want french fries and two
coconut pies.
Thats what I want for
supper.

Dana
I want chicken thats
delicious and very nutritious
Thats what I want for
supper.

Milledge
I want a hot dog thats
fat but not with a rat
Thats what I want for supper

Sandra
I want spaghetti thats hot
and a little too hot
Thats what I want for
supper.

Tammy M
I want macaroni and cheese
and small green peas
Thats what I want for
supper.

Roger
I want a hamburger on a roll but
not in a bowl
Thats
what I want for supper

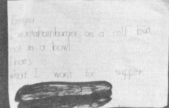

Is Mark here?   Here is Mark.

Is Susan here?   Here is Susan.

At first, only a few should be used at a time, and the contrast in each word should be enough so that none will be confused. Again, we want success, not failure.

Here is an example of how six words

the	house	at
is	doll	my

may be manipulated to form the following:

my doll

the doll

my house

the house

my doll house

the doll house

my doll is at my house.

My doll is at the house.

My doll is at the doll house.

The doll house is at my house.

These are merely a sample of how a very few words with *contrasting shapes* and *no common elements* may be used for practice in whole-word learning. Words with similar or identical elements, however, may easily confuse the beginner. For example, *mother, father, faster, water, where* are very difficult for a beginner to differentiate because they are sufficiently alike to be confusing.

Flashcards are another means of repetition. They should not be used as a means of competition in a reading "Shoutdown," but for individual or small-group practice in seeing differences and special characteristics of whole words. They can also be used to construct phrases and/or sentences on the table, floor, chalk rail, or flannel board.

Some years ago, Dr. Donald D. Durrell, then professor of education at Boston University, developed what he called "every-pupil response cards." His purpose was to achieve "high intensity learning," with every child in the learning group participating in the activity, rather than just one child responding while the others in the group remain passive.

In the beginning of whole-word instruction, each child in the group is given a lined card on which the child copies a word, for example, *doll*. As the teacher reads, the children raise the card with *doll* printed on it every time the word *doll* is heard. Later, a second word card—for example, *house*—is prepared by the children. Now each child has two cards and must discriminate between them as the words *doll* and *house* are read. More cards are added, and the lesson is completed when the child can make the necessary auditory and visual discriminations quickly enough to select among five or six cards the correct one to hold up in response to the teacher's oral cue.

BUILDING A BANK OF WHOLE WORDS

We have found that one of the most effective methods of commencing beginning reading is to help young children develop a sight vocabulary of 32 basic words composed of those sixteen in the Houghton-Mifflin *Getting Ready to Read* list and those on Richards and Ogden's list of 18 basic verbs. The verbs, *go* and *will* appear on both lists, hence 32 altogether. We call them "Starter Words."

32 Basic "Starter Words"

a	as	in	I
go	to	you	will
not	on	and	we
she	the	he	it
be	come	do	get
give	have	keep	let
make	may	put	say
see	can	send	take

We print those words on 3 × 5 cards to serve both as flash cards (on an individual teacher-pupil basis) and as individual practice cards. They can also be used with "buddies" working in groups of two or three. Perhaps because of the influence of *Sesame Street* and the *Electric Company* T.V. programs, we find many children can do better with words printed in capitals rather than in lower-case.

As children begin to learn these sight words, they seem pleased to "discover" (with our help) that they can string several of them together in meaningful clusters. For example, *in, I, go, not, will, can, make* can form the basis for a number of different groupings. For example:

I can not go.

I can go.

I will not go.

I can make . . . (whatever)

I will not make a boo-boo (or whatever).

I can go in the . . .

or using the child's own name or someone else's name in the blank:

_____ can go in the water (or whatever).

Inasmuch as many of the children have learned initial consonant sounds, it is usually better to start the whole-word learning with a few words beginning with initial consonant sounds rather than with vowels. We have found that the following are frequently learned by sight first:

see,   you,   keep,   be,   and   *say*

Why not start, then, with these easy ones, giving the child an immediate taste of reading success.

A PHONICS APPROACH

Those interested in teaching phonics as the prime focus in reading insist that children can master the language by learning the "sounds" of the five vowel graphemes, *a, e, i, o, u* and the consonants, followed by some practice on words containing diphthongs, consonant digraphs and blends, and vowel digraphs. They assume that English can be segmented that way and so, when a child has learned the sounds represented by those letters and letter combinations (called phonics correspondences), words can be deciphered by "sounding out" the parts and then blending the sound segments together into a word that, hopefully, is known and is in the child's speaking vocabulary.

Just how many different sounds children would have to learn to associate with alphabet letters is difficult to say. There are probably seventeen vowel sounds, including diphthongs. Here is the way the phonetic features of vowels in standard English are frequently presented by those who support what they call a "pure" phonics approach:

a	apple	*e*	elephant	*o*	hot
a	ate	*e*	key	*o*	open
a	father	*i*	indian	*o*	gone
a(r)	care	*i*	ice cream	*u*	cut
		i (r)	pier	*u*	use
				u (r)	fur

Those opposed to a pure phonics approach claim it is too simplistic for English which contains such a large number of irregularities.

Debating whether a whole-word approach or a phonics approach is best is likely to get us nowhere. In fact, such a debate is largely "academic," for we

A phonics lesson may be conducted with a selected group of children who need special help on a particular phonics element. The experienced teacher can invoke techniques that have been successful in the past. What preparation should a beginning teacher make for such a help session? Note the features in this classroom environment that indicate that reading is an important segment of day-to-day learning.

know that children must learn to utilize both strategies. Whole-word vocabulary must be buttressed with a strong background in phonics, and we believe that it should be done through direct, structured instruction and not left to chance.

Because of the importance of phonics in beginning reading instruction, the methods and materials for teaching phonics are discussed in detail in Chapter 5.

TEACHING THE ALPHABET

Many claim that our language is "alphabetic" and, therefore, children should learn the pronunciation of the names of all alphabet letters in order to be ready for reading. The *Sesame Street* T.V. program seems to proceed on that notion. Although a large body of research has been assembled at Boston University, much of it done to prove the point rather than to investigate its validity, it seems more likely that children who know the alphabet before learning to read are children who have other faculties for learning to read that account for their superiority in both alphabet and reading. We cannot accept the idea that there is a causal relationship.

LEARNING-BY-DOING STRATEGIES

Some children in the beginning reading classroom will be very eager to learn to read. Others will come along more slowly. The eager students should be encouraged to "read" on their own if they wish to do so, even though other children may not yet have reached the same state of readiness. Sometimes the eager-to-read children can be grouped together to read on their own, each reading the same story. As other children "get the bug," so to speak, they, too, should be encouraged to join the group. Let the children in the reading group help one another. However, be careful that the good reader is not exploited to the extent that the child virtually becomes a tutor to the slower children.

Children reading on their own are, in effect, learning by doing—an old and honored learning strategy. In such learning by doing, the child advances at his or her own pace. The child is also self-motivated when learning by doing, a distinct advantage in the learning process. (So-called "individualized reading" is based on the principle of learning by doing. This method for learning to read is discussed in Chapter 9).

Learning-by-doing strategies are not, however, completely unstructured. To be truly effective, such learning should be guided by the teacher—although guided with a light hand. The teacher, will, of course, provide the kinds of books and stories best suited to the child's learning. The teacher should also be ready to "coach" the child whenever coaching is needed. Children may need help with pronunciation of a word that puzzles them, or help with a new word they may not have encountered before.

Teacher aides and volunteers can help children in small groups. But they must not be turned loose without training and instructions. They need to be coached on the following:

How to help the child figure out a word that has already been encountered before.

How to provide the pronunciation of a word for a child.

How to help the child make an educated guess based upon context.

How to control the group so one child does not monopolize the reading.

How to "hold back" and allow other children in the group help each other.

When to call on the teacher for help.

How to keep a record of progress of each child.

How to "observe" and report observations to the teacher.

Limits on the involvement of teachers aides and volunteers must be set so they and the teacher know the exact areas in which they operate and for which they are responsible.

It seems relevant here to consider whether under such do-it-yourself conditions, pupils are learning to read *correctly*. We prefer to "beg the question" and, in place of an answer, propose another question: When a young child is brimming over with the urge to sing, should we say, "No. Not until you have been taught to sing correctly!"?

Learning by doing is, in a sense, a "private" process. But children are social creatures, as every teacher soon learns. They will, in fact, insist upon involving the teacher in their "private" learning. They will bombard the teacher with questions. "What is this word?" "What does this word mean?" They will insist that you join them in their excitement as the magic of learning to read by reading takes hold upon their minds and imaginations. This is the way it should be. Encourage and cherish these magic moments as harbingers of learning delights to come.

KINESTHETIC/TACTILE TECHNIQUES

It has long been known that tracing the forms of letters and words reinforces the visual memory component of reading. Through the ages, even before paper was available, tutors coached students by having them write symbols with pointed sticks in the sand. We recall the story of Archimedes drawing his mathematical symbols in the sand, and of Jesus enscribing a Hebrew phrase in the sand. At the turn of our own century, Dr. Maria Montessori encouraged slum children of Rome to draw letters with sticks in the sand. Even today, we have observed "teachers" with groups of children in primitive societies tracing their alphabet symbols and words in the sand with their fingers.

Our early ancestors sensed to be true what psychologists centuries later would prove to be true. Tracing, which involves kinesthetic and tactile modes of learning, reinforces visual and auditory modes of learning. (As we discussed in an earlier chapter, all four modalities, visual, auditory, kinesthetic, and tactile—VAKT—are necessary for optimum learning.) In more modern times, the kinesthetic and tactile modes of learning were sometimes neglected as tools for learning to read. In the early 1930s, however, Dr. Grace Fernald revived interest in these modes through her successful employment of them in remedial-reading techniques. Although tracing is but a part of the "Fernald Method," it is to her that a large part of the credit should go for contemporary "rediscovery" of the importance of tracing in learning to read.

Letter manipulation is another kinesthetic/tactile technique and is also a first step toward the ultimate goal of *encoding* (putting letters together to form words). Although we usually think of encoding as synthesizing phonics—in other words, spelling words with the letters that represent the sounds—small children can learn to spell words long before they know the sounds of the letters.

Conversely, some children can encode according to the sounds of letters before they know the letter (alphabet) names. In either case, letter manipulation is a valuable technique and a first step towards writing—a substratum of beginning reading.

Movable Manuscript Letters   The alphabet blocks of early childhood have long been a playtime means of learning alphabet letters and of constructing short words. In the long run, however, with all but the most persistent children, these six-sided blocks are likely to discourage rather than encourage word learning. They are, for each block contains six different letters, cumbersome and confusing. Moreover, the letters are usually all capital letters. Blocks do have a place, however, in the language development of toddlers and often are the child's first introduction to the printed symbols of our language.

Better than alphabet blocks are the several varieties of manuscript letters available from school supply houses. However, let the buyer beware: some are too small and are easily scattered around the classroom to be lost and swept away by the custodian, and some are marketed in flimsy cardboard boxes that soon break apart. The letter components of a *Scrabble* set are excellent for letter manipulation. (Discarded *Scrabble* sets can occasionally be purchased at rummage sales.)

Specialists working with the perceptually handicapped are acquainted with the Norrie Composing Letter Case, developed a number of years ago by the late Edith Norrie at the Ordblinds Institut in Copenhagen. It is modeled on the "upper case" and "lower case" trays that compositors once commonly used in hand-setting type in a printing establishment. The Norrie Letter Case is well constructed of cabinet woods and is, consequently, very expensive. It is not likely to be a part of the usual equipment of very many classrooms, but adequate trays can be made much more cheaply by utilizing some of the materials and equipment readily available. It would be wise for every education student who intends to teach reading to construct some kind of letter case for use in the classroom.

Here is one method for doing so:

1. Obtain from a variety store or other supply shop compartmentalized plastic or metal trays used to keep nuts, bolts, and screws sorted and separated.
2. Using alphabet letters cut from paper, paste (preferably with rubber cement or Elmer's glue) one lower-case letter on the "floor" of each compartment, being sure to use a left-to-right sequencing through the alphabet. These letters on the "floor" of each section act as cues to sorting. If possible, use the same type face for your letters as that of the letters to be used by the children. If the letters are on cardboard bases, steam each cardboard and peel off the face so it can easily be glued to the floor of each compartment.
3. Fill each compartment with at least five identical lower-case letters, so that the children may compose a number of words using the letters. Have one compart-

ment available for blank cardboard tabs on which the child can print additional letters if needed to augment the five complete alphabets that are already in the case.

The child is now equipped with a letter-sorting case for composing words. Some capital letters will be needed, as will periods and question marks. These can be set up in a separate composing case. Three complete capital alphabets are all that are likely to be needed for beginning reading.

In New South Wales, Australia, we observed a new word-composing system (from England) that is producing remarkably good achievement in both reading and spelling. It is called *Breakthrough* (not to be confused with Allyn & Bacon reading series of the same name). The chief components of *Breakthrough* are letters on tabs, words on tabs, and punctuation marks on tabs. Each child has a composing box and a rack (similar to a Scrabble rack) that is long enough to hold a sentence of five or six words. Children must know twelve sight words before starting to use the "Sentence Maker" in the Breakthrough kit. They are: *home, mum* (the Australian equivalent of the word *Mom)*, *dad, bed, television, baby, brother, sister,* and four verbs. In addition, they must know the articles *the* and *a* plus the conjunction *and.* A few prepositions are used in the set, along with preprinted suffixes and prefixes for the verbs. The child can either construct words, using the letters in the kit, or sentences using the words.

Manuscript letter manipulation by children as young as three is successfully practiced in many American Montessori-type schools. In most such schools, children are not taught the names of the letters, but the most common sounds that they represent. The youngsters are able to "encode" words according to the "sounds of the letters." In the Montessori schools we have visited we noticed that sometimes the word is spelled correctly and sometimes not, but the important thing is that the word be spelled "as it sounds" to the child.

In most classrooms for beginning readers, however, letter manipulation is expected to be accompanied by reasonably correct spelling. At some point in the learning-to-read process, children must begin to associate correct spelling with the correct word. However, this does not mean that you should expect the beginner to spell each and every word correctly each and every time. Some children will have more difficulty than others in spelling words. None of the children, at this stage of instruction, will have had enough training in phonics or spelling rules to spell perfectly. (Even mature readers are sometimes notoriously poor spellers.) Be satisfied with and applaud reasonably accurate spelling when the child is manipulating letters to construct words.

MANUSCRIPT PRINTING AND COPYING

Spelling (or encoding) through manipulation of movable letters should be followed by practice of writing in manuscript (printing letters by hand). Manuscript approximates machine-printed reading materials more closely than does cursive penmanship. Hence transfer of learning from manuscript lettering to printed lettering is easier and more direct.

One excellent early exercise in manuscript lettering is to have the child copy his or her name in manuscript. This accomplishment will be hailed with pleasure by the child and will also encourage the beginner to apply this new skill to the lettering of other words.

Almost all early exercises in manuscript lettering will likely be copying exercises. Copy books, which offer models for the learner to emulate and which provide a day-by-day record of achievement, have been a staple of the primary school classroom for generations.

Rote copying, however, can be carried to extremes. We can attest to that fact, having observed children in other countries engaged in enormous amounts of rote copying of stories that teachers had laboriously printed on chalkboards. In many cases, children were copying entire stories from books or from handouts. All this is evidence that copying per se can easily reach the point of diminishing returns, at which it becomes meaningless and unproductive.

Copywork should be as personal and experiential as possible—the copying of the child's name, for example. Copying that utilizes the child's "special words" is another effective technique.

Copying and getting it "just right" is serious business to many children. What kind of reward do you think would be appropriate for such intense effort? Can every child attain perfection at this (or at any) age? How does one accommodate for individual differences?

Each child is encouraged to choose a number of words that are especially meaningful to the youngster. The child is then directed to copy these particular words in manuscript. (A group discussion can later be generated about why the child chose the words and about how words have special meanings for all of us.)

Word-copying can also be used to focus attention on an idea or concept. A particularly apt title of a story, for example, could be copied to help focus attention on the tale's story line.

Copying phrases is a good technique for helping children become better acquainted with how patterns of language look in print. Prepositional phrases are naturals for beginners: "at the circus," "to the store," "over the hill," "under the tent," and so on. Children who practice phrase copying are less likely to run into difficulties later on because of reliance on word-by-word reading.

LANGUAGE-EXPERIENCE STORY BOOKLETS

In Chapter 2 we discussed the importance of language-experience activities in the readiness classroom—that is, strategies for learning based on the child's own experiences. Language-experiences story booklets provide a similar strategy for the beginning-to-read classroom. Indeed, they can provide an almost foolproof strategy to generate beginning reading.

Initial construction of the booklets involves a bit of innocent deception. Most children come to the classroom willing and eager to tell stories about themselves and their experiences to teacher and classmates. (As teachers soon learn, the youngsters are sometimes *too* willing and eager.) The trick is to secretly record any particularly exciting tale, either by taking notes or by use of a tape recorder. The child should be kept unaware that the story is being recorded. Some young children may be inhibited if they are aware they are being recorded and their stories may lose *spontaneity*. Other children may become verbal show-offs in future sessions.

Once the child's story has been recorded on paper or taped by the teacher, it is then written in manuscript (still without the knowledge of the child). It is printed on small sheets that can be assembled into a booklet. The story may consist of only a few sentences, or it may be relatively long. Its length will be determined by the teacher according to the ability and attention span of that particular child.

One good procedure is to "manufacture" the booklets so that the pages, when folded over, are 4 × 6 inches. A blank cover should be reserved to be filled in later after the teacher and child have discussed the story and decided on its title. Five half-sheets, folded over and stapled together in the middle provide an 18-page booklet. The teacher should print the story lines in manuscript on one page, leaving the opposite page to be filled later with an illustration by the child. Other formats may, of course, be devised by the creative teacher.

There is always a right time, and, perhaps more frequently, a wrong time to do things when working with young children. A sense of timing is essential in all teaching. Experience with children and sensitivity to the feelings and moods of each child help you sense when the timing is "just right" to present to the child the language-experience story booklet you have made.

In a sense, the booklet is a gift from you to the child. Therefore, treat it as a gift: "I liked your story yesterday about the fire engine. I liked it so much that I made something for you!" or "You know that big people write books for children. Sometimes, little children can write books if a big person helps them." "You told an interesting story yesterday, and I have made your story into a book just for you!" This approach almost never fails to make the child feel very important and special.

After the "presentation," the teacher should read the child's story privately with the child. The immediate reaction is almost certain to be one of surprise, pleasure, and joy. Sometimes, however, the joy may be accompanied by tears of embarrassment, boisterousness, and boastfulness. Some children may even react initially with fear or resentment. However, if the sensitive teacher has selected "just the right time" for presentation, the booklet will be received positively with joy and laughter and, perhaps, with hugs and kisses!

To repeat: language-experience booklets can provide an almost fool-proof strategy for generation of beginning reading. The words in the story are the child's very own and recognized as such by the learner. Motivation to "read" the words in the story is strong indeed. Reading booklets "authored" by other children in the class will also provide a highly motivated learning experience for the child. After all, it's a story by "someone I know."

You will discover that recording and hand-printing booklets throughout the year for a classroom of children requires an enormous amount of time—much of it after-school time. But once you have seen how children react to language-experience booklets, you will probably, somehow, find the time to prepare them. It's hard to ignore those joyful hugs and kisses.

"LITTLE" BOOKS

"Little" books have been popular for many years in the English-speaking countries of the British Commonwealth: England, Scotland, Ireland, Canada, New Zealand, and Australia. Their origin, perhaps, was dictated by the economics of scarcity and frugality. "Little" books of American origin are now beginning to appear on the market.

They are, indeed, *little* books by anyone's standards, being only 4 × 6 inches and usually containing 18 to 24 pages, half of which contain pictures illustrating the story lines. When we first came upon them in the New Zealand schools, our first impression was that they are really *nothing!* But later we came to realize that they serve the key purposes stated in the objectives at the beginning of this chapter, namely "success and the achievement of self-satisfaction."

Of course, this does not happen automatically. There must be an effective "directed reading lesson" (DRL) such as described later in this chapter.

With the "little" books, the child becomes an "instant reader" by listening to the teacher read the book while following along in his or her own copy. Then everyone reads a sentence in chorus. The same story is read several days in a row until many of the children in the group have actually memorized the story. The pictures accompanying each page of the text cue the readers to the story lines.

There are obvious advantages and disadvantages to this strategy of story memorization. With this technique, the child is helped to learn whole words. More important, the child is enjoying immediate success in completing a "whole book." This generates tremendous satisfaction and motivation to go on to the next story. On the negative side, however, there is the probability that children will develop the habit of guessing at words and will rely entirely upon whole words, neglecting to develop other word-identification skills. There may also be undue reliance on the illustrations to carry the story lines. (In Chapter 9 we discuss how "little" books are used in an individualized reading program.)

A FULL BAG OF TRICKS

Every teacher of very young children needs "a full bag of tricks" to keep a roomful of lively youngsters productively busy. (Anyone who thinks otherwise has obviously never had such a task.) In a sense, the teacher must be a kind of magician, ever ready to dip into this bag of tricks whenever the attention of the classroom "audience" falters. But rabbits do not just come out of hats—they must be carefully put in the hat to start with. The teacher's bag of tricks must likewise be carefully planned if it is to add variety and zest to the task of learning to read.

Here are some examples of successful "tricks of the trade."

Decks of picture cards are standard equipment in most classrooms. Some decks are designed for matching pictures with words; others are for matching pictures with beginning graphemes or with beginning sounds. The cards can be used by one child alone, but provide more fun and better learning when two or three children play with them together, each reinforcing the other through double check and feedback.

The post-office game (played in pairs) also uses cards. Postal slots are cut into a stand-up cardboard front. One child sits "inside" the post office, and one "mails" cards into the properly labeled slots. The teacher can add variety to the game by providing cards with initial consonant sounds, vowel sounds, or words as the criteria for correct "sorting" and "mailing." If, for example, short vowel sounds are to be learned, five slots would be labeled: $\breve{a}$ $\breve{e}$ $\breve{i}$ $\breve{o}$ $\breve{u}$.

If a is being taught, the child mailing the cards would have a pack of picture cards, some depicting a words: *apple, astronaut, are,* and so on. As the cards are placed in the slot, the "postmaster" can verify them by checking to see if the same pictures are on his or her $\breve{a}$ list. In this manner, both children share in the learning process.

Puppets can be excellent motivational devices. The creative teacher can use them to applaud correct responses or to express sadness at incorrect ones.

Puppets are also useful to draw out the bashful or reluctant youngster. Some bashful children will speak through a puppet, whereas otherwise they might remain almost nonverbal.

Spinner boards are another source of excitement and variety. The board is constructed with a spinner pointer in the center and words or phonics elements around the outer edges. When the spinner points to a word, the child holds up the matching letter or word card. For further variety, the child who has the matching card puts it into a discard pile and the one who discards all cards first becomes the winner of the game.

Bingo games are popular for small-group play. They may either be "phonics bingo" or "word bingo." Constructing enough bingo cards for a group of children is quite a task because there must be a variety of combinations and no more than two winners for each game. However, once constructed and laminated with contact paper, they will last for many years.

The picture-card game is played with four to eight picture cards in the pack, each of which depicts an object starting with the same phonics element: for example, *bell, bed, bug, ball, bat, button,* and so on. Several phonics elements should be practiced during each game, but more than eight elements per game will likely confuse the youngsters.

Four to eight cards are dealt to each player. The rest of the pack is placed on the table. Children take turns drawing a card from the pack and must decide to discard it or keep it and discard another card. One card must be discarded each time. Each child attempts to complete a "book" of four to eight cards of pictures of items that all begin with the same sound.

If the children are playing without the supervision of an adult, they can double check the correctness of the card by looking at the letters printed on the back of each picture card.

The listening post is another engaging item for your bag of tricks. It utilizes a cassette tape recorder and a distributor box with recepticals for several earphone jacks. The children are shown how to turn the cassette off and on. They are also given printed copies of the story which they read along with the recording. A story or other material is recorded on the cassette and listened to by the children through the earphones.

The teacher must select the story or other material to be recorded and arrange to have it read onto the cassette. You can record it yourself, or you may wish to enlist the aid of someone better trained for this kind of task—perhaps a friend who has had theatrical or other kind of public-speaking experience. The prime requisite is that the recording reflect careful pronunciation and enunciation and some sense of dramatic values. You must also, of course, arrange to have printed copies of the recorded material available for use with each set of earphones. (These printed materials are often referred to as "talking books.")

The cassette recording may be interrupted at strategic points for direction and instruction. For example: "See the picture at the top of this page. Does it show how Alice feels? Now, on your worksheet, find the word *Alice.* It begins with the same sound as *apple* and begins with the same letter as *apple* does. Now, copy the word *Alice* on the line just below. Now, see if you can read the sentence: '*Alice* . . . is . . . happy.' Now, after you have stopped the tape recorder, write "Alice is happy" on the line below the sentence. Remember, you are going to copy the sentence, "Alice is happy." on the line. Now, read that sentence—"Alice is happy." Now stop the tape recorder and copy it."

A variety of worksheet activities may be devised by the teacher to take advantage of the high-intensity learning provided by the listening post. The teachers' manuals of the basal reader are one good source of ideas for such activities. In fact, stories from those basal readers can be put on tape with appropriate directions for the child recorded along with the story. With all recorded instructions, attention must be given to the amount of time necessary to carry out the recorded direction. If the time needed for the task is relatively long, the child should be directed to "stop the cassette while you do this."

Listening posts are sold commercially under several different brand names. Many schools have them on hand, either in the classroom or in storage. If your school is without one, you may be fortunate enough to have friends (or perhaps some parents of the children) who are knowledgeable enough in electronics to improvise a listening post for your use. Listening posts have been made from discarded electronic components and equipment and have even utilized old telephones (which the children love to use) in place of commercial earphones. Needless to say, any such makeshift listening post should be checked carefully for safety by an electronics expert.

The tachistiscope is another aid to learning. Basically, it is a projection machine that flashes words onto a screen, using a shutter device for controlling speed of exposure. It is intended for practice in whole-word identification.

With some cardboard, glue, and a sharp knife, you can construct a device to serve much the same purpose as the commercial tachistiscope. Strips of cardboard with words printed on them are passed through a cardboard sleeve with a "window" cut in it. The window is just large enough to expose one of the words on the strip. The speed of exposure is, of course, hand controlled. Here's how to construct the device:

The cardboard sleeve is about 4 inches wide and 9 inches long. This requires an $8\frac{1}{4}$-inch-wide cardboard, 9 inches in length, folded on dotted lines shown in the illustration.

The strips for the words to be studied should be cut to shape and lined by the teacher. But each child should be allowed to choose his or her own words (within the lesson plan) that are to go on the strip and to do their own printing of the words. This not only provides practice in word printing but also provides the reinforcement factor of personal involvement. If the strips are to be used extensively, it is a good idea to help preserve them by a covering of transparent contact paper. The plasticity of the paper will also help reduce friction and allow the strip to slide more easily in the sleeve.

Most children love to work this simple device and to identify the words as

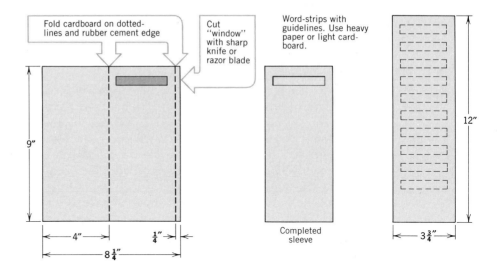

they appear in the "window." If they cannot identify them, most children will not be at all hesitant about asking for help from the teacher. In any case, do not overly encourage the child to pass the strip through the sleeve quickly. The primary objective at this point is not speed, but reinforcement of whole-word recognition.

Rebuses and ideographs also belong in your bag of tricks. Rebuses are pictorial representations of words or phrases. The word *doorman,* for example, would be represented by the picture of a door and a man. Children love to puzzle out rebuses. In doing so, they are "painlessly" learning new words and word parts that they may not yet have encountered on the printed page. Rebuses are commonly used in beginning reading programs.

Ideographs are pictorial representations designed to be closely associated with the letters for which they stand. The word, *ideograph,* was coined to depict the notion that a symbol on paper (a *graph*) can stand in place of some idea, hence *ideo-graph*. Although there have been attempts to devise ideographs for all alphabet letters, we have found only a few basic ones to be at all effective with beginning readers. Here are some examples of ideographs:

THE DIRECTED READING LESSON

The directed reading lesson (DRL as it is commonly called in the profession) is a somewhat structured and highly motivational procedure. It has been in use as a teaching device for as long as basal reader teachers' manuals have been in existence. In spite of the fact that it is an old-established technique, it has so

many advantages and so few disadvantages that every teacher of reading should know the routine and what it purposes to accomplish.

As in the case of all good lessons, the DRL has objectives and includes plans to meet them. It also consists of a series of sequential steps designed for developmental learning. Basically, the technique consists of five sequential steps 1. preparation, 2. reading, 3. discussion, 4. skill reinforcement, 5. enrichment) designed for developmental learning.

A Simplified Directed Reading Lesson for Teaching Beginning Reading.

Part 1

Preparation

Objectives

To set the thinking of the young learner as readiness for the story.

To suggest ideas that will trigger the learner's own experiences, so that meaning is brought to the reading.

This form of readiness usually starts with discussion about the picture, illustrations, or artwork that is used to give mood, setting, and feeling to the story. The artwork usually provides clues to some of the questions: who? what? where? when? Here is an example:

The picture shows a boy and girl flanking an adult woman, all standing with their backs to the viewer, looking into the window of a store. In the window we can see a toy boat, train, balls, sand pail, doll, and tea set. The woman is wearing a long, heavy coat and the children are wearing winter jackets.

"What do we see in the picture?"
The usual answer is "toys" (a too generalized response).
"What kinds of toys?" (calling for a more detailed response)
"What else do we see in the picture?"
"Children." "Children looking in the window of a store."
"What kind of children? What kind of store? What else do we see?"
"A mother."
"It might be a mother, but are we sure it is the mother of the children?"
"It might be their grandmother."
"What makes you think so?"
"Because her coat is long."
"She has gray hair."
"Maybe you think she's their grandmother because *your* grandmother has gray hair." "Is that why you think this is the children's grandmother?" (Note that the child's answer is not directly contradicted.)
"What do you think the boy is saying?" (The boy in the illustration is pointing to the train. This question calls for direct involvement in the feelings of

the boy—that is, for "identification" with the character in the story.) Similarly: "What do you think the little girl is saying?"

"What time of the year do you think it is?" (This calls for inference.) "What makes you think so?"

These are the types of factual, inference, and thought questions that are used in the so-called, "Preparation" stage. They help the child relate to the story's setting, mood, and characters. Even before reading, the child knows *who, where, when, what* in a generalized way. In addition, the teacher or parent can print some of the sight words that will be found in the story. These should be the words that have been elicited from the children during the introductory perusal of the picture. In this case they could be: *toys, boy, girl, grandmother, store, train, doll,* and so on.

Obviously, the teacher has to be well-prepared, with a thorough knowledge of the story and its vocabulary to make the preparation stage a successful stepping-stone to reading.

Directed Reading Lesson

Part 2

Reading In beginning reading, children need constant support and encouragement, someone to respond and to praise their success. Most of all, they need someone to keep them from failing. This is a crucial time in their educational experience.

In very beginning stages of the DRL, the teacher or parent reads the story *for* and *with* the child, pointing to each word and making left-to-right *sweeps* with the pointing fingers *across short phrases*. When it can be done without a negative reaction from the child, the child's fingers may be held and used as pointers. Some teachers prefer to use a strip of cardboard to cover the reading material up to the line being read. Any such method helps achieve what psychologists call "visual tracking." It is imperative that the child in the beginning reading stages develop the habit of eye movement from left to right and, later, to develop a smooth flow of word and phrase processing. This cannot be done if the child's attention is allowed to float all over the page, or if the teacher insists on absolute perfection in the beginning.

The Directed Reading Lesson in a Whole-Word Approach Whole-word learning in the reading stage of the directed reading lessons may be generated on a one-to-one basis or by working with small groups. In the one-to-one approach, the teacher sits with the child and both work together from a single book. The teacher pronounces words and phrases slowly and the child is encouraged to echo these elements as spoken by the teacher.

Working with small groups rather than one-on-one requires a somewhat different technique. The teacher of small groups necessarily loses a certain amount of direct control over the learning process. Visual teaching, for example, cannot be kept under constant supervision. But if the group is small enough (and it *should* be kept small), the teacher can still monitor learning to the extent that any gross deviation from the left-to-right process can be corrected. As a further control of small-group activities, the teacher may now and then ask each member of the group to designate a "special" word for group discussion about its meaning and function in the sentence and its identifying characteristics. Of course, as with one-to-one teaching, children in the group should be encouraged to echo story words and phrases as they are read by the teacher.

Whether working one to one or in a group, children should be encouraged to "read" the story on their own after several teacher/child readings. At this point, a considerable amount of the story will have been memorized, but the teacher should stand by to supply troublesome words and to help out with a phrase or sentence if the reader appears to be tiring or becoming a bit discouraged.

The Directed Reading Lesson in a Phonics Approach   If, instead of or in addition to a whole-word approach, the teacher wishes to employ a phonics approach, the reading stage of DRL will progress more slowly because it will more often be interrupted with questions such as, "How does the word begin?" "What vowel letters do you see in the word?" "What might the word be if it starts with . . .?" In the phonics approach, there are more breaks in continuity and there is likely to be a loss in comprehension of the flow of language.

In addition, too much emphasis on phonics skills at this early stage of reading may arouse anxiety in the child. It may also deprive the beginner of the reinforcing achievement of the more immediate success inherent in the whole-word approach. Nevertheless, phonic skills do lead to greater accuracy in word identification and some phonic skills can be very useful even in the beginning stages of learning to read, including the reading component of the direct reading lesson.

Directed Reading Lesson

Part 3

Discussion   The discussion phase of DRL is intended to test for and develop cognitive learning, or comprehension. The word *cognitive,* as we have previously noted, has the same Latin base *(cognitio; cognoscere)* as the word *recognize.* In learning, however, cognitive means more than recognizing. In reading, it means more than merely recognizing a word as one that has been previously seen and memorized. It means *knowing* the word because we *know* its meaning. This kind of knowing is personal and intimate and is based upon one's own experiences. The mature reader, of course, has developed this kind of comprehension over years of reading. The beginner, however, must be carefully coached along the road to word comprehension.

The Comprehension Check The comprehension check-up after reading is conducted orally by the teacher in just about the same way as the prereading picture discussion. Questions concerning who? what? when? where? why? how? how much? how many? call for *literal* answers of facts derived from the reading. There are also questions to check deeper ("cognitive") meanings, all predicated upon *knowing,* rather than merely repeating verbatum what the author has said (literal).

This *cognitive* level of reading has been popularly referred to as the *interpretive* level (discussed fully in Chapter 7, comprehension) during which the teacher poses questions to elicit "interpretation" of what has been read. The interpretation is based upon the past experiences of each child:

"What do you think Mary did with the money she found?"
"Why do you think she did that?"
"How do you think Bugs Bunny felt when Mr. Owl told him that the seeds he had planted were not carrot seeds?"
"What do you think Louise really meant when she said that she 'couldn't stand it another minute'?"
"Do you think that sports are important to Billy?"
"What makes you think so?"
"Sports are important to you, aren't they?" (support helps the child feel *right*)
"Why do you think it is springtime in the story?"

These latter three questions are the type that help draw out interpretations based upon implied meanings. This is possible when the details in the story convey enough information for each child to attempt some interpretation, limited, of course, upon the past experiences of each. Some interpretations, therefore, will be elaborative and reflect rich experiences; others will be minimal, at best.

Another cognitive skill that is developed through the directed reading lesson is the ability to sequence. This is more than a mere recitation of an order of events such as: this happened, then this happened, and then this happened. With the help of special questions, the teacher can elevate the thinking to an awareness of causal relationships:

"What caused this to happen?" ("Why did it happen?")
"If the dog hadn't barked, what would have happened?"

Cause-and-effect relationships such as this may be extended to a chain of events, each a precursor of the next. In that way, a child is led to understand that acts have consequences. This leads to *knowing*—the essential element in cognitive reading.

Here are the subfactors of comprehension that we hope a child can demonstrate after the basic essentials of beginning reading have been mastered:

1. The meaning of a word, a phrase, and/or a sentence.

2. Following the story plot.
3. Knowing who, what, when, where, how, why.
4. Sensing implied meanings.
5. Able to predict future actions, based upon previous situations in the story.
6. Seeing cause-and-effect relationships.
7. Feeling emotional reactions to persons and events.

Directed Reading Lesson

Part 4

Skills Reinforcement During the preparation, reading, and discussion phases of DRL, the child has been slowly developing certain skills. Now is the time to reinforce those skills.

For example, there are always certain phonics elements to be reinforced. The beginning consonants and beginning sound groupings of letters can be reviewed and applied to one or two new words. Several words can be used as examples of bases upon which two or three new words can be constructed by changing the initial consonants. One word can serve as a phonogram or base to be added to a few selected initial consonants.

Story words such as *store, train, toys, boy, girl* could be used to build new words (but only a very few new words should be taught at this point). *Toy* and *boy* could be compared. Some flashcard practice on story words might be helpful. By all means, children should be encouraged to print story words on lined paper or in workbooks.

Directed Reading Lesson

Part 5

Enrichment The final phase of the direct reading lesson consists of enrichment activities. Perhaps the story can be acted out by some of the children with the rest as "audience." Perhaps a poem or jingle on much the same topic as the story's could be read aloud. Perhaps the teacher could construct an "experience story" based upon a child's comments about a personal experience similar to that of a character in the story. The enrichment stage may also be used to lead into a new story (and a new DRL): "We liked that story, didn't we? Now I have another one very much like that one. Would you like to have me read it for you?" Whatever enrichment activities the teacher decides upon, it is essential that they be creative, varied, and fun for the children.

BEGIN WITH THE CHILD

This, our final "How Do I Begin?" item, might just as well have been our first, for it is the keystone of the entire beginning-to-read program. Each and every activity and technique we have enumerated above can succeed only if we *begin with the child*. Remember always that you are not just teaching a subject, you are teaching children.

Observation   Pay attention to the child. As we pointed out in Chapter 2 and at the beginning of this chapter, children signal their readiness to read in a variety of ways: the questions they ask ("What does that word say?" Does this word begin like my name?"), their interest in and ability to handle story books, and so on. They send other signals also. They signal their need for help and their need *not* to be helped, their need for attention and their need not to be noticed. The creative teacher will be ever alert to all such signals. Let the child learn at his or her own pace. What that pace is can be read in the child's own signals.

Motivation   We have throughout this chapter noted scores of devices and techniques to help motivate the child to read. However, all such devices and techniques are basically extrinsic and can succeed only if they arouse the child's intrinsic desire to learn to read. Motivation must come from within if it is to be truly effective. The teacher's desire to teach is indeed important—but not nearly as important as the child's desire to learn. Study the children for evidence of self-motivation and foster its further development. Help those who signal a lack of self-motivation to achieve it.

Study the children to learn what interests them. Talk with the children to learn the experiences they have had. Use materials and techniques relevant to their interests and experiences. In short, begin where the child is, not where you, or some other adult, might like the child to be.

Self-Actualization   Let us assume, now, that we are dealing with children who have exhibited all of the signals that indicate they want to learn to read. What features of *self* are most significant in helping determine "How do I begin?"

Self-actualization is the immediate goal. The intrinsic drives may be many and varied. Some children we have known have had intense drives to read to find out information. Others have had equally intense drives to learn to read just to master that skill and to accomplish the mere goal of mastery. Their self-actualization is similar to that of the mountain climber who was asked, "Why do you climb mountains?", and answered, "Because they are there." We believe that some children want to learn to read just because reading is a challenge in itself. They are likely to read anything and everything they can, regardless of its cognitive or affective worth.

Some children are determined to learn to read for the pleasure of being in the company of a particular adult who takes the time to work with them. A teacher sometimes finds herself in such a position, acting *in loco parentis*, thus satisfying the child's need to have had a mother or father reading to him/her at home.

Attention-getting may occasionally be self-actualizing for some children, and learning to read may be the medium for achieving that goal. If this is what they need, should we deny it to them? Similarly, some children love to perform, not especially for attention, but as a medium for self-expression. The ability to read a story orally with expression and an occasional "sound effect" is pure joy to them.

Gifted children seem to be universally motivated to learn to read to find out, to excel, to learn more vocabulary, and even to compete with their peers. Their urge for excellence manifests itself early, and learning to read is one essential means for self-actualization.

Finally, all children who want to learn to read will say that they want to do so because "it is *fun*." That is their way of generalizing our psychological term, "self-actualization."

Relevance   This is an overworked term of the last decade, yet what better word is there to refer to the real interests of five- and six-year-olds who are beginning to learn to read?

A number of reports have been published on the reading interests of children and adolescents, but we know of none that delineate the reading interests of beginners. Consequently, we must rely on our own experience, on that of other first-grade teachers, on that of librarians, and on that of parents.

Children's interests at this age are individualized and quite varied. Much depends upon the exposures they have previously had: T.V., movies, books, stories, toys, play, trips, conversation, and so on. Nevertheless, there seem to be some features that have some universality among five- and six-year-olds in our cutlure today.

The interests of children, therefore, serve as clues to relevance. By the time children have reached readiness, they have acquired a number of story "friends." Mickey Mouse is a universal favorite. Many can even spell, "M-I-C K-E-Y M-O-U-S-E," in the Mickey Mouse song. Children love animals and pets, real and imaginary. They love scary stories, the imaginative, and the ridiculous. They enjoy repetition and alliteration. For example, in *The Gingerbread Boy*, "Run, run, as fast as you can! . . ."; in *Chicken Little*, "The sky is falling!"; in "There's a goblin lives at our house, at our house, at our house."; in *The Three Bears*, "Who's been sitting in my chair?" . . . ; in *Pinocchio*, "And his nose grew and grew and grew!" . . . ; in MUD! MUD! MUD!; and in the nonsensical alliteration in the Dr. Seuss stories.

These imaginative tales are, perhaps, more relevant to the beginner than are the realities of everyday life. Yet, most of our beginning-level reading materials are in different modes. The new basal readers have taken great steps toward providing children with more relevant beginning reading materials than those of the past decades. Individualized reading selections can be found (through careful and diligent search) that are relevant and also at a beginner's level of difficulty.

Finally, children themselves, are the keys to relevance. They will soon let us know what they like and what they don't like; what they want to learn to read and what they don't; what they want you to read to them again and again.

If one will but listen to children, one will soon learn one more answer to the question, "How do I begin?"

One can scarcely imagine a more important or rewarding task than starting

What could be more *relevant* than an impending trip to the hospital (perhaps for a tonsillectomy) for a six-year-old? Putting it down in print makes it possible for this child and others in her group to read something that is very meaningful at that moment.

a young child on the yellow-brick road to learning, knowing that the wizard who dwells at the end of the road has a lifetime of unimagined wonders in store for the traveler who completes the journey. But remember always that learning to read is a child-centered process. Study the child. Listen to the child. Learn from the child.

SOME ESSENTIAL ELEMENTS OF A SUCCESSFUL BEGINNING READING PROGRAM

1. Surround children with an environment for reading.
2. Tell and read good stories and poems to the children.
3. Encourage a few early-bloomers to read some little stories on their own (with the help of adults).
4. Produce some language-experience story books, individualized for each child.

5. Teach some basic consonant and vowel sounds.
6. Employ some read-along books and stories, emphasizing "how the word begins" when an unknown word is encountered.
7. Coach the children in learning how to print in good manuscript.
8. Begin the learning of "service" sight words, using Dr. Jerry John's list or Dr. William K. Durr's list as a guide.
9. Work with three-letter words, emphasizing the CVC pattern (consonant-vowel-consonant) because they are most apt to be phonetically regular.
10. Hold sessions with small groups to elicit each child's "personal feelings" words, and print those words on word-cards for each child.
11. Arrange for each child to have an individual word book, alphabetized, and containing words that the child wishes to use in composition of stories.
12. Encourage the composition of stories, having each child utilize his or her word book. (This phase of the program requires an aide or volunteers. One teacher is not enough!)
13. Teach a *few* phonics "rules" and syllabication strategies to help the child in word identification. (Details in Chapters 4 and 5.)
14. Conduct some rote repetition practice, using flash cards or other means of practice.
15. Demonstrate how words can be built upon graphemic bases, emphasizing the letter clusters that constitute each base.
16. Use movable letters and words to help children construct words, phrases, and sentences.
17. Use gadgets, games, special equipment, and so on for development and reinforcement of reading skills.
18. Use directed reading lesson procedures for each major story used in the classroom.
19. Remember that you are teaching children as well as teaching reading.
20. Feel good about yourself, remembering that you are involved in a tremendously important educational activity—helping children open the windows of the world through reading!

BIBLIOGRAPHY

Allington, Richard, "An Evaluation of the Use of Color Cues to Focus Attention in Discrimination and Paired-Associate Learning," *Reading Research Quarterly* **10**:2 (1974–1975), 244–247.

Askland, Linda C., "Conducting Individual Language Experience Stories," *Reading Teacher*, **27**:2 (November, 1973), 167–170.

Aukerman, Robert C., *Approaches to Beginning Reading*, New York: Wiley, 1971.

Aukerman, Robert C. (Editor), *Some Persistent Questions in Beginning Reading*, Newark, Delaware: International Reading Association, 1972.

Ball, Samuel, and Gerry Ann Bogatz, *Reading With TV: An Evaluation of the Electric Company*, Princeton: ETS, 1973; see also the follow-up 1973 ETS report.

Barr, Rebecca C., "Instructional Pace Differences and Their Effects on Reading Acquisition," *Reading Research Quarterly*, **9**:4 (1973–1974), 526–554.

Barr, Rebecca, "The Effect of Instruction on Pupil Reading Strategies," *Reading Research Quarterly*, **10**:4 (1974–1975), 555–582.

Barrett, Thomas C., "The Relationship Between Measures of Prereading Visual Discrimination and First-Grade Reading Achievement," *Reading Research Quarterly*, **1** (1965), 51–76.

Batinich, Mary Ellen, "Language-Experience Activities," *Reading Teacher*, **23**:6 (March (1970), 539–546.

Belmont, Ira, "Requirements of the Early Reading Task," *Perceptual and Motor Skills*, **38** (1974), 527–537.

Bettelheim, Bruno, "Learning to Read: A Primer for Literacy," *Harpers Magazine*. (April, 1979), 56–58.

Bogatz, Gerry Ann and Samuel Ball, *A Summary of the Major Findings in the Second Year of Sesame Street*, Princeton: ETS, 1971.

Briggs, Chari and David Elkind, "Cognitive Development in Early Readers," *Developmental Psychology*, **9** (1973), 279–280.

Brittain, Mary M., "Inflectional Performance and Early Reading Achievement," *Reading Research Quarterly*, **6**:1 (1970), 34–48.

Burke, Elizabeth, "A Developmental Study of Children's Reading Strategies," *Education Review*, **29**:1 (1976), 30–46.

Burt, Velma, "A Daily Story Approach to Beginning Reading," *Reading Teacher*, **23**:6 (1970), 507–510.

Boarks, Nancy, and Amy R. Allen, "A Program to Enhance Peer Tutoring," *Reading Teacher*, **30**:5 (1977), 479–484.

Chall, Jeanne, *Learning to Read: The Great Debate*, McGraw-Hill Book Co., New York, 1967.

Christina, Robert, "Learning Sight Words," in *Language Face to Face*, Margaret Early (Editor), Syracuse University, 1971, 109–114.

Chomsky, Carol, "Stages in Language Development and Reading Exposure," *Harvard Educational Review*, **42** (1972), 1–33.

Church, Marilyn, "Does Visual Perception Training Help Beginning Readers?" *Reading Teacher*, **27** (1974), 361–364.

Conrad, R. "Speech and Reading," in *Language by Ear and by Eye,* J. F. Kavanagh and I. G. Mattingly (Editors), Cambridge: MIT Press, 1972, 205–240.

Dahl, Patricia R., and S. Jay Samuels, "Teaching Children to Reading Using Hypothesis/Test Strategies," *Reading Teacher,* **30**:6 (1977), 603–606.

Denburg, Susan D., "The Interaction of Picture and Print in Reading Instruction," *Reading Research Quarterly,* **12**:2 (1976–1977), 176–189.

Dietrich, Dorothy M., "New Approaches to Easing Word Attack at the Beginning Reader Levels," *Reading Teacher,* **23**:6 (1970) 511–515.

Dolch, Edward W., "Basic Sight Vocabulary," *Elementary School Journal,* **31** (1936), 456–460.

Dolch, Edward W., and B. R. Buckingham, *A Combined Word List,* Boston: Ginn, 1936.

Dreyer, H. B., "Rx for Pupil Tutoring Programs," *Reading Teacher,* **26**:8 (1973), 810–813.

Dunn-Rankin, P., "The Similarity of Lower-Case Letters of the English Alphabet," *Journal of Verbal Learning and Verbal Behavior,* **7** (1968), 990–995.

Durkin, Dolores, "Children Who Read Before Grade One," *The Reading Teacher,* **14** (1961), 163–166.

Durkin, Dolores, *Children Who Read Early;* Teachers College Press, Teachers College, Columbia University, 1966.

Durr, William "Computor Study of High-Frequency Words in Popular Trade Juveniles," *Reading Teacher,* **27**:1 (1973), 37–42.

Ehly, Stewart W., and Stephen C. Larsen, *Peer Tutoring for Individualized Instruction,* Boston: Allyn & Bacon, 1980.

Elliot, Arthur, "Student Tutoring Benefits Everyone," *Phi Delta Kappan,* **54** (1973), 535–538.

Estes, W. K., "The Locus of Inferential and Perceptual Processes in Letter Identification," *Journal of Experimental Psychology,* **2** (1975), 122–145.

Evans, James R., and Linda J. Smith, "Psycholinguistic Skills of Early Readers," *Reading Teacher,* **30**:1 (1976) 39–43.

Fadiman, Bernard, Presented to the annual conference of the Reading Reform Foundation, Scottsdale, Arizona, May 23, 1975.

Feeley, Joan T., "Television and Reading in the Seventies," *Language Arts,* **52** (1975), 797–801.

Feeley, Joan T., "Reading with TV: British and American Approaches," *Reading Teacher,* **30**:3 (1976), 271–275.

Foley, Louis, "Something of What English Owes to French," *Reading Horizons,* **15**:3 (1975), 135–141.

Frager, Stanley, and Carolyn Stern, "Learning by Teaching," *Reading Teacher,* **23**:5 (1970), 403–417.

Freshour, Frank W., "Beginning Reading: Parents Can Help," *Reading Teacher,* **25**:6 (1972), 513–516.

Frith, Uta, "Why Do Children Reverse Letters?" *British Journal of Psychology,* **62** (1971), 459–468.

Gates, Arthur I., "The Necessary Mental Age for Beginning Reading," *Elementary School Journal,* **37** (1937), 498–508. This is the "classic" report by Dr. Gates that generated the notion that a child must have a *mental age* of *6-years; 6-months* to be successful in beginning reading.

Gleitman, Lila R., and Paul Rozin, "The Structure and Acquisition of Reading I: Relations Between Orthographics and the Structure of Language," in *Toward a Psychology of Reading,* Arthur S. Reber and Don L. Scarborough (Editors), Hillsdale, NJ: Erlbaum, 1977, 1–53.

Gold, Patricia and Adele M. Taylor, "Of Course, Volunteers," *Reading Teacher,* **28**:7 (1975), 614–616.

Goodacre, Elizabeth J., *Reading in Infant Classes.* The Mere, Upton Park, Slough, Bucks, Wales: National Foundation for Educational Research in England and Wales, 1967.

Goodacre, Elizabeth J., and Margaret M. Clark, "Initial Approaches to Teaching Reading in Scottish and English Schools," *Reading,* **5**:2 (1971), 15–21.

Goodman, Kenneth S., "Analysis of Oral Reading Miscues," *Reading Research Quarterly,* **5**:1 (1969), 9–30.

Goodman, Kenneth S., and Yetta M., "Learning to Read is Natural," in *Theiry and Practice of Early Reading,* Vol. 1, Lauren B. Resnick and Phyllis A. Weaver (Editors), Hillsdale, NJ: Erlbaum, 1979, 137–154.

Goodman, Yetta M, and Burke, Carolyn L., *Reading Miscue Inventory,* New York: Macmillan, 1972.

Groff, Patrick, "A New Sequence for Teaching Lower-Case Letters," *Journal of Reading Behavior,* **5**:4 (1972, 297–303.

Groff, Patrick, "The Topsy-Turvy World of 'Sight' Words," *The Reading Teacher,* **27**:6 (1974), 572–577.

Groff, Patrick J., "Sight Words: The Humpty Dumpty of Reading Instruction," *Reading* (U. K. Reading Assoc). **8** (1974), 11–16.

Groff, Patrick J., "Long Versus Short Words in Beginning Reading," *Reading World,* **14** (1975), 277–289.

Groff, Patrick J., "The Mythology of Reading: Sight Words," *Reading Horizons,* **15**:4 (1975), 208–211. This is a sequel to Dr. Groff's "Topsy-Turvy World of Sight Words," In *Reading Teacher,* **27**:6 (1974), 272–278.

Groff, Patrick J., "Limitations of Context Cues for Beginning Readers," *Reading World,* **16**:2 (December, 1976), 97–103. Presented six reasons why context clues are not necessarily the best means for identifying words.

Guralnick, Michael J., "Alphabet Discrimination and Distinctive Features," *Journal of Learning Disabilities,* **5** (1972), 428–434.

Hall, MaryAnne, *Teaching Reading as a Language Experience,* Columbus: Charles E. Merrill, 1970.

Hall, Mary Anne, "A Language-Experience Perspective," *Reading World,* **15**:4 (1976), 196–202.

Hardy, Madeline, I., "The Development of Beginning Reading Skills: Recent Findings," in *Reading and Related Skills,* Margaret Clark and Alastair Milne (Editors), London: Ward Lock Educational, 1973, 46–56.

Hardy, M., R. G. Stennett, and P. C. Smythe, "Auditory Segmentation and Auditory Blending in Relation to Beginning Reading," *Alberta Journal of Educational Research,* **19** (1973), 144–158.

Harris, Albert J., and Milton D. Jacobson, "Basic Vocabulary for Beginning Reading," *Reading Teacher,* **26**:4 (1973), 392–395. This article contains the Harris and Jacobson "Core Words" list.

Harris, Albert J., and Milton D. Jacobson, "Some Comparisons Between Basic Elementary Reading Vocabularies and Other Word Lists," *Reading Research Quarterly,* **9**:1 (1973–1974), 87–109.

Harzem, P., M. I. Lee, and T. R. Miles, "The Effect of Pictures in Learning to Read," *British Journal of Educational Psychology,* **46**:3 (1976), 318–322.

Hillerich, Robert L., "Word Lists—Getting It All Together," *Reading Teacher,* **27**:4 (1974), 353–360.

Hook, J. Nick., *History of the English Language.* New York: Ronald Press, 1975. This is, in our opinion, one of the best resources for teachers. It is up-to-date, easy-to-read, and contains an excellent bibliography and a list of almost 3500 American/English words, indexed for reference to pages on which they are discussed.

Hoskisson, Kenneth, "Successive Approximation and Beginning Reading," *Elementary School Journal,* **75** (1975), 442–451.

Jennings, Robert E., "Teaching Reading from Children's Language Experience Stories, *Kansas Reading Quarterly,* **7**:3 (1974), 134–139. (Part I), Part II appeared in **7**:3 (1974), 172–177. These are excellent articles on the practical use of language-experience stories.

Johns, Jerry L., "Should the Dolch List be Retired, Replaced, or Revised?", *Elementary School Journal,* **74** (1974), 375–380.

Johns, Jerry L., "Updating the Dolch Basic Sight Vocabulary," *Reading Horizons,* **16**:2 (1976), 104–111.

Johns, Jerry L. and DiAnn W. Ellis, "Reading: Children Tell It Like it Is," *Reading World,* **16**:2 (1976), 115–128. Most of the 1600 children surveyed had little or no understanding of the reading process.

Johnson Dale D., "The Dolch List Reexamined," *Reading Teacher,* **24**:5 (1971), 449–457.

Johnson, Dale D., and P. David Pearson, "Skills Management Systems: A Critique," *Reading Teacher,* **28**:8 (1975), 757–764.

Johnson, H., D. R. Jones, A. C. Cole, and M. B. Walters, "The Use of Diacritical Marks in Teaching Beginners to Read," *British Journal of Educational Psychology,* **42** (1972), 120–126.

Johnson, Marjorie S., and Roy A. Kress, "Task Analysis for Criterion-Referenced Tests," *Reading Teacher,* **24**:4 (1971), 355–359.

Jones, Daisy Marvel, *Teaching Children to Read,* New York: Harper and Row, 1971, 46–47. Presents 62 subfactors of readiness under six categories: physical, social, psychological, intelligectual, linguistic, and general.

Kasdon, Lawrence, M. (Editor), *Reading Teacher,* **26**:3 (1972). This entire issue on testing is an excellent source of information on informal reading inventories, criterion-referenced testing, etc.

Kenkins, Joseph, R. Barker Bausell, and Linda Jenkins, "Comparisons of Letter Name and Letter Sound Training as Transfer Variables," *American Educational Research Journal,* **9** (1972), 75–86.

LaBerge, David, "The Perception of Units in Beginning Reading," in *Theory and Practice of Early Reading,* Vol. 3, Lauren B. Resnick and Phyllis A. Weaver (Editors), Hillsdale, MJ: Erlbaum, 1979, 31–52.

Laird, A. W., and Joseph P. Cangemi, "When Are Children Ready to Learn to Read?" *Reading Improvement* **12** (1975), 47–49.

Livo, Norma J., "Reading Readiness Factors and Beginning Reading Success," *Reading Teacher,* **24**:2 (1970), 124–129.

Lloyd, Bruce A., "P-V-S, a New Approach to Teaching Communication Skills," *Reading Horizons,* **14**:2 (1974), 69–74. This article presented a detailed how-to-do-it procedure for the Picture-Vocabulary-Story, in which the pupil matches vocabulary to form a picture from which a story is developed.

Lott, Deborah and Frank Smith, "Knowledge of Intraword Redundancy by Beginning Readers," *Psychonomic Science,* **19** (1970), 343–344.

Lowe, A. J., and John Follman, "Comparison of the Dolch List with Other Word Lists," *Reading Teacher*, **28**:1 (1974), 40−44. All five word lists contained the same 150 most-common words. "Regardless of type of material, level of (difficulty of) material, or whether sampling or word counts were made, basic words are essentially the same."

Mason, George E. and William E. Blanton, "Story Content for Beginning Reading Instruction," *Elementary English*, **48 (1971), 793**−796.

Mason, Jana M., "Overgeneralizations in Learning to Read," *Journal of Reading Behavior*, **8**:2 (1976), 173−182.

McNeil, John D., "False Prerequisites in the Teaching of Reading," paper presented at AERA Annual Meeting, Chicago, April, 1974.

McNinch, George, "Auditory-Perceptual Factors and Measured First-Grade Reading Achievement," *Reading Research Quarterly*, **6**:4 (1971), 472−492.

Mangieri, John N., and Michael S. Kahn, "Is the Dolch List of 220 Basic Sight Words Irrelevant?" *Reading Teacher*, **30**:6 (March, 1977) 649−651.

Meltzer, N. S., and R. Herse, "The Boundaries of Written Words as Seen by First Graders," *Journal of Reading Behavior*, **1** (1969), 3−13.

Mickelson, Norma I., "Associative Verbal Encoding (a/v/e): a Measure of Language Performance and its Relationship to Reading Achievement," doctoral dissertation, abstracted in *Reading Research Quarterly*, **9**:2 (1973−1974), 227−230.

Montgomery, Diane, "Teaching Prereading Skills Through Training in Pattern Recognition," *Reading Teacher*, **30**:6 (1977), 616−623.

Muehl, Siegmar, and Marie C. DiNello, "Early First-Grade Skills Related to Subsequent Reading Performance: A Seven-Year Followup Study," *Journal of Reading Behavior*, **8**:1 (1976), 67−82.

Neidermeyer, Fred C., "Effects of Training on the Instructional Behaviors of Student Tutors," *Journal of Educational Research*, **64** (1970), 119−123.

Neuman, Susan, B., "Television: Its Effects on Reading and School Achievement," *Reading Teacher*, **33**:7 (1980), 801−805.

Otto, Wayne, and Robert Chester, "Sight Words for Beginning Readers," *Journal of Educational Research*, **65** (1972), 435−443.

Pflaum, Susanna W., "Diagnosis of Oral Reading," *Reading Teacher*, **33**:2 (1979), 278−284.

Pidgeon, Douglas, "Logical Steps in the Process of Learning to Read," *Educational Research* (Windsor, England), **18**:3 (1976), 174−181.

Pienaar, Peter T., "Breakthrough in Beginning Reading: Language-Experience Approach," *Reading Teacher*, **30**:5 (1977), 489–496.

Prescott, George A., "Criterion-Referenced Test Interpretation," *Reading Teacher*, **24**:4 (1971), 347–354. The author presented a clear explanation of the nature, use, and value of criterion-referenced tests.

Rauch, Sidney J. (Editor), *Handbook for the Volunteer Tutor*, Newark: International Reading Association, 1969.

Read, C., "Pre-School Children's Knowledge of English Phonology," *Harvard Educational Review*, **41** (1971), 1–34.

Robinson, Helen M., Visual and Auditory Modalities Related to Methods for Beginning Reading," *Reading Research Quarterly*, **8** (1972), 7–39.

Rodenborn, Leo V., "Determining, Using Expectancy Formulas," *Reading Teacher*, **28**:3 (1974), 286–291.

Ross, Ramon R., "Frannie and Frank and the Flannelboard," *Reading Teacher*, **27**:1 (1973), 43–47.

Ryckman, David B., Rosemarie McCartin, and Sam Sebesta, "Do Structured Reading Programs Hamper Intellectual Development?" *Elementary School Journal*, **77**:1 (1976), 71–73. Answer: "No."

Samuels, S. Jay, "The Effect of Letter-Name Knowledge on Learning to Read," *American Educational Research Journal*, **8** (1972), 65–74.

Samuels, S. Jay, "Hierarchial Subskills in the Reading Acquisition Process," in *Aspects of Reading Acquisition*, John T. Guthrie (Editor), Baltimore, Johns Hopkins University Press, 1976, 162–179.

Samuels, S. Jay, and Roger H. Anderson, "Visual Recognition Memory, Paired-Associate Learning and Reading Achievement," *Journal of Educational Psychology*, **65** (1973), 160–167.

Savin, H. B., "What the Child Knows About Speech When He Starts to Read," in *Language by Ear and by Eye*, J. F. Kavanagh and I. G. Mattingly (Editors), Cambridge, MA: MIT Press, 1972.

Schwartz, Robert M., "Strategic Processes in Beginning Reading," *Journal of Reading Behavior*, **9**:1 (1977), 17–26.

Sebesta, Sam Leaton, "The Art of Storytelling" in *Some Persistent Questions on Beginning Reading*, Robert C. Aukerman (Editor), Newark, DE: International Reading Association, 1972.

Segal, Marilyn, "An Experimental Study in Perceptual Modality Training," *Journal of Reading Behavior*, **3**:4 (1970), 22–34.

Shankweiler, Donald and Isabelle Y. Liberman, "Misreading: A Search for Causes," in *Language by Eye and By Ear*, J. F. Kavanagh and I. G. Mattlingly (Editors) Cambridge: MIT Press, 1972.

Shedlock, Marie L., *The Art of the Story-Teller*, New York: Dover, 1915. (One of the old classics on the art).

Shy, Roger W., "The Mismatch of Child Language and School Language: Implications of Beginning Reading Instruction," in *Theory and Practice of Early Reading*, Vol. 1, Lauren B. Resnick and Phyllis A. Weaver (Editors), Hillsdale, NJ: Erlbaum, 1979, 187−207.

Silverston, Randall A., and John W. Deichmann, "Sense Modality Research and the Acquisition of Reading Skills," *Review of Educational Research*, **45** (1974), 149−172.

Smith, Lewis B., and Glen D. Morgan, "Cassette Tape Recordings as a Primary Method in the Development of Early Reading Material," *Elementary English*, **52** (1975), 534−538.

Smythe, P. C., R. G. Stennett, Madeline Hardy, and H. R. Wilson, "Developmental Patterns in Elemental Skills: Knowledge of Upper-Case and Lower-Case Letter Names," *Journal of Reading Behavior*, **3**:3 and **3**:4 (1970−1971).

Spache, George D and Spache, Evelyn, B., *Reading in the Elementary School*, Allyn & Bacon, Boston, 1973, p. 76. List twenty-eight items in a "Readiness Checklist" under five main headings: Vision, Speech, Listening, Scoial and Emotional Behavior, and Interest in Learning to Read.

Speer, Olga B., and George S. Lamb, "First Grade Reading Ability and Fluency in Naming Verbal Symbols," *Reading Teacher*, **29**:6 (1976), 572−576.

Staten, Marge, "Teaching a Basic Sight Word Vocabulary," *Reading Horizons*, **13**:1 (1972), 16−22.

Stauffer, Russell H., *The Language-Experience Approach to Teaching Reading*, New York: Harper and Row, 1970.

Telegdy, Gabriel A., "The Effectiveness of Four Readiness Tests as Predictors of First Grade Academic Achievement," *Psychology in the Schools*, **12** (1975), 4−11.

Templeton, Shane, "Young Children Invent Words: Developing Concepts of 'Word-ness,' " *Reading Teacher*, **33**:4 (1980), 454−459.

Timko, Henry G., "Configuration as a Cue in the Word Recognition of Beginning Readers," *Journal of Experimental Education*, **39** (1970), 68−69.

Tway, Eileen, "Language Experience: All Together," *Reading Teacher*, **27**:3 (1973), 249−252.

Wardhaugh, Ronald, "Theories of Language Acquisition in Relation to Beginning Reading Instruction," *Reading Research Quarterly,* **7**:1 (1971), 168–194.

Wattenberg, William W., and Clare Clifford, "Relation of Self-Concepts to Beginning Achievement in Reading," *Child Development,* **35** (1964), 461–467.

Weber, Rose-Marie, "First-Graders Use of Grammatical Context in Reading," in *Basic Studies in Reading,* Harry Levin and Joanna P. Williams (Editors), New York: Basic Books, 1970, 147–163.

Whisler, Nancy G., "Visual-Memory Training in First Grade: Effects on Visual Discrimination and Reading Ability," *Elementary School Journal,* **74** (1974), 51–54.

White, William F., and Margaret Simmons, "First Grade Readiness Predicted by Teachers' Perception of Students' Maturity and Students' Perception of Self," *Perceptual and Motor Skills,* **39** (1974), 395–399.

Young, F. A., and D. B. Lindsley, (Editors) *Early Experience and Visual Information Processing in Perceptual and Reading Disorders,* Washington, D.C.: National Academy of Sciences, 1970.

Zirkel, Perry A., and John F. Greene, "Measurement of Attitudes Toward Reading the Elementary Grades: A Review," *Reading World,* **16**:2 (1976), 104–113.

UNIT THREE

Only the most obstinate would deny that reading is a skill, and few would dispute the statement that no skill is learned without drill. Research in skill training during the last half-century has regularly shown that blind repetition is not as effective as drill supported by knowledge of causation and of results. This is particularly true of the learning of motor skills. How much more true it must be in the acquisition of the skill of reading. A teacher, therefore, who sets forth to teach a child to learn to read should be prepared to help that child with an understanding of some of the means for acquiring that skill so that drill will be within the cognitive mode and not just within the repetitive mode.

The skills of reading are many-faceted, but not so many that they cannot be segmented and delineated as separate, yet related, subskills. It is possible (indeed, some have done it) to fragment reading into more than one hundred identifiable subskills; each to be tested, prescribed, taught, learned, and retested. This we refer to as the "nitty-gritty" of reading. We do not deny that somewhere in the process and somehow the child who would become an efficient, mature reader must internalize most of these nitty-gritty subskills.

We believe it is helpful, first, to devise a logical framework of categories upon which the many subskills can be arranged. The five chapter titles in this unit serve that purpose; these categories briefly restated are (1) the skill of word recognition; (2) phonics; (3) vocabulary, (4) comprehension, and (5) study. To elaborate on them at this point would be repetitious of the extensive treatment given each category in its own chapter. The point here is that we must know how to teach word-recognition skills, phonics skills; comprehension skills; vocabulary skills; and reading/study skills, for they are the fundamental functions of the process of reading. Without them all, there is no finished "product."

SKILLS

Unit Three, therefore, may be considered as the heart of the reading-learning process. No one segment of the unit should be thought of as more important than any of the others. Neither should it be thought that their sequence implies a hierarchy, albeit that the sequence, admittedly, is consciously arranged on what we are prepared to contend is a logical order.

Whereas at one time reading specialists maintained that reading/study skills would not be taught until the intermediate grades; that some of the "advanced" phonics' skills and word analysis skills were appropriate for the fourth grade; and, in fact, that a structured ordering of these skills could and should be designated for "introduction" by grades, it is now the consensus that there is much interrelatedness between these skills and it is neither logical nor realistic to attempt to program their introduction.

Even so, it is hardly realistic to ignore that first things come first and form the foundation for further learning. It would seem irrational, for example, to expect a first grader to engage in reading for main ideas before having acquired a good battery of word-recognition skills. Similarly, it seems logical that vocabulary development can be a part of word-recognition skill training, and *vice versa*.

There are those who advocate (or seem to do so) that children will learn to read "just by reading." Some children may appear to do so. Yet, upon close scrutiny, they frequently carry on their own skills-learning simultaneously. We suspect that their superior abilities equip them to be able to seek the right kind of help at the right moment of need; to internalize the generalizations quickly; and, thus, to build a quality of reading skills far in excess of those that have been formally taught to them and their peers. We do not accept the notion that they have learned to read "just by reading" any more than one learns to play an instrument just by playing. To perfect any skill, be it reading or running, requires more than just doing it. The help of a trained coach who knows what help to give and when to give it is as essential in reading as in tennis, golf, piloting a plane, surfing, or whatever.

The strategies suggested in the five chapters in this unit on skills are intended to help prepare you to be that "reading coach."

CHAPTER FOUR

How Do I Teach
Word-recognition Skills?

Preschool Communication Skills
Recognition of Familiar Words in Print
   Definition of "Word Recognition"
   From Known to Unknown
   Exposure and Repetition
Recognition of Words in Isolation
   Nouns: The Names of Things in the Environment
   Teaching Verb Recognition
Teaching Word-Analysis Skills
   Definition of Word Analysis
   Phonics in Word Analysis
   Syllables in Word Analysis
   End-of-Word Technique
   Recurring Structural Patterns
   Contractions
   Letter Configuration
   Compounds
Teaching Word-recognition Skills in Context
Conclusion

PRESCHOOL COMMUNICATION SKILLS

As we have indicated throughout this text, children do not enter the learning-to-read classroom with what philosophers call *tabula rasa*—that is, with minds free of previous impressions. In truth, their minds have already absorbed basic linguistic patterns and language habits. Children come to the classroom with a "speaking vocabulary" quite adequate to communicate among themselves and with adults. In addition, they may have a "listening vocabulary" of literally thousands of words. (The extent of each child's linguistic development will, of course, depend upon the child's previous social and cultural environment.) Teaching reading skills does not, then, begin in a vacuum. The foundation for learning these skills has already been laid.

That foundation is as yet, of course, a somewhat shaky one. The ever-active minds of normal youngsters are capable of absorbing a good deal more than they can accumulate. At this stage, for example, word recognition is likely to be merely at the visual and/or auditory level—which may lead to errors in usage that can be very amusing to the adult and sometimes instructive to the teacher. Many a loud young voice has piously poured forth in song at Christmas with "Round John Virgin" replacing "round yon Virgin" or "Gladly, the cross-eyed bear" instead of "Gladly, the cross I'd bear."

Then there is the five-year-old who proudly displayed his "Christmas" drawing of what appeared to be an airplane with four persons on board. When asked, "Tell me about your picture," the child replied that the people in the picture are Mary, Joseph, and the baby Jesus. "Who, then, is the fourth person?" "Oh, that's the 'conscious pilot,' and he's taking them on the flight to Egypt!"

Smile as we will, the child's logic is unassailable. The youngster has heard the Biblical story of the Holy Family's "flight into Egypt." Is it not logical for the modern child to assume that, if you're going to take a flight, you need an airplane to take it in? And isn't it reasonable to have a "conscious pilot" to fly it? The point is, of course, that the teacher must base strategies for teaching reading skills upon the child's own experiences.

Mistakes, logical or not so logical, aside, normal preschoolers and youngsters just entering school have a remarkable ability to recognize the meanings of thousands of words and to use many of them with reasonable correctness in conversation. Your job as a teacher of reading is to build upon this ability and move the child along the road to recognition of words in point.

Two Cornell University psychologists, Professors Eleanor Gibson and Harry Levin, who have worked primarily in the field of psycholinguistics, suggested that word-recognition should be considered from five points of view:

1. *Graphically,* inasmuch as they are composed of sequences of spaced letters surrounded by larger spaces before and after.

2. *Phonologically* because they are subject to analysis of their phonemic units.
3. *Orthographically,* for there are accepted rules that certain letters may appear together in a certain way in certain words, whereas others may not. (This may explain why words that are incorrectly spelled "just don't look right" to the mature reader.)
4. *Morphemically,* inasmuch as words do trigger some meaning or meanings (morphemes) by themselves outside of context. For example, the word *baseball* contains two meanings regardless of whether or not it is used in connection with *bat, field, player, uniform, score, fan,* or whatever. The word has a morphemic characteristic.
5. *Syntactically,* for usually words do not appear by themselves, but as units in a sentence in which they have functional tasks to perform, which give them their cognitive meaning.

The reader of this text will recognize that it is precisely these elements that have been emphasized throughout our previous discussions of word recognition and other facets of learning to read. You have met them before and you will meet them again.

RECOGNITION OF FAMILIAR WORDS IN PRINT

DEFINITION OF "WORD RECOGNITION"

Word recognition (sometimes called "word identification," "word analysis," or "word attack") is the ability to differentiate a particular printed word symbol from all others and to understand its most common meaning in isolation and/or in the setting (context) in which it is used.

FROM KNOWN TO UNKNOWN

As noted above, teaching word recognition should begin with what the child already knows—in other words, you should proceed from the known to the unknown. For example, many youngsters come to beginning reading already able to recognize words commonly seen in their environment—*A & P, McDonalds, Dairy Queen, Sesame Street, Mister Rogers,* and so on. Many such already familiar words can be used as a basis for further word recognition.

Most children can also recognize their own names in print (or, if not, they can rather quickly be taught to do so). Children's names, therefore, are logical starting points for teaching word recognition skills.

EXPOSURE AND REPETITION

As previously noted, one very effective technique for use with beginners is for the teacher to take attendance by holding up flash cards containing the printed names of the children. In less than a month of such routine, many children will have developed word recognition techniques adequate for differentiating and pronouncing the names of many, if not most of their classmates. When children are asked, "How do you know that is Jimmy's, or Ellie's, or Tommy's name in print?" the answers vary: "Because it starts the same as mine." "Because it has that little twisty thing at the end." "Because it's like my brother's name." Or maybe the answer will be something seemingly irrelevant, such as "because I like Jimmy," or maybe "just because." The exact components of this learning process remain a mystery. Obviously, different children use different clues.

At this point it should suffice to say that the words children already recognize in print are the logical and most effective starting points for teaching whole-word recognition. From them, children transfer initial sounds related to initial graphemes to other words that "begin like my name," or they find internal graphemic characteristics in their own names that also appear in new words. Thus they move from the known to the unknown, with at least some small units of learning being transferred, provided of course, that the children are encouraged and helped to make the transfer.

As also previously noted, drill on sight words is essential in the beginning stages of word recognition. The flash card technique should be used extensively in the beginning classroom to generate familiarity with sight words. Methods and devices for this technique have already been detailed in Chapter 3.

High-frequency sight words should also be practiced through individualized reading of materials containing these words. When such words become automatically recognized in context, they indeed become, as Dolch called them, "service words"—that is, words of repeated service to the reader.

Special writing exercises designed to use as many sight words as possible provide further practice in the learning of these essential high-frequency words.

RECOGNITION OF WORDS IN ISOLATION

As we know, words are learned both in isolation and in context. Even though the two skills are essentially different, there is no real dichotomy between them. Both are essential to learning to read and both must be taught.

Many children, even by the age of three or four, have already learned to recognize letter clusters as printed symbols that signal pronunciations. They have, in fact, learned such letter clusters (words) in isolation. By the time they reach school, such children are eager to learn more of them and more about them. "What is this word?" "What does that word mean?" Although they may be quite adept at speaking in phrases and sentences, beginning readers never ask "What does this phrase say?" or "What does this sentence mean?" Such semantic entities are as yet a bit too complex for them.

Let us, then, begin where the child begins—with recognition of words in isolation. Later in the chapter, we will discuss recognizing words in context.

NOUNS: THE NAMES OF THINGS IN THE ENVIRONMENT

Teaching Noun Recognition   As the two-year-old moves from the pointing stage to awareness that every object has a *name,* nouns become a major point of attention in language acquisition. Body words and the names of people and things in the immediate environment are usually learned first: *nose, eyes, ears, tummy, dog, cat, bird, book, bed, Mommy, Daddy, car, TV,* and so on.

The small child's first book is likely to consist of illustrations of persons and objects (nouns), and the child's first "dictionary" is not so much a book of definitions as it is an alphabetically arranged series of pictures illustrating nouns.

Even before the child has much command of spoken nouns, parents are likely to encourage noun recognition by asking, "Where is the cow in the picture?" "Point to the tree," and so on. Later the small child will be heard privately repeating the noun over and over until it is fixed in memory. All this is done through intrinsic motivation with no outside compulsion or reward, for the child already recognizes that names of things are a significant part of communication.

It seems logical, but without any more than pragmatic proof, to suppose that the more nouns in one's speaking vocabulary, the more ready for recognizing nouns in print. Throughout the entire school day, you as a classroom teacher help children acquire a vocabulary of nouns in a purposeful, directed learning manner. It can be subtle, but should convey the message that "everything has a correct name, and we will learn it." A turtle is a *sand turtle,* or a *box turtle.* A "bug" is something that has a special name. A flower has a name, and so on. This is especially effective later on in the grades when children begin to learn the parts of moving machines; the parts of larger wholes. They can learn that streets also can be more specifically called by such names as *Avenue, Lane, Alley, Crescent, Circle, Boulevard, Way, Place, Plaza, Drive,* etc. By the time children commence to learn names such as these, they will already be reading at some level of proficiency. But we cannot wait until they commence to read to begin to help them build a large store of nouns in their speaking vocabulary. Throughout their entire school life, children should have purposeful planned instruction emphasizing correct nouns for things.

Recognition of Nouns in Print   Because nouns are so basic in the development of the child's speaking and reading vocabulary, our discussions in previous chapters of whole-word learning and word recognition in general have been necessarily and deliberately focused on nouns. Consequently, we have already detailed numerous techniques, methods, and materials for teaching noun recognition skills and will not repeat them here. Suffice it to reiterate at this point that no opportunity to build noun recognition in the beginning classroom should be neglected.

Pictures of noun objects, together with the printed nouns should permeate the room, and they should be used frequently for practice. Here are some effective strategies for doing this as a means of fostering whole-word recognition of nouns in print:

1. Three-dimensional word-picture cards can be made and used to help the child remember initial sounds. We have a listing of such words (that can be illustrated in 3-D) provided for you in Chapter 5 (following). Although 3-D picture cards were originally meant to be used only as cues to beginning sounds, they can also be used effectively for almost any noun for which a 3-D object can be obtained.
2. Pictures of things can be obtained from catalogs, and there is almost no end to the picture cards, picture sheets, picture notebooks, and picture dictionaries that can be made by children who are learning whole-word recognition. Old *Sears,*

Ward, and *Spiegel* catalogs are the richest source of nouns. Similarly the scores of Christmas catalogs that are distributed each season can be "recycled" for use this way. Farm catalogs, automobile catalogs and promotional literature, seed catalogs, "sale" catalogs, and so on are all readily available to us. In any case, as the collection of pictures (with whole-word names) grows, each child should begin to classify them alphabetically. This is the beginning of the child's individualized word resource book (dictionary).

Children cannot go through the elementary years with reliance upon picture/word cards as clues to words. Somewhere the picture clue must be dropped. In fact, some research indicates that children learn nouns as easily without pictures. We hold the position that, if pictures seem to help, use them. However, if the children seem to be relying on the pictures entirely as crutches to word identification (as is often the case) they should gradually be eliminated (psychologists call this "cue reduction") for sooner or later, this must happen, anyhow.

Observation, supported by some research, seems to convince one that children can just as easily learn the words *airplane, monster,* or even *dinosaur* as the word *cat.* To be sure, we do not know *how* this is possible, but we can speculate on *why* it takes place. We suggest that children learn most easily that which is most relevant to them at any point in time. For example, the child who has just visited Disneyland or Disneyworld has a readiness to learn *Cinderella, Mickey Mouse, Pluto, bears, ghosts, pirates,* and perhaps, even *Caribbean,* although the latter is much more abstract. Similarly, television programs induce a readiness for learning nouns in print, depending, of course, upon the particular TV program that is popular "right now." Most examples would be "dated," but there are some universals such as *parade, bands, Christmas, Sesame Street, neighborhood* (Misterogers' Neighborhood), *Big Bird, football, hockey, basketball, sports, mystery, Electric Company, Sylvester and Tweety, Donald Duck, Bugs Bunny, Fat Albert,* and *Woody Woodpecker.*

Whether we like it or not, these are the names of things that children watch on TV, and they are ready-made for teaching printed nouns. Similarly, as the names of things, places, and people are brought up for discussion in class, the printed nouns representing those concrete things can be learned first in isolation and then immediately in use in printed sentences. Children who are being helped to develop their own printed language-experience story booklets have constant need for using nouns. For example:

We Visited the Mall

Last *night* my *mother* and *father* took me to the *Mall.* There were many *people* there. We went into *stores* and my *mother* bought a new *coat.* There were *fountains* and *birds,* and a *man* played the *organ.* We had a *hamburger* and *Coke* and came *home.* I rode the *escalator,* too.

TEACHING VERB RECOGNITION

Some fifty years ago, two of America's pioneer linguistic scholars, I. A. Richards and C. K. Ogden, discovered that our language has only 850 basic words—the tap-root words for all the thousands of other words we speak and write. Of these basic words, only *18* are verbs. In other words, an individual could conceivably communicate somewhat adequately throughout a lifetime with mastery of only these 18 verbs:

be	come	do	get	give	go
have	keep	let	make	may	put
say	see	seem	send	take	will

"Make the car go"; "Come, and let me see what you have."

"Put it here where I can get it." (*Can* is now substituted for *may* in common usage).

"Will you have some more supper?"

"This ice cream doesn't seem to keep too well."

"Have your say, and then go!"

Observation will attest, however, that children come to beginning reading with a speaking verb vocabulary a good deal higher than 18.

The action words that describe the activities of people, animals, machines, and the work of nature in the child's immediate environment, including the vicarious environment provided by television and movies, constitute the stock of verbs that a child usually learns. As with *all* learning, the acquisition of verbs is influenced by the breadth and depth of each child's experience; by the awareness of the child of his/her environment (one subfactor of intelligence); and by purposing to learn the actual words that describe the actions (motivation). These individualized factors largely account for the range of differences in the acquired verbs in children's communication. Yet, we believe there is a common core of words that most average five-year-olds are able to acquire in our environment.

Through a study of the day-to-day conversation of a total of 575 kindergarten children over a period of ten years, we determined the 400 most-common verbs used by those five-year-olds. They are as follows.

The 400 Verbs Most Commonly Used by Five-Year-Olds

look	see	jump	run	eat	laugh
cry	go	is	(any form of *to be*)		hurt
hit	went	sit	stand	fall	drink
turn on	gone	talk		fly	crawl
turn off	break	drive	wash	clean	buy
give	take	read	ask	tell	find
get	make	burn	cut	shoot	kill (cont.)

The 400 Verbs Most Commonly Used by Five-Year-Olds (cont.)

practice	pray	rescue	bandage	ring	promise
pump	work	fight	steal	race	tune in
rake	raise	smash	crash	shake	rattle
fit	move	rest (on the floor)		sleep	back-up
rock (the boat)		roll	row (the boat)		save
slip	scold	screw	scrub	sell	send
get-set	serve (a meal)		shake	fry	bake
stir	shave	fix	show	sharpen	sink
skate	skid	slap	slice	smash	smell
smoke	smooth	sneak	sneeze	drip	soak-up
soften	sort	speed	spell	spend	spit
spill	spoil	split	spray	spread	hide
squeeze	squirt	squash	squirm	squish	start
stop	stand	step	stick	sting	straighten
stretch	string	suck	dive	sweat	swing
change	pour	nail (it)	bring	take	tackle
tap	teach	taste	tease	tear (up)	thank
think	(it's) thundering		(it's) snowing		(it's) raining
tip	toast	tow	tramp	trip	climb
try	unbutton	upset	untie	use	visit
dig	put	load	pay	miss	hear
say	change	chase	cheat	play	chew
spit	swollow	paint	write	splash	chop
choose	let	grab	hold	lock	close
open	shut	color	lick	pour	dump
copy	count	cover	dance	don't	draw
put	drag	dress	drop	wet	dry
dump	duck	watch	listen	say	—said
count	finish	sing	bust	(burst)	blow
blow-up	die	dying	feed	fill	empty
fish	fix	show	bounce	color	build
smile	grin	howl	have	help	hide
hold	keep	dance	skip	turn	hop
bang	hug	hunt	hurry	touch	wiggle
keep	button	snap	unload	land (the plane)	
ski	share	buy	talk	learn	leave
print	lies	lay	pretend	live	shine
	(tells lies)				
leave	lost	(lose)	mark	mash	meet
mess	ring	milk	mind (the baby)		miss
mix	give	moo	quack	meeow	move

The 400 Verbs Most Commonly Used by Five-Year-Olds (cont.)

name	need	sleep	wake up	can-have	
sweep	shovel	hoe	sew	sow	pick
do	pack	paddle	sail	decorate	
dip	park	pass	pat	pound	screw
twist	peel	peck	peek	pet	wind (the clock)
pick	pile	pin	pitch	plan	think
plow	plant	poke	point	dive	mail
scare	hit	blow	light	can do	can't do
tell	like	hate	let	not allowed to	
yell	have	think	know	come	
pull	push	lift	bump	bet	kick
throw	catch	swim	sail	ride	cough
bark	beat	win	love	feel	break
tie	button	zip	bend	shine	born
bite	melt	bring	slide	kiss	wave
wag	wiggle	wait	waddle	walk	
wave	waste	(wasting)	water (the flowers)		
wax	wear	weigh	wet	wish	
freeze	twist	pile	float	turn around	
back up	work	wreck	yawn	scoot	
dust	mop	wham	zoom	run (the vacuum) (the water)	

It is of great significance that little easy-to-learn words such as these verbs are at the heart of our language and, therefore, should be the words that children should master in print as soon as possible. Some can be learned as printed whole words in isolation; others can be learned in the course of spoken conversation, with special attention to a special printed word; and others will be mastered as part of larger linguistic entities such as printed phrases and/or sentences.

Many of the methods and techniques already detailed for teaching word recognition skills are applicable to verb identification—sight-word drill, flash cards, picture cues, and so on. As to picture cues, however, verbs, because they describe actions rather than objects, may be somewhat difficult to illustrate—or at least require more detail than picture cues for nouns. Still, it can be done. Sports pictures on commercial flash cards or culled from magazines or old books can provide excellent picture cues for learning to recognize verbs such as *throw, hit, run, jump, dive, tackle, catch, race, sail, pull,* and *swim.*

In the intermediate grades, the teacher can use ingenuity to develop picture cues for verb-recognition reinforcement and for initiating awareness of the multiplicity of meanings and uses an already-recognized verb may have. For example, the verb *drive* for most children will be initially recognized in conversation (and in print) as having to do with "driving a car." A picture of someone driving a bargain (a customer and a street peddler haggling over price), or cowboys driving cattle across the plains, or a driveway, drive for funds, or of a drive-in movie, etc. will add new dimensions to the simple verb *drive.* How would you illustrate "drive me crazy"?

"Scanning" is a useful technique for verb-recognition training. Here is one source: The old 1950s and 1960s basal reader series used controlled vocabulary and repetition as the means for beginning reading. If it is possible to find old preprimers and primers from one or more of those old basals, they can be used for scanning for the appearance of verbs in their "controlled" vocabularies. The listing of words that are repeated many times will be found in the last pages of those readers. Verbs such as *jump, run, see, look, come, go, get, give, find, ride, hide, fix, show, bring, try, work, stop, take, open, keep, put, watch, have, play, help, said, pull, hit, let, slide, climb,* and, perhaps, others were very common in the controlled vocabulary. Lessons can be devised in which children are asked to scan the page for any one of those verbs. The verb can be printed on the chalkboard, or displayed on a flashcard, and the children can attempt to match it with "finds" in the old storybooks. The teacher, of course, must be certain that the word appears several times on the pages designated.

Whatever specific techniques you use for teaching verb-recognition skills, whenever possible let the children suggest the words they wish to study (learn to recognize).

Many related verbs can be suggested during group discussions. For example, discussion may center on words that "tell about something we do with our legs and feet." The verbs that are suggested will most likely be *run, jump, dance, kick, slide, bend, walk, jog, climb.* These words will be printed on the chalkboard or on "flashcards" that will be used for word recognition.

In more advanced stages of learning, children can generate such extended forms as past tense and participles: *jumped, jumping; walked, walking;* and so on, and even *playfully, helpfully,* may be suggested, even though they have their origins as verbs used as nouns. If they are suggested, they must not be rejected.

In the autumn, it is usual that conversation turns to the change of seasons. What verbs could the teacher expect children to use and what additional verbs may the teacher generate for purposes of discussion and whole-word learning? Here are a few that children will use: *turning* (color); *flying* (flights of birds); *falling* (leaves), resulting in discussion of the *Fall* and in the verb, *to fall; hiding* (squirrels hiding nuts). The teacher can embellish the verb vocabulary with words such as *storing, harvesting, preparing, gathering,* and *changing* (seasons). These words are studied to observe their roots and the *-ing* ending and the fact that it makes them require a "helping word" (from the verb, *to be*) such as *is, are, was, will be,* and *have been.* With such a set of concepts, the entire discussion can develop into a study of these aspects of verbs. This is usually done in the third and fourth grades.

It is helpful to have these words printed on flocked cardboard so they can be shifted around on the flannelboard during discussion and, later, by the children during their individual learning sessions in which they are studying and learning them in isolation.

Be on the alert to spot especially vivid verbs used by the children. They love such words and are particularly receptive to techniques for recognizing them in print. For example, let us suppose a child comments during a science lesson that "our hamster wiggled out of Betsy's hands." The perceptive teacher will immediately recognize *wiggle* as a verb well-suited for practice in recognition. The ensuing discussion might go something like this:

"Amy told us something about our hamster. Who can repeat what she said?" Several children will repeat: "Our hamster wiggled out of Betsy's hands."

"Do you like that word, *wiggled?*"

("Yes!")

"Who wants to show us what it is like to *wiggle?*"

"Now, let's everyone stand up and *wiggle.*" (After the wiggling is over, it is time to "strike while the iron is hot.")

"There is something about that word, *wiggled,* that may help us remember it when we see it in a book." (Print *w i g g l e d* on chalkboard making the letters "gg" wiggly. Slowly pronounce the word, with emphasis on the /gg/ sound.)

"What is there about this word that might help us remember it?" (Help the children find special features of the word: the /gg/ feature; it begins with *wi;* it has an /l/ sound in it.)

After you have helped the child identify features of *wiggled,* print *b i g g e r* on the chalkboard, leaving *w i g g l e d* on for comparison.

"Is this the same word as *wiggled?*"

"Why not?"

At this point, recognition in print of the verb *wiggled* will have developed in many of the children. Now reinforce its recognition by printing it in the original sentence, "Our hamster wiggled out of Betsy's hands."

TEACHING WORD-ANALYSIS SKILLS

To this point in the present chapter, we have concentrated on recognition of whole words as if words were indivisible entities. We know, of course, that they are not. Words are divisible into sounds and letters and combinations of sounds and letters. Letter combinations can be added to or subtracted from words to form new words. In short, words have parts and these parts constitute the "internal structure" of words.

DEFINITION OF WORD ANALYSIS

Word analysis is the study of the internal structure of a word—that is, the study of whole-word parts. Whole-word recognition skills enable the child to acquire a basic reading vocabulary. As learning progresses, however, the words to be read necessarily become more complex and more numerous. Additional skills are needed to facilitate recognition of these new and relatively complex words. Consequently, we turn now to a discussion of word-analysis ("word attack") skills and how they function as aids to recognition.

PHONICS IN WORD ANALYSIS

You will remember that we have several times throughout this text discussed the use of simple phonics in whole-word recognition—for example, the role of initial consonant sounds as clues to identification ("It begins like . . ."). Since phonics is essentially the study of the sounds of the letters and letter combinations of words—there is, so to speak, a natural affinity between phonics and word analysis, per se.

Analytic Phonics   The use of initial consonant letter/sounds described above is the first step in establishing analytic phonics as a method of word analysis. In analytic phonics, the pupil literally "takes the word apart" and then attempts to apply what he/she knows about phonics pronunciation; stringing out a sequence of sounds for each letter or letter combination in an attempt to recreate the word vocally.

This sort of word analysis works fairly well on simple words, on words of one syllable, and on long words that are composed of regular phonics elements. But the irregular words (that used to be known as the "spelling demons") may also be thought of as the "phonics demons." About 20% of our English words fall into this category.

Inasmuch as the entire chapter following this one is devoted to teaching phonics, we will postpone full discussion of the subject until then.

SYLLABLES IN WORD ANALYSIS

It is frequently suggested by classroom teachers that the children "tap out" the syllables that they hear in a spoken word. It has been adequately demonstrated that this is not a difficult task; in fact, it may be almost a "natural." But, how can one tap out the syllables in a word that one does not know how to pronounce? Moreover, if one can pronounce the word well enough to tap out the syllables, of what use is the tapping? In answer to this question, it has been demonstrated that, when skilled readers are presented with nonwords, they immediately segment them into probable syllables in an attempt to pronounce them. In addition, when a skilled reader encounters an unknown word in print, an attempt is made to segment the word into syllables until its correct pronunciation can be verified in the dictionary. There appears, therefore, to be a need to syllabicate unknown words as a means of entry into pronunciation. Consequently, we suggest that, as children encounter multisyllable words in their reading, they be alerted to the probability that those words can be divided into pronounceable segments; by so doing, many unknown words in print can emerge as known words in the child's listening and speaking vocabulary.

Count-the-Vowels Technique   Children close eyes and listen to the teacher pronounce a multisyllable word. They try to identify the number of vowel *sounds* that they hear, for each syllable contains but one vowel (or vowel diphthong) sound. As children become proficient in this skill, they will be able to repeat the vowel sounds that were contained in the word.

With more practice, they will be able to print the word with reasonably correct spelling, using the voice units as guides. To aid in more accuracy, teachers should be particularly careful not to dictate the spelling/reading demons. There is no need to confuse children . . . there are plenty of regularly spelled words that may be used for children.

Examples of Spoken Syllabication

ab-sent	act-ing	a-go
air-plane	air-lin-er	air-port
am-bu-lance	A-mer-i-can	an-i-mal
an-oth-er	ap-ple	(pronounced a-pl)
at-ten-tion	au-to-mo-bile	as-tro-naut
a-way	band-age	bar-be-cue
bas-ket	bat-ter-y (sometimes pronounced bat-tree)	
straw-berry	be-gin	be-hind

Ben-ja-min (if there is one in the class . . . or any other classmate's multisyllable name)

be-witched	bo-lo-ney	bot-tom

at-tack (pronounced a-tak)   at-tend-ance (pronounced a-ten-dance)

bro-ken	as-pir-in	bro-ther

(the dictionary gives the syllabication as broth-er, but that is not the way the children pronounce it)

but-ter (pronounced bu (t) ter)

	can-dy	cannon (ca-non)
col-or	cop-y	cos-tume
		(Halloween)
dan-ger	dent-ist (the dictionary syllabication is den-tist)	

(cont.)

Examples of Spoken Syllabication (cont.)

dif-fer-ent	di-vide	dol-lar
dri-ver (dictionary syllabication is *driv-er*)		fath-er
e-lec-tric	emp-ty	e-rase
fas-(t)-en	feath-er (perhaps, fea-ther)	
gas-o-line	gro-cer-ies	
fill-ing	fool-ish	freez-ing
ham-mer	hap-py	in-side
let-ter	luck-y	re-mem-ber
morn-ing	moth-er	
mon-ey	mon-ster	nurs-er-y
o-cean	o-pen	or-ange
out-side	paint-er	pa-rade
pen-ny	peo-ple	per-son
pick-le	play-ing	po-ta-to
pre-tend	pus-sy-wil-low	ra-di-o
sep-a-rate	som-er-sault	sug-ar
Sun-day	sur-prise	tab-le
sweat-er	tel-e-vi-sion	thanks-giv-ing
Ses-a-me	to-mor-row	veg-e-ta-ble
win-dow	win-ter	

END-OF-WORD TECHNIQUE

Our language is full of words that are built on word patterns in which the endings can easily be identified. For example, verbs that are converted into *agents* are called *agentives*. They are usually formed by ending *-er* to the action . . . thus making a word that designates a doer of the action. For example: *farm + er = farmer*. Agentives are easily spotted by the technique of "look at the end of the word for a possible clue." (Beware of such words as *butter*.) Practice should be on verb agentives that have become nouns: *farmer, singer, swimmer, painter, driver, walker*, and so on.

Consider how you would teach end-of-words with *-le*. Here are a number of common words in that pattern that third graders can more easily recognize after they have spotted the *-le* ending.

handle	tackle	apple	double	puddle	toddle
simple	freckle	uncle	peddle	buckle	beetle
table	cable	fable	staple	cradle	maple
eagle	people	needle	noodle	bugle	bridle
rifle	noble	cycle	stable	speckle	poodle

RECURRING STRUCTURAL PATTERNS

The process of reading would be miserably slow if we had to read each new word and analyze it with no antecedents for guidance. Fortunately, most words have internal elements that conform to regular structures in our language. The intraword features recur over and over again and consist of regularly recurring structural patterns of roots and affixes, possessives, plurals, past tense, present tense, derivatives (adjectives derived from verbs and adjectives derived from nouns), adjective comparisons, contractions, compounds, and adverbs.

Suffixes   English-language prefixes and suffixes recur again and again as potential guides to word recognition. The beginning reader may have scant awareness of these common word-segments, but, with the help of the teacher, will gradually become acquainted with them. By the time they reach third-grade level, most children will have learned to recognize the more common prefixes and suffixes and to use them as guides to word recognition.

Study of a few of the more-reliable suffixes provides extra reinforcement for advanced word-analysis work. Here are those that we have found most helpful:

-able	-er	-ize	-ship	-most
-ance	-ful	-less	-tion	-ness
-ation	-hood	-ly	-ward	-age
-en	-ion	-ment	-ive	-ology
-ence	-ish	-ous	-ant	-wise
	-ist			-ward

Common Prefixes

ab-	(not)	fore-	(in front of) (before)	mis-	(wrong)
anti-	(against)	hyper-	(more)	non-	(not)
ante-	(before)	hypo-	(less)	post-	(after)
circum-	(around)	il-	(not)	pre-	(before)
con-	(together)	im-	(not)	re-	(back again)
counter-	(against)	in-	(not)	pro-	(toward)
de-	(take away from)	ir-	(not)	sub-	(under)
dis-	(take away)	inter-	(between)	super-	(greater)
ex-	(from)			trans-	(across)
				un-	(not)

Present-Tense Derivatives   *Walking, swimming, riding, rubbing, batting, hopping,* and so on are not problems in reading, even though some may cause concern for children in knowing when to double the consonant in spelling. Third-person-singular forms are also easy for most children: for example, *come—comes,—*

hammer—hammers. But the *-en* form, used by itself or with a "helping" verb may need special attention near the end of the primary years. It is a form not common to children's speech and when found in print may appear "strange," even though the child may be able to pronounce it. A few examples may illustrate this point:

The book was *taken* during the night.

Please *loosen* my belt.

Help me *tighten* this bolt.

The child most likely will be able to handle those, but will probably be blocked by these:

He was closely *shaven*.

The address *was given* to the Senate.

This tragedy *may hasten* the decision.

Adjectives Derived from Verbs   Forms of descriptive, picturesque speech, fabricated to create mental images are frequently abstract and need special study for word identification. For example: a *running* nose (which children usually hear in conversation as "a *runny* nose"; *waving* fields of grain; *drifting* clouds; the *rising* tide (which in conversation is usually, "the tide's coming in.")

Adjectives Derived from Nouns   Our language is full of adjectives that modify nouns, yet are derived from other nouns. In a sense, therefore, the new word combination is a double noun. Let's look at a few examples that lend themselves to study for purposes of word analysis:

friend — friendly   *fire — firey*
bird — birdlike   *blue — bluish*

Adjective Comparisons   Another intraword structure that is so common to children's speech is the adjective comparison such as *big, bigger, biggest,* and *small, smallest.* Those that are regular in construction present no problem. Those that are irregular have to be learned as separate entities, with little or no transfer.

Contractions   Most children have mastered contractions in their everyday speech. *Ain't* is probably the most popular, with *can't* a close second. When children see contractions in print, few, if any, problems are encountered. The following examples should suffice to prove that:

The teacher *isn't* here yet.

Isn't the teacher here yet?

Can't we go out to play?

Hasn't it been fun?

Verbs to be Made into Contractions

is not	was not	are not	were not	are not
can not	have not	had not	could not	do not
should not	ought not	does not	did not	
must not	has not	would not	will not	

Dare not is sometimes pronounced daren't and in some geographical regions its common contraction, especially among children, is *dassen't:* "I dassen't come out to play." This usually means, "I'm not *allowed* to come out to play." How would you deal with that one?

Pronouns to be Used in Contractions

I am	we are	you are	it is	I will
he is	she is	they are	you will	we will
they will	he will	she will		

Inasmuch as most contractions are common in the average first-grader's speaking vocabulary, it is no problem to work with them in second grade where we help the children understand their printed construction. We cannot improve on "learning by doing."

Letter Configuration   Although, strictly speaking, letter configuration is a letter-analysis rather than a word-analysis skill, it may be well to note that letter shapes as well as word segments may offer internal clues to word recognition, as pointed out in an earlier chapter. Ascenders and descenders (especially ascenders) can play a prominent role as clues to recognition. Note, for example, what happens when you try to scan a line of print that has been cut exactly in half. Which half-line is easier to read?

It is highly unlikely and equally improbable that

It is highly unlikely and equally improbable that

Compounds   Compound words (linguists like to call them "a union of free morphemes") lend themselves naturally to word analysis, for each segment of the compound may also be recognized as a separate word. Recognition of new compounds comes easily if at least one of its segments has already been learned.

Most English compounds are made from straightforward, logical, simple combinations of words. We may be thankful that we do not have compounds-upon-componds, such as the German

lebensmittelgeschaft
(life + means + a shop for buying)

transposed into English: *a shop for purchasing the means of life* = a grocery store!

Some Compounds Useful for Practice in Structural Analysis

baseball	ballbat	hairpin	supermarket
baseball bat	shoelace	carwash	highway
bedroom	fireplace	ironingboard	teakettle
armchair	typewriter	schoolbus	airport
boxcar	bedtime	popcorn	catfish
grasshopper	cartwheel	padlock (this needs explaining)	
grandstand	pancake	starfish	wishbone
pigpen	sandbox	postcard	sunshine
campfire	mailbox	horseback	drivein
tiptoe	bulldozer (this needs explaining)		

TEACHING WORD RECOGNITION SKILLS IN CONTEXT

Up to now, we have been discussing a number of means that are usually used with children for purposes of helping them recognize words in isolation. We hold that these are necessary skills, not only for beginners, but also for more advanced elementary school children and even adult readers who, from time to time, are confronted with a new word in print and who need word-analysis skills for identifying, pronouncing, and recognizing it.

Children tend naturally to look for contextual clues when puzzling out the meaning of new words in print. Research indicates that children in the beginning stages of reading guess at the meaning of a new wording according to the meaning's contextual probability. Such initial guesses are, of course, often wildly inaccurate. As the learning process progresses, however, the guesses become "educated guesses" and increase in accuracy. The beginning reader, then, should be encouraged to guess at the meaning of a new word according to whether or not it "makes sense" to the child in context.

Psychological experiments have shown that an individual who is shown a partially completed figure (of a square, for example) immediately completes the figure in his mind. The explanation for this is that the person already has the mental picture of a complete square stored in the visual memory and the partial square immediately activates that mental image. A similar process occurs in reading. A partial phrase, clause, or sentence can immediately activate whatever portions of the memory bank contain the reader's mental image of the whole phrase, clause, or sentence. The mind leaps ahead to "enclose" the entire word sequence within its contextual meaning.

Psychologists call this mental process "contextual clozure." The principle of contextual clozure has long been used by classroom teachers to develop skills in word recognition through context. The technique involves both auditory and visual memory. For example, the teacher might say: "I'm going to read a sentence right up to the last word. You can tell me what the last word will be. But it must begin with the same letter as *bug* (or whatever word the teacher chooses for the lesson)."

"He went around the corner so fast he fell off his b_____."

Restricting the possible answers to words beginning with a specific consonant sound (in this case /b/) helps eliminate wild guessing. But the real point of the drill is to develop awareness that context gives clue to meaning. The final word might be *bike,* or *bicycle,* or even *board* (for skateboard), but context rules out words such as *bed, bag,* or whatever.

The routine that is helpful in teaching children to use semantic clues when they are reading is as follows:

1. Start the sentence or phrase again and read more quickly up to the unknown word.
2. The child is then asked to listen and think while the teacher rereads that same sentence or phrase up to the unknown word.
3. "What do you think the next word should be?"
4. When the child makes his/her "educated guess" of what it might be, then there are several questions needed to verify that word:
   a. Do you think that word makes sense?
   b. How does the word begin that you have supplied?
   c. Look, now, at the sentence and see if the word you thought you didn't know begins with ____.
   d. Is that the word you thought it should be?

You may, of course, devise your own reading materials for use with this technique, but commercial workbook-type materials are readily available for the purpose.

(We will have more to say about the importance of context in learning to read in later chapters of this book.)

CONCLUSION

We have presented the various strategies that we have found to be effective in helping children recognize words in print, both in isolation and in context. Moreover, we claim that there should be no conflict between the learning of single words and learning to identify those same words in context.

It is no contradiction to maintain that words not only can represent meanings by themselves, much as a dictionary defines meanings; but also that words depend upon their contextual settings to indicate the shades of meaning and/or the special meanings that they are intended to generate. Hence, we recommend that words learned in isolation be put into printed contextual settings for the elaboration of meanings and for more sophisticated practice in word recognition.

The end product of word recognition is comprehension; word recognition is one means to that end.

BIBLIOGRAPHY

Allington, Richard, "Cue Selection and Discrimination Learning," *Academic Therapy*, **10** (1975), 339–343.

Allington, Richard L., and Anne McGill-Franzen, "Word Identification Errors in Isolation and in Context: Apples vs Oranges," *Reading Teacher*, **33**:7 (1980), 795–780.

Ames, W. S., "The Development of a Classification Scheme of Contextual Aids," *Reading Research Quarterly*, **2** (1966), 57–58.

Anastasiow, Nicholas, *Oral Language: Expression of Thought*, Newark, Delaware: International Reading Association, 1971.

Artley, A. Sterl, "Words, Words, Words," *Language Arts*, **52**:8 (1975), 1062–1072.

Atkinson, Richard C., and John D. Fletcher, "Teaching Children to Read with a Computer," *Reading Teacher*, **25**:4 (1972), 319–327.

Baron, J. and I. Thurston, "An Analysis of the Word-Superiority Effect," *Cognitive Psychology*, **4** (1973), 207–228.

Barr, Rebecca C., "The Influence of Instructional Conditions on Word Recognition Errors, *Reading Research Quarterly*, **7**:3 (1972), 509–529.

Barrett, Lincoln *The Treasure of Our Tongue*, New York: Knopf, 1964.

Biemiller, Andrew, "The Development of the Use of Graphic and Contextual Information as Children Learn to Read," *Reading Research Quarterly*, **6**:1 (1970), 75–96.

Blanton, William E., and Terry Bullock, "Cognitive Style and Reading Behavior," *Reading World*, **12** (1973), 276–287.

Bloom, L., *One Word at a Time*, The Hague: Mouton, 1973.

Blumenthal, A. L., *Language and Psychology; Historical Aspects of Psycholinguistics*, New York: Wiley, 1970.

Bormuth, John R., John C. Manning, Julian W. Carr, and David P. Pearson, "Children's Comprehension of Between- and Within-Sentence Syntactic Structures," *Journal of Educational Psychology,* **61** (1970), 349–357.

Brooks, Lee, "Visual Patterns in Fluent Word Identification," in *Toward a Psychology of Reading,* Arthur S. Reber and Don L. Scarborough (Editors), Hillsdale, NJ: Erlbaum, 1977, 143–182.

Charlotte K. Brooks, "Some Approaches to Teaching Standard English as a Second Language," *Elementary English* **42** (1964), 728–733.

Burger, Natalie S. and Charles A. Perfetti, "Reading Skills and Memory for Spoken and Written Discourse," *Journal of Reading Behavior,* **9**:1 (1977), 7–16.

Canney, George F., "A Study of the Relationship Between Pupils' Aural Vocabulary and Their Ability to Apply Syllabication Rules or to Recognize Phonogram Patterns to Decode Multiple-Syllable Words," *Journal of Reading Behavior,* **8**:3 (1976), 272–288.

Carroll, John B., Peter Davies, and Barry Richman, *The American Heritage Word Frequency Book,* Boston: Houghton Mifflin, 1971. They found, upon an analysis of 5,000,000 running words in school books used in grades three through nine, that there are 87,000 *different* words, but that 5000 accounted for 90% of the context. However, 90% means that one in every ten words is an unknown. Moreover, that tenth word will most likely be a noun or verb that cannot be guessed from context!

Cazden, Courtney, *Child Language and Education.* New York: Harcourt Brace Jovanovich, 1972. Especially good on theories of language acquisition by children.

Cazden, Courtney, *Play With Language and Metalinguistic Awareness,* paper presented at the Second Lucy Sprague Mitchell Conference, New York: Bank Street College, May 19, 1973.

Chomsky, Carol, "Reading, Writing, and Phonology," *Harvard Educational Review,* **40** (1970), 287–309.

Christina, Robert, "Do Illustrations Hinder or Assist Sight Vocabulary Acquisition?" in *Diversity in Mature Reading, National Reading Conference Yearbook,* Phil L. Nacke (Editor), 1973, 185–189.

Clark, Eve V., "Non-linguistic Strategies and the Acquisition of Word Meanings," *Cognition,* **2**:2 (1974), 19–23.

Clymer, Theodore A., "The Utility of Phonics Generalizations in the Primary Grades," *Reading Teacher,* **16** (1963), 252–258.

Cohn, Alice S., and Elaine Schwartz, "Interpreting Errors in Word Recognition," *Reading Teacher,* **28**:6 (1975), 534–537.

Crary, Helen L., and Robert W. Ridgway, "Relationships Between Visual Form Perception Abilities and Reading Achievement in the Intermediate Grades," *Journal of Experimental Education*, **40**:1 (1971), 17−22.

Crutchfield, Marjorie, *Individualized Reading: A Guide for Teaching Word-Analysis, Skills*," Los Angeles: Gramercy Press, 1975.

Dale Philip, *Acquisition of Language*, 2nd edition, New York: Holt, Rinehart, and Winston, 1976.

Daniel, Patricia N. and Robert S. Tacker, "Preferred Modality of Stimulus Input and Memory for CVC trigrams," *Journals of Educational Research*, **67** (1974), 255−258.

DeStefano, Johanna S., "A Sociolinguistic Investigation of the Productive Acquisition of a School Language Instruction Register by Black Children," unpublished Ph.D., dissertation, Stanford, CA: Stanford University, 1970.

Downing, John, "Children's Concepts of Language in Learning to Read," *Educational Research*, **12** (1970), 106−112.

Downing, John and P. Oliver, "The Child's Conception of a Word," *Reading Research Quarterly*, **9** (1973−1974), 568−582.

Dulin, Kenneth L., "Using Context Clues in Word Recognition and Comprehension," *Reading Teacher*, **23**:5 (1970), 440−445.

Emans, Robert, "When Two Vowels Go Walking and Other Such Things," *Reading Teacher*, **21** (1967), 262−269.

Frederick, E. Coston and Beverly Hackleman, "An Investigatinn of First-Grade Children's Use of Language Structure," *Reading Horizons*, **12**:1 (1971), 14−17.

Fromkin, Victoria and Robert Rodman, *An Introduction to Language*, New York: Holt, Rinehart, and Winston, 1974.

Gamsky, Neal R., and Faye W. Lloyd, "A Longitudinal Study of Visual Perceptual Training and Reading Achievement," *Journal of Educational Research*, **64** (1971), 451−454.

Garman, Dorothy, "Comprehension Before Word Identification, *Reading World*, **16**:1 (1976), 279−287.

Gipe, Joan P., "Use of Relevant Context Helps Kids Learn New Word Meanings," *Reading Teacher*, **33**:4 (1980), 398−402.

Gleitman, Lila and Paul Rozin, "Teaching Reading by Use of a Syllabary," *Reading Research Quarterly*, **8** (1973), 447−483.

Goodacre, Elizabeth, J., "Reading Research," in *Reading*, Vols. 7, 8, 9, 10 (1973−1976). An excellent summary of reading research in Britain annually done by Dr. Goodacre.

Groff, Patrick, "The Topsy-Turvy World of 'Sight' Words," *Reading Teacher,* **27**:6 (1974), 572—578. Cited research to indicate that children discriminate *parts* of words from the time they begin to learn to read.

Groff, Patrick, "Some Semantics of Basic Word Lists," *Reading Horizons,* **16**:3 (1976), 160—165.

Groff, Patrick, "Long Versus Short Words in Beginning Reading," *Reading World,* **14** (1975), 277—289.

Hall, Edward T., *The Silent Language,* Garden City, NY: Doubleday, 1959.

Hanna, Paul R., Richard E. Hodges, Jean S. Hanna, and Edwin H. Rudorf, Jr., *Phoneme-Grapheme Correspondences as Cues for Spelling Improvement,* U.S. Office of Education Bureau of Research Publication No. 32008, Washington, DC: 1966.

Hartley, Ruth N., "Effects of List Types and Cues on the Learning of Word Lists," *Reading Research Quarterly,* **6**:1 (1970), 97—121.

Hillerich, Robert L., "Word Lists—Getting it All Together," *Reading Teacher,* **27** (1974), 353—360.

Holden, M. H., and W. H. MacGinitie, "Children's Conceptions of Word Boundaries in Speech and Print," *Journal of Educational Psychology,* **63** (1973), 551—557.

Hunt, Kellog, *Grammatical Structures Written at Three Grade Levels,* Champaign, Ill: National Council of Teachers of English, 1965.

Ives, Josephine P., Laura Z. Bursuk, and Sumner A. Ives, *Word Identification Techniques,* Chicago: Rand McNally, 1979.

Johnson, Dale D., and Edward Merryman, "Syllabication: the Erroneous VCCV Generalization," *Reading Teacher,* **25**:3 (1971), 267—270.

Johnson, Dale D., and P. David Pearson, "Skills Management Systems: a Critique," *Reading Teacher,* **28**:8 (1975), 757—764.

Johnston, J. C., and J. L. McClelland, "Visual Factors in Word Percepion," *Perception and Psychophysics,* **14** (1973), 365—370.

Johnson, N. F., "On the Function of Letters in Word Identification: Some Data and a Preliminary Model," *Journal of Verbal Learning and Verbal Behavior,* **14**:1 (1975), 17—30.

Jones, Margaret B., "The Effect of Specificity of Reading Purpose on Childrens Reading Achievement," *Journal of Reading Behavior,* **8**:4 (1976), 405—414.

Jorm, Anthony F., "The Effect of Word Imagery on Reading Performance as a Function of Reading Ability," *Journal of Educational Psychology,* **69**:1 (1977), 46—54.

Jorm, Anthony F., "Children's Reading Processes Revealed by Pronunciation Latencies and Errors," *Journal of Educational Psychology,* **69**:2 (1977), 166–171. "Syllables and letter clusters are probably *not* processed as units for any type of word, but there is some evidence that letters may function as units."

Katz, Leonard L. and David A. Wicklund, "Word Scanning Rate for Good and Poor Readers," *Journal of Educational Psychology,* **61** (1971), 138–140.

King, Ethel M. and Siegmar Muehl, "Different Sensory Cues as Aids in Beginning Reading," *The Reading Teacher* **19** (1965), 163–168.

Kiraly, John and Alexandra Furlong, "Teaching Words to Kindergarten Children with Picture, Configuration, and Initial Sound Cues in a Prompting Procedure," *Journal of Educational Research,* **67** (1974), 295–298.

Klein, Helen A., Gary A. Klein, and Mary Bertino, "Utilization of Context for Word Identification Decisions in Children," *Journal of Experimental Child Psychology,* **17** (1974), 79–86.

Klumb, Roger and Wayne Otto, "Effect of Three Teacher—Feedback/Incentive Conditions on Pupil's Reading Skill Development in an Objective-Based Program," *Journal of Educational Research,* **70**:1 (1976), 10–14.

Knafle, June D., "Word Perception: Cues Aiding Structure Detection," *Reading Research Quarterly,* **8**:4, (1973), 502–523.

Knafle, June D., "Children's Learning of Words as a Function of Minimum Contrasts in Variable Letter Positions," *Journal of Reading Behavior,* **8**:2 (1976), 205–220.

Kuenne, J. B. and Joanna P. Williams, "Auditory Recognition Cues in the Primary Grades," *Journal of Educational Psychology,* **64** (1973), 241–246.

Larkin, Willard, and David Burns, "Sentence Comprehension and Memory for Embedded Structure," *Memory and Cognition* **5**:1 (1977), 17–22.

Lefevre, Carl A., "Comprehensive Linguistic Approach to Reading", *Elementary English,* **43** (1965), 657.

Liberman, Isabelle Y., "Segmentation of the Spoken Word and Reading Acquisition," paper presented at the meeting of the Society for Research in Child Development, Philadelphia, March, 1973. Reported that, up to age six, it is much easier for children to recognize syllables in spoken words than to recognize phonemes as segments.

Loban, Walter D., "The Language of Elementary School Children," National Council of Teachers of English, Research Report No. 1, 1963.

McClelland, James L., "Letter and Configuration Information in Word Identification," *Journal of Verbal Learning and Verbal Behavior,* **16**:1 (1977), 137–150.

Macworth, Jane F., "Some Models of the Reading Process: Learners and Skilled Readers," *Reading Research Quarterly,* **7**:4 (1972), 701–733. It is refreshing to find a professional researcher who recognizes that there are two quite distinct aspects of reading: learners and skilled readers, and that research on the latter has limited value for understanding the process involved in the former. The author's proposals hold considerable interest to the reading specialist, especially her discussion of certain psychological aspects of reading acquisition.

Mackworth, Norman H., "Seven Cognitive Skills in Reading," *Reading Research Quarterly,* **7**:4 (1972), 679–700.

McFeely, Donald C., "Syllabication Usefulness in a Basal and Social Studies Vocabulary," *Reading Teacher,* **27** (1974), 809–814.

Malmquist, Eve, "An International Overview of Primary Reading Practices," *Journal of Reading,* **18** (1975), 615–624.

Marzano, Robert J., Norma Case, Anne DeBooy, and Kathy Prochoruk, "Are Syllabication and Reading Ability Related?" *Journal of Reading,* **19** (1976), 545–547.

Mason, Jana M., "Suggested Relations Between the Acquisition of Beginning Reading Skills and Cognitive Development," *Journal of Educational Research,* **70**:4 (1977), 195–199. "Word-learning is the best measure of a cognitive component (that underlies learning to read) being related both to classification and to reading abilities."

Meltzer, Nancy, S. and Robert Herse, "The Boundaries of Written Words as Seen by First-Graders," *Journal of Reading Behavior,* **1** (1969), 3–14.

Menyuk, Paula, "Relations Between Acquisition of Phonology and Reading," in *Aspects of Reading Acquisition,* John T. Guthrie (Editor), Baltimore: Johns Hopkins University Press, 1976, 89–110.

Meyer, D. E., R. W. Schvanveldt, and M. G. Ruddy, "Functions of Graphemic and Phonemic Codes in Visual Word Recognition," *Memory and Cognition,* **7** (1974), 309–321.

Mickelson, Norma I., "Meaningfulness in Children's Verbal Learning," *Western Psychologist,* **2** (1970), 71–75.

Miller, Ethel B., "You Want to Read? Listen!" *Reading Teacher,* **26**:7 (1973), 702–703.

Nelson, Katherine, "Some Atributes of Adjectives Used by Young Children," *Cognition,* **4**:1 (1976), 13–30.

Nelson, Keith E., "Facilitating Children's Syntax Acquisition," *Developmental Psychology,* **13**:2 (1977), 101–107. A study of the effects of adult's verbal intervention in helping children with spoken language.

Nodine, Calvin F. and James V. Hardt, "Role of Letter-Position Cues in Learning to Read Words," *Journal of Educational Psychology,* **61** (1970), 10–15.

Packer, Athol B., "Ashton-Warner's Key Vocabulary for the Disadvantaged," *Reading Teacher,* **23**:6 (1970), 559–564. An application of Sylvia Ashton-Warner's key vocabulary method in four cities: Jacksonville, Philadelphia, Yakima, and Jonesboro.

Page, Willaiam D., "Pseudocues, Supercues, and Comprehension," *Reading World,* **15**:4 (1976), 232–239.

Pearson, P. David, "The Effects of Grammatical Complexity on Children's Comprehension, Recall, and Conception of Certain Semantic Relations," *Reading Research Quarterly,* **10**:2 (1974–1975), 155–192.

Perfetti, C. A., "Retrieval of Sentence Relations: Semantic vs. Syntactic Deep Structure," *Cognition* **2**:1 (1974), 1–7.

Pikulski, John, "Effects of Reinforcement on Word Recognition," *Reading Teacher,* **23**:6 (1970), 516–522.

Quandt, Ivan, *"Investing in Word Banks,"* *Reading Teacher,* **27**:2 (1973), 171–173. Quandt presented an adaptation of Sylvia Ashton-Warner's strategy for developing individual word booklets, together with follow-up games with words.

Rayner, Keith and George W. McConkie, "Perceptual Processes in Reading: The Perceptual Spans," in *Toward a Psychology Reading,* Arthur S. Reber and Don L. Scarborough (Editors), Hillsdale, NJ: Erlbaum, 1977, 183–206.

Rozin, Paul and Lila Gleitman, "The Structure and Acquisition of Reading II: The Reading Process and the Acquisition of the Alphabetic Principle," in *Toward a Psychology of Reading,* Proceedings of the CUNY Conference (Spring, 1974), Arthur S. Reber and Don L. Scarborough (Editors), Hillsdale, NJ: Erlbaum, 1977, 55–141.

Rosinski, Richard R. and Kirk E. Wheeler, "Children's Use of Orthographic Structure in Word Discrimination," *Psychonomic Science,* **26**:1 (1972), 97–98.

Sapir, Selma G., "Auditory Discrimination with Words and Nonsense Syllables," *Academic Therapy,* **7** (1972), 307–313.

Seymour, Dorothy Z., "Word Division for Decoding," *Reading Teacher,* **27**:3 (1973), 275–283.

Shankweiler, Donald and Isabelle Y. Liberman, "Misreading: A Search for Causes," in *Language by Eye and By Ear,* Kavanagh and Mattlingly (Editors) Cambridge, MA: MIT Press, 1972, 314.

Shapiro, Lewis, Nicholas Anastasiow, and Dennis Hoban, "The Mature Reader as an 'Educated Guesser,' " *Elementary English,* **49** (1972), 418–421.

Shuy, Roger W. "Detroit Speech: Carless, Awkward, and Inconsistent, or Systematic, Graceful, and Regular?" *Elementary English,* **45** (1968), 565–569.

Shuy, Roger W. Walter A. Wolfram, and William K. Riley, *Linguistic Correlates of Social Stratification in Detroit Speech,* Cooperative Research Report, Project 6-1347, U. S. Office of Education, Washington, DC, 1967.

Singer, Harry, S. Jay Samuels, and Jean Spiroff, "The Effect of Pictures and Contextural Conditions on Learning Responses to Printed Words," *Reading Research Quarterly,* **9**:4 (1973–1974), 555–567.

Singer, Harry, "Sight-Word Learning With and Without Pictures," *Reading Research Quarterly,* **15**:2 (1980), 290–298.

Smith, Frank and Deborah L. Holmes, "The Independence of Letter, Word, and Meaning Identification in Reading," *Reading Research Quarterly,* **6**:3 (1971), 394–415.

Strickland, Ruth in "Linguistics and Language," *Proceedings,* First Annual Forum in Reading, Texas Women's University, 1965. Dr. Strickland stated that the child "has a vocabulary of something like 3,000 words when he comes to Kindergarten."

Taylor R. L. and S. Reilly, "Naming and Other Methods of Decoding Visual Information," *Journal of Experimental Psychology,* **83** (1970), 80–83.

Terry, Pamela R., S. Jay Samuels, and David LaBerge, "Word Recognition as a Function of Letter Degradation, Spacing, and Transformation," *Technical Report,* Center for Research in Human Learning, Minneapolis: University of Minnesota, 1976. The researchers reported that beginning readers process *each letter* of a word prior to recognizing the word, whereas skilled readers recognize the words as single units, utilizing some minimal cues.

Theios, J. and J. Gerard Muise, "The Word Identification Process in Reading," in *Cognitive Theory,* Vol. 2, N. Castellan, Jr., D. Pisoni, and G. Potts (Editors), Hillsdale, NJ: Erlbaum, 1977.

Timko, Henry G., "Configuration as a Cue in the Word Recognition of Beginning Readers," *Journal of Experimental Education,* **39** (1970), 68–69.

Vandever, Thomas R. and Donald D. Neville, "Modality Aptitude and Word Recognition," *Journal of Reading Behavior,* **6** (1974), 195–201.

Venezky, Richard L., and Dominic W. Massaro, "The Role of Orthographic Regularity in Word Recognition," in *Theiry and Practice of Early Reading,* Vol. 1., Lauren B. Resnick and Phyllis A. Weaver (Editors), Hillsdale, NJ: Erlbaum, 1979, 85–107.

Wardhaugh, Ronald, "Theories of Language Acquisition in Relation to Beginning Reading Instruction," in *Theoretical Models and Processes of Reading,*

Harry Singer and Robert B. Ruddell (Editors). Newark, DE: International Reading Association, 1976, 42−65. Wardhaugh clearly differentiated six conditions in which learning to read is significantly different from learning to speak our language. Briefly restated, they are:

1. Learning to read is usually commenced abruptly, whereas learning to speak is so developmental that it is almost subconscious to the child.
2. There is a certain level of anxiety in parent, teacher, and child when reading begins; but not so with talking.
3. Reading instruction is formal and deliberate; spoken language acquisition is informal with little, if any, instruction necessary.
4. Learning to speak has its own intrinsic rewards, but extrinsic rewards (and motivation) are frequently imposed on learning to read.
5. Learning to read involves visual discrimination in addition to the auditory discrimination necessary for normal speech production.
6. Reading materials are more formalized and dissimilar from natural speech of children.

Waugh, R. P. and K. W. Howell, "Teaching Modern Syllabication," *Reading Teacher,* **29**:1 (1975), 20−25.

Weber, Rose-Marie, "A Linguistic Analysis of First-Grade Reading Errors," *Reading Research Quarterly,* **5**:3 (1970), 427−451.

Wheeler, D. D., "Processes in Word Recognition," *Cognitive Psychology,* **1** (1970), 59−85.

Williams Joanna P., "Some Experiments on Visual and Aural Word Recognition," in *20th Yearbook,* National Reading Conference, 1971, 78−84.

Williams, Joanna P., Ellen L. Blumberg, and David V. Williams, "Clues Used in Visual Word Recognition," *Journal of Educational Psychology,* **61** (1970), 310−315.

Wolpert, Edward M., "Length, Imagery Values, and Word Recognition," *Reading Teacher,* **26**:2 (1972), 180−186. Among other findings, Wolpert reported that high-imagery words were learned with amazingly more ease than were low-imagery words (the *t*-value was 7.28 and greatly exceeded the 0.001 level of confidence). High imagery words are those of deep meaningfulness, concreteness, goodness, emotionality.
This research supports the strategy of Sylvia Ashton-Warner.

Woodcock, Richard *Rhebus Reading,* Circle Pines, MI: American Guidance Services, 1970.

CHAPTER FIVE

How Do I Teach Phonics?

INTRODUCTION

For much of our relatively recent past, the teaching of phonics has been surrounded by controversy. Some of this controversy has been productive. Sequence of instruction and proper teaching techniques, for example, have been and remain legitimate subjects of productive debate. Too often, however, the controversy has reached ridiculous proportions, especially when it has raged around such questions as "Should we or should we not teach phonics?" or "Which is superior, the whole-word method of teaching reading or the phonics method?" Actually, such questions are really nonquestions: they cannot be answered logically in their own terms. We do teach phonics, whether or not we recognize that fact. Phonics as a fundamental word-recognition skill is always part of a successful reading program, whether phonics learning be "planned" or "incidental." As to which is superior, the whole-word or the phonics method, that's a bit like asking "Which is superior, air or food?" Just as both air and food are necessary for life, both whole-word techniques and phonics are necessary to a truly effective reading program.

In 1967, Dr. Jeanne Chall published an educational bestseller on phonics aptly titled *Learning to Read* and even more aptly subtitled *The Great Debate.* In her work, in which she traced the pro's and con's of the phonics controversy, she made a distinction between a "meaning-emphasis" and a "code-emphasis" approach to reading. Unfortunately, some specialists have misread her research findings to conclude that there is a distinct dichotomy between the two approaches, thus adding a bit more fuel to the on-going controversy.

In the 1960s, many severe and often unjustified attacks were launched against the nation's school system. This was the era of the our-schools-are-an-educational-wasteland and the why-Johnny-can't-read brand of extremist criticism. Some of this era's criticism was, however, justified, and educationalists began various reforms to improve the system. One such reform, known as a "system approach" had renewed emphasis on establishing specific goals for the educational process, setting up specific programs to reach these objectives, and testing for specific proof that the goals had been reached.

The teaching of phonics was soon affected by all this. A movement has now emerged toward:

1. Identifying the phonics skills necessary for word analysis proficiency.
2. Delineating the specific performance objectives for each phonics element.
3. Establishing systematic sequential patterns for criterion-referenced testing-teaching-retesting on all phonics skills.
4. Utilizing the major contributions linguistics scientists have brought to the field of reading.
5. Reactivating the concept of individual differences by providing for continuous progress of each child at his or her own rate in learning phonics.

The trend of this movement is based upon the logical assumption that (a) phonics skills are elements of efficient word-recognition, (b) phonics skills can be identified and to some degree isolated, (c) phonics objectives can be stated, (d) children can be tested for acquisition of specific phonics skills, especially through performance in using those skills, and (e) children who lack certain skills can be grouped for special instruction.

THE PLANNED PHONICS PROGRAM

As has been emphasized throughout this text, good learning requires good planning. The phonics program is no exception. Specific materials and strategies must be planned. Specific goals must be set and specific time periods scheduled for attaining these goals. Tests must be designed for ease of instruction.

All this requires that a sequence of instruction be established. The sequence you will discover below in this chapter is not, of course, the only possible one, but it seems to be a reasonable one and is close to what many successful teachers have been following for years. You will note that the sequence is not inflexible as to grade level. You will find no specific set of phonics elements designated as *the* elements to be taught in, say, the second grade or fourth grade. With continuous progress and individual differences as guiding factors in reading instruction today, children will (or should) move through the sequence at their own optimum pace.

Before leaving this general introduction to phonics and getting into the nitty-gritty of "How Do I Teach Phonics?," a word of caution:

The specifics of a planned, sequential phonics program such as that set out below can easily lead to overemphasis on repetitive and deadening drill and, occasionally, phonics for phonics sake; abuses that had much to do with neglect of phonics in earlier years. Good teachers should not need to be reminded that phonics is not an end in itself. Nor will the acquisition of phonics skills in itself guarantee the ability to read, for reading is far more than rote decoding or mastery of phoneme-grapheme relationships. It involves a gestalt of intellectual, psychological, experimental, and emotional processes far more complex than any one of its subskills, including the very important subskill of phonics.

READINESS FOR PHONICS

Most children will have reached readiness for phonics at about the same time they reach readiness for reading—that is, at the completion of the readiness year. They will be able to recognize similarities and differences in speech sounds (recognize words that begin alike and end alike). They will be able to use initial consonant substitution in oral construction of word families. They will be able to identify identical writing-system units (graphemes) and to differentiate between units that are not identical. They will be able to discriminate between words that are identical and words that are different. They will be able to recognize most letters of the alphabet and reproduce the sounds commonly associated with them. Finally, most children by the end of the readiness year will have learned to print their own names and some letters of the alphabet. Given these skills—or most of them—the child is ready to enter a basic phonics program.

PRONUNCIATION SYMBOLS

Throughout this chapter on phonics and elsewhere in the book where we discuss letter-sound correspondences, we use the simplified pronunciation symbols found in the *American Heritage Dictionary of the English Language* (1969–1977). Our reason for using these simplified symbols is to provide a guide for prospective teachers of reading that is devoid of terms that are not easily understood. Few university students or nonspecialist teachers are well-enough acquainted with the symbols of the International Phonetic Alphabet or those of the Trager-Smith linguistic scheme to profit from their use in a volume of this type. In addition, we occasionally use strikes / / to indicate pronunciation where their use seems to aid in setting off pronunciation from printed letter symbols. We are aware that this is inconsistent with scholarly linguistic practice, but this text is directed to juniors and seniors in elementary methods classes, and not to linguistic scholars.

Spellings	*Pronunciation Symbol*	*Spellings*	*Pronunciation Symbol*
pat	ă	noise	oi
pay	ā	took	o͝o
care	âr	boot	o͞o
father	ä	out	ou
bib	b	pop	p
church	ch	roar	r
deed, milled	d	sauce	s
pet	ĕ	ship, dish	sh
bee	ē	tight, stopped	t
fife, phase, rough	f	thin	th
gag	g	this	th̲
hat	h	cut	ŭ
which	hw	urge, term, word, heard	ûr
pit	ĭ	valve	v
pie, by	ī	with	w
pîer	īr	yes	y
judge	j	zebra, xylem, vision, pleasure, garage	zh

Spellings	Pronunciation Symbol	Spellings	Pronunciation Symbol
kick, cat, pique	k	about, item, edible, gallop, circus	ə
lid, needle	l	butter	ə
mum	m		
no, sudden,	n		
thing	ng		
pot, horrid	ŏ		
toe, hoarse	ō		
caught, paw, for	ô		

OBJECTIVES, MATERIALS, AND STRATEGIES OF A PHONICS PROGRAM

PHONICS OBJECTIVE 1

MASTERY OF CONSONANT LETTER/SOUND CORRESPONDENCES

The correspondence of letters to sounds is considerably more regular for consonants than for vowels, although there is not, even with consonants, a complete one-to-one correspondence. Children must learn to match consonant phonemes (sounds) with consonant graphemes (alphabet letters). This is called the skill of *letter-sound correspondences*. It is more simple with consonants than with vowels, because consonant sounds are considerably more regular. So we start with consonants.

Strategy 1. Initial Consonant Letters

The program usually commences with an easy consonant letter-sound relationship; one that is fairly consistent and regular. The consonant letter *m* is popular as a beginner. The teacher frequently commences consonant work by using a "key picture card," showing an object whose "name" begins with the letter *m*. Although it is technically incorrect, the child is often told that "the sound of this letter, *m*, is the same sound we hear at the beginning of the word *man*." (It should be emphasized here again that letters *do not have sounds*.) The teacher then repeats the *m*-sound in sequence "/m/, /m/, /m/; *man*." "Now let's hear *you* say *"man."* "mmmm . . . *man*." "Mmmm is the sound we often make when we are enjoying something we eat and like." "Do you say 'mmmm' when you are licking an ice cream cone?" "Mmmmm." "That is the sound we hear at the beginning of the word, *man.*" "Who knows another word that begins with the same sound as the mmm in *man?*"

When the children in the group have established the letter/sound correspondence in this warmup session, they can then be given a worksheet or their pupil workbooks for reinforcement exercises on *m* and /m/. The worksheet will likely contain pictures of objects whose names begin with letter *m* and have the /m/ sound, "as in *man.*" Moving from the key picture and key word to the workbook is no problem if the teacher has previously showed children how to use a workbook, how to find pages in it, and so on.

The lession on the *m*-/m/ letter/sound relationship should not run for more than fifteen minutes. On a subsequent day, a review of "/m/, as in *man*" is followed with a similar lesson on another consonant letter/sound relationship, and so on through the fourteen regular consonants: *b, d, f, h, j, k, l, n, p, r, t, v, w, z.* The two ("hard" and "soft") sounds represented by the initial consonant *c,* and those represented by initial consonant *g* require special treatment. *Qu* is usually treated with the consonant blends, inasmuch as *q* never appears alone. *X* is learned in the word *X-ray* or *exit,* and also is learned as a final sound in *box* and *fox* (which children hear as identical to /ks/). Initial consonant *y* is taught first, but final *y* is left to be learned along with vowels.

Although some beginning reading programs teach all of the consonants first (and in isolation), it is probably better practice to limit the number of consonants at first to a few. The main drawback to this approach is that it is difficult to find reading materials that contain words beginning with only those few selected consonants. (They most likely would be devised sentences in phonics workbooks.) The teacher, occasionally, may develop sentences containing words beginning with the selected consonants. Here are a few sample sentences that provide practice on the beginning consonants: *b, f, h, m,* and *t.*

> Ben had to hunt for his mitt. He found the mitt behind his barn.
> "Mother," he said, "I found my mitt behind the barn, and now I can hit
> the ball and play baseball tonight with the team." "Take the bat, too,"
> his mother said.

Some reading programs teach a few of the most-used consonants first, encouraging children to use them as cues to determine how the word begins (ignoring words beginning with other consonants). This is another instance of the "Can you think of a word that begins with that sound and makes sense in the sentence?" approach. In beginning reading instruction, most teachers tend to simplify instruction by equating one sound with only one consonant letter, temporarily ignoring the fact that some phonemes are represented by two consonants, such as *sh, th* (as in *thin*) or *th* (as in *though*), *ch* as in *chin,* (or *ch* as in *Christmas*), *ff* as in *off* (and *f* as in *of* compared with *f* as in *fish*), and *gh* as in *enough.* In reading, those "irregularities" are usually left to be handled as "exceptions" at about the third-grade level, although, of course, they are encountered earlier in "sight words" without being analyzed.

A sequence for introducing consonants, based upon their frequency of use and upon the principle of contrast, has been proposed by Dr. Patrick Groff, who justified his preferred sequence on the basis of eight research studies of letter sequence and on the four criteria below:

(a) on the need to contrast letters with different graphic features, (b) on the frequency with which consonant letters appear at the beginning of high-frequency monosyllabic words or syllables, (c) on the relative difficulty children have in learning to copy, write, name, and associate sounds with these letters, and (d) on the need to provide for contrasting sounds (that letters represent).

Groff's sequence of consonants is as follows:

t contrasted with s
l contrasted with c
f contrasted with m
b contrasted with r
h contrasted with w

Along with the teaching of these pairs of contrasting consonants, Groff included instruction in the vowels on the supposition that there is an appropriate place for introducing each one. For example, he suggested that after the t/s contrasting pair is taught, the *a* should be taught in contrast with the *t*. Similarly, *o* with *l*, *i* with *f*, *u* with *b*, and *e* with *d*. The rest of the consonants are taught in contrasting pairs thus: p/v, d/n, k/g, j/z, g/x and y.

Groff's sequence for introducing consonants would seem to be the best one so far devised.

Children who have prior knowledge of particular consonant sounds should be exempted from having to "learn" them again in group instruction. This will, of course, leave unfinished pages in such children's workbooks, and, undoubtedly, some little six-year-old perfectionists who can not tolerate such ommissions will be very upset. (Pity them, for they are going to be hard to live with as they grow older!) You might suggest to these little compulsive overachievers that "You can zip through those pages and fill them in anytime it suits you, either now or later." Or, you may *try* to convince them that, inasmuch as they already know those sounds, they can invest their time more productively in other pursuits:

"You are more lucky than most of the class. You already know these, don't you? (They won't dispute that.) You really don't need to do this—unless you want to—so you can look at this book or have fun doing something else (something constructive) while the rest of us have to work."

Assuming that the phonics workbooks "skill book," or worksheets you have selected are the work of knowledgeable and reliable reading specialists, you can be sure they contain the distillation of many good ideas accumulated through years of successful teaching. Well-prepared phonics workbooks and worksheets can provide you with an immediately available collection of sequenced practice materials. Used properly, and with common sense, the workbook can be a resource that will save you countless hours of unnecessary spade work.

Here is a sample of a routine frequently used with a phonics workbook:

"Put a mark like this (teacher demonstrates how to mark an "X") on each picture that you think has a name that begins with /m/, like in *man*."

"What is this a picture of?"

"Yes, it is a picture of a monkey (or money, etc.)."

"Does that word begin with /m/ as in *man*?"

"Yes it does begin with /m/, so we can put this X mark over the picture. As we do this, we say /m/ and *monkey*." Everytime we put a mark (X) on a picture of something that begins with /m/ like in *man*, we say the beginning sound /m/. And, to be sure we are right, we say the name of what is in the picture, too."

Strategy 2. Generalizing from Sight Words

Teachers frequently find it useful to present several known sight words that all begin with the same initial consonant. For example, *m* words could be *man*, *mother*, *mat*, *my*, *me*. The children pronounce them at the same time that the teacher displays the printed words. This double stimulus—hearing the word and seeing the printed words—helps impress upon the children the fact that the words "all begin with the same sound and with the same letter." After they have "generalized" this fact, they are ready to work on sound/letter correspondences and to do workbook exercises as previously described. Generalizing (working from the known to the unknown) is deservedly favored by many teachers. Although either approach works well if the teacher is comfortable with it, generalizing has the added advantage of conforming with the principle of "discovery learning."

Initial Consonant Reinforcement Activities

Young children enjoy phonics games, not only for the fun games bring to what otherwise could be dreadfully dull, but also for the challenge they afford.

Riddles or guessing games are an old standby. For example:

"I am thinking of an animal that walks like /m/man, has hands and feet like /m/an, looks little like a /m/an, and whose name begins with the same sound as /m/an."

"Which animal is it?"

After the correct answer (monkey) is elicited, the followup is to have the children write the word, use it in a sentence, and copy the sentence for practice in using the word in context.

Completing the sentence is another good game which children can play with words having the same initial consonant. This, too, utilizes contextual clues as well as providing initial consonant constraint.

"I am going to say something and leave out a word. And you are going to know what the word is because you know the first sound of that word. You already know that it begins like /m/an.

"Mother lit a candle with a _____ ."

Here are a few more examples:

"I couldn't buy two comic books because I didn't have enough _____."
"When we had the table all set for breakfast, we discovered that we didn't have any _____ to pour on our cereal."
"Joe spilled his soup on the lunchroom floor, and I went to find the _____ to clean it up."

In some instances children will supply words that fit the context but do not begin with the consonant sound being studied. When this happens, their contributions should be accepted (for it shows comprehension and involvement), but acceptance should be followed with a comment such as:

"Yes, that *is* a good word and makes sense, doesn't it? Now, let's see if we can think of another good word that also makes sense, but is one the begins like /m/an."

Object sorting games utilizing small plastic objects representing fish, dishes, boat, baseball bat, monkey, boy, saw, and so on, were popularized by the Houghton-Mifflin *Getting Ready to Read* program. Houghton-Mifflin's initial consonant sorting unit can be purchased as a separate module from the publisher. Similar small plastic representations can often be found in large variety stores. Cottage cheese boxes may be used as containers for the objects, with each box labeled with one consonant letter and key picture.

If, for example, the group is studying *f* and has completed the study of *m, b, c,* and *d,* five cartons labeled with these five letters would be presented to the children. A number of small plastic objects representing things that begin with one of these simple consonant letters would be assembled. Children, working in pairs or in groups no larger than four, would take turns calling the name of the object and pronouncing its initial consonant sound while placing the object in the correct container.

The accuracy of the performance of each child is monitored by the others in the group. This frees the teacher for individualized work elsewhere. (If adult supervision is needed, this is a good project for a teacher's aide or volunteer helper.)

Consonant wall charts may be constructed by the children under adult supervision. Lack of perfection in the charts will be outweighed by the stimulus to learning engendered by the personal involvement of the children. Moreover, such charts can be tailored to the particular phonics elements being studied at the moment. More importantly, they will include pictures of objects that are relevant to the children who selected them.

Phonics recordings are available commercially for use with some phonics workbooks, or independently with worksheets. Such recordings generally contain directions to the student and pronunciation of the words and consonant sounds. However, recordings especially made by the teacher for a particular group are frequently *much* more effective than those produced commercially. On tape, the teacher can direct certain children within the group by name to perform certain tasks. Moreover, the teacher can modify the phoneme correspondences to the children's dialect system. In addition, we have found that some of the commercially available tape recordings of phonics practice move along much too rapidly, and others may contain theatrical and/or stilted speech patterns that are difficult for some children to understand.

Phonics devices (which the British call "apparatus") are available in several forms: phonics word wheels, phonics sliderules, phonics matching cards, and so on.

What preparation should you give to a child that would make this phonics learning device most effective?

A teacher-made consonant and vowel chart can be very effective, especially if it is developed with the help of the children.

Board games can be homemade or purchased from publishers. Commercial board games (such as the *Phonics We Use* games produced under the supervision of Dr. Arthur Heilman and available from Rand-McNally) are generally to be preferred over the homemade variety.

PHONICS OBJECTIVE 2

TO TEACH MASTERY OF SHORT VOWEL SOUNDS

Many teachers and reading specialists prefer to commence phonics instruction with "short" vowel sounds, and there is good justification for this approach. One justification for this preference is that most of the one-syllable words that children encounter in the consonant-vowel-consonant (CVC) pattern are pronounced with the short vowel sound. The short vowel sounds therefore, are much more common and, hence, considered more useful than other phonics elements. Moreover, there are only five short vowel sounds, and once they are learned, children will have the basis for synthesizing them with a few consonants to make many words they already have in their speaking vocabulary. For example, with the five short vowel sounds and three consonants, *t, n,* and *p,* we can print: *at, an, in, it, on, up, pan, pin, tan, ten, tin, tap, tip, top, net, not, nut, pen, pat, pet, pit, pot, pep, pop, pup, tot, nap, nip.* Note that the short vowel constraint does not permit such words as *no, ton, to,* and so on. If we were to add the other consonants, it would be possible for the children to construct 73 regular CVC words using the short-a as the medial vowel; 39 using the short-e; 56 using the short-i; 51 using the short-o; and 51 using the short-u, making a total of 270 phonemically regular CVC words. The utility of this approach in this early stage of learning to read would seem to be obvious.

It also seems obvious that whether to teach consonants or vowels first is purely an academic question, inasmuch as there are only a handful of words (such as *I* and *a*) that do not contain both consonants and vowels. Therefore, since we are concerned that children transfer phonics learnings to whole-word identification as soon as possible, vowels *and* consonants should be brought together for study as soon as a few of both have been learned.

Bringing vowels together with consonants is sometimes referred to as "tucking the vowels in." Reading specialists refer to the process as *synthesizing* the sounds; hence the expression *synthetic phonics.* This process is contrary to word analysis, in which a word is "decoded" to attempt to discover its phonetic makeup and, hence, pronounce it. The process of phonetic decoding is called *analytic phonics.*

Most advocates of back-to-good-old-phonics have in mind both synthetic phonics and analytic phonics, their assumption being that children should first learn letter/sound relationships, and when they then meet a new word they can analyze it and synthesize the sounds into correct pronunciation. There are many valid bases for such an argument. On the other hand, there are many irregular elements and words in our language that do not lend themselves to this kind of simple decoding. Moreover, phonics and pronunciation are not the only constituents of the complex process of reading. Too exclusive reliance upon "pure phonics" can create miserably slow and ineffectual readers.

Short-Vowel Rule

The short-vowel rule tells us that where there is a one-syllable word in the CVC pattern, the vowel in the middle usually has a short sound. Children can easily be led to awareness that the letter "tucked in the middle" of short words usually has a "short" sound. (Somewhere along the line, children will learn that those *a, e, i, o, u* letters and ă, ě, ĭ, ŏ, and ŭ sounds are called *vowels,* just as they have already learned that some other letters are *consonants.*) In fact, many children will come to state the short-vowel rule in their own words. For example:

"Little words with only one vowel in the middle are short."

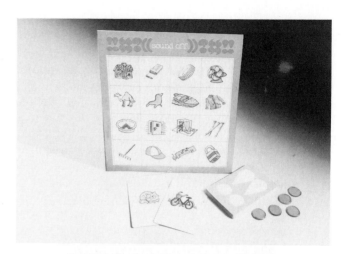

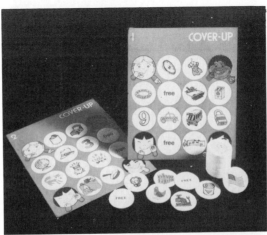

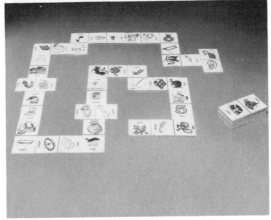

These board games are illustrative of those available commercially for use in phonics practice or just for fun.

"Short words with only one vowel in the middle are pronounced with short vowel sounds."

"The vowel in a CVC word is almost always short."

The short-vowel rule can be extended to cover the few words that begin with a vowel: *egg, and, it, is, up, on, at, an, in,* for example. "The one vowel at the beginning of a one-syllable word is almost always short." (Words like *ate* and *ice* are subject to the "final-e" rule.)

Short-Vowel "Key Words"

Many pure phonics systems use the same key words as cues to five short vowel sounds: a—*apple*; e—*elephant*; i—*indian*; o—*ostrich*; and u—*umbrella*. (In some instances, *astronaut* has replaced *apple*.) Occasionally, the key words used contain the short-vowel sound *within* the CVC pattern; for example, *hat, bed, lid, cop, cup.* It is considerably more difficult to find key words suitable for illustration that begin with the short-vowel sound. Here are a few that are sometimes used: *ant, egg, imp, exit, umpire.*

Key Pictures and Nouns for Short-vowel Sounds

Astronaut	Elephant	Indian	Ostrich	Umbrella
Ant	Egg	Imp	Exit	Umpire
Hat	Bed	Lid	Cop	Cup

Words with either *beginning* or *medial* short-vowel sounds may be used as key words. We believe that practice with both is most productive, for short vowel sounds are regularly found in both positions.

Short-Vowel Techniques

Should you teach *one* short vowel at a time, or all five at once? One-at-a-time teaching may lead to greater mastery and less confusion. Moreover, although children frequently learn to pronounce ā, ē, ī, ō, ū as long vowels together in rapid succession, very seldom does anyone learn to pronounce the short vowels ă, ĕ, ĭ, ŏ, ŭ, in this fashion. Try it. See how halting your efforts are at first. However, since short vowels occur more frequently than the long, teaching five short-vowel sounds together is probably best.

At least two beginning reading programs teach the five short-vowel sounds together and the five long-vowel sounds together. Some approaches teach three sounds for the letter *a* (ă, ā, ä) together; two for the letter *e* (ĕ, ē); two for the letter *i* (ĭ, ī); three for the letter *o* (ŏ, ō, ōō); and two for the letter *u* (ŭ and ū). Children using such programs face the task of deciding which of the sounds is the one that results in a recognizable word that "makes sense" in a sentence.

Using the Principle of Minimal Differences

With the children, investigate the minimal differences between words containing *t, r, p, m*, and short vowels ă and ĭ in this manner:

Place these two words on the chalkboard or flannel board:

> *tap*
> *rap*

Discuss how they are alike and their minimal differences. (The initial consonants are the only differences.) Leave the words on the board and add *tip* and *rip*.

> *tap*   *tip*
> *rap*   *rip*

Discuss the minimal differences left-to-right across from one word to the other, comparing the *medial vowels*. At this point, two sets of minimal differences will have been introduced: initial consonants and medial vowels.

Leave the words on the board and add *Tim* and *rim*:

> *tap*   *tip*   *Tim*
> *rap*   *rip*   *rim*

Point out to the children that now the final consonants are the "differences."

Add *tam* and *ram*, noting that now the final consonant has changed and the medial vowels is ă.

> *tap*   *tip*   *Tim*   *tam*
> *rap*   *rip*   *rim*   *ram*

At each change, the word analysis is concentrated on the *one* new element and on the language pattern that has been created.

PHONICS OBJECTIVE 3

TO IDENTIFY WORDS THAT END WITH THE SAME FINAL CONSONANT SOUND, AND DISTINGUISH THEM FROM WORDS WITH OTHER ENDINGS

Identifying final consonant sounds is usually a relatively simple operation, but it does call for attending and listening, the basic requirements of auditory discrimination. The teacher pronounces a series of words that, for example, end with the /t/ sound, including a few "distractors." The children are requested to respond to the words in any one of several different ways:

Thumbs up is a traditional method of response. The teacher pronounces pairs of words that end with the same consonant sound, but do *not* rhyme. For example: fat/fit; sit/sat; bat/boy (distractor); fan/fat. Children put thumbs up if the words end alike. Emphasis in this exercise is on the last *consonant* sound; not whether the words rhyme or not.

Final consonant training, like all phonics work, should move from auditory discrimination to visual discrimination and on to reinforcement. One useful scheme is to have each child print, say, the letter *t* on one piece of tagboard and the word *no* on another. When the final consonant *t* is heard in both words of the pair, each child holds up the card with the grapheme *t*. The *No* card is held up when one of the distractors is pronounced.

Cards with sandpaper letters are even better for they provide visual-auditory-kinesthetic-tactile (VAKT) practice. The teacher stands in the rear of the group and pronounces the pairs of words. When *t* words are pronounced, each child holds up the *t* and then traces over the *t*, pronouncing the sound while doing so.

Although there is little research on the learning value of using rhyming words, teachers and children both enjoy them. Enjoyment aside, however, rhyming exercises should be used with caution. Some five- and six-year-olds have considerable difficulty grasping the concept of rhyming. They seem, at this stage of their development, unable to connect rhyming exercises with jingles or nursery rhymes (assuming they have been exposed to them in the home). They may also confuse rhyming words with words that merely end with the same sound. Further, some children may speak in dialects that do not lend themselves to the rhyming patterns of standard English. All in all, the teacher of very young children would do well to be skeptical about the value of rhyming exercises in early phonics work.

PHONICS OBJECTIVE 4

TO LEARN PATTERNS OF LANGUAGE (PHONOGRAMS)

Word families, or *phonograms,* have long been popular as guides to learning in reading instruction. Although they do rhyme because of their common language pattern, they are not, technically rhyming words. It may not be linguistically correct to refer to language patterns as *phonograms,* but that is what teachers have been calling them for a century or more.

At the beginning of phonogram practice, it is wise to move from the simple to the complex, commencing with one-syllable CVC patterns using the VC bases, such at *-at* and *-an.* This routine employs *initial consonant substitution* and, in this instance, a collection of phonograms based on *-at* and on *-an:*

>*-at—cat, mat, bat, hat, sat, rat, fat*
>*-an—can, man, fan, tan, Ann, ran, Dan*

Children are fond of these elementary language patterns, for they are regular and introduce just one linguistic element (Minimal Contrast) at a time.

Some bright children will undoubtedly suggest more complicated words with initial and final consonant blends and/or digraphs. Accept their suggestions, even though some of the "lesser lights" among the children may not comprehend them. Also, some children will have fun proposing sentences that are close to nonsense but contain some of the elements they are studying. Here is one that emerged in one of our phonogram sessions:

"How, now, you old cow?"

There are scores of phonogram bases. Here are some simple ones to be used as starters:

>*-ad, -ad, -ag, -am, -ap, -eg, -ell, -et, -ig, -ill,*
>*-in, -ob, -ot, -ug, -un, -op, -ut, -en, -it, -ub*

Inasmuch as reading is but one part of a total language-arts cluster of skills and depends upon VAKT sensory input, we can expect very little, if any, reading skill to be developed by verbal practice alone. Children need to utilize the other sensory domains: to see the words, to write them, touch them, as well as pronounce them. This calls for practice in all aspects of VAKT.

Sometimes, however, the teacher neglects to plan for such practice. If, for example, one phonogram base is printed on the chalkboard and, as rhyming words are suggested, the initial consonant letter is erased each time during initial consonant *substitution,* the original consonant letter is visually lost. There is nothing left (because it has been erased) for comparison. Two psychological learning principles are being violated when that is done: First, visual memory needs *reinforcement* through visual symbols. Children quickly forget the symbols after they are erased. Second, original learning is subject to *retroactive inhibition.* When a new initial consonant or whole word that looks like the previous one is introduced, it is apt to wipe out the visual image of the original one. Consequently, there are good reasons for keeping both symbols in view on the chalkboard: (a) they provide a basis for quick and immediate review, (b) they provide the means for visual discrimination and contrast, and (c) they provide models for the child to copy during the kinesthetic-tactile segment of the learning process.

Here, again, planning is necessary. Before beginning the lesson, the teacher must print the phonogram base a number of times on the chalkboard. The base should be printed in a vertical column, with a space to the left of each phonogram base for an initial consonant or consonant diagraph to be chalked in. Using a different colored chalk, the teacher inserts the proper consonants as the children propose new words. If the group is small and the children are able to print letters quickly, they should be allowed to insert the graphemes themselves.

Here is an example of how the -*ob* base would look on the chalkboard:

> —ob
> —ob
> —ob
> —ob
> —ob
> —ob
> —ob
> —ob
> —ob
> —ob

As a teacher of youngsters you will soon become conditioned to expect the unexpected. There is always the possibility that some child, drawing upon the language of home and community, will provide the word *slob* to complete, for example, an -*ob* base. What do you do with that? There is only one correct teaching procedure: you accept it as a word that is common in today's culture. In this case, the word might even lead into a discussion of human relationships: "None of us wants to be called a 'slob,' do we?" Or perhaps, "It isn't nice to see a person eating like a slob, is it?" (By the way, the word comes from the Dutch word *slobbern,* meaning to eat slovenly).

The point, of course, of this little aside is that you should always be alert to the teaching potential of unexpected responses from your imaginative charges. Exploit such responses to create incidental but satisfying learning experiences whenever possible. It is in the exercise of such creativity that teaching—whether it be instruction in phonics or any other aspect of reading—becomes an art. Think about that for a while. . . .

Now, back to the nitty-gritty of phonograms.

Phonogram bases printed on tagboard can be flocked with "Christmas snow" or have cotton wadding rubber cemented to the backs. They can then be used on the flannelboard and shifted about us convenient. (Commercially printed phonograms are available at school supply companies). The initial consonants should be displayed at the left in a vertical column. Enough graphemic base cards should be available to attach to the initial consonants to complete words. (All this of course takes planning by the teacher, but what effective lesson doesn't?)

Here is an example of a display for the bases *-ake* and *-ick:*

	-ake **base**	*-ick* **base**
b-	bake	
d-		Dick
f-	flake	flick
g-		
h-		
j-		
k-		kick
l-	lake	lick
m-	make	
n-		nick
p-		pick
qu-	quake	quick
r-	rake	
s-	shake stake	sick stick slick
t-	take	tick trick
v-		
w-	wake	wick
x-		
y-		
z-		

Other useful grapheme bases beginning with *short* vowels are:

-ab	-ad	-ag	-am	-an	-ap	-and	-as -at -ack -ank	
-ed	-eg	-en	-et	-end				
-ib	-id	-ig	-in	-it	-ick	-ing		
-ob	-od	-og	-op	-ot	-ock			
-ub	-ud	-ug	-um	-un	-ut	-ust		

PHONICS OBJECTIVE 5

TO COPE WITH CONSONANT BLENDS AND CONSONANT DIGRAPHS

Although *consonant blends* and *consonant digraphs* both consist of digraphs (two letters) there is a difference between them. A consonant blend is two sounds blended together. To produce a blend, the voice mechanism emits two separate sounds in extremely aspid succession. A consonant digraph, on the other hand, produces one sound and this sound is different from the sound of either of the two letters spoken separately. For example, *gn* as in *gnaw*, *ph* as in *phone*, and *ps* and *ch* as in *pychi* are consonant digraphs. *Sh* as in *shine*, *st* as in *stop*, and *fr* as in *fresh* are consonant blends.

One way to distinguish between the two types of digraphs is to remember that the word *blend* itself starts with a consonant blend/bl. But, in any case, the distinction is not of primary interest so far as teaching youngsters to read is concerned. Your task is simply to help children pronounce two adjacent consonants.

The digraphs most commonly used to start with are:

> *ch-, wh-, sh-,* and *th-* in initial position, and
> *-ch, -sh, -th, -ck,* and *-lk* in final position

Some phonics programs also have the children study double consonants in final position: *-ll* and *-ss* being most common as starters. Obviously, double consonants cause little trouble, and you can treat them as though they were single letters, with very little additional ado.

The most common consonant blends in initial position should be studied first, leaving the more difficult blends and most triple-consonants (known as trigraphs) until later. Here is a sequence of blends we have found to be satisfactory:

> *bl-, st-, sl-, pl-, fl-, tr-, gr-, fr-, sp-, gl-, sm-,*
> *dr-,* and *cr-*

It is simple matter to move from these blends to three trigraphs: *str-, spl-,* and *spr-.*

Blends to be studied first in final position are:

> *-st, -sk, -ld, -nd, -nk, -lk, -mp, -ng*

All of the methods previously suggested for initial consonant substitution and some of those suggested for phonograms can be used in teaching and learning consonant blends. Actually, however, few children need much practice on pronunciation of blends. They merely need work on recognizing the blends in print.

Place known words on the chalkboard or feltboard and have the children substitute blends in initial or final positions, thus:

Initial Position			Final Position		
back	+ bl-	= black			
tack	+ st-	= stack	dum	+ -mp	= dump
lack	+ sl-	= slack	thin	+ -ng	= thing
lace	+ pl-	= place	an	+ -nd	= and
lame	+ fl-	= flame	as	+ -sk	= ask
rain	+ tr-	= train	men	+ -nd	= mend
rap	+ str	= strap			
rip	+ gr-	= grip			
lash	+ spl	= splash			
litter	+ gl-	= glitter			
mall	+ sm	= small			

Here are some groupings of consonant blends and consonant digraphs that are most commonly taught:

Classes of Initial Consonant Blends

The "1" Blends:	bl-	cl-	fl-	gl-	pl-	sl-	
The "r" Blends:	br-	cr-	dr-	fr-	gr-	pr-	tr-
The "w" Blends	dw-	tw-	sw-				
Trigraphs							
as Blends	scr-	spr-	squ-	str-	spl-	shr-	thr-

Final Consonant Blends

-ct	-dk	-dt	-ft	(-ght)	-ld	-lk	-lf	-lt
-lp	-mp	-nc	-nch	-nd	-pt	-br	-rd	-rg
-rk	-rl	-rm	-rn	-rp	-rd	-rt	-rv	-rz
-sk	-st	-sp	-xt					

Consonant Digraphs (Single Sound)

ch-	(cherry)	-ck	(block)	th-	(this)	th-	(thistle)
-ng	(sing)	sh-	(ship)	wh-	(whale)	qu-	(queen)
gn-	(gnaw)	-gh	(laugh)	ph-	(phone)	ps-	(psychic)
wr-	(write)	kn-	(know)				

PHONICS OBJECTIVE 6

TO LEARN LONG-VOWEL SOUNDS AND TO APPLY THE "FINAL-E" RULE

Long-vowel sounds are probably the easiest of all phonics elements to learn in isolation because they are identical to their letter names. Inasmuch as most children in the United States have learned the alphabet names through children's TV programs or instruction in the home before coming to formal reading, the transfer of letter names to long vowels is a simple task. What is not so simple is the ability to know when a vowel letter is pronounced "long" or "short" when it appears in a word. This one problem alone causes more trouble in reading than any other. (To compound the problem, there are several alternative vowel pronunciations with which to contend.) An additional problem with long-vowel sounds arises when two vowels are found side-by-side in a word. Which is pronounced? Or do they together represent a different sound than either vowel would standing alone?

One time-honored method is to convert a known three-letter CVC word into a four-letter long-vowel word by adding a *final-e*. List the three-letter CVC words on the chalkboard and to the right of each print the four-letter word. This is coded CVC+e. Move from the word in the left column to the new word with the final-e. Soon the children will be able to generalize the "rule" and state it in their own words. Here are some words to start with:

mad	made	pal	pale
cap	cape	tap	tape
rat	rate	mat	mate
hid	hide	rob	robe
rod	rode	not	note
hop	hope	rid	ride
tot	tote	rip	ripe
bit	bite	kit	kite
fin	fine	fad	fade

Rag, sag, wag, since the *g* changes from hard to soft when *e* is added, cannot be used here. Note, too, that in the list above there are no *e* words. There are *few* instances where the e can be easily changed to long-e by the addition of final-e. It usually requires a double-*e*, -ea, -ey, or -y to effect that change.

Working with words such as those above, children will soon come to formulate their own final-e, "magic-e", "silent-e", or CVC+e rule. In their own words, it usually comes out something like this:

"When we add the letter *e* to the end of a small word, it usually makes the vowel in the middle 'long'."

Phonics Rules and Generalizations

In 1963 Dr. Theodore Clymer published an important study of the value of phonics rules. His findings indicated that there are very few cases in which a particular phonics rule operates 100% of the time. Other researchers have largely substaniated Clymer's findings. There has, consequently, been a tendency among some reading specialists to play down the importance of phonics rules.

However, merely because rules are not 100% operative is no reason to ignore them in beginning reading instruction. Rules and generalizations have their uses, especially for beginners. Dr. Mildred Henderson, for example, found that about 44 of Clymer's generalizations were useful when their objective was word identification.

Irregularities in the English language are often cited as an argument against the usefulness of phonics rules. Dr. Paul Hanna, however, has shown that our language is not nearly so irregular as is sometimes claimed. In his monumental study of phoneme/spelling correspondences, Dr. Hanna and his associates fed 17,000 words into a computer programmed with the spelling rules of the English language. The words were spelled phonemically and the computer's task was to spell them out correctly according to the rules. The resulting printout was 80% accurate. But we can readily claim that children are not computers (see the delightful little book, *Don't Push Me; I'm not a Computer!*).

In a more recent study, Ralph Turner and Sandra Roth of West Virginia University investigated the consistency of phonics generalizations in words occurring in running text rather than in isolation. When word frequency in running text is taken into consideration, the usefulness of the generalizations is altered, as shown in the chart below. The authors found that, "when the rule was a simple one-to-one correspondence (i.e., *ch* is always pronounced as in *chair*), then direct rule-learning was most effective." They also found that, even though the two-vowel rule is correct less than 30% of the time, there are subelements of the rule that are very useful; for example, *au* as in *sauce* is pronounced ô 83% of the time. (*Laugh* and *beauty* are exceptions to be learned as sight words.)

Consistency of Phonics Generalizations: Results of Five Research Studies*

Consonant Generalization	*Study*	CW[1]	TW[2]	%	FCW[3]	FTW[4]	%
C followed by *e* or *i* sounds like *s*	Clymer	66	69	96			
	Bailey	260	284	88			
	Emans	79	88	90			
	Turner	1065	1152	92	27,541	29,100	94
C followed by *o* or *a* sounds like *k*	Turner	1783	1784	99	42,412	42,419	99

Consistency of Phonics Generalizations: Results of Five Research Studies*

Consonant Generalization	Study	CW[1]	TW[2]	%	FCW[3]	FTW[4]	
Ch is usually pronounced as in *kitchen*,	Clymer	99	104	95			
not as in *machine*	Bailey	196	225	87			
	Emans	35	52	67			
	Turner	431	601	71	19,361	16,004	82
When *c* and *h* are next to each other, they	Clymer	103	103	100			
make only one sound	Bailey	225	225	100			
	Emans	53	53	100			
	Turner	596	598	99	19,164	19,171	99
When a word ends in *ck*, it has the same	Clymer	46	46	100			
last sound as in *look*	Bailey	80	80	100			
	Emans	9	9	100			
	Turner	83	83	100	3,011	2,011	100
The letters *c* and *g* before *y* are soft	Turner	74	74	100	998	998	100
The letter *g* often has a sound similar to	Clymer	49	77	64			
that of *j* in *jump* when it preceeds the	Bailey	168	216	78			
letters *i* or *e*	Emans	60	75	80			
	Turner	601	734	81	12,133	16,622	72
G before *n* is silent	Turner	40	96	41	1,083	1,989	54
When *ght* is seen in a word, *gh* is silent	Clymer	30	30	100			
	Bailey	40	40	100			
	Emans	3	3	100			
	Turner	133	135	98	5,418	5,463	99
When a word begins with *kn*, the *k* is	Clymer	10	10	100			
silent	Bailey	17	17	100			
	Emans	3	3	100			
	Turner	28	28	100	1,925	1,925	100
When a word begins with *wr*, the *w* is	Clymer	8	8	100			
silent	Bailey	17	17	100			
	Emans	4	4	100			
	Turner	32	32	100	1,038	1,038	100
In *ph*, one hears the sound of *f*	Turner	188	194	96	2,209	2,423	91

Vowel Generalization							
When *y* is the final letter in a word, it	Clymer	169	201	84			
usually has a vowel sound	Bailey	462	518	89			
	Emans	265	270	98			
	Turner	1505	1620	92	49,613	60,302	82
When the letter *i* is followed by the letters	Clymer	22	31	71			
gh, the *i* usually stands for its long sound	Bailey	25	35	71			

Consistency of Phonics Generalizations: Results of Five Research Studies*

Consonant Generalization	Study	CW[1]	TW[2]	%	FCW[3]	FTW[4]	
and the *gh* is silent	Emans	3	3	100			
	Turner	109	139	78	4,551	5,230	87
When *a* follows *w* in a word, it usually has	Clymer	5	47	32			
the sound of *a* as in *was*	Bailey	17	78	22			
	Emans	5	18	28			
	Turner	29	246	11	112,481	17,721	63
Final *e* makes the preceeding vowel long	Clymer	80	288	63			
	Bailey	330	578	57			
	Emans	37	59	63			
	Turner	941	2212	42	40,886	102,292	39
When *a* is followed by *r* and final *e*, we	Clymer	9	10	90			
expect to hear the sound heard in *care*	Bailey	23	24	96			
	Emans	2	2	100			
	Turner	26	27	96	843	5,238	16
When two vowels are together, the first is	Clymer	309	686	45			
long and the second is short	Bailey	586	1732	34			
	Emans	87	480	18			
	Turner	1728	6508	26	54,204	185,215	29
In *ay*, the *y* is silent and the *a* is long	Clymer	36	46	78			
	Bailéy	44	50	88			
	Emans	6	6	100			
	Burmeister	21	21	100			
	Turner	238	241	98	15,147	15,387	99
Words that have *ee*, have a long *e* sound	Clymer	85	87	98			
	Bailey	148	171	87			
	Emans	24	24	100			
	Burmeister	31	35	89			
	Turner	285	325	87	11,245	14,222	74
The two letters *ow* make the long *o* sound*	Emans	18	18	100			
or the *ou* sound as in *out* (* first half not	Burmeister	31	31	100			
used)	Turner*	151	277	54	6,466	12,445	50
In *ie*, the *i* is silent and the *e* is long	Clymer	3	47	17			
	Bailey	27	88	31			
	Emans	5	22	23			
	Burmeister	3	31	26			
	Turner	292	558	52	5,615	11,119	50

[1]number of words consistent with the rule
[2]total number of words containing the elements of the rule
[3]frequency in running text of the words consistent with the rule
[4]total frequency in running text of words containing the elements of the rule

SOURCE Turner, Robert R. and Sandra R. Roth, ''Reconsiderations of Phonic Generalizations,'' paper presented at the annual meeting. American Psychological Association, Chicago, August, 1975. Used by permission of the authors.

PHONICS OBJECTIVE 7

TO IDENTIFY THE LONG-VOWEL SOUND IN CERTAIN VOWEL DIGRAPHS, AND TO APPLY THE TWO-VOWEL RULES WHERE APPLICABLE

The next phonics objective is to practice converting known words with medial short-vowel sounds to words with long vowel sounds. This is most easily done by merely adding another *e* to words already containing the medial vowel *e*. This double-*e* in English is always pronounced with the long-*e* sound. Only words that can be converted into real words having double-*e* as the medial vowels should be used in this exercise. Here they are:

bet	beet	met	meet	bled	bleed
fed	feed	red	reed	fell	feel
wed	weed	step	steep		

Two-Vowel Rule 1

From these few examples alone, children can learn to generalize that "When the two vowels *e-e* (or double-*e*) are together, the first one says its name and the second is silent" or, more simply, "two *ee*s together are pronounced e."

The e-a Vowel Digraph   Practice with long-*e* in combination with *a* is the next step in long-vowel study. Here are words that are appropriate for this segment of phonics instruction:

beach	cheap	leaf	neat
bead	dream	leak	peak
beam	heat	lean	peace
beast	feat	leash	peat
beat	heath	leave	pea
beaver		mean	reach
cream	heap	meat	read
sea	stream	tea	weave
seat	season		wheat
seam	team	gleam	

One effective strategy is to derive words for practice from known CVC words by "tucking in" the letter *a*. Here are some useful words for this purpose:

bed	bead	met	meat
best	beast	net	neat
bet	beat	pet	peat
led	lead	red	read
men	mean	set	seat

Another similar method is to start with CVC words that have the short-a sound and "tuck the vowel *e* in" changing the first vowel to long-e and making the a "silent".

bad	bead	man	mean
lash	leash	rap	reap
pat	peat	fat	feat
bat	beat	mat	meat
sat	seat	nat	neat
		Sam	seam

These are tricky words, but they are encountered in children's reading and must be learned somehow. It is better to learn them as belonging to these spelling patterns than to try to learn them all by rote.

The a-i Vowel Digraph There are enough incidences of the *ai* combination to warrant practice on this vowel digraph. Here are twenty examples:

bait	daisy	laid	saint
daily	dainty	maid	wait
faint	main	chain	brain
paint	grain	strain	raid
gain	pain	raise	rain

Of course there are exceptions, such as *said, aisle,* and so on but these exceptions do not negate the value of learning this spelling pattern. In addition, exceptions can be used to alert children that there is diversity in the language and that exceptions to pronunciation patterns must sometimes be dealt with.

Words for comparison may also be made by inserting *i* in known words to show that the insertion of the vowel-*i* changes the short vowel a to long-a.

bat	bait	bit	bait
mad	maid	chin	chain
ran	rain	man	main
grin	grain	fan	faint
rid	raid	pan	pain
string	strain	pin	paint

The o-a Vowel Digraph The long-o, followed by *a*, may be studied with the following few words:

boat	moat	float	road
coat	foam	goat	toad
roam	loan	moan	groan
			load

Some of these may be derived from known CVC words:

bat	boat	cot	coat
flat	float	rod	road
cat	coat	mat	moat
got	goat	man	moan
ram	roam	lad	load

Two-Vowel Rule 2 (for e-a, a-i, and o-a Vowel Digraphs)

After some practice with vowel words above, the spelling patterns should reveal enough regularity that the children can generalize a two-vowel rule that might be stated:

"When the two vowels, *e-a, a-i,* and *o-a,* are together, the first is *usually* pronounced with its long vowel sound and the second is silent." Or, more simply:

"When *e-a; a-i;* or *o-a* are together, the first is *usually* long and the second is silent." Always have children emphasize *usually* by underlining, printing in red, or some other device. "Usually" is emphasized to alert them that there are other exceptions that must also be learned.

Exceptions to the Two-Vowel Spelling and Pronunciation Patterns

Work with two-vowel spelling exceptions must come sooner or later. Depending upon the ability of each group of children, you may wish to defer working with exceptions until later. They are presented at this point, however, because their study proceeds logically from work with the vowel digraphs.

When *ai* and *ea* are followed by *l* or by *r,* pronunciation may be a problem for children. For example, *fear* may be pronounced *fir,* and *near, hear,* and *gear* mispronounced similarly. In some dialects, *deal* is pronounced with a schwa sound. In others, it is pronounced *del,* and such words as *meal, seal, steal, real, heal,* and *squeal* may have similar *dialectic* variations.

The *ai* pattern, followed by *l* or by *r,* is another situation that may present a dialectic exception. Regardless of a child's dialect, however, the *ai* (plus *l* or *r*) pattern can be practiced with the following words (this instruction is most often given in the second grade):

chair	bail	snail	fail
hail	jail	mail	nail
quail	rail	sail	pair
pail	wail	tail	frail
stair	fair	hair	lair
trail	flair		

What About the "When-Two-Vowels-Go-Walking . . ." Rule?

For decades, the clever little vowel rule "When two vowels go walking, the first one does the talking" has been a favorite of teachers and children. It has been repeated so often that we are sometimes inclined to forget that it applies only in some cases: *e-e; e-a; a-i;* and *o-a* (when not followed by *l* or *r*). It is much better, in our opinion, to teach patterns with words that do help the child learn to pronounce *ea, ai,* and *oa* than to work with a so-called "rule" that is not a generalization. Here are a few examples of words to practice with: *beat, bait, boat, heat, hail, goat, meat, main, mail, moan, nail, pail, soak, team, wheat.* Avoid *dea*- words for you'll run into *dead, death, dear, deal,* and so on.

One Procedure for Applying Vowel Rules

The six-step procedure proposed for applying vowel rules in word identification by Dr. James B. Carlin is intriguing. Carlin claimed that his method of using vowel rules and exceptions would account for 92% of all the words in a beginning reader's reading materials! He suggested that only *two* vowel spelling patterns need to be considered:

1. Long-Vowel Spelling Pattern The two-vowel rule, in which the first vowel of the pair "says its long sound," and cases in which one-vowel at the end of a word or syllable "says its long sound."

2. Short-Vowel Spelling Pattern When one vowel letter in a word is followed by a consonant, that vowel "says its short sound."

The steps suggested by Carlin are as follows:

1. Apply the appropriate spelling pattern rule, either the *long* or *short* rule. See if it works. If so, no further steps are needed.
2. If the appropriate vowel spelling pattern rule does not work, try the other one.
3. If steps 1 and 2 do not solve the problem try the schwa (/ə/) sound. (Example: *does.*)
4. If the first three steps do not solve the problem, reverse the order of the vowels and try again. (Example: *great.*)
5. If the problem is still unsolved, try special spelling patterns:
    oo as in *food* and *good*
    ou and *ow*
    aw, au, all, or
    oy, oi
    final syllables such as *-age, -ate, -ace.*
6. As a last resort, use the dictionary.

PHONICS OBJECTIVE 8

TO DEAL WITH THE SCHWA SOUND

Over the last two decades or so, reading specialists have adopted the schwa symbol ə (upside-down-e) to represent the indeterminate sound of vowels in unstressed syllables. Some specialists think of the schwa as representing a neutralized sound. Children, however, do not need to know the schwa per se to pronounce words like *about, banana, sofa, today, tomorrow, autograph, automobile, automatic,* and so on. Regardless of dialect, children use the schwa sound naturally according to their individual speech patterns. The schwa may be a useful phonics symbol, but it has little else to contribute to the classroom phonics program.

PHONICS OBJECTIVE 9

TO LEARN VARIANT PRONOUNCIATION OF VOWELS "CONTROLLED BY -R AND BY -L"

In cases where a vowel is followed by *r* or by *l,* children often become bewildered because neither the short vowel sound nor the long vowel sound serves their needs in word identification. A third alternative vowel choice needs to be learned.

Key pictures and key words can serve as cues to pronunciation. Here are a number of possibilities listed by vowel:

a ar	—	car, farm, yard, arm, jar, star, arch, cart
e er	—	her, herd, fern, germ, jerk, term
i ir	—	girl, bird, shirt, dirt, skirt, stir, first
o or	—	fork, horn, cork, fort, born
u ur	—	fur, nurse, curl, curb, urn

Some of these words may be beyond the ability of children to decode, but work on spelling patterns in which the vowel is controlled by *r* may begin with a few words that are known and the work continued to include other words as the child moves up through the primary years.

A second strategy is to have the children underline the *ar, er, ir, or,* and *ur* elements in words on a worksheet and/or in the printed material. Underlining is not, of course, a learning process, but it does provide practice in identification of words containing vowel + r and vowel + l words.

Classification is another means of identifying these spelling patterns. As words are encountered that demonstrate vowels controlled by *r* they are placed under the correct one of five columns headed *ar, er, ir, or,* and *ur.* For l-controlled vowel words, use three columns headed *al, ol,* and *ul.*

Practice in Relating Printed and Spoken Vowels

Rote memorization is one direct and effective means of learning the sounds represented by each of the vowel letters in various spelling patterns, but memorization of sounds should be coupled with seeing the letters that represent the sounds in print. Moreover, seeing the phonics elements in print in a structured reading context is also essential for transfer of learning. Immediate use leads to immediate transfer. To help in this process of relating sounds to print, a set of matching flashcards containing the elements listed below can be used.

a			o			
ă	apple		ŏ		ostrich	
ā	gate		ō		only	
ä	-ar	car				
â	care					
e						
ĕ	elephant		u			
ē	she		ŭ		umbrella	
			ū		use	
			û	-ur	fur	
				-er	her	
i				-ir	first	
ĭ	indian					
ī	ice		ə	schwa	today	

Dozens of additional word cards for practice in relating long, short, and schwa sounds to words should be prepared for individual, "buddy," or small group practice. The following words are a few of the starters that may be put on category cards:

astronaut	art	edge	equal	motor
ask	lost	egg	just	roller
ate	age	even	hammer	ivory
absent	am	elf	father	idea
arm	end	moth	important	burn
old	over	open	use	nurse
offer	odd	actor	up	purse
on	only	doctor	under	turn
first	girl	inch	into	ivy
must	turkey		off	inch

When the plain vowel cards are shown to the group, the children should be asked to respond with the three common sounds that each letter represents. When the category cards (with the names suggested above) are sorted into categories by the child (or team), each child should then print them under category headings, and, finally, use them in sentences copied onto category sheets. The category sheets might look like this:

a	e	i	o	u
a a ar	e e r	i i r	o o r	u u ur r

PHONICS OBJECTIVE 10

TO LEARN TO RECOGNIZE AND PRONOUNCE MORE DIFFICULT CONSONANT DIGRAPHS AND BLENDS

It should always be kept in mind that the ultimate purpose of and justification for phonics learning is to aid the child in approximating the pronunciation of unknown words. Once that is accomplished, language patterns and context will engender word identification. The final check is "Does it make sense?" Thus, phonics is a word-identification skill based on comprehension. The phonics objectives discussed so far are simple skills to aid identification of simple words. However, as words to be learned throughout the primary years become progressively more complicated, more advanced phonics skills are needed for identification and comprehension. Recognizing and pronouncing difficult consonant digraphs and blends and the remaining phonics objectives in this chapter are representative of these more advanced phonics skills.

Consonant digraphs and blends have been presented previously as whole spelling patterns. More advanced study with blends and digraphs employs developmental transfer techniques in which the initial consonants from each of two known words are united to form a digraph that represents the beginning blended sound in a new word. Here is the list of words we have developed for practice on blends:

Initial Consonant from

First Known Word		Second Known Word		Blend	New Word
(b)	all	(r)	at	br	brown
(c)	ar	(1)	ast	cl	class
(c)	ar	(r)	at	cr	crash
(d)	og	(r)	at	dr	dress
(f)	ast	(r)	at	fr	friend
(f)	ast	(l)	ast	fl	flash
(g)	o	(r)	at	gr	grass
(g)	o	(l)	ast	gl	glass
(p)	an	(l)	ast	pl	plan
(p)	an	(r)	at	pr	prize
(s)	ad	(c)	ake	sc	school
(s)	ad	(k)	ite	sk	sky
(s)	ad	(l)	ast	sl	slap
(s)	ad	(m)	e	sm	small
(s)	ad	(n)	o	sn	snap
(s)	ad	(t)	op	st	stop

(t)	op	(r)	at	tr	trip
(t)	op	(w)	ill	tw	twist

With this strategy, the "difficult" blends become much less difficult, inasmuch as learning them emerges directly from prior learning stored in memory cells.

Blending digraphs in final positions may also be accomplished by selecting final consonants from two known words and, in the manner described for initial consonant blends, forming a digraph. The digraph should then be immediately used in a new word ending with a consonant digraph or blend.

The main emphasis should be on the use of the newly acquired phonics skill in whole-word identification in writing and reading context.

PHONICS OBJECTIVE 11

TO RECOGNIZE AND BE ABLE TO PRONOUNCE CONSONANT TRIGRAPHS AND CLUSTERS

Trigraphs and *clusters* are two terms for the same thing. Some reading specialists prefer to use *cluster* for all multiple consonants in order to simplify terminology. In any case, words containing three consonants together really cause very little confusion after consonant digraphs and blends have been mastered.

The trigraph clusters to be learned as "sight" letter patterns are: *str- thr- squ- spr- spl- sch-* and *shr-*. Sight words for use in practice in learning trigraph clusters include the following:

string	strain	straight	strap	strange
straw	stray	streak	street	stream
stretch	strict	strike	strip	strong
splash	split	splice	splint	splinter
school	scheme	schedule	scholar	schooner
sprain	sprang	spray	spread	spree
spring	sprint	sprout	spruce	sprinkle
shred	shriek	shrill	shrimp	shrine
shrink	shrivel	shrub	shrunken	shrug
squad	squall	square	squash	squeak
squeegee	squeeze	squelch	squirrel	squirt
thread	threat	three	thrift	thrill
throng	throat	thriller	through	throw

In the following boxes we present the words most common in children's language usage according to these trigraph "families": scr- spl- str- spr- shr- spl- and thr-.

Scr- words	**Spl words**	**Str-words**	**Thr- words**
Scrabble	splash	straddle	thrash
scram	splatter	strait	thread
scramble	splendid	strand	threat
scrap	splice	strange	threaten
scrape	splint	strap	three
scratch	split	straw	thrift
scream	splinter	stray	thrill
screen	splotch	stream	thriller
screech	splurge	street	throat
screw	splutter	strength	throb
scribble		stress	throng
scrimmage	**Spr- words**	stretcher	throttle
script	sprain	strict	through
scrub	sprang	strike	throw
	sprawl	string	thru
	spray	strip	thrust
Shr- words	spread	stripe	
shrank			
shread			
shrew	spring	stroke	
shriek	sprinkle	strong	
shrill	sprint	struggle	
shrimp	sprout		
shrine	spruce		
shrink	spry		
shrivel			
shrub			
shrug			
shrapnel			

PHONICS OBJECTIVE 12

TO LEARN TO RECOGNIZE AND PRONOUNCE DIPHTHONGS

Diphthongs, which we have already discussed, need special attention as advanced phonics elements. The word is derived from the Greek, *diphthongos*, literally meaning "two sounds." In actual practice, however, the two vowel sounds are "glided" from one to the next. There seems to be some difference of opinion among specialists concerning which are pure diphthongs and which are quasidiphthongs. However, for the purposes of teaching primary children to read, any distinction between the two is unimportant. Here is a list of glided vowel pairs (dipthongs):

oi—boil

oy—boy

ou—out

ou—you (for contrast with *out*)

ow—now, cow

ew—few

ai—mail

ai—chair (influenced by *r*)

oa—coal (influenced by *l*)

ie—pie

oo—soon

aw—saw (possibly)

One strategy of long standing that has been used by teachers for many kinds of phonics practice is the use of envelope pockets into which children sort specific phonics cards. This is a particularly effective scheme for diphthong drill.

Eight pocket envelopes are prepared as shown below:

oi   oy   ou   ow   ew   ai   oa   ie

At first, these pockets may have a small cut-out key picture to aid children in identifying the sound—a cow, for example, for *ow*. Later the key pictures can be removed, with only the vowel digraph representing the diphthong remaining.

Here are some words, we use for diphthong identification and sorting into category pockets:

boy	afraid	now	gear
coil	joy	die	near
brown	how	tie	real
cow	clear	deal	hear
frown	seal	rear	snail
chair	bail	pair	wail
pail	rail	mail	tail
fail	hail	jail	fear
meal	coal	toil	soil
spoil	out	oil	shout

| found | house | town | frown |
| toy | south | mouse | clown |

Distractors should be added to the list and put on a discard pile when they are found not to fit into any category.

The spelling patterns of the most common diphthongs, *oi, oy, ou,* and *ow,* should eventually be learned as sight elements. The *-ail* and *-ear* patterns should be memorized next. Children who have mastered these six spelling patterns and who can identify them in words in isolation and in context will have a good command of diphthongs.

Be careful not to overstress difficulties arising from regional pronunciation of such words as *dear, cow, oil, mouse,* and so on. In New England or the Deep South children may diphthongize certain words or drop the r-sound in others. They will, nevertheless, manage to learn to deal with common diphthong sounds resulting from certain spellings, as easily as children whose pronunciation is more "standard."

PHONICS OBJECTIVE 13

TO BE ABLE TO DIFFERENTIATE PHONICS CONTRASTS

We have identified ten phonics contrasts as important elements to our language. By the end of the second year, most school children will have been exposed to all ten and will have mastered most of them. The discussion of these contrasts that follows is based upon the learning principles that items that go together should be learned together and that similar items and contrasting items are often learned best in pairs.

Phonics Contrast 1

Hard c and Soft c

By the time they reach the hard and soft *c* lesson, most children will have already encountered *cat* and *cent*. A rule that is often taught for hard and soft *c* is:

C, followed by *e, i,* or *y* is usually pronounced "soft," like *sss.*

To teach hard and soft *c*, set up sheets of paper for children to use in a dictation lesson. Three headings are necessary: hard-c, soft-c, and c followed by
_____.

hard c	**soft c**	**c followed by**
cat	cent	e

The first two words on the sheet are dictated as samples. They are *cat* and *cent*. The *c* in *cent* is followed by *e;* therefore it is soft. If the children have memorized the hard *c*-soft *c* rule, they will be looking for words in which the initial consonant *c* is followed by *e*, *i*, or *y* to put in the "soft" column.

The following words can be used for dictation. As each is pronounced by the teacher, the children should print them in the proper columns. Children who are not able to follow dictation and who cannot spell adequately should be given the list on paper to work with.

city	circle	cap	canon	cane
center	candy	cell	cold	cinema
Cinderella	came	cork	color	calf
cement	cycle	connect	cop	cut
cigar	Cynthia	come	circus	

(The last word on the list, *circus*, is a hard one because it has two different sounds of *c* in it. How should the children categorize it?)

Phonics Contrast 2

Hard g and Soft g

G followed by *e*, *i*, or *y* is usually pronounced as soft-g, or as /j/.

The same format used for dictation practice on hard and soft *c* is also effective here:

hard g	**soft g**	**g followed by**
gas	giant	i or y

The following words may be used for dictation:

gas	giant	game	Gipsy	go
giraffe	gem	generous	gate	goat
gala	gun	gyp	guppy	ginger
gentle	gum	gallon	George	germ
good	gold	gym	gone	gentle
got	guess	gull	garden	general
German				

Get, gear, geese, gift, girl are some of the exceptions to the rule.

Although children may be taught the hard *c*-soft *c* and hard *g*-soft *g* rules more or less by rote, practice with the dictation sheets will also lead most youngsters to inductive discovery of the basis for and proof of these phonics rules.

Following mastery of the "soft-g" sound, the next logical step is to help the children learn that there are two ways to spell the soft-*g sound*. Set up two phonics pages as follows:

Soft g sound Spelled with j

ja	je	ji	jo	ju
Jack	jet	Jim	job	jump

Here are some words for use in dictation with the above form:

Jack	jet	Jim	job	jump
June	John	just	jam	jog
jig	jewel	jug	judge	jolly
just	joy	jar	jerk	jersey
jungle	Joe	jelly	jaw	jeans
jigsaw	Joey	junk	join	jiffy
Jay	jazz	jail	jiggle	jockey

A simple contrast page can now be prepared for practice:

soft-g	j
gem	jam

Dictate the contrast words without the use of contrast cards and have the children try to place the words under the correct headings. Do not use too many contrast words. If you do, you may overwhelm some of the children. The following words should suffice:

gem	jam	job	gentle
germ	jeans	Joe	general
George	jig	jail	ginger
Jacket	Japan	giant	gipsy
joy	junk	gym	gyp
juice	juggle	just	jury

This will, no doubt, be a frustrating exercise for many children. Some will be able to visualize the initial consonants after very little practice. Others will not get the idea, let alone recall the letters. The only way to learn these kinds of words is through drill and repetition. As far as we know, there is only one rule for soft g and it is not very reliable. It states that "Whenever *g* is followed by *e, i,* or *y,* it is usually soft." The rule *usually* works (as in the the examples above) but note that we have purposely excluded from the list such words as *get, give, gear, giddy, girdle,* and so on.

Eventually, most children will be able to use visual memory to verify whether or not the printed word "looks right." Visual memory can be stimulated and fortified kinesthetically through tactile copying and then closing the eyes and visualizing and selecting the form that "looks right." For this purpose, sheets containing two sets of spelling may be prepared. For example:

gem	jem	gunk	junk	gail	jail
gam	jam	gipsy	jipsy	gury	jury
Jeorge	George	juggle	guggle	ginger	jinger
gacket	jacket	Japan	Gapan	guice	juice
joy	goy	general	jeneral	giant	jiant

Ask the children to judge which word "looks right." If necessary, have them prove their choice by using the dictionary.

Phonics Contrast 4

y Pronounced as i and as e

The problem of deciding what is the actual sound represented by the final-y in words has bothered reading people for some time. Some "authorities" claim that it is to be pronounced $\bar{i}$; *some insist on* $\bar{e}$, and a few that it is $\breve{e}$. The rule that is often quoted is:

In words of two or more syllables, if the final-y is preceded by a consonant, it is *usually* pronounced like long-e. Another rule is: In words or syllables where *y* is the only vowel, it is *likely* to be pronounced like long-i. The word "likely" is used because, in unaccented syllables, the *y* is usually pronounced short *i.* as in *bi/cy/cle.* Yet, in some sections of the country it is pronounced long *i.*

Some dictionaries still insist on the short-i sound for the final-y in an unaccented syllable that ends a word. Thus, according to them, the pronunciation of baby would be $b\bar{a}b\breve{i}$. We have lived in most geographical regions of the country and have never heard that pronunciation in common speech.

In any case, do not make too big a fuss about this particular contrast. Teach it in an oral practice session. (It might also be pointed out to the children, who by this time are about seven years of age, that English words that are usually pronounced with the final i sound, are usually spelled with a final y, and that words we have borrowed from the Italian and Spanish are usually spelled with final-*i*, but are pronounced with final-e, as in *spaghetti.*)

Here are some final-y words for practice use:

baby	cry	fry	merry
city	spaghetti	only	pry
any	many	pretty	by
carry	why	every	macaroni

funny	very	sunny	try
July	guy	spy	my
sky	hairy	fairy	spry

You can point out to the children that in all but one of these 28 words, the final-*y* is preceded by another consonant. In all of these cases, most reading teachers treat the final-*y* as a vowel sound, even though children have previously learned it as a consonant letter representing an initial consonant sound.

Phonics Contrast 5

The Two Pronunciations of -ow

Words containing the spelling pattern *-ow* frequently create pronunciation problems for children, inasmuch as there are two pronunciation alternatives. Diphthongs such as *now, cow, down,* and so on, usually create no problem after they have been learned as diphthongs, but children are not always certain of the pronunciation of the following -ow words:

sow	now	know	row
low	glow	blow	snow
throw	crow	grow	mow
tow	bow	bow-wow	how

This is another situation where *context* can provide the clue to pronunciation. For practice, therefore, children should be asked to write these words in their own sentences and note how their *ow* sound may vary with context. For example:

"It is time to mow the grass."

"In the spring, the old sow had little piggies."

"In the spring we sow seeds."

"Now he does not know what to do."

"Now, you know."

"You now know what to do."

"The seats are in a row."

"They stood in a row."

"They lined up and started a new row."

"They argued and started a row."

"After she sang, she made a bow."

"For her hair, she made a bow."

Phonics Contrast 6

Several Spellings of the /u/ Sound

Confusion is often generated by the several spellings of the /u/ sound (this is especially discouraging to students learning English as a second language). For example:

ew as in *new*	*ue* as in *blue*
oo as in *moon*	*u* as in *rule*
ui as in *fruit*	*o* as in *do*

Practice in these /u/ sound spellings should at first be done with words in isolation. The pronunciation of such words is less a problem to native speakers of English than is the encoding (writing the words). Spelling is further complicated by such phonics contrasts as *blew* and *blue, do,* and *due, new* and *knew, no* and *know,* and so on. Here is another case where the pronunciation given to each word is determined largely by context. Consequently, the children should practice using these words over and over again in their writing.

Phonics Contrast 7

Six Pronunciations of the Vowel·Digraph -ou

In addition to the regular pronunciation of the *ou* as a diphthong *(out),* there are five additional pronunciations regularly recognized as common in the English-speaking world. The *ou* contrasts are:

-ou	ou	*out ouch*
-ou	ō	*soul*
-ou	oo	*soup*
-ou	ŏŏ	*could would should*
-ou	ŭ	*touch rough*
-ou	ô	*cough ought*

There seems to be no way that a primary pupil can learn to differentiate these contrasts by means of word analysis or phonics analysis. This leaves only rote learning.

For practice in these words, have the children engage in a "write/say" exercise, led by the teacher. Flocked stimulus cards should be prepared for the teaching unit. Here are some words that may be used to start:

much	moon	hole
such	soon	pole
touch	soup	soul

The teacher can ask questions and make comments such as the following:

"How is this one different?"

"Why is this one different?" You don't know. I don't know why, either. It just is different, and we must learn it this way."

"What do we see in the third word in each column that is the same?"

"Yes, the *ou*. But the *ou* is pronounced differently in each word!"

"The only way we are going to remember these *ou*-words is to practice, so, when we meet one in a sentence, we can say, 'Hello, I know you' 'I know who you are'."

At this point, distribute paper (or notebooks) for work on *ou, ou*-words, and *ou*-words *in context*. Use the flocked *ou*-word cards for this write/say exercise. Here are some words to use:

touch	soup	soul	cough
could	would	should	
out	shout	about	
pout	stout	young	

Note that *-ough* is a different spelling pattern and should not be introduced at this point, except in the word *cough,* which has the same vowel pronunciation as does *coff* in the word *coffee*.

Phonics Contrast 8

Long-Vowel Homophones

There are quite a number of words that contain that might be called "long-vowel homophones" (different spellings for the same vowel sound). Although we have discussed some of these previously, we have found that it is fruitful to provide special sessions in the second and/or third grade in which these phonics contrasts are usually studied and mastered.

Here are some words to use on display cards for practice in long-vowel homophones.

bake	main	break	lake	pail	pale
weight	rake	Mae	nail	fail	glue
beet	beat	seat	wheat	treat	blue
me	key	eagle	eat	lay	lei
meet	meat	hay	say	maid	my
week	weak	sail	sale	made	bite
plain	plane	steel	steal	know	no

heel	heal	hole	whole	sow	so
knight	night	great	grate	feat	feet
write	right	rite	aisle	isle	hoe
hi!	high	eye	I	lone	loan
lite	light	pain	pane	suit	flew
to	too	two	pair	pare	pear
read	reed	red	read	hear	hare

Some of the above words are not homophones, but are included as "distractors." The number of homophones and the kind that children can identify will depend largely on age and past vocabulary experience.

Children should first make up sentences using each word in its correct context. Where there are two spellings that indicate different meanings, parallel sentences are helpful:

> She filled the *pail* with water.
>
> She is sick and looks *pale.*
>
> The boat has a large *sail.*
>
> The store has a big *sale.*

Use of such contrasts in context through writing seems to us to be the most effective way, perhaps the only way of reinforcing awareness of these contrasts so they can be recognized easily in reading. As noted previously, Dr. Harry Levin wisely suggested that in addition to teaching children the regularly recurring patterns, we would also teach them what he termed a "set for diversity," the anticipation that there are many alternatives in meaning, in spelling of sounds, and in interpreting the sounds represented by written symbols. The child must be helped toward awareness that the meaning of a word may be influenced by syllabication, stress, and the addition of prefexes and affixes as well as by context.

Phonics Contrast 9

Special Trigraphs

As we have mentioned before, trigraphs cause little trouble, but there comes a time during the primary years when it is profitable to study special trigraphs and to contrast them with consonant digraphs and blends.

Let us take, for example, the trigraph, *sch*, which is usually pronounced /sk/ in words such as *school, scheme, schooner,* and *schedule.* (In regions where British pronunciation is reflected, such as New Zealand, Ireland, Scotland, and Australia, the *sch* is pronounced /sk/ in *school,* but /sh/ in *schedule.*)

Fortunately, there seems to be only four words with *sch* that are commonly found in primary-grade reading materials. They are *school, scheme, schooner,* and *schedule. School* is most common, of course, and is easily learned as a sight word. *Scheme* is frequently found in junior novels. *Schooner* is common in tales of the sea, even at the second-grade level. And, since *schedule* is a common day-to-day word of teachers and school officials, children will no doubt have heard it frequently before they are very far along in the first grade.

Four things can be done to help fix these contrasts (trigraphs contrasted with digraphs and blends) in the visual memory of children, *First,* the children should write them in manuscript; *second,* the words should be used in sentences; *third,* the words should be illustrated by drawings or cutouts; *fourth,* the following words may be used for dictation with three every-pupil-response cards: *sc, sh,* and *sch.* The children hold up the card with the appropriate spelling for each word dictated by the teacher.

scale	show	shake	shadow	school	shape
sheep	scarce	shallow	schooner	shawl	share
schedule	shamrock	shark	scare	shave	she
shear	sheer	sheet	scooter	shelf	shine
ship	short	shoe	shoot	shook	shop
short	shore	shot	show	shovel	scheme
shock	shell	sharp	shame	scold	scoot

Other initial consonant clusters might be studied to complete this phase of phonics, but their application is very limited, as can be seen from the following lists of the most common words in each category:

Christians	fry	hybridize	syllable	lunch
chronical	fly	hydrogen	symbol	lymph
chromatic	glycerin	hygiene	sympathy	lyric
chrysanthemum	phase	hymn	symphony	myriad
crypt	phrenology	hyper-	synchronize	myrrh
crystal	Phyllis	hypo-	Synagogue	myrtle
type	physical	hysterical	syndicate	mysterious
typical		hydrant	synonym	myth
typhoon	pygmy	hydro-	system	
tyrant	pyramid			
	Pyrex			

It might be noted that most of these consonant clusters are of Greek origin and, actually, when they contain the letter *y*, it is used as a vowel. The *ch* is a representation of /k/, and the *ph* is pronounced /f/. Although these are advanced phonics elements, they generate very little trouble for average or above-average students in the upper-elementary grades. Consonant clusters are contrasts learned by comparison with related consonant digraphs and blends. Since children move from the known to the unknown in working these phonics elements, they have little problem in mastering them.

Phonics Contrast 10

The -are Spelling Pattern

Long before working on the *-are* spelling pattern, children will have learned *are* as a sight word. Now they are confronted with a phonics contrast, for, when the three letters *a r e,* are used as a base for phonograms, the pronunciation changes.

Mastering this contrast is accomplished through initial consonant substitution. Most children need only minimal drill to do so. The first two words to be contrasted may be *are* and *care.* In neither case does the final-*e* rule apply, for we are dealing with a situation that does not lend itself to "rules" that elementary school children can or should worry about. The following words, therefore, should be learned as sight words in a group:

are	—care	are	—spare	are	—mare
are	—bare	are	—square	are	—pare
are	—dare	are	—scare	are	—rare
are	—fare	are	—share	are	—hare
		are	—blare		

In the process of learning these words, many children will accumulate a few new words and should be encouraged to write and use them in sentences. If possible, have the children write them in sentences in which they use the word *are* and one of the words with the *-are* base.

Phonics Objective 14

TO BE ABLE TO IDENTIFY AND UNDERSTAND THE USAGE OF "SILENT" LETTERS

When children ask, "Why do they have that letter there if we don't say it?", we always explain that "Long ago, people really did say that letter, and so they spelled it that way." This simple explanation has always been adequate.

Near the end of the second year, it is common practice to engage in some work with words containing silent letters such as *kn-, wr-, -ck, gn-, -ln, -mb, -sl,* and *-tch.*

For more than a century, teachers have used the strike (/) through a letter to demonstrate that it is not to be pronounced. In fact, many readers of the past century printed the strikes on all silent letters as aids to learning.

LESSON X.

1. The Hâré and the Tortøisé.

determined

1. A hâré and a tortøisé once ran a race. You may think it was a foolish thing for a tortoise to race with a hare. It is true that the hare is fleet, while the tortoise can go but slowly.

2. The tortoise knew this, but determined to do his best. He stärted off in his plödding way and lost no time in reaching the goál.

3. The hare, however, lay down for a nap. He thôụght there was plenty of time, the tortoise being a slow wạlker. When he awoke, he lēápéd forwârd on the track. He expĕcted soon to overtake the tortoise.

4. But the hare had slept too long. On reaching the goál, he found the tortoise there awạïting him.

————————

2. The Ărab and the C.amél.

1. An Ărab lay down in his tent one cold night, expĕcting to go to sleep. His camél looked in and asked if he might put his head inside for wạrmth. The Arab said he might.

2. But this was not ēnøŭgh for the camel. Soon he asked if he might not also put his foré féét inside the tent. The Arab said he might.

3. Before long, the camel squēézéd his body in and asked if he might stay there. The tent was small, but the Arab møvéd a little to make room. He thought the camel would surely be satisfïéd now.

4. But the camel now felt that he would like the tent to himself. So he asked his master to step outside and make more room.

Another and better method of coping with letters that are not to be pronounced is to have the children learn a collection of sight words containing the various silent letter patterns.

A third method is to alert children to be aware of consonant digraphs and to consider two questions: 1. "Can the digraph be pronounced as a blend?" and 2. If not, which letter should be pronounced? Here are some common words along with pairs for children to work with:

not — gnaw	night — knight	(how many silent letters)
not — gnat	no — know	(two silent letters)
not — gnash	nick — knick	(two silent letters)
go — gnome	rock — knock	(two silent letters
nice — knife	ring — wring	go — ghost
net — knit	Tom — palm	off — laugh
not — knot	home — comb	bath — laugh
I'll — aisle	it — which	(this is a tricky one)

Fortunately, instances of words beginning with silent letters are rare in reading materials for children. Below are listed the only *gn-*, *wr-*, and *kn-* words that we could justify having a primary pupil learn:

gn —	gnarl	gnash	gnaw	gnome	
wr —	wrap	wreath	wrench	wriggle	wrestling
	wring	write	wrist	wrong	wrote
kn —	knack	knee	kneel	knife	knapsack
	knight	knit	knob	knock	knoll
	knot	know	knuckle		

After drill on such words, the children can reach a generalization of their own: Every time a word begins with *gn-* or *kn-*, only the *n* is sounded and the *g* or *k* silent. The same type of generalization can be developed by children from drill with *wr-*, which appears frequently enough to warrant special attention. Here are some more common *wr-* words along with pairs:

rap	wrap	hen	wren
ran	Wrangler	(children are acquainted with this name on jeans)	
rat	wrath	teath	wreath
ring	wring	wiggle	wriggle
mist	wrist	rest	wrestle
kite	write	gong	wrong
bench	wrench	vote	wrote

Silent letters in final position also create some problems for children. In fact, it appears that they are lifelong annoyance to many people. The most common silent letters in final position are:

-ck, -lm, -mb, -sl, -gh, and *-tch*

Here is a list of *-ck* solo-digraphs for practice:

tack	back	neck	deck	lack
quack	rack	sack	pack	dock
flock	clock	rock	sock	pick
sick	trick	kick	lick	knock
quick	stick	tick	wick	buck
duck	luck	tuck	struck	flick
tock	(or *tic-toc,* or *tick-tock*)			
nick	(or Good Old Saint Nick)			

Most children will have encountered whole words in which there is a *-tch* consonant trigraph at the end. They probably have read stories in which the "old witch" has been a character, or a story of baseball in which the words *pitch* and *catch* are common sight words. Consequently, they are ready to examine this spelling pattern and to consider the silent *t* in such words. Here are words for practice of the *-tch* pattern:

itch	hitch	ditch	stitch
match	batch	catch	latch
patch	fetch	wretch	notch
pitch	Dutch	hutch	watch

(and perhaps satchel)

In this lesson, some children will find it helpful to make comparisons, such as we have suggested previously. They can compare *much* and *such* with *Dutch* and *pitch,* noting the silent letters.

Some "silent" letters are particularly difficult for children to learn because of inherent inconsistencies in letter/sound correspondence. The best way to deal with such problems is for both teachers and children to face up to the fact that some solo-digraphs are, indeed, "stinkers" and are sure to present difficulties. One way to do so is to boldly label them for what they are: "Nasties," "Stinkers," "Wierdos," "Bummers," "Freaks," for example. Children react positively to this kind of humorous honesty. Once they are candidly labeled for what they are, these troublesome spellings seem to present less problem for many youngsters.

High on the "Stinker" list are *-lm* and *-mb.* Consider, for example, the change in vowel pronunciation in words such as *comb, bomb,* and *tomb.*

Here are some common *-lm* and *-mb* words to be mastered:

calm	balm	psalm	lamb
dumb	numb	comb	bomb
jamb (door jamb)	limb	palm	thumb
tomb			

The combinations *-sl, -gn,* and *gh* might also be placed in the "Stinker" category, although children soon discover that the *-gh* usually represents the /f/ sound except in *weight* and *weigh.* Only a few words are needed for practice in this category:

island	aisle	enough
tough	weigh	cough
rough	sign	reign

Special study is also necessary for the six words in the *-ough* phonogram that are "look alikes," having almost identical shape and common phonic and graphemic elements:

tough	through	trough
thought	thorough	though

Those six words contain all of the requisites for creating total confusion for children who know only the "look-say" method of whole-word reading.

In work with "silent" letters, the following sequence of strategies is usually employed:

1. The children write the words in manuscript.
2. They underline the "silent" letter combinations.
3. They strike out the silent letters.
4. They learn the meanings of new words encountered.
5. They note similarities and contrasts.
6. They use the words in sentences.
7. They identify the words in sentences and in paragraphs that have been prepared by the teacher.
8. They read the paragraphs orally for a check on their skill in coping with "silent" letters.

PHONICS OBJECTIVE 15

TO LEARN TO PRONOUNCE WORDS CONTAINING THE QU- BLEND

Special attention should be given to the *qu-* digraph and the spoken blend it represents. You should point out that *q* is *always* accompanied by *u;* that it never is alone in our language.

Here are common words for practice on *qu-*:

quack	quarter	quake	quality
quantity	queen	question	quick
quarrel	quail	quiet	quilt
quite	Quaker		

PHONICS OBJECTIVE 16

TO COPE WITH SOUNDS AND SPELLINGS OF HOMOPHONES AND HOMOGRAPHS

Homophones are words or parts of words that sound alike but are spelled differently.

Homographs are letter groups or whole words that are spelled alike but pronounced differently.

Although the incidence of homophones and homographs is quite small when one considers the thousands of words that elementary school children learn to read as sight words, these examples of diversity are important enough to warrant special lessons. The few times they do occur may be just enough to cause a complete breakdown in reading unless children have learned them in special lessons directed toward their special characteristics.

Many phonics sequences completely ignore these special cases, in the hope that the child who is learning to read will somehow absorb knowledge of homophones and homographs as he or she goes along and will be able to use this knowledge when it is needed. However, this laissez-faire attitude may, as noted above, lead at best to a slowing down and at worst to a complete breakdown of the learning-to-read process.

Not all children will, of course, be able to cope with all of the homophone and homograph elements discussed in this section. The point is, however, that children should be made aware that such special problems will sooner or later be encountered and must sooner or later be mastered.

The Three Sounds of *ear* Words

Words containing *ear* present a problem because they may be pronounced as *learn*, as *near*, or as *bear*. Differentiating *ear* words can best be taught through stimulation and reinforcement of the visual memory process. Display cards showing the spelling of the *ear* words should be shown to the children. The children should be provided with paper containing three column headings:

ear   *learn*   *bear*

As the words are displayed, the children copy them under the proper heading.

Some words for the display cards are:

ear	fear	pear	bear
learn	dear	gear	yearn
hear	near	wear	smear
tear	tear	clear	earl
earn	earth	early	year
hear	rear		

Contextual clues are the only means by which a child may be sure of the pronunciation of many of these words, for example:

"The little boy tried to be brave, but a tear came to his eye."

"The little girl was mad and began to tear the paper."

The Three Sounds of *ch* Words

When a child encounters *ch-* as an initial digraph, it is likely to be rendered /ch/ as in *church*. *Church* is a good key word for practice because *ch* occurs in it twice. Other pronunciations of the *ch-* pattern are found in words such as:

chorus	choir	Christ
chalet	Chevron	Christmas
Chicago	chemical	Charlotte

Charles could be included in the above list for contrast.

The great majority of words with the initial consonant digraph *ch* are regular. Many are of Greek origin. Here are some of them:

chimes	church	chair	child
cherry	checkers	chicken	check
Charles	chart	cheek	chalk

The *ch* as /k/ and the *ch* as /sh/ must be memorized as exceptions and must be used in writing. In our experience, we have found consistency in the types of sentences the children construct. They usually run something like this:

"At Christmas the choir sang in St. Charles Church."

"The child stood on the chair to mark the chart with chalk."

"The children played checkers at the Christmas party."

"The Christmas chimes rang from the church tower."

"Charlotte and Charles went to Chicago for Christmas."

"At Christmas it is summertime in Christchurch." (N.Z.)

The Three Spellings of the Sound /f/

English spelling over the centuries has been affected by importation of words from the Continent, especially from Greece, parts of France, and parts of Germany. The *ph* spelling of the /f/ sound is an example of such "imports." (Older primary-grade children may be interested to learn where such words came from.) Here is a list of *f*-sound words that have this "irregular" spelling. They are just about the only ones that will be encountered by the elementary school child:

phantom	pharmacy	phrase	pheasant
Phillip	phobia	Phyllis	Philadelphia
philosopher	phony	phonograph	Philippines
phosphate	photograph	photoflash	physics
physical	phlox	phonics	phase
phone	physician	physique	physical

A few words that end with the *-ph* and *-gh* as symbols for /f/ should also be specially taught. They can serve as further examples of the diversity that is to be expected in the study of the English language. Here are some *-ph* and *-gh* words for drill:

enough	cough	photograph	trough
autograph	philosophy	hydrophobia	

Some teachers find it helpful to encourage children to devise modernized spelling for such words, and to write contrasting sentences with the words spelled in both traditional and phonics forms. For example:

"Phillip took a photograph of Phyllis standing in front of a phony pheasant in Philadelphia."

"Filip took a fotograf of Filis standing in front of a fony fesant in Filadelfia."

"In physics she tried to photograph the phantom pharmacist with a photoflash made with phosphorus."

"In fizix she tryd to fotograf the fantom farmacist with a fotoflash made with fosforus."

Of course most primary children, even eight and nine year olds, will not be able to construct such complex sentences themselves, but some will be able to construct simple sentences along the same lines. When this exercise is completed, an effective conclusion of the lesson is to have the children convert sentences written in modernized spelling back into traditional spelling, using the various spelling of the phoneme /f/.

Five Spellings of the /sh/ Sound

The peculiar spelling of the /sh/ sound in *ti, si-, ci-, ch-,* and *su-* words comes to us from the Latin word element *tia* by way of English borrowings from the Italian and French languages. Here are some English words that reflect this migration and which may be used for phonetic analysis:

attention	mention	pension	nation
emotion	patience	ambitious	sugar
sure	chalet	gracious	

This is one of the most difficult phonetic elements to master, primarily because there are very few instances of this spelling peculiarity found in the vocabulary of primary-school children. A few like *sugar, sure,* and *nation* are ordinarily learned as sight words. Others must be learned through phonetic analysis, using the special elements *si-, ci-, ti-,* and *su-* as the signals for the /sh/ sound.

The Four Sounds of -*ough*

The words *cough, enough, dough,* and *bough* illustrate the confusion that can arise when pronunciation of the cluster -*ough* is being learned. Students with superior abilities seem to be able to handle this diversity, whereas others seem to have unending trouble. (The occurrence of those words in elementary school reading is so very small that some teachers feel that practice on the alternative pronunciations is a poor investment of time, which may be true.)

Assuming that there is time to work with these differences, the only method that seems to work reasonably well is to have the children memorize the words as whole-words in a look/say approach. Here are words for practice:

cough	enough	borough	bough
thorough	dough	nought	rough
trough	wrought	bought	trough
through	tough	thought	slough

The latter word, *slough*, is probably the most troublesome, for it can be pronounced sloo or sluf, depending upon context, and is rarely in the elementary child's listening or reading vocabulary.

One effective look/say technique is to have the children convert *-ough* words into compounds or combine them with nouns to make two words. For example:

cough becomes *cough medicine*

thorough becomes *thoroughfare*

wrought becomes *wrought iron*

dough becomes *donut* or *doughnut*

rough becomes *rough house*

trough becomes *watering trough*

through becomes *thru street* or *thruway*

The Three Sounds of *-augh*

The vowel digraph *-au* is frequently followed by the consonant digraph *gh*, which, instead of always signalling the /f/ sound, tends to be a silent digraph in some words. This is a difficult diversity to explain to eight and nine year olds.

Practice on some of the few words containing the *augh* cluster may help the perceptive child to recognize it as a signal of diversity, and to determine which of the three sounds it stands for in a particular word.

Consider the word *caught*. It is a phonetic monstrosity! There is only one regular consistent phonics element in the word, the *final-t*. The initial consonant is hard-c. There are three silent letters, *u, g,* and *h*. The *au* is pronounced ô, the third alternative pronunciation of *au*. Yet, since most children know the word, it is a good one to start with.

Fortunately there are very few English words that contain the *-augh* spelling pattern. The six base words below are the only ones commonly used throughout the English speaking world.

laugh	caught
laughter	haughty

daughter   taught
draught

(The word *draughtman* might possibly be added, but today the word is more commonly spelled "draftsman.")

You can be the judge as to which, if any, of these rare words should be used for study of *-augh.*

The Three Pronunciations of *cu*

As previously noted, the *q* in English is *always* followed by *u*. On the other hand, the sound kyoo is also designated by *cu;* the sound ku also by *cu;* and the sound ku when the *cu* is followed by *r*. Here are some Kyoo words:

cute	cubic	cucumber	cube	Cuba	curiosity
cue	Cupid	cure	(curious curio)		

For study purposes, the pronunciation of those words should be contrasted with those having the short-vowel sound, ku:

cup	culture	cub	cuddly
cunning	custodian	custard	

When the *cu* is followed by *r,* the vowel change is identical to the single vowel *u,* controlled by *r,* for example:

curse	current	currency	curry
curved	curtain	curtsy	curve
curl	currant		

Curio and *curiosity* are exceptions to the categories listed above.

Many children will be able to pick up these slight differences in pronunciation merely by hearing the words spoken or read aloud in story line context.

PHONICS OBJECTIVE 17

TO RECOGNIZE AND PRONOUNCE THE REMAINING PHONOGRAM CLUSTERS

As children progress upward through the grades, they encounter more and more phonogram clusters. In Phonics Objective 4, (To Learn Patterns of the Language), we presented simple two-letter phonogram bases such as *-an, -at, -op,* and so on. We now conclude our phonics sequence with an introduction to the more advanced phonogram bases. These are the relatively regular clusters upon which hundreds of words are built. Here are those advanced phonogram bases that our research indicates are most significant:

-igh	-ight	-ive	-unny
-ing	-eigh	-ief	-ould
-udge	-ind	-ump	-old
-ong			-stle

Consonant substitution in word building has long been accepted as a technique for internalizing linguistic patterns. (Phonograms are recurring spelling patterns.) You will find that most children enjoy working with word building on phonogram bases. Even very able children, although they do not really need this kind of practice, will derive intellectual satisfaction and pleasure from the challenge phonogram work gives them.

The assumption of phonogram exercises is that, if children can build words on phonogram bases, they will be able to recognize these words and the bases upon which they are built when encountered in their reading.

Here are some of the possibilities for practice on word building from phonogram bases.

-igh	-ight	-eigh	-ive	-unny
high	night	weigh	five	funny
nigh	bright	eight	dive	sunny
sigh	might	eighty	wives	bunny
	mighty	neighbor	jive	runny
	fight	or		
	sight	neighbour		

-ing	-ief	-ould	-old	-ong
sing	belief	could	fold	long
fling	relief	would	mold	song
bring	grief	should	hold	dong
ring	fief		cold	bong
king			told	gong
linger			bold	klong
finger			gold	
singer			sold	
ringer				

-udge	-ind	-ump
nudge	find	jump
budge	hind	hump

budget	rind	rump
grudge	mind	bump
sludge	bind	mumps
fudge	kind	crumpets
	wind	dump
		grumpy
		lump

After lists of words are constructed by each child, or by two working as a pair, the proof of understanding the phonics element of phonograms and their proper usage is in the sentences they devise as they use the words in context. This must always be the culminating test. If children can demonstrate such understanding in their own writing, they will have no problem in transferring the learning to the process of reading from the printed page. It matters not at all whether the reading is from a basal reader series, a reading scheme, individualized tradebooks, or so-called linguistic materials. The child who has mastered these language patterns will have no trouble transferring this learning to the story lines therein.

BIBLIOGRAPHY

Ackerman, Margaret D., "Acquisition and Transfer Value of Initial Training with Multiple Grapheme-Phoneme Correspondences," *Journal of Educational Psychology,* **65**:1 (1973), 28–34.

Artley, A. Sterl, "Phonics Revisited," *Language Arts,* **54**:2 (1977), 121–126.

Aukerman, Robert C., *Approaches to Beginning Reading,* New York: Wiley, 1972. Chapter on "The Pure Phonics Approach."

Beck, Elsie, *Don't Push Me; I'm Not a Computer,* New York: McGraw-Hill, 1976.

Bernbach, H. A., "Stimulus Learning and Recognition in Paired-associate Learning," *Journal of Experimental Psychology,* **75** (1967), 513–519.

Bickley, Rachel T., A. C. Bickley, and Harry Cowart, "Oral Language Responses and Reading Performance in the Intermediate Grades," in *20th Yearbook,* National Reading Conference, 1971, 11–13.

Brown D. L. "Some Linguistic Dimensions in Auditory Blending," *20th Yearbook,* National Reading Conference, 1971, 227–236.

Burmeister, Lou E., "Final Vowel-Consonant-e," *Reading Teacher,* **24**:5 (1971), 439–441.

Burmeister, Lou E., "Content of a Phonics Program Based on Particularly Useful

Generalizations," in *Reading Methods and Teacher Improvement,* Nila B. Smith (Editor), Newark, DE: International Reading Association, 1971.

Calfee, Robert C., and Patricia Lindamood, "Acoustic-Phonetic Skills and Reading—Kindergarten through Twelfth Grade," *Journal of Educational Psychology,* **65**:3 (1973), 293–298. This research report concludes that "There is a need for more concerted attention to the development of phonological skills in the early grades, and a need to continue training on those skills at the syllable level until each child has reached an adequate criterion of mastery."

Canney, George, and Robert Schreiner, "A Study of the Effectiveness of Selected Syllabication Rules and Phonogram patterns for Word Attack," *Reading Research Quarterly,* **12**:2 (1976–1977), 102–124.

Carlin, James B., *"Four-Step Process for Vowel-Attack Problems,"* *Reading Teacher,* **26**:8 (1973), 802–822.

Carnine, Douglas W., "Phonics Versus Look-Say: Transfer to New Words," *Reading Teacher,* **30**:6 (1977), 636–640.

Caroline, Sister Mary, *Breaking the Sound Barrier,* New York: Macmillan, 1960.

Chall, Jeanne S., *Learning to Read: The Great Debate,* New York: McGraw-Hill, 1967.

Chomsky, Carol. *The Acquisition of Syntax in Children from 5 to 10.* Cambridge: MIT Press, 1969.

Chomsky, Carol, "Reading, Writing, and Phonology," *Harvard Educational Review* **40** (1970), 287–309.

Clark, Eve V., "Non-Linguistic Strategies and the Acquisition of Word Meanings," *Cognition,* **2**:2 (1974), 39–44.

Clay, Marie M., "A Syntactic Analysis of Reading Errors," *Journal of Verbal Learning and Verbal Behavior,* **7** (1968), 434–438.

Clay, Marie M., and Robert H. Imlach, "Juncture, Pitch, and Stress as Reading Behaviour Variables," *Journal of Verbal Learning,* **10** (1971), 133–139.

Clymer, Theodore F., "The Utility of Phonics Generalizations in the Primary Grades," *Reading Teacher,* **16** (1963), 252–258.

Conrad, R., "Speech and Reading," in *Language by Ear and by Eye,* J. F. Kavanagh and I. G. Mattingly (Editors), Cambridge, MA: MIT Press, 1972.

Davis, Joel J., "Linguistics and Reading," *Language Arts,* **54**:2 (1977), 130–134.

Dzama, Mary Ann, "Comparing Use of Generalizations of Phonics in LEA, Basal Vocabulary," *Reading Teacher,* **28**:5 (1975), 466–472.

Emans, Robert, "Linguists and Phonics," *Reading Teacher,* **26**:5 (1973), 477–482. This is an excellent discussion of the several issues in phonics, linguistics, grapheme-phoneme approaches, and other misconceptions in beginning reading.

Emans, Robert, and Jeanne Harms, "The Usefulness of Linguistically-Based Word Generalizations," *Elementary English,* **50** (1973), 935–936.

Farmer, A. R., "Sound Blending and Learning to Read: An Experimental Investigation," *British Journal of Educational Psychology,* **47**:1 (1977), 155–163.

Fleming, James, T., "Alternative Interpretation of Evidence of Phonemic Recoding in Visual Word Recognition," *Journal of Reading Behavior,* **8**:1 (1976), 7–18.

Ferguson, C., and D. Slobin (Editors), *Studies in Child Language Development,* New York: Holt, Rinehart, and Winston, 1973, 4–167.

Gibson, Eleanor J., and Harry Levin, *The Psychology of Reading,* Cambridge, MA: MIT Press, 1975.

Glass, Gerald C., and Elizabeth H. Burton, "How Do They Decode? *Education,* **94** (1973), 58–64.

Gleitman, Lila R., and Paul Rozin, "Teaching Reading by Use of a Syllabary," *Reading Research Quarterly,* **8**:4 (1973), 447–483.

Golinkoff, Roberta M., and Richard Rosinski, "Decoding, Semantic Processing, and Reading Comprehension Skill," *Child Development,* **47** (1976), 252–258.

Goodman, Kenneth S., "Reading: A Psycholinguistic Guessing Game," paper presented to the annual meeting of the American Educational Research Association, New York, February 16, 1967 and printed in *Journal of the Reading Specialist* (publication of the College Reading Association), **6** (1967), 126–135.

Groff, Patrick J., "Sequences for Teaching Consonant Clusters," *Journal of Reading Behavior,* **4** (1971–1972), 59–65.

Groff, Patrick, J., "A Phonemic Analysis of Monosyllable Words," *Reading World,* **12** (1972), 94–103.

Groff, Patrick, J., "Reading Ability and Auditory Discrimination: Are they Related?" *Reading Teacher,* **28**:8 (1975), 742–747.

Groff, Patrick, J., "The New Anti-Phonics," *Elementary School Journal,* **77**:4 (1977), 323–332. Presents a four-point rebuttal against the recent writings of Frank Smith and Kenneth Goodman on how young children learn to read.

Groff, Patrick, J., *Phonics: Why and How.* Morristown, NJ: General Learning Press, 1977.

Gutherie, John T., and S. Jane Typer, "Psycholinguistic Processing in Reading and Listening Among Good and Poor Readers," *Journal of Reading Behavior*, **8**:4 (1976), 415–426.

Hanna, Paul R., Richard E. Hodges, Jean S. Hanna, and Edwin H. Rudorf, Jr., *Phoneme-Grapheme Correspondences as Cues to Spelling Improvement*, U.S. Office of Education Publication 32008, Washington, D,C, 1966.

Hartley, Ruth M., "A Method of Increasing the Ability of First-Grade Pupils to Use Phonetic Generalizations," *California Journal of Educational Research*, **22** (1971), 9–16.

Hay, Julie, Charles E. Wingo, and Mary C. Hletko, *Reading With Phonics*, Philadelphia: Lippincott, 1967.

Henderson, Mildred K., Doctoral dissertation, University of Tulsa, 1969.

Jenkins, Joseph R., R. Barker Bausell, and Linda Jenkins, "Comparisons of Letter-Name and Letter-Sound Training as Transfer Variables," *American Educational Research Journal*, **9**:1 (1972), 75–86.

Johnson, Dale D., and Edward Merryman, "Syllabication: The Erroneous VCCV Generalization," *Reading Teacher*, **25**:3 (1971), 267–270.

Karlsen, Bjorn, and Margaret Blocker", Black Children and Final Consonant Blends," *Reading Teacher*, **27** (1974), 462–463.

Kibby, Michael W., "The Effects of Certain Instructional Conditions and Response Modes on Initial Word Learning," *Reading Research Quarterly*, **15**:1 (1979), 147–171.

Lamb, Pose, "How Important is Instruction in Phonics?" *Reading Teacher*, **29**:1 (1975), 15–19.

Liberman, Isabelle Y., "Segmentation of the Spoken Word and Reading Acquisition," *Bulletin of the Orton Society*, **23** (1973), 65–77.

Liberman, Isabelle Y., Donald Shankweiler, William F. Fischer, and Bonnie Carter, "Explicit Syllable and Phoneme Segmentation in the Young Child," *Journal of Experimental Child Psychology*, **18** (1974), 201–212.

Liberman, Isabelle Y., Donald Shankweiler, Alvin M. Liberman, Carol Fowler, and F. William Fischer, "Phonetic Segmentation and Recoding in the Beginning Reader," in *Toward a Psychology of Reading*, Arthur S. Reber and Don L. Scarborough (Editors), Hillsdale, NJ: Erlbaum, 1977, 207–226.

Mason, Jana M., Elizabeth Kniseley, and Janet Kendall, "Effects of Polysemour (multiple-meanings) Words on Sentence Comprehension," *Reading Research Quarterly*, **15**:1 (1979), 49–65.

McClelland, J. L., "Preliminary Letter Identification in the Perception of Words and Non-Words," *Journal of Experimental Psychology*, **2** (1976), 80–91.

McNeill, D., and K. Lindig, "The Perception Reality of Phonemes, Syllables, Words, and Sentences," *Journal of Verbal Learning and Verbal Behavior,* **12** (1973), 419–430.

Menyuk, Paula, "Relations Between Acquisition of Phonology and Reading," in *Aspects of Reading Acquisition,* John T. Guthrie (Editor), Proceedings of the Fifth Annual Hyman Blumberg Symposium on Research in Early Childhood Education, Baltimore: Johns Hopkins University Press, 1976, Chapter 3, 89–110.

Moskowitz, B. A., "On the Status of Vowel Shift in English," in *Cognitive Development and the Acquisition of Language,* T. E. Moore (Editor), New York: Academic Press, 1973.

Muller, Douglas, "Phonic Blending and Transfer of Letter Training to Word Reading in Children," *Journal of Reading Behavior,* **5** (1973), 212–217.

Railsback, Charles E., "Consonant Substitution in Word Attack," *Reading Teacher,* **23**:5 (1970).

Read, Charles, *"Pre-School Children's Knowledge of English Phonology,"* *Harvard Educational Review,* **41**:1 (1971), 1–34.

Rentell, Victor M., and John J. Kennedy, "Effects of Pattern Drill on Phonology, Syntax, and Reading Achievement of Appalachian Children," *American Educational Research Journal,* **9** (1972), 87–100.

Rinsky, Lee Ann, "A, E, I, O, U, but also OO," *Reading Teacher,* **29**:2 (1975), 146–149.

Rosner, J., "Phonic Analysis Training and Beginning Reading Skills,"*Proceedings of 79th Annual Convention, American Psychological Association,* **6** (1971), 533–534.

Ruddell, Robert B., *Reading-Language Instruction: Innovative Practices,* Englewood Cliffs, NJ: Prentice-Hall, 1974.

Rystrom, Richard, "Perceptions of Vowel Letter-Sound Relationships by First-Grade Children," *Reading Research Quarterly,* **9**:2 (1973–1974), 170–185. Rystrom found that dialect (Black English versus Standard English) made no difference in the abilities of children in first grade to learn letter-sound relationships.

Seymour, Dorothy Z., "Word Division for Decoding," *Reading Teacher,* **27**:3 (1973), 275–283. Seymour pointed out some specific errors in teaching syllabication: One cannot syllabicate words that one does not already know; the borders of syllables are indeterminate and cannot be precisely assigned to visual separation points between particular letters; auditory syllables and printed syllables are frequently not identical; linguists usually consider the final -*le* and -*re* as a recognizable suffix not needing anything else attached to it.

The author proposed three simple generalizations:

1. In CVC words, the vowel is generally short;
2. In CV words (such as *go, me, by*) the vowel is usually long;
3. Vowel letters in assorted *left-over* word parts are usually decoded with a schwa sound.

Those three generalizations can be applied to multisyllable words.

Smith, Frank, *Understanding Reading: A Psycholinguistic Analysis of Reading and Learning to Read,* New York: Holt, Rinehart, and Winston, 1971.

Tovey, Duane R., "Children's Grasp of Phonics Terms vs. Sound-Symbol Relationships," *Reading Teacher,* **33**:4 (1980), 431–437.

Venezky, Richard L., *Language and Cognition in Reading,* Madison: University of Wisconsin Research and Development Center for Cognitive Learning, Technical Report 188, 1972.

Wallach, Lise, Michael A. Wallach, Mary G. Dozier, and Nancy E. Kaplan, "Poor Children Learning to Read Do Not Have Trouble with Auditory Discrimination But Do Have Trouble with Phoneme Recognition," *Journal of Educational Psychology,* **69**:1 (1977), 36–39. "Lack of phonemic analysis skills plays a significant role in poor children's frequent difficulties in learning to read."

Winkley, Carol K., "Why Not an Intensive-Gradual Phonic Approach?" *Reading Teacher,* **23**:7 (1970), 611–620.

CHAPTER SIX

How Do I Provide For Vocabulary Development?

INTRODUCTION

Vocabulary development is an area of classroom reading instruction that is all too frequently slighted. Sometimes it is assumed that vocabulary development is something of an "automatic" process, a byproduct of other areas of reading instruction. (A perusal of the literature indicates, for example, that even some experts seem to confuse vocabulary development with word identification, tending to concentrate on the latter area at the expense of the former.)

Sometimes it is assumed that little or no classroom attention need be paid to reading vocabulary because it will, in any case, develop outside the classroom environment, in the home or elsewhere, in much the same way preschoolers develop listening and speaking vocabularies. The importance of home environment and parental attention to the development of reading skills has been stressed time and again throughout this text. But even if all home environments were as ideal in this respect as one might wish, this fact (or, rather, this fantasy) would not preclude the necessity for specific classroom attention to vocabulary development. Vocabulary development is an integral part of the learning-to-read process. As such, it must be an integral part of the classroom learning-to-read program.

WORD LISTS FOR VOCABULARY DEVELOPMENT

Vocabulary development in a child's early years is chiefly experiential. The child's vocabulary is more or less limited to words associated with people, things, places, and conditions with which the child has had experience. When a child says "I'm cold," "I'm hungry," "I'm tired" or "I'm happy," "cold," "hungry," "tired" and "happy" are not abstractions. They are concrete expressions of reality as experienced by the child.

Vocabulary development in the classroom, then, should be firmly based on the experiences of everyday living. To this end, the twelve vocabulary lists that immediately follow have been categorized according to twelve specific areas of everyday living. Each list contains common sight words frequently found in out-of-school reading material (books, newspapers, periodicals) pertaining to the living areas covered by the list.

Not so many years ago, it was the policy in reading instruction to suppose that small children could cope only with small words, and older children (commencing about third grade) could begin to deal with longer words. Vocabulary lists in those days were very limited in first grade and not until about the end of third grade did they contain multisyllabic words or compounds to any great extent. Even simple observation today indicates that such a notion is not based upon reality. By some unknown means, children can and do master unbelievably long words. Perhaps the most exaggerated current example of this feat is children's ability to pronounce *super-cal-a-fragil-istic-expi-ali-docious* from the Disney film, *Mary Poppins.* Many children learn long words in print with the same ease that they learn short, so-called "easy words." When asked, "How do you know that word?", a variety of answers points to two probabilities: (a) that motivation to learn the particular "big" word was a compelling factor; and (b) that each child devises a particular scheme for identifying and remembering the word. In the latter case, it may be that "it begins like . . ."; it has a particular part in it that is recognizable; or "I don't know . . . I just know it."

Further research by experimental psychologists may someday provide definitive explanations of the magic by which children perform this learning task. In the meantime, we can proceed upon the knowledge that, properly motivated to learn whole words, children will generally be highly successful, regardless of the length of the words.

Twelve Areas of Everyday Living and Reading

1. People
2. Home
3. The Things We Eat
4. The Clothes We Wear
5. The Earth on Which We Live
6. Sports and Vacations
7. Travel and Transportation
8. The World of Work
9. The Performing Arts
10. Society and Government
11. Health and How We Feel
12. Science and Invention

1. People Words

head	hands	feet
arms	fingers	toes
legs	eyes	ears
body	nose	mouth
hair	knee	teeth
tongue	throat	belly
shoulder	abdomen	ankle
knuckle	fingernail	eyebrow
eyelash	stomach	bowels
thigh	lungs	heart
blood	sinus	skin
digestion	bones	ribs
pulse	breath	muscles
boy/girl	man/woman	people

2. Home Words

house	home	apartment
flat	trailer	mobile home
project	room	kitchen
bedroom	toilet	bath
mother	father	brother
sister	baby	Mom/Dad
phone	telephone	sink
door	garage	bed
yard	fence	bushes
trees	grass	furnace
window	television	heater
washer	dryer	stove
range	refrigerator	fireplace
sofa	chair	table
rug	floor	ceiling
wall	sidewalk	walk
furniture	radio	bookshelves
cupboards	ironing board	iron
pots	pans	dishes
knives/forks/spoons	dishwasher	freezer
light	lightswitch	plug
doorknob	hinges	tub
sewing machine	drain	faucet
water	basement	cellar
roof	outside	inside
downstairs	upstairs	stairs
railing	insulation	storm windows/storm door
screens	shutters	well
gutters	downspouts	patio/terrace
mailbox	lobby	elevator
hall	lock	mixer
clock	lamp	dresser
drawers	chest	desk
railing	balcony/lanai	porch
air conditioning	dehumidifier	vacuum
frypan	blender	toaster
oven	burner	counter
hamper	incinerator	trash
garbage	wastebasket	disposal
drapes	curtains	hi-fi
record player	stereo	tape recorder
records	tapes	doorbell

night latch	dead bolt	broiler
barbecue	closet	nightlight
chimney	doorman	guard
laundry	dining room	living room
bedroom	nursery	recreation room
garden	pool	alley
neighbors	electric	gas
janitor	stoop	walk-up
manager	caretaker	deliveries

3. The Things We Eat Words

food	drink	eat
cereal	meat	eggs
chicken	hamburger	pork
steak	chops	roast
milk	cartons	fruit
orange	apple	banana
peach	pear	grapes
lemon	grapefruit	strawberry
cake	cookies	pie
coffee	coke	soda
vitamins	raisins	salt/pepper
salad	Jello	yoghurt (yogurt)
cottage cheese	cheese	bacon
ham	bagels	lox
pizza	spaghetti	macaroni
lasagna	tortillas	enchalada
hotdog	rolls	bread
toast	jelly/jam	butter/oleo
ice cream	muffins	cupcakes
chop suey	chow mein	dessert
breakfast	dinner	supper
lunch	sandwich	soup
crackers	vegetables	deli
corned beef	dairy	casserole
potluck	leftovers	pickups
nuts	brunch	fish
gravy	pancakes	waffles
pasta	icing	candy
potatoes	rice	honey
apple sauce	baked	stewed
sausage	prunes	pineapple

rhubarb	heat	boil
burn	brown	tomato
pea	bean	corn
carrots	onions	spinach
peppers	salt/pepper	sugar
cream	grits	bacon
tetrazzini	tuna	noodles
ravioli	pudding	scrambled
boiled	poached	pickles
tamale	stuffed	turkey
dressing	hash	lobster
BLT	bread	asparagus
pot roast	chili	biscuits
bologna/boloney	cabbage	celery
chocolate	cinnamon	tea
cream	dressings	oil
French	Italian	Chinese
juice	fresh	frozen
canned	dried	dehydrated
freeze-dried	Graham cracker	whole wheat
rye	spices	lamb
liver	lettuce	oatmeal
molasses	mushrooms	oysters/clams
pastries	sauces	relishes
salad dressings	sauerkraut/kraut	shrimp
shish-ka-bob	sour/sweet	vanilla
vinegar	shortening	

4. The Clothes We Wear Words

shoes	pants	trousers
dress	skirt	blouse
shirt	tie	sweater
zipper	button	snaps
snowsuit	bikini	swimsuit
underpants	panties	girdle
stockings	pantyhose	bra
shorts	collar	cuffs
sox	belt	scarf
coat	jacket	carcoat
overcoat	jams	jeans
dungarees	bluejeans	sweatshirt
gloves	rubbers	galoshes

boots	pantsuit	slacks
overblouse	knickers	vest
halfslip	slip	suit
muumuu	caftan	robe
negligee	nightie	pjs/pajamas
briefs	shoe laces	slippers
parka	sport shirt	leisure suit
chaps	sombrero	hat
cap	Stetson	formal
gown		

5. The Earth We Live On Words

world	earth	globe
river	lake	stream
pond	ocean	bay
swamp	bog	water
waterfall	falls	geyser
desert	island	continent
mountain	hill	volcano
wind	temperature	weather
meteorology	glacier	iceburg
map	equator	hemisphere
latitude	longitude	celcius
fahrenheit	season	tropics
subtropics	arctic	temperate
zone	air flow	westerlies
trade winds	degree	climate
Pacific	Atlantic	Arctic
Indian	Mediterranean	plains
plateau	Alps	Antarctica
Europe	Asia	America
belts	tundra	currents
Pampas	valley	canyon
high country	plantation	sheep station
ranch	locks	farm
rocks	lava	pumice
molten	faults	wind
rain	weathering	dunes
sandstone	granite	erosion
beds	erupt	clay
shale	sand	coal
petroleum/oil	sediment	salt

iron	copper	uranium
stone	floods	mineral
fossil	strata	tilt
truck farm	mine	quarry
forest	drilling	continental shelf
depths	altitude	grasslands

6. Sports and Vacation Words

skateboarding	hiking/tramping	cricket
baseball	tennis	football
soccer	basketball	hockey
skiing	iceskating	boating
swimming	golf	championships
Olympics	winner/loser	contest
league	game	team
teammates	players	rules
club	court	basket
base	racquet	equipment
score	standing	tourney/tournament
defeat	swamped	trimmed
edged out	opener	contestants
doubles	doubleheader	regulations
sportsmanship	jump	leap
hit	run	mitt
bat	putt	course
speed	horse	race/sprint
sail	trophy	cup
major	minor	farm
leisure	camp	trailer
scooter	snowmobile	camper
fishing	campsite	cottage
lodge	instructor	coach
stocked	fishery	national
state	reservations	natural
surfing	resort	recreation
skating	rink	pool
track	diamond	stadium/arena/stands

7. Travel and Transportation Words

train	bus	plane
boat	ship	monorail
camel	elephant	subway

airplane	helicopter	streamliner
jet	jetliner	jumbojet
airport	station	metro
surface	air	speed
electronic	rapid	public
highway	thruway	expressway
toll roads	interstate	truck
truckers	truck stop	international
seaport	terminal	port
authority	forwarding	trailer
horse	unions	hijack
rest stop	weigh stations	patrol
diesel	tailgating	shipment
storage	cartage	express
freight	cargo	longshoremen
pilot	navigator	control tower
steward	stewardess	reservation
booking	seating	hold
tonnage	intercoastal	waterways
interstate	inspection	commerce
regulation	commission	storage
elevator	warehouse	dock
container	containerized	pilferage
ticket	loading	ramp
hoist	bales	passenger
big rig	"Smoky Bear" (police)	citizen-band radio

8. The World of Work Words

factory	mill	plant
mine	bank	finance
company	produce	make
worker	management	union
orders	product	packaging
selling	advertising	money
payroll	costs	sales
prosperity	depression	recession
jobs	work	welfare
unemployment	interest	insurance
benefits	fringe	manufacture
commerce	merchant	store
shopping	mail	outlet
discount	markup	raw materials
finished	machine	automatic

automation	electronic	control
computer	assembly	assembly line
seasonal	cost	price
value	surplus	closeout
markdown	clearance	season
special	fashion	introduce
latest	model	repair
replacement	parts	service
customer	layoff	hiring
seniority	strike	market
exchange	broker	certificate
invest	speculate	develop
regulation	contract	shipment

9. The Performing Arts Words

art	fine art	painting
sculpture	oil	canvas
frame	studio	gallery
museum	institute	artist
painter	musician	orchestra
band	pose	model
hall	concert	recital
organ	piano	instrument
notes	easel	brush
paints	landscape	portrait
picture	piece	play
theater	television	artist
perform	actor	scenery
stage	curtain	audience
ticket	program	composer
display	exhibit	clay
print	draw	costume
sound	conduct	member
admission	reservation	opera
opening	review	practice
rehearsal	performance	guest
chorus	ensemble	Broadway
center	performing	modern
classical	theme	spectacular
bowl	troupe	summer
colony	tryout	circus
acrobat	clown	side show
midway	big tent	trainer
carnival	ballet	makeup

10. Society and Government Words

politics	government	law
legal	bills	introduce
committee	legislature	senate
house	representatives	state
federal	party	campaign
election	run	ticket
office	lawyer	governor
police	ordinance	enforce
judge	jury	case
versus	decision	amend
finance	taxes	register
document	country	city
mayor	jail	prison
citizen	crime	safety
criminal	protection	service
benefits	parks	recreation
highways	schools	hospitals
public	private	license
inspection	control	President
training	education	patrol
cabinet	budget	ballot

11. Health and How We Feel Words

afraid	unhappy	happy
mad	glad	tired
hungry	little	big
lost	sick	hospital
cavities	aspirin	doctor
dentist	nurse	operation
tonsils	chicken pox	mumps
measles	cold	hot
sniffily	ache	hurt
bad	good	angry
friendly	uncertain	inadequate
confident	upset	apprehensive
anxious	worried	concerned
desirous	incapable	independent
dependent	indifferent	unconcerned
concerned	involved	defeated
dejected	excluded	included
loved	medication	recovery

12. Science and Invention Words

chemistry	physics	astronomy
biology	botany	material
elements	experiment	inventions
discovery	chemicals	space
electronic	research	power
energy	solar	lungs
nuclear	patent	laboratory

USING WORD LISTS

Here is one technique for using "living area" word lists for vocabulary development:

1. Type up each list for duplication by machine or by some other copying method.
2. Run off twice as many copies of each list as you have students, plus a few extras.
3. Stack as many copies of each list as you have students and cut these stacks into strips, one word to a strip.
4. Staple all identical word-strips together so that you have one bundle for each word on each list.
5. Collect twelve containers, one for each living area, label them for identification.
6. Place the stapled bundles of word-strips from each list in these proper containers.
7. Display uncut copies of each word list on a bulletin board or in some other convenient classroom location.
8. Give each child an envelope with his or her name on it.
9. Give each child a copy of each of the twelve lists.

As each child masters a living area word in print, he or she is allowed to go to the storage box, obtain the strip containing that word, and place it in his or her own envelope. The word is also checked on the child's uncut list as a sign that the word has been learned.

How does the child "prove" to the teacher that the word has been mastered? Here are some examples of "proof" that children find reasonable and fun to offer: The child might present a picture cut from a magazine or newspaper that illustrates a word. A written sentence using the word correctly might be offered as proof of mastery. The child might present a newspaper or magazine clipping with the word encircled, or copy the word and its definition from an elementary dictionary. As an additional and final "proof," the child might be required to identify the word in a multiple-choice setting.

Another technique suitable for older children for vocabulary building in the living areas is to use the predetermined twelve categories and have the child build his or her own list of words for each category. Each day, the child decides which category will be worked on and selects (with the help of the teacher, if necessary) reading materials likely to provide new words in that area.

For example, if the child chooses "sports and vacations," the day's reading could be in the weekly classroom newspaper, in *Sports Illustrated,* or in a sports novel. On another day, the child might choose another living area with new reading materials selected according to the new choice.

As each new word in a given area is learned, it is added to the child's list for that area. Proof of learning is provided through the same techniques noted in the section above.

This alternative approach to vocabulary development in the living areas has the advantage for the teacher of requiring less preparation time and less individual guidance. Since it is less structured, it allows the child more freedom of choice and more opportunity to move at his or her own pace. It also provides added motivation in that it allows initial concentration on areas of particular interest to the child—another example of the recommended practice of "beginning with the child."

The Vocabulary Savings Bank Book   The "Vocabulary Savings Bank Book" can provide additional motivation for vocabulary development. The "bank books" consist of 28 sheets of lined paper, one for each letter of the alphabet, plus a cover sheet with the name of each child in the class printed on it, stapled together at the top. Each child is given his or her book and instructed to label each sheet of the book with one letter of the alphabet, consecutively from A to Z.

When a new word is learned, it is "deposited" in the child's account under the proper letter. Later, the words can be "withdrawn" for use in writing exercises assigned by the teacher.

Children like this device and enjoy seeing their bank account grow day by day. In addition, it helps dramatize the value of having a "rich vocabulary" for everyday reading and writing.

OTHER CATEGORIES OF EVERYDAY LIVING

The twelve specific areas of everyday living suggested above for use in vocabulary development are not, of course, the only possible categories for building and working with lists of common sight words found in everyday living. You may wish to work with somewhat less inclusive categories, such as the examples listed below. Strategies and techniques used with the "twelve areas" may also be used or adapted for use with the less-inclusive areas of your choice.

1. Actors and actresses
2. Artists
3. Birds
4. Cars
5. Cats
6. Cities
7. Composers
8. Diseases
9. Dogs
10. Explorers
11. Energy
12. Fish
13. Flowers
14. Holidays and Holy Days

15.	Insects	23.	Presidents
16.	Inventions	24.	Rivers
17.	Islands	25.	Seas and Oceans
18.	Lakes	26.	Space
19.	Minerals	27.	Television
20.	Mountains	28.	Trees
21.	Nuts	29.	Vegetables
22.	Pioneers	30.	Workers

USING STRUCTURAL COMPONENTS FOR BUILDING VOCABULARY

In Chapter 4 we suggested that primary children be alerted to recognize a large number of common prefixes and common suffixes as aids to structural analysis. Now we will repeat some of those prefixes and suffixes, with emphasis on their cognitive characteristics and their contribution to vocabulary development. But first, a few "do's" and "don'ts" when working with roots and affixes:

1. Limit the study of roots and affixes to those that are fairly regular in meaning and that make sense to the child.
2. It is unproductive to spend a great amount of time in the elementary grades (or even in the secondary school) on Latin and Greek roots.
3. Use only English words and foreign words that are in common usage as the bases for vocabulary development.
4. Use only those roots and affixes that have meaning in themselves and that, together, create a word in common usage. (Example: under + coating.)
5. Don't waste children's time developing vocabulary that they already know and already can recognize and pronounce from print.

SUFFIXES

Suffixes are in general much more useful and meaningful than prefixes in vocabulary building. It is good practice to spend a considerable amount of time in the intermediate grades on suffixes. But you need not wait until the intermediate grades to begin working with them. Younger children can handle some suffixes very well. Two suffixes that can usefully be worked with as early as the second grade are *-ing* (the doing of something) and *-er* (a doer of something). They can be learned together and should be studied in parallel columns, using identical verb bases for each pair, thus:

farm	-er	farm	-ing
bake	-er	bake	-ing
teach	-er	teach	-ing
preach	-er	preach	-ing

drive	-er	drive	-ing
play	-er	play	-ing
run (n)	-er	run (n)	-ing
learn	-er	learn	-ing
skate	-er	skate	-ing
plan (n)	-er	plan (n)	-ing
surf	-er	surf	-ing
sing	-er	sing	-ing
manage	-er	manage	-ing
ranch	-er	ranch	-ing

Other easy-to-learn suffixes are:

-ful (full of)

pain + ful = painful

joy	joyful
hope	hopeful
power	powerful
thank	thankful
taste	tasteful
help	helpful
delight	delightful
bounty	bountiful
event	eventful
dread	dreadful
plenty	plentiful
rest	restful
sin	sinful
play	playful

-less (lacking; being without something)

pain + less = painless

joy	joyless
hope	hopeless
power	powerless
thank	thankless
taste	tasteless
help	helpless
event	eventless
rest	restless
sin	sinless
life	lifeless
food	foodless
tooth	toothless
end	endless
top	topless

-like (appears to be similar or like something)

life + like = lifelike

fern	fernlike
child	childlike
rough	roughlike
fool	foollike
girl	girllike

-ish (appears to be similar or like something)

child	childish
rough	roughish
red	redish
fool	foolish
girl	girlish

man	manlike
boy	boylike
baby	babylike
home	homelike

man	mannish
boy	boyish
baby	babyish
sweet	sweetish

-y (being replete or "filled" with something)

sun + y =	sunny	fun (n)	funny
hill	hilly	run (n)	runny
stone	stoney	smell	smelly
rain	rainy	dirt	dirty
frost	frosty	scratch	scratchy
chill	chilly	bug	buggy
snow	snowy	star	starry
scare	scarey	hair	hairy

noun + ist = (one who performs in a specific capacity)

piano + ist = pianist

organ	organist
violin	violinist
art	artist
drama (t)	dramatist
hypnotic	hypnotist
psychology	psychologist
psychiatry	psychiatrist
bigamy	bigamist
sorcery	sorcerist
journal	journalist

-way (a path of travel)

high + way = highway

road	roadway
sky	skyway
fly	flyway
path	pathway
walk	walkway
bike	bikeway
free	freeway
entry	entryway
drive	driveway
run	runway

-en (made from or make like)

gold + en = golden

wool	woolen
wood	wooden
silk	silken
red	redden
soft	soften
hard	harden
sweet	sweeten

-ness (having or being)

good + ness = goodness

kind	kindness
mean	meanness
sloppy	sloppiness
glad	gladness
happy	happiness
sad	sadness

As children progress through the intermediate grades, they can be challenged with more difficult suffixes. For example:

-itis   (inflammation of a bodily organ)
tonsilitis
appendicitis

-port (to carry)
transport
import
export
deport
support

-ous   (full of being)
poisonous
glamorous
scandalous

able   (capable of)
workable
singable
likeable

PREFIXES

Most prefixes are of little use in teaching vocabulary development because most prefixes are "irregular" in the sense that they do not give us sharply defined clues to word meaning and word identification. Take, for example, the prefix *ab-* (away from). Will awareness of the meaning of *ab-* help a child learn words such as *abduct, abbreviate,* or *abstract?* Not likely. In the case of *ab-*, there is also the risk that the child might confuse this prefix with the *ab* in words such as *abode, abide, abrupt,* and *abortion.*

There are, however, a few more "regular" prefixes that can be used with profit in vocabulary development. Research by the authors of this text indicates that the following prefixes are the most useful for teaching vocabulary development.

Most Useful Prefixes in Vocabulary Development, Based Upon Incidence of Occurrence and Regularity of Meanings	
anti-	opposed to, against
hyper-	too much
hypo-	too little
in-	not (the prefix *in-* is not "regular," but it occurs often enough in its "not" meaning to make it useful)

inter-	between
multi-	many
non-	not
over-	too much, on top of
pre-	before
post-	after
pro-	in favor of
pseudo-	false, pretending
quasi-	almost, not quite
re-	again
self-	the person himself or herself, the thing itself
semi-	half
sub-	under, below
super-	above, better, more than
un-	not, to perform an opposite act
well-	good, well done

When working with *un-* in vocabulary development, you also have the opportunity to impress upon the children that a prefix may have more than one meaning. Give the students a list of *un-* words, in some of which the prefix means "not" and in some of which it means "to perform the opposite act" and then challenge them to discover which *un*-s have which meaning.

Un Words for Discrimination in Meaning

unable	unhappy	unlock	unbroken
unlike	unload	unlace	unscrew
unzip	unreal	unfold	unwind
uncover	unfortunate	unheard of	undone
unstuck	uneven	unkind	untrue
unkept	untidy	unnecessary	unarmed

This is a good exercise, even for first- and second-graders. In the higher grades, words such as *unattended, uncontrollable, unannounced,* and *unconscious* may be listed.

Un- is not, of course, the only prefix useful in vocabulary development. But, would you believe, the unabridged *Random House Dictionary of the English Language* lists approximately 11,500 words having the prefix *un-!*

Children, even as early as second grade, have many prefix words in their speaking vocabularies but are not, of course, aware that such words illustrate a pattern or "family" of words. One method for teaching this awareness is to have the children begin by calling out words they know that begin with various prefixes. The teacher then prints the words on the chalkboard or, using a felt pen, on large sheets of paper. Each word is listed under its proper prefix heading. Seeing the words so arranged in print will help the children to recognize that the words belong to "families" and eventually to acquire them for their reading vocabularies. Here is a sample of some words which might be used in this kind of exercise:

over-		**super-**	
overcome	overrun	superman	superbowl
overboard	overthrow	superstar	superburger
overcoat		supermarket	

inter-		**pre-**	
intercity	interact	pregame	prepay
interracial	interschool	predawn	preschool
international	interstate	preview	prewar
interchange			

post-		**mis-**	
postgame	postwar	misspell	mistake
		misuse	misfortune
		misinformation	

tele- (far away)		**sub-**	
telephone	telegraph	submarine	subway
television	telescope	subdivide	subsoil
telegram		substation	

USING THE DICTIONARY IN VOCABULARY DEVELOPMENT

When used correctly, and with due respect for readiness of the children, dictionaries are an excellent resource for vocabulary development. There are some excellent dictionaries designed for the primary grades. They are well-illustrated, printed in large typeface, and have simplified definitions. Most have the phonetic pronunciation spelled out. Some have word derivations. These "beginner's" dictionaries are easy to use and children should be encouraged to use them. More important, they should be *taught* to use them correctly, so that the dictionary's potential as a vocabulary-building resource can be fully realized.

Every child in the classroom should have quick and easy access to a dictionary, which means that each classroom should have several copies of the dictionary being used. It is also a good idea to have a more advanced, somewhat larger dictionary on hand to help impress upon the child that not all the words in our language can be contained in one small book.

Do not use small "pocket" dictionaries for primary grade children. They contain too many words beyond the level of those children, and their definitions are not relevant to the needs of six- to eight-year-olds. Moreover, the print is very small.

A whole-class lesson on learning how to use the dictionary is appropriate at every level, but it is especially important for first-graders who are just being introduced to this resource. Whenever possible, use the "discovery technique" to help the child become familiar with the dictionary and its uses. Let the child "discover" its value by handling the book and asking and answering questions about it. Start simply, perhaps by asking the children how they think this "book of words" might help them to deal with words. The answers will probably be something like: "It will give us lots of words to read." "It might tell us what the words mean." "It will show us pictures of words." "Maybe it will help us say the words." As the lesson progresses, the youngsters will discover more and more about the dictionary and its uses and come to the general conclusion that "When we need help with words, our dictionary will help us."

NONPRODUCTIVE DICTIONARY STRATEGIES

Never use the dictionary as a kind of teaching crutch or as a substitute for meeting the child's individual needs. For example, merely telling a child to "Go home and look up these words" is a mistake on two counts. First, it assumes that the child *has* a dictionary at home (an assumption too many teachers make because they themselves were fortunate enough as children to have a dictionary at home), and further assumes that the child knows how to use a dictionary. Second, such a blunt command provides little or no motivation for the child, and what motivation it does provide will certainly not be child centered.

A variation on the ineffective go-home-and-look-it-up routine is, "If you come across a word you don't know, just look it up in the classroom dictionary." Such an injunction is discouraging to the child, who is very likely to need guidance and assistance in this procedure. It is, simply, passing the buck from teacher to child.

And do not fall into the trap of asking children who are not ready for such an exercise to "look up these ten (or whatever number) words in the dictionary and write sentences using them." Here is what you may get:

Word	Dictionary Definition
absolute	free

The judge absoluted the criminal.

economy	thrift

The girl wanted to have economy and put the money in the bank.

> *glorify*   to give high honor to a person

The President should have glorify when he comes to our city

> *pursuit*   following; seeking

The bus was pursuiting the truck when the accident happened.

> *nebulous*   cloudy; hazy; indistinct

Today is nebulous.

TEACHING AND LEARNING THE ALPHABET IN SEQUENCE

Knowing the alphabet in sequence is, of course, necesary for locating information in dictionaries, encyclopedias, phone books, and other sources. To this end, children must learn the alphabet in sequence. Does any more need to be said? Yes. The *relative position* of each letter within the alphabet must also be learned. A child must be able to make an educated guess as to whether or not a word beginning with *s*, for example, is to be found near the front or end or middle of the alphabetical listing.

Sorting exercises may be used for practice on relative position of letters within the alphabet. Here are two such exercises that work well.

Ask the children to separate the pages of the dictionary into three equal parts, putting card markers between the parts. The children will discover that there are many more words beginning with some letters than with other letters (for example, there are more *s*-words than any others and very few words beginning with *qu-, j, k, x, y*, and *z*. Have the children then make letter strips containing the alphabet letters in each one-third of the dictionary.

| a b c d e f g | h i j k l m n o | p q r s t u v w x y z |

The first exercise with the three letter strips as guides involves the separation of a stack of letter cards alphabetically into three piles. After the letters have been sorted into three groups, the children then should arrange them further in alphabetical order.

A second procedure with the three alphabet strips as headings involves the sorting of word cards in the same manner as the letter cards in the previous exercise. The words should be nouns, or the names of children in the class. Noun word cards can be made or may be purchased from Garrard Publishing Co., Champaign, Illinois.

As children progress in alphabetizing skills, they can eliminate the alphabet guide cards. They can also move on to alphabetizing to the second and third letter in words. Development of these latter skills may take three years or more.

FINDING SPECIFIC WORDS IN THE DICTIONARY

To find a specific word in the dictionary the child must, of course, master elementary skills in alphabet sequence as noted above. Knowing where in the dictionary (beginning, middle, or end) the word is likely to appear will further facilitate the process. Looking up words in the dictionary can also be made easier and quicker by teaching the child the function of the top-of-page guide words found in all good dictionaries. Children can be taught to use these guide words as indications that the word they wish to look up will or will not likely be found on a particular page of the dictionary.

Here is a game that can add a bit of fun to instruction in using dictionary guide words:

Children in a small group (all of about the same ability) are given dictionaries. The teacher displays a flocked word card on the flannel board and children compete with each other to see who can first find the *page* in the dictionary where that word will probably be found. In this part of the game, the task is not to find the word itself, but the page. The child must also explain, with reference to the guide words, why it is likely that the word will be found on that page.

In the next step of the game, the children compete with each other to locate the actual word. The teacher should observe any miscues that lead to difficulties in finding the right word and use such miscues in subsequent corrective teaching.

PRONUNCIATION SYMBOLS

Learning to handle dictionary symbols for word pronunciation is an ongoing task for elementary school children. The time to begin instruction in this skill is now, when the children are first learning to use the dictionary. Help the child acquire at least some basic familiarity with the meaning of accent, syllabication, and other such marks and how they function as aids to pronunciation. More formal instruction can be left to a later stage.

MULTIPLE DEFINITIONS OF DICTIONARY WORDS

Vocabulary development means not only learning new words but also discovering new meanings of words already learned. Here the dictionary is both a boon and a bane. A boon because the dictionary may give a number of meanings for a single word. A bane because multiple meanings may confuse the child who consults the dictionary for the meaning of a word he or she has met in a specific

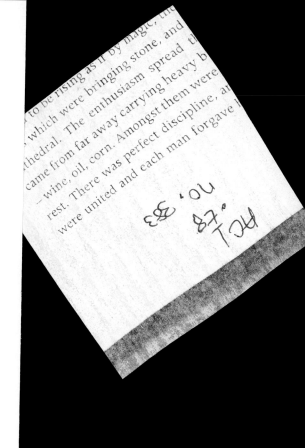

context. For example, a child might come across the unknown word *cast* in the sentence "Daniel was cast into the lion's den." If the child consults an average-size dictionary, he or she would probably have to read halfway through a score of definitions before finding the one that fits the desired context:

1. cast—to throw (cast a net)
2. cast—to send (cast a glance) (cast one's eye around).
3. cast—to throw down (as in wrestling) (cast his hat in the political arena)
4. cast—to shed (the snake cast off its skin)
5. cast—to imprison (someone is cast into a cell)
6. cast—to send away (they were "castoffs" from society)
7. cast—to shape (cast a vase in clay)
8. cast—to deposit (cast a ballot in an election)
9. cast—the mold or form for pouring a plaster cast (the die was cast)
10. cast—to toss (cast the dice)

This can be frustrating for many children. It is up to the teacher to minimize this frustration by guiding the child to the correct meaning and by pointing out to the child that using the dictionary can, so to speak, give us several "new words" for the price of one.

You may also reinforce this lesson concerning the value of the dictionary in vocabulary building by devising lists of various meanings for common words in the children's vocabularies. For the word *run*, for example, you might list some or all of the following variations:

run down the street	run against (counter to)
run a race	run for office
have a run of good luck	run down in health
on the run	make a run for it
in the long run	run dry
a newspaper run	a dry run
run off a few copies	run its course
run a blockade	
run across a friend	run off at the mouth
run off (an overflow)	run on (chatter)
run together (as in	run afoul of
birds of a feather)	
the color runs	the designs run together
run around with	run through (to stab)
	run through (to look through
	papers or a book rapidly)
run the risk	run according to plan
run out of something	run aground
have the run of the yard	run circles around
run riot	run up (sew up)
	a run (a brook or mountain stream)

Merely pointing out to the children that the dictionary gives various meanings of a single word or merely listing various usages of common words will, of course, be of little value without practical application. Children should be encouraged to practice these variations in content, orally, and in writing.

USING ETYMOLOGIES IN VOCABULARY DEVELOPMENT

Dictionary etymologies (word origins) can be used successfully to build vocabulary, especially with children who have more advanced reading skills. Unusual compounds are very useful in this regard. A word such as *limelight,* for example, is not commonly found in the speaking or reading vocabularies of intermediate-grade children, but its etymology as noted in the dictionary could well be "unusual" enough to remain in the child's memory, thus stimulating the child to retain the word in his or her working vacabulary. *Gooseflesh* is another such word whose etymology contains and explains its meaning.

Another etymology technique is the use of cartoon drawings to depict unusual and interesting word origins. First have the children find words in the

"How It Began" was a popular newspaper daily cartoon feature in the 1920s and 1930s. You could duplicate the idea in your classroom. What planning and routine would you have to establish to make it most effective? (© 1937 by United Features Syndicate, Inc.)

dictionary that are suitable for this kind of exercise. Then have the children draw simple cartoons depicting the origin of the chosen words.

ENCYCLOPEDIAS

Although encyclopedias will be discussed in some detail in the next chapter in connection with reading comprehension, a word should be said here about their value in vocabulary development. Because of their natural curiosity, children are likely to be attracted toward encyclopedias for information and answers to questions about the wonders of the world they see unfolding about them. Encourage this attraction as a source of vocabulary development.

Fortunate is the child who has an encyclopedia to browse in at home. Those less fortunate should at least have access to an encyclopedia in the classroom. *Childcraft Encyclopedia, World Book, Book of Knowledge,* and *Compton's Pictured Encyclopedia* are among those particularly useful for children of elementary school age.

USING SYNONYMS IN VOCABULARY DEVELOPMENT

Practicing with synonyms can be a most rewarding exercise in vocabulary building. Young children frequently refer to synonyms as "substitute words," indicating a keen insight into the nature and purpose of such words.

Since we are concerned primarily with building a reading vocabulary, practice with synonyms should involve the children seeing the synonym in conjunction with the printed word or words for which it can serve as a substitute. First, choose a few "main words," *big, little, friend,* for example. Then shuffle together a number of word cards, each containing a substitute for one of the main words. Have the children go through their deck of word cards and put each card under the correct main word. For example:

big	**little**	**friend**
large	small	buddy
huge	tiny	pal
great	wee	chum

As the child's reading skills develop throughout the grades, more "difficult" words can be used to help familiarize the child with synonyms in point. Here are examples of some "main words" and synonyms that may be used with older children:

old

antique
ancient
worn
elderly
aged
venerable
olden
archaic
obsolete

change

alter
vary
modify
transform
convert

trouble

discord
strife
conflict
clash
dissention
argument
bother
inconvenience
vex

kind

helpful
thoughtful
friendly
gentle
considerate
sympathetic
pleasant

costly

expensive
dear
precious
priceless
valuable
invaluable

trip

journey
tour
expedition
safari
excursion
charter
jaunt
outing
cruise
flight

slowly

leisurely
deliberately
dilatorily

foolish

silly
ridiculous
absurd

hard

difficult
intricate
troublesome

great

big
enormous
immense
stupendous
huge
super
tremendous
gigantic
colossal
mammoth
gargantuan
vast

home

house
dwelling
building
flat
tenement
abode
residence
apartment
mansion
condominium
quarters

single

alone
sole
solitary
individual
separate

THE "IN OTHER WORDS" GAME

In this synonym game, a simple sentence is printed or written on the chalkboard with one word underlined. For example, "The children were *loud*." The class might respond with "In other words, the children were *noisy*," or *boisterous*, *thunderous*, *roaring*, and so on. The new words should be printed below the original word as they are offered by the children. It is up to the teacher, of course, to see to it that the preferred in-other-words synonyms fit the context of the original sentence.

What might be called "synonym ping-pong" is another technique, especially useful with youngsters, for teaching synonym recognition in print. A card with a word printed on each side, each word synonymous with the other, is held aloft between two children. One child reads aloud the card-word facing him or her. The other child "returns the serve" with the synonym on his or her side of the card.

Here is another synonym word-card game, which older children like. Each child in the game is dealt six word cards. A stack of cards containing synonyms for these words is placed face down on the table. Each child, in turn, draws a card from this pile. If the word drawn is synonymous with one of the player's six words, the child keeps the card to create a pair. If not, the card is discarded face up. The next player is free to take this card if it is needed to make a pair. If not, the player can draw a face-down card from the center stack. The object of the game is to be the first child to pair up all six of the words originally dealt to the players.

In all work with synonyms, it should be impressed upon the children that although we may call synonyms "substitute" words, they are very seldom *exact* substitutes. Indeed, their principle value as vocabulary builders lies in the fact that they represent different shades of meaning for similar concepts and, consequently, lend richness and variety to vocabulary.

Obviously, words learned as synonyms must be read and used in context if they are to become part of the child's reading vocabulary. Only in context can their special shades of meaning be conveyed and expressed. Children should be encouraged to construct phrases and sentences using synonyms in context. They should also be encouraged to collect their own lists of synonyms gleaned from their own reading to be used as a source of a more accurate and picturesque working vocabulary.

USING ANTONYMS IN VOCABULARY DEVELOPMENT

Although antonyms do not provide the richness and variety of synonyms in vocabulary development, they nevertheless can be used with profit in the development of vocabulary skills. Usually in the elementary grades, we single out antonyms that are so far as possible exact opposites, using only one word that is the opposite of another word. Many of the same techniques used for practice with synonyms can be used with or adapted for use with antonyms. Here are some simple opposites useful for antonym practice:

black	white	sick	well
morning	night	summer	winter
first	last	good	bad
up	down	left	right
rich	poor	more	less
same	different	north	south
fast	slow	pull	push
on	off	help	hinder
stop	go	sad	happy
front	back	hot	cold
empty	full	above	below
open	shut	near	far
give	take	big	little
soft	hard	save	spend
girls	boys	stand	sit
east	west	easy	difficult
late	early	succeed	fail
light	dark	asleep	awake
weak	strong	plenty	shortage

FURTHER STRATEGIES AND TECHNIQUES FOR VOCABULARY DEVELOPMENT

THE ONE-A-DAY MULTIPLE WORD GAME

Each child is given a large empty plastic bottle in which to "collect" the new words the child has added to his or her vocabulary during the school year. When proof has been given that a word has really been learned, the word is printed or typed on a slip of paper and given to the child for deposit in the child's bottle. Many children will have collected 150 or more words for their bottles by the end of the school year.

"NEWS" BULLETIN BOARD

All elementary school rooms can effectively make use of a *News Bulletin Board* on which are printed some different news items or notices each day. In so doing, the teacher strives to introduce new vocabulary words. Here are some examples that we have used in the readiness year:

"It is time to clean up for *lunch*."
"Maryellen takes *attendance* today."
"This is Albert's *birthday*."
"Don't forget your *lunch* money tomorrow."
"Bring an *empty* paper bag soon."

In the kindergarten, the purpose is merely to get children used to seeing vocabulary that they know in print. By some magic, certain children are able to recognize those words even in different settings. In the first grade, the *News Bulletin Board* serves as the vehicle for new vocabulary to be practiced, copied, and used in printed sentences by the children. They easily become sight words; recognized again in subsequent notices, such as:

"We will not have *lunch tomorrow*."
"We have perfect *attendance* today."

In the intermediate grades, the *News* may tell:

"A *magician* will *perform* at a *special assembly* in the *auditorium* tomorrow."
"There will be a field trip to the *planetarium* next Tuesday. Study *astronomy* topics; *especially* the *solar system, galaxies,* and *constellations*."

WORD MOBILES

In the primary grades, children enjoy adding new vocabulary words to a classroom "word mobile." It is most effective to have several mobiles, each one holding words of a single category. For example, there might be one mobile for happy words, one for dangerous words, and so on. When the group decides a word is new enough to hang on a mobile, it must also decide which category it comes under. Suppose the word is *delightful*. It would be hung on the "happy" word mobile, which already may have such words as *pleasant, charming, vivacious, smiling, entertainment*.

THE "MAYBE" ADJECTIVE GAME

In this game, the teacher selects a noun and the children suggest adjectives that "maybe" modify it. For example, the teacher might say, "The word is *car*." The children would then respond with "Maybe it's a *green* car," or "Maybe it's a *foreign* car," or *sports* car, or *freight* car, or *flat* car. Since the teacher can more or less anticipate which modifiers the children are likely to choose for a given noun, these words can be printed up ahead of time on slips of paper for display to the children when they say their "maybe" word. If the children outguess the teacher in this respect (and they probably will), the word can be printed on a blank strip of paper kept especially for such an eventuality.

IDENTIFICATION OF PARTS OF WHOLES

Every workable machine, process, or complex thing has parts that have names. A huge vocabulary can be developed by learning the correct names of those parts. Some things are more appropriate for elementary school children than are others. For example, it would be quite irrelevant to expect and require that children learn the names of the bone structure of the body or any other sophisticated collection of complex and interassociated parts. However, we have found that there are a good number of children who are sufficiently interested in learning the names of the parts of some of the things in their environment: for example, the parts of a bike, a motorbike, a dress, a spaceship (TV oriented), sports equipment, a rescue van, big trucks, and so on.

The technique for this is very simple. All that is needed is a large diagram of a process or a cutaway diagram of the interior—let us say, of a *spacecraft* or a *big truck*. Some children will show unusual concentration in labeling the parts accurately.

There are just as many opportunities for developing vocabulary this way as

Naming the part helps a young reader to acquire vocabulary. However, inasmuch as *the whole is greater than the sum of its parts*, the process of "getting it all together" results in an understanding of relationships and a deeper comprehension of each vocabulary word's relationship to the whole.

there are machines, processes, and complex things in our environment and within the knowledge of the children in our class. We start with simple things, like the parts of a bike, with first graders, and progress through the grades to more complicated and more sophisticated things and more advanced vocabulary.

PREPLANNED IN-CLASS OBSERVATIONS

Throughout any school year and in every grade, there are countless opportunities for preplanned language experiencing through in-class observation of scientific phenomena such as the hatching of chicks, the freezing of water, the creation of steam, lifting iron with magnets, the transformation of polywogs into frogs, lifting weights by means of pulleys, the mixing of colors, and so on. The list of in-class scientific and technological observations is almost unlimited; it is circumscribed only by the resourcefulness of the teacher and by time.

As the vocabulary is learned, it is printed on tagboard by the teacher and is copied and used by the children. It is better, of course, to preplan the entire project, and that involves printing the vocabulary on the tagboard strips beforehand. The words may then be displayed immediately within the observation period at the appropriate time. In addition to saving class time, this makes use of the principle of learning, *contiguity* (Chapter 1), where the visual symbol is learned immediately with the pronunciation of the new word and the observation of its meaning.

In the many instances where observation must depend not upon actual in-class experiments or demonstrations but upon *vicarious* experiencing through films or filmstrips, the same procedure for learning the new vocabulary applies, except that the vocabulary lesson must wait for the review period after the showing of the film.

PREPLANNED FIELD TRIPS

As with in-class observation, first-hand experiencing on field trips provides reality to the words that describe the operations and environment being observed, but it must all be preplanned.

Example of Vocabulary Development on a Zoo Field Trip　Most field trips to the zoo, at least as far as we have observed, are excursions "to see the wild animals," with but minimal residual learning. We suggest that it is much better to explore only one section of the zoo and to capitalize on the several facets of knowledge that are inherent in it, one of which is vocabulary. Although we do not expect elementary school children to learn the technical names of the animals and/or their habitat, we do know that most second- and third-grade children can learn the following terms in a field trip to observe, for example, *the* *animals of the tall grasslands:* elephants, rhinos, tigers, leopards, gazelles, tall grass, lion, monkey, gorilla, zebra, safari, anteaters, hippos, wild game, antelope, buffalo, herd, jungle, rainfall, desert, villages, huts, tribes, savanna, crocodiles, plains, plateau, cattle, pasture, grazing, thatched-roofs, prairies, predators, burrows, migration, adaptation.

These words would not all be learned at the zoo, of course. But the exposure to the zoo animals of the grasslands of Africa can motivate interest in learning their names. That would be the language-experience base upon which the vocabulary of the animals' native environment would be developed. Thus, the field trip to the zoo provides the first-hand experience for the beginning of a constellation of words—all related to the original language-experiencing—that will be learned as the unit on the animals of the tall grasslands is developed. Vocabulary, thus learned, is reinforced through the reading of stories, travelogues, encyclopedias, newspaper accounts of safari adventures or exploration, and *National Geographic World* (written for elementary school pupils).

SPONTANEOUS LANGUAGE-EXPERIENCING FOR VOCABULARY DEVELOPMENT

As we are writing these words, sitting in the sunshine of a clear, crisp October day, we see the flight of wild geese overhead, an event that brings thrill and wonderment to children of all ages. In the classroom, when the honking of the geese is heard, we all rush to the windows or outdoors to observe one of the greatest mysteries and wonders of nature. When the awe and excitement has subsided, we talk about what we have seen—the *who, why, how, when,* and *where*—and another constellation of new words emerges, supported by cognitive and affective experiencing.

This is spontaneous . . . well, not quite, for, as teachers we know that every October the same wonder of nature will take place, and we are prepared. We "just happen to have" some pictures of wild geese in flight and some words already prepared on strips of tagboard.

> *nature   migration   flyways   migratory   instinct*
> *earth's magnetic field   feeding grounds   seasons   banding*
> *conservation   endangered species   annual   flight*
> *temperature zone   Antarctica   wildfowl   tropics*
> *range   breeding   continent   destination   homing*
> *navigation   seasonal   phenomenon   refuge   fledglings*
> *coastal marshes   wintering   populations   colonies*

But there are times, of course, when happenings are really spontaneous. It is at such times that we have the opportunity to prove that teaching is truly an *art.*

CONCLUSION

Throughout this chapter, we have emphasized two concepts: *first,* that vocabulary development is a total language-arts effort in which new words are adopted into one's speaking and writing vocabulary as essential parts of learning to identify them in print as written words; and, *second,* that successful and developmental vocabulary learning and enrichment must not be incidental, but must be preplanned.

So that vocabulary development may be organized and orderly, we have suggested twelve areas of everyday living into which words may be categorized and have listed hundreds of basic starter words. We have also listed thirty categories for the classification of new vocabulary words. These categories may serve as guides for the broad and balanced enrichment of children's speaking, writing, and reading vocabularies as they move upward from kindergarten through sixth grade.

We are convinced that much enlightenment comes from a knowledge of basic roots and affixes and that many new words may be easily learned by applying such knowledge. Therefore, we have suggested many strategies for using structural components for building vocabulary.

Dictionaries and encyclopedias are, of course, essential sources for knowledge of words, but children must be taught how to use them for vocabulary development in addition to the usual search for definitions.

Finally, we have described a number of successful strategies for vocabulary enrichment in the elementary school, grades K through 6.

We leave this chapter with these words of advice:

The learning of vocabulary does not "just happen"; it must be purposefully preplanned. It can be made to happen!

BIBLIOGRAPHY

Barnhart, Clarence L., Sol Steinmetz, and Robert K. Barnhart, *The Barnhart Dictionary of New English Since 1963,* New York: Harper and Row, 1973.

Bush, Clifford, L., and Mildred H. Huebner, *Strategies for Reading in the Elementary School,* New York: Macmillan, 1970.

Carroll, John B., Peter Davies, and Barry Richman, *The American Heritage Word Frequency Book,* New York: American Heritage/Houghton Mifflin, 1971.

Dale, Edgar, Joseph O'Rourke, and Henry Bamman, *Techniques of Teaching Vocabulary,* Palo Alto: Field Educational Publications, 1971.

Draper, Arthur G., and Gerald H. Moeller, "We Think With Words," *Phi Delta Kappan,* **52** (1971), 482−484.

Follett, Wilson, *Modern American Usage,* New York: Warner Books, 1966.

Gates, Arthur I., *A Reading Vocabulary for the Primary Grades,* New York: Bureau of Publications, Teachers College, Columbia University, 1935. This is one of the classics in the field.

Greet, W. Cabell, William A. Jenkins, and Andrew Schiller, *In Other Words, A Beginning Thesaurus,* Chicago: Scott, Foresman, 1968.

Harris, Albert J., and Milton D. Jacobson, *Basic Elementary Reading Vocabularies,* New York: Macmillan, 1972.

Horowitz, Edward, *Words Come in Families,* New York: Hart, 1977.

Johnson, Dale D., and P. David Pearson, *Teaching Reading Vocabulary,* New York: Holt, Rinehart and Winston, 1978.

Kurth, Ruth J., "Building a Conceptual Base for Vocabulary Development," *Reading Psychology,* **1**:2 (1980), 115–120. Presents twenty categories of meaning for vocabulary development.

Lundsteen, Sara W., "On Developing Relationships Between Language Learning and Reading," *Elementary School Journal,* **77**:3 (1977), 192–204.

McCracken, Robert A. and Marlene J., *Reading is Only the Tiger's Tail,* San Rafael, CA: Leswing Press, 1972. Read it. You'll like it!

Manzo, A. V., and John K. Sherk, "Some Generalizations and Strategies for Guiding Vocabulary Learning," *Journal of Reading Behavior,* **4** (1971–1972), 78–89.

Newman, Edwin, *Strictly Speaking,* Indianapolis: Bobbs-Merrill, 1974. The subtitle is revealing; *Will America Be the Death of English?*

Newman, Edwin, *A Civil Tongue,* New York: Bobbs-Merrill, 1976.

Otto, Wayne and Robert Chester, "Sight Words for Beginning Readers," *Journal of Educational Research,* **65** (1972) 425–443.

Roget's International Thesaurus, New York: Thomas Y. Crowell Co. Perhaps the most widely-used, listing 250,000 words!

Slobin, Dan I., "They Learn the Same Way All Around the World," *Psychology Today,* **2** (1972), 72. After studying the research on 25 languages, Slobin determined that, in at least 18 languages, children always use one-word "sentences" (invariably *nouns*) at first.

CHAPTER SEVEN

How Do I Teach
for Reading
Comprehension?

Introduction
Levels of Comprehension
Six Modes of Comprehension
    Literal Mode
    Interpretive Mode
    Assimilative Mode
    Applicative Mode
    Critical Mode
    Affective Mode
250 Patterns of Comprehension Questions
    Cause-and-Effect Questions
    Sequence of Events
    Value Judgments
    Characterization
    Sensitivity to Problems and Feelings of Others
    Literal Information
    Main Ideas/Details
    Problem Solving
    Imagination/Reality
    Implied Meanings, Evidence, and Generalizations
    Vocabulary, Meanings, Synonyms, and Loaded Phrases
    Picture Evidence
    Extending the Story

Each facet of instruction in the reading program has its specific objective or objectives. Together, however, they all have one common objective—*comprehension*, the ultimate reading skill. The word "comprehension" means the act or process of understanding the nature or meaning of something, the act or process of *grasping with the mind*. It is, then, a mental process, and, as we shall see, a far from simple one.

Comprehension is not (as reading is not) "getting meaning from the printed page." There is no "meaning" on a printed page. There are only lines and curves that we happen to call letters and from which we build words. Meaning resides not on the printed page but in the mind of the person who wrote the words. Comprehension will not be found on the printed page, but in the mind of the reader who reads the words.

Throughout this text we have constantly stressed the importance of experience in the reading process. In reading comprehension, experience is vital. The meaning of words read by a child must correspond in some fashion with the memory and meaning of experiences, real or imagined, stored in the child's mind.

This basic psychological truth should be kept constantly in your own mind as you go about teaching for reading comprehension. Many words do, of course, have generally accepted meanings; otherwise spoken and written communication of any kind would be impossible. But each child brings to words connotations and denotations that are based on the child's individual experience. The experiences of any two people in the whole world can never be alike, not even when experienced together!

We tend to generalize and to assume that our own experiences equip us to comprehend the experiences of others. However, we cannot assume such commonality of comprehension. For example, what do *we* mean and what do *you* mean when we say, "We are going for a holiday at the seashore"? Do you visualize the seashore as a long, uninhabited sandy beach lined with coconut palms, gently washed with a warm surf, or do you visualize it as a seaside resort filled with sun-worshipping bathers, lifeguards, blaring music—a place "where the action is"?

Years ago we might have been justified in assuming some degree of commonality of children's experiences. In a rural school, for example, we could safely have assumed that a farm child would have had experiences with horses, chickens, cows, pigs, and, perhaps, sheep and goats. But today, specialized farming makes such an assumption invalid.

Be prepared, also, to take into account the fact that the experiences of all children are relatively limited. They cannot yet "know" all that you do. They are wonderingly and wondrously grasping for *new* meaning. They are, in a sense, like the fabled blind men trying to "comprehend" the elephant.

The Blind Men and the Elephant

It was six men of Hindostan,
To learning much inclined,
Who went to see the elephant,
(Though all of them were blind):
That each by observation
Might satisfy his mind.

The first approached the elephant,
And happening to fall
Against his broad and sturdy side,
At once began to bawl,
"Bless me, it seems the elephant
Is very like a wall."

The second, feeling of his tusk,
Cried, "Ho! what have we here
So very round and smooth and sharp?
To me 'tis mighty clear
This wonder of an elephant
Is very like a spear."

The third approached the animal,
And happening to take
The squirming trunk within his hands,
Then boldly up and spake;
"I see," quoth he, "the elephant
Is very like a snake."

The fourth stretched out his eager hand
And felt about the knee,
"What most this mighty beast is like
Is mighty plain," quoth he;
"Tis clear enough the elephant
Is very like a tree."

The fifth who chanced to touch the ear
Said, "Even the blindest man
Can tell what this resembles most;
Deny the fact who can,
This marvel of an elephant
Is very like a fan."

The sixth no sooner had begun
About the beast to grope
Than, seizing on the swinging tail
That fell within his scope,
"I see," cried he, "the elephant
Is very like a rope."

And so these men of Hindostan
Disputed loud and long,
Each of his own opinion
Exceeding stiff and strong,
Though each was partly in the right,
And all were in the wrong!

John Godfrey Saxe

LEVELS OF COMPREHENSION

From pioneer studies in educational taxonomy (classification of objectives) and other widely esteemed educational works the reading profession has garnered an indeterminant collection of labels (some useful, some useless) the most popular of which have been three that have been applied directly to reading comprehension:

1. The *literal level* of comprehension.
2. The *interpretive level* of comprehension.
3. The *critical level* of comprehension.

The *literal* level has been described as that "level" at which facts can be repeated or supported directly from information garnered from the printed page. It is implied that this is a very elementary level of comprehension requiring only the ability to repeat facts.

How can one be certain that each child has the same concept of a word, a phrase, or an idea as you have? Really, now, is that ever possible? What steps are necessary to assure that some meeting of minds and general consensus of understanding has been achieved?

The *interpretive* level is conceived as a higher level thought process involving a recognition of causative factors (cause and effect), making inferences from facts, and reaching conclusions and generalizations.

The *critical* level denotes a reader's ability to think in a critical manner concerning the materials being read. This may involve analysis of propaganda by applying one's own value judgments, and so on. In short it is subjective thinking as opposed to objective thinking. Even though it may be subjective in nature, critical reading also might call upon objective data to support a point of view.

This three-level notion of reading comprehension has its uses. It is, however, simplistic, and can be misleading. It is misleading in the sense that it implies a hierarchy of comprehension skills, each more valuable than the other. It suggests that teacher and child should move as quickly as possible from less-worthy literal (factual) level upward to the more-valued higher levels. In practice, such a philosophy could easily lead to the encouragement of guessing and subjective generalizing as being more valuable than the ability to work with substantiating facts.

The three-level notion is, furthermore, simplistic in that it suggests reading comprehension is a much less complex process than it actually is. There are factors in comprehension not easily categorized under one or the other of these three levels.

SIX MODES OF COMPREHENSION

Instead of levels of comprehension, we propose the concept of *modes* of comprehension. Our emphasis will be on the mode or "manner" in which comprehension occurs, rather than on levels of comprehension. All of the six modes of comprehension we discuss are of equal importance. Each is related to and reinforces the others. Development of skills in all six modes is essential for successful instruction in reading comprehension. The six modes are as follows:

1. Literal mode.
2. Interpretive mode.
3. Assimilative mode.
4. Applicative mode.
5. Critical mode.
6. Affective mode.

THE LITERAL MODE OF READING COMPREHENSION

In teaching for comprehension within the literal mode, we are concerned primarily with the literal meaning (or meanings) of words and, by extension, with the literal facts and information contained in reading materials. Comprehension within the literal mode has been an underlying concern and implied objective of many of the strategies and techniques—labeling of classroom objects, word-differentiation games, exercises in dictionary use, and so on—discussed throughout this text, particularly those discussed in the previous chapter on vocabulary development.

Definitions   A first step toward fostering literal comprehension is to guide children toward an understanding of some of the complexities involved in arriving at literal definitions. They must be taught that a label on an object—the word *table* pasted on a piece of classroom furniture, for example—merely tells us what we *call* the object. It does not tell us what the word means. Asking for verbal definitions of common object names is a good technique for teaching awareness of this distinction. For example, let's say you ask the children to define the word *table*. In defining *table*, most children will eventually conclude that "It is a piece of furniture." But before they arrive at this point, they will have progressed through several levels of cognition. Most children will begin trying to define the word with something like, "A table is something you have in a room." They must be led to observe that "something" doesn't really tell much about a table. After all, *candy* is "something," *milk* is something. "Is it candy?" will elicit a loud "no!." "Well then, what *kind* of 'something' is a table?" Eventually, it will be classed as a "piece of furniture." *Classification* is a first step in definition. *Distinguishing its features* is the next: A child might say,

> "A table is a piece of furniture with legs." "But, so is a chair. What makes it different?"

Finally, the children will conclude that "A table is a piece of furniture with four legs and a flat top." After further experience, they may "discover" that some tables have three legs and some have five or six, some tables fold up, some don't, and so on. The children will, in short, have taken some important first steps toward literal comprehension.

In the intermediate grades, children can learn to handle definitions of abstract terms. This process requires more sophisticated mental processes and must be introduced gradually. Begin with definitions of simple qualities that are generally familiar, such as: *hard, happy, late, warm, hungry.* As children become more proficient in defining abstractions in their own words, challenge them further by suggesting they compare their definitions with the definitions in a beginners' dictionary.

Questions and Questioning   Because the literal mode of comprehension involves literal meanings and literal facts, instruction in this mode lends itself naturally to "simple" question and answer techniques, with the questions calling for restatement or recall of facts: "List the five parts of. . . ." "State the four reasons for. . . ." *Simple* questions and answer techniques? Not really. Not if your questions are, as they should be, structured to *teach* comprehension and not merely to test for it. Being able to recall facts and regurgitate them on cue is indicative of potential for comprehension but it is by no means proof of comprehension, even of simple comprehension in the literal mode.

For example, let us suppose that an elementary school geography book in a unit on the Netherlands states that "The Dutch built polders to protect their land." Let us further suppose that following the reading, the teacher asks:

> "What did the Dutch build?"
> Answer: "Polders." (100% literally correct.)
>
> "How do you spell it?"
> Answer: "p-o-l-d-e-rs" (100% literally correct.)
>
> Or the teacher could ask, "Who built polders?"
> Answer: "The Dutch" (100 % literally correct.)

"Why did the Dutch build polders?"
Answer: "To protect their land" (100% literally correct.)

Do these 100% correct answers prove comprehension? Of course not. The child has no idea why polders are necessary to protect the land, or even what a polder is. (Indeed, most people not living in an area such as that of the Netherlands would have to hustle to the nearest dictionary in order to define *polder*.)

We would hope, of course, that no teacher would be satisfied with this kind of pointless questioning while instructing for comprehension in the literal mode. But studies of the nature of questions asked by elementary school teachers in comprehension exercises indicate that this kind of questioning may be more prevalent than one would like to think.

For example, Dr. Frank J. Guszak tape-recorded 1857 comprehensive questions asked by second-, fourth-, and sixth-grade teachers. Upon analysis, he found that about 60% of the questions called only for literal recall of facts; 13.5% for recognition (also repetitive); 6.5% for conjecture; 7.2% for explanation; 15% for evaluation; and less than 1% asked for restatement of facts in the child's own words. On the positive side, Dr. Guszak did find that questions calling for simple recall of facts decreased from 66.5% in the fourth grade to just under 50% in the sixth grade.

In a similar study of teacher questioning strategies made by the U.S. Office of Education it was found that 68% of all questions asked called for regurgitation of facts and that more than half of the remaining questions merely called for embellishment of facts previously elicited. An earlier study by Dr. Mary Jane Aschner showed an almost identical situation prevaling in the classrooms tested.

Questions calling for simple recall of literal facts do, of course, have a place in your arsenal of questions for testing and teaching for comprehension in the literal mode. But a wide variety of questions is needed if such exercises are to be truly effective. Skill in questioning will come with experience. It is a good idea for you to keep a log of your first efforts at constructing comprehension questions, noting successes and failures. (As an aid to your efforts, you will find later on in this chapter an extensive list of sample comprehension questions, arranged by categories.)

Copying   The physical act of copying, as has been previously pointed out, is not to be highly recommended as a teaching or learning technique. It can, however, be used with success if some kind of cognitive dimension is added to the exercise. For example, literal comprehension may be fostered by an exercise such as the following:

Give the children a word list of objects commonly found in a supermarket. Then have them copy each word according to the product classification system normally used in supermarkets—that is, under headings such as "Fresh Produce," "Dairy Products," "Meats," and "Cleaning Aids." Similarly, literal facts (or events) found in an article or story may be copied in sequence or according to categories chosen by the teacher.

Filling in the Blanks   Filling in the blanks is an older method than the cloze procedure (which is a test of a child's ability to comprehend written context well enough to be able to supply the missing words that have been deleted at regular intervals.), but is somewhat related to it. It is a useful technique for reinforcing comprehension in the literal mode. Here is a sample of a fill-in-the-blanks paragraph for use in this kind of exercise.

The Fox and the Grapes

One hot summer _____, a Fox was walking down a dusty _____. He was thirsty. He found some grapes hanging on a _____ way up in a _____. He thought that, if he could get those grapes, he would _____. But he couldn't _____ the tree no matter how hard he _____. So he _____ ed and _____ ed as loud as he could, but the _____ didn't _____ down. Finally, after all that, he _____ and said to himself, "I _____ want the grapes, anyhow. They probably are _____. He was a _____ Fox.

THE INTERPRETIVE MODE OF READING COMPREHENSION

Unlike the literal mode, the interpretive mode of comprehension involves understanding of causative factors, making inferences, and drawing conclusions. At the risk of considerable oversimplification, one might say that the literal mode involves *what* happened, and that the interpretive mode involves *why* it happened.

The question of *why?* underlies *all* human decisions and all human actions. To miss the *why?* is to miss the impact of the story, the impact of history, biography, and the daily news. *Why?* is the key to the deep meanings of reading material.

After reading *Jack and the Beanstalk*, a child can demonstrate literal understanding of the story by correctly answering questions such as "Who is the boy in the story? Where was he going? Whom did he meet? What did he sell? What did he climb?" But for interpretive comprehension, the reader must be led to formulate and answer *why* questions. *Why* did Jack sell the cow for some bean seeds? *Why* was Jack's mother unhappy? Only then does the child begin to read within the interpretive mode of comprehension.

Questions and Questioning   As with the literal mode, questions play a very important role in strategies for teaching for comprehension within the interpretive mode. Interpretation involves understanding of cause-and-effect relationships, ability to anticipate, ability to differentiate time, ability to make inferences, ability to recognize characterization, and ability to interpret figurative

Comprehension: Detecting Word Meanings From Context

Children love to "earn" badges. Here, we suggest a "Word Detective" awarded to children who develop the habit of sleuthing for word meanings.

language. Good questions are required to stimulate acquisition of each of these skills.

Cause-and'Effect Questions Understanding the relationship between cause and effect is basic to interpretive reading. If the child is unable to sense this relationship in reading materials, the child is not reading within the interpretive mode. Careful questioning and careful guidance toward correct answers can help to foster awareness of the relationship between cause and effect. What caused Rip Van Winkle's wife to do what she did? What happened to make Huck Finn and Tom Sawyer wish they were somewhere else? What caused the car in this story to run down the hill? Cause-and-effect questions are, of course, essentially "Why did it happen?" questions.

Prediction Questions One of the most fruitful strategies of teaching reading comprehension is the exploration of predictions in the plot of stories. In some ways, this is related to cause-and-effect. To predict, one must be aware of causes and their effects. When the situation is identical or similar, the same causes are likely to result in the same effects, and the results can be reasonably predicted. Prediction questions call for "educated guesses" based on knowledge acquired earlier and on what has been read so far in the story at hand. Whether or not the "guess" is a good one is learned by further reading of the story. Here are some samples of prediction questions:

"Ponies are trained to be mounted from the left side. What do you think will happen if Jimmy mounts the pony from the right side?"

"The Yankee in King Arthur's Court knows that a total eclipse of the sun occurred on that very day in that year. How do you think he can use that information to help himself?"

One of the chief functions of the teacher is to help a child in interpretation. What preparation must you make to be able to ask the "right" questions that lead a child to satisfying interpretation?

"What do you think the policeman will do with the mother duck and her ducklings who want to cross the busy street?"

All such questions and answers are followed up with, "Let's read on and see if we are right in our prediction (or guess)."

Inference Questions The ability to make inferences is essential to comprehension in the interpretive mode. The reader must make explicit what the writer has left implicit. Children must be guided toward understanding that literal statements may mask true meaning and that writers sometimes deliberately do this to make a point or to make reading more exciting and enjoyable. They must be taught to "interpret" the writer by making the inferences the writer wishes them to make.

Here is a paragraph from Mark Twain with a sample of the kind of questions that might be asked to sharpen inference-drawing skills:

"Yes, and you done more than that," said Injun Joe, approaching the doctor, who was now standing. "Five years ago you drove me away from your father's kitchen one night when I come to ask for something to eat, and you said I warn't there for any good, and when I swore I'd get even with you if it took a hundred years, your father had me jailed as a vagrant. Did you think I'd forget? . . ."

Tom Sawyer, Mark Twain

What can you infer about Injun Joe's character from this passage? What can you infer about Joe's reputation in the community? What can you infer about the social standing of the doctor and the doctor's father?

Time Questions Generally speaking, young children have a problem with the concept of time, as revealed by the kinds of questions they ask about "time." "How fast are seconds? Do they go like this: 12345678?" "When is it going to be tomorrow?" "Why didn't yesterday last longer?" "When were the olden days?" "What was it like way back when I was little?" "When am I going to be grown up?" "When are we going to be almost there?"

In reading, children often have difficulty in conceptualizing time span in a story line and, indeed, in differentiating the "then" of a story and the "now" of reading a story. Herein probably lies the basis for the time-honored convention of beginning children's stories with "Once upon a time . . ." or "Long, long ago . . ." Children seem to be able to handle very indefinite time concepts easier than definite ones.

Here are some samples of the kind of probing a teacher can use to help children interpret time elements in reading materials:

"Just then, a snarling dog appeared" ("When was 'just then'?" If this probe draws a blank, try "What was *happening* just before the dog appeared?'

"Now, there were shepherds abiding in the fields, watching their flocks." ("Does 'now' mean right now? Or does it mean 'then'? How can you tell?")

"Before he opened the door, he peeked in the window." ("Why doesn't the author tell us 'how long' before?" If this draws a blank, try "Does it matter in the story how long before he opened the door he peeked in the window?")

Characterization Questions Comprehension within the interpretive mode calls for attention to the literary device of "characterization." This device is found in all types of reading materials, but especially so in fiction. Children should be guided toward understanding how characters can "come alive" through interpretation of the written word.

Note, for example, how Booth Tarkington used characterization:

A bitter soul dominated the various curved and angular surfaces known by a careless world as the face of Penrod Schofield. Except in solitude, that face was always cryptic and emotionless; for Penrod had come into his twelfth year wearing an expression carefully trained to be inscrutable. Since the world was sure to misunderstand everything, mere defensive instinct prompted him to give it as little as possible to lay hold upon. Nothing is more impenetrable than the face of a boy who has learned this, and Penrod's was habitually as fathomless as his hatred for literary activities . . .

Penrod, Booth Tarkington

Is Penrod really a "bitter soul," a boy likely to grow up to be a bitter sour man?

How does the author use facial expressions to characterize Penrod and his reaction to a world that is "sure to misunderstand everything?"

Pick out the specific words used by the author to denote how Penrod's face reflects his "defensive instinct against a "careless world."

The extract below from Washington Irving's *The Devil and Tom Walker* is another example of the kind of writing exceptionally suitable for sharpening awareness of a characterization as a tool of interpretive comprehension.

. . . there lived near this place (Boston) a meagre, miserly fellow, of the name of Tom Walker. He had a wife as miserly as himself: they were so miserly that they even conspired to cheat each other. Whatever the woman could lay hands on, she hid away; a hen could not cackle but she was on the alert to secure the new-laid egg. Her husband was continually prying about to detect her secret hoards, and many and fierce were the conflicts that took place about what ought to have been common property. They lived in a forlorn-looking house that stood alone, and had an air of starvation. . . . no smoke ever curled from its chimney; no traveller stopped at its door. A miserable horse, whose ribs were as articulate as the bars of a gridiron, stalked about a field. . . . Tom's wife was a tall termagant, fierce of temper, loud of tongue, and strong of arm. Her voice was often heard in wordy warfare with her husband; and his face sometimes showed signs that their conflicts were not confined to words.

The Devil and Tom Walker, Washington Irving

"If the author had not used the word *miserly* in this passage, what else in the passage would lead us to believe that Tom and his wife were, indeed, miserly characters?"

"How does the author's characterization of Tom's house reflect and reinforce his characterization of Tom and his wife?"

"How does the author's description of Tom's wife help establish her character?"

"What does the reference to Tom's face in this description tell us about Tom's wife?"

"How does the word *termagant* help us to know what kind of person Tom's wife was?" (This will be a dictionary lesson: a violent, turbulent, brawling shrew; fierce; temper, loud; waring; tough; fighter.)

Interpretation of Figurative Language Figurative language, by its very nature, cannot be taken literally. It can be understood only within the interpretive mode of comprehension. Most children have little or no difficulty with this concept, for they understand that when we speak of the *legs* of a chair, the *eye* of a needle, a river *bed,* or a *fork* in the road, we are not using these words in their common literal meanings. When they read ''Her eyes were stars, bringing happiness to everyone,'' they know that eyes are not stars.

Figures of speech provide the reader with comparisons that stimulate interpretation. When a person or object or situation is described as being *like* something else, the supposition is that the reader has had experience with the ''something else.'' For example:

> Like a breath of wind on a smoldering fire, her anger became fierce-burning again.
>
> *The Princess and the Vagabond*

> A man with the mouth of a mastiff, a brow like a mountain, and eyes like burning anthracite—that was Dan'l Webster in his prime.
>
> *The Devil and Dan'l Webster,* Stephen Vincent Benét

Adroit questioning can help bring out the nuances of simile and metaphor which the child might otherwise overlook.

One simple strategy for teaching children to interpret figurative language is to have them construct similes and metaphors of their own and to justify their aptness. A few examples can get them started, for example ''cool as a cucumber,'' ''you're a good egg.''

By asking the question, ''What is it really saying to us?'' we are asking the child to define meaning through interpretation.

THE ASSIMILATIVE MODE OF READING COMPREHENSION

In the assimilative mode of comprehension, the reader takes information and facts found in reading material and assimilates them into a larger, more meaningful whole. In a sense, the reader ''processes'' information by categorizing and/or organizing it so that it is comprehended not as a single unit of meaning but as part of an entire complex of meaning. ''The whole is greater than the sum of its parts.''

We cannot just pour knowledge into a child, as it was rumored was done in the Medieval town of Nurnburg. In her interesting book, *Don't Push Me, I'm No*

Computer, Helen Beck relates the legend of the "Nurnberger Trichter," a huge funnel used by the town fathers to pour instant knowledge into the dense heads of the citizens of Nurnberg. The German word, *eintrichtern,* means literally "to pour in through a funnel." After the knowledge is "funneled in," it must be assimilated and categorized. This is done by helping children develop classifications and by aiding them in sorting out new ideas. As new information, ideas, concepts, and the like are encountered in a child's reading, the child who has been taught to categorize will be constantly and simultaneously sorting out the identifying elements and placing them in proper perspective.

Cateogrizing   Categorizing (or classifying) is a first and essential step toward reading comprehension in the assimilative mode. Categorization helps develop in the child a sense of the "relatedness" of words and concepts to a general subject—in other words, the relationships of parts to wholes, the essence of assimilation.

We have already discussed many techniques and strategies for teaching categorization skills in relevant sections of this text and will discuss further strategies to this end in Chapter 8. Suffice it to say here that just about all classroom reading materials—fiction, nonfiction, biography, newspaper, and periodical articles—lend themselves readily to exercises in classification. Even book titles and poetry can be classified according to subject matter, a process most children thoroughly enjoy.

Devote as much classroom space as you possibly can to display of general headings under which the children can list (categorize) new concepts and new information gleaned from classroom reading. As the number of headings and the listings below them grow, you and the children will have a visual record of your students' progress in acquiring classification skills.

Categorizing by Constellation of Ideas   A more sophisticated kind of categorization employs the concept of *constellation of ideas,* a concept discussed in Chapter 1 as a basic principle of learning: things that go together should be learned together. Unlike simple categorization, the constellation of ideas concept does not merely illustrate the relationship of parts to whole, it also illustrates relationships between wholes.

Let's suppose you are involved with a fourth-grade geography unit on the Midwest. As reading in this area progresses, a large number of "information units" begin to emerge. If you had the children note these units on the chalkboard as they emerged from their reading, the board would soon be filled with a clutter of seemingly unrelated items and would probably look something like this:

> Great Lakes, corn belt, soybeans, cattle, grasslands, network of canals, rivers, Mississippi, Missouri, Ohio, Wabash, Indiana, Illinois, Michigan, Wisconsin, Iowa, Missouri, Minnesota, Kentucky, Ohio, Arkansas, railroads, stockyards, sunflower seeds, cattle, white-face Herefords, farm implements, Detroit, automobiles, iron ore, steel mills, lake freighters river locks, dairyland, cheese, grain, barge traffic, grain exchange (the Pit), Big Ten football, universities and colleges, Highway I-80, "Little Red Schoolhouse," Old Northwest Territory, Indian country, Ordinance of 1787, George Rogers Clark, Black Hawk War, War of 1812, pioneers, Mormons, immigrants, Germans, Swiss, Poles, Italians, railroads, Chicago, airports, trucking, Blue Grass, horse-racing, politics, Blacks, minority groups, Kentucky Derby, Kansas City, Minneapolis, Cleveland, St. Louis, St. Paul, Toledo, Schlitz, Budweiser, "Windy City," baseball, hockey, football, urbanization, suburbs, and so on.

Of course no real comprehension of the Midwest can come from this kind of clutter. The first step toward comprehension would be to categorize the items under general headings (wholes) such as Agriculture, Cities, Transportation, People, and History. A "constellation of wholes" can then be displayed to the class to illustrate how understanding relationships between and among wholes is as essential to comprehension within the assimilative mode as is understanding relationship between wholes and parts.

Ordering and Sequencing   Recognition of the importance of order and sequence is a further essential skill for comprehension (and recall) within the assimilative mode. The order and sequence in which information units appear in reading materials is a vital clue to total meaning.

One simple strategy for teaching this skill is to print the principal events in a story on cardboard strips, mix up the strips, and ask the children to arrange them according to story sequence: "These cards tell us all the things Emily did. But they are all mixed up. See if you can arrange them so they tell us what Emily did first, what she did second, and so on in the same order she did them in the story." For some stories, an effective follow up might be to have the children deliberately put some of the strips out of sequence and then discuss how this new ordering might affect the outcome of the story.

Outlining   A formal outline involves detailed ordering and sequencing of information according to main headings, subheadings, and so on, a topic we discuss in Chapter 8. Here we are interested simply in teacher use of some of the more basic principles of outlining as an aid to instruction in comprehension within the assimilative mode. Thus:

Print the main points and principal subpoints of a story or article on strips of flocked tagboard. (Flocking will allow the strips to be rear-

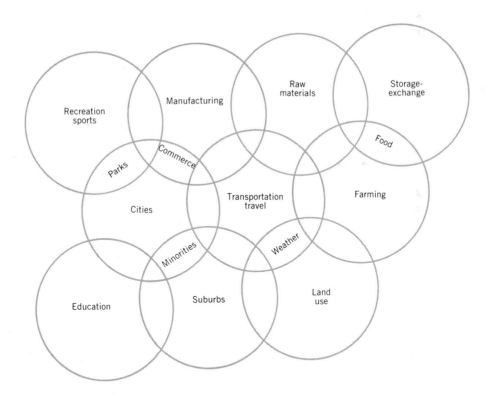

The Midwest—A Constellation of Concepts

Cut-up cartoon strips may be used to help children develop a sense of story sequence. What cautions should you set for yourself in the selection of cartoons? What means can you use to make the cut strips durable? What directions would you give to an aide for using this learning device?

ranged if necessary after they have been placed on a flannel board.) Also print the title of the story or article on a tagboard strip.

Begin the exercise by asking one of the children to read the title of the story aloud. (It is good practice to choose one of the poorer readers for this task. Titles are not likely to be difficult, especially if there has been some discussion of the material beforehand. Thus, a poor reader may gain a bit of encouragement from successfully reading the title to the class.) Place the title strip at the top of the flannel board. As the exercise progresses, you may have occasion to refer to the role of titles as aids to comprehension. At times, titles may play an important role in this respect.

Ask the children to read the material silently. Tell them to look for "main points" in the material and, when they find them to let the teacher know. Tell them to do the same for "subpoints" that are details of main points. When a child suggests a correct main point, place the corresponding tagboard strip on the flannel board. When a child suggests a correct subpoint, the corresponding subpoint strip is placed on the board beneath its main point.

Although only correct main points and subpoints will be put up on the board (only correct points, of course, will have been readied in advance), be prepared to accept incorrect ordering and sequencing initially if the class seems to agree that such listing is satisfactory. As the lesson progresses, guide the children to have "second thoughts" about suggested incorrect listings and to "advise" you how to rearrange the tagboard strips to make them coincide with the correct order and sequence in the article or story. This kind of trial-and-error approach can help the child realize that correct order and sequence requires and deserves careful attention.

Below is the first part of an article on bridges. Following the article is an "outline" of the article as it might appear on a classroom flannel board. (The outline has been expanded to include two other parts of the article not reprinted here.)

Bridges

Men have made and used bridges for a very long time. It is hard to say just when they began to do so. Maybe hundreds and hundreds of years ago a man needed to cross a stream. He might have seen a log that had fallen across it like a little bridge. So he ran across the log and reached the other side. He did not get the least bit wet.

This may have happened a number of times. Then the man might have placed a log across a small stream himself when he didn't want to get his feet wet. Then, much later, men began to fasten logs together to make longer and wider bridges.

In jungles men of long ago might have crossed streams by swinging on long, strong vines. The vines hung from trees on the river banks. After a bit, these people began to use thick vines or rope to make bridges. Rope bridges are still in use in a number of places. They make some people feel dizzy, for they swing back and forth as you cross on them.

SOURCE. Adapted from *Take Flight,* Level G., *The Merrill Linguistic Reading Program,* published by the Charles E. Merrill Publishing Co., Columbus, Ohio. Copyright, 1975, The Bell & Howell Company. Reproduced by permission.

BRIDGES

LONG AGO

Old log across stream
Logs fastened together
Vine bridges in jungle
Rope bridges

TODAY
Wood
Stone
Steel
Concrete
Lift up
To let boats go past
Swing

BRIDGES ARE FOR
People
Cars
Trucks
Trains
To cross water
To connect hills

The teacher should have extra strips of tagboard and a felt marker available to add other ideas that emerge during or after the outlining session. For example, a child in the cattle or sheep country may want to add that bridges are to let a drove of sheep or cattle cross. Another child who has crossed a long suspension bridge may want to add that some bridges are "made with big wires." To bring reality to the comprehension lesson, pictures of the various types of bridges may be brought for inspection and discussion.

Follow up of Outlining Activities   There are at least two follow-up lessons that may be used to reinforce comprehension of outlines. First, the children can copy the outline and illustrate each detail or those they elect to illustrate. Second, the flocked strips could be shuffled and children working in pairs or very small groups could reassemble the outline on the flannel board during their work session. A third possible expansion of the lesson would be within the so-called "creativity" segment of the unit and could include the reading of poems about bridges or singing songs about bridges, or bringing in more pictures of famous bridges. These could then be interspersed with an expanded outline that would include the poems and the songs in printed form, as well as the pictures.

Organizational Patterns   Most reading material falls into one or the other of a few common organizational patterns. Recognition of these patterns can aid the child in comprehending idea and detail as an interrelated whole, first by separating main idea from details and then mentally recombining them.

Here are five common organizational patterns. To help familiarize the child with these recurring patterns, print them on the chalkboard or post them on the bulletin board, or, perhaps, have the children make their own individual copies. Alert the children to be on the lookout for the patterns in their reading. Copies of the patterns may also be used in exercises wherein the children match sentences and paragraphs from their reading with one or the other organizational pattern.

1. *main idea* first, then
    detail
    detail
    detail

2. detail
   detail   first, then statement of *main idea*
   detail

3. *main idea* then
    detail
    detail   then *main idea*, restated
    detail

4. detail
   detail   then *main idea* then more   detail
   detail   detail
                                           detail

5. *main idea* then   detail   then *main idea* then   detail
   (part one)   detail   (part two)   detail
               detail   detail

In a story, novel, biography, or play, main ideas may be identified by filling in a sentence consisting of: *Who did what, when, where, how, with whom, and why?* or may be filled into an outline, thus:

    Who?   Did what?

      When?   Where?

          How?

    With Whom?   Why?

THE APPLICATIVE MODE OF READING COMPREHENSION

The applicative mode of comprehension involves the ability to apply information gleaned from reading to one's own pursuits, purposes, and problems. It involves ability to transfer previously attained knowledge to new situations and ability to arrive at generalizations and draw conclusions. Again, adroit questioning can help inculcate and sharpen these essential skills.

For example, children can be guided toward recognition of the possible transferability of previous learning to new situations with questions such as the following:

"What have we learned before that we can make use of here?"

"Have we ever learned something that is just about the same as this? How did that situation turn out?"

"What do we already know that we can use here?"

"Do we see anything here that is almost exactly like something else that we have read about? Does that help us know what might be going to happen here?"

"What things in this story are similar to those in another story we have read? Do these things help us understand the setting of this story and the people in it?

Skills in making generalizations and drawing conclusions can be fostered by probes and questions such as the following:

"In all these cases, the same thing happened. Why?"

"What conclusions can you draw from what you've read so far? Let's read on and see if the author draws the same conclusions."

The fact that comprehension of what we read can help us in our everyday pursuits, purposes, and problems seems obvious to most adults, but children must be guided toward realization of this fact. They must be led to an understanding that much of what they read has "practical" applications, and that almost everything they read can enrich their personal lives. Here are some strategies and techniques for teaching comprehension in the applicative mode.

Following Directions   Learning to follow printed directions is a basic skill of comprehension in the applicative mode. In fact, instruction in direction skills should, properly, begin even before the child learns to read. For example, a kindergarten teacher can print directions on slips of paper and have the children take turns selecting slips for the teacher to read aloud. Each child then tries to follow the "direction." Directions might be something like "Go to a child who is wearing the same color dress as you are and ask her to change places with you," or "Go touch the child farthest away from your place and then come back and touch the child nearest to your place." The objective of such a "game" is, of course, to develop skills in following verbal directions which can be carried over into following printed directions.

Later, when children can read, pairs of children can play a similar game, with one child reading the directions to and checking on the accuracy of performance of the other child.

It is not too difficult to devise reading materials specifically designed to foster skill in following directions in a real-life situation, for example, you might give the child the following printed instructions for assembling three gears.

> Put the largest gear on a peg, and insert small end of the peg into the hole marked 7.
>
> Place the smallest gear on a peg and insert the small end of the peg into the hole marked 3.
>
> Place the middle-sized gear on a peg and insert the small end of the peg into the pegboard in a position between the two gears, so that all its teeth mesh with the teeth of the other two gears.
>
> If you follow these directions, all three gears will move when you turn one of them.

Of course, the child must reach a certain physical and mental maturity to follow these particular printed directions, and you should have on hand working facsimiles of the gears for the child to handle.

Printed directions for fostering reading comprehension in the applicative mode can be devised for any number of operations, from rules for games, to cooking recipes, to operating a tape recorder, and so on. The important thing is to teach the children that directions must be correctly comprehended before they can be correctly followed.

It is fun and productive to discuss with older children why some people, even adults, have so much trouble following printed directions. Is it because some people are just plain stubborn and want to do things "their way"? "When all else fails, then try reading the directions" seems to be the motto of a lot of do-it-yourselfers. Or could it be that some printed directions just aren't very clear (even when they're not written in Japanese)? Here is a chance to remind the youngsters that comprehension is a two-way street, that it depends on the writer as well as the reader. Bad writing makes for bad comprehension; a lesson to keep in mind in their own writing exercises.

Problem Solving Actions have consequences, and sometimes these consequences present problems that must be solved. Children are aware of this truism, but they need to be taught that reading materials can sometimes supply answers to personal problems or at least lead to a better understanding of them. Again, they need to be made aware that what they learn in their reading may be applied to their own everyday lives and that, indeed, in many cases there may be specific reading material designed to aid in solving specific problems. This, of course, can be a powerful incentive for reading in general. More to the point here, it can provide the teacher with many opportunities for reading instruction within the applicative mode of comprehension.

Elementary school children do have many problems to solve, some more serious than others. Here are some of the problems children in the elementary grades frequently face: "What if I get a pet?" "What if I go swimming alone?" "What if I get a paper route?" "What if I try out for the team and don't make it?" "What if I go to the new skateboard park?" "What if I leave home?" "What if I stay out nights with older boys?" "What if I cheat?" "What if I steal?" "What if I deface or destroy something?" "What if I copy someone else's homework?" "What if I repeat rumors?" "What if I try drugs?" "What if I 'take off' in someone's car without permission?" "What if my mother and father get a divorce and we have to move somewhere else?" "What if I don't report a crime I know about?" "What if I don't attract boys?" "What if I'm too fat or too skinny?" "What if I don't know how to dance?" "What if I feel uncomfortable with girls?" "What if I don't seem to fit in with the crowd?" The list could go on and on.

Reading may not supply instant answers to such "what if's," but it can help the child to see how other people handle or handled similar problems and to anticipate probable consequences of doing or not doing this or that or of being or not being this or that kind of person.

Encourage the child to look for solutions to and better understanding of their own personal problems through reading. In other words, help them to apply their reading to their everyday lives. This requires that an abundance of varied reading resources be available to the child. It also requires a creative and resourceful teacher.

Let us suppose that one of the older children in your class is in the "what if?" stage about buying a motor scooter or Moped. The child already knows that there are certain consequences involved in buying, owning, and riding a motor scooter and is looking for answers to questions about these consequences. Ask the child what kind of questions he or she has in mind and then guide the youngster toward reading materials that can help answer them. For example:

"How heavy a scooter do I want?"
(Reading about horsepower, weight, velocity, maximum speed of scooters, etc.)

"What will happen when other people ask for rides or to 'try out' my scooter?"
(Reading stories about borrowing, about losing fair-weather friends when one no longer has anything to share.)

"What maintenance chores are necessary? Will I be able to do these myself? How much will maintenance cost?"
(Reading maintenance manuals and repair manuals.)

"What are the traffic ordinances that control operation of a motor scooter by one of my age?"

(Reading of traffic ordinances.)

"What about antinoise ordinances that prohibit revving up scooter motors? (Reading of antinoise and environmental ordinances.)

"What risks are involved? What is the safety record of motor scooters?"

(Reading of newspaper accounts of accidents, bulletins from the National Safety Council, etc.)

"How much will insurance cost, *if* I can get it?"

(Reading insurance regulations and insurance company brochures.)

"How can I secure my scooter from theft?"

(Reading articles on the incidence of such thefts, methods used to steal scooters, and problems of security.)

"How much will it really cost to own a motor scooter? Can I afford it?"

(Readings on costs of time payments, finance charges, resale value, cost of accessories, etc.)

The child may not need or want to read *all* these specific materials. The child might, indeed, find materials better suited to his or her purpose than the ones you've chosen. If so, rejoice. You have succeeded in teaching the child the value of reading for comprehension within the applicative mode.

THE CRITICAL MODE OF READING COMPREHENSION

Critical is derived from the Greek, *krites* (a judge), and, thus, implies judgment. Comprehension within the critical mode involves making value judgments about information gleaned from reading. It involves questions of "right" and "wrong," of "truth" and "falsity." At its simplest level, it involves separating fact from fiction.

Children are inclined to take what they read literally. They must be guided toward realization that the printed page may contain more (or sometimes less) than meets the eye. In short, they must be taught that comprehension involves judgment of what is read.

Value judgments are, of course, based on experience and sophisticated value judgments come only with maturity. But even very young children can and do make simple judgments, which are no less valid for being "simple." Your task as a reading teacher is to help the child sharpen his or her judgmental skills by teaching the child to apply them to reading.

Fairy tales and similar highly imaginative stories provide excellent opportunities for teaching young children to read within the critical mode of comprehension. Most such stories are basically good-versus-evil stories, a universal theme readily understood even by very young children. Teach the children to go beneath the surface of the story; to bring their critical judgment to bear on the story:

"Did the wicked witch deserve to perish?"

"Did the good fairy deserve to triumph?"

"Was it right for the king to shut the princess up in the tower?"

Help the children judge the story characters in light of their own experiences:

"Do you know anyone who sometimes acts like the bad wolf in this story?"

"Do you ever act like one of the wicked stepsisters in this story?

In short, help the children see that storybook judgments have relevance to real-life judgments.

"Are the facts as presented here consistent with your understanding of the subject?"

"Does the writer present both sides of the question?"

"Does the writer leave out facts that might otherwise weaken his or her argument."

Questions in this vein will help the children realize that reading is not a passive process, that it is, in a sense, a dialogue between writer and reader in which the reader passes judgment upon what the writer has written.

Materials for instruction in the critical mode of comprehension should not, of course, be limited to fairy tales and argumentation pieces. Critical judgment must be brought to bear on all reading—fiction, nonfiction, poetry, and so on. Teach the child to be on the lookout for hidden meanings, inferences, and other such subtleties in all reading materials. Teach the child to be aware that a writer's background may be relevant to reader judgments. (Is the writer a consumer advocate? A labor leader? A clergyman?) Help the child develop a critical mind-set toward all reading. Without such a mind-set, comprehension is stunted at its source.

Here are some questions illustrative of those used in the critical mode of reading comprehension:

"Is this like I know it?"

(Is this consistent with experience?)

"Is this important?"

(Is this relevant or irrelevant?)

"Is the writer really answering the question, or is the writer just saying words to mix us up?"

"Is the writer evading the question?

"Is the writer trying to get us off the track and mix us up?"

"Is the writer creating a 'smokescreen' or a 'paper dragon' to divert thinking from the main issue?"

"Are these real facts or just what the author thinks?"
(Is this fact or opinion?)

"What is the writer really saying without saying it?"

"Are the writers trying to sell us on their idea?"
(Is this a promotional "snow job"?)

"I think maybe the writer is being paid by someone to write these ideas."
(What are the motives behind this?)

"Do you agree with the writer . . . do you think the writer is telling the truth?"
(Does this violate my own values?)

These are key questions that would have to be restated in simple language for children. The child is not asked to criticize the author's credentials, but to analyze and compare the content of the reading material with the child's own knowledge of reality and his/her values.

"What other story does this remind you of?"

"What are the good points that the author brings out?"

"What things did the author say that you can agree with?"

"What things can you add to what the author has said?"

"The author is writing against the idea . . . what can you say in favor of the idea?"

"What things in the author's life made him/her write this article (or story)?" . . . "If those things had happened to you, could you have written a story like this, too?" . . . "What would you have put into your article (or story)?"

"Can you understand why the author wrote as he/she did?"

"Do you think this article will help the cause?"

"Is it good to have another side of the story?"

"Suppose we had only read the other side of the story, what wouldn't we have known?"

THE AFFECTIVE MODE OF READING COMPREHENSION

We come now to the last of our six modes of comprehension, the affective mode. In our discussion of the first five modes, we have concentrated primarily on the "analytic" aspects of comprehension. In this section we will discuss its "emotive" nature. When we speak of the affective mode, we are speaking of feelings and emotions triggered by the mental process we call reading. Just how this occurs, we can leave to future research. That it does occur, there can be no doubt. What we read can make us clench our teeth, can increase our heartbeat, make us tense our muscles. It can make us smile or frown, laugh or cry. Our topic, however, is not the physiological manifestations of emotion, but its role in fostering and/or intensifying comprehension.

Can we really "teach" comprehension within the affective mode? Can we really "instruct" children how to "feel"? Strictly speaking, of course not. Emotions are very personal and, for some children, very private experiences. What we can do is expose the children to a wide variety of emotionally appealing reading materials, encourage their emotional involvement with what they read, encourage their open expression of this involvement (when appropriate), and help them channel their feelings and emotions toward a better understanding of the values, attitudes, and beliefs of the world in which they live.

Materials for Reading Comprehension in the Affective Mode   Finding reading materials with which children can become emotionally involved is not a difficult task. Professional writers of literature for children are well aware that their work must be relevant to the interests of children if it is to be accepted by them as something other than a chore to get through. Children, as do all of us, respond to the universal themes—love and affection, overcoming of obstacles to success and happiness, the triumph of good over evil, and so on—that are found in most of the reading designed specifically for use in kindergarten through the elementary school years. If we want children to be *affected* by the books they read, shouldn't we concentrate on the selection of books that speak in *universals?*

Stories must be about goals and desires that correspond to those of the young readers. For example, children, even in the readiness year, know that money can buy things that are nice to have; hence, money is to be desired as a means for enriching the quality of life. (A recent survey indicates that money is at the top of children's lists of values.) Children's desires are similar to those of adults and run a wide range of needs and wants: wealth, happiness, love, attention, success, acceptance, popularity, and so on. However, the younger the child, the more *concrete* is the desire: a particular kind of toy, ice cream, candy, fun at a particular place such as a ride on the carrousel, a particular kind of pet, a particular kind of trike, bike, wagon, skates, or "wheels."

The desires of other children may be concentrated on the "things" of their culture; especially the "things other kids have." Depending, of course, upon the peculiarities of geographic region and/or season, these can be such things as specific sports equipment (baseball, football, soccer, Rugby, skating, basketball, hockey, fishing, snorkeling, skiing, surfboarding, etc). Sports stories, consequently, are high on any list of older children's favorites.

To be liked and to have friends is a universal desire of normal individuals, especially young children, and this theme may account for the perennial popularity of the little story, *Will I Have a Friend?* with preschoolers just about to enter Kindergarten.

The elementary school child's need for affection and love finds expression in a number of ways, especially by his or her affection for animal pets. This is reflected in preferences for reading about animals and the popularity of the animal "classics": *Blaze; Rudolph, the Red-Nosed Reindeer; Bambi; Lassie; Black Stallion; My Friend, Flicka; Silver Stallion; Lightning; Sounder; King of the Wind; The Incredible Journey; Big Red; The Yearling;* and the New Zealand award-winning book, *David of the High Country.* The love theme is largely the reason for the popularity of *Heidi, Grandfather and I; Grandmother and I; My Mother is the Most Beautiful Woman in the World;* and *Swiftwater.*

Series Books A large percentage of children become enamoured with books in a particular theme or in a series, becoming avid reader-fans of the *Hardy Boys, Cowboy Sam, Morgan Bay Mysteries, Nancy Drew, Bobbsey Twins* (yes, they are still around! and are updated), *American Adventure Series, Childhood of Famous Americans, Cherry Ames, Sue Barton,* and so on.

Every children's librarian knows scores of boys and girls who have become so fixated on the fabulous achievement of the characters in their favorite series that they have devoured every book in the series before moving on to something else. Such dedication to what, obviously, is a recurring theme and almost-identical plot should reveal to parents, teachers, and librarians that the child has an enormous *need* to be satisfied and satiated. Older children's needs are many: adventure, excitement, achievement, importance, status, success, acceptance as an equal with adults, self-fulfillment, a coming-of-age.

These are *real* needs, even though they seldom, if ever, can be verbalized by children; indeed, they should not be! They are real needs that are not being satisfied in the normal activities of everyday life. Therefore, they must be satisfied vicariously. How better it is for the child to be living these experiences through books in series such as listed above than through violent TV, movies, or crime, itself!

How often, too, do parents, teachers, and librarians fail to realize that children's needs, like hunger, gnaw at the very center of their beings; all the while, the child must remain silent, afraid to cry out, "I'm hungry; I need . . . I need . . .!" Society, in its blundering efforts to polish children with a facade of maturity forces boys and girls to hide these essential psychological, emotional, and experiential internal urgencies:

"Why don't you read something else for a change?"

"Haven't you read enough *Nancy Drew* mysteries?"

"Stop bringing home those trashy books . . . they're all alike!"

"We don't read series books in *our* classroom . . . they are *not* good literature!"

"You will become lopsided if you read more of those awful *Bobbsey Twins* books!"

Consider how incongruous it is that those who criticize series books for children may be those same adults who maintain a rigorous weekly TV ritual with their "favorite series," are regular purchasers of the latest in their favorite mystery series, attend the same Bridge club weekly, golf with the same cronies on the same course regularly, and/or spend specific never-to-be-interrupted periods viewing the weekly sports program on TV year-in-and-year-out! The regularity of *series*, like vitamins, apparently provides children with their "minimum daily requirements" for normalized, healthy mental and emotional homeostasis.

Children's series are popular because they satisfy needs that otherwise would be repressed, only to find outlet through less desirable channels. Consequently, we must not depreciate the role that series books play in the affective mode. How do we know what children yearn to read and/or experience? We know that the motivation for reading (as for all learning) is self-improvement. The child must see himself or herself as being something better, greater, more effective, more acceptable, more knowledgeable, more skillful, more powerful, more loveable, more *something*. Without this desire for self-fulfillment, learning is but an empty ritual, a fraud, a travesty. Reading materials must, therefore, be relevant to the interests, problems, desires, and lifestyles of today's children and youth. Inasmuch as children's interests undulate with the winds of time and especially with current TV offerings, today's listings of children's interests will not likely be accurate for tomorrow.

There are, however, some common elements in the interests of children that appear to be timeless, even though emphasis this year may be more on one facet than on all equally. Those currently most common are:

Money; pets; animals (especially horses and dogs); *sports; love* (not Hollywood style); *strength* (admiration of friends); *excitement; adventure; good character* (few want to be "bad guys"); *peace in the world; travel.*

These are the prime interests that we have researched and identified. You may wish to survey children today to see the *specific* interests that are current under each of these categories. The following survey will help in that effort. It will provide clues to what their reading interests will be, too.

SELF-SATISFACTION QUESTIONNAIRE

What subjects do you like best in school? (If none, write "NONE")

1.
   Why?
2.
   Why?

What three things do you do almost every day after school; or in your spare time, or during holidays?

1.
2.
3.

If it were possible for you to get your wish, what things would you *rather do* after school, or in your spare time, or during holidays?

1.
2.
3.

What three TV programs do you like best?

1.
2.
3.

Name three books that you have read and liked.

1.
2.
3.

Name three magazines (or comic books) that you like best.

1.
2.
3.

What are the three best movies you have ever seen?

1.
2.
3.

Humor and Satire Humor depends entirely upon comparison for its effectiveness. The grossly distorted and ludicrous has to be compared with the child's own awareness of reality. The child subconsciously is answering the question, "What is so funny?"

"Why is this funny?"

"Would you think it was funny if it happened to you?"

"Is it only funny when it happens to someone else?"

Teachers must be alert to new books that provide humor for children. A child who lives entirely in the world of serious facts, never enjoying the humorous, the ludicrous, or the incongruous, may become an individual who is stern, severe, unflinching, and hard to live with.

Values, Standards, and Attitudes Psychologists sometimes use the term "significant others" to refer to those who serve as primary models for behavior—parents, teachers, close peers, and so on. Our values and attitudes are also influenced by such persons. In reading within the affective mode of comprehension, characters in novels and stories can become "significant others" for the child. Affective reading can help a child comprehend what it means to be loved, detested, lied to, bullied, appreciated, scorned, what it means to be an only child, a sick child, a Black child in a White society, and so on. With such empathy comes a widening of the reader's moral and ethical horizons.

Indeed, if we had to sum up reading for comprehension in the affective mode in a single word, *empathy* might well be that word. Encourage the child to empathize with characters and situations in stories and novels. Encourage them to explore how they "feel" toward what they have read. Probe, gently if need be, but probe. "Did it make you feel angry to read how the white storekeeper treated Tommy just because he was a black child?" "Were you happy when Jane finally got the new dress she wanted?" "Did you feel like crying when Mary was so sick?" "Did you feel guilty when Bob's mother and father worried why he didn't come home on time because sometimes *you* don't come home when you're supposed to?"

Factual Materials in Affective Reading Reading in the affective mode is not, of course, confined to reading of fiction. Nonfiction materials can also be used effectively, especially with older children. Children can and should become emotionally involved in all reading. Factual materials about tragedies and triumphs, about disasters and about disasters avoided, about happy occasions and sad occasions must all be read within the affective mode for full comprehension. Help the child to realize that facts need not be dull. Facts are dull only when they fail to excite the emotions.

Bibliotherapy The relatively new discipline of *bibliotherapy* is based upon the reasoned assumption that carefully guided reading can be a therapeutic tool in the treatment of personal inadequacies and other emotional problems. A story or factual piece about a handicapped child, for example, can help a handicapped child deal with the personal problems and emotional stress that may accompany a physical handicap—*if* the reader strongly identifies with the character or situation that is being read about.

Reading has also been used as an adjunct to psychiatric treatment for its cathartic effect in helping to ameliorate psychological maladjustment. Here again the key to success is the patient's ability to identify with situations and characters in the reading material used in the therapy.

The very fact that such therapy can be effective should lead us to conclude that what we guide children to read and how we guide them to comprehend what they read can obviously have important and lifelong consequences.

The Significance of the "Affective Domain" Everything a child hears, sees, reads, or otherwise experiences, is part of him or her forever, provided it *affects* him or her. The recall of hidden past feelings is the basis for effective therapy by psychoanalysis. Brain surgeons, such as the noted Dr. Wilber Penfield, have demonstrated that meaningful experiences in an individual's life lie deeply buried in one's memory bank, ready to be retrieved under proper conditions.

This is, indeed, scary! For its significance lies in the fact that the experiences a child has can *affect* him/her for life whenever those experiences are meaningful enough to foster *feelings*. This is the *affective* domain. Because attitudes, concepts, values, and beliefs (and prejudices, as well) spring from feelings, we adults should be constrained by our better judgment to assure that children have the finest affective reading materials. This does not imply that all stories should portray a rosy picture of life. In fact we would be distorting reality and doing an injustice to limit available reading materials to a diet of "They lived happily every after" stories.

Great literature is the result of long hours, days, months, years of work by a great artist! It is "great" because it addresses itself to the realities of life and the emotions that they generate.

Into stories, poems, and plays are woven words and phrases that denote mood, tone, imagery, and rhythm. Some teachers attempt to create literary appreciation by analysis and dissection of the artist's art. Such efforts are, of course, futile, for mood, tone, imagery, and rhythm are psychological stimuli; not mechanical devices.

Children sense mood, tone, imagery, and rhythm, especially when a story is skillfully read to them. That is why poems should *always* be read to children, and plays should be done orally.

You will find that when you have selected just the *right* story; have practiced it to perfection so that mood, tone, imagery, and rhythm can be *felt*; and have done a perfect job of reading it to the children, it will end in a hushed, enthralled silence which must not be violated with some stupid question, for, invariably, a little voice will break the spell, almost in a whisper, saying, "Read it again, Teacher!"

It is *then* that you will *know* that you have *arrived* as a great teacher!

There is but one measure of the *quality* of the reading experience, and that is the depth of feeling that results as the reader identifies with the experiences and feelings of a storybook character.

Comprehending within the affective mode is entirely a physio-psychological phenomenon. It is a transactional process in which the author ascribes experiences and feelings to the storybook characters, which, in turn, are experienced and felt emotionally by the reader who identifies with his/her favorite character. Because of this transaction, reading materials have the potential for affecting children's personalities, attitudes, concepts, beliefs, prejudices, and values for life!

250 PATTERNS OF COMPREHENSION QUESTIONS ARRANGED ACCORDING TO CATEGORIES

1. Cause and Effect—Consequences

When _____ happened, then what happened?

What happened that made _____ happen?

Why do we sometimes do things without thinking about what might happen?

Can you think of reasons why _____ happened?

　Lets read on to find out if you are right.

Why did _____ try (to do something)?

Did _____ make plans just in case _____ happened?

If _____ had _____ (done this or that) would _____ have happened?

What was the reason that _____?

What is the reason for _____?

What did _____ do in order to (do something)?

What did _____ do in order to (get something)?

What did _____ do in order to (keep something from happening)?

Why did _____ decide that _____?

Why did _____ say that _____?

What did _____ say he would do if _____?

Although (such-and-such happened), what (good came out of it)?

Although (such-and-such happened), what worse could have happened?

2. Sequence of Events

What did _____ do when _____?

What happened first? Then what happened? etc.

What was the first thing she did? Then, the next thing?

What should she have done next? And then what should she have done?

If she had done that, how would things have turned out differently?

When this happened and that happened, then what would probably happen next? Lets read on to find out.

3. Value Judgments

What did _____ do that was selfish?

Was what _____ did to _____ a nice thing to do?

What would have been better to do?

Was _____ right to (punish so-and-so)?

Was _____ right to run away from home?
What would you have done instead?

What happens when we say we will do something and then don't do it?

How does it affect us? How does it affect others?

Do we always _____?

When is it good to pretend?

When is it good to make plans?
What happens when we make impossible plans?
What is impossible?

What happens if we pretend all the time?

What happened to _____ in the story when she daydreamed?

What happens if we daydream *all* the time?

Did she like to __(do that)__? Why? (Why not?)

Would you have done that?   (reasons).

When someone gossips like _____ in the story, what happens?

Now that we have learned about (something from a factual article), what should we do about it? (What action can we take?)

Now that we have read the article, which side is right?

When someone quotes someone else ''out of context'' (without telling everything that she said) what is the purpose?
Is that an honest thing to do?

Are the people in the story ''different''? How?
Are we better than people who are different?
What can we learn from people who are ''different''?

When we watch TV, or see a movie, or read a book, how do we know that the story is ''good''?

Why do some people like one story and others do not?

What kind of story do you feel is "good"?

4. Characterization—Types of Persons

What kind of a person was _____?

Who in the story showed the greatest kindness for animals?

What are some of the things that _____ did that made him/her disliked by the others?

Who in the story would you most like to be with?

Who in the story was brave? What did he/she do that was a brave thing?

Why was _____ such a mean character?
   What changed him/her?

Can human nature be changed? What in the story makes you think so (not)?

What was _____ pretending to be in the story?
   Do people really believe him/her?

What happens when we are "found out" to be pretending to be something we really aren't?

When _____ said he/she would <u>do something</u>, did he/she have any intention of doing it?

How do we know that a person is really trustworthy?

What are the things that _____ did that showed lack of dependability?

Select a child to read a sequence containing conversation, with the purpose of showing the characterization of the persons speaking in the conversation.

5. Sensitivity—Identification with Another's Problems/Feelings

How did _____ feel when _____?
   How could you have made him/her feel better?

What did _____ want? How could you have helped him/her to get it? Would it have been good if he/she had been able to get it?

Why did _____ want to _____?

How did _____ in the story make you feel?
   What did you want to do because of it?

Does _____ make you feel happy?

Does _____ make you feel sad?

Does _____ make you feel excited?

Does _____ make you feel disappointed?

Would you like to be like _____ in the story?

What do you think can be done about _____?
   (This calls for a sensitivity for a problem explained in an informational article.)

How did _____ "poke fun" at _____?
   What happens to us when we "poke fun" at another person?
   Why do people try to belittle others?
   What happens to the other person?
   What do people think who hear us "poking fun" at another?

How can we have a joke without belittling another?

Do ethnic jokes belittle others?

What kind of person will feel better (more self esteem) by reading this book?

Can you remember when you felt like the character in the story? What did you do to overcome that feeling?

How did _____ try to make _____ feel badly?
   (feel good; feel guilty; feel a nuisance;
   feel a bother; feel important; feel naughty)?

Why do we like (or not like) animal stories?
   (*or* fairy tales; stories about adventure; love; sports; excitement; crime; murder; mystery; horror; boys; girls; families; problems; inner city ghetto; gangs; long-ago; poor people; rich people; etc)?

6. Literal Information

Who?   What?   When?   Where?

How many? How much? How?

How many (people; things; etc) were there?

When did _____?

What did (so-and-so) do?

Where was the _____ found?

Where was _____ taken?

How did _____ discover _____?

What took so long?

How did _(so-and-so)_ in the story train to be a champion?

Why did _____ give up?

Why does it take so long?
   Is it worth it?

If you want to become a _____, what training is necessary?

Where did they find the _____?

When did _____ see the _____?

How long will it be until _____ happens?

Where did _____ live?
    What kind of a place was that?

How did _____ hurt _____?

7. Main Ideas—Details

What is the main idea in the article we just read?
    (See components of main idea described in
    Chapter 8, "Reading/Study Skills")

What are the details that tell us more about the main idea?

How many main ideas are there in the article?
    How can there be more than one?

Suggest a title that states the main idea.

Read the sentence that states the main idea.

8. Problem Solving

_____ in the story had a problem. How did he/she solve it?

What would have happened if he/she hadn't solved it that way?

We see in this story how _____ solved the _(problem)_.
    How can that help us when we have the same problem?

Is it possible that we may someday have the same problem that _____ had in the story?

Why didn't _____ believe that _____ would happen to him/her?

What do we often think will happen to other people, but won't happen to us?
    Why don't we think it will happen to us?

Why did _(this happen)_?

Why did _(person)_ do _(the same thing)_ every day at the same time?

Do you know anyone who got into the same trouble?

What should a person do to avoid getting into such trouble?

How could that problem have been different?

How could that problem have been avoided (prevented)?

How could that problem have been stopped?

How could that problem have been changed?

How could the situation have been improved?

What can we do to solve our own problems?

What can we do to prevent problems from happening to us?

9. Imagination/Reality

Is this a true story?

Are the people in this story "real"?

Could the people in the story have been real people?

Why do fairy tales always turn out good?
    Is life like that?
    If life isn't like that, why do we like fairy tales?
    What other stories do we like for the same reasons?

How do we know that _____ is true (probably true)?

What things in the story tell us what life was like in <u>(place)</u> (or time)?

Would you liked to have lived there (then)?

When and where was (is) (will be) the best time and place to live?

Is there a Utopia?
    What is it like?

What do you imagine it was like to have lived in _____? (or time)?

Is it possible that _____ could happen today?
    What would you do if it did?

What kind of stories do grown-ups read that are like fairy tales for them? (escape, identification, etc.)

What really are *giants, fairys, goblins, ghosts, elves, witches, sorcerers, Brownies, gnomes, Menihunis* sprites, *Pixies*?

What stories have you read in which they were characters? What did they do?

Do you think they ever existed? Do you think they exist now?

How are they used in stories that you like?
    What do they really mean to us?

10. Implied Meanings; Evidence; Generalizations

What proof do we have that _____ is true?

Are there such things as _____? Proof? Hearsay?

Do you agree that _____?

Why do you think _____ was surprised?

How did it happen that _____ (did this) rather than what was expected?

What makes you think that _____ was a "bad guy"?

If we know <u>(this)</u> and <u>(this)</u> and <u>(this)</u>, then what can we conclude? (Generalizations)
    Would that *always* be true?

Why is _____ willing to take this risk?

Would you?

Why did _____ help that person?
Do you think you would under the circumstances?

Why do you think _____ was willing to give up _____?
Do you think you would, too?

What makes you think that _____ will (do something) ?

In your experience, do you think that _____ was acting sensibly? Why? Why not?

Why do you think that people didn't like what he did?
Who do you think was right? Why?

How do you think that _____ could have acted against what the majority of the people thought he/she should do?

Who was right?

Do you think _____ liked to _____?
(do something)
What proof do you have of that conclusion?

How can you tell that a certain person is from a different place or different part of the world?
In the story, where do you think _____ was from?

How do you suppose that _____ knew _____
(person)   (something that was supposed to be

_____?
a secret)

What do you think happened to the _____?

Where would you start to look for it if you were asked to find it?

What makes you think that _____ had outside help?

At this point in the story, who do you think is the murderer?

11. Vocabulary, Word Meanings, Synonyms, Loaded Phrases

What does that word mean to you?

When _____ used the word, _____, what did he/she really mean?
(word)

When we hear the word _____, what ideas, places, scenes, and/or people come to mind?

What words are "sound" words that create a feeling when we hear them pronounced all in a string? (Onomatopoeia).

Read from the story some set of words and tell what or how they made you feel.

Do you think the author put them in for that purpose?

Compare _____ with _____.

Contrast _____ with _____.

    Can you see why the author used (*that word*) instead of _____?

In what ways are _____ and _____ similar? (Different)?

    (This question can be used to develop synonyms)

Read this word alone. What does it mean alone?

    Now read it in the sentence in the story. What does

    it mean in the sentence? Why are they different meanings?

What happens when people quote words and/or sentences

without telling the whole story?

    Is that a form of lying? Deceit? Omission?

    Why do people do this?

Why, in the story (or article) is _____ a most important word?

Why is _____ an important symbol? What does it mean to _____

                                                               (a particular

_____?

group of people)

What in their experience makes it have a special meaning?

    What other words could you use to say the same thing?

What does it mean to (do something)?

    (Interpretation of an idiomatic expression)

    Example: "Bump the bell" (Ring the doorbell).

Why do we use _____ to mean _____?

                (word)

    Example: Why do we call ground beef in a bun, a "hamburger"?

What words of ours do people in other places in the world (with other languages) use just like we do?

    Why do you think they use our words?

What does it mean "to _____"?

What is the different between _____ and _____?

Where did _____ come from?

              (word)

    What did it originally mean? How do we use it today?

    Why do you think the meaning changed?

What is a _____?

            (slang or coloquialism)

    What word could we use instead and still mean the same?

What is _____?   Homophone?

    What is another word that sounds the same,

    but has a different meaning?

    Here are two words in the story that are spelled

exactly alike. Why are their meanings different?

What word in the story is the opposite of _____?

What word in the story is the real key to the _____?
(situation or mood)

What is the significance of this word as the author used it?

Why did the author repeat _____ several times?

What words did the author use that came from other places in the world?

What words in the story convey meanings, moods, motives?

What words are put into the article to make us have "feelings"? What do we mean by "Loaded words"?

What are the words "loaded" with? (Hostility, feelings, untruths, half-truths, hate, etc.)

What is propaganda? How can we detect propaganda?

12. Picture Evidence

How does the picture tell us what time in the year it is?

What season of the year is it?

Where in the world does the picture show the story will take place?

From the picture, what do you think the story (or article) is about?

What is unusual about the picture?

What are the people doing in the picture?

Does the picture make you want to read the story (or not)?

Is the picture of something real or something we just think about?

Is it the way you think things should look?

At what point are we "standing" as we look at the place (or things that are happening) in the picture?

What clues does the picture give us?

Would you enjoy the story more (or less) if it didn't have pictures?

13. Creative Reading—Extending the Story

What was the most exciting part of the story?

How would you have felt if the story had turned out differently?

What do you think will happen next?

Let's turn the page and read on to find out.

How could this story be made into a play? (Movie)?

Could this poem be expressed in a picture, or sculpture?

Could this story be made into a poem (song)?
> What kind of song (Country music, etc?)

What other stories (poems) have been made into works of art to express the same feelings?

When the author wrote the story, what kind of experiences do you think he/she had had as background for the story?

If you had had the same experiences, could you have written a story like this?

How would you have changed the story? Why?

The story ended . . . but, if it was to go on, what things do you think would probably happen?

Would you like for the story to have gone on?
> Or did it end just at the right time?

Why doesn't this story end by telling what really happened to the characters in the end?

What did you already have to know to have enjoyed (or (understood) the story (poem; article; play)?

If you were to write a story something like the one you just read, how would it be different?

If you were to write a story on the same subject (theme) as the one you have just read, what would your story be?

Use the story you have just read to think of some good titles for other stories. (They don't have to be on the same theme; just whatever comes to mind).
> Which of those titles would be your favorite?

If you like to read stories, perhaps someday right here in this class, *you* will begin to write one yourself!

BIBLIOGRAPHY

Agrast, Charlotte, "Teach Them How to Read Between the Lines," *Grade Teacher*, **85** (1967), 72–74.

Anderson, Richard C., "How to Construct Achievement Tests to Assess Comprehension," *Review of Educational Research* **42** (1972), 145–170.

Aschner, Mary Jane, "An Analysis of Verbal Interaction in the Classroom," in *Theory and Research in Teaching*, New York: Columbia University Press, 1963.

Aukerman Robert C., *Approaches to Beginning Reading*, New York: Wiley, 1971.

Aulls, Mark W., "Relating Reading Comprehension and Writing Competency," *Language Arts*, **52**:6 (1975), 808–812.

Barclay, J.R., "The Role of Comprehension in the Remembering of Sentences," *Cognitive Psychology,* **4** (1973), 229–254.

Barrett, Thomas C., "Taxonomy of Cognitive and Affective Dimensions of Reading Comprehension," in NSSE Yearbook, Part II, University of Chicago Press, 1968, 19–23.

Beck, Helen, *Don't Push Me, I'm No Computer,* New York: McGraw Hill, 1976.

Brooks, Penelope H., Drew J. Arnold, and Maria Iacobbo, "Some Cognitive Aspects of Reading Comprehension," *Peabody Journal of Education,* **54**:3 (1977), 146–153.

Ruth K. Carlson, *Folklore and Folktales Around the World,* Newark, DE: International Reading Association, 1972.

Carroll, John B., "Defining Language Comprehension" in *Language Comprehension and the Acquisition of Knowledge.* Washington, DC: Winston, 1972, 1–29.

Carroll, John B., and Roy O. Freedle (Editors), *Language Comprehension and the Acquisition of Knowledge,* Washington, DC: Winston, 1972. This is one of the important current compendiums of collected essays on language, memory, and comprehension.

Clay, Marie M., *A Diagnostic Survey: The Early Detection of Reading Difficulties* Auckland: Heinemann Educational Books, 1972.

Cognition: International Journal of Cognitive Psychology, Elsevier Sequoia SA, P.O. Box 851, Lausanne 1, Switzerland.

Culhane, Joseph W., "CLOZE Procedures and Comprehension," *Reading Teacher,* **23**:5 (1970), 410–413.

Cunningham, James W., "Metaphor and Reading Comprehension," *Journal of Reading Behavior,* **8**:4 (1976), 363–368.

Davis, Frederick B., "Psychometric Research on Comprehension in Reading," Project No. 2, U. S. D HEW, Washington, DC, 1971, Project 0.9030, pp. 8–60.

Davis, Frederick B., "Psychometric Research on Comprehension in Reading," *Reading, Research Quarterly,* **7**:4 (1972), 628–678. For almost 40 years, Davis has been researching within the field of reading. This is a significant summary of much of the research in the area of comprehension. Davis concluded that comprehension is "largely dependent on knowledge of word meanings and on ability to reason in verbal terms." (p. 663)

Davidson, Jessica, *Is That Mother in the Bottle?* New York: Franklin Watts, 1972.

Downing, John, "The Cognitive Clarity of Learning to Read," in *Literacy at All Levels,* Vera Southgate, (Editor), London: Ward Lock Educational, 1971.

Edwards, Violet, *Group Leader's Guide to Propaganda Analysis*, New York: Institute for Propaganda Analysis, 1938.

Ekwall, Eldon E., "Informal Reading Inventories: The Instructional Level," *Reading Teacher*, **29**:7 (1976), 662–665.

Elkind, Davis, "Cognitive Development and Reading," *Clairmont Colleges Reading Conference Proceedings*, 1974.

Epstein, Sam and Beryl, *The First Book of Words*, New York: Watts, 1954.

Ernst, Margaret S., *Words*, New York: Knopf, 1954.

Estes, Thomas H. and Joseph L. Vaughan, Jr., "Reading Interest and Comprehension: Implications," *Reading Teacher*, **27**, (1973), 149–153.

Fagan, William T., "Transformations and Comprehension," *Reading Teacher*, **25**:2 (1971), 169–172.

Funk, Wilfred, *Six Weeks to Words of Power*, New York: Pocket Books, 1955.

Funk, Wilfred and Norman Lewis, *30 Days to a More Powerful Vocabulary*, New York: Funk, 1942.

Funk, Charles Earle, *Horsefeathers and other Curious Words*, New York: Harper and Row, 1958.

Gerhard, Christian, *Making Sense: Reading Comprehension Improved Through Categorizing*. Newark, DE, International Reading Association, 1975. This is actually a guide to writing paragraphs, reports, and essays, but is excellent in its suggestions for categorizing.

Geyer, John J., "Comprehension and Partial Models Related to the Reading Process," in *The Literature of Research in Reading With Emphasis on Models*, Frederick B. Davis (Editor), New Brunswick: Rutgers University School of Education, 1973, 167–199.

Glenn, Hugh W., "The Effect of Silent and Oral Reading on Literal Comprehension and Oral Reading Performance," Unpublished doctoral dissertation, University of Southern California, 1971.

Golinkoff, Roberta M., "A Comparison of Reading Comprehension Processes in Good and Poor Comprehenders," *Reading Research Quarterly*, **11**:4 (1975–1976), 623–659.

Golinkoff, Roberta M., and Richard Rosinski, "Decoding, Semantic Processing, and Reading Comprehension Skill," *Child Development*, **47** (1976), 252–258.

Gonzales, Phillip C. and David V Elijah, Jr., "Rereading: Effect on Error Patterns and Performance Levels on the IRI," *Reading Teacher*, **28**:7 (1975), 647–652.

Green, Richard T., *Comprehension in Reading: An Annotated Bibliography*, Newark, DE: International Reading Association, 1971.

Guthrie, John T., "Reading Comprehension and Syntactic Responses in Good and Poor Readers," *Journal of Educational Psychology*, **65**:3 (1973), 294–299. Guthrie reported that his research indicates that "the comprehension of verbs and function words in silent reading is determined by syntactic clues, while the comprehension of nouns and modifiers appears to rely upon semantic clues." (p. 298)

Guthrie, John T., Mary Seifert, Nancy A. Burnham, and Ronald I. Caplan, "The Maze Technique to Assess, Monitor Reading Comprehension," *Reading Teacher*, **28**:2 (1974), 161–168.

Guthrie, John T. (Editor), *Cognition, Curriculum, and Comprehension*, Newark, DE: International Reading Association, 1977. This is a compendium of the talks given by the research scholars who presented papers and rebuttals at the seminar on research on reading comprehension in 1975, held in Newark Delaware. Because of the backgrounds of the presenters in cognitive psychology and psycholinguistics, the contents of this volume are not recommended for undergraduate students in the first course in reading.

Guszak, Frank J., "Teacher Questioning and Reading," *Reading Teacher*, **21** (1976), 227–234.

Guszak, Frank J., "Questioning Strategies of Elementary Teachers in Relation to Comprehension," *Reading and Realism, Proceedings of the International Reading Association* **13**:I (1968), 110–116. For a more detailed analysis of the types of questions used with low, average, and high groups, see:

Guszak, Frank J., *Relations Between Teacher Practice and Knowledge of Reading Theory in Selected Grade School Classes*. Madison, WI: U. S. Office of Education Report S-437, 1967,

Hunkins, Francis P., *Questioning Strategies and Techniques*, Boston: Allyn and Bacon, 1972.

Hunkins, Francis P., *Involving Students in Questioning*, Boston: Allyn and Bacon, 1976.

Hunt, Lyman C., Jr., "The Effect of Self-Selection, Interest, and Motivation upon Independent, Instructional, and Frustrational Levels," *Reading Teacher*, **24**:2 (1970), 146–151.

Jongsma, Eugene, *The Cloze Procedure as a Teaching Technique*, Newark, DE: International Reading Association, 1971.

Kender, Joseph P., "Informal Reading Inventories," *Reading Teacher*, **24**:2 (1970), 165–166.

Kennedy, Dolores, "The Cloze Procedure, Use It to Develop Comprehension," *Instructor* **84** (1974), 82–86.

Kintsch, Walter, and others, "Comprehension and Recall as a Function of Content Variables," *Journal of Verbal Learning and Verbal Behavior,* **14** (1975), 196–214.

Kintsch, Walter, "Reading Comprehension as a Function of Text Structure," in *Toward a Psychology of Reading,* Arthur S. Reber and Don L. Scarborough (Editors), Hillsdale, NJ: Earlbaum, 1977, 227–256.

Kintsch, Walter, "On Modeling Comprehension," *Educational Psychologist,* **14** (1979), 3–14.

Kleederman, Frances F., "Linguistic Applications to Reading Comprehension," *Reading World,* **15**:3 (1976), 151–160.

Lamb, George S., and John C. Towner, "The Portents of Reading," *Reading Teacher,* **28**:7 (1975), 638–642.

Lanier, Ruby Jeanne, and Anita P. Davis, "Developing Comprehension Through Teacher-Made Questions," *Reading Teacher,* **26**:2 (1972), 153–157.

Loftus, Elizabeth F., and Geoffrey R. Loftus, "On the Permanence of Stored Information in the Human Brain," *American Psychologist,* **35**:5 (1980), 409–420.

Lundsteen, Sara W., "Levels of Meaning in Reading," *Reading Teacher,* **28**:3 (1974), 268–272.

Mussen, Paul, Rosenzweig, et al. *Psychology,* Lexington, MA: Heath, 1973.

Neuwirth, Sharyn E., "A Look at Intersentence Grammar," *Reading Teacher,* **30**:1 (1976), 28–32.

Oaken, Robert, Morton Wiener, and Ward Cromer, "Identification, Organization, and Reading Comprehension of Good and Poor Readers," *Journal of Educational Psychology,* **62** (1971), 71–78.

Ohanian, Vera, "Cherished Books of Children: What Makes Them So?", *Elementary English,* **47** (1970), 946–952.

Oliver, Marvin E., "The Effect of High-Intensity Practice on Reading Comprehension," *Reading Improvement,* **10** (1973), 16–18.

Page, William D., and Gay Su Pinnell, *Teaching Reading Comprehension,* ERIC Clearing House on Reading and Communication and The National Council of Teachers of English, 1979.

Peller, Lili, "Daydreams and Children's Favorite Books," in *The Psychoanalytic Study of the Child,* **14** (1959), 414–433.

Penfield, Wilder and P. Perot, "The Brain's Record of Auditory and Visual Experience," *Brain,* **86** (1963) 595–596. Penfield's conclusions have been challenged by Loftus and Loftus.

Perfetti, Charles A., "Retrieval of Sentence Relations: Semantic Vs. Syntactic Deep Structure," *Cognition* **2**:1 (1974).

Perfetti, Charles A., and Thomas Higaboam, "The Relationship Between Single Word Decoding and Reading Comprehension Skill," *Journal of Educational Psychology*, **67** (1975), 461–469.

Perfetti, Charles A., and Susan Goldman, "Discourse Memory and Reading Comprehension Skill," *Journal of Verbal Learning and Verbal Behavior*, **15** (1976), 33–42.

Potter, Thomas C., and Gwenneth Rae, *Informal Reading Diagnosis,* Englewood Cliffs, NJ: Prentice-Hall, 1973.

Powell, William R., and Colin G. Dunkeld, "Validity of the IRI Reading Levels," *Elementary English*, **48** (1971), 637–642.

Raynor, Keith, "The Perceptual Span and Peripheral Cues in Reading," *Cognitive Psychology*, **7** (1975), 65–81.

Reid, Virginia M. (Editor), *Reading Ladders for Human Relations*, Washington, DC: American Council on Education, 1972. This excellent annotated bibliography is already in its 5th edition. It is a basic book in this area of affective mode of comprehension. Every teacher and librarian should have it!

Rowell, Elizabeth H., "Do Elementary School Students Read Better Orally or Silently?" *Reading Teacher*, **29** (1976), 367–370.

Ruddell, Robert B., and Arthur C. Williams, *A Research Investigation of a Literacy Teaching Model: Project DELTA.* Washington, DC: U. S. Office of Education, EDPA Project No. 005262, 1972.

Rystrom, Richard, "Toward Defining Comprehension; A Third Report," *Journal of Reading Behavior*, **3**:1 (1970–71), 20–28.

Sanders, Norris M., *Classroom Questions*, New York: Harper & Row, 1966.

Schaefer, Paul J., "The Effective Use of Questioning," *Reading World*, **15**:4 (1976), 226–231.

Schell, Leo M., "Promising Possibilities for Improving Comprehension," *Journal of Reading*, **15** (1972), 415–424.

Sherman, Jay L., "Contextual Information and Prose Comprehension," *Journal of Reading Behavior*, **8**:4 (1976), 369–380.

Schwartz, Elaine, and Alice Sheff, "Student Involvement in Questioning for Comprehension," *Reading Teacher*, **29,** (1975), 150–154.

Siler, Earl R., "The Effects of Syntactic and Semantic Constraints on the Oral Reading Performance of Second- and Fourth-Graders," *Reading Research Quarterly*, **9**:4 (1973–1974), 583–602.

Simons, Herbert D., "Reading Comprehension: The Need for a New Perspective," *Reading Research Quarterly,* **6**:3 (1971), 338–363.

Smith, Arthur E., "The Effectiveness of Training Students to Generate Their Own Questions Prior to Reading," in 22nd *Yearbook,* National Reading Conference, 1973 (Phil L. Nacke, Editor), 71–77.

Spearritt, Donald, "Identification of Subskills of Reading Comprehension by Maximum-Likelihood Factor Analysis," *Reading Research Quarterly,* **8**:1 (1972), 92–110.

Swenson, Ingrid, and Raymond W. Kulhavy, Adjunct Questions and the Comprehension of Prose by Children," *Journal of Educational Psychology,* **66** (1974, 212–215.

Thorndyke, Perry W., "Cognitive Structures in Comprehension and Memory of Narrative Discourse," *Cognitive Psychology,* **9**:1 (1977), 77–110.

Thorndike, Robert L., "Reading as Reasoning," *Reading Research Quarterly,* **9** (1973–1974), 135–147.

Valmont, William J., "Creating Questions for Informal Reading Inventories," *Reading Teacher,* **25**:6 (1972), 509–512. This article presents twenty guidelines for developing good effective questions for teacher-made informal reading inventories.

Weaver, Phyllis A., "Improving Reading Comprehension: Effects of Sentence Organization Instruction," *Reading Research Quarterly,* **15**:1 (1979), 129–146.

Willows, Dale M. "Reading Between the Lines: Selective Attention in Good and Poor Readers," *Child Development,* **45** (1974), 408–415.

Wolf, Willavene, Charlotte Huck, and Martha King, "The Critical Reading Ability of Elementary School Children," in *Critical Reading,* Martha L. King (Editor), Philadelphia: Lippincott, 1967. Similar article in *Reading Research Quarterly,* **3** (1968), 435–496.

Wolfram, Walt, "Extended Notions of Grammar and Reading Comprehension," *Journal of Reading Behavior,* **8**:3 (1976), 247–288.

Wulz, S. Vanost, "Comprehension Testing: Functions and Procedures," *The Reading Teacher,* **33**:3 (1979), 295–299.

CHAPTER EIGHT

How Do I Teach Reading-Study Skills?

Motivation
Getting Acquainted with Textbooks
  Titles
  Author
  Copyright
  Table of Contents
  Index
  Visuals
  Running Heads
  Appendix
  Glossary
  Meaning-Bearing Signals
Strategies for Teaching Reading-study Skills
  Survey
  Advance Organizers and Directed Reading Questions
  The 3-Rs
  Skimming
  Scanning
  Structure and Organization; a Reading-Study Skill
  Reading Rate
  Library Skills
Making Reading-Study Materials Available to Elementary School Children
Some Classroom Strategies for Helping Elementary School Children Utilize
    Informational Reading Materials and Reading-Study Skills

There are, in our opinion, three ultimate objectives for learning to read: for *enjoyment;* for *self-acutalization,* and for *information.* It is difficult, if not impossible, to draw a sharp distinction between those three, for reading for enjoyment is certainly self-enriching; reading for information is self-enriching and may also be enjoyable.

Reading for information requires some special reading skills and, consequently, some special teaching strategies for helping children acquire what are commonly called reading-study skills. In this chapter we present some of the means by which you may help children utilize previously learned reading skills to make their informational reading more efficient and more enjoyable.

MOTIVATION

Most young children seem to be obsessed with the desire to find out, to discover, to learn the why and wherefore of everything. We who daily communicate with young children are constantly bombarded with "Why?" and "How come?" Because children are thus self-motivated to learn, it should be a simple matter to transfer that motivation to reading an informational book that answers their questions of "Why?" and "How come?"

The first exposure some children have to an informational book is the moment a subject-matter textbook is distributed in the classroom. That moment can be one of discovery or one of disaster! In the latter case, we have all experienced occasions when we got the message: "This is it, get busy now and read your lesson."

It is certainly more effective if the first exposure to an informational textbook can involve some real sense of positive anticipation. To help this happen, you can anticipate what a child may expect in terms of what the book promises. Whether or not the new textbook appears to be a threat or a promise depends largely on what the teacher is able to do when it is first introduced to the children. Here is a suggestion of what seems to work quite well:

"Isn't this a *beautiful* book!"

"Look at those beautiful pictures! Each picture tells us something."

"We will know so much more and be a lot smarter by reading this book, for it tells us so many new things."

From this type of introduction, we move to having the children express personal anticipation of what the book or informational material will likely mean to them. Self-improvement is the personal goal to be sought. Anticipation of self-improvement is the intrinsic factor in motivation.

GETTING ACQUAINTED WITH TEXTBOOKS

TITLES

Some (perhaps most) textbook titles and chapter titles within the text are more or less prosaic, indicating merely the specific subject matter covered. Some, however, show a good deal of originality and can be used for classroom discussion to spark interest in the book.

"Why do you suppose this author calls her book *How We Were* instead of just plain *American History?*" "Why is Chapter 6 called 'The Iron Horse' when it's really about America's railroads?" "If you were writing a book about American History (or science, or government) what title would you give it?"

AUTHOR

Sometimes, knowledge about the author or authors of a book may help spark interest in a book. "This science book was written by an elementary school science teacher. Do you think this shows he has a good background for writing such a book? Do you suppose some famous scientist might write a textbook you'd like better? Why? Why not?" "This book about sports was written by two ladies. Do you think women know enough about sports to write such a book? What qualifications do the authors have for writing such a book?"

Information about the background and qualifications of textbook authors is ordinarily included in promotional materials distributed by the publishers. If such information is not on hand, have the children write to the publisher and request it. Most publishers will quickly furnish the author's vitae sheet. Some authors will respond with a personal letter to the children.

COPYRIGHT

Even copyright data may provide significant information about a specific book. Year of publication, for example, may be significant. Most textbooks used in today's classrooms are more or less "up to date." However, even up-to-date books will probably lag behind in today's fast-moving world. For example, a book on transportation published just a few years ago is likely to be totally silent about our "energy crisis." Nor would a science book of 1970 have anything to say about men landing on the moon.

Children may also profit by some instruction in the meaning of "copyright" as it applies to legal ownership of an author's work. Here are a few suggestions:

"What is a copyright?" "What do you think that word means?" "Is it made up of any words we know?" "What is a copy?" "What is a right?" "What do we mean when we say, "I have a *right* to do something?" "So, what does it mean to have a 'right to copy'?" "Who do you think gives a copyright?" "Who do you think has the right to copy our book?" "What might happen if *we* made copies of our whole book?" "Could we copy parts?" "Could we sell the parts we copied?" "Why not?"

TABLE OF CONTENTS

A textbook's table of contents provides a preview of what will be covered in the text. In addition, it gives the reader an overview of the relationship between the parts and the whole of the book—that is, it provides a kind of "outline" of the book's content, showing Parts (Units), Chapters, and Subsections, each in its relationship to the other. This can be a directed-discovery lesson from about Third Grade upward. Here are some guidelines:

1. What does the word, *contents,* mean? What is another word like it that we know?
2. What does it tell us about our book?
3. How many parts or units is the book divided into?
4. What is the main idea that each part (unit) is going to cover?
5. Take the units from the table of contents and rearange them *across* the page instead of up-and-down . . . like this (demonstrate).
6. Then copy the title of each chapter under the unit heading.

INDEX

Although the Index is in the back of the book, it is usually examined immediately following discussion of the Table of Contents, the reason being that both Contents and Index are useful guides to locating information within the book. In fact, the Index is even more useful to elementary school children.

Here are some typical procedures:

"On what page of the book does the author tell us about the Santa Fe Railroad? Let's look at the index and see." "Does the author have anything to say about the Erie Canal: Yes, Erie Canal is listed in the index, page 73."

Some training, especially for older children, should also be given in cross referencing and differentiation between major and subtopics as indicated by index format. Also, alert the children that they should not immediately "give up" if they cannot find a particular topic in the index. It may be listed as a subtopic under a major topic.

"Does the author of this sports book cover hand ball? Let's see. No, handball is not listed under the letter *H.* But wait. The table of contents has a section on Court Games. Yes, here it is in the index, listed in the *C* column, indexed under Court Games—handball, pp. 90–91."

VISUALS

Picture books are, of course, a staple of the readiness-to-read process. By the time the child is ready for development of reading-study skills, he or she is (or should be) already attuned to the function of simple illustrations (pictures) commonly found in early reading materials—for example, the relationship between illustrations and story line.

Visuals are what make our textbooks so colorful and beautiful. They cost tremendous amounts of money, for most are prepared especially for the books in which they appear. They are done by the best artists that can be put under contract. They are there for purposes . . . not just to fill up pages. Make use of them in this manner:

Training for Optimum Use of Pictures

1. "Do you like books that do not have pictures?"
2. "Why not?"
3. "What do pictures do for you?"
4. "Let's look through our book . . . what kind of pictures do you find?"
5. "Since you like pictures in books . . . and have told why you do . . . will the pictures in our book help that same way?"
6. "What, then, do we think the pictures in this book will do?" (Make a list of the things that the children in the group propose that pictures will do for them.)
7. "Now, lets find some pictures that do some of these things." (Stop before this session becomes boring.)

Besides pictures, however, textbooks and other informational materials contain other kinds of visuals with which the child may not be so familiar—charts (and tables), graphs, maps, and the time lines. Help the children to understand that these visual devices can be "read" just as the printed word is read.

Charts, for example, can provide classification information that is more easily and quickly grasped than if this information were presented in sentence form. An author might choose to write: In 1981, doctors earned x number of dollars per year; lawyers, earned x number of dollars; movie stars earned x number of dollars; baseball players earned x number of dollars; and so on. However, such information might be easier and quicker to grasp in chart form:

1981 Earnings

Profession	Earnings
Doctors	$_____
Lawyers	$_____
Movie Stars	$_____
Baseball Players	$_____
_____	$_____
_____	$_____

To help familiarize the children with the function of charts, you might supply them with data out of which they can construct their own simple charts. (Tables are similar to charts in that they provide information in succinct tabular form. Instruction for the use of tables is similar to that for use of charts.)

Similarly, line graphs, bar graphs, and pie graphs can be "read" as substitutes for or supplements to printed sentences.

Reading Line Graphs   "On graphs, we read two things together: *First,* the information along the bottom line; and, *second,* the information along the left-side line."

Distribute some very simple facts and have children construct simple graphs for application of this reading/study skill.

Reading Bar Graphs   "Bar graphs are easy ways of telling the same information."

"Rainfall is collected in tubes that show how much rain has fallen. Pretend those tubes were lined up.

Discuss how a bar graph shows exactly the same thing as a line graph shows. "Which is easier to read?"

Pie Graphs   "When we want to find out how much of our money goes for different things, it is easy to see if the information is presented in a pie graph. It is called a pie graph because . . . can anyone guess?"

Maps   Some basic instruction in map reading should be given if the textbook contains this visual device. Tracing of printed maps and constructing simple maps from textbook data can be helpful in such instruction. More sophisticated instruction in map reading is available from commercial publishers.

Time lines   Time lines in a text or other informational reading are helpful for many youngsters. Such devices can help the child grasp the concept of time—a difficult concept for many children, as we have previously noted. One very effective technique for instruction in time lines is to have the children (with the aid of the teacher, of course) construct their own. The one on the next page was constructed for second graders:

RUNNING HEADS

The specific format of running heads may vary from book to book. Some texts will use part (or unit) titles across the top of one page and chapter titles across the top of the facing page. Others may have chapter titles on one page and section or subsection titles on the facing page. Others may employ some further variation of titles and headings as running heads.

S	Started school — Some were afraid
O	Went for nature walks
N	Visited Fire Station
D	Worked in workbooks
J	Had Christmas Party for Mothers
F	Learned songs and rhythms
M	Learned how to count and alphabetize
A	Put on play in auditorium
M	Didn't want to leave Kindergarten
	Summer Vacation
S	Made new friends
O	Started to learn to read
N	Started to learn to do arithmetic
D	Had a weekly science lesson
J	Visited a museum
F	Went on field trip to the Zoo
M	Summer Vacation
A	We read books all by ourselves
M	Play in the Second Grade Band
S	Are writing stories about out trips
O	We have a science fair in our room
N	It is now time to learn Metric

Kindergarten 1979 — First Grade 1980 — Second Grade 1981

In any case, children should be taught awareness of running heads as locational devices and as aids to study—that is, as reminders of the specific subject matter under discussion.

APPENDIX

Appendices are included in factual books for one significant reason, namely, as a resting place for facts that would otherwise complicate line-to-line reading in chapters. The informational materials are placed in the appendix to "uncomplicate" the reading. Children can discover that the appendix contains great amounts of valuable information that one might have to spend hours searching for.

GLOSSARY

If the book has a glossary—and many of the newer elementary school texts do—it should be used as the dictionary for the subject. Two purposes of glossary are, *first,* to provide definitions to fit words as used in the text, and, *second,* to make the definitions more conveniently available.

Children can easily *discover* the reading/study value of the glossary.

MEANING-BEARING SIGNALS

Editors give special attention to the following *meaning-bearing signals:*

type face

symbols

numerization

color, shading, overlays

punctuation

marginal notations

So that the impact of this effort will be captured, the following comparison is effective:

"Let's look at the way they have printed our book. . . . The person who planned it is called 'the editor.' " "The editor puts many things into the book that help us." "We could call them signals or signs . . . just like signs on the road that tell us to be careful . . . or to stop . . . or that there is a curve ahead."

"Let's think of each line of words in the book as a road." "What signs can you find that tell us to look, or be careful . . . or start . . . or stop . . . along the road of reading?"

Type face and Symbols   Children generally respond with such answers as: "black letters" (*boldface* type); "big letters" (*capital* letters usually for titles of sections); "colored parts" (where *color* is used for emphasis or overlay); "numbers" (*numerals*); "little slanted letters" (*italics*); "stars" (*asterisks* *); "squares" (material *boxed* off from the rest).

Color, Shading, and Overlays   Color, shading, and overlays are lavishly used today not only to make the textbooks more attractive but, more importantly, as signals to the importance of certain topics or concepts within each chapter. With a little guidance, your children can become aware of the help such visual aids can be in their informational reading.

Punctuation Signals   Children do not readily recognize that *punctuation marks* are also meaning-bearing signals. Those need to be explored and the chief punctuation marks learned:

> *period; exclamation mark; interrogation point* (commonly called a "question mark" by the children); *colon; semicolon; comma; apostrophe; dash; quotation marks; parentheses; brackets; elipses marks* (the children call them "dots") . . . to indicate materials left out; *hyphen.*

Although they are all listed here, they will not be "learned" all at once, nor, probably, all in one school year.

The *comma* deserves very special attention in reading, for it signals the *smallest interruptions* in the flow of thoughts through a sentence. Commas are our most frequently occurring meaning-bearing signs. They are also our most important signals, for they "frame" conceptual entities. Our objective is to have children discover that commas are used as signals to set off ideas, and that those ideas between the commas should be read as one idea regardless of the number of words involved.

Marginal Notations   Many newer elementary school textbooks have marginal notations as study aids! These useful devices may be in the form of questions, such as "What do you think this means?", "Where did you read about this before?", "Is this the same as _____?" They may take the form of directions. For example, "Find the low countries on this map," "Look at the chart on this page and see which year had the most rainfall."

Help the children to understand that such devices have a purpose, that they are intended as aids to study and guides to interpretation of text content.

STRATEGIES FOR TEACHING READING-STUDY SKILLS

Members of primitive cultures have passed on skills, legends, and useful information to their offspring through rituals, talk-stories, and demonstrations. Although we in our own culture do much the same thing, such a process is extremely limited to verbal communication. The difference between the primitive culture and our own is to be found largely in the storing of information and its availability to present and future generations. The ability to read the record of mankind and to share in the progress of society is enriched many times over because we are the beneficiaries of the written records of many great civilizations before us. To want to know and to want to learn to read to find out are basic traits of today's children. But just learning to read is not enough to equip children to cope with the enormous amounts of informational materials that are generated daily and yearly. Neither should a child have to go about blindly in his/her effort to read informational materials. There are some strategies that work much better than trial-and-error methods and, because of the success we have had with them, they should be passed on to our children as reading-study skills.

The method used by anyone when reading informational materials is determined by two variables: (1) type of material, and (2) purpose of the reader. This idea may be visualized in this formula:

$$\frac{\text{Material}}{\text{purpose}} = \text{method}$$

If it is a long, well-organized discourse, such as a chapter or informational article, a preview, called a *survey*, is very helpful. If the material is very easy and/or in a field in which the child already is acquainted with the terminology, it can be read faster than material that is loaded with new and difficult vocabulary. However, if the child's purpose is to learn every detail, then a different reading/study method is used. If it is to skim over for a general idea, *skimming* is the technique indicated. If some particular fact is sought, the material should only be scanned for it.

THE SURVEY

What should the child consider in making a preliminary survey of a chapter to be read in a content area textbook (or other kind of informational study book— biography, historical novel, a how-to book, a book on sports, etc.)? Begin with the title. Certainly, the chapter title should give us a good idea of the chapter's overall content.

Headings and subheadings can serve as cues to principal points covered in the material. Numbered statements and lists provide further cues to main ideas, as do italicized and boldface words, phrases, and sentences. Visuals, such as charts, graphs, and illustrations, may also highlight important information contained in the chapter. If the chapter in question has a detailed introductory section and/or a detailed summary section, round out the survey by having the child read these sections carefully, word-by-word before proceeding to read the chapter in its entirety.

You, of course, must be thoroughly familiar with chapter content yourself before instructing the child in making his or her own survey. Questions and comments should be readied in advance to help guide the children. For example:

"What does the picture on page 6 tell us about what is covered in this chapter? What does the numbered list on page 9 tell us? Why is the last sentence on this page italicized?"

Reading-Study Skills are Usually Indicated in
Teacher's Editions of Basal Readers

This excerpt shows part of the lesson plans for use with the informational article, "Storms, Nature's Powerhouses." Note that the teacher's plans contain a reduced-sized page from the pupil's reader.

As the children become used to survey-prompting questions from the teacher, a productive extension of this strategy is to have them construct similar questions of their own to be answered in group session.

Another helpful strategy for developing survey skills is to mount on a display board oak tag strips containing chapter title, heads, and subheads. These may be put on display as the children discover them in their survey of the material or they may be posted in advance as an aid to previewing the material. Word-strips may also be similarly utilized for vocabulary peculiar to chapter content.

ADVANCE ORGANIZERS AND DIRECTED READING QUESTIONS

Another method of organizing prereading is through what psychologists call *advance organizers.* It was described by Smith and Hesse as being a period of general information about the topic or material and previews of the sequence of events. It is similar to the *survey* in the S-Q-3R technique; a form of motivational readiness; a warm-up of ideas related to the topic. Although their investigation was done with secondary school students, it is pertinent to note that the use of what Smith and Hesse called "cognitive organizers" resulted in greater retention of main ideas.

Dr. Larry Andrews compared the results obtained from the use of *cognitive organizers* and *directed reading questions,* the former being bits of advance organization—a briefing, so to speak—and the latter being the questions and/or problems the teacher expects the students to be finding answers for as they read the selection. The *cognitive organizer* method, according to Andrews, yields significantly better results. His investigation was also done with Seventh Graders, but the method is just as valid for older elementary children. Information in the form of *cognitive organizers* has always been used by superior teachers.

Anticipating through Questions   It is productive for children in a group to devise a few questions that they can reasonably anticipate will be answered from their reading. Developing such questions is part of the *survey* of the chapter. These may be questions of their own, subheadings that can be turned into questions, or actual questions found at the end of the chapter.

$$\frac{\text{factual material}}{\text{what to look for}} = \text{questions}$$

The one trick to be prevented is children's tendency to search for answers to the questions rather than working for a more comprehensive understanding of the chapter.

The 3-Rs

In Robinson's SQ3R technique and in others similar (PQRST, PAR-4), various notions are included in structured style. They are such things as *read, review, recite, test, summarize, rewrite,* and, perhaps, others. The main idea is that, after the child has read the chapter, the parts should be *related* to *each other,* to the child's *past experience,* and to the *whole.* This may be visualized by the following formula:

$$\frac{\text{factual materials}}{\text{putting it all together}} = \text{the 3-Rs}$$

Dr. Russell Stauffer, long an advocate of reading as a *thinking* process, proposed a routine designed to foster increased comprehension. He called it Directed Reading-Thinking Activities (D-R-T-A) and described it fully in his book of the same name. He also cited (page 77) a study by Petre, one of his doctoral students at the University of Delaware, that compared the usefulness of the D-R-T-A and Directed Reading Activity (DRA) strategies. Stauffer cited evidence that "the D-R-T-A appears to allow more quantity, higher quality, and wider variety in pupil responses as a group-directed reading instructional procedure," as opposed to the Directed Reading Lesson (DRL), which is a teacher-directed routine. He also indicated that his research showed that boys and girls do equally well and that the D-R-T-A works with reading groups at all levels, but especially well with the better readers. Stauffer cited other studies that verify the superiority of the D-R-T-A.

It is, therefore, worthwhile to consider the three basic steps in Stauffer's D-R-T-A routine:

1. *Predicting.* This phase is directed by the teacher in the same manner as an *introduction* or *motivation* lesson with such questions as, "What do you think the story is about?" "What does the title mean?" "From the picture, can you guess where it happened?" "From the art work, can you predict that it is a happy or sad story?" This phase is referred to as "setting purpose."
2. *Reasoning.* While reading the story, the children then become responsible for verifying their predictions, adjusting, or changing. They are held to reasoning on cause-and-effect situations, making further predictions, and involving themselves in judgments based upon details in the story checked against their own past experiences.
3. *Proving.* In this third phase of the D-R-T-A, the children cite excerpts from the story that prove their assumptions and/or what caused them to change their predictions.

SKIMMING

Skimming is an effective technique for quick comprehension of main ideas in relatively easy-to-read informational materials. One of the prerequisites to skimming is the determination of purpose, that is, the reader's choice. When the choice is to obtain a general idea in easy material, skimming is the reading/study skill that should be used.

$$\frac{\text{easy, factual material}}{\text{looking for general idea}} = \text{skimming}$$

Children even in the First Grade can be taught to skim. For example, the teacher can distribute to the group several of the small excellent little books on science written for First-Grade students. Let us suppose that the reading and pictures describe the manner in which a turtle burrows down into the ground in preparation for winter. This general idea cannot be verified entirely from the pictures. The child should be able to prove from words picked up during skimming that this is what is happening. The words *turtle, digs, down, sleep, winter* are the key meaning-bearing words. By this means, the child learns that skimming is the process of picking out word signals that give clues to meaning.

In the primary grades, skimming can be very effective when the reader has considerable background in the subject. To teach this skill, select a small group of students who have some knowledge of a particular subject. Do not include in the group anyone who is unknowledgeable of the general area. Select an informational article on that subject.

One danger in skimming (and in scanning, discussed below) is that some children may begin to believe that this technique (or something like it) is all that is needed for productive study of informational material.

Reading-study skills are intended to foster comprehension, and true comprehension does not come with simple understanding of "main ideas" (see Chapter 7.)

SCANNING

Scanning is a locational as well as a reading skill. It involves quick location of a specific fact within the informational material being read. By the time the children are ready for development of reading-study skills, they will already have used some form of scanning for a particular word in dictionaries, encyclopedias, indexes, and other kinds of alphabetical listings (even, perhaps, with their personal use of telephone books).

$$\frac{\text{informational material}}{\text{search for specific fact}} = \text{scanning}$$

As a technique for quickly locating and absorbing specific facts in study materials, scanning involves details such as who, what, where, how, how many (or how much), and why. The child should be taught to look for textual and typographic signals indicating location of such information. For example, "who" presupposes a proper name, and hence a word beginning with a capital letter. "Where" may also involve a capitalized place name (although not necessarily). "When" may involve a word indicating day of the week, or a word indicating a month, or a season, or the part of a day, and so on. It may possibly involve clock time or a date and hence be signaled by numerals. Similarly, "how many" or "how much" may be signaled by numerals or spelled-out figures or by words or signs expressing amounts or measures—"big," "small," "scanty," "Inches," "feet," dollar signs, etc. "Why" is often signaled by words and phrases such as *because* and *in order to* or by infinitives beginning with *to*, such as "to accomplish," "to solve the problem of . . . ," "to outsmart the enemy," and so on.

STRUCTURE AND ORGANIZATION: A READING-STUDY SKILL

If the concept of memory cells (Chapter 1) is accepted, then it is logical that the input into those cells could be haphazard or could be planned and structured. If the objective of reading is to be able to sort out main ideas, details, sequence, classification, categorization, structural relationships, and so on, then input must be structured.

It is not reasonable to expect that informational material that is read and stored in the memory cells will be retrieved in any manner or form other than that in which it was stored!

Here are some strategies for helping young people improve their reading-study skills through awareness of the structure and organization of informational reading materials:

Main Ideas and Details   The most important single skill in the reading/study group is the ability to determine what is the main idea of an article, paragraph, or section.

The following framework, when put to use as a regular routine, has proved to be very helpful:

What is the main idea?

Who?_____

did what? _____

when? _____where?

how? _____

why? _____

details:

how much? _____

how many? _____

what else? _____

what next?_____

That format applies to informational material in which some living thing (man or animal) does the action.

In descriptive material in which processes are described, the following framework is effective:

Main Idea in Cause-and-Effect Relationships

What happens? _____

when this _____and

this _____

do this _____

In directions, here is the format that has been helpful:

Main Idea: Following Directions

Do this: _____

and this: _____

and this: _____

then this will happen: _____

_____

Sequence   Ideas in sequence should be organized in one of several ways, depending upon the nature of the material: If the ideas are in time sequence, this form will help the child visualize them in relationship to each other:

Sequence

first _____

second _____

third _____

etc. _____

or

this happened _____

then_____

then_____

finally _____

or

a long time ago _____

more recently _____

today _____

    or

yesterday _____

today _____

but tomorrow _____

    or

formerly _____

now _____

in the future _____

Classification   The child who can devise categories is well on the road to independence in the reading/study skill known as *classification*. To classify or "sort out," one needs to understand the main types of groups. If the child devises his/her own headings, the process will be more cognitive than if the teacher determines the headings.

Outlining   Outlining of informational reading can be an aid to revelation of organization and structure and hence an aid to meaning and comprehension. The purpose of the outline is to extract main ideas and supporting details from the material and to place them in a format indicating logical relationship of part to part and whole to whole. Various formats may be used in formal outlines for designation of main heads, subheads, sub-subheads, and so on. Here is one such format:

Formal Outline

I _____

  A _____

  B _____

    1 _____

    2 _____

      a _____

      b _____

      c _____

Some informational materials, especially science and technology materials in the intermediate and later grades, use numerical headings throughout and hence lend themselves to decimal-system outlining. For example, an outline of Chapter 7 in a science text might have the following format:

$$
\begin{array}{l}
7: \quad\underline{\qquad(title)\qquad} \\
\quad 7{:}1 \\
\qquad 7{:}1{:}1 \\
\qquad 7{:}1{:}2 \\
\qquad\quad 7{:}1{:}2{:}1 \\
\qquad\quad 7{:}1{:}2{:}2 \\
\quad 7{:}2
\end{array}
$$

Rewriting   Like outlining, transcription of main ideas and supporting details into the reader's own words highlights and aids comprehension of these ideas and details. Unlike outlining, however, it allows (even forces) the child to "internalize" the information—that is, to relate it to previously learned information and experience and thus enhance long-term retention. Transcribing information into one's own words does not, of course, mean that the child is expected to "rewrite" an entire informational work. In fact, cue-reduction is an essential principle of this reading-study skill. Informational cues are reduced as the child transcribes the *gist* of the material into words specifically meaningful to the child, words that then become personal cues to stimulate recall (see Chapter 7.)

Encouraging the children to transcribe reading-study materials into their own words is an extremely effective strategy for development of basic reading-study skills. (In our experience, it is perhaps the single most effective such strategy at any and all grade levels.)

$$
\frac{\text{informational materials}}{\text{rewrite}} = \text{long-term retention}
$$

READING RATE

As teachers, you will often hear comments such as "Billy is a fast reader," or "Sally is a slow reader," and will, no doubt, find yourself making similar judgments. We must, however, keep in mind that "fast" and "slow" are relative, not absolute concepts. Some kinds of informational material must, of necessity, be read more slowly than other kinds. New and/or difficult materials, for example, require a slower pace than familiar and/or easy materials. Reading rate is relative also to individual differences among the children—experiential development, vocabulary skills, ability to phrase-read, general mental development, and so on.

This being said, the fact remains that most, if not all, children need instruction in and encouragement toward increasing their reading speed as an essential reading-study skill. The first step is to develop awareness in the children that they are, perhaps, reading more slowly than they need to. Most children are unaware that they are reading all materials regardless of difficulty at approximately the same rate of speed. Many will be pleasantly surprised (and reassured) to learn that they can and should read faster under certain circumstances; that reading pace depends not only on the reader but also on the type of material being read and on the purpose of reading it.

One useful analogy for reinforcing such awareness is to compare reading with traveling in an automobile, with the driver of a car who varies the speed of a car according to road conditions and the purpose of the trip.

$$\frac{\text{road conditions}}{\text{purpose}} = \text{speed}$$

Just as the driver of a car drives at a slower speed under difficult travel conditions, so should the reader move at a slower rate through difficult textual materials. Conversely, when the going gets easier, speed can safely be increased. As to purpose, the driver of a car may drive slowly if the trip's purpose is to absorb as many scenic details as possible along the way, or the driver may speed up if the main purpose of the trip is to move quickly from one place to another. Similarly, the reader may read more slowly if the purpose of reading is to absorb as many specific details as possible and read faster if the purpose is to get from one main informational point to another.

Fortunately, merely pointing out to the children that their reading rate is slower than it need be is often enough to start them on the road to speedier reading.

Increased reading rate must, of course, be accompanied by adequate comprehension. Increased rate with a drop in comprehension leads to no actual improvement in reading-study skills. The efficiency of increased reading rate is directly related to degree of comprehension, according to this formula:

$$\text{rate} \times \% \text{ of comprehension} = \text{reading achievement}$$

If a child reads at 80 words per minute with 100% comprehension, reading achievement is said to be 80. At 100 words per minute with 80% comprehension, achievement is still 80. However, if the child doubles words-per-minute reading from 80 to 160 and comprehension drops from 80% to 40%, reading achievement drops to 64—hardly a gain in overall reading-study skill!

Doesn't it appear reasonable that *purpose* is really the controlling factor in speed? If the reader is satisfied with fairly good achievement, it pays to cover 50% more reading material (at 70% comprehension) and achieve a higher achievement score as a result.

Again, the comparison with driving a car seems to be valid. If one is on a vacation trip, one can go slowly and see everything, or, one can travel 50% faster and see quite enough. Actually one may see more in the same space of time.

Older children are pleased with the fact that teachers are not insistent on them getting everything at 100% comprehension. In fact, it is more realistic (and, therefore, more motivating) to suggest that, "We don't need to know *everything* there is to know about everything we read, do we?" "So why don't we try to read a little faster and to try to remember what each of us thinks we should know." That strategy really works well; for, as we know, many children will set higher objectives for themselves (when left alone to do it) than those *required* by teachers.

Rate of reading, being subject to individual differences and types of materials being read, is not a fixed entity, but a variable that should be encouraged as children are learning to become efficient in reading/study skill.

LIBRARY SKILLS

"Getting the library habit" is often advised by those who want children to go to the library for the purpose of "getting books." This is but one step toward exploiting library resources to their fullest.

Getting the library habit begins in Kindergarten as children are taken by groups to explore and to hear stories of their own choosing read by the librarian. Today, elementary school libraries contain many media of learning in addition to books, and, as a consequence, are called "multimedia learning centers." Consequently, we are directing our attention in this segment of the chapter only to those informational materials that are to be read, and are calling them library materials, for want of a better name. Skills in locating and using such resources are valuable reading-study assets.

Organization of School Libraries Within Multimedia Learning Centers   Most multimedia learning centers contain library materials on open shelves, readily available to children. By exploring and through guidance, children can learn that reference books are separated from the informational books, and that all are separate from "stories" (fiction) and biography.

Card File   The card file is the first step in learning to use the library as a source of reading/study materials. Library of Congress cards and the older Dewey decimal system cards cross reference materials in three ways:

> 1. author;   2. topic;   3. book title

For elementary school children, however, the foremost help is the topic card. That is the first fact children should *discover*. To be certain that they do, they should be guided in their library experience with questions such as: "If you are looking for books on *sports,* which of these would you look for first: O. J.

Simpson, football, Babe Ruth, tennis, or just *sports?"* "Why?" "If you were looking for a book about Pete Rose, which of these would you look up first: *baseball, home runs, world records, Pete Rose,* or *sports?"* "Why?" If you were looking for books on baseball, which of these would you look for first: *Pete Rose, sports, spring training, farm teams, baseball?"* "Why?" How would you look for a book on baseball rules?

"Make a list of the things that file cards tell us." "Which are most important in finding a book?" Through this technique, children usually discover that file cards contain considerable information that they can express in their own words:

> "It tells us the title of the book."
> "It tells us what the book is about."
> "It says who wrote it."
> "It tells what's in it." (Topics are listed.)
> "It tells what number to look for." (Call number.)
> "It tells how big the book is." (Number of pages.)
> "It lets us know how old it is." (Copyright date.)
> "Does it have pictures."

The children will eventually discover that, if they find one book by a certain author that is especially good, they can look under that author's name and find others listed on additional cards.

Numerical System Children need help in learning the manner in which the numerical system is organized. One should not expect them to memorize the system. One thing they can do, however, is to make a "map" of the library in their school, showing in a general way where informational books on various subjects are to be found.

Reference Materials

Encyclopedias The first reference books that children know are usually the encyclopedias written especially for children: *Compton's;* the *Book of Knowledge, World Book* and, possibly, *Brittanica Junior* (for advanced readers). The encyclopedia habit appeals to many children, because they can find information without having to bother with card files and searching through books. In addition, encyclopedias today are beautiful and inspiring.

Special Reference Books Most special reference books are written for adults and are at high readability levels. Nonetheless, many elementary school libraries have some of the most popular, such as *World Almanac* and *Guinness Book of Facts,* and they are intriguing to imaginative children.

News Magazines Several excellent news magazines specially written for elementary school children are available for classroom use. Subscriptions to them are usually on a semester or school-year basis. The technique of using a weekly classroom news magazine commences in the Kindergarten and is developed throughout the elementary years, whereas use of the daily newspaper in the library requires special training, often provided by the librarian.

MAKING READING-STUDY MATERIALS AVAILABLE TO ELEMENTARY SCHOOL CHILDREN

As we stated at the beginning of this chapter, our special attention has been directed toward strategies for helping children learn those reading-study skills for "finding out"; for using reading to discover answers to "Why?" and "How Come?" No discussion on this topic would be complete without further attention to those informational reading materials that should permeate every elementary school classroom. Consequently, we conclude this chapter with an overview of the types of informational materials that you can use most successfully right in your classroom for immediate answers to immediate questions. You will want to keep some in the room and others you will want to have referenced for quick retrieval from the school library.

In reviewing the variety of resources that are currently available to children for "finding out," we have set up a few categories that seem logical and, hopefully, are inclusive enough for our purposes. Books in most of these categories are also categorized as *trade books* to distinguish them from textbooks. Children tend to view trade books as "pleasurable" and textbooks as "work."

A science hall display case can show books on many subjects at several different readability levels. How can you cooperate with the librarian to develop such a display?

PRIMARY-LEVEL INFORMATIONAL BOOKS

Several publishers in America, New Zealand, Australia, and England have made special efforts to develop very small beginners books on factual, informational subjects. These books frequently describe "how things work," a special event, a place, an episode in some famous person's life, or are beginners informational books on classes of things.

Such booklets are, in one sense, encyclopedias treating a variety of subjects, but each self-contained in one very small booklet. Larger books of the same nature, containing more advanced and more detailed information are available and should be the next step after the child has learned the basics of reading.

HISTORICAL NOVELS

The deep meaning of history is to be learned through historical novels, certainly not in history textbooks which, unfortunately, are recitations of historical facts, rather than the living portrayal of people and movements that have had their impact on the destiny of people and nations.

The main feature of the historical novel is not that it conveys relatively accurate information about historical facts (although it does that), but that it creates for the reader a *feeling* for the times (in German, a *Zeitgeist*—spirit of the time). It recreates the horrors of war; the smell of rotting bodies during the Bubonic Plague, and all the other sensory stimuli that are the concomitants of a well-written historical novel. They are part of the stuff that distinguishes good historical writing from commonplace textbook history. They help make it possible for the reader to relive the past within the *affective* domain.

Because of the nature of historical novels, they are primarily for older children in the intermediate grades and in junior high school. They require some sense of historical time and historical perspective, as well as acquaintance with geography for their full enjoyment and impact.

Identification with heroes and heroines who are the historical characters in a story is dependent on the child's urge to have lived and to have taken part in the history-making events of a prior time and different environment. The need to escape from the dull present and to achieve that which one cannot achieve under present circumstances seem to be the two pervasive psychological factors that are satisfied by historical novels.

There are hundreds of good historical novels especially written for children. They contain not only the art of the storyteller, but the persistent scholarship of the research historian. Such a combination of talents is difficult to find, but, fortunately, some of our best writers have chosen this field.

Because of the care with which the authors of historical novels depict the spirit of the times and develop their tales of pseudoreality, we hold the position that historical novels are one of the prime sources of informational reading.

BIOGRAPHIES

Biography is the informational vehicle by which young readers can vicariously experience the problems, challenges, decisions, and successes of some *significant other*. As in the case of the historical novel, the spirit of the times in which that person lived is recreated through description, speech characteristics, values, manners, customs, events, food, clothing, and shelter. An individual can read *about* foods, clothing, shelter, political events, economic problems, issues, and so on in history books and in factual accounts, but the spirit of the times has to be *felt* through the senses of a real person. It has to be responded to by the thoughts and decisions and actions of a real person. This is what sets biography apart from history. Through biography history can live, and through *identification* the reader can relive history.

There are good biographies for children in almost every area of interest: spies, sports, music, art, social service, politics, science, adventure, the professions, and so on. As in the case of historical fiction, biographies are usually for readers of age 10 or 12 and up. These are the years when young people are looking for lifetime significant others. During these preadolescent years, they

These children, together with their teacher, are fortunate to have been able to "experience" the environment of a colonial schoolhouse and to reenact an early learning session. How can such a project enhance comprehension? List the pros and cons to the questions, "Is it worth the trouble?."

are seeking to *become.* They are aware of themselves, of their hopes and secret aspirations, and the need to find great inner peace by reading about others who have succeeded against difficult odds.

Biographies help the young preteens and adolescents envision themselves in roles that are significant both to them and to society.

REGIONAL NOVELS

Regional novels, like biographies and historical novels portray people against a background of time, place, and environment so accurately that the end-result for the reader is the vicarious experience of having lived in that region at that particular time in history. The regional novel, thus, not only provides the enjoyment of fiction, but also exudes the feeling of the times.

The marvellous novels by Sterling North, Jack London, Paul Annixter, and others are of this type, portraying life in the north country wilderness, recreating that life for the reader. Other American writers set their stories in the homelands of their childhood: Meindert DeJong's *Wheel on the School: Journey from Peppermint Street,* and others of Holland; or Isaac Singer's stories of Warsaw ghetto life. Some authors seek out regions and live for a period of time to internalize the spirit of the time and place before they write about it. This was especially true of Lois Lenski who wrote about *Strawberry Girl* only after she had lived with such a girl and her family in Florida; *Blue Ridge Billy; Cotton In My Sack* (life among the Arkansas share-cropper children); *Judy's Journey* (a migrant worker's child); and *Prairie School* (a blizzard sweeps across South Dakota and traps children in school for four days). These are just a few.

Other writers appropriately write about life in their own little part of the world: the Cumberland Mountains, the American Southwest; India; Japan; city life; the lands of their birth, or some region that they have adopted.

As is the case of historical novels, most regional tales were developed by their authors for older children who have acquired a sense of geography and the historical events indigenous to a particular region. They serve a definite need . . . namely, to escape, to travel, to live somewhere else, to experience different things. They help the young reader transcend time and space and vicariously sense a real "somewhere else" to which we all, at times, have yearned to go.

INFORMATIONAL BOOKS ABOUT THE "HERE-AND-NOW"

When a child selects a book about something real today, we assume that the purpose is to "find out." Yet, it may also be that the urge to "find out" is generated by the stronger, intrinsic desire to *become.* So, if a book about baseball is chosen, it may be that the reader wants to learn more information about the sport but also about one of its players to reinforce the inward dream of becoming a baseball great.

This brings us to a consideration of the psychology behind the selection of *any* book. Why does a child select a book? Assuming that the selection is totally voluntary, it seems to be for two reasons: to find out and to become. All life's choices—books, or otherwise—are based upon self-satisfaction of self-felt needs.

In this section of the chapter, we attempt to identify the areas that are essentially thought of as "finding out" about things in the here-and-now and to discuss them briefly. Every classroom or learning center must have plenty of informational materials to help the children who want to find out about certain places, people, or things in the here-and-now. (See our description of interest-based reading in Chapter 9). To emphasize this point may seem strange, but our observations convince us that too much stress is placed on the past, slighting the present . . . hence, we hear so much flack about school not being *relevant*. What young people mean, we have concluded, is that much of their studies does not relate directly to the here-and-now; especially, to life as they are experiencing or envisioning it. We suggest, therefore, several categories of reading materials in the here-and-now that should be filled with informational reading materials that make learning to read worthwhile.

Sports   Sports is the Number-1 all-time universal interest of children and youth, and there is no dearth of good informational books on sports. Here are a few subcategories to keep up-dated as the years go by and as times and sports heroes and heroines come and go.

Biography of Sports Figures

1. The All-Americans
2. Olympic winners
3. The Pro's

Rules of the Game

1. Rules and regulations
2. Layouts and dimensions

History of Sports

1. How it began: The Olympic games, etc.
2. How the game has changed: Modern Olympics.
3. Sports arenas:
    a. of the Ancients
    b. of the early days in america.
    c. Mid-America (1920's, etc.)
    d. modern arenas, here and abroad

Professional Sports vs. Amateur Sports

1. College sports
2. The Olympics
3. The Leagues of Professionals
4. Sports Clubs.
5. Sports and Gambling: Undue influence on players.
6. Sports and Drugs: Illegal drugging of participants.
7. Financial support of Amateur sports.

Organized Sports for Children

1. Pros and Cons.
   a. Little League
   b. Soccer
   c. Babe Ruth League
   d. Baby Hockey
2. Making play areas available to all children.
3. Participation of all vs. team sports.

Competition

1. World records
2. World Series
3. International competition

Sports by Classification

This is a huge area in itself.

Spectator Sports, and Individual Participation

Economics of Sports

1. Equipment
2. Club dues
3. Coaching
4. Cost of participation
5. Professional contracts and salaries

We have frequently heard youngsters bemoan the "fact" that "There ain't nothin' to read." But, as soon as they are surrounded by the wealth of reading materials on sports, you can be certain that complaint will cease. The most interesting and elaborate bulletin boards and display cases may be developed around the theme of sports and books that relate to sports.

We have noticed great enthusiasm for reading about surfing by youngsters and young adolescents in Ohio—more than a thousand miles from the surf, and of figure skating by youth in Hawaii—half-a-world away from ice. Interest in sports seems to transcend space and chronological age, thus making it one of the "universals" that makes learning to read worthwhile.

How Things Work   Reading "to find out" is more often than not directed to finding out how things work. There are good books in this field, and there are some bad ones. The good ones have the attributes of relevance; they are up-to-date, describing things as they are now, and they are readable by young readers. They have been written with particular age groups in mind and edited with attention to average reading abilities. There are some such books "written down" to the level of first graders. They frequently are titled "First Book of _____" or some such title.

Science, Technology, and Mechanics are the areas that usually are considered as those dealing with "how things work". Even at the Kindergarten and First-Grade levels there are excellent books on science: on turtles, bugs, hamsters, fire, growing things; magnets, magnifying glasses, and the whole world simplified in pictures and explanation.

Your elementary classroom "science table" not only will contain exhibits and realia of how things work, but also will have a collection of books related to the special themes—changed as the collections of things are changed. The presence of books motivates children to "find out" more. The ability to read becomes worthwhile because they are worthwhile things to find out and worthwhile books immediately available for the task. You will continually be helping the children to use their reading-study skills in the finding-out process.

In the broader spectrum of the here-and-now there are other phenomena to be investigated to find out how things work: How does a kite fly, or an airplane, or a rocket? How does a doctor perform an operation, or a researcher conduct an experiment? How do we choose a president, or a beauty queen? How does an automobile work, or a State legislature? What happens at the hospital or at the airport? How does a supermarket get food from all over the world, or how does the world get food? How does the United Nations work, or a labor union. How do we tell time, and how does time treat us? What makes things grow, or the Northern Lights glow?

When children learn that informational books contain the answers to these and to many of the other questions about how things work in the here-and-now, they will develop the habit of seeking out books and opening them as windows to the mysteries of the world. When an adult joins the child in "finding out" through books, the joy of discovery is more than doubled. Try it, and see!

Wheels We have designated *wheels* as one of the newer universal themes. Fortunately, the interest has been so manifest that it has motivated many good writers of children's books to concentrate efforts in producing some good books in this area. Books about building cars; racing cars; driving cars; dune buggies; hot rods; antiques; trucks; screaming demons; motorbikes; foreign cars; the Indianapolis 500; Daytona; Monte Carlo; Jags, Mercedes, and Ferraris, drag racing, LeMons, skateboards, dirt racers, street dragging, funny cars, vans, wheels, wheels, wheels! Try and stop them from reading about wheels! And who wants to stop them? Isn't that what reading is for?

Animals Animals, especially pets, are universal in appeal. So, there are books on how to care for pets, what kind of animals make good pets, and what kind are wild and should be left to nature. Conservation of endangered species is a currently relevant theme for older readers.

Children tend to transfer their love of pets in a generalized way to all animals, tame or wild. This myth has been perpetuated by hundreds of books about friendly bears, possums, crocodiles, kangaroos, alligators, and the like. In the world of here-and-now, there are a good number of excellent books on the habits and habitats of wild animals. There are informational books, all designed to enlighten young readers not only of the habits of wild things, but the need to preserve them for a balance of nature in a world fast becoming unbalanced!

There are also great books about special animals. For example, Marguerite Henry's classics about horses—most are "almost" true stories such as *Misty of Chincoteague* (roundup of wild ponies on Chincoteague Island), A Newbery Honor Award book, *King of the wild* (race horse), the 1949 Newbery Medal winner; *Brighty of the Grand Canyon; Justin Morgan Had a Horse; Mustang: Wild Spirit of the West!;* (the true story of a girl who led the fight to save the wild mustangs).

Here we are talking about factual books about animals in contrast with those mentioned under novels. Of course, novels can be factual and still carry the interest of a plot and characters. Factual books about animals and their place in the here-and-now are important parts of every good reading program. There must be books about dogs, and cats, racoons and bears, zoos and circuses, hunting and fishing, mating and offspring, and all the other wonderful things about nature that young readers will discover in books and in *Ranger Rick,* that wonderful little full-color nature magazine published especially for children by the National Wildlife Federation.

How to Do It When one elects to do something, to make something, be it a garden, a birdhouse, a glider, a kite, or a computer, the purpose and the act become one of creating. By creating, the creator is self-actualizing. It may be impossible, therefore, to separate the many do-it-yourself and how-to-do-it

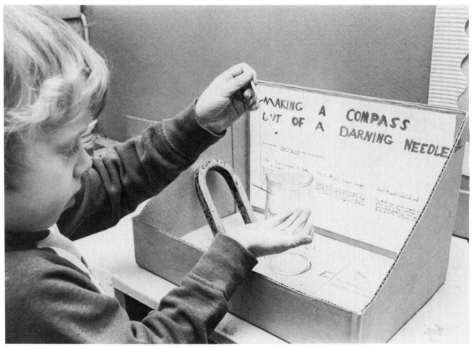

Not only can one read to learn how to do something, but one can also write up the directions in one's own words for others to read and follow.

books from the category of books for self-fulfillment and classify them merely as books for finding out. Why should it matter?

The main point is that the environment for reading be filled with books on how-to-do-it, for children don't just want to read *about* the world of the here-and-now; they want to *become* a part of that world by making things that work, thus helping them become part of the present.

There are how-to-do-it books in every avocation and hobby, and, consequently, there is no need to list them here. In fact, any listing would most likely soon become obsolete as fads and fancies change almost as fast as new years roll around. What is "big" this year will, perhaps, be superseded next year with something different.

Making things seems to be a universal drive experienced by children. It obviously starts in the toddler years . . . stacking blocks, fitting puzzles together, and later working with construction kits and other put-togethers from the toy store. Children who live in the mainstream culture observe parents making pies and cakes and cookies and dresses and tinkering or painting in home workshops or at community recreation workshop classes.

Free creativity eventually gives way to more structured activity. At that point, the child almost certainly needs information from experts on how-to-do-it. That is where books come in.

But the wise teacher should not wait for that moment. The environment for reading should contain many books covering a wide variety of fields . . . ready to be read as new vistas of creativity begin to dawn on children. In fact, the awareness of a book may be just what a child needs to activate a latent urge to create the very article that is described in the book. Many children we have known never thought of doing the things that they found (through books) that they really could do. It works both ways. Books can motivate the activity; the activity can call for the reading of a book.

The child who, early in life, has been led to creativity by being surrounded with how-to-do-it books will not likely become an adolescent with nothing to do! How-to-do-it books open up new vistas of creativity, leisure-time hobbies, avocations, and even lifetime vocations and inventions.

The Arts   It may seem far-fetched to suggest that children might read books in the arts. Our experience is just the opposite. We believe that the answer lies in the fact that children are intrinsically interested in the beautiful. A beautiful toy or doll captivates the six-year-old just as fully as it does the adult who purchases it.

Children feel the beauty of springtime, the rolling surf, fallen leaves in autumn, holidays, new clothes, shiny toys, a new bike, or a handsome jack-o-lantern.

Few children, however, have been led to books about beauty—the arts.

One way to do it is through poetry. A poem is read, and children are "set" to artistic expression generated by the poem. Then, we just "happen to have" some books that fit the theme. Books on sculpture—beautiful fountains that are man's waterfalls carved in stone; on buildings that are architects' dreams for enhancing the quality of living; on paintings and painters and how they worked to achieve perfection in their art; on music and composers who translated their emotions through instruments to stir the emotions of listeners.

Books about art and artists are natural concomitants in the environment of informational reading.

Our Country   Americans are not alone in the belief that America is the finest place on earth. As we have traveled around the globe, others constantly remind us that we are a favored people in a favored land, and that they yearn to come to share the blessings of America with us. We have been stopped in the Bazaars of Damascus; in the Old City of Jerusalem; on the back byways of Taiwan; in the airport in Cairo; on a jungle road in Mindanao; and on a South Sea island, all with the same question: How can I get to America? Please help me!

There are beautiful books about our country, but we are convinced that we have been negligent in helping our youth to internalize the greatness and beauty of this homeland of ours. We had to travel afar to be brought to the realization that many of America's problems today stem from this neglect.

Geography books are, probably, the first books about our country that elementary school children encounter. Some of the new basal reader series carry informational excerpts about many respects of American government and life in the United States, as well as elsewhere in the world. There are several outstanding series books that have been written specifically for elementary school children on topics relating to our country: Vignettes of history; true stories of episodes in American life, enjoyed renewed interest and appreciation during the Bicentennial celebration. Informational articles, based upon historical events abound in children's literature. Most of these are *before* the "here-and-now", but children enjoy them because most are written with a flair for excitement, adventure, and bravery.

SOME CLASSROOM STRATEGIES FOR HELPING ELEMENTARY SCHOOL CHILDREN UTILIZE INFORMATIONAL READING MATERIALS AND READING-STUDY SKILLS

The manner in which one utilizes the resources that have been assembled is, in a large measure, the determining factor in the success of children in "finding out." Here are some strategies that we recommend:

INTEREST CENTERS

We have previously suggested specific areas of interest: sports, how things work, wheels, animals, how to do it, the arts, and our country. Special interest centers set up in various locations in the room are very effective. Each center will contain books, realia, and picutes relating to the special category. For example, a sports interest center would have blown-up photos and posters of active participants in sports, books about sports, biographies of sports "greats," novels with sports themes, and so on. There should also be a card file of informational books, novels, and biographies that are available in the library. A more elaborate center might have articles or short stories that have been cut from magazines and laminated in plastic, together with some reading-study questions to spark and/or verify comprehension of main ideas and details in the informational reading of that article or short story.

We recognize that many elementary school rooms are not large enough for seven separate interest centers operating simultaneously. In such cases, the

A listening center may be used to provide "read along" materials on any informational topic. Children can be motivated to want to discover what new and interesting things they can learn at the listening center each day. This takes planning, too.

interests can be changed and alternated through the school year, or they may be separate segments of one larger interest center.

PROPAGANDA ANALYSIS

The ultimate of critical reading is the analysis of propaganda—be it advertising, political or religious. Reading for information provides the background of facts for the critical reading of propaganda in the search for truth. Many of today's youth are dedicated to finding out "what it's all about." They want to "get to the bottom of things," meaning *truth*.

The job of the public school in a democracy is not to tell students *what* to think, but to provide informational materials that will help them reach their own decisions. This means reading materials from many points of view, for almost all large organizations have propaganda machines turning out selective reading material that favorably presents one side of an issue. Finding out what propaganda is all about is one of the essential skills that youth must learn in school if, indeed, that schooling is to be "relevant." Teaching children and youth to read propaganda materials critically is one of the ways we make learning to read worthwhile.

DECISIONMAKING

The essence of freedom and, indeed, democracy is the right to consider alternatives and to make decisions. Through informational reading materials, we are able to provide children and youth with the facts for educated decisionmaking. We have discussed *problem solving* in Chapter 7, but mention it here again because it is so relevant to the urge to find out and because it necessitates the application of reading-study skills to informational reading. It is dependent upon the availability of informative reading materials that provide facts for answering these two questions:

1. What if (this happens)?
2. What if it doesn't (happen)?

In more personal terms, those two questions can be stated: "What if I do?" and "What if I don't?"

Specifically, those two questions could be applied to all of life's decisions and problems. A few will suffice:

What if I do? . . . What if I don't? . . .

smoke cigarettes . . .

purchase a new car . . .

leave home . . .

take this job . . .

go out in this weather . . .

quit school . . .

skip school . . .

take someone else's homework . . .

deface someone else's painting . . .

steal someone else's idea for a science fair project . . .

do my homework . . .

set this priority instead of that . . .

The above-mentioned real-life problems are very personal problems for many elementary school children, and are by no means unusual. Others have faced them and have written about them. Reading the experiences of others and identifying with their feelings; reading the facts and advice of experts; and honestly setting the facts in the perspective of the two basic questions are the essential elements in decision-making.

Constellation of Concepts   In Chapter 7 we discussed the fact that "things that go together should be learned together" as one of the principles of the psychology of learning. It is appropriate that we discuss it again in the context of reading-study skills.

One of the exciting experiences in learning is the expanding of a constellation of concepts around one specific theme or idea. The mention of one thing leads to another and to another and another, *ad infinitum.* Why? Because the individual has read about all of these related concepts, perhaps individually, without much thought of relating them.

We frequently jest about teachers spending an entire year on *Indians.* Yet, the development of a constellation of concepts around the theme, *Indians,* has merits. Here are some of the related concepts that are in the constellation whose nucleus is *Indians:* Pilgrims, Puritans, Mayflower, Plymouth Plantation, religion, Mayflower Compact, government, ocean voyages in small ships, hardships of voyage in the Seventeenth Century, planting of corn, Thanksgiving, early churches, architecture, the Common, the New England town, town meetings, and so on. Have we strayed away from Indians? Yes, but behind all of these related concepts, the shadow of the original theme, *Indians,* lurks. Mention of Indians could have triggered thoughts in other directions: for example, frontier skirmishes, log forts, Indian raids, treaties, and Roger Williams. The point here is that every one of these related ideas is a worthy subject for informational reading (and recreational reading, as well).

So a year on Indians could very easily lead to a year's reading of fascinating informational materials on almost all of the facets of life in early Colonial America. How much more history, economics, politics, government, religion, environment, and spirit of the times, would be acquired and brought together in a *constellation of concepts* this way, compared with the sterile memorization of facts as usually presented in so-called "history" books!

Mention of any theme leads the creative and active mind to begin exploring the constellation of ideas that revolve around the nucleus. Try a few:

The Midwest

Pollution

The environment

poverty

brotherhood

liberation

ecology

time

power

family

Learning to read is worthwhile when children and youth can be given a choice of a wide variety of reading materials on all of the facets in the constellation of concepts surrounding any or each of such themes as these.

Through informational reading, learning becomes *discovery.* Freedom to read and the wherewithall for reading transport the individual from ignorance to knowledge, which, in turn, reveals more ignorance and the resultant search for *more* knowledge.

We are quite aware of the fact that some of the suggestions in this chapter are repeats of those made previously under other chapter headings, but their inclusion here seemed to be important. Our experience convinces us that, if the skills delineated in this chapter are taught purposefully and at appropriate times during the elementary years, the reading-study skills of the children will be significantly enhanced, and their abilities to locate informational materials and organize them will be developed for lifetime use.

There is no easy road (that we know of) to the development of reading-study skills. But there are better ways than those that emerge from hit-or-miss, trial-and-error efforts. We have found those presented here are the most effective and appropriate for elementary children who are learning *"how to read to learn."*

BIBLIOGRAPHY

Andrews, Larry, "Reading Comprehension and Three Modes of Prereading Assistance," *Journal of Reading Behavior* **5**:4 (1972), 237−241.

Ausubel, David P., "The Use of Advance Organizers in the Learning and Retention of Verbal Material," *Journal of Educational Psychology,* **51** (1960), 267−272.

Calder, Clarence R., and Seleiman D. Zalatimo, "Improving Children's Ability to Follow Directions," *Reading Teacher,* **24**:3 (1970), 227−238.

Dahl, Patricia R., "A Mastery-Based Experimental Program for Teaching High-Speed Word-Recognition Skills," *Reading Research Quarterly,* **9**:2 (1975−1976), 203−211. The study, done with Third Graders indicated the need for *overlearning* in order that the skills in reading become automated, thus permitting them to operate as a holistic process.

Dishner, Ernest K., and John W. Readence, "A Systematic Procedure for Teaching Main Idea," *Reading World,* **16**:1 (1976), 292−298.

Foreman, Dale I., "The National Assessment of Elementary Reading Project," *Reading Teacher,* **28** (1972), 292−298. An important report on the NAER project that tested word meanings, reading and interpreting reading aids, following written directions, knowing and using reference sources, recognizing significant facts in passages, drawing inferences, reading critically, and reading rapidly.

Gerhard, Christian, *Making Sense: Reading Comprehension Improved Through Categorizing.* Newark, DE: International Reading Association, 1975.

Glynn, Shawn M., and Francis J. DiVesta, "Outline and Hierarchial Organization as Aids for Study and Retrieval," *Journal of Educational Psychology,* **69**:2 (1977), 89−95.

Moore, W. E., "The Effects of SRA Laboratory Usage With Fifth-grade Children," *Technical Report Research Bulletin,* No. 29, New South Wales, Australia: Department of Education, 1968.

Morton, J., "The Effects of Context Upon Speed of Reading, Eye Movements, and Eye-Voice Span," *Quarterly Journal of Experimental Psychology,* **16** (1964), 340−354.

Pikulski, John J., and Margaret B. Jones, "Writing Directions Children Can Read," *Reading Teacher,* **30**:6 (1977), 598−602. This article contains some very useful suggestions and examples for structuring *directions* that are to be used for reading practice into forms that are easy to read and are not confusing for beginners.

Proger, Barton, and others, "Advance and Concurrent Organizers for Detailed Verbal Passages Used With Elementary School Pupils," *Journal of Educational Research,* **66** (1973), 451−456.

Readence, John R., and David Moore, "Strategies for Enhancing Readiness and Recall in Content Areas: The Encoding Specificity Principle," *Reading Psychology,* **1**:1 (Fall, 1979), 47−54.

Robinson, Helen M. (Editor), *Improving Reading in the Intermediate Years,* Glenview, IL: Scott-Foresman, 1973.

Rowell, Elizabeth H., "Do Elementary Students Read Better Orally or Silently?" *Reading Teacher* **29**:4 (1976), 367−370.

Schneeberg, Helen, and Marciene Mattleman, "The Listen-Read Project: Motivating Students Through Dual Modalities," *Elementary English,* **50** (1973), 900−904.

Smith, R.J., and K. D. Hesse, "The Effects of Prereading Assistance on the Comprehension and Attitudes of Good and Poor Readers," *Research in the Teaching of English.* **3** (1969), 166−167.

Stauffer, Russell G., *Directing the Reading-Thinking Process,* New York: Harper and Row, 1975.

Swalm, James E., "A Comparison of Oral Reading, Silent Reading, and Listening Comprehension," *Education,* **92**:4 (1972), 111–115.

Tribble, Gloria, "Research and Word-Development Skills," *Ohio Reading Teacher,* **6**:1 (1971), 3–4.

Vacca, Richard T., and Joanne L. Vacca, "Consider a Stations Approach to Middle School Reading Instruction," *Reading Teacher* **28**:1 (1974), 18–21. The Vaccas shared their experiences with learning stations by suggesting the following: (1) a tape recorder/typewriter station for language-experience stories; (2) a word-mix station for sequencing skills; (3) DRTA station for directed reading-thinking activity (See Stauffer) that is teacher-led; (4) main idea station using pictures and paragraphs mounted to illustrate main ideas; (5) cloze cards station stressing comprehension clues; (6) tutoring station using peers as "buddies"; and games station.

UNIT FOUR

Which approach to the teaching of reading has proven to be the best single means for all children? Our task would be much more simple if we could find the answer to that question. Yet, when we consider the fact that there are more than 100 approaches to beginning reading, we are quickly brought back to the realization that there are many media through which children learn to read. The main points to be remembered are that most, if not all, have good features; that children have learned to read through one medium or another, and that no one medium appears to be universally or equally efficacious for all.

The conclusion that any reasonable person should reach, it seems to us, is that the teaching of reading should utilize the best features of any and all alternatives. The resulting strategy and media will comprise an *eclectic* system; the best of all worlds!

Unit Four serves as an introduction to the two major means: *individualized reading* and the *basal reader approach*. Neither chapter will *fully* equip you to handle the individual reading approach or the basal reader approach, but, by reading them and doing some of the activities suggested by your professor, you will have the foundation for the development, refinement, and utilization of both techniques.

We believe that every teacher of reading must be acquainted with both the individualized approach and the basal reader approach, for, as we emphasize in the two chapters in this unit, it is not a matter of "either/or" but a need for *both*. Both have advantages and both have disadvantages, but the advantages of *both* approaches are strong evidence that superior teachers of reading will be using both.

MEANS

CHAPTER NINE

How Do I Manage
Individualized Reading?

What is Individualized Reading?
Advantages of Individualized Reading
Disadvantages of Individualized Reading
Basic Strategies for Individualized Reading
   How Can I Begin an Individualized Reading Program?
   Continuing an Individualized Reading Program
     up through the Primary Grades
   Selecting and Organizing Materials for the
     Individualized Reading Program
     Types of reading materials
     Organization of individualized reading materials
   The Independent Reading Period
   The Teacher–Pupil Conference
   Record Keeping
Chief Features of Individualized Reading

WHAT IS INDIVIDUALIZED READING?

Individualized reading is many things, all integrated into a unified classroom mechanism for reading. It is a way of thinking about teaching and learning. It is a way of thinking about individuals. It is a way of thinking about self.

A definition—if one is possible—might be something like this: "Individualized reading is a way of organizing a classroom learning situation in which all children are selecting and reading books of their own choice at their own comfortable rates; and, in the same class, are grouped for skills instruction according to their observed needs."

In a truly individualized reading situation, the teacher is expediter of learning, planning for learning to take place. In modern educational terms, the teacher is *manager* of learning. Thus, the role shifts from one in which the teacher is the dominant character to one in which he/she is organizer and helper, moving around the room as an ever-present source of encouragement and advice, and a reactor to children's needs and comments.

Individualized reading should *not* be confused with *individualized instruction*—the latter being a one-to-one teaching-learning situation necessitated by situations where a child is retarded in reading and needs intensive individual remedial work: one teacher—one child. On the other hand, in a classroom in which individualized reading is taking place 25 to 30 children all may be reading different selections and the teacher will be giving each child some individual attention from time to time.

Two strategies are paramount: (1) to provide a wide variety of relevant and appropriate books from which children may individually choose according to their likes and interests; and (2) to observe each child in a normal reading situation to ascertain instructional needs and assign each child to a group for training in a specific deficient skill.

If one can visualize an "open" classroom in which children have the opportunity to move about and select books from the classroom library; sit in small groups and listen to one of their classmates reading from a favorite book; share a synopsis of a book with a friend; sit with the teacher and discuss a book and read portions so the teacher can observe progress and/or needs, then one can probably appreciate the advantages and disadvantages of individualized reading as a means of helping children learn how to read, and or having children enjoy books after they have acquired basic reading skills.

ADVANTAGES OF INDIVIDUALIZED READING

SELF-SELECTION

In the individualized reading program, the teacher may guide the child toward choice of reading materials but does not interfere with such choice. No attempt is

Can children be "turned loose" during the book selection phase of individualized reading? What preplanning must you do as the teacher? What preplanning should you do with the pupils? What controls and/or restraints must be operational to prevent chaos? What responsibilities do you, as the classroom teacher, have when your pupils are in the library for book selection?

made toward establishing a "well-balanced" diet of reading. No stigma is attached, for example, to reading only about sports, or only about animals. No attempt is made to get the child to "broaden" his or her outlook by switching from one juvenile-book series to another, or to some other type of materials. The child's current interest dictates what is currently being read.

SELF-PACING

Some children work fast; others are dilatory. "Average" speed for reading in any grade is probably a figment of imagination. Individualized reading is a system in which books are to be enjoyed at whatever pace each individual chooses. In fact, pace is never really a consciously planned element in reading in an individualized reading classroom.

DIFFICULTY LEVELS

There is no stigma for anyone reading "below grade level." Indeed, there is no "grade level" placed on the trade books, although a good teacher may have a fairly accurate notion of the approximate difficulty of the material. The main feature is that children can read at what they, themselves, determine to be their own *comfortable* levels.

In helping children select books that are not too difficult for their abilities, teachers need to know both the approximate reading ability of each child and the approximate readability level of each book. Regardless of teachers' suggestions, children are free to attempt to read books beyond their own reading levels; and, finding those books too difficult, they are free to admit a mistake without incurring sarcasm or censure.

LEARNING CENTERS AND THE OPEN CLASSROOM

Learning centers and the concept of the "open classroom" are essential features of the individualized-reading classroom environment. The basic learning-center unit is the classroom library. In larger rooms, it is possible to set up centers for special kinds of reading: novels in one area; informational books—including encyclopedias, yearbooks, and books on science, social studies, etc., in another; biographies and autobiographies; talking books, listening tapes, recordings, and so on, in other areas; a center for sharing; one for learning skills in groups with teacher; and a workshop corner for individual work for reinforcing skills in workbooks or worksheets.

The concept of the "open classroom" is, of course, integral to individualized reading. It is impossible to imagine an individualized-reading classroom wherein children are confined to seats fastened to the floor. Freedom to move about the room is essential for children and teacher alike.

GROUPING

Individualized reading is not intended to isolate children from one another. Indeed, working in pairs and groups is likely to be far more prevalent in well-run individualized-reading classrooms than in traditional classes. However, children are not grouped according to age or grade level but according to specific skills to be learned or strengthened. In addition, grouping is used to enable the children to share their reading experiences with one another; perhaps to listen to a favorite story read by one of their peers; or maybe just to share their enthusiasms and interests.

THE TEACHER IS "EXPEDITER"

In individualized reading, the teacher's role shifts to that of an expediter of learning. The teacher, during the individual conference time, listens to a child

A small group of children who are working on the same skills may successfully be guided by means of taped directions. In this photo, the tape apparently is directing the children's attention to the cover of the book and, perhaps, to the title, *Winnie the Pooh and Tigger.* What skills might this session be designed to develop?

read. As the teacher circulates around the room, the teacher consults, suggests, advises, encourages. The teacher *plans* for learning to take place. The learning that does take place is largely in direct relationship to the breadth and depth of the teacher's plans. The teacher is even more important as the dynamo in the individualized-reading classroom than teachers ordinarily are in other types of reading instruction. Here, indeed, it is the *teacher* that makes the difference!

DIAGNOSIS/PRESCRIPTION

Diagnostic-prescriptive learning is the basic method of teaching skills in the individualized reading classroom. In fact, this has been an essential component from the very beginnings of the individualized reading movement (1960s) long before "diagnostic-prescriptive" became the "in word," along with mastery learning in the mid 1970s.

Efforts were made to popularize individualized reading as early as the 1950s. Dr. May Lazar was one of the early leaders of the movement; describing practices that she had introduced into the New York City schools. What is now called the diagnostic-prescriptive element is accomplished in the individual teacher-pupil conference, described later in this chapter.

CUMULATIVE RECORDS

Accurate day-to-day records of each child's achievement and needs in reading skills are kept. They are the heart of the individualized reading approach, for they serve as guidelines for teaching each new reading skill. Certainly, just reading books on an individual basis does not assure that a child will learn to read well. The records that a teacher keeps on each child's performance are the reference points for grouping and for instruction in skills that appear to need strengthening. Without records, individualized reading would just be free reading with neither goals, directions, nor verification of progress.

INTRINSIC MOTIVATION AND SUCCESS

It has often been said that "Nothing succeeds like success." In the individualized reading approach, each child succeeds somewhat approximating his/her own potential. Some, obviously, achieve more than others. Some are reluctant readers; others are avid bookworms. In no instance is any child a "failure."

Children who experience the freedom of reading under this method have frequently been known to read almost unbelievable numbers of books; as many as one hundred in a school year. Yet, the number or variety of books read is not used as a competitive ruse to pit one child against another. Bribes or rewards (now called "token reinforcement") are not necessary. The intrinsic reward that accompanies the completion of a story usually is all that is necessary.

An *environment of books* surrounds everyone in an individualized reading classroom. As environment affects all of us, so does the environment of books affect the children. In that environment are beautiful books to look at; children learn that books can be beautiful. Informational books convey the message that one can learn many things from books. Children who are thus surrounded with books begin to realize that books can do something to enhance their own quality of life; can make them more knowledgeable, more valuable as persons, can help them reach their own goals.

DISADVANTAGES OF INDIVIDUALIZED READING

There is no doubt that the individualized reading approach to teaching reading can be extremely effective, nor is there any doubt that it has been used with great success by some teachers. However, this is not to say that it is without difficulties and disadvantages. It is, perhaps, more ideal than practical. Indeed, given the conditions in many schools today, it may be quite impractical for certain teachers to attempt such a program in some schools. In any case, before discussing strategies for implementing the program, let us take a rather hard look at the difficulties involved in setting up and utilizing this approach to the teaching of reading.

PREPARATION TIME

Individualized reading strategies require enormous amounts of preparation time that may or may not be available to you. Anyone contemplating an individualized reading set-up must dedicate several hours each day at the outset for planning and preparation of room and materials.

Getting the program started is just the beginning. Large blocks of preparation and planning time must be set aside daily and weekly to keep the system working. Teachers who are not willing to invest at least two hours per day for planning, record keeping, and prescriptive materials should not undertake individualized reading. Time is of the essence!

TIME FOR INDIVIDUAL CONFERENCES

Running an individualized reading program also requires an enormous amount of *time* for *individual conferences*, far more, in fact, than most proponents of individualizing admit. In a class of 30 children, meeting five days per week, how much time could be given to each child for a conference and still run the remainder of an elementary school curriculum including spelling, writing, arithmetic, science, art, music, and physical education? Additional time, of course, is needed for attendance, notices, health checks, all-school activities, lunch, toileting, and arrival and departure routines.

Let us assume that the reading periods can last, at most two full hours per day (a rather large amount of time for some schools). During those two hours, the teacher helps pupils select books, responds to enthusiastic comments from children, helps arrange pupils in pairs for independent skill practice on phonics games, stops to listen to some child reading to several friends, and is involved in other routine activities inherent in an open classroom. How many individual conferences can one hold per day? Four is a good average; sometimes five.

That means that, with careful planning, each child may possibly have a conference with the teacher once every two weeks. At the beginning of the school year, the conferences will probably be shorter and more frequent. By mid-year, they will become more lengthy; less frequent. Many teachers view this as a disadvantage that limits their effectiveness.

MANAGING AN OPEN-CLASSROOM ENVIRONMENT

The individualized-reading environment and the nature of the program itself may present serious classroom management problems. It is not an easy task to maintain direction of groups of mobile children in an open-classroom situation.

"Well, so much for the open-classroom experiment."

Cartoon by Glasbergen/Phi Delta Kappan, December, 1977.

Indeed, teachers of upper grades often complain that their students arrive without mastery of basic skills because lack of order and direction in the open classroom has precluded their learning these skills. This, of course, need not be. A properly run open classroom is not chaotic, nor does it lack proper direction and guidance. Nevertheless, it would be folly to deny that some teachers lack the expertise or temperament to manage the open classroom or that such classrooms do degenerate into chaos.

Individual conferences may also present classroom-management problems. Such conferences totally engage the attention of the teacher to the exclusion of other members of the class. If the conference lasts ten minutes, which it frequently does, there can be trouble in unsupervised parts of the room. Careful planning and good classroom organization is necessary to assure that the other children remain constructively employed during individual conferences. Chaos during the teacher-pupil conference has been the "undoing" of many inexperienced teachers.

Another strain on classroom management is the very fact that the program is essentially self-motivated. Ideally, self-motivation and self-direction should be at the heart of all learning, but some youngsters, especially very young children, will need extra guidance in this direction—another management problem. Some teachers, unfortunately, are tempted to assume that development of self-motivation is automatic. It is not.

The elaborate and time-consuming record keeping essential to a successful program may also lead to mismanagement. When record keeping becomes overly burdensome, the temptation is to turn this task over to teacher aides or other helpers. This, in turn, can lead to lack of personal awareness of a child's progress in the classroom. There is danger that the child may cease to be an individual to the teacher and become little more than a recorded number.

DIAGNOSTIC "KNOW-HOW"

To run a successful individualized reading program, a teacher has to be acquainted with the diagnostic techniques generally used during such conferences and must certainly know most of the phonics and word recognition skills expected of children in a reading program.

In recent years, considerable emphasis has been placed upon what is called "mastery learning." This has come about as a result of several factors: Bloom's Taxonomy of Educational Objectives, "diagnostic/prescriptive" teaching; "criterion referenced" teaching; and such structures as the "Wisconsin Design." Most of these are predicated on the assumption that each teacher will know the various reading skills and will have some sequence in mind. Furthermore, it is assumed that each teacher will be able to check on *each* child and, as a result of that short check, will be able to assign children to *ad hoc* groups for special instruction in *specific* basic skills.

The expectation that all teachers will be competent to do this, will have the time and commitment to do it, and will, in fact, do it does not seem to be founded on reality. This time-consuming and sophisticated task requiring much training and practice seems to preclude the probability that many individuals will undertake it.

SEQUENCE OF SKILLS

Skills sequencing for each individual child is, undoubtedly, one of the most difficult aspects of maintaining an individualized reading program. In other approaches to reading, skill sequence is frequently provided for the teacher. For example, it is detailed in the teacher's manual for basal reader series and in phonics workbooks. In programs based upon skills-assessment and prescriptive teaching, skill sequence is "prepackaged," together with pretests, instructional techniques and materials, and criterion-referenced post-tests.

Although these resources are available to teachers using the individualized approach, most individualized reading programs prefer to rely on the teacher to conduct individual diagnosis and subsequent individually prescribed instruction. This may lead to an erroneous assumption that skill sequence is basically irrelevant to the program. However, although there may be no rigid hierarchy of reading skills, there is certainly some validity in sequencing. For example, it would not be sensible to teach vowel digraphs before individual vowel sounds nor to teach consonant blends before individual consonant sounds.

Skill sequencing in the individualized reading program requires that the teacher plan an entire sequence for each child and follow it for each child. However, deficiencies that become apparent during individual conferences will almost surely not correspond exactly with the sequence devised by the teacher. Somehow, the teacher must be able to determine whether or not each child has mastered the skills appropriate to a particular span of the school year. If trouble with a specific skill does not manifest itself in an individual conference, can the teacher assume the child has mastered that skill and is ready to proceed to a sequential one?

QUESTIONING DURING THE CONFERENCE

Throughout this text (particularly in Chapter 7), we have emphasized the importance of proper questioning in the teaching of reading. Other approaches to reading provide a good deal of "prepackaged" help in formulating questions. Some materials used in the individualized reading program may provide this aid. Most, however, will require formulation of questions related directly to the story each child has chosen and the objectives of the conference. At one time, the purpose of the conference might be to determine whether or not a child has been able to discover main ideas and supporting details. At another conference, the type of book being discussed might lend itself to a discussion of characterization, values, commitment, priorities, or any number of qualities of life. Questioning, to be useful and effective, should be directed toward a positive goal. The teacher must know *why* each question is asked; *what* is to be gained by asking it; and *where* the answers lead. To this end, the teacher must know each story or selection and be able to ask the "right" questions. This takes *some* doing!

READABILITY LEVELS

Although the child in an individualized program is encouraged to choose reading material without specific restrictions as to readability level, some guidance may be necessary. So-called trade books are prominent in most individualized programs and most of these do not indicate the book's grade-level readability. Of course, readability level is not indicated for many other types of materials used in the program. Lack of such information may pose problems for the teacher when asked to recommend or suggest materials for reading in the individualized program.

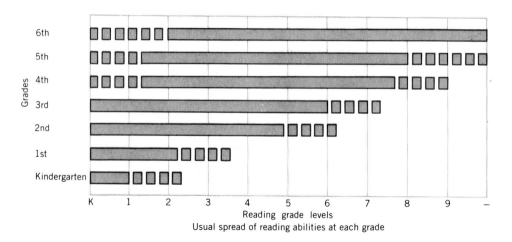

Usual spread of reading abilities at each grade

LOSS OF GROUP REINFORCEMENT

Common reading experiences have for years been a part of most group reading lessons. It is seldom that this happens in a truly individualized situation, for the essence of individualized reading is found in the fact that each child is reading something different. *Lack* of common reading experiences is a disadvantage some believe to be quite serious. They point to the fact that social interplay of ideas, sharing feelings about story characters, discussing cause-and-effect situations, and making predictions together are all part of group thinking and problem-solving techniques. They do not see this happening in an individualized reading situation.

NEGLECT OF SUPERIOR CHILDREN

There is a temptation to release children who demonstrate superior work habits and high intelligence to learn *on their own*. It may be true that generations of children with high intelligence have learned in school in spite of teachers. However, an individualized reading program should never lose track of students by sending them forth with little or no guidance or control. Superior children need the freedom that individualized reading affords, but they also should not be *neglected*. In fact, personal experience with classes of such children supports our contention that planning for them to operate at their maximum potential requires far more effort than most teachers realize. An individualized reading approach provides that opportunity, while, at the same time, is a challenge and responsibility that is just too much for some teachers.

THE TASK OF BOOK COLLECTION

It takes months and even years to accumulate a *collection of reading materials* adequate for the various reading abilities and interests of 25 children in a classroom. That may seem to be a fatalistic viewpoint; however, it can be and is done. But it is a chore which, in the end, is a rewarding one.

Trade books, articles, magazines, pamphlets, poems, short stories, biographies, and so on that are relevant to the interests and needs of children of the age, environmental backgrounds, abilities, and self-concepts of your entire class would have to be assembled! Hundreds of items must be available either in a self-contained library within the class, from the school learning materials center, and/or from the local public library or state lending library.

Books and other reading materials must be available and on hand for special days, the seasons, holidays, special events, to correlate with TV programs, and to conform to the common interests of boys and girls of the age and backgrounds of the children in class.

This is a monumental task. Just thinking about it drives some teachers right back to the basal readers where a team of reading experts has already done the job for them. Other, more energetic individuals, accept it as a challenge and do the job admirably, but, admittedly, with great expenditure of time and effort.

PUBLIC RELATIONS

Explaining and *justifying* the program to parents is one of the disadvantages that must be recognized. It is not only a public relations job, it is an educational project in which parents must be retrained to think about a new concept of education, involving a *non*basal reader approach, an open classroom, self-selection, self-pacing, and no tests to indicate grade-level achievement. It is easy for parents to conclude that this is a program where little or no teaching takes place. Moreover, many parents have been trained to think in terms of grade-by-grade progress with grades based upon comparative norms.

It takes a good person to reeducate parents and community concerning the merits of individualized reading. Moreover, very little research supports any claim that children who have had individualized reading are superior readers to those who have had other methods. The "selling job" is a difficult one, especially in times when parents and revolting taxpayers are equating academic achievement with a structured classroom and failure with a *laissez faire* classroom. Teacher performance and accountability are on the spot!

COLLEAGUES

Suspicion and *jealousy* often attend a situation where one teacher succeeds with individualized reading and gets publicity in press and on TV. Other teachers who, perhaps, are just as dedicated to their particular approach to reading may wonder why one teacher is thus singled out for recognition, while they plug along day-after-day with equally good results as measured by their student's performance on reading-comprehension tests. A few teachers have been known to abandon individualized reading because of the negative feelings expressed openly or covertly by their colleagues.

CONCLUSIONS—ADVANTAGES AND DISADVANTAGES

This lengthy recital of advantages and disadvantages is meant to delineate the common reactions of thousands of teachers toward individualized reading.

A few conclusions seem obvious:

1. It is a time-consuming operation.
2. It requires uncommon dedication.
3. It is different from the traditional.
4. It requires a tolerance for movement within a classroom.
5. Because it is "different," it generates criticism.
6. It necessitates structure, planning, and a knowledge of skills beyond that ordinarily found in most beginning teachers.
7. It frees children to select and read materials of their own liking. As a result, much more reading takes place.
8. It is *not* for everyone. Some children need more structured sequence and pace than individualizing provides. Some teachers need the security of prepackaged materials and method devised by "experts." Some teachers do not have the physical and/or emotional capacity to mount and manage such a huge undertaking.
9. It demands an ability to communicate with children and to respond to their

needs, feelings, and expressions of self-concept. In this, it demands utmost sensitivity.

BASIC STRATEGIES FOR INDIVIDUALIZED READING

Having observed the pros and cons of the individualized reading approach, we may now turn to a more detailed description of how a program works.

HOW CAN I BEGIN AN INDIVIDUALIZED READING PROGRAM?

An individualized reading program can be begun in the First Grade, or even in Kindergarten. A first step in such a program is the construction of the individualized experience story. The teacher (or teacher's aide) constructs this story for the child from the child's own experiences as elicited from discussion with the child. The teacher also constructs very short and simple stories for the child to copy and helps the child begin an individualized word list. Eventually, the child is encouraged to make up and print out his or her own stories. (These techniques have been described fully in Chapter 3.).

Individualized reading materials for children just learning to read can be culled from old basal reading series and other preprimer sources—a simple cut-and-paste job. For example, a story of three or four pages in a preprimer can be stretched out to eight or ten pages by cutting out pictures and story lines and placing them so that they face each other on double-page spreads.

Certain conditions are, of course, necessary if this early individualized program is to succeed. For example, reading materials ("little books") must be very short and simple so that they can be read over and over and, in effect, memorized. Stories must be individually tailored for each child. The teacher must be ready to help with new words, for the child has not yet begun to acquire word-analysis techniques. The children should be encouraged to believe that they will begin to "read" as soon as they enter the program. Finally, classes must be small enough so that the teacher can give the individual attention to each child demanded by such a program.

CONTINUING AN INDIVIDUALIZED READING PROGRAM UP THROUGH THE PRIMARY GRADES

If we envision children in the kindergarten or first grade commencing to read by just learning a whole-word method, we may be prone to extend this notion and concept up into the second and third grades by imagining that the children continue to progress merely by enlarging their memorized sight vocabulary. To carry this concept one step further, we would naturally assume that those same children would be allowed (even encouraged) to read whatever they wish and at whatever pace they choose, and that's it! Although this may, indeed, be a somewhat accurate description of what goes on in some so-called individualized reading programs, it is certainly a corruption of the basic philosophy of individualized reading. Underriding the general concept of individualized reading is the recognition of individual differences and the fact that there are specific and identifiable skills that must be mastered, that the teacher must know those and have a technique for identifying children who exhibit deficiencies in the various factors, and that children should be grouped for instruction in the skills that they need.

There is no conflict between proponents of individualized reading and those who insist on teaching children basic reading skills. First, in a complete, authentic individualized reading program, the teacher/pupil conference time is essentially a period of diagnosis of reading deficiencies and needs. Second, grouping for skills instruction is employed for purposes of instructing several children who need to learn the same specific reading skill. Third, comprehension skills are developed by exactly the same questioning strategies that are used in any good basal reader program.

The main difference, therefore, is not one of reading skills but that a basal reader series is most frequently used in a traditional structured approach, and a collection of booklets and/or stories is used in an individualized reading approach, with each child reading something different from that being read by any or most of his/her classmates.

Many teachers have not been trained in teaching beginning reading skills through an individualized reading routine and, therefore, do not feel confident that they can accomplish satisfactory results with such a collection of multifaceted materials and seemingly unstructured sequence. They seem to fear that, under ordinary classroom conditions, they might inadvertently skip many of the basic reading competencies necessary for developing skillful readers.

Those same teachers believe that, after children have mastered basic word-recognition and comprehension skills in a structured learning-to-read program, individualized reading (which they equate with individual selection and individual pacing) is a fine thing.

As a result of this widely current (but inadequate) idea of individualized reading, many if not most schools that profess to have an individualized-reading program in operation, actually have one starting in grade two or in grade three and extending upwards *after* the children have learned specific reading skills. In such situations, the work in the first grade is largely phonics, word recognition, and comprehension strategies, followed in the second grade and third grade with self-selection, self-pacing, teacher-pupil conferences, grouping according to deficiencies, and skill-sessions that might be viewed as "remedial" or, at best, "corrective."

SELECTING AND ORGANIZING MATERIALS FOR THE INDIVIDUALIZED-READING PROGRAM

As previously noted, the individualized-reading program requires that a multiplicity of reading materials be available for selection by the children involved in the program. The principle of self-selection also requires that these materials represent various levels of reading difficulty and that they be relevant to the interests of the children.

The children must, of course, have access to materials within their reading competencies. Since the spread of reading ability increases from first grade onward, the range of reading-level materials must also increase as the child progresses through grades one to six. For example, in first grade, your collection of reading materials should range from picture books (for nonreaders) through books at second-grade readability. In fourth grade, the range should be from first grade through fifth grade readability, and so on. It is possible that some children in a particular grade may be able to read at a somewhat higher readability level than the available materials provide. This, however, need not be a serious problem. Children (and, indeed, adults) can enjoy and profit from reading at a "comfortable" level even though, if taxed, they are capable of reading more difficult materials.

As to relevancy, overworked as this word has become in contemporary pedagogy, relevancy is nevertheless vital to productive self-selection of reading materials in the individualized program. Materials must be of interest to the child if the child is to be properly motivated to read. (Do you willingly read what is not of interest to you?)

But how can we know what interests a particular child? We can listen. We can observe. Let the children themselves tell you what they would like to read about. Most will be forthcoming. If not, try something like the "three-wishes" test. "If you could do anything you want, what three things would you do?" "If you could be anyone you wish, what person would you want most to be? What would be your second and third choices?" Also, observe the children. Is the child attentive when reading certain materials? Or restless? Does the child go more often to one type of materials then another in making his or her selection?

There are, of course, materials of almost universal appeal, tested and proven by time to interest almost any child. Needless to say, such materials should always be included in your individualized reading collection. In addition, be sure to keep your collection current. A popular TV program, for example, may spark special interest in space travel, or in surfing, or monsters or whatever. (TV stations supply advance programming sheets for months ahead.) Be prepared by having materials on hand to satisfy interests growing out of these and special events (the baseball World Series, for example, or the Olympic Games) and upcoming holidays.

Types of Reading Materials   We have detailed elsewhere in the book the wide variety of reading materials that should be available in the learning-to-read classroom and/or school learning center. Suffice it to say here, that variety is, if possible, even more important in the individualized-reading program. The principle of self-selection requires that no avenue of interest be closed. Almost all types of books should be on hand—short stories, novels, biographies and autobiographies, fun books (cartoons, jokes, etc.), poetry books, science books, and so on.

In addition, your collection might include newspaper and magazine clippings, elementary-school periodicals, mail-order catalogues, direct-mail advertisements, even comic books. Also it definitely should include encyclopedias and other source materials appropriate for use by children.

Variety can also be added to your collection by inclusion of books from so-called Hi-Lo or easy reading series—that is, books specially constructed for high interest and low readability levels. Although such works are generally used with children needing remedial instruction, they can also be a valuable asset to the individualized reading collection. Spache's reference works, *Good Books for Poor Readers* and *Good Reading for Disadvantaged Readers* (both published by Garrard Press) are excellent guides to selection of these types of materials.

A special word should also be said here about prepackaged materials for individualized reading, the best known and most widely used of which are probably the *SRA Reading Laboratories*. These so-called "laboratories" are actually boxed materials, consisting of cards on which are printed interesting stories and articles in a progressively more difficult sequence. After selecting a card (which is color-coded according to level of difficulty) the child tests himself or herself on comprehension and a few other study skills, makes a record of accomplishment in his or her pupil record book, and works on one or more special skills before going on to the next story or to the next higher level. They are do-it-yourself materials appropriate for self-selection, salf-pacing, and self-evaluation. They are available for differing levels from about second grade up through secondary school.

A collection of short stories can easily be assembled by using stories in childrens old weekly and/or monthly magazines and periodicals, and by selecting good ones from out-dated basal readers. Two copies of each magazine or book are needed to provide the total story. The parts should be assembled with pages back-to-back, and then laminated between sheets of contact paper. They can then be filed (as in the Interest-Based Reading Plan) under headings such as *horses, pets, fishing, baseball, nurses, travel*, and *swimming*.

Poems are universally enjoyed by children. There just never seem to be enough available, and, often, not at the right time. Consequently, poems from old basal readers should be clipped, mounted, and laminated. Children's magazines and classroom newspapers are also sources of poems that should be clipped and preserved. Poems, too, should be filed under headings that will permit their use when the occasion arises.

Advertisements provide a rich source of reading material. They may be used as the media for comparisons between years and eras in history . . . prices, styles, modes of living, and so on. They may also be used to assess truth-in-advertising, motivational techniques, propaganda, generation of wants and desires, values, and/or necessities and luxuries.

Organization of Individualized Reading Materials   Proper organization of reading materials is extremely important in the individualized reading classroom. The children must have some relatively quick and easy way to find materials that are to their specific interests. Otherwise the open-classroom atmosphere of the program could lead to chaos. Since the program is interest-based, whatever organizational pattern you use should be based as far as feasible, on the childrens interests.

In Chapter 7, "Comprehension," we suggested that one way to organize is to adopt and adapt the interest-based reading program that was devised in the early 1970's by Bryan McQuillan and his staff in the Curriculum and Research Branch of the Education Department in Melbourne, Victoria, Australia.

The main feature is the designation of all materials in the collection according to interests of children. The whole plan is based upon the assumption that these are, indeed, the true interests of children. Such an assumption has to be made to get this type of program started. Adjustments can be made later as new interests develop.

The Interest-based plan is implemented in the classroom by means of boxes, each carrying the label of the interest. In one school in Melbourne that we visited, three boxes were being used for each interest theme. Each box was color-coded and the booklets within it were also coded with stickers of the same color. Each color represented a readability level. For example, the data in the boxes are designated as level A, level B, and level C (most difficult).

All level A materials and the boxes containing them could have red stickers; level B could be blue; and level C could be yellow . . . or any other colors that are conveniently available.

The headings for each interest category are:

Home and Family	Science
School	Occupations
Children's Activities	Houses
Toys	Festivals, holidays
Farm	Space
Animals	Baby
Zoo	Food
Sea	Legends, Fantasy, Folk Tales
Shops	Communication
Birthdays	Machines

Circus, Fairs, Shows	Other Lands
Insects, Reptiles, Spiders	Prehistoric Animals
Transportation	Clothing
Size, Shape, Color, Number	Weather and Seasons

A creative teacher, however, will find ways of adapting this interest-based reading plan and will find that, by color-coding the materials (both clippings and booklets), and storing them in color-coded holders or boxes, children will make great use of them as part of the individualized-reading approach.

Several additions can be made to bring the system within the American culture. Here are a few suggestions:

Sports Australian children appeared to be just as fascinated with sports as are American children . . . but the "interest" plan did not include "sports" as one category. We think it should be added.

Vacations Vacation travel . . . especially by camper has become such an important part of the lives of many children that this should be a good category. In this same connection, perhaps *National Parks* could also be added. Road maps, camping brochures, resorts, and so on could all have a place under this large category.

Adventure This is another category that should be added to make a place for clipped short stories of adventure that will fast fill up a container.

Self Self is a special category that seems to be very important. It would include a person's body, manners, how one feels about self, comparisons with "norms," friends (how to make and keep them), values and so on.

Money This is another major interest of all children.

Sea This may not be as relevant in Arizona as in San Francisco (which faces the sea). It may be that other categories such as *Mountains, Desert, Great Lakes,* and so on should be added, depending on where your school is located.

Farms Farmland constitutes a huge part of America, and it is a basic interest of millions of children. In this same connection *Food* seems to be an appropriate addition.

Wheels In the last chapter, we cited "wheels" as a most relevant topic for informational reading. We observe that almost all children look to the day when they can own and ride a two-wheeler, skateboard, motor scooter, motor bike, and/or Moped. Every individualized reading room must have plenty of "wheelies" books.

THE INDEPENDENT READING PERIOD

Depending upon classroom conditions and the total day's schedule, the amount of time given to concentrated independent reading will vary from 15 minutes to an hour. Another variable may be the "independent reading" abilities of the children—that is, the level at which a child reads comfortably with few errors, at a smooth pace, and with reasonably good comprehension. Even within class-rooms where children have been homogeneously grouped, there will most likely be a wide range in ability to read independently, and this difference must be allowed for. Fifteen minutes may be too much time for the child who has not yet learned to sit and attend to the task of reading a book. On the other hand, this pittance of time may frustrate the child who is an extremely slow reader.

Children can be "conditioned" to attend to books during independent reading time. This may well be commenced during the kindergarten year, even though most of the children are not yet able to "read" the words in the traditional manner. They can, however, be taught to "read" a picture book of their own choosing and to concentrate on that book for an extended period of time.

In their delightful little book, *Reading is Only The Tiger's Tail*, the Mc-Crackens described "Sustained Silent Reading" (SSR) in Kindergarten Classes. They cited numerous Kindergarten classrooms where silent "reading" of books is "sustained" by all Kindergartners for 15 to 20 minutes daily. Better, still, they described how it is done.

The main element in the success of the independent reading period is individual responsibility. Inasmuch as children will be reading "on their own," they

Individualized reading is successful when children are reading relevant materials of their own choosing at their own rate. Is reading such as this adequate proof that children are efficient readers? How does one know?

should have the opportunity of making their own plans for reading. This is a natural follow-up of the self-selection process. Freedom of choice need not mean lack of goals nor unstructured disorganization. Success in learning is dependent largely upon planning, and that planning should be directed toward self-fulfillment. Each child, consequently, will achieve a higher degree of satisfaction if the plan for independent reading is directed toward a specific goal.

If, on the other hand, the child feels that it is necessary to be reading a book just because it is book-reading time, the independent reading period will be anticipated daily as a chore and its purpose will be defeated.

All goals for reading a book or any other bit of reading material during the independent reading period must be selfish . . . self-actualizing, that is. There must be some anticipated self-satisfying rewards. For example, a child decides on *Horses* as the subject of special interest. His/her goals may be to learn about different kinds of horses, about a special breed of horses, how horses are trained, a famous horse in history, or, perhaps, the child is interested only in a novel or adventure story in which a horse is the hero. The child then should be able to set a goal by answering the question: "What's in this book for me?" (It doesn't have to be a book . . . it can be an article or some other informational source). With a goal, the child reads independently with purpose that is self-directed and self-fulfilling . . . the opposite of reading something that the teacher wants read.

In such an independent reading period, does the teacher have the right to ask, "What are you reading that book for?" or "Why didn't you select *this* article instead of the one you are reading?" or "Don't you think you are wasting your time on that?" What responsibilities does the teacher have? What restraints must be observed?

THE TEACHER–PUPIL CONFERENCE

Some versions of individualized reading include only self-selection and independent reading; and, to be sure, those might suffice, but it is a very inadequate notion, for it makes no provision for structured and purposeful learning and followup. The teacher/pupil conference is the heart of the learning segment of the individualized reading program. It is a structured, yet informal, discussion and planning session. It is a business meeting during which ideas are shared, assessments are made, decisions are agreed upon, and plans for further development are consummated.

Planning for the Conference   In the primary grades, the teacher must review the child's record and note especially the comments and plans made at the previous conference, for the child during those years is still likely to be quite dependent upon the teacher for guidance.

The teacher-pupil conference is the heart of the successful individualized reading programs. How can you know the "right" questions to ask, the needs to be met, and the effective skills practice to be prescribed?

Here, then, are some of the facts that the teacher should have at hand when the child arrives for the conference:

1. Reading level of child . . . independent level.
2. Theme that the child is pursuing.
3. Name of book the child is reading.
4. Type of story . . . general story theme.
5. Why child selected that particular book.
6. Specific reading problems, if any, that the child is working on.

7. Special vocabulary that the child needed to master (according to last conference).
8. Specific skills group that the child is now working in.
9. Special interest of the child.
10. Other books that the child has read. What reading pattern is developing?

Timing the Conference   The average time spent in teacher/pupil conferences appears to be about 8 to 10 minutes. And the realities of present-day classrooms seem to indicate that each child can expect to have a conference once every two weeks. That is not enough, of course, but it may be 8 to 10 minutes more of undivided attention than a child gets under other approaches to reading.

In addition to the 8 to 10 minute conference, each child receives time in a group for specific skills instruction and time in whole class sharing of reading experiences.

Interaction During the Conference   The individualized reading conference is one of the few times when child and teacher get to know each other as persons. Personal relationships are developed because the teacher learns of the deeper interests of each child, interests that would not be revealed publically before the entire group. The pupil learns that the teacher is also interested and enthusiastic about the child as a person, and that the child's goals and selection of books are of value. It is a time when the teacher learns to know the self-concepts of each child.

In addition to being a time of "getting-to-know" each other, the conference is a sharing time. The teacher does not need to know each book completely. Given the chance, the child will share the main ideas, the plot, the characters, the mood of the story. All the teacher needs to do is to exercise great restraint and let the child do the talking. This is also a rare event in a child's school life, a chance to spend an uninterrupted period of time telling a teacher a story. In a sense, it provides the same psychological rewards to the older child that show-and-tell-time does for the four and five-year old.

The teacher's reaction to the child who shares the story during the conference must be positive and supportive. Such comments as the following are appropriate:

"You liked the story, didn't you?"

"You liked _____ (name of character), didn't you?"

"I think maybe you wished that you could have been with _____ (name of character)."

"It must have been fun to have lived where _____ (name of character) lived."

"That was a good story, wasn't it?"

"_____ (Name of author) writes good stories, doesn't he/she?"

"I think you might like to read another good story by that same author, _____ (name)."

If, on the other hand, the child indicates a dislike for the story, comments such as the following prove to be very supportive:

"You didn't like tht story, did you?"

"A story like that makes one feel bad, doesn't it?"

"You don't like sad stories, do you?"

"I like stories that make me feel good, don't you?"

"I don't think I would like that story, either."

By positive affirmation of a child's feelings, the teacher can learn a great many things about children's books and their influences on book selection.

During the conference, the teacher can also learn much about children's current interests. This is extremely important, for nowhere else can we find an up-to-date listing of children's interests. Those that have been published from time to time are at least two years old when published, and they are frequently the result of responses to predetermined check lists of what someone thought children should be interested in. All printed check lists of children's interests are not only obsolete, but, upon comparison with children's actual expressed interests, are likely to be inaccurate. The teacher/pupil conferences keep the teacher up-to-date on the current interests of children. Next year there will be some new and different interests.

Diagnosis During the Conference   In addition to the personalized features of the conference, there is also one element that both teacher and pupil understand . . . that is that the teacher is to pick up any apparent problems that the child exhibits and is to help make plans to correct them. In a sense, the teacher/pupil conference is akin to the piano lesson. The child performs and the teacher points out difficulties and prescribes exercises to correct the problem or to strengthen a skill.

The type of diagnosis done during the conference is, of necessity, a discovery of gross errors and omissions. It is not meant to be the type of diagnosis of reading disability carried out by a trained reading specialist. The children operating in an individualized reading program are not likely to be those that are laboring under severe reading disabilities. Should such a child appear, the conference is not the place for him/her; but rather the reading clinic where diagnostic testing can be done with more elaborate instruments.

The child's performance is not compared to that of the whole class nor to a national norm. The teacher merely observes that the child needs help with this phonics element or with this particular phrasing. Perhaps the child is not reading with adequate comprehension. The teacher then plans some prereading questions that will help direct the thinking of the child as the rest of the book is read, or will assign the child to a small group that will be working on the phonics element that needs to be learned.

Follow-up   After the diagnosis/assessment/check-up, teacher and pupil talk about progress and plan for more progress. Individual assigments can be made—sometimes in a programmed reading text or in a specific phonics or word-analysis program—for working on a specific skill, or the child may be put into an *ad hoc* group that is being formed for group work on a special problem.

If there are no specific skill deficiencies evident during the conference, the plans will turn toward the next developmental step in reading—perhaps a more difficult book on the same theme, some articles giving factual information on some aspect of the story, another book on the same theme, but written in a different style, or another book by the same author.

Another follow-up activity is to group several children together who have been reading books on the same theme, and to have them share their book experiences. This requires some adult supervision, and that should be planned for as part of the grouping.

Some teachers require that every book be followed with some type of "creative" activity, for example the writing of a sequel, drawing a picture, or make up sentences using special vocabulary from the book. This can be "creative," but, as a steady requirement, may become countercreative.

Adroit follow-up questions about past reading selections can help the child develop improved selection skills, skills essential to a successful individualized reading program:

"Was this the kind of book you expected it to be?"

"Did the cover help you make up your mind about it? Did the cover fool you?"

"Did the illustrations give you a good idea what the book was about?"

"Did you look to see if there were a lot of big words in the book?"

"Do you think you should have asked the teacher to read some of the book to you before you chose it?"

"Did someone recommend the book to you? Were they right?"

"Was the book too long? Too short?"

"Did you notice who the author of the book was before you picked it?"

RECORD KEEPING

As previously pointed out, record keeping is a very time-consuming but very essential element of the individualized-reading program. In the lower grades, it must be done entirely by the teacher. In the upper elementary grades, the children may help in this task by keeping their own records of progress and development.

A record of books and other materials, fiction and nonfiction, read by each child should be kept. This file should include the dates the work was commenced and finished and the child's response to the material. Did the child find the work especially satisfactory, fairly so, not satisfactory at all? Did the subject matter and/or theme seem right for this particular child? It may also be useful to record a short summary of the plot or theme of the material and new vocabulary encountered.

Individual and Group Records for Word Recognition   Phonics and other word-recognition skills have been thoroughly described in Chapters 4 and 5 that they do not need repetition here. Inasmuch as they are very essential in the teaching of reading, there must be some definite strategies for assuring that they are taught and learned within the framework of an individualized-reading program. It seems that most individualized-reading set-ups depend upon the teacher's ingenuity to accomplish this goal. By that, we mean that teachers must be constantly on the alert to detect indications that a particular child needs special training in this or that word recognition skill.

Without records, it is probable that only gross deficiencies will be apparent enough for discovery and remediation. In this same manner, there is the possibility that children may become so deficient in skills that remedial situations of many types will be created just because of lack of adequate detection skills and devices. It has always been and always will be the better teaching strategy to prevent reading deficiencies rather than allow them to develop and then attempt to remediate them. Therefore, in any individualized-reading program, a record of each child's word-recognition skills is kept; and group records are, essentially, the total of individual records and serve the purpose of visualizing groupings that are needed from time to time for special skills development.

There are several kinds of individual record sheets that serve the purpose just as well in the individualized-reading classroom as they do in more traditional reading arrangements. They usually take the form of check or tick (British) sheets, upon which each skill is checked off as the child masters it, and skills needing to be strengthened are circled. The value of the group sheet is that, when several children show evidence of needing help in a certain skill, an *ad hoc* group can be formed for that purpose. The circles on the sheet show which children are to become members of that special training group.

There is evidence that some children can and do learn some phonics skills without direct instruction. As children read to the teacher during their individual teacher-pupil conferences, the teacher can double check on mastery and can check off those skills without further instruction.

Without further discussion of the advantages and limitations of check sheets, we present one here that we have used successfully. As can be imagined, it requires considerable time and effort to make it perform its task. There is no half-way or easy way to mastery.

Sample Word-recognition Skills Checksheet

PHONICS ELEMENTS VOWELS	Mary Arnold	John Archer	Billy Briggs	Anne Colotti	Deanne Duncan	Fred Finegold	Henry Higgins	Jennie Jenkins	Kay Kato	Lena Lambrina	Maku Maori
"Short" Vowel Sounds											
a						a				a	
e				e		e		e	e	ẹ	
i			i	i		i			i	i	i
o				o		o			o	o	
u		u	u	u	u	u			u		
"Long" Vowel Sounds											
a											
e											
(pie) i											
(toe) o											
oo u											

One word of caution should be stated here. It is that the check sheets should indicate *phonemes* (if that is what is being checked) and not *graphemes.* In other words, if you are checking on pronunication skills, the chart should reflect that and not spelling skills.

The sample check sheet contains information that indicates that four separate *ad hoc* groups should be formed: short-e, short-i, short-o, and short-u. The children who will constitute each group are indicated with circles around particular symbols. It may be that Fred and Lena are the only children left who need help with short-a sound. If so, they will have a group especially for them.

It might appear that children in an individualized-reading program would need help in the entire gamut of word-recognition and phonics skills, ranging from those taught early in the first grade to those generally taught in third grade. Such a conclusion may not be too far from the truth, for children who are in a true individualized-reading program have the privilege of selecting any reading materials of their liking, and, by so doing, they are most apt to select from the thousands of books on the "trade book" list, few of which are written with a controlled vocabulary. The obvious result is that the children will be confronted with the entire range of phonics elements and word-recognition problems from the very start. It is not realistic to suppose that they all can be handled simultaneously, or even within one year of instruction.

Fortunately, when given the opportunity of self-selection, self-pacing, and self-evaluation, an amazing percentage of children succeed to at least a relatively acceptable level of performance in reading, without much special training in phonics skills. Such performance, however, may mask some deficiencies that, if left uncorrected, may have the effect of limiting the child's progress beyond a certain point in reading. Records help prevent this.

CHIEF FEATURES OF INDIVIDUALIZED READING

In this chapter, we have presented an overview of the process and materials used in an individualized-reading program. However, anyone who contemplates undertaking individualized reading is urged to read the several books listed in the bibliography to this chapter and to observe as many individualized-reading classrooms in operation as possible.

This overview has delineated the usual complaints against individualized reading and the positive features as well. It should be recognized that individualized reading is, at least theoretically, an ideal method, but that there are many provisos preventing it from becoming universal.

The positive features of the individualized reading strategy are those very same features that *any* sensible approach to reading would ordinarily have.

1. Concern for individual differences.
2. A wide and varied collection of reading materials.
3. Self-selection in keeping with each child's needs and interests.
4. Self-pacing.
5. Teacher/pupil conferences with individual children.
6. Data-keeping on records for use in grouping.
7. Small-group instruction on skills, directly related to pupil needs.
8. Sharing; follow-up; creativity.
9. Each child in a continuous-progress plan, with success and optimum development the goal.

When the right circumstances prevail, and if the program is properly planned and implemented, the individualized-reading program can be extremely effective, well deserving of its high rank as one of the two major approaches to the teaching of reading.

BIBLIOGRAPHY

Introductory Comments

Individualized reading, as we know it today, was introduced during the 1950s as an alternative to the lock-step of the basal readers that were in use at that time. The strategies and routines that were developed then are as viable today, and, hence, there is little "new" concerning methods. Therefore, we do not apologize for including references here to some of the old "classics" in the field, dating back several decades.

Abbott, Jerry L., "Fifteen Reasons Why Personalized Reading Instruction Does Not Work," *Elementary English*, **49**:1 (1972), 33–36. Presents ways disadvantages may be converted into positive means for promoting individualized reading.

Allington, Richard, "Sustained Approaches to Reading and Writing," *Language Arts*, **52**:6 (1975), 813–815.

Atkinson, Richard C., and John D. Fletcher, "Teaching Children to Read with a Computer," *Reading Teacher*, **25** (1972), 319–327.

Baily, A. V., and G. Housekeeper, "Does Individualized Reading Affect Other Subject Areas," *Elementary English*, **49**:1 (1972), 37–43.

Beretta, Shirley, "Self-Concept Development in the Reading Program," *Reading Teacher*, **24**:3 (1970), 232–238. This article presented a convincing plea for individualized-reading procedures as a means for developing self-concepts in children.

Birch, Jack, and Jane Birch, *Preschool Education and School Admission Practices in New Zealand*, University of Pittsburgh, Center for International Studies, 1970.

Brogan, Peggy, and Lorene K. Fox, *Helping Children Read: A Practical Approach to Individualized Reading*, New York: Holt, Rinehart, and Winston, 1961. One of the excellent early discourses on the subject.

Cain, Mary A., "The Literate Children of British Primary Schools," *Elementary English*, **52** (1975), 84–87.

Cox, William F. Jr., and Thomas G. Dunn, "Mastery Learning: a Psychological Trap?" *Educational Psychologist*, **14** (1979), 24–29.

Deep, Donald, "The Computer Can Help Individualize Instruction," *Elementary School Journal,* **70** (1970), 351–358.

Duker, Sam, *Individualized Reading: An Annotated Bibliography,* Metuchen, NJ: Scarecrow Press, 1968. 648 items are annotated in this valuable resource volume.

Duker, Sam, *Individualized Reading,* Springfiled, IL: Thomas, 1971. Dr. Duker provided a wealth of personal experiences with individualized reading in an attempt to convince his readers that it is not only possible, but practical and effective.

Dunn, Rita, and Kenneth Dunn, *Teaching Students Through Their Individual Learning Styles: A Practical Approach.* Reston, VA: Reston Publishing Co, Inc., 1978. This is the very best treatment of modern individualized-instruction techniques and materials. Like our own book, this is a *how-to-do-it* and *why* practical approach.

Fadiman, Clifton, presented to the Reading Reform Foundation Annual Convention, Scottsdale, Arizona, May 1975.

Feeley, Joan T., "Television and Reading in the Seventies," *Language Arts,* **52**:6 (1975), 797–881.

Feeley, Joan T., and Blanche Rubin, "Reading in the Open Classroom," *Languagae Arts,* **54**:3 (1977), 287–289.

Fletcher, John D., and Richard C. Atkinson, "An Evaluation of the Stanford CAI Program in Initial Reading," *Journal of Educational Psychology,* **63** (1972), 597–602.

Glasser, Joyce F., *The Elementary School Learning Cernter for Independent Study,* New York: Parker, 1971.

Harris, Larry A., and Carl B. Smith, *Individualizing Reading Instruction: A Reader,* New York: Holt, Rinehart, and Winston, 1972.

Hollingsworth, Shirley, "Tuck in a Poem or Two," *Language Arts,* **54**:2 (1977), 180–181.

Hosey, Joseph G., "Oral Reading—Misused?" *Elementary School Journal,* **77**:3 (1977), 218–220.

Howes, Virgil M., *Individualizing Instruction in Reading and Social Studies,* New York, Macmillan, 1970.

Hunt, Lyman C., Jr., "The Effect of Self-Selection, Interest, and Motivation upon Independent, Instructional, and Frustrational Levels," *Reading Teacher,* **24**:2 (1970), 146–158.

Johns, Jerry L., "Strategies for Oral Reading Behavior," *Language Arts,* **52**:8 (1975), 1104–1107.

Kohl, Herbert, *Reading, How To,* New York: Dutton, 1973. One of Kohl's delightful observations of the reality of classroom teaching with individualized reading.

Laughlin, Rosemary M., "The State of School Dictionaries," *Language Arts,* **52**:6 (1975), 826–830.

Lamme, Linda L., Self-Contained to Departmentalized: How Reading Habits Changed," *Elementary School Journal,* **76** (1976), 208–218.

Lazar, May, "Individualized Reading: A Developmental Approach," *New York Supervisor,* New York City Board of Eduction, Fall, 1957, 15–17.

Lazar, May, "Individualized Reading: A Dynamic Approach," *Reading Teacher,* **11** (1957), 75–83.

Lazar, May, *A Practical Guide to Individualized Reading,* New York City Board of Education, Bureau of Educational Research, Publication, –40. 1960. This was the "Bible" for Individualized Reading in its early years. . . . A real "classic" in the field.

Majer, Kenneth, "Computor-Assisted Instruction and Reading," in *Reading Process and Pedagogy,* William Blanton and J. Jaap Tuinman (Editors), *Indiana University School of Education Bulletin,* **48** (1972), 77–98.

Mark, Theodore A., "The Ability of Children to Select Reading Material at Their Own Instructional Reading Level," in *Assessment Problems in Reading,* Walter H. MacGinitie (Editor), Newark, DE: International Reading Association, 1973, 87–95.

McCracken, Robert A. and Marlene J., *Reading is Only the Tiger's Tail,* San Rafael: Leswing Press, 1972. This is a delightful and beautifully composed book filled with actual examples of children's writings and drawings (many in full color). It is an excellent resource (as well as inspiration) to anyone commencing individualized reading through the language-experience approach. Everyone ought to read it, anyway!

McMillan, Dorothy, The *PM Instant Reader Series,* Wellington: KEA Press, 1970.

Miller, Wilma H., "Organizing a First-Grade Classroom for Individualized Reading Instruction," *Reading Teacher,* **24**:8 (1971), 748–752. This is a practical proposal for organizing the First-Grade classroom into the following centers: book center, communication center, science center, art center, and arithmetic center. Specific directions are given for the supplies for each center for individualized reading.

Moore, Jesse C., Clarence J. Jones, and Douglas C. Miller, "What We Know

After a Decade of Sustained Silent Reading,'' *Reading Teacher,* **33**:4 (1980), 445–450.

Povey, Gail, and Jeanne Fryer, *Personalized Reading,* Encino, CA: International Center for Educational Development, 1972.

Raymond, Dorothy, *Individualizing Reading in the Elementary School,* West Nyack: Parker, 1973. Dr. Raymond presented a step-by-step description of exactly how individualized reading has been done for the past 10 years in the public schools of Waterville, Maine, where she is currently Reading Consultant. The book is full of pictures, charts, forms, and examples. It is a handbook especially valuable for the beginner. Don't overlook this one!

Reeves, Harriet R., ''Individual Conferences—Diagnostic Tools,'' *Reading Teacher,* **24**:5 (1971), 411–415. Specific suggestions were made by the author for how to arrange for individual diagnostic conferences within the school week, the keeping of individual records, and how to set up skill groups based upon information obtained in the conferences. This is a very practical article.

Reid, Virginia, *Individualizing Your Reading Program,* New York: Resources for Learning, 1970.

Rudman, Masha K., ''Using Children's Books in a Reading Program,'' in *Children's Literature: An Issues Approach,* Lexington, MA: D Heath, 1976, Chapter 10.

Sanders, Stanley, and Jean P. Wren, ''The Open-Space School—How Effective?'' *Elementary School Journal,* **77**:1 (1976), 57–62.

Sartain, Harry W., ''What are the Advantages and Disadvantages of Individualized Instruction?'' *Conference Proceedings of the International Reading Association,* **13**:2 (1969), 328–356. An excellent delineation of problems and how they may be overcome.

Sinoes, Antonio Jr., ''The Myth of the Open Classroom,'' *Education,* **97**:2 (1976), 183–186.

Spache, George D, *Good Reading for Poor Readers,* Champaign, IL: Garrard, 1978 (revised regularly).

Spache, George D., *Good Reading for Disadvantaged Readers,* Champaign, IL: Garrard, 1975.

Stauffer, Russell G., and Max M. Harrell, ''Individualizing Reading-Thinking Activities,'' *Reading Teacher,* **28**:8 (1975), 765–769.

Thiel, Norma A., ''An Analysis of the Effectiveness of the Teaching of Reading by Individual Prescription,'' ERIC/CRIER, ED, 061–690, 1972.

Thompson, Richard A., and King, Merritt, Jr., ''Turn On to a Reading Center,''

Reading Teacher, **28**:4 (1975), 384—388. Thompson and Merritt described a sequence of steps that they found effective in establishing a reading/learning center. It is a straightforward how-to-do-it discussion.

Veatch, Jeannette, *How to Teach Reading With Children's Books,* New York: Teachers College, Columbia University, 1964. An interesting little cleverly illustrated paperback.

Veatch, Jeannette, *Reading in the Elementary School,* 2nd ed. New York: Wiley, 1978. Although this is an overview of many facets of reading instruction its major emphasis is on individualized reading. Chapters 2—7 are of great assistance to anyone starting such a program.

Wheeler, Alan H., "A Systematic Design for Individualizing Reading," *Elementary English,* **53**:3 (1973), 445—449.

Wright, Robert J., "The Affective and Cognitive Consequences of an Open Education Elementary School," *American Educational Research Journal,* **12** (1975), 449—468.

CHAPTER TEN

How Do I Teach
Reading With a
Basal Reader Series?

Definition
The Physical Components
    "Levels" in the Series
    Teacher's Manuals
    Workbooks
    Ancillary Materials
The Literary Component
    Diversity of Content
    Authorship
The Graphic Arts Component
Instructional Components
Reading Research and Study Skills
    Self-fulfilment—An Instructional Objective
    Creative Thinking
    Word-Identification Skills Strand
    The Directed Reading component
    Follow-Up Activities
    Development of Reading skills
    Enrichment
The Management Component
Provisions for Individual Differences
Disadvantages of Basal Readers
Advantages of the New Basal Series
How to Judge a Basal Reader Series

We turn now to the second major approach to the teaching of reading to be discussed in this unit—the basal reader approach. Although the basal approach usually includes some elements of the individualized—reading program, it is much more elaborate and structured. Just as the individualized program may be said to be characterized by individual selection and self-pacing, the basal reader approach may be said to be characterized primarily by the materials used in the program—that is, by what has come to be known as the basal reader *series*.

The elaborate sets of books, workbooks, manuals, tapes, transparencies, and boxes of gimmicks and gadgets known as the *basal reader* series are a strictly American package deal. But their fame has spread throughout the English-speaking world, and elsewhere, too. The American basal readers, themselves, are the largest, most beautifully illustrated, most multifaceted, most literarily-diverse, most expensive, and most talked-about materials for reading found anywhere in the world. A definition is in order as a start in comprehending the breadth of these multimedia reading resources:

> A set of elementary school readers for Kindergarten through Grade Six; arranged so that each successive book contains materials of increasing difficulty, complexity, and length—each reader being accompanied by a correlated pupil workbook and teacher's manual—is referred to as a *basal reader series*; frequently shortened to *basals*.

There are actually six parts to a full-fledged basal series:

1. The physical components.
2. The literary components.
3. The graphic-arts components.
4. The instructional strategies components.
5. The directed reading activities components.
6. The management components.

At this writing, there are fifteen American basal reader series, listed here alphabetically according to publisher, together with the name of the series and copyright dates:

Allyn & Bacon, PATHFINDER Series, c. 1982

American Book Company, AMERICAN READERS, c. 1980

Economy Company, KEYS TO READING, c. 1980

Ginn & Co., 720 SERIES, c. 1980 RAINBOW EDITION

Harcourt Brace Javanovich, Inc., BOOKMARK READING PROGRAM, c. 1980

Harper and Row, READING BASICS PLUS, c. 1980

Holt, Rinehart and Winston, Inc., HOLT BASIC READING, c. 1980

Houghton Mifflin Co., HOUGHTON MIFFLIN READING PROGRAM, c 1981

Laidlaw Brothers, LAIDLAW READING PROGRAM, c. 1980

J. B. Lippincott Co., LIPPINCOTT BASIC READING, c. 1981

The Macmillan Co., SERIES r: MACMILLAN READING, c. 1980

Charles E. Merrill Co., THE MERRILL LINGUISTIC READING PROGRAM c. 1980

Open Court Publishing Co., THE HEADWAY PROGRAM, c. 1979

Rand McNally and Co., RAND MCNALLY READING PROGRAM c. 1981

Scott, Foresman and Company, SCOTT, FORESMAN READING, c. 1981

THE PHYSICAL COMPONENTS

Any basal reading series that intends to "make it" in today's highly competitive market contains what might be thought of as a standard collection of physical components. These are the pupil books, teachers' manuals (or teachers' editions of the pupil books), student workbooks, reading improvement materials, reading enrichment materials, cards, pictures, boxed materials, and tests.

Nowhere else in the world can there be found such an array of carefully-planned and beautifully-executed sequential materials in reading.

"LEVELS" IN THE SERIES

A "series" implies that the books are sequential in difficulty as well as in content, being planned to fit the reading abilities and changing interests of children as they progress upward through the elementary school.

Most teachers today have grown up "through the grades" in elementary school. In America, the "grades" start with five year olds in Kindergarten and proceed through the elementary primary grades (1, 2, and 3) through the so-called "intermediate" grades (4, 5, and 6), with one grade for each 9-month academic year. In other parts of the English-speaking world, a similar arrangement exists. Most Australian, Canadian, and Scottish schools are similar to the American graded plan. Some of the English and New Zealand schools are structured with the Infant Room for five- and six-year-olds, followed by "standards" and later by secondary school "forms." Regardless of designation, the majority of schools have placed children in graded categories, and basal reader series have in the past designated the books according to grade-level, from readiness through grade six.

Most, if not all, publishers now recognize the trend toward emphasis on a "continuous-progress curriculum." Consequently, they now designate the progressively-more-advanced books according to *"levels."* Because there are no

"Levels" are not standard designations for the difficulty of basal readers. Each publisher is free to label the book alphabetically or numerically, but most publishers provide a chart indicating the equivalent "grade level" of each book in the series.

criteria for "levels," each publishing firm uses its own arbitrary divisions. The result is that some series are divided into ten, twelve, and as many as thrity-six levels designed for continuous progress from Kindergargen through Grade Six. Teachers, administrators, and parents still want to know "what grade level" the child is on. Consequently, most publishers now have conversion tables to show "levels" and "grade-level-equivalents" in parallel columns. For example:

TEACHERS' MANUALS

All publishers provide complete lesson plans, together with suggestions for enrichment and follow-up activities, either in separate teacher's manuals or in teacher's editions of the pupil books. The latter usually have the designation "T.E." affixed somewhere on the covers.

Some teacher's editions have the manuals bound in the front half, followed by the complete pupil's reading book. Others have just the pupil's reader which has been *overprinted* with directions and suggestions. Most teacher's manuals now contain reduced (and, in most cases, full color) reproductions of the pages in the pupil's books, the purpose being to have a ready reference for the suggested strategies in each lesson plan. The following example from the Teacher's edition, Level 7 of the *Young American Basic Reading Program* illustrates this feature:

tence and try to figure out the contraction *don't*. . . . Have *don't* underlined in the sentence, then traced in the writing space. . . . Repeat the procedure for *won't*. Make sure that pupils understand that *don't* stands for *do not* and that *won't* stands for *will not*.

Recognizing new words Call attention to the two columns of words in the box. Have pupils draw a line from each contraction to the two words it stands for.

Using new words For the exercise on the lower part of the page, have pupils complete each sentence by underlining the word that means the opposite of the underlined word in the sentence.

▶ NOTE: *Jeff, Billy, Peter Rabbit*, and *Mr. Mc-Gregor* are four names introduced in the next story. Show word cards 268–71 or write the names on the chalkboard. Tell pupils that these are names of four characters in the next story.

Introducing "The Peter Rabbit Play" (Pages 40–45)

In this story, children read about another classroom activity—staging a play. They will identify with the situation and will recognize the play that the children create based on Beatrix Potter's The Tale of Peter Rabbit.

Setting purposes for reading Have pupils turn to page 40 and read the title of the story. . . . Say: In this story the boys and girls put on a play at school. Can you tell from the title who the play is about? . . . What costumes might the boys and girls use in putting on a play about Peter Rabbit? . . . What parts might there be in the play? . . . We will find out the answers to these questions as we read the story.

DIRECTED READING

Silent Reading

—Read the first three pages to find out who will be in the play and what they remember about the story of Peter Rabbit.

Pages 40–42

—Who was going to be Peter Rabbit? Who was going to be Mr. McGregor?
—What did Jeff have to remember about his part? What did Billy have to remember?
—Do you think that other boys and girls were needed in the play? You will find out as you finish the story. You will also find out something funny that happened when one of the actors got mixed up. Finish the story now.

—Who was going to play Peter Rabbit's mother? Was she going to treat all her rabbit children the same way? Why not?
—What did the children wear for costumes?
—What funny thing did Billy do?
—Who came to see the play?

Story Interpretation and Extension

Discuss with pupils how the children in the story put on the Peter Rabbit play. Make sure that, during the discussion, these ideas are developed:

—Plays at school are put on for fun.
—Each character in a play knows what he is to say and do.
—The boys and girls in the Peter Rabbit play wore simple costumes, but costumes are not always necessary.
—Putting on a play requires actors and an audience. (In the Peter Rabbit play, the children from the next classroom were the audience.)

Tell pupils that they will have an opportunity to put on their own play when they read the next selection in *Together We Go*.

Rereading the Story

Recalling story sequence Have pupils turn to page 41. Say: **Before the boys and girls put on the Peter Rabbit play, Jeff's teacher asked some questions to help them remember what to do. Find the question the teacher asked Jeff on this page.** . . . Have the sentence (*last*) read aloud. . . . Then have pupils turn to page 42 and read Jeff's answer.

Continue: **After Jeff finished speaking, what did the teacher ask?** . . . Have someone read the sixth sentence aloud. Then ask: **Who answered the question?** . . . **What did Billy say he would do when he saw Peter Rabbit eating in the garden?**

Continue having pupils find each question that the teacher asked and the answer given. In each sentence note that, although what the teacher asked is not a complete sentence, it makes sense as a question. When all questions have been read and answered, pupils should understand that in answering the teacher's questions, the children in the story related not only what they were to do but also the order in which they were to do these things.

Enjoying oral reading Have pupils read the story as a play. Choose pupils to read the parts of Jeff, Billy, the teacher, and the tall girl. Have other pupils assume the role of narrator, letting each child read the narrative sections on one full page. Tell each child with a character's part to read only *what* the character said (the words inside quotation marks), omitting the *said* phrase.

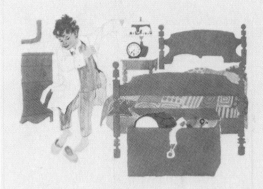

The Peter Rabbit Play

Jeff jumped from his bed.
This was the day for the Peter Rabbit
play at school.
And Jeff's teacher was going to let
him play Peter Rabbit.

Jeff dressed very fast that morning.
He got something to eat.
Then he ran from his apartment.
Soon he was at school with all the
other boys and girls.

"Boys and girls," said the teacher.
"You won't forget what to do in
the play, will you?
Jeff, what are you in the play?"

"I won't forget," said Jeff.
"I am Peter Rabbit, and I am bad.
I run away from the rabbit house.
I get hungry, and so I go into
Mr. McGregor's garden.
I eat and eat and eat."

"What comes next?" said the teacher.

Billy's hand went up.
"I run after Peter Rabbit," he said.
"I am Mr. McGregor, and I yell at him.
I don't like rabbits eating things in
my garden."

"Then what?" said the teacher.

"I jump into a big can," said Jeff.
"But the can has water in it, and
I get all wet.
So I jump from the can when
Mr. McGregor is not looking.
He won't get his hands on me!
I run away as fast as my legs can go."

"And then?" said the teacher.

"I go back to my mother," said Jeff.
"And my mother gets after me.
And, boy, do I get it from her!"

"I am the mother," said a tall girl.
"Peter was very bad.
He has to go to bed hungry.
The other rabbits get something to
eat, but not poor Peter.
Bad rabbits must go to bed hungry."

"Very good," said the teacher.
"Now, rabbits, get the ears and put
them on."

The children went to a box and got
the rabbit ears they had made.

44

The teacher looked at the children.
"Billy," she said, "are you a little
mixed up?
You are the man, Mr. McGregor.
You don't need rabbit ears."

"What am I thinking of!" said Billy.
He put the ears back in the box.

Then the children from the next room
came to see the play.
The play was good, and the children
liked it.
It was fun when Peter hid in the can.
It was fun when Mr. McGregor yelled.
But the best fun of all came when
Mr. McGregor put on rabbit ears.

45

BUILDING AND EXTENDING SKILLS

Teacher-directed Activities

Understanding contractions Write the sentences below on the board and have them read silently. . . . Ask: **Do these sentences mean the same thing?** . . . **How are the sentences different?** . . . **How are the words *don't* and *do not* different?** . . . Pupils should understand that in the word *don't* the letter *o* in *not* has been left out and an apostrophe mark is written in its place.

> I don't like to go to bed.
> I do not like to go to bed.

Follow the same procedure with these pairs of sentences, having children compare the contractions *won't* and *can't* with the words *will not* and *can not*:

> I won't forget.
> I will not forget.
>
> I can't come to the party.
> I can not come to the party.

To challenge pupils, extend the exercise, explaining that contractions can be used for other words children know. Write the sentences below on the board, underlining *didn't* and *wasn't* as

shown. Say: **The underlined word in one of these sentences means the same thing as *did not*. Can you say the word and point to it in the sentence?** . . . Write *did not* above *didn't* and have pupils tell how the words are different. . . . Repeat for *was not*.

> Ben <u>didn't</u> come with me.
> Wendy <u>wasn't</u> at the party.

Extending knowledge of *-ing* forms Before you begin this activity, write these sentences on the chalkboard, underlining the *-ing* words, as shown:

> Mother did some <u>gardening</u>.
> Mr. McGregor has a <u>watering</u> can.
> Dad is <u>backing</u> up the car.
> The girls are <u>dressing</u> for the party.

Begin by displaying *paint* and *painting* (word cards 250 and 250a) and having the words read. . . . Ask someone to tell what has been added to *paint* to make *painting*. . . . Then have the root word, *paint*, framed.

Explain that *-ing* can be added to other words pupils know. Display the words *back*, *garden*, *dress*, and *water* (word cards 136, 214, 219, 242). Have pupils find the *-ing* form for each displayed word in a sentence on the chalkboard and then read the sentence aloud. . . . Point out how the *-ing* word and the root have different meanings.

Understanding cause-effect relationships Write the sentences below on the chalkboard. Explain that each of these sentences has two parts and the parts are separated by a comma. Have pupils read the first sentence silently. . . . Then ask: **Which part of the sentence tells what Peter Rabbit did?** . . . **Which part tells** *why* **Peter Rabbit went into Mr. McGregor's garden?** . . . Continue the same procedure with the second and third sentences, asking pupils to read the part of the sentence that tells what Peter Rabbit had to do, then the part that tells why he had to do it.

—Peter Rabbit got hungry, and so he went into Mr. McGregor's garden.
—Peter Rabbit was bad, and so he had to go to bed hungry.
—Mr. McGregor ran after Peter Rabbit, and so Peter jumped into a big can.

FOLLOW-UP PRACTICE

Using *Reading Skills Four*, Page 28

Drawing inferences This exercise requires pupils to read statements carefully and interpret sentence clues in order to draw correct inferences. Have pupils read the story in each box and underline the word that correctly completes the last sentence of the story.

After pages 40-45. Together *We Go*.

"Mother, can I go and play in the snow?" asked Wendy. "I won't run into the street. I will play in the ____." clouds house yard	"Ben has a very bad cold," said the teacher. "He can't come to school. He must stay in the ____." rain house bus
"My friend has a big dog," said Penny. "I don't like her big dog. He ran away with my ____." hat pond leg	"I made a cake for Stan," said Mother. "But don't tell him. It is a surprise for his ____." car party ears
"I won't forget to bring it," said Greg. "I will let you play with my ____ in the park." plane lunch bed	"I am not very hungry," said Candy. "But I wish that I had some ____ to drink." paint eggs water

28   ► Drawing inferences.
        • Using sentence clues, underline the word that correctly completes each sentence. (See T.E. for complete directions.)

Using Duplicating Masters 12, 13

Recognizing sequence In Duplicating Master 12, pupils match pictures with the sentences of a story. This exercise provides an opportunity to read *gardening* and *watering* in story context (see "Extending knowledge of *-ing* forms" under "Teacher-directed Activities").

Drawing inferences In Duplicating Master 13, pupils use story clues and personal experience to judge outcomes. This exercise reinforces the skill focused on in the follow-up workbook page.

Providing for Individual Differences

Recognizing contractions Prepare this challenging exercise for pupils who successfully completed "Understanding contractions" (page 70). Pupils are to read each sentence, noting the underlined words, and then underline the word below the sentence which means the same as the underlined word.

Mother said, "Do not play in the street." Don't   Didn't
Greg's toy car will not go. won't   was not
The children did not ride on the bus. don't   didn't
Jeff's house was not far from school. won't   wasn't
Billy and Jeff did not see the frog. don't   didn't

Finding sentences that answer questions Prepare the exercise below. Pupils are to read each question on the upper part of the sheet and find its answer on the lower half. They should mark each question and its answer with the same color crayon. Note that there are five questions and six answers.

_____ "Do you have my hat?" asked the man. _____ "Will you get the frog?" asked the boy. _____ "Can you see my hat?" asked the girl. _____ "Do you help Mother?" asked the teacher. _____ "Are you in the play?" asked Pam.
_____ Ben said, "No, I won't get a frog." _____ Billy said, "Mom and I go to the park." _____ Wendy said, "No, I can't see a hat." _____ Jeff said, "I am Peter Rabbit in the play." _____ Wendy said, "I don't have the hat." _____ Billy said, "Yes, I like to help my mom."

It can be noted that in this instance, the teacher's edition is spiral bound, for ease of use. Several publishers make this feature available to teachers.

A few examples of the other parts of the physical component of a basal series should suffice to illustrate the multifaceted nature of a complete basal series:

WORKBOOKS

The old basal reader "workbooks" earned the connotation of "seatwork" and/or "busywork," for they were frequently used for that purpose. Consequently, some publishers today use such terms as "skill books," "study books," "activity books," and "pupil books," but the majority still refer to the paperback booklets that pupils use for reinforcement of skills as "workbooks," which, indeed, they are.

ANCILLARY MATERIALS

In the past, a number of large publishing firms developed an extensive variety of reinforcement, improvement, and/or enrichment materials to be purchased as an entire package or separately. Included were such extras as pupil practice sheets, flash cards, matching lotto games, boxed spinner games for skills practice, picture/word card packs, bingo-type games, tape cassettes, tape recorders and earphones, audio filmstrips, and projectors, tachistoscopes for flashing words and phrases on screens, controlled reader projectors with boxed filmstrips, 35-mm slides, "talking books," 45-rpm recordings, boxed story booklets for "free reading," and so on.

In recent years, however, increased attention to cost-effectiveness by school administrators and by the general public has led to curtailment of production and purchase of such materials. At present, the only such axcillary materials as are considered essential to the success of the program are likely to be found in the classroom.

THE LITERARY COMPONENT

DIVERSITY OF CONTENT

Almost any type of reading material may be found in a typical series: fiction, nonfiction, plays, poems, and so on. Almost any topic may be addressed: from life in the big-city slums to life on a secluded island, from how the American Revolution began to how the Korean War was settled, from how a spinning wheel works to how a space vehicle is launched.

Every effort is made to exclude racism and sexism from basal materials. Harmful stereotypes are avoided. Gone are the days when members of racial and national minorities were depicted only in menial or stereotyped positions. Gone are the days when all little girls were "dumb" about mathematics and totally incapable of understanding the simple process of engine combustion. Gone are the days when all little boys wanted only to play rough-house games and never could understand how to run a vacuum cleaner or change a baby's diaper.

AUTHORSHIP

Inasmuch as fine literature is one good reason for learning to read, most basal readers are planned to include a selection of the works' of many of our foremost contemporary writers for children as well as selections from the old, so-called "children's classics."

The array of authors whose works have been negotiated for use in many of the new basal readers reads like a listing of "Pulitzer Prize Winners": In fact, many of the authors represented in the basals have been winners of the Newbery awards and other literary citations. Here are the names of but a *few* of the many outstanding writers of children's stories and poems whose works are now found in many of the basal series:

Leland B. Jacobs	Liliam Moore
Aileen Fisher	Sara Teasdale
Langston Hughes	Dorothy Aldis
Charlotte Zolotow	Laura Ingalls Wilder
Michael Flanders	Patricia Lauber
James Holding	Roy Chapman Andrews
Rosemary and Stephen	Sterling North
Vincent Binét	Louis Untermeyer
John Ciardi	Langston Hughes
Cornelia Meigs	Mabel Leight Hunt
Wanda Gag	and scores of others . . .

The variety and excellence of the literary works provided at virtually every level of most of the new basal reader series would be difficult, if not impossible, to match through any other means. The reason, of course, is that the materials for each level are selected carefully by a team of knowledgeable reading specialists and childrens literature experts who, through many months of discussion and in-class research, determine which selections meet the criteria of excellence and, at the same time, are appropriate for average readers at each level of the elementary school.

THE GRAPHIC ARTS COMPONENT

We have already stated that today's basal readers are the most beautiful ever! This is not just a value judgment, it is a reality. A comparison of our American basals with the readers in the series and "reading schemes" of other countries quickly supports this statement. Moreover, comparison with those series of two or more decades ago provides vivid proof of the difference between those old uninspiring renditions that "carried the story lines" (showing mother cooking and Rags shaking water on baby) and today's representations of excitement and beauty.

Almost every type of graphic representation is included: fanciful and realistic, impressionistic, modernistic, charts, diagrams of processes, maps, comic strips, montage, vignette, and so on. Almost every type of graphic medium is reproduced: pen and ink, oils, water colors, brush, charcoal, pencil, acrylic, photography, airbrush, and so on.

Design, layout, typography, and use of space are all planned to provide an "environment" for the story, poem, or other type of selection, just as a stage setting is planned and executed to provide mood, feeling, and environment.

No longer does the "picture" help the child "figure out" the story, but, on the other hand, the graphic arts components are designed to contribute a background of time, place, and feeling *surrounding* the story and *surrounding* the printed words, as well.

INSTRUCTIONAL COMPONENTS

THE TEACHER'S MANUAL LESSON PLANS

The teacher's manual is the instructional heart of the basal reader approach to the teaching of reading.

The best routines and suggestions from countless scores of teachers and reading specialists are collected and distilled by the authors of the basals; the result being that a somewhat standard collection of procedures is followed, even though the sequence may be quite different from series to series.

Note, the over-printing in this teachers edition.

Teacher's manual lesson plans include most or all of the following features:

1. Specific objectives are stated for each lesson, delineating as exactly as possible what learning and reading skills the lesson is intended to foster.
2. Suggestions for motivating interest in the reading materials are set forth. These may include examples of interest-arousing questions, suggestions for presentation and discussion of realia connected with the reading, use of filmed materials and recordings, reading of related materials, field trips and so on.

A Travel Tale

The Ridge City Zoo was getting a second baby chimp. Mr. Hines was (bringing) this one with him from (Africa) by ship and then by train.

Mr. Hines was a good manager and had no (problems) on the ship. He engaged a little room called a cabin, and he kept the chimpanzee in it with him. Three times a day, the (ship's) cook sent meals to the cabin for Mr. Hines. He sent three different meals for the little animal. Each time, the baby chimp ate till his sides (bulged.)

After they left the ship, they went by (taxicab) to get a train for Ridge City. Mr. Hines had to have a (chain) on the chimp for this ride. The little (chap) did very well on the way, but he did manage to steal the (driver's) cap. He did not want to hand it back. At last he (tossed) it from the taxicab. Mr. Hines had to pay the man for the cap. He said " Bad boy ! " to the chimp. But he had to smile when the little animal (snuggled) up to him and wanted to be (petted.)

80

3. Suggestions for introducing new vocabulary, for example questions, references to previously learned words having similar elements, phonetic clues, word families, and word patterns.

4. Directed reading lessons. (The directed reading lesson is described in detail later in this chapter.)

5. Specific follow-up activities for each lesson plan are included in most manuals. Suggested activities may include group discussion, vocabulary, and comprehension enrichment exercises, creativity projects, related language arts work, and so on.

6. All teacher's manuals for primary level basal readers (K through 3) present various suggestions for development of phonics skills and structural analysis skills, including word-building exercises and use of context clues. Workbooks are often the principal vehicle for development of phonics and word-recognition skills in the basal approach.

THE WHOLE-WORD APPROACH TO WORD RECOGNITION

One distinguishing feature of the basal series approach to reading is its use of the whole-word method for teaching word recognition. This method has been thoroughly discussed previously in this text. Suffice it to repeat here that research and experience indicates children can and do recognize many whole words without decoding them letter-by-letter. Most children make remarkably fast progress in learning to "read" (pronounce words found in story lines) in basal preprimers and first readers. The children remain good reading performers so long as their reading material does not contain words they have not encountered before. In the basal program, each new lesson contains words previously mastered (at least, that is the expectation). New words contained in the material are previewed and learned as whole words *before* the children begin to read the new lesson.

The whole-word method has, as previously noted, come in for a good deal of criticism. Critics justly note the alarming number of reading failures that have resulted from exclusive use of this approach. However, no modern basal series approach even hints that the whole-word method should be used to the exclusion of all other techniques. It is employed only as one useful beginning segment of the complex process of learning to read.

SCOPE-AND-SEQUENCE CHARTS

Some publishers of basal reader series provide oversize charts as an instructional guide, showing the scope of the elements covered in the program and the sequence in which they are introduced. These scope-and-sequence charts list all the phonics elements, comprehension skills, and language arts activities to be found in the series and the levels at which the various skills are introduced and developed. One such chart is reproduced here to illustrate the extent of the information provided. Note that only a few skills are introduced at first, followed by increasingly more increments in the Second Grade. By the Third Grade, most of the phonics skills have been introduced and, in fact, scheduled practice on them is usually reduced and finally dropped after the Third Grade.

COMPREHENSION STRATEGIES

The objective of all reading, be it fostered by basal readers, individualized reading, synthetic phonics, reading machines, or whatever, is understanding—comprehension. We have devoted an entire chapter (Chapter 7) to this topic. Virtually every basal series suggests questions similar to the 250 patterns we developed in Chapter 7. It should be noted that such questions are the foundation of *any* developmental program. This should help reinforce the idea stated previously that:

"Good reading methods are effective regardless of the media."

Rather than repeat here any of the comprehension strategies used with basal reader stories, we believe that a few applications will be adequate to suggest the type of strategies used:

Let us suppose that the basal reader article is about the "Tall Ships" that came to America for the Bicentennial celebration. The questions would most likely be:

"What are the 'Tall Ships'?"

"Why did the 'Tall Ships' come to America?"

"Where did they come from?"

"What were the 'Tall Ships' originally used for?"

"What are they used for now?"

"What do the crews of today's 'Tall Ships' learn?"

"What are some of the navigation problems on a 'Tall Ship' today?"

"Are they different from the problems of long ago?"

"How big are the 'Tall Ships'?"

"How many 'Tall Ships' are there still sailing the seas?"

"How is a 'Tall Ship' made?"

"What happens when there is no wind?"

"How do the crew members furl and unfurl the sails?"

"What do you think it would be like to be a crew member on a 'Tall Ship'?"

BASIC READING 1975
SCOPE AND SEQUENCE CHART

J.B. Lippincott Company
Educational Publishing Division
East Washington Square
Philadelphia, Pa. 19105

Numbers refer to pages where skills are first introduced.

	BOOK A T.E.	A W.B.	A D.M.	BOOK B T.E.	B W.B.	B D.M.	BOOK C T.E.	C W.B.	C D.M.	BOOK D T.E.	D W.B.	D D.M.	BOOK E T.E.	E W.B.	E D.M.	BOOK F T.E.	F W.B.	F D.M.	BOOK G T.E.	G W.B.	G D.M.	BOOK H T.E.	H W.B.	H D.M.
STRUCTURAL ANALYSIS																								
SINGULARS					48			19			36					36	46							
PLURALS					48			19		72	36					36	46							
COMPOUND WORDS							34	27	17	30	44	26	45	37		36	38	2	22	9				
SYLLABICATION				5	4	3	34	43			45	32	8	36	25	2	76	5	2	7	22	2	30	1
ACCENT													10			5			2	7		2	55	
PREFIXES																			22	14	9	56	4	
SUFFIXES				6			38		16		87		8	39		28	17		68	55		27	8	10
BASE WORDS							37		18			25	8	7		28	44	39	22	3		7	73	
CONTRACTIONS							70			58		22	67	84		35	47	11	26	22		11	27	7
POSSESSIVES							63													48		22	28	14
COMPREHENSION																								
RECALLING STORY DETAILS	38	27			2	30	4	7		12	40		12	28	6	96	3		45	4	23	6	9	
USING CONTEXT CLUES	78	13		68	23		42	18		10	23		16	13		133	7		9	1		4	39	
UNDERSTANDING MAIN IDEA		42	40							47	50		15		9	9			11		2	37	63	
INTERPRETING FIGURATIVE LANGUAGE	104													57		117			36		19	4		32
PREDICTING OUTCOMES													53						8			14		9
SEQUENCING	55	24	9		18		33	81		8	13	4	28	11		42			5	63	1	13	1	
CLASSIFYING IDEAS AND INFORMATION	7			41	61		94	50	7	31	8	11		18		78	13		30	27	14	20	19	
MAKING INFERENCES	38	31		19			94			21			24	20	3				8			3	83	
DRAWING CONCLUSIONS	30			19	53		76	60		7	35			9		6	3		8	45	4	3	12	26
EXPRESSING AND JUSTIFYING OPINIONS	63																8		34	49		5	62	
PICTURE INTERPRETATION	18	9	20	4	18	4	5		32	6			11			13			3			10		
UNDERSTAND POETRY	98			4			22			9			25			17			15			15		
INTERPRETING EMOTION	60			11			15						11	29		49			13	16	5	6	5	
SENTENCE STRUCTURE																								
SIMPLE SENTENCES	18		7	2	49		74	22		3	72		7	9		33	15					66	22	
COMPOUND SENTENCES																			74			66		
SUBJECTS										49	40		33	17	28	126	92		31	36	15	57	15	3
PREDICATES										49	40		33	17		126	92		31	36	15	57	15	3
DIRECT OBJECTS													121			31	18	7	31		15	8	7	3
PHRASES	31			79	55	9	74	45	16	2	24		103	78		47			10	24		37	10	
WRITTEN COMMUNICATION																								
CAPITALIZATION	3			50			4									22								
PERIODS	18			50			5			16		32				24	70							
COMMAS	30								9	16						24								
QUOTATION MARKS				14						16						24								
EXCLAMATION POINTS	30			11			5		9							23			26	28	12		76	
APOSTROPHES							63			54		22	67	84		35	47		26	22		28		
HYPHENS							23			54										73		22		
CREATIVE WRITING	51			15			31			13			23			48			16			9		
PARAGRAPHING				79			16				74		25	88					60		1	20	78	
QUESTION MARK	53								9	16						24	70							
ORAL COMMUNICATION																								
CREATIVE EXPRESSION	24			2			24			5			26			11			6			9		
GROUP DISCUSSION	2			14			5			16			12			8			14			4		
VOCABULARY BUILDING																								
SYNONYMS						23	75	21	21	14	2	4	68	84	32	34		22	26	23	11		13	
ANTONYMS							75	8	21	14	7	4	91	70	32	76	5	39	9	19		58	4	30
HOMONYMS				52			75			19	22		10	68		46	6	19		1		28	39	17
RHYMING WORDS	74		29	22	45	23	30	9	21	11	54	4	43	16	15	11	82							
WORD STUDY	15	23	39	2	19	24	2	1	21	1	2	9	10	4	6	6	7	4	11	15	27	2	11	8
WORD GROUPS																								
NOUNS	25			80	49		36						33	66	27	27	1		14	10				
VERBS	25			80	49		38	28		27			33	60	27	27	11		31	10		7		
PRONOUNS				48		28	63		5	32		13	93	72	37	25	1	10	57			38	57	
MODIFIERS				50			113			12			28	71	27	15	10		20		30	7	2	
PREPOSITIONS																46	32			90		40	46	31
STUDY SKILLS																								
READING CONTENT MATERIAL										72			13			17			10			66		
USING A TABLE OF CONTENTS	2			1			4			12	93		13			5			2			1		
USING THE LIBRARY													24			30			10			9		
USING THE GLOSSARY													10			5			2					
SKIMMING AND SCANNING							42						109			116			3			2		
READING FOR SPECIFIC INFORMATION				14			4			6			11			8	34		3			3	24	34
ALPHABETIZING			19				88			12	3	4	10			5	79		2	18		2	34	
READING MAPS AND CHARTS	53												14			97			6			30	87	36

1. Why were the girls called the Clover Street trio?

2. What kinds of things did the girls enjoy doing?

3. Does a four-leaf clover really bring good luck?

What planning must one do to assure that the basal reader lesson is in the cognitive and affective modes?

"What would it be like to be the Captain?"

"Why aren't there more 'Tall Ships' today?"

Comprehension questions on fiction will likely emphasize the cognitive and affective modes, with special attention to personal involvement in plot and theme. For example:

"Why did Maryellen say that?"

"Where in the story does it tell us how Peter felt when his skateboard was stolen?"

"What did Alex try to do to get the dog free?"

"Did Sammy like his new home? What makes you think so?"

"Can you think of any reasons why Alissa ran away?"

Scope and sequence charts such as this are provided by publishers to aid educators in visualizing which reading skills are introduced and reinforced and the sequence in which they are taught to the pupils.

"What would you have done? Why?"

"Why did the monster attack the automobile?"

"Where was the space ship headed when it ran into trouble?"

"What do you think the passengers should do to correct the trouble?"

"Will they be able to survive until help arrives?"

"How long will that be?" What might happen in the meantime?"

"Would you like to be on that space ship now?"

"If you were on the space ship, what would you do?"

THE LITERARY APPRECIATION STRAND

Inasmuch as the pupils' books in a basal series are, essentially, literary anthologies of high-quality selections from many genre (stories, poems, plays, biography, vignettes from novels, journal reports, informational articles, legends, myths, speeches, autobiography, how-to-do-it directions, historical novels, science fiction, etc.) the instructional component includes, from the earliest preprimers up through sixth grade, a literary appreciation strand, during which children are led to appreciate the authors craft and the use of literary devices to achieve effect and feeling.

The clever employment of "the right word in the right place" is one strategy used to call attention to this facet of literary skill. From it, children are encouraged to enlarge their useful vocabulary to be more expressive in their oral and written language usage. Thus, vocabulary development wells from reading and takes on the element of habit through usage. This aspect of the instructional component also has to be planned.

READING RESEARCH AND STUDY SKILLS

One facet of the instructional strategies in a planned basal reading lesson is the development of habits and skills in "finding out" and "remembering." Children are helped to learn where to find answers, where to look for ideas, how to organize thinking, how to sort out main ideas and details, sequence of plot and/or process, how to use graphic aids for understanding, and how to organize and outline for information storage and recall. We described these fully in Chapter 8, "Reading-Study Skills."

SELF-FULFILLMENT—AN INSTRUCTIONAL OBJECTIVE

It is likely that one cannot instruct another individual to be "self-fulfilled," yet newer instructional strategies have been significantly influenced by recent trends in education that emphasize self-needs, self-fulfillment, awareness, problem solving, coping, and so on. The new basal readers include much material that is selected for the above purposes; to aid the child to identify with the problems and situations in which story characters find themselves, and to internalize the solutions to such problems.

Through identification in good literature, children may find self-fulfillment. It is not automatic, however, just as transfer is not automatic (see Chapter 1), but must be "arranged for" as part of the instructional strategies, making use of significant and relevant literary content. The objective is identification, catharsis, empathy, and/or self-fulfillment.

CREATIVE THINKING

One of the ultimate objectives of reading is to extend one's cognitive functioning beyond the facts of the printed page to the fancies of the creative mind. The instructional component seeks to do just that by encouraging young readers to take mental "trips" beyond the stories and to imagine different outcomes, extensions of the story, and so on, as well as to write their own stories, poems, and/or express the inspirations that the story or poem has generated in some other art form. This is creativity. It cannot be structured by a teacher, but it can be anticipated and time can be planned for creativity to flourish.

WORD-IDENTIFICATION SKILLS STRAND

Phonics and other word-identification skills are a completely separate strand of learning that flows through the first three grades and is outlined in the teachers' manuals. The newer basal reader series include work on both analytic and synthetic phonics, thus responding to recent trends "back to basics".

The phonics and/or word identification lesson is a skills-development session that usually takes place entirely removed from the reading lesson. Nevertheless, every reading lesson contains some word-identification work, such activities as noting words that are compounds of previously learned words, guessing words from context and initial graphemes, predicting words because of the natural flow of language, observing words that have been altered by affixes, tense, number, and employing previously learned phonics know-how in analyzing new words in print (analytic phonics).

THE DIRECTED READING COMPONENT

The Directed Reading Lesson The directed reading lesson (DRL) has been a feature of basal readers for decades. It is at once one of the strengths and one of the weaknesses of the basal reader approach. Its strength lies in its elaborate array of directions and references to resources for each textbook lesson. Novices to teaching find the directed reading lessons in the teacher's manuals to be a valuable teaching guide and an aid to confidence. Critics, however, note that rigid adherence to this highly structured routine may negate teacher and pupil originality and creativity. Knowledgeable teachers will, of course, learn to exploit the good and avoid the bad, knowing that the DRL as outlined in the teacher's manual is a collection of good suggestions, not commands.

In the preparation phase of the reading lesson, new words are introduced and previously learned words are reviewed. What part does the pupil's workbook play in this activity?

The typical directed reading lesson is likely to include most or all of the following ten sequential elements:

Summary of story   A summary of the story or article is provided as a preview for the teacher.

Preplanning for the materials:

visuals: filmstrips, overhead transparencies, pictures, charts, maps, diagrams.

equipment: models, toys, dolls, aparatus

workbooks: cards for "place-holders," pencils, crayons

recordings: poems, stories, sounds, music, machines

games: equipment, playing equipment

follow-up: materials, costumes, "props," and so on.

Objectives   They are usually delineated in the manual, but each teacher will want to add special objectives. Objectives when stated specifically serve as mental maps, guiding the teacher through the lesson.

Preparation for Reading.   The teacher's manual provides plenty of suggestions for the "Presentation" stage, in which the teacher reviews old concepts with the children; presents a new one or two; reviews old vocabulary that may be found again in the story; may have children draw pictures of an animal (if the story is about an animal) or write a short paragraph about an animal; may play a word game, a riddle ("I'm thinking of . . ."; or discuss a place (zoo, park, etc.) that is the setting of the story.

The purpose of the preparation period is to orient the children to vocabulary, things, people, places, and environment that relate to the type of story to be read, without direct reference yet to the story in the book. Specific *new* whole-word vocabulary is usually introduced at this stage, but many teachers now make a point of analyzing the new words phonetically wherever possible within the abilities of the children at that point.

Independent Silent Reading   The children in the reading group are not dumped into the story "cold," but are "readied" by questions such as:

"Who would like to read the title of our story?"

"What do you think the story will be about?"

"Why do you think so?"

"Who are the people in the picture?"

"Where do you think they live?"

"When we read the story, let's try to find the answers to these two questions: 1. _____ 2. _____ (which should be placed on the chalkboard).

"We will start on page —, but, before we start, take your cardboard markers and place them between pages — and —. That is where we will stop first."

When the children in the reading group have reached the place marked, the teacher then leads a *brief* discussion dealing with comprehension, feelings, details, or whatever seem important enough to *stop* at that point. The only reason for stopping is to solidify a concept that is necessary for better comprehension and/or enjoyment of what is to follow. Stopping just to ask questions is an annoying procedure, unproductive, and even counterproductive.

Discussion Following the reading of the selection, several types of discussion ensue. The artwork may be discussed first if it provides the setting and mood of the story, which it usually does. Comprehension questions should be judiciously preplanned, not just spur-of-the-moment questions that are meaningless and without purpose.

The comprehension discussion should not drag on past the "point of diminishing returns." Teachers, with practice, can learn to sense when interest has reached a peak—and STOP! "Stop while you are ahead" is a good rule.

Oral Reading Some teachers find it useful to have children reread parts of the selection orally. There are several good reasons for this to be done occasionally. For example, if there is a word that should be understood from context, it may be that some children may not get its meaning. If there is a word that is a "look-alike," it may be confused and mispronounced. For example, in one story, children are playing house together and are making a little dish "out of a gourd." When children are asked to read that part, someone invariably reads, "They made a dish out of ground." This is reasonable and understandable to children who have made mud dishes and mud pies. Oral reading reveals that the word is not *ground* but *gourd*. The teacher then should have a gourd available to show how a dish could be made from it.

Oral reading should be purposeful to reveal problems or for listening enjoyment. It may be justified for the entertainment and/or information of the child's classmates and for practice in oral expression. In the first instance, a child may read orally when he/she has discovered something special that should be shared with others who have not had the opportunity of reading it. This is a normal adult behavior, for how frequently we are reading something in a magazine or newspaper and we suddenly look up and say, "Listen to this! Here's something new: . . ." Children should be encouraged to do likewise as a normal, everyday activity in reading. Second, we are justified in encouraging children to read orally as a means of improving their skills in oral expression. This has been an aspect of education sadly neglected in recent decades.

There are two prerequisites for oral reading: First, the child should have something worthwhile to share. Second, the child should not read orally to classmates until he/she has developed the skill to make such reading a pleasurable listening experience to the audience. This latter can be achieved through practice on the excerpt by reading it onto a tape recorder until teacher and pupil are satisfied with the performance. We are not expecting perfection, but we should strive for enjoyment of both reader and listener.

Follow-up Activities   Some of the many follow-up activities to a basal reader story may be art work; the writing of a follow-up sequel, writing a paragraph with the new vocabulary of the story; reviewing special sounds in the story; syllabication practice; reading aloud a poem that is related to the story; reading another story by the same author; listening to a recording; and so on.

Development of Reading Skills   This segmemt of the lesson is usually done in the pupil's skillbook (workbook) or worksheets. It usually will deal with phonics, structural analysis, blending, syllabicataon, word-building, phonograms, likenesses and differences, or selecting the proper word. It may also be a review for those who need additional practice.

Children should be grouped according to diagnosed needs for the development of reading skills. This need not be done daily, nor for each different story. A teacher who keeps adequate records on each child will set diagnostic periods when progress will be assssssed and new groups formed. Slow children tend to remain slow, and they need additional help and *encouragement*. Moreover, they need tasks at which they can know success.

An advanced group may be given additional tasks or games (not for reinforcement) for enjoyment. Children who already know phonics skills are bored with the usual workbook activity, but enjoy competition in phonics games.

Enrichment   All children, regardless of reading ability, need enrichment commensurate with the ability of each. This is the one place where the imagination and dedication of the teacher makes a difference! It takes tremendous amounts of time to plan and collect enrichment materials. The librarian can be most helpful in this effort, but the teacher must *know* the potentials, limitations, and special interests of each child. That knowledge is the basis for success in planning enrichment reading.

Reading enrichment takes many forms, chief among them being stories by the same author; stories about the same subject (sports, horses, etc.); related poems; plays (dramatize the same story or another similar one); reading in encyclopedias to satisfy curiosity about some person, place, or thing in the story just read (this should be specially recommended to gifted children who are always wanting to know more); reading orally in a small group of equally good readers who have the same interest in a particular story; listening to a tape or recording of an author or poet, reading his/her own works; listening to a speech by a famous person whose biographical vignette has just been read; and listening to a song written about conditions such as were described in the selection just read.

One can readily envision the planning and work necessary to mount this segment of the reading lesson! But this is what reading is all about. Let us repeat: "Learning to read opens windows of the world."

THE MANAGEMENT COMPONENT— PROVISIONS FOR INDIVIDUAL DIFFERENCES

THE OPEN CLASSROOM

In the previous chapter on individualized reading we discussed in some detail the open-classroom concept and its contribution to the related concepts of individual selection of reading materials and self-pacing. Suffice it to say here that much the same management opportunities and difficulties occur when the open classroom is the setting for the basal series reading program.

Obviously, when reading skills are to be learned, there must be structure and planning for the effort to be successful. Even in an open classroom, where children may move from one learning station to another, the reading skills station must be rigorously planned, and the activities must be directly related to the skill that is being taught. Consequently, a basal series may be used in an open classroom that is structured for learning just as well as in an individualized reading set-up. It is very sequential in nature, segmented into levels, and, therefore, helps as a framework for groups to move at their own speed.

CONTINUOUS PROGRESS

Educators for decades have deplored the practice of locking children into academic-year time blocks, called "grades," regardless of the abilities of each individual child. Some children need longer to master materials, some need less time, and some, unfortunately, never master some subjects in a whole lifetime. The concept of "continuous progress" finally was popularized and became somewhat of a reality in some schools in the early 1970s, and some publishers of basal series quickly sliced their books into smaller volumes, labeled "Levels."

Other publishers just changed the covers and, instead of the traditional grade-level designations, the books then became "levels," without further ado. We have previously noted that there is no *standard* for "levels" but that most publishers now show the approximate grade placement for each level.

Continuous progress implies that each child will progress from one level to the next, then through the work of that level and on to the next, regardless of school days, weeks, or months spent on a particular level. A gifted learner might cover four or five levels in a basal reader in one academic year, whereas a student less able might feel comfortable progressing through only one level. In either case, "continuous progress" is taking place. No one is being held back and no one is moving ahead only on the basis of time spent in the classroom.

As is the case with individualized reading, a tremendous amount of record-keeping is involved in a continuous-progress classroom. Each child's progress must be monitored daily. Each child's daily instruction must be individually prescribed. However, the structured and sequential nature of the basal series and the testing program that is built into most series make establishment of a continuous progress curriculum and individually prescribed instruction (I.P.I) much less arduous than it otherwise would most certainly be.

MASTERY LEARNING

Mastery learning is a concept that naturally grew out of the *performance-objectives* movement that swept through education in the 1960s. Criteria were set up as part of the objectives that guided every minute step in the learning sequence. The theory was that, when an objective was met, it could be substantiated by testing, based upon criteria of excellence (i.e., 80%, 90%, etc.). It was argued that each step should be delineated with a specific objective, detailing the performance to be anticipated. This, then, would be paralleled with a measure or test of performance to determine whether or not the individual had mastery of that skill segment. If so, the learner would move to the next subskill. If the test revealed that the child was lacking that particular skill, then the child was placed in a special group with others who, also, were in need of training in that skill. These were frequently referred to as *ad hoc* groups (set up temporarily for that specific purpose).

After "teaching to the needs" (called "criterion-referenced teaching") had taken place, criterion-referenced testing was done to determine whether or not the child had attained sufficient mastery of that subskill to move on to the next. The result was that the testing programs in several of the basal series became "criterion referenced," and the term "mastery learning" apeared in some of the teacher's manuals. Tests accompanying the elaborate phonics and word-recognition skills lesson plans contained in teacher's manuals make it possible for teachers to operate a successful *mastery learning* curriculum in reading, using the basal series as the basic framework.

DIAGNOSTIC-PRESCRIPTIVE TEACHING

In the preceding chapter on individualized reading we discussed the problems and rewards of successful diagnostic-prescriptive teaching. Diagnosis of difficulties in the basal series program is somewhat similar to diagnosis in the individualized program (close observation and careful record keeping). Prescriptive teaching is comparatively easier in the basal program in that the basal materials provide built-in suggestions and instructions for teaching to specific needs. In addition, many basal programs now include diagnostic tests.

At one time, computer-assisted instruction was considered to be the answer to the prayers of every teacher burdened with the perplexities of prescriptive instruction in any reading program. It was hoped that the computer could be used to store literally thousands of instructions and assignments for the myriad of skills and subskills needed for learning to read and that these instructions and assignments could be matched with the needs of individual children in the classroom. Major porblems, however, have arisen in writing programs to encompass all the skills and subskills relevant to reading. In addition, budgetary cutbacks have resulted in a slackening of research in the area and in troubling questions about the cost effectiveness of such expensive electronic aids to teaching.

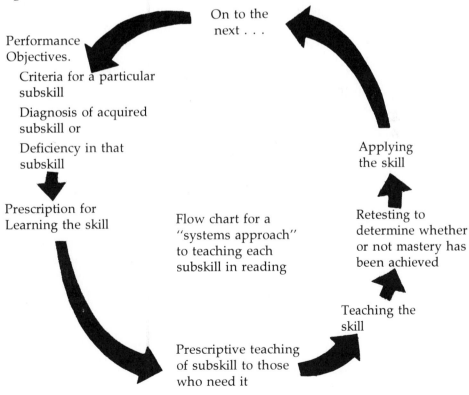

On to the next . . .

Performance Objectives.

Criteria for a particular subskill

Diagnosis of acquired subskill or

Deficiency in that subskill

Prescription for Learning the skill

Applying the skill

Retesting to determine whether or not mastery has been achieved

Flow chart for a "systems approach" to teaching each subskill in reading

Teaching the skill

Prescriptive teaching of subskill to those who need it

In any case, teachers always have and will continue to set up their own "systems approach" to diagnostic-prescriptive teaching. The flow chart illustrates the essential elements of any such approach.

MANAGEMENT MATERIALS

Many basal reading series programs now include a prepackaged management component. Such components may consist of materials boxed separately for each series level containing unit tests, level tests, prescriptive practice exercises on duplicating masters, scoring sheets, answer keys, plus a management guide to using the component. Tape cassettes for one-to-one reteaching or reading improvement may also be included in the basal series management materials.

DISADVANTAGES OF BASAL READERS

In spite of the care with which a basal reader series is planned, developed, and finally brought together as a final multi-million-dollar publishing achievement, it still seems to be the "in thing" to criticize basal readers. Yet, in our experience, we have noted that many who think they are criticizing the basals are actually basing their remarks and objections on old outdated series that are no longer being published, or on unimaginative and/or inadequate teaching methods employed by teachers using the basals. Nevertheless, there have been and there probably always will be some weaknesses potentially inherent in the basal reader approach. Here are some that frequently have been expressed:

1. Memorization of whole-words that called for a very limited, controlled vocabulary in the beginning stories.
2. Uninteresting stories that were contrived for First Grade preprimers and primers. These utilized the "controlled," and repetitious vocabulary.
3. Stories that were "unreal," depicting story children and story families that were not in keeping with the environment in which many children live.
4. Repetition that became boring. In some basals, the authors set up a formula calling for each new word to be repeated twelve to fifteen times in the succeeding six or eight pages. That practice was based upon an old research study that purported to prove that children needed that many repetitions to assure learning. The result of such structured repetition was:

> Oh, Oh, Oh,.
> Look, Mother, Look, Look!
> Oh, Mother, Look at Tom.

5. One whole series was bought and used for all children throughout the school. The result was that *all* children in any designated grade had the one basal book for that grade, regardless of whether they were reading above *grade level,* at *grade level,* or below *grade level.*

6. All children in the class read the same story during whole-class instruction, regardless of whether they could progress faster or were not ready for that level of reading. There was little, if any, provision for individual differences.

7. Children were not allowed to take their basal readers home to read to their parents "for fear they might *read ahead* before they were ready," or foul up tomorrow's lesson in class by already knowing the story.

8. Teachers repeated word-for-word mechanically the routine *suggested* in the teacher's manual. In fact, in some school systems, the reading supervisor insisted upon strict compliance with the questions and directions verbatum form the teacher's manual.

9. The three-group classroom structure became almost universally standard, because suggestions in the manuals provided for specific drill work with one group while the other two groups did assigned "seat work" designed to "keep them busy" . . . hence the term, "busy work". Some of the older manuals had blocks of time for the daily activities divided into work assignments for each of the three ability groupings for each day of the school year.

10. Oral reading was the daily routine, with children being called upon in "round-robin" sequence to "stand and read" to the group.

11. Many basal series relied almost exclusively on stories, with little variety in reading materials. Few poems or plays were included; little, if any, informational reading in the sciences, social studies, and so on. The result was that children learned to relate only to the cause-and-effect relationships in story plots, characterization, and so forth with little training in reading in content areas.

12. Some basals—to save money on royalty payments—confined their selections to old, out-of-copyright materials. The results were that few, if any, of the best current children's stories and poems were included.

13. Some basals, claiming to be a return to the "good old children's classics," provided selections far-too-advanced for the children who were to read them. This situation resulted where the content of the basals was not "graded," which often was the case when a publisher did not include reading specialists on the team of senior authors.

14. Vocabularies in various basals did not conform to a standard set of words for each grade level. There was no uniformity of vocabulary from one series to another. This led to a serious question as to whether or not there actually is a valid measure of grade-level reading materials.

15. Designating grade levels on the books encouraged some children to ridicule their less-able classmates who were reading books labeled for lower grades.

16. The use of graded materials (basals) convinced some school administrators that a "good" teacher would have every child reading *at grade level*; and,

consequently, teachers were judged on whether or not their children were reading at grade level.

17. Some administrators issued ultimatums to the effect that "no child is to be promoted unless he/she is reading at grade level." Such pronouncements, of course, led to dishonest testing . . . or to discouragement in those whose potentials were less than average.

18. Because of the large investment in a basal reader series for an entire elementary school, the use of the series tended to extend over many years; far beyond the point of obsolescence. Many of the stories became outdated, and teachers became bored from year-after-year repetition.

19. As children became more sophisticated through television, the basal series became less interesting or challenging . . . yet, they "were stuck with it."

20. Perhaps the most serious and often-repeated criticism was that the basal series just doesn't teach children how to read! Of course, we could say that no book, by itself, "teaches" children to read. Behind that criticism was the complaint that teachers using the basals went through the question-and-answer sessions with the children; taught them whole-word vocabulary; but did not teach them phonics and other word analysis skills. It is, no doubt, true that this happened in a large enough number of cases to bring on this criticism.

It should be noted here that these disadvantages and criticisms are stated in past tense, inasmuch as they referred to basal series of the 1960s and early 1970s.

ADVANTAGES OF THE NEW BASAL SERIES

Despite the disadvantages noted above at least some of which are not so much inherent in the program as they are the result of inappropriate teaching and administration, the modern basal reading program has noteworthy advantages when properly implemented and taught.

When used with judgment, most new basal reader series provide the following positive increments in the total reading program:

1. Beautiful, exciting format of stories and art interwoven in full color—each story presented in a different layout.
2. A carefully selected anthology of stories, biography, poems, and informational articles, written at high interest grade-level readability.
3. A sequential program of vocabulary development.
4. A developmental plan of word-analysis techniques.
5. Teacher's manuals embodying the best classroom practices oriented directly to each story, poem, and article.
6. Coordinated pupil study-books, filmstrips, independent reading bibliographies, enrichment materials, and so on.

7. An extensive collection of fine children's literature and informational articles appropriate for children in the intermediate grades, together with suggested strategies for transferring basic reading skills to those materials.
8. A developmental sequence of comprehension skills, throughout the entire elementary grades.
9. A well-developed management system assuring mastery learning.

These, we believe, are the reasons why basal reader series will continue to be the nucleus of the most primary level reading programs for years to come. Good teachers will appreciate the strengths of the new basals and will exploit their good qualities, adding features from other sources in an eclectic approach to reading instruction.

HOW TO JUDGE A BASAL READER SERIES

On the surface, all basal reader series may appear to be very much alike. That is understandable, for any that is too unusual or maverick will stand little chance of success in the market place. On close inspection, however, there are some significant differences; some dictated by philosophy, some by financial restric-

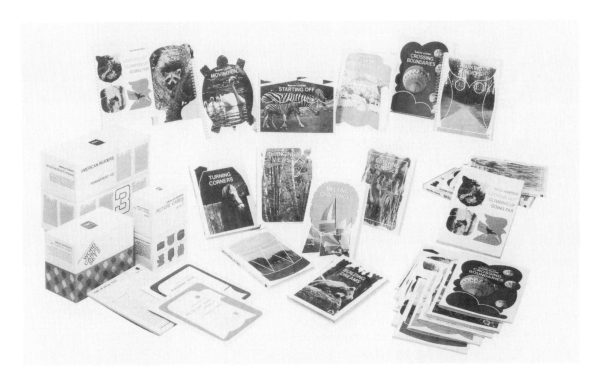

tions, some by differences in the editorial teams, and some by expediency. As an aid for comparison and, perhaps, for selection of the basal series that best fits certain situations and particular learners, the following check sheet is presented.

In addition to checking "yes" or "no," you may wish to make some subjective qualitative judgments as well. For example, it may not be enough to check "yes", that the series includes cassettes for individual listening. A value judgment may well be in order to answer the questions, "How appropriate is the cassette material?" "Does the cassette material go slowly enough for my particular pupils?" "How easy to understand is the voice on the cassette?"

Other value judgments are certainly appropriate when judging art work, the literary selections and the appropriateness of the selections for children in a particular economic and/or geographic region.

The following check sheet is not meant to yield a definitive score, but to highlight the many facets of the basal reader series and to make comparisons possible on these many standard features.

Components of Pupil Texts   YES   NO

Are the covers attractive?

Are the book titles meaningful?

Are the covers easy to clean?

Is there a library binding that allows the book to lie open flat?

Is the "level" coded on the spine?

Is the "level" coded on the back?

Are the books easy to stack?

Which of the following literary genre are included:
   short stories?
   plays?
   songs?
   poems?
   informational articles?
   vignettes from longer novels?
   legends and myths?
   letters and speeches?
   newspaper reports and journal excerpts?
   science fiction?
   advertisements, flyers, etc.?
   directions, recipes, etc.?
   biography and autobiography?
   historical fiction?

Is there a balance of informational articles from: YES NO
    social studies?
    science?
    health and sports?
    arts and artists?
    travel and adventure?
    home economics?
    recreation?
    business, commerce, etc.?
    invention, technology, etc.?
    careers and the world of work?

Is there an adequate balance of selections in the "real" and "make believe"?

Is there a satisfactory balance of selections from the "children's classics" and from contemporary children's literature?

Are many of contemporary award-winning authors' works represented?

Are the stories "devised" by a group of relatively unknown writers?

Are the literary selections "relevant" to today's young readers?

Do the selections represent an adequate cross-section of contemporary living?

Does the artwork provide an environmental setting and mood for the story or article?

Does the artwork illustrate the action in the story?

Are realistic male/female roles in keeping with the conditions existing at the time and place of the story or selection?

Are positive cultural images of socio-ethnic groups today adequately presented?

Where there is cultural bias and/or propaganda is it made clear that this is the case and the purpose for including it?

Are the following literary devices adequately developed in the pupil texts and in the teacher's edition plans:
    plot?
    characterization?
    simile/metaphor?
    sounds (alliteration, onomatopoeia, etc.)?
    rhythm and rhyme?
    imagery?
    implied, "deep" meanings?
    verbal description?
    loaded language, sales pitch, "snow" job?

Materials for Individual Differences   YES   NO

Are the following materials available:
  Boxed collection of books arranged and coded for various reading
    levels?
  transition books?
  pupil workbooks for reinforcing skills?
  pupil workbooks or sheets for reteaching skills to slower learners?
  games for small-group activities?
  individual game-type activities?
  cassettes for individual listening?
  pupil-progress record charts or sheets?
  self-corrective materials?
  every-pupil response cards?

Ancillary Materials to Enhance Skills Learned

                                                            YES   NO

Are these available:

games?

filmstrips?

flashcards?

wall charts?

picture-word cards?

tachistoscopic programs?

alphabet letters?

puppets and other gimmicks and gadgets?

Authorship and Editorship   YES   NO

Are the senior authors well known as distinguished reading authorities?

Does the team of authors include:
  a children's literature specialist?
  a reading supervisor?
  a classroom teacher at each level?
  a child-development specialist?
  an elementary education specialist?
  a testing and evaluation specialist?
  a graphic arts specialist?
  a language arts specialist?
  a linguistics specialist?

Was the series developed by the publisher's in-house group of editors?

Relevance and Viability of the Series

YES   NO

Are the selections in the books relevant to today's children?

Are the selections appropriate for the interests and abilities of the particular children in your school?

Is the readability of the books
too difficult?
too easy?
just right?

Are the selections "dated", so they will be out-of-date in five years?

Is the artwork attractive and relevant to the environments of today's children?

Are the selections "old-fashioned"?

Are the books of the series in traditional sequence so children may transfer in and/or out easily?

If you had to select a series that you would have to stay with for ten years, would this one do?

Storage of Components

YES   NO

Are books standard size for shelf storage?

Do the workbooks have a place *on* the cover for the pupil's name?

Are the books color-coded according to level?

Are there self-contained boxes for
filmstrips?
cassettes?
games?
flashcards and flipcards?

Are the container boxes sturdy?

The Instructional Program

YES   NO

Do the teacher's editions (or manuals) contain:
story synopsis?
suggestions for introduction and motivation for each selection?
comprehension questions?
notations highlighting special details?

objectives for each lesson?

list of materials to be assembled prior to teaching each lesson?

oral reading suggestions?

review of previously learned skills?

suggestions for follow-up activities?

list of related "enrichment" reading materials?

specific information on location of those enrichment materials?

reproduction of pages from the pupil's reading book?

information on the authors of the stories, poems, and other selections?

background information on the region and/or environment that is the setting of the selection?

suggestions for diagnostic/prescriptive teaching?

realistic continous-progress planning?

practical plans for *ad-hoc* grouping?

plan for vocabulary development and enrichment?

a total language-arts program or strand?

thorough plans for a sequential phonics program?

a reading study-skills developmental program?

suggestions for oral speaking and dramatics?

a composition and expository writing sequence?

a planned use of the library?

a plan for information search using library skills?

a thorough sequential word-recognition program (phonics, word structure, contextual clues, etc.)?

Do the lessons in the teacher's edition (manual) all follow the same routine?

Are the lessons in the teacher's edition (manual) varied for interest?

Could a novice teacher work successfully with the plans in the teacher's edition?

Is there a definite identifiable phonics strand?

Does the phonics strand, if any, follow a developmental sequence?

Does the phonics strand, if any, appear to be "helter-skelter"?

Is it possible to know which word-recognition skills are covered in the First Grade and which are covered in the Second Grade (within reason, that is)?

Is there undue repetition from one level to the next and to the next?

Would you be happy using the materials of this Series?   YES   NO

Would this be your first choice?

Would this be your middle choice?

Would this be your last choice?

BIBLIOGRAPHY

Aukerman, Robert C., "Look at Dick and Jane Now!" *Reading Informer*, **3** (1975), 9–11.

Aukerman, Robert C., *The Basal Reader Approach to Reading*, New York: Wiley, 1981. This volume presents the only complete description of all fifteen current basal reader series.

Barnard, Douglas P., and James DeGracie, "Vocabulary Analysis of New Primary Reading Series," *Reading Teacher*, **30**:2 (1976), 177–180.

Britton, Gwyneth E., "Danger: State-Adopted Texts May be Dangerous to Our Future," *Reading Teacher*, **29** (1975), 52–58.

Bruton, Ronald W., "Individualizing a Basal Reader," *Reading Teacher*, **26**:1 (1972), 59–63.

Fishman, Anne S., "A Criticism of Sexism in Elementary Readers," *Reading Teacher*, **29** (1976), 443–445.

Freedman, Glenn, and Elizabeth G. Reynolds, "Enriching Basal Reader Lessons with Semantic Webbing," *The Reading Teacher*, **33**:6 (1980), 677–684.

Gonzales, Phillip A., "What's Wrong with the Basal Reader Approach to Language Development?" *The Reading Teacher*, **33**:6 (1980), 668–673.

Kelly, Ann Marie, "Sight Vocabularies and Experience Stories," *Elementary English*, 52 (March, 1975), 327–328.

Lutz, John, "Some Comments on Psycholinguistic Research and Education," *Reading Teacher*, **28**:1 (1974), 36–39.

Pikulski, Edna C., review of *Houghton Mifflin Reading Series*, *Reading Teacher*, **30**:5 (1977), 558–560.

Rodenborn, Leo V., and Earlene Washburn, "Some Implications of the New Basal Readers," *Elementary English*, **51** (1974), 885–888.

Rudie, Helen N., "Poetry in Basal Readers: Perished or Cherished," *Elementary English*, **52** (1975), 136–140.

Samuels, S. Jay, "Effects of Pictures on Learning to Read, Comprehension, and Attitudes," *Review of Educational Research*, **40** (1970), 397–407.

Wartenberg, Herbert, review of *Reading Basics Plus*, *Reading Teacher*, **30**:5 (1977), 552–555.

Weintraub, Samuel, "The Effect of Pictures on the Comprehension of a Second-Grade Basal Reader," Unpublished doctoral dissertation, University of Illinois, 1960.

UNIT FIVE

If there is a single feature common to all elementary school classrooms it is the reality of the individual differences. To contend that all children have equal potentials in reading is (a) to ignore more than a century of psychological, psychiatric, neurological, and educational research; (b) to be oblivious to the day-to-day experience of countless teachers; and (c) to reject common sense. Throughout this book we have constantly emphasized the importance of individual differences in learning in general and in the teaching of reading. Why, then, this final unit on "differences"?

The answer is that in this unit we will stress what might be called "special differences"—differences based on intellectual, psychological, socioeconomic-cultural-linguistic, physical-emotional, and educational factors that vary significantly from the general norms. These special differences may be peculiar to a particular group within the school population or they may occur only in particular individuals.

To the uninitiated, the children of suburbia may appear to be an homogenized lot from "good" homes, advantaged, clean, honest, well-imbued with society's values, or whatever one might imagine. What about the children of the inner city? Can we also generalize about them as an homogenized lot? Points of view, prejudices for or against a socioeconomic-ethnic-cultural group, and misinformation about inner-city children all militate against positive concepts and color our generalizations about one group or another.

Almost every classroom contains children from the neighborhood majority group and some children from minority groups. Children from any identifiably different group are

SPECIAL DIFFERENCES

apt to have special needs because of their "differences." There are also "exceptional" children. For some of them, communities have designed and mounted special programs of "special education" directed toward "intervention" treatment of those most severely handicapped and, in some cases, special opportunities for those who are extremely gifted. In fact, at this writing, there is much attention to the handicapped as a result of Public Law 94-142 (1977) "Education for All Handicapped," which provides for large sums of Federal money to aid programs designed for "mainstreaming" such handicapped children.

Another point should be made clear. It is the fact that there are large numbers of children who have not learned to read and, yet, are *not* "remedial" reading cases. We are speaking of those who have never yet had consistent, adequate, sequential reading instruction. For all intents and purposes, they have never been taught to read. For them, it is never too late to begin. Some can be handled in the regular classroom. Others will need a special "late-starters" room. They are children with special needs.

In this unit, we have devoted one chapter addressed to the understanding of children with special needs; how to identify them, and what have been found to be the most effective ways of teaching them to read within the resources of the ordinary classroom so all may learn.

It should be clear that we are not discussing "remedial" or "corrective" reading; neither are we ignoring it. It is our position that remedial reading is more properly within the realm of advanced courses in professional training in reading and has little justification in an introductory course on "How do I teach reading?"

It should also be emphasized that, although special differences may be caused by factors that vary significantly (in fact or in intensity) from the general norm, the children, themselves, are in no way "abnormal." We are concerned here with children who, despite their "special differences" can and should remain in the regular classroom.

The final section of this single-chapter unit is devoted to the subject of assessment. Testing for reading achievement is, of course, an essential element of all learning-to-read instruction. We have already considered this subject at various points throughout this text, but some reiteration of and elaboration on this important topic is particularly germane at this point. Assessment, particularly for the discovery of reading deficits, is vital to the success of instruction designed to alleviate skill deficiencies rooted in special differences.

CHAPTER
ELEVEN

How Do I Teach Reading
So All May Learn?

The aphorism that children are as alike as thumbs and as different as thumbprints is worth repeating here—and very much worth remembering throughout your teaching career. Without constant consciousness of individual differences, your effectiveness as a teacher will be a good deal less than desired. Dealing with individual differences calls for alertness in detecting individual difficulties and for patience and skill in handling them, as noted throughout this text.

In the regular classrooms in which we have taught and in those in which you will teach, there are those who are:

1. Intellectually different.
2. Psychologically different.
3. Socioeconomically-culturally-linguistically different.
4. Physically-emotionally different
5. Educationally different.

But how do you handle the children in your regular classroom who vary from the norm to the extent they can be considered as having "special differences"? How do you teach reading to children who are intellectually gifted, or to children who are significantly slow to learn? How do you teach children who are linguistically different from the general school population? How do you teach those who are physically or emotionally handicapped? How do you teach children who have been educationally deprived? In short, how do you teach reading so that all may learn? One basic tenet is uppermost: rather than deplore the differences, our task is to accentuate the positive, at the same time attempting to provide whatever special help is needed to get each child on the road to reading success. In current educational jargon, we are to "teach to their strengths."

HOW DO I TEACH READING TO CHILDREN WHO ARE INTELLECTUALLY DIFFERENT?

We are convinced beyond a doubt that the children at both extreme ends of the psychointellectual spectrum are most neglected, are frequently left to be on-their-own, and, as they move upward through the grades, they become acutely aware of their postion in the pecking order. Two examples from my own experience should suffice:

My *first* class was the *lowest* eighth grade group in a large metropolitan school. When the children seemed to face failure at even simple tasks, they would glibly remind me, "Mr. Aukerman, we are the *dumbest* class this school ever had. You can't teach us anything!" (At times, it seemed that they set about to prove it!) My fourth grade class frequently reminded me that, "We are the *smartest* class in this school. You can't teach us anything!" The average I.Q. of that class was 136!

Obviously, someone had informed those two groups of their intellectual status, and they had become conditioned to what they thought was expected of them.

THE INTELLIGENCE FACTOR

We have previously in this book discussed the controversy surrounding the use and misuse of I.Q. testing. Setting aside for the moment just how fair such tests are and how accurately they measure that elusive characteristic we call "intelligence," it is neither sensible nor realistic to ignore functional intelligence as a factor in individual differences. In every population of children, we can anticipate that about ten percent will test out at or below 80 I.Q. and about ten percent at 130 or above. Whatever the specific I.Q. spread of your classroom, you are likely to encounter some children who are at or near the bottom of the intellectual heap and some who are at or near the top.

A USOE reading study concluded that "reading is a unitary accomplishment . . . and is best interpreted as a manifestation of general intelligence." This and other research on the relationship of intelligence to reading indicates that most children with high I.Q. scores (130 and above) can easily be taught to read (many of them learn to do so on their own), and that most children with low I.Q. scores (80 and below) have difficulty learning to read and, as a group exhibit a high incidence of poor reading achievement and failure.

What can you do to help the intellectually gifted child to reach his or her full reading potential in the normal classroom setting? What can you do for children who are significantly below average intellectually to help them overcome their difficulties?

THE INTELLECTUALLY GIFTED

Most intellectually gifted children are early readers. Many will have taught themselves to read before entering the first grade, with or without significant familial aid or formal pre-first-grade instruction. Most of these children may have developed a few undesirable or incorrect habits that will need to be unlearned. Some may have completely bypassed some basic reading skills, the undetected absence of which may lead to difficulties in reading later elementary-grade materials. Early reading ability does not *per se* guarantee automatic and continued superiority. Even with gifted children, much, very much, depends upon the teacher. Incidentally, most early starters are also eager to begin learning to write, which involves learning to spell as well as learning to form letters—further tasks for the teacher of gifted children in the early grades.

Longitudinal research by early-reading specialist Dr. Dolores Durkin indicates that gifted children who learn to read early will continue to make exceptional progress if this head-start is exploited throughout the grades. Durkin pointed out that early reading leads to very satisfactory accomplishments and does not, *per se*, as some critics contend, lead to later reading problems. She insisted, however, that early starts in reading are significant only when they are taken advantage of in subsequent school years. When schools introduce reading in kindergarten, they must plan their subsequent reading program so that it builds upon what has been learned in early reading instruction.

Only through observation and introspection can we surmise how gifted children teach themselves to read or so easily learn to read with a minimum amount of help. Somehow, they seem to devise their own system of phonics generalizations. Nevertheless, they do need some special phonics training to help them become most efficient in reading. One thing they can do is to work cooperatively with a tutor in deductively developing phonics generalizations: "Generally, this and that happens . . ." or "Usually, when this-or-that happens, then . . ." are the ways gifted children make such statements about what they observe about our language.

A gifted child can greatly benefit by a one-to-one relationship in the first stages of reading. A four-year-old or a kindergartner should have a teacher's aide or a volunteer, or an older child (the latter is called a "cross-age" tutor) at hand to help with first efforts at reading, pronouncing difficult whole words, printing the child's own name and other words of interest, responding to the child's questions, reading along with the child, and discussing what has been read.

Recognizing the Intellectually Gifted   It is not difficult to recognize the intellectually gifted child in the classroom. As noted, it is probable that such a child will have already learned to read before entry to the first grade. Those who haven't will show exceptional eagerness to do so. A large vocabulary is another very reliable measure of early giftedness.

Gifted children are likely to pursue interests far beyond those of their more average classmates. Indeed, their cognitive maturity is likely to exceed that of ninety percent of their chronological-age peers. They prefer to deal with more complicated and abstract ideas than do their peers. They regularly show eagerness to explore information and ideas related to their reading interests.

Total concentration on whatever they are reading is another characteristic of the intellectually gifted. This tendency may lead some children to persist in finishing "to the bitter end" what they happen to be reading regardless of whether or not they can really comprehend the material or even whether or not the material is interesting to them or enjoyable to read. In short, they may be inclined to drive themselves harder than is desirable. Group discussion may present problems for the gifted. Such children may become bored with discussion geared to the less-sophisticated interests and abilities of their average peers.

They may also evince irritation with their classmates' inability to understand and appreciate their discussion comments.

Grouping the Gifted   If gifted children are fully to develop their superior potentials, they must be handled in small homogeneous groups. Only thus can we teach to their strengths. Only thus can they fully profit from instructional association with their peers because only thus can peer-motivation be fully operative. The gifted should not be individually isolated and allowed to "go ahead on their own." Nor should their superior potential be diluted or stymied by "mainstreaming" them with no attention to their special needs.

Reading Materials and Methods for the Gifted   A few observations from our experience may be helpful in anticipating what to do with the gifted children in your reading class:

1. Their reading interests are as multifaceted as life, itself. Therefore, they need freedom of choice, depending upon their particular interest at the moment.
2. They tend to "over-do" a particular theme, apparently driven by the desire to learn *everything* there is to know about it. Don't decide their needs for them, but provide them with reading resources on that theme until they are satisfied.
3. They are avid encyclopedia fans. Have plenty of the new encyclopedias for children available, especially *World Book, Book of Knowledge, Comptons Pictured Encyclopedia,* and the new (1977) *Random House Encyclopedia* (a one-volume monster, but beautifully done).
4. In their unrelenting search for information, have plenty of other reference works, books of facts, and so on.
5. Their thinking is global, resulting in the need to explore most, if not all of the related facets of a subject. Therefore, they are good candidates for early instruction in reading-study skills (Chapter 8).
6. They are vocabulary buffs. In fact, their superior use of vocabulary is an almost foolproof means of identifying a gifted child even in the preschool years. In reading, they love to work with homonyms, antonyms, synonyms, word origins (etymology), and so on (Chapter 6).
7. They are not satisfied with the *who?, what?, when?, where?* type of facts, but are eager to learn the *whys?* and *hows?* of events, processes, etc. What must you provide for them?
8. They enjoy discussing what they have read with others who are an intellectual challenge to them. Provide time and place for talk sessions and sharing in homogeneous groups.
9. They are highly creative. Help them in their desire to create stories of their own. At first these are "talk stories," to be captured and written down by the teacher for reading tomorrow or some other time. A tape recorder may help.
10. By the third and fourth grades they will want to be reading novels that you might

ordinarily consider appropriate for older children. What criteria would you use in providing such advanced reading for eight- and nine-year-olds?

SLOW LEARNERS

Children who are significantly below average intellectually are sometimes referred to by educational psychologists as "high risk" children—that is, there is a high risk that teachers will fail to teach such children what they should be taught and that the children will fail to learn what they should learn. It is much better, however, for the classroom teacher to consider such children as opportunities for creative teaching rather than as potential failures. Children in the tenth to twentieth percentile (I.Q.'s ranging from about 80 to 85) can be taught to read in the average classroom—*if* you are willing to spend the necessary time with them and to exercise patience and understanding. Most significantly, slow learners can attain third- or even fourth-grade reading abilities by the end of the elementary years. Not the most ideal of accomplishments, perhaps, but at that reading level they will at least be able to function productively in mainstream society.

Some Features that Make Slow Learners In Need of Special Reading Help

1. They are concrete learners (as opposed to abstract). They need to deal with concrete ideas.
2. Those in the 10th to 20th percentile (I.Q.'s ranging from about 80 to 85) are usually educable in reading *if* we are willing to spend time, patience, and understanding.
3. Many slow learners can memorize a few simple phonics rules that give them some concrete guidelines.
4. They generally can memorize the basic sounds represented by constant letters, and can apply those sounds at the beginning of words.
5. They learn best with short whole-word phrases rather than memorizing a vocabulary of whole-words in isolation.
6. Rote learning is better than analysis of language structure.
7. They spend a disproportionate amount of time watching TV. Their reading materials can capitalize on that. *Sesame Street* stories are a good start.
8. Their environmental exposure is likely to be circumscribed. Most of them know little of the world beyond their own neighborhood.
9. They have very limited concepts of history or geography.
10. Their vocabulary of standard English is likely to be severely limited.
11. Their cognitive skills are usually underdeveloped compared with others of the same chronological age.
12. Their attention span is very limited.
13. They will pretend to finish a story that they know they can't read. This feat may

be accomplished "before you have time to turn around." What signal do you think they are giving by doing this?

14. Sports is one area of universal interest. You can capitalize on that.
15. They are easily distracted.

Grouping Slow Learners   As important as homogeneous grouping is for gifted children, it is even more so for slow learners. Our experience with them provides us with the basis for our position that they either "languish by the wayside" or become behavior problems when forced to endure failure, frustration, and/or feelings of stupidity when heterogeneously grouped with a whole class of peers who, obviously, are smarter than they. How would you feel?

We are after success in developing a reading skill. Grouping for reading, therefore, is the most efficient and most practical way to achieve that goal. The slow learners may be "mainstreamed" later in nonacademic activities; certainly not in reading.

Some Hints for Helping Slow Learners in Your Classroom   Slow pacing is a must for slow learners. Be patient. Hurry them and you are likely to lose them.

Emphasize rote learning rather than analysis of language structure. Slow learners do not find it inordinately difficult to memorize the basic sounds represented by consonants and to apply these sounds to the beginning of words. They can also learn simple vowel sounds by rote. Memorizing whole words in isolation is likely to be difficult for slow learners. Try rote learning of whole-word phrases instead.

After the children have mastered some whole-word vocabulary, start them on "high-low" materials geared to their interests. Simple stories in which animals are personified appeal to most children. Materials about sports will also be well received. Since today's slow learner is likely to spend a disproportionate amount of time watching TV, capitalize on that fact by giving them reading materials related to TV presentations—*Sesame Street* materials, for example. Don't neglect language-experience stories. Such stories, of course, will be necessarily circumscribed by the limited experiences most slow learners bring to the classroom. After the children have mastered teacher-constructed experience stories, they can go on to write their own under the guidance of the teacher or an aide. Remember, too, that the slow learners are more at home with the concrete than with the abstract. Choose materials and methods geared to this preference.

Slow learners are capable of memorizing a few simple phonics rules upon which to build rudimentary reading skills. Each such phonics element should be reinforced through practice and writing.

Above all, give the slow learner as much one-to-one attention as humanly possible. Ideally, the school budget should allow for at least some individual coaching by specialists. Volunteers may also be helpful in this respect.

INTELLIGENCE AND THE ESTIMATION OF READING POTENTIAL

As noted previously, intelligence measurement is a highly controversial area. However imperfect as I.Q. scores may be, they can be useful as a tool for an estimation of reading potential. Below is a formula of our own devising for measuring reading expectancy at various intellectual levels. Unlike other formulas found in the literature, the I.Q. scores in our formulas are not used as percentages (a totally inaccurate concept), but are, rather, converted into *percentiles*. We have found the formula to be very accurate throughout the entire I.Q. range.

Our reading expectancy formula is based upon the following factors:

1. We expect an average achiever to be at grade level.
2. I.Q.'s should be converted into percentiles (%iles),
3. Percentiles can then be related to a midpoint (50th percentile), which is the point at which an I.Q. of 100 is said to be.
4. A percentile should have 0.50 subtracted from it and then multiplied by 2 *to determine the percent above or below normal* of any particular I.Q. rating.
5. The percent above or below normal indicates that particular individual's relationship to the norm for his or her grade. The grade, therefore, should then be multiplied by that percentage.
6. If the child's I.Q. places him or her above average, a plus amount is indicated; if below average, a negative amount is indicated. This means, therefore, that the child's grade-level is either to be augmented or diminished to indicate expectancy.

THE AUKERMAN READING-EXPECTANCY FORMULA

$$\text{Reading Expectancy} = \text{Grade} + \{\text{Grade} \times [(\text{I.Q. percentile} - 0.50) \times 2]\}$$

Examples of the Reading-Expectancy Formula in Use

I. A 4th Grader; I.Q. = 100 = 50th %ile.
R.E. = Grade + {Grade × [(%ile − 0.50) × 2]}
         4 + {4 × [(0.50 − 0.50) × 2]}
         4 + {4 × [0]}
R.E. = 4 + 0 = Grade 4 Reading Expectancy

II. A 4th-Grader; I.Q. 120 = 90th %ile.
R.E. = 4 + {4 × [(0.90 − 0.50) × 2]}
         4 + {4 × [0.40 × 2]}
         4 + {4 × [0.80]}
R.E. = 4 + 3.20 = Grade 7.2 Reading Expectancy

III. A 4th-Grader: I.Q. 80 = 10th %ile.

$$R.E. = 4 + \{4 \times [(0.10 - 0.50) \times 2]\}$$
$$4 + \{4 \times [-40 \times 2]\}$$
$$4 + \{4 \times [-0.80]\}$$
$$R.E. = 4 \times -3.20 = \text{Grade 1.80 Reading Expectancy}$$

IV. A 2nd-Grader: I.Q. 125 = 95th %ile.

$$R.E. = 2 + \{2 \times [(0.95 - 0.50) \times 2]\}$$
$$2 + \{2 \times [0.45 \times 2]\}$$
$$2 + \{2 \times [0.90]\}$$
$$R.E. = 2 + 1.80 = \text{Grade 3.8 Reading Expectancy}$$

Method of Converting I.Q. Scores Into Percentiles

I.Q. (approximate)	Percentile (approximate)
130 and above	97th and above
125	95th
120	90th
115	80th
110	75th
105	60th
100	50th mean
95	40th
90	25th
85	20th
80	10th
75	6th
70	3rd

Although these are approximations, they are good enough for our purposes of estimating where to begin and what to look for in estimating reading potentials.

HOW DO I TEACH READING TO THE PSYCHOLOGICALLY DIFFERENT?

SELF-CONCEPT

We hold the position that many psychological "differences" are generated by the erosion of a positive self-concept. We have written much already, and more could be said about the effect of a positive self-concept on a child's achievement in school for it is directly related to motivation. In the great majority of cases, good readers are highly motivated and poor readers have already developed a negative self-concept. Their anticipation of learning to read has already been negated.

After reviewing much of the research, Quandt concluded: Sufficient evidence has been found . . . and enough support from authorities in education and psychology has been accumulated to suggest that many disabled readers can be helped by improving their self-concepts.

Four types of conditions have been suggested for improving self-concepts and, thereby, reading ability:

1. Establishing a positive atmosphere in the classroom.
2. Making the child feel accepted.
3. Providing him/her with success.
4. Encouraging a positive environment at home.

The success and acceptance built into these conditions are the best means known for improving self-concepts. However, it must be remembered that success and acceptance are not products of a set of materials or of a program or of a classroom organization. *They are products of the most influential factor in all teaching—you, the teacher.*

MOTIVATION: A PSYCHOLOGICAL FACTOR

Motivation for reading commences long before a child undertakes the task of reading by himself/herself. It is part of the listening habit, and a teacher can soon detect those children who have not learned to listen to stories. Listening to stories and wanting to read are both motivated by the same objectives.

Teachers can observe those who are self-motivated (intrinsic motivation) and those who are not. Extrinsic motivation must be planned for the latter, usually through relevant rewards and incentives.

AVOIDANCE AND READING

Children who avoid having to read may be covering one or more facets of failure. Reading may be painful to them. They may be embarrassed by their errors when asked to read aloud. Some children, even in the first grade have been verbally humiliated and punished for reading failure. They successfully retreat into avoidance, and in many cases they do not offer excuses . . . just shrug their shoulders and appear stupid. Other children may demonstrate inability to read only while in the classroom in order to sidestep the reading materials prescribed by the school and/or teacher. This is a common ploy used by children and youth who are smart enough to put on an act of incompetence, which actually is a cleverly devised scheme of avoidance. Other "avoiders" may learn tremendous amounts of information from classroom, TV, radio, and visual presentations and feel no need to learn to read. One solution to this problem is to provide a wealth of reading materials relevant to their special interests. These have been discussed at length in Chapter 9.

EMOTIONS AND READING

Some of the basic dimensions of personality have their roots in so-called "emotions." Theories of personality describe some of these in the following ways, many of which can be detected in the classroom:

Self-Pleasure Although some may reject the notion, pleasure-seeking includes selfishness. One who seeks pleasure is responding to an emotional need. Freud referred to the *ego* and *super-ego* as labels for pride, self-enhancement, achievement, and the need to build up ones self-image. The *super-ego* is frequently equated with doing what one *ought to do*, rather than what one really wants to do.

In reading, these two facets of self often clash. The child may feel compulsion to read what the teacher suggests, at the same time wanting to read something else. When the teacher observes the child surreptitiously reading something in place of prescribed reading, it is time to reassess what has been prescribed. Obviously it is not meeting the needs of the child, but may be creating guilt feelings when the child is "caught." Self-pleasure should be a guide to the type of reading materials that "different" children need.

Fear, Pain, Anger, and Aggression These emotions are all part of a bundle of complex emotions that may be both originators and resultants of behavior. The child who is fearful (whatever be the reason—or no reason at all) is a child whose emotional condition stands in the way of successful learning. Similarly, the child who exhibits anger (whatever be the known or hidden reason) is apt to engage in aggressive behavior that is disruptive to others. It is totally antagonistic toward reading and tends to build up to an explosive point. These emotional conditions are easy to detect: "I hate . . .! " or "I'm going to kill so-and-so!" or "I'm afraid!" The child who can verbalize those feelings in this manner is in better shape than the child who hides them and later lashes out suddenly at society. The child who verbalizes fear, hate, aggression, and anger is asking for help!

SOCIAL PRESSURE AND READING

In our society, environmental factors have a tremendous affect upon behavior, upon a child's need to learn to read. Many learning theorists refer to *imitation* and *modeling*. Following an adult model (*a significant other*) is a strong generator of emotion. The child who imitates the behavior of some *significant other* tends, without being aware of it, to assume some of the emotional characteristics of the hero model. Abraham Maslow and Carl Rogers have both been proponents of self-actualization, especially in terms of the expectations of society, for *belongingness, acceptance,* and *love*. Learning to read is an achievement highly regarded by our society. Children and youth who have not learned to read are often labeled as somehow "different."

HOW DO I TEACH CHILDREN WHO VARY FROM THE SOCIOECONOMIC-CULTURAL-LINGUISTIC NORM?

Given the cultural variety of American society and the mobility of its members, it is likely that at least some children in your classroom will vary widely from the socioeconomic-cultural-linguistic norm. Some of your children may speak a culture-based dialect other than or in addition to that of standard American English. Others may be bilingual, with English as a second language. Some may speak little or no English at all. Indeed, in not a few American classrooms today, the majority or even all of the students may be outside the socioeconomic-cultural-linguistic mainstream.

Some, but by no means all, of such children may also exhibit differences other than linguistic; differences stemming perhaps from their culture and perhaps from their socioeconomic backgrounds. Some such children may exhibit signs of improper or inadequate nutrition and poor health care. They may lack generally accepted social graces. Poor home and community environments may have depressed motivation and fostered defeatist attitudes toward learning. Because of their lifestyles, many suffer from cumulative sleep loss and chronic fatigue. Their value systems (even their sexual mores) are apt to be markedly different from those of mainstream children. Most have marginal experiences beyond home and immediate neighborhood. They may be inordinately suspicious of authority figures, including teachers. In any case, all such children need your special help and understanding. As Professor William Steward has observed:

> When a standard-English-speaking child learns to read, his task is essentially one of decoding graphic representation of a language that is very much like the one he already uses. For him, the reading problem is just that—a reading problem. However, when a child who has not learned to speak standard English is asked to learn to read in it, his task will be infinitely more difficult—and, perhaps, even senseless. For, even if he succeeds in decoding the written forms of individual words, such a child may find that they do not go together in any pattern that is familiar or meaningful to him.

BIDIALECTICAL AND BILINGUAL CHILDREN AND READING

Although we tried and found it impossible to separate the effects of economic deprivation, culture, environmental experiences, language patterns, dialects, behavior patterns, and values—all of which are inextricably related—we, nevertheless, think it expedient to concentrate this discussion on the strengths of two main groups (leaving concern for children who speak only a foreign language to special teachers):

1. Those who speak two English dialects (bidialectical).

2. Those who are bilingual, a foreign langage with English as a second language (ESL).

By the very nature of the fact that a "different" langauge separates individuals somewhat from the mainstream, isolation is a product of dialect and or of the foreign language which is one's primary means of communication. On the other hand, isolation, itself, tends to produce dialectical variations.

ISOLATION, DIALECTS, AND READING

Learning to read is neither a function of color, nor is it bounded by geographic constraints. Nevertheless, isolation, however imposed, be it by mountains, valleys, islands, ghettos, reservations, race, color, politics, economics, or society, or any combination of these is certain to result in "different" speech patterns, attitudes, concepts, values, motivation, and experiential backgrounds that tend to militate against reading achievement. Perhaps, instead of being concerned about dialects and isolation and those concomitant differences, we should be working on the larger problem of *isolation from the mainstream*, for that is what makes schools, teachers, textbooks, and curricula so *foreign* to countless numbers of children.

READING AND CHILDREN WHO ARE
BIDIALECTICAL

There are many groups of children of isolation who live in communities where a special dialect of English has developed over several generations. For example, *Southern Mountain Children* have characteristics of behavior that are culturally imbued through generations of isolated living in *Appalachia*. Poverty is not the only factor that seriously affects school aspirations and achievement. Superstitions and distrust of "outsiders" augment differences. Parental attitudes toward the rest of society are largely negative and, in addition, the White children of Southern Appalachia are apt to be imbued at home with the concept that "I'm jist as good as inny-body else;" and "Nobody ain't-a-gonna' tell me nuttin."

"These mountain dwellers exhibit fierce independence as a result of their long and continuous fight for survival," wrote Alvin L. Bertrand. He also observed that these poor White children "are generally reared impulsively by their parents, with relatively little of the conscious training practiced in middle-class families . . . punishment is always physical punishment."

"Rates of school absenteeism are high, primarily because many parents do not value education and, therefore, do not compel their children to attend school." In essence, Bertrand concluded, "the children of the subsistence level poor (Whites) in rural areas are monumentally deprived—of a full social life, of many of the basic necessities of life, of a chance to improve themselves, and of an understanding of the behavior necessary for getting along in and contributing to society at large." (Be sure to read Catherine Marshall's beautifully-written story of *Christy,* and see the film *Coal Miner's Daughter*).

Our own experience with Cumberland Mountain children leads us to believe that many White children of Southern Appalachia reflect parental fears that the school represents outside middle-class values; the type of "larnin' that ain't-a-gonna-do-ya-no-good!" On the other hand, one of the "strengths" of many of the poor Whites of the Appalachian region is their devotion to "old-time religions" and to fundamentalism. Although they are many generations removed from their Gallic ancestors, they retain strong respect for the Holy Word of God and the necessity of *learning to read* in order to interpret it first-hand. That much of education (learning to read) they support, but they expect the schools to do that. Indeed, many we have observed and talked to in Appalachia strongly resent any home projects involving parental help. "Teachin' them young-uns t'read is that teacher's job."

Appalachia has developed a distinct dialect, reflecting many words and expressions retained from the England and Scotland from which their ancestors came before the American Revolution. We have listed children from this region as bidialectical because they can understand standard English even though they do not speak it. Moreover, parents do not think it strange or "foreign" to have their children learning to read in standard mainstream English. Their dialect is merely a means of communication, and has little, if anything, to do with he printed word.

Such children, and children from other similarly isolated communities, will, of course, require special help in learning to read. (Incidentally, merely because you may be teaching in a school far removed from an isolated area is no reason to expect you will not encounter such children. In recent years, for example, poverty has driven many Appalachian families to seek work and to live in industrial cities of the North and elsewhere.)

BLACK ENGLISH AND READING

Black English has received more attention and discussion than any other cultural-linguistic difference. As a result, there are more definitive facts known (as well as more misconceptions) about Black English and its relationship to reading than about any other nonstandard dialect group. Not everything, of course, is presently known about the relationship of learning to read and the use of Black English, but much has been learned through the research and work of dedicated scholars and teachers. The brief account of this important topic set forth below is based upon this scholarship (William Labov, Joan Baratz, Kenneth R. Johnson, Walt Wolfram, Dorothy Strickland, and others).

In 1969, Baratz reported that there was a larger percentage of Black children failing in school than non-Black children. There is no indication that the situation has changed. William Labov (Department of Linguistics, Columbia University) stated that "One of the most extraordinary failures in the history of

American education is the failure of the public school system to teach Black children in urban ghettos to read. . . . We are plainly dealing with social and cultural events of considerable magnitude in which the linguistic factors are the focal points of trouble or centers of difficulty rather than the primary causes."

There appears to be considerable agreement among researchers into the characteristics of Black English on one point, at least. It is that there are definite *systematic differences* between Black English and standard English. Some of those differences have been identified and serve not only as a means of identification of children who speak the dialect, but, more importantly, as explanations of the nature of their "differences."

So that you will not make gross errors in judgment but will, on the other hand, capitalize on their strengths, we summarize a number of misconceptions about children who speak Black English.

Misconceptions About Children Who Speak Black-English Dialect

1. *They are making "errors" as they speak and read English.* It is true that, to one who is trained in standard English grammar, pronunciation, and enunciation, speakers of Black English are making "errors." However, linguistic scholars point out that these so-called "errors" are actually "consistent differences" that are essential built-in features of "standard Black English." Anyone who would attempt to correct those errors by substituting standard English forms would actually be introducing gross errors into the dialect.

2. *Black English is inferior.* Black English is no more intrinsically inferior than any other American dialect. True that it is a dialect of English, but we do not label Texas and Oklahoma drawl as being inferior, nor do we denote southern White pronunciation as inferior, even though each is "different."

3. *Children who read standard English with Black English translations are guilty of miscues.* Even those who at one time believed this was the case have now concluded that, what appear to be miscues, are actually very clever *translations* of foreign (standard English) ways of expressing things into Black dialect. It is now believed that children who do this instant translating are demonstrating a high level of comprehension of the original material as well as exceptional intellectual gymnastics.

4. *Black children are nonverbal.* This notion was generated by researchers in the 1950s and 1960s when a massive effort was mounted to try to improve the education of inner-city children. It may be true that in some classrooms, Black children tend to be less verbal for several reasons: teacher rejection of their dialect, fear of making "errors," and conflict between dialect and mainstream English that is too great for them to sort out. More recent studies, including just common-sense observation of Black children at play, certainly reveal highly verbal youngsters communicating and fabricating "talk stories" replete with fascinating verbal imagery.

5. *Speakers of Black English are lip-lazy.* Any "outsider" who has attempted to

imitate Black English soon finds that it takes a fair amount of lip manipulation to accomplish the task. The slurring that is dubbed "lip-laziness" is as much a feature of the dialect as is the nasal characteristics of spoken French.

6. *Black English is merely simplified standard English.* Black-English speakers do simplify standard grammatical forms. For example, for standard English, "He goes," Black English would be "He go." There is also an almost-universal use of present tense for past tense. The speaker of Black English knows it is past by means of the context and certain time markers such as *yesterday, last week,* and so on.

    Yesterday they went . . . emerges as *Yestaday, they go* . . . . This does not mean that speakers are simplifying English; they are speaking the dialect as it is.

    There probably was a time when the African slaves were learning Plantation English that this simplification was the best they could manage. Exactly the same condition prevailed in Hawaii when Chinese, Japanese, and Portugese were imported to work on the sugar and pineapple plantations. A simplified Plantation English emerged, known and spoken today as Pidgin English. Even though the original need to simplify our grammar no longer exists, these simplified forms have become standard in Black dialect and in Hawaiian Pidgin.

7. *Speakers of Black English have something wrong with their hearing.* Speakers of Black English do not pronounce the final consonant /r/ in many words. But neither do folks from certain parts of Maine, Boston, and Rhode Island! *Four* becomes *fo-'ah* in Southern Rhode Island English . . . both drop the /r/, but, in the latter case, speakers go one step more and create a two syllable word. There is nothing wrong with their hearing.

8. *All Blacks speak Black English.* This, of course, is not true. Black English is not due to skin pigmentation.. . . . It is a product of the subculture in which it is the primary means of communication. Moreover, many Puerto Ricans who have migrated near Blacks in the inner city have learned and now speak Black English, perhaps with a slight Spanish overtone.

9. *Black English is the cause of reading failures of massive proportions in inner city schools.* It is true that current research suggests that, "the greater the use of Black dialect, the higher the incidence of reading failure." But, like much research, the failure to take into consideration other variables that are coexistent may lead one to reach incorrect conclusions. Is Black English the cause of the poor performance in reading, or is it the poverty and cultural differences of the Black inner-city slums that produce children with low motivation to learn to read and significant physical, cognitive, and experiential deficiencies? May it also be a lack of understanding on the part of teachers and a lack of relevant reading materials in the Black idiom that stand as barriers to learning to read?

10. *Black English should be replaced with standard English.* At one time, this was prescribed as the cure. It didn't work! A child's home and environmental language is never replaced, but a second language should be learned for survival and achievement in "outside" situations, such as in the schoolroom and in the larger mainstream society.

From this survey of misconceptions, it should be clear that children who speak in Black dialect (be they Black, Puerto Rican, or White) have learned a dialect that is culture-centered and is the primary means of communication at home and in their culture. Black dialect contains deviant *consistencies* that cannot be veneered with standard English forms.

Common Linguistic Characteristics of Black English   Here are some common linguistic characteristics peculiar to Black English:

1. Elimination of final consonants in many words:
    pas for *past*   *be* for *bed*
    cu for *cup*   *m ä* for *my*
2. Dropping /r/ as a final consonant:
    sto for *store*
3. Dropping possessive forms:
    Bobo ha for *Bobo's hat*
    the boss' c ä for *the boss's car*
4. Dropping plural forms:
    all m ä friend goin' for *all of my friends are going*
5. Dropping *-ing* and replacing it with /n/
    goin' for *going*
6. Dropping prepositions:
    all ma friend for *all of my friends*
7. Dropping /s/ in third-person, singular, as above.
8. Elimination of the copula (helping verb):
    all ma friend goin' for *all of my friends are going*
9. Introduction of helping verbs, especially *be*, in places where they are not used in standard English.
    He be gonna' go for *He will go.*
10. Using double-negatives (not exclusively a characteristic of Black English).
    He don't got no money.
    Ain't nobody seen it.
11. Addition of /s/ in the first person singular.
    Ah lives 'n Brooklyn.
12. Replacing final /-th/ with /f/.
    mouth pronounced as *mouf*
13. Dropping final /l/ sounds.
    I need some he(l)p (pronounced *hep*).
14. Use of ä for final /y/ sound in word *my*.
    Have it m äa way.

We might summarize some of those common characteristics with the following:

Ah see d' man (yesterday). *He goin' pah d' sto, whe(n), alluva sudd'n, he whip audda naaf an(d) come aftah me. Ah take off fas(t), man, fas(t)!*

This is an attempt to reproduce on paper some Black dialect without using IPA (International Phonetic Association) symbols. It is, admittedly, a stereotype of standard Black dialect; an attempt to delineate those features that are fairly consistent in the speech of children who speak in Black English.

Bidialecticalism and Reading   It should be obvious that neither isolation nor dialect should be a major hinderance to reading acquisition, inasmuch as children who speak English dialects understand standard English. They are bidialectical.

Why, then, is it that huge percentages of children with these cultural-linguistic differences are found in the lowest levels of achievement in reading, as a recent survey of reading achievement in one of our largest school system showed?

The study was a comparison of the reading achievement of sixth graders in schools having at least 80% Anglos with that of sixth-graders in schools predominately Oriental, Black, or Mexican-American. The Caucasian students of European ancestry scored above the national norm. The others scored in the range between 10th and 20th percentile; more than 60% *below* the national average!

Is it teacher indifference, teacher rejection of pupils with "differences" (prejudice?), environmental discouragement, physical malnutrition, inner-city disorganization, dialect, isolation, or what? We suggest that a combination of some of these factors conspires against many of these children.

What, then, can we do? What strengths can we capitalize upon?

1. First and foremost we must keep in mind that the intelligence-distribution among bidialectical youngsters is the same as that of children who speak only standard English. This means that at *least* 80 percent of such children can, with your help, learn to read within the regular classroom.
2. Children who speak dialects do not need reading instruction contrived in dialectical materials, because, as Kenneth Goodman finally concluded, the so-called miscues that occur in their reading are actually evidence of their unusual ability to make instant translations from book English into their own dialect.
3. They have a wealth of "different" experiences in their own subculture that can be used as the subjects of many relevant "talk stories" and language-experience stories.
4. They know that standard English exists and that it is expedient to learn to use it at appropriate times. In fact, Professor Johanna DeStefano found that, even in first grade, 56% of children who ordinarily spoke in Black dialect made classroom responses in standard English, and, that, by the fifth grade, over 70% of the

in-class responses of that type of children were in standard English. Similarly, Judy Gay and Ryan Tweney found that:

Production of Black English forms decreased significantly from kindergarten to sixth-grade. The findings suggest that, at least in a school setting, older Black children have the ability to respond orally to a language task in standard English if they perceive the situation to be one in which they should do so. This finding also supports the concept of code-sliding suggested by Skupas and Tweney (1975).

They reported further that Black children already know the basic contrasts in both Black and standard English when they first enter Kindegargen. They are, by that time, largely *bidialectical*.

5. These children view the same TV programs as do mainstream children, and, therefore, have some vicarious experiences and background in common.
6. The interests of children, regardless of culture, are largely the same—sports, pets, and so on—and serve as categories of interest in reading.
7. Even though the surface grammar is "incorrect," the deep meaning is retained, regardless of dialect. This fact points to the probability that, as long as meaning is within the bounds of relevancy for the child, dialect is little or no hindrance to the child learning to read in standard English.

BILINGUALISM AND READING

America is still viewed as the land of freedom and opportunity, attracting in the decades since World War II millions of immigrants, bringing their cultures, languages, and children with them. This migration has created monumental problems for our schools, and it is impossible in the space here to elaborate on the problems, suffice it to say that, in the State of Hawaii, alone, the Department of Education has identified 44 *different home languages!*

Because of the conditions in the homelands from which the great majority of the families have come, they were able to bring few possessions. According to immigration sources, most come penniless, relying on relatives or friends here to vouch for their keep. Moreover, according to welfare department records in ports of entry, most come with only common laborer skills. They all seek a new start in life, and are anxious that their children succeed in school. This is a strength.

The largest immigrant groups are the Spanish-speaking Cubans, Puerto Ricans, and Chicanos; the Portuguese; Asians from the rim of the Pacific, including huge numbers of Filipinos and the "Boat People" from Vietnam; and the Polynesians and Micronesians from the South Pacific. In addition to those four categories, there are the much-smaller numbers of Native Americans speaking a great diversity of tribal Indian languages. Regardless of where you teach, it is more than likely that you will have some children from homes where a foreign language is the primary language of communication. Here are a few examples of "differences," knowledge of which may help you cope with these children in your reading class.

CHILDREN FROM SPANISH-SPEAKING HOMES

Chicano-English has several unique characteristics. Yet some of these are also recognized as standard deviations used by speakers in other Spanish or Creole dialects of English. Future tense "helping words" are often omitted:

I will not go.   Don't come tomorrow.
I no go.   *You no comma tomorrow.*

Use of long $\bar{e}$ in place of short $\check{i}$
    heem for him

Use of comparatives *more* and *most* for suffixes -er and est.
Use of *he* in place of *she*.

She is the smaller girl.
He more leetle girrl.

We specially commend to your consideration the excellent studies of Mexican/American Chicano speech done by Dr. Miles Zintz (University of New Mexico). He emphasized the idea that culture, values, and the deeper meanings of language are all interrelated, and that there is more to nonstandard English than merely the dialectical differences. Many of his writings stress the point that Chicano children who have to adjust to a different culture while, at the same time, attempting to use a different language, "experience extreme frustration" and *appear* to be inferior in intelligence and to lack cognitive skills; becoming "nonlingual."

Bilingual Chicano children in the Las Cruces (New Mexico) school system were reported by Mary T. Keith to have scored significantly below Anglos in readiness, reading, and total achievement in spite of a number of special programs targeted to them. She noted that, over a period of three years of testing, "the percentage of children scoring *below* the 25th percentile on the *Metropolitan Reading Readiness Test* from English-speaking backgrounds was only 0.02 percent, whereas those from Spanish-speaking backgrounds was 30.7 percent."

In another study of children from bilingual backgrounds, Gaarder's findings support our previous comments on self-image, especially as it relates to a feeling of inferiority in many Spanish-speaking children. Children with such low self-esteem were found to have "rejected self, school, parents, their native culture and its values, and society in general."

Few people outside the Southwest are aware of the enormous impact the

Chicano problem is having on the schools. Because of the inability of the U. S. Immigration Service to control migration from Mexico and the high birthrate of Mexicans, a recent projection indicates that the Mexican-American population living in the United States by the year 2000 will reach 75,000,000! Schools should be gearing up to face the problems this will generate, especially reading instruction.

Some teachers tend to stereotype Chicanos as being lower-class, less-intelligent, less-motivated, and high-risks in education. Such a generalization diverts attention from those Spanish-speaking children from middle-class homes, whether they be in Miami (Dade County) where hundreds of thousands fled from Castro's Cuba, or in the Southwest.

One of the best descriptions of the characteristics of middle-class Spanish-speaking children has been provided for us by Dr. Ruth H. Mattila, who has worked for over a quarter-century in teacher education for Spanish-speaking children in Northern New Mexico. Comparing them with middle-class English-speaking counterparts, she lists thirteen characteristics, briefly excerpted as follows:

1. Not being able to read is normal.
2. Not nervous when unable to read.
3. More social relationships to adults, due to extended-family experiences.
4. Very sensitive to anyone who does not like them because of their Spanish culture.
5. Less verbal; less concerned with need to read.
6. Work well together—work poorly alone.
7. New members of group must be assimilated before any work can move forward.
8. More politically astute.
9. Forceful and fluent in public speaking.
10. Authoritarian and male-oriented.
11. More demanding of proper form and ritual.
12. When they have set reading goals, they have patterns of accomplishment that are not distinguishable from Anglos.
13. Once started in reading, they are just as competitive as Anglos, but are more responsive to praise and more sensitive to criticism.

Spanish-speaking children whose families migrated from Cuba or Puerto Rico appear to have acquired a mongrelized English linguistic pattern caused primarily because of the fact that most have been forced to find housing in the Black ghettos of our large cities. The bilingualism of these children, consequently, is comprised of their home language (a Spanish dialect in itself) and a dialect of English, affected largely by the Black English of the community in which they live. They must learn some standard English, thus making them trilingual.

Children From Portuguese-Speaking Homes   Portuguese-speaking families are found in huge numbers concentrated in two or three regions, the largest of which is, probably, the Fall River-New Bedford (Massachusetts) and East Providence (Rhode Island) area.

Most of their children come to school from families with little or no educational tradition. Yet, most whom we have observed are eager for education and, in spite of their language handicap, assimilate into their English-speaking environment very quickly, becoming bilingual with the special teachers provided for them. But, as is the case so often with foreign groups, there are those who exhibit what we sometimes think of as "typical" (stereotyped) foreign behavior: low self-image, inability to speak even a modicum of English, fear of being ridiculed for errors, disruptive behavior, ganging up with peers who have the same problems, and unwillingness to try to identify objects in English even after much effort on the part of their special bilingual teachers.

Children who exhibit these characteristics have, according to their ESL teachers, a difficult time learning to read even in their native Portuguese. Such children also experience severe reading problems in English and do not belong in the regular reading classroom.

Children from Asian and Southeast-Asian Homes   We are indebted to Dr. Doris Ching for her excellent description of some of the linguistic "differences" common to Chinese/American children who have the problem of becoming bilingual:

1. Chinese (Cantonese) does not have the initial consonant digraph /th/ as in *than*.
2. Chinese does not have initial consonant sounds /n/ and /r/. It is difficult to produce these sounds.
3. When the Chinese indicates a number such as *two*, the noun is not pluralized. Example:, *two book*.
4. Chinese often does not use "helping verbs" when the meaning is evident. Example: *Mountain big*. (Not necessary to say "The mountain is big."
5. Chinese/American children often add a vowel at the end of English words that should end at the consonant /f/. Example: *day off* is pronounced *day offu*.

The staff of the Washington State University's Right-to-Read Center produced an excellent report on the relationship of reading to factors characteristic of several types of Asian/American children. With the Center's permission, we have extracted the following details:

1. . . . The Asian community consists of Filipinos, Chinese, Japanese, Koreans, Samoans, and peoples of the Pacific isles as well as the Asian continent; thus a great range of behaviors and cultural differences . . . both inter- and intra-cultural differences in classroom behavior. For example, a third generation Japanese-

American will behave in a much different manner than a Japanese child who has just arrived from Japan.

2. Japanese-American children come from families that exhibit strong efforts to adapt: high achievement orientation, and, sometimes increased identification with Japanese culture.

3. Japanese-Americans attach a high value to the process of learning: keeping extensive notes, long hours of study, and so on, which may be almost as important as the learning, itself.

4. Most Filipino-American children (second behind Mexico in immigration) are not achievement-oriented. They frequently are ghetto dwellers, emulating their ghetto neighbors in lifestyle.

5. Most first-generation Filipino-Americans continue to communicate in their native dialects: Ilocano, Tagalog, Visayan, etc. In Hawaii, where tens of thousands of Filipino arrivals speak only Ilocano, a massive effort has been mounted in the schools on their behalf. At this writing, it appears to be moving in the direction of producing reading materials in Ilocano as the means of introducing those children to reading.

6. The Chinese-American child is likely to live in a family culture in which failure to behave in a proper manner brings immediate punishment through the use of shame and guilt.

7. The Chinese-American child expects the teacher to maintain a "status" role, and to remain aloof from the students, not touching them or making overt gestures of friendliness. As the child becomes more a part of the mainstream culture, all this changes.

8. Asian Americans have great difficulty with our English alphabet symbols, because one character in Chinese, for example, may stand for a total word or even a phrase. Moreover, Asian languages are largely tonal to convey shades of meanings and even different meanings to a far greater extent than does English. The language symbols and patterns of the Vietnamese language present additional problems to the children of the "Boat People" when they begin to learn to read in English.

9. Federally financed centers for the development of reading materials for Asian-American children and for children in the American Trust Territories are presently in a dilemma: whether to encourage the learning of reading in English or in their native languages. We will later in this discussion enumerate the pros and cons of that.

10. Up to the present, it has been mandated that all children who have English-language deficits must have special help in the schools, especially with their reading.

Compensatory Instruction in English   To assure that national origin minority students receive compensatory instruction in English, the U.S. Supreme Court upheld the class-action suit of Kinney K. Lau (a minor) to compel the San Francisco Union School District to provide *all* non-English-speaking Chinese children with bilingual *compensatory education in the English language* (January 24, 1974).

In reversing the lower court's decision, the Supreme Court opinion read in part:

Basic English skills are at the very core of what these public schools teach. Imposition of a requirement that, before a child can effectively participate in the educational program, he must already have acquired those basic skills is to make a mockery of public education. We know that those who do not understand English are certain to find their classroom experiences wholly incomprehensible and in no way meaningful.

Lau vs. Nichols

It was indicated during the case that:

At least 2,850 Chinese-speaking students were unable either to understand or communicate in the English language sufficiently to function in the classroom. Two-thirds of those students (approximately 1,800) received no special instruction or help in English. The other 1,050 Chinese-speaking students did receive special instruction in the English language, but only 500 received such instruction in full-time specially-designed classes.

Beezer cited other cases (U.S. vs. Texas 1970; Sera vs. Portales Municipal Schools, 1972; Guadalupe vs. Tempe, Arizona Elementary School District, 1972) to indicate the trend toward court-ordered instruction in English for national-origin minority students. He noted that "School districts enrolling a 'sizeable' number of non-English-speaking students may have to establish a bilingual program or lose all federal funds they are now receiving." This means, of course, that instruction in reading would be in English, but would have to be adjusted to the needs of those non-English-speaking children.

Children from Native-American-Indian Homes   *Native-American* is the label now being used for all American-Indian peoples, regardless of whether they be Chippewa, Apache, Cheyenne, or even members of an Alaskan tribe. Consequently, it may be impossible to generalize or to briefly delineate any common language characteristics of children from such backgrounds. Several researchers who are closely associated with certain groups of *Native Americans* help us some with their findings. Our best resource is the relatively-new *Journal of American Indian Education*. We highly recommend it to anyone who will be teaching in schools having children from Native-American families.

One characteristic that is common to several reports is that children give outward evidences of being "passive and unexpressive, accepting their environment which is usually hard and dangerous." Also, as is the case in less-mechanized cultures, there is little, if any, concern for *time*. Punctuality is not a "virtue" in Amerindian culture. Neither is women's liberation a part of that way of life. Native-American boys, therefore, are said to reflect the adult male attitude toward work, and this, obviously, has considerable influence on their attitude toward the need for academic effort in the classroom.

Language is also a problem. Because of the number of tribes there is no common primary language. Hopkins pointed out that there is a great diversity of languages and language combinations spoken by Native-American children, and that this "is a source of educational frustration for the professionals who have the responsibility for instructing Indian children and youth." He also alluded to the "several possibilities of language instruction, including:

1. Tribal language only.
2. Bilingualism, that is, English and the tribal language.
3. A dialect of the tribal language, which occurs with any large diverse population such as the Navajo.
4. Trilingualism, including the tribal language, English, and Spanish.
5. A combination of the tribal language and English (spoken concurrently, not separated).

It is estimated that there are 100,000 Navajo, and between twelve and twenty-one groups speaking other tribal languages, some groups numbering only a few hundred. This fact presents an impossible problem to those who suggest that reading be taught in the native language first. In many cases, English has been imposed (for various reasons) on the inhabitants of the reservations. The result is what has become known as *Reservation English.* Indeed, as the old people who speak the tribal languages die out, the languages fade with their passing, and the children adopt an English dialect that serves them adequately. There is no doubt that localized dialects of English will soon supplant the tribal languages.

Other Non-English-Speaking American Children In addition to those already cited, there are American families and enclaves of families who for various reasons persist in speaking their native language in the home and whose children may not be bilingual when they enter school—children of recent European immigrants, for example, or children from traditional German or Scandinavian families in the rural Midwest, or French-speaking children in certain areas of New England, especially along the Canadian border.

All in all, no matter where you teach in the United States today it is not at all unlikely that you will encounter children who vary from the cultural-linguistic norm in that they are bilingual. In which of their languages should they begin to learn to read?

Should Beginning Reading Be Taught in English or in the Child's Primary Language? The question of whether children whose primary language is not English should begin learning to read in their primary language or in English is debatable. There are advantages and disadvantages in either approach.

Advantages of Beginning Reading in the Foreign Languages

1. The child already knows the structure of his/her "home language."
2. The child can probably already recognize some printed words in the foreign language.
3. The child probably feels *comfortable* in using the grammatical sequences (syntax) of the primary language.
4. In a class where there are several children with similar foreign language backgrounds, they can work as a group and thus avoid the feeling of being "foreign."
5. Family members can help by listening to reading and, if literate, can provide at-home reinforcement and help.
6. Bilingual reading teachers may be available in areas having a high concentration of foreign-speaking children and there is federal money for special help for such teaching.
7. The words and realia of the foreign culture are portrayed and illustrated in some foreign-language reading texts and reflect the characteristics of the child's home life and culture. Holidays and Holy Days are usually part of the story-content of the foreign-language readers. The child feels more "at home" with such books.
8. Children who do not speak English fluently find the grammatical constructions in their own primary language much easier to handle than those of English.
9. The child's cultural values are not upset by the sudden imposition of middle-class Anglo-American ethics and mores.
10. This approach conforms to the psychological principle that we should "start where the learner is; moving from the known to the unknown."
11. Reading success will, generally, be achieved much faster than in cases where the child must learn English and reading simultaneously.
12. Reading in the primary language will help the child proudly to identify with his/her rich culture that is part of our total American *pot pourri* of cultures.

Disadvantages of Teaching Beginning Reading in a Foreign Language

1. It is difficult for a child to *transfer* his/her language learning from the structure of a foreign language to reading in English. Unlearning will have to be done because of confusion where syntax is different.
2. It is difficult for most school systems to locate bilingual teachers qualified to teach reading in a foreign language.
3. Obtaining books is difficult. In most instances they must be imported or specially developed. This takes time and a staff of specially trained experts. As this book goes to press, the Federal government-financed centers for the development of such materials are just beginning to function. Several such materials-development centers have been established where needs are greatest. The Hawaii Bilingual/Bicultural Education Project has now become known as the Pacific Area Language Materials Development Center and is producing

Should the schools in America teach this boy in the language of his ancestors if it is still the home language? In a recent case (July 12, 1979) Judge Joiner of the U.S. District Court (Michigan) in the case of the Martin Luther King Elementary School Children *v* Ann Arbor School District Board (Civil No. 7-71861) indicated that schools must take appropriate action to "teach them to read in the standard English of the school, the commercial world, the arts, science, and professions.

materials in some of the languages spoken in spots in the Pacific, namely Ilokano, Palaou, and so on. Some of their materials are bilingual. The process is costly and extremely time-consuming.

4. The children in a foreign-language beginning-reading program may be branded as "second-class citizens" by teachers who do not understand the need to acknowledge differences.

5. Citizens who are resenting spiraling taxes voice an increasingly loud criticism of the use of tax monies to support foreign-language reading programs for children who are living in our English-speaking society and, according to the critics, "should be learning English."

6. Learning to read in a foreign language and exclusive exposure to foreign-language reading materials may hinder the child's entry to mainstream American society and culture. Furthermore, setting the children apart in the classroom situation may reinforce their feelings of alienation from the mainstream American educational system.

How Do I Teach Reading to Bilingual Children? Most of the methods and materials that have been described in Chapters 2 and 3 are appropriate for beginning reading with bilingual children, with special consideration for the language handicap which they must overcome.

Bilingual children generally need a longer and slower readiness program, regardless of the age at which they enter the reading-in-English program. After they have learned beginning reading techniques, they usually can be "mainstreamed" for the special skills described in Unit Three: word-recognition, phonics, vocabulary development, comprehension, and reading-study skills.

Because of their feelings of insecurity, it is best to have bilingual children work in pairs ("buddy system") even though one child in the pair is able to speak only English. If both members of the pair are bilingual, so much the better. Rely heavily on langauge-experience stories (Chapters 2 and 3) when working with bilingual children. Seeing their own real-life experiences transcribed into printed English by the teacher will strengthen their motivation for learning to read. Such "talk stories," which are so much a part of their own culture, will help them realize that reading is alien neither to themselves nor their culture. Dr. Virginia French Allen suggested experience stories composed of simplified statements she called "Tarzan Talk" in what we might call "telegram" style. The example she presented is sufficient to illustrate the content:

> Big crocodile swim river. Pretty girl swim river. Girl see crocodile. Crocodile see girl. Crocodile hungry. Crocodile open mouth. Eat girl?
> From this restricted mode, the children then develop the English sentences in an elaborative mode, suggesting possibilities for completing and expanding the sentences with articles, adverbs, adjectives, and subordinate clauses, and so on.

The features of their primary language will spill over into their reading of English as miscues, but must be recognized as their normal thought patterns. For example, the Chinese-American or Japanese-American child may use the singular number where standard English calls for the plural: "The boy sold eight newspaper." "It was many day since I come here." It is best not to "correct" such misuses until after the child has established satisfactory reading skills. The niceties of the language are not a major priority for the bilingual child learning to read English.

Teaching such children to read requires several extra efforts. First, whole words that are relevant to their particular isolated subculture must be learned as sight words. Second, language-experience charts must carry the children's dictated experiences, but should tactfully and gradually be changed from street language dialect or reservation English to a very simplified standard English. Third, the known phonics elements that are common to both the dialect and standard English should be practiced and learned first. Fourth, writing by each child should be begun by having the child keep a booklet of his/her "own"

Children who need special language help deserve special, individual attention. What preplanning would have to be done to make this effective?

words; those that are of greatest relevance and/or interest; and then by helping the children write their stories, using those word booklets as resources. Fifth, many materials that are set in a background similar or representative of the culture in which the children live should be obtained and read to them. Sixth, easy materials with stories set in the culture which the children know should be obtained for children to begin to read. Seventh, language-experience booklets should be made for the children, based on their *talk stories,* and illustrated by sketches, illustrations, cut-out pictures, or actual photographs taken for the occasion.

In the following five groupings we suggest supplementary support strategies for helping the bilingual child to cope with reading instruction in English.

1. The visual: using objects and realia for identifying objects with names, both spoken and printed;

2. The physical: using actions and the body movements in space. This makes it possible for children to see, hear, and read prepositions indicating position and directionality (*before, under, toward, on, to,* etc.);

3. The active: using drama, songs, mime, games, and poetry; all with action;

4. The syntactical: using the natural grammatical sequences or *our* language. This means phrasing. "Many naive teachers think of language learning merely in terms of acquiring new vocabulary." But Gleason indicated that a speaker of a new language can get along with less than 1% of the vocabulary of that language, but needs 50% to 90% of the grammatical structures to be effective in it;

5. The multi-media: using tape recorders, pictures, slides, filmstrips, diagrams, charts, stick figures, puppets, field trips, mock-ups and models, Language Master (two-track audio cards), and the like.

HOW DO I TEACH READING TO CHILDREN WHO HAVE PHYSICAL AND/OR EMOTIONAL PROBLEMS?

Children who suffer from severe physical or emotional handicaps should, of course, receive professional assistance in special classrooms and/or in appropriate clinical settings. However, as a teacher you are likely to encounter at least some children whose physical, health, or emotional problems are such that they may be compensated for in your regular classroom.

VISION PROBLEMS

Much research has been done in recent years on the relationship between visual perception and reading achievement. Poor vision may make learning to read somewhat more arduous, but there is little or no evidence to suggest that vision difficulties will, *per se,* prevent a child from learning to read. (After all, blind children can be taught to read.)

Children with severe vision difficulties should, of course, be referred for professional help. Below is a checklist published by the American Optometrical Association that can help you identify children in your classroom who may be visually handicapped. (A single check is placed alongside a symptom appearing occasionally, two checks if it appears frequently.)

Observational Check-List for Possible Vision Problems

THE ABC'S OF VISION DIFFICULTY

A's—Appearance of the Eyes:

Eyes crossed or turning in, out, or moving independently of each other. __ __

Reddened eyes, watering eyes, encrusted eyelids, frequent styes. __ __

B's—Behavioral Indications of Possible Vision Difficulty:

Body rigidity while looking at distant or near objects or while performing in class:

Avoiding close work. __ __

Unusually short attention span or frequent daydreaming. __ __

Turning of head so as to use one eye only, or tilting of head to one side. __ __

Placing head close to book or desk when reading or writing. __ __

Frowning or scowling while reading, writing or doing blackboard work. __ __

Using unusual or fisted pencil grasp, frequently breaking pencil, and frequent rotation of paper when writing. __ __

Spidery, excessively sloppy, or very hard to read handwriting. __ __

Excessive blinking or excessive rubbing of eyes. __ __

Closing or covering one eye. __ __

Dislike for tasks requiring sustained visual concentration.

Nervousness, irritability, restlessness, or unusual fatigue after maintaining visual concentration. __ __

Losing place while reading and using finger or marker to guide eyes and keep place while reading. __ __

Saying the words aloud or lip reading. __ __

Difficulty in remembering what is read. __ __

Skipping words and re-reading. __ __

Persistent reversals after the second grade. __ __

Difficulty remembering, identifying and reproducing basic geometric forms. __ __

Difficulty with sequential concepts. __ __

Confusion of similar words. __ __

Difficulty following verbal instructions. __ __

Poor eye-hand coordination and unusual awkwardness including difficulty going up and down stairs, throwing or catching a ball, buttoning or unbuttoning clothing or tying shoes. __ __

Displaying evidence of developmental immaturity. __ __

Low frustration level, withdrawn, and difficulty getting along with other children. __ __

C's—Complaints Associated With Using the Eyes:

Headaches, nausea, and dizziness.

Burning or itching of eyes. __ __

Blurring of vision at any time. __ __

Some Hints for Helping Children with Vision Problems   Children with vision problems may need reading material printed in large type. Teacher-printed experience stories may need to be done in larger letters than usual or typed on large-face "Primary type" typewriters.

Special attention should be given to classroom lighting when working with visually handicapped children. Be sure they have sufficient light for their needs. Eliminate glare. If necessary, provide them with nonglare writing paper. Use glare-proof yellow chalk for chalkboard work.

Try the buddy system. Pair a child having poor vision with a child having normal vision. The latter child may act as a prompter and can help "correct" mistakes stemming from poor vision.

They can be encouraged to read with their "favorite" eye. They do not need binocular vision to learn to read.

Use of pretaped stories (done by teacher, teacher's aide, or volunteer) is very helpful for "read-along" sessions. The pretaped story is turned on and the child singly or in a group of others with vision problems can read along in his/her own book while listening to the story being read.

HEARING PROBLEMS

Most children who are deaf or hard-of-hearing do learn to read, but it takes extra effort to accomplish the task. Auditory acuity (the ability to hear sounds distinctly) is related to auditory discrimination; a significant factor in learning to read. There are numerous research studies that indicate that "auditory processing problems are among the most significant factors differentiating between normal and poor learners."

Hearing problems of the kind likely to be encountered in the regular classroom may be more difficult to detect than comparable visual problems. Here are some common symptoms of auditory acuity deficiencies that may be serious enough to affect learning:

Symptoms of Possible Auditory Acuity Deficiencies

1. Can the child differentiate between initial consonant sounds and between final consonant sounds, especially between /p/, /b/, and /t/; between /j/ and between /s/ and /f/? Hearing loss in the higher ranges causes children to confuse these consonant sounds.
2. Does the child repeat words and phrases with similar-sounding words, but incorrect ones?
3. Does the child continuously misinterpret spoken directions?
4. Does the child seem to turn one "good ear" toward the speaker?
5. Does the child appear to be inattentive?
6. Does the child frequently say, "I don't understand" or "I don't know"?
7. Does the child regularly ask to have things repeated?

---

8. Does the child complain of noises" in the ear?
9. Does the child speak abnormally loud?
10. Does the child read and/or talk in a monotone?

Any child showing evidence of serious hearing impairment in the classroom should, of course, be referred for professional diagnosis and treatment. Barring total or near-total deafness, most hearing-impaired children can remain in the regular classroom and can be taught to read.

Some Hints for Helping Children with Hearing Problems Whenever possible, group hearing-impaired children together for reading instruction.

Whenever possible, face the child directly during instruction sessions.

If necessary, slow down the pace of instruction.

Use facial expression and gestures to reinforce meanings and instructions.

Enunciate carefully, especially when working with consonant sounds, blends, and digraph correspondences.

If necessary, speak in a louder than usual tone of voice.

Control unnecessary and distracting classroom noise.

Make full use of available audio devices such as audio-gain recordings and earphones.

NUTRITION AND READING

Inadequate nutrition has long been recognized as a debilitating factor associated with, if not actually a major cause of poor school performance, and, rightly so, for nutritionists have voluminous data to prove the relationship between protein deficiency and low mental achievement. Physiological chemists have been accumulating data and reporting on the relationship of protein, RNA, and DNA, in the transmission of stimuli transferred from the external sensors to the brain. They also show a definite positive relationship between protein and the retention of learning.

There is little that the classroom teacher can do to remediate poor nutrition. Some schools have provided breakfasts for children from disadvantaged homes where an adequate diet is missing and poor performance in the classroom is common. The school hot-lunch program should be promoted by the classroom teacher, together with discussion of the importance of consuming the entire daily portions of a balanced school lunch.

Referrals of children who appear to be deficient in nutrition should be made to proper school authorities, and the classroom teacher should keep a tight overview of the remediation strategies to assure that they are being continued by both school and pupil.

If possible, parents should become part of the remedial effort. We recognize that this, frequently, is an unreal expectation. It takes considerable effort!

In-class demonstrations of lack of vitamins and protein deficiency can be carried out under the guise of "The Science Corner." Guinea pigs and hamsters can be isolated and fed different diets, with observable results. Children can read about nutrition in simple science texts written at first-grade levels. Similarly, plants can be grown and fed various amounts of fertilizer (plant *food*), and the effects of poor nutrition can become vivid.

Finally, teachers of undernourished children must muster patience and compassion, for, at this writing, teachers are prohibited from administering supplementary vitamins, minerals, protein, and so on, to children who obviously need food supplements and who could do better in school achievement if they had adequate daily amounts.

Symptoms of Possible Nutritional Deficiencies

1. Is the child lethargic?
2. Does the child have frequent illnesses, colds, and other respiratory troubles?
3. Is the child underweight?
4. Is the child short-of-stature compared to his/her peers?
5. Does the child have frequent sores on the body?
6. Does the child have bad teeth?
7. Is the child unable to engage in strenuous physical activity, normal for his/her peers, without excessive fatigue?
8. Does the child have breakfast before coming to school?
9. What does the child report as the usual home diet?
10. Does the child recieve a free hot-lunch program?
11. Is the child's family supported by welfare, aid-to-dependent children, or some other agency?
12. Does the child ask for (or "steal") candy or goodies from other children?
13. Does the child's body show other signs of severe malnutrition (bloated stomach, sunken eyes, skin-and-bones appearance, etc.)?
14. Has the child been referred to medical care? What is the program, if any, for treatment?
15. Does the child have lung trouble (coughing) that might signal tuberculosis?
16. Is the child overly aggressive, troublesome, and/or overactive? Nutritionists have evidence that his may be due to a high-sugar and "junk food" diet!

CHRONIC SLEEP DEFICITS

Huge numbers of otherwise-healthy children come to school with chronic sleep loss due to late hours, television, parental negligence in getting them in "off the street" at night, or a combination of all three. The best evidence of this is to be found in the classroom at mid-morning. Such children are yawning and/or

Regardless of the cause, be it nutritional deficiency, chronic sleep loss, or tranquilizers, the child who sleeps in class needs special help. What plans would be necessary to provide special reading instruction for this child? Whose responsibility is it?

sound asleep. A mininap revives them until lunchtime. Moreover, countless numbers of children are on tranquilizing drugs administered by physicians and/or by parents. In either case, we point to the obvious fact that a child must be awake to learn to read.

There is little difference between the effect of absenteeism and of chronic sleep loss except that, in the latter, the child is physically present but cognitively absent.

How do you teach children who are asleep? You don't. But you can make some provision such as:

1. Enlist the cooperation of the parent in monitoring the sleep patterns of the child.
2. Provide a rest area for a mininap.
3. Suggest a checkup by the school nurse and/or doctor, with a report to the parents.
4. Plan reading skills sessions for such children at times when they are most alert. This is usually in the first hour of the morning.
5. Stop instruction or reading practice as soon as yawning is noticed.
6. If possible, provide an exercise session with plenty of fresh air inhaled and stale air exhaled from the lungs.

DYSLEXIA AND READING

Over the past decade a great amount of information and misinformation has been generated under the term *dyslexia*. Dozens of otherwise-reliable professionals have attempted to postulate on what it is or what it is not. The result has been much talk and considerable publication of articles, leaving the teacher of reading with either confused notions or totally inaccurate concepts of this physical condition that prevents an individual from learning to read. Medical doctors have presented their guesses. Optometrists have prescribed "visual exercises." Psychologists have suggested brain lesions. Physical therapists have set up trampolines and crawling strategies. And reading teachers have been confronted with the totally unreasonable notion that everyone who cannot or has not learned to read is a *dyslexic*.

At this writing, more research is being conducted on dyslexia abroad than in the United States. Much of it, too, is confusing, ranging all the way from those, such as Schlee in Germany, who deny the very existence of dyslexia to those who claim that they have discovered as many as 20% of a population of children with dyslexia. Apparently, someone is wrong; perhaps both. We are convinced that there is such a conditon as dyslexia, and we define it thus:

Definition of Dyslexia

A physical condition causing an individual who has normal intelligence and who is able to remember the names of objects to be unable to retain the connection (correspondence) between the printed symbol (visual memory) and the spoken word (auditory memory) which it represents.

There is much solid evidence to indicate that dyslexia is a physical condition and should be treated as such by a physician before reading instruction is effective.

The Dyslectic Individual and Reading

1. The dyslexic is, otherwise, an intellectually unimpaired individual.
2. The dyslexic cannot recall previous associative learning between printed words and spoken words.
3. Dyslexics have EEG (electroencephalograph) brain wave patterns quite similar to those EEGs of individuals who have *petit mal* (a mild form of epilepsy).
4. The epileptic-type EEGs indicate that the brain is "short-circuiting," eliminating the associateve connections made during learning.
5. By administering nonconvulsant drugs (such as are given to patients suffering from epilepsy) the brain waves become normal.
6. Once the physical condition is alleviated, the patient is sent to a reading teacher and is able to learn to read!

These facts have been confirmed by several psychiatrists whom we have interviewed among them, Dr. David Clouston of the Porirua Hospital, Wellington, New Zealand. He explained that the *petit mal* condition is usually so slight as to be undetectable in a normal physical examination. It is revealed only through the EEG. He indicated that he remedies the condition with nonconvulsant drugs, and the dyslexic child then responds normally (without short-circuiting) to reading instruction. It is as simple as that!

Equally exciting is the more recent report (1978) that motion-sickness drugs have also produced positive results with dyslexic children.

We relate these findings here for two reasons: First, we hope they will prevent you from going through meaningless and ridiculous motions and strategies as sorcerers in the Dark Ages. Second, the reading profession should seriously consider dyslexia as a physical condition that may easily and successfully be alleviated so we may teach reading so all may learn.

How Do I Teach Reading to a Dyslexic Child?   One problem is that children do not show signs of dyslexia until they have been in school reading programs for two or more years. If they do not learn to read in grade One, they are usually considered to be children with learning problems, and are often mistaken for slow-learning children with low I.Q.s. Perceptive teachers including their kindergarten teacher, can easily refute such notions. But it frequently takes two or more years before it is evident that the dyslexic child has normal or above-normal intelligence but cannot retain the correspondences between graphic symbols and spoken words or letters. Two years of instruction have gone by and the child has not begun to learn to read!

Here are the things that yield results in teaching the dyslexic child to read:

1. Identify him/her as a dyslexic. Our research on this subject convinces us that there is only one way that we can be certain that a child is a true dyslexic. Work with parents and physician to have an EEG (electroencephalogram) taken and compared by a competent specialist to the typical EEG of *petit mal*. If the pattern is similar or the same, but at reduced intensity, the individual is a true dyslexic, but does not have the overt behavior of *petit mal* (a mild form of epilepsy).
2. The physician can reduce the condition with anticonvulsant drugs or anti-motion-sickness drugs and stabilize it under his/her supervision.
3. The individual is now ready to learn. Because the child is likely to be at least several years behind his/her peers in reading by the time the condition has been diagnosed and treated, initial reading instruction will have to be on a one-to-one catch-up basis.
4. Beginning reading instruction will commence as though the child had never had instruction previously. A group of dyslexic children who, at the age of eight, were treated with anticonvulsant drugs and then sent to a special reading teacher for instruction had no knowledge of the alphabet, highway stop-and-go signs, or any of the other visual symbols of an ordinary environment. They had

to start with letters and phonics simultaneously with whole words. Nevertheless, they progressed rapidly. Some were up to expected level within a year of one-to-one instruction—a three-year gain in one year!

DISRUPTIVE BEHAVIOR

It is unrealistic to ignore the fact that, in a large number of classrooms, there are children who exhibit disruptive behavior. In fact, this is by far the greatest problem for beginning teachers.

There is little question that such children "disrupt" their *own* learning as well as that of others. We have included a discussion of it here, because we share the opinion of nutritionists and other psychologists that it frequently (but, of course, not always) is a physical expression of unmet needs and/or of a severe nutritional imbalance. Furthermore, many children who are diagnosed as "disruptive" are children with actual physical conditions that generate movement and nonconforming behavior.

Children suffering from physical or emotional problems leading to extremely disruptive behavior should be referred for professional attention. Most

When a confrontation takes place, how can it be resolved so the child restores his/her self respect? Behavior problems are time consuming and disrupt reading instruction unless special plans are made to prevent problems from occuring. Can success and self-satisfaction be preplanned for each child?

disruptive children can, however, be handled in the regular classroom. Disruptive behavior is a particularly pressing problem in many inner-city schools, for obvious reasons (poverty, poor home and community environment, etc.). It has been estimated that in some inner-city schools teachers may spend as much as 80 percent of the school day dealing with students exhibiting such behavior. However, disruptive behavior is by no means confined to children from low socioeconomic areas. No matter where you teach, it is a problem with which you will undoubtedly have to deal.

There are probably many causes and few cures. For example, children with so-called "growing pains" may be told that "there is no such thing as growing pains;" nevertheless, they actually suffer from pains in the arm and knee joints! A small amount of relief from those pains is obtained by movement, stretching, walking, cracking joints, and so, all of which some teachers may interpret as disruptive and defiance of "rules." Some researchers have proceeded on the assumption that "growing pains" are the result of the deposit of calcium nodules in the arm and knee joints at a faster rate than the body can absorb. The condition may be alleviated by drugs. This is a project for the medical clinic, and, therefore, calls for referrals from the classroom teacher.

Many disruptive children have unpredictable and recurrent emotional flare-ups. These may be the result of over-permissiveness, poor self-image, resentment, massive sugar intake, junk foods in place of a balanced diet, and any number of other causes. They may even be caused by threatening learning situations with which the child cannot cope.

Although it is easy to identify a child who is physically disruptive, it is quite another thing to identify the cause. Moreover, without identification of the cause, very little, if anything, can be done to alleviate the situation or to teach him/her in the normal classroom setting.

You are not, of course, expected to play the role of professional therapist in the classroom, searching for deeply hidden roots of disruptive behavior. You will have neither the time nor the expertise for such a role. You can, however, often discover some of the more obvious causes of disruption through observation and gentle probing. It does little or no good to confront the child directly with "Why are you causing this trouble?" Almost certainly, the child has no idea why.

Basically, the disruptive child is likely to be a frightened child masking fright with untoward aggression ("I *won't* sit where you tell me!" "I hate you!" "I wish I could kill everybody!"). What is the child afraid of? Is it some seemingly unresolvable home or environmental conflict? Is it expectation of failure? Is it the learning situation itself? Observe. Listen. You may be able to alleviate the situation. The disruptive child is a child pleading for help.

Some Hints for Helping the Disruptive Child   If the disruptive child is to learn, he/she must somehow be made nondisruptive (which may take the patience of Job and the compassion of a saint, but perhaps this, too, goes with teaching).

Here are some techniques that have been found to be useful in eliminating or alleviating disruptive behavior. (For a more detailed discussion of such techniques, see Swift and Spivak, as cited in the bibliography at the end of this chapter).

Reinforce appropriate behavior with rewards. Consistent reinforcement such as a smile, pat on the back, a wink, or a good word from the teacher for appropriate behavior may serve the purpose but tangible rewards such as stars, toys, or candy are likely to be even more effective.

Try negative reinforcement for misbehavior: exclusion from a prized activity, quiet reprimands, and so on, which call attention to the fact that the behavior is not acceptable.

Be sure the child is fully aware that his or her behavior is disruptive (some children may not really realize this). A useful technique is to have the child keep his/her own record of incidences of disruptive behavior as indicated by the teacher. You might also keep a record of the number of times the child is away from his/her prescribed place in the classroom as an indication of at least the potential for disruptive behavior. The assumption behind these and similar techniques is that the greater the child's awareness of behavior, the greater the potential that he/she may determine to control it.

Be very clear and precise in your statements as to what constitutes disruptive behavior and what its consequences will be. It is essential that the child knows "the rules of the game."

Keep reading sessions short. The attention span of disruptive children is likely to be unusually short. In addition, such children are likely to be easily distracted.

Give step-by-step instructional directions rather than rely on a sequential set of directions more appropriate for less easily distracted children.

Whenever possible, use one-to-one instruction. Two or three disruptive children may be handled in a group, but keep in mind that children tend to reinforce each other's behavior. Disruptive children often like to "show off" their antics to peers who respond positively to them.

Try "anticipatory cueing." Inform the child that he/she will be called upon at some point in the instructional session. This technique will help stimulate the child to pay attention and thus lessen the potential for disruptive behavior.

Individualize and vary your techniques and procedures as much as possible when dealing with disruptive children. What may work with one child may not work with another. What may work under one set of circumstances may not work under another. There is no one "correct" method for helping the disruptive child.

If necessary, call on outside assistance for help in dealing with disruptive classroom behavior. Many school systems have at least some such assistance available: observer-consultants, behavior specialists, school psychologists, health professionals, and so on. A team approach is better than trying to "go it alone."

In our experience, there is but one conclusion that is a priority: Disruptive children must be made *nondisruptive* (by whatever means prove effective) before they can be taught to read. When that has been accomplished, they are taught to read by techniques and materials appropriate to their intellectual abilities and self-motivation.

SEX DIFFERENCES AND READING ACHIEVEMENT

For more than three decades (long before the women's liberation movement) researchers have been attempting to equate sex differences in children with achievement in reading. It appears that this effort arose from the often-repeated claim that girls mature earlier than boys and are superior achievers during childhood. A cause-and-effect relationship, apparently, was assumed. Today we find far more evidence that superior or inferior reading achievement of boys or girls is related directly to social expectations imposed as sex roles from early childhood through adolescence.

Socially Imposed Expectations on Boys and Girls and Reading Achievement   It is pertinent here to refer to an older classic study in which Anderson, Hughes, and Dixon reported that, although girls learned to read earlier than boys, their rate of reading development was the same as boys when I.Q. was held constant. Also, Balow reported that, when reading readiness was held constant, no significant differences in reading between boys and girls were apparent.

In a longitudinal study of boys and girls, grades four through eight, Dakin found no signnficant differences, and Sinks and Powell concluded, after studying children in the same grade-span, that no generalization could be made concerning the effect of sex differences on reading differences. Dwyer also found that, when age, intelligence, types of reading materials, and so on are accounted for, there is little to support the notion that boys are worse readers than girls just because they are boys.

When boys and girls are free to select for themselves, there are few real differences in their tastes. A poll, conducted by the *Ladies Home Journal* in 1975 revealed that *sports,* which is supposed to be male oriented, captured the top position for both boys and girls, with O. J. Simpson, the current football hero at that time as number-one choice. The top heroes and heroines in 1975 were:

O. J. Simpson, football; Elton John, British rock singer; Neil Armstrong, astronaut; the late John Wayne, movies; Robert Redford, actor; Chris Evert, Olympics medal winner; Mary Tyler Moore, TV; Billie Jean King, tennis heroine; Henry Kissinger, then Secretary of State; and Joe Nameth, football. In addition to those, Katherine Hepburn made the girl's list and President Gerald Ford was on the boy's top-ten list out of a total of 50. Chris Evert and Mary Tyler Moore were on the boy's list.

In studies where sex differences were found related to differences in reading achievement, there is considerable agreement that the differences are

A male teacher or tutor helps in many instances where boys are experiencing reading difficulties.

not sex, *per se,* but probably are differences that a particular society imposes on its boys or on its girls. To support this conclusion, we point to Preston's study of reading achievement in German schools and in American schools. He found that American girls scored higher in reading achievement but that German boys were higher, and attributed the apparent sex difference to differences in cultural expectations. A decade later, Johnson concluded that cultural factors were responsible for differences in reading ability related to sex. His study was done with boys and girls in the United States, Canada, Nigeria, and England. In 1961, Gates, in his monumental study of more than 15,000 boys and girls also suspected an environmental rather than a physical explanation of sex differences.

HOW DO I TEACH CHILDREN WHO ARE EDUCATIONALLY HANDICAPPED?

Besides children who need special help in the regular classroom for the various reasons (intellectual, cultural-linguistic, physical, emotional) discussed above, you will undoubtedly encounter some children who need compensatory reading instruction because somehow, somewhere along the line, they have become victims of inadequate reading instruction. Such children will show evidence of gaps in reading skills which must be identified and ameliorated. Once the gaps have been filled, the children can proceed with normal step-by-step skill development. Most such compensatory instruction can be carried out in the regular classroom.

It should be useful at this point to be a bit more specific concerning the nature of each cause so we can determine the best approach to teaching reading to such children.

INADEQUATE CLASSROOM INSTRUCTION

Inadequate classroom instruction means that the child has not been *taught* the basics of reading, the end result being that the child has gaps in his/her reading skills. Those gaps must be identified, and this can be done with one of the newer criterion—referenced tests. This is a simple, although, admittedly, a time-consuming process. If you can get the reading specialist to do this testing, good!

EXCESSIVE FAMILY MOBILITY

When families move, the sequence of reading instruction of the children is very likely to be disrupted. In addition, a child who moves from one school to another may find himself/herself in a completely new instructional system. For example, a child who has become used to a basal reader program may suddenly be required to cope with an individualized program. Or the new school may emphasize whole-word reading instruction whereas the old school emphasized structured isolated phonics or the i.t.a. alphabetical system.

Such "switches in signals" will obviously be confusing for the child and detrimental to learning to read, especially when the move is made during the school year. In today's highly mobile society, an increasing number of children in the regular classroom are found to be educationally handicapped because of excessive family mobility and consequently in need of special attention and remedial measures.

Migrant Children Children of migrant farm workers are likely to be particularly educationally handicapped because of excessive family mobility. Large numbers of such children are constantly being switched from one school to another as their families follow the seasonal planting and harvesting of the nations' crops. For most of these children, continuity of instruction is an impossible dream. Without remedial and compensatory instruction they are almost certain to become deficient in reading skills and remain so throughout their school years. (Many of these children are doubly handicapped in learning to read in that their home language or dialect is likely not be be standard English).

Several states have now undertaken a cooperative project to help teach migrant children to read. Extensive use of tutors is part of the program. Migrant children are assessed skill-by-skill through the use of the *Criterion reading Assessment Program.* Their reading needs are computerized into the *Migrant Data Bank* in Little Rock, Arkansas. As the child moves from place to place with the family, following the crop planting and harvesting, the Data Bank provides each new school with information, allowing the school to pick up instruction where the last school left off.

In spite of this cooperative innovation, it is found that migrant children need more than just spotty skills instruction. As is the case with other children, they need time to retain the skills, and to transfer them to real reading situations. Family moves frequently cancel such reinorcement. Mary Jassoy described the features of a program for such children in the Palm Beach County, Florida schools.

Features of the Palm Beach County Migrant Children Reading Program

1. The migrant child program is compensatory. It is in addition to the regular classroom program.
2. The classroom teacher notifies the tutorial teacher of the needs of the child.
3. The tutorial teacher then teaches the skills to a group of eight to ten tutors.
4. Each tutor (under the supervision of the tutorial teacher), works with no more than three children at a time.
5. Tutors are trained for four weeks.
6. Tutors are hired only after showing success in the tutorial training program.
7. Tutors create *home packets* for the migrant children. They contain games, minibooks, puzzles, paper, crayons, and clay. The child signs out a packet and may keep it for a designated length of time. When leaving the school, the child may take one packet along on the road to the next school.
8. Tutors are encouraged and have been successful in developing and creating games and new materials directly related to the experiences of migrant children.
9. Photos are taken and used as illustrations for language-experience stories and booklets.

It is reported that, by means of this cooperative system of assessment and the use of trained tutors with very small groups, migrant workers' children can experience some degree of continuity in reading instruction.

EXCESSIVE ABSENTEEISM

Absenteeism is another major cause of systematic instructional deficit, for, in schools where it is excessive, reading achievement scores are among the lowest recorded in the country. In some of our inner-city elementary schools, absenteeism reaches 35 to 50 percent at times during the year.

It cannot be determined if absenteeism, *per se* is the total cause of the poor reading achievement, or whether it be the total global socioeconomic-cultural milieu that underlies it. Nevertheless, absenteeism is the visible factor that may be the symptom of deeper causation. The effects are much the same as those caused by family mobility.

LACK OF CONSISTENT ARTICULATION IN THE READING CURRICULUM

One common cause of school-induced reading deficiency is lack of articulation within the system's reading instruction program. Poor curriculum policies may result in one teacher using one set of materials and one method in a classroom and another teacher in another classroom using an entirely different approach, or just "doing her own thing." In such a situation, a child moving from one classroom to another or one grade to the next is almost certain to suffer from confusion and skill gaps.

ADMINISTRATIVE EXPEDIENCY

Administrators maintain their positions largely based upon their ability to engender "progress." This frequently involves the acquisition of federal funds for "innovative" projects. Innovation requires novelty of instruction and/or materials. Children in so-called "experimental" reading groups usually make progress in reading that is superior to those in the "control" (do-nothing-different) groups. It would seem that this special attention should accelerate the children in the experimental groups, and that they would stay ahead, yet we know of no longitudinal study that shows this happens *unless* careful planning is made to capitalize upon the progress already made and to adjust the subsequent reading instruction as well.

On the other hand, countless numbers of schools have "tried" this-and-that in an effort to give teachers the privilege of "experimentation." Such short-term detours have, in our experience, frequently been holidays from the more strenuous business of learning reading skills. But, while the experimentation is going on, the administrator can point with pride that his school is experimentally oriented. Ths seems to imply progress! Or is it a year of wasted reading instruction?

NEGATIVE EDUCATIONAL ENVIRONMENT

Probably the most inexcusable cause of systematic instructional deficit is a negative educational environment. This is found in many forms, such as teacher bickering, jealousy, unprofessionalism, degrading teacher attitudes toward children or toward their ethnic background and their primary language, teacher strikes, lack of adequate supplies (especially up-to-date reading materials), let-the-other-fellow-do-it attitude, lethargy, frustration on the part of teachers due to lack of administrative support, chaotic discipline, lack of home/school rapport, excessive noise within the school, disrupting gangs of intruders from the outside, lack of supportive services (such as psychologist, reading teacher, multimedia specialist), dirty or antiquated school facilities, inadequate lighting, political interference, and, perhaps others.

Even though we may all agree that such factors are inexcusable, the facts show that they do exist. And their existence militates against optimum progress in reading.

RECOGNIZING THE EDUCATIONALLY HANDICAPPED CHILD

Here are some clues to help you recognize the educationally handicapped child:

Does the child rely solely on the "look" of a word for recognition?

Is the child unable to pronounce any whole word not previously learned?

Is the child unable to differentiate between initial-consonant letter/sound correspondencies?

Is the child able to start a word correctly but unable to complete it without guessing?

Is the child unable to handle vowels?

Is the child unable to handle consonant digraphs and blends and vowel digraphs?

Does the child know long-vowel alphabet sounds but not short-vowel alphabet sounds?

Does the child know the soft /s/ sound but is unable to pronounce the /s/ sound in words like *sure* and *sugar* without prompting?

Does the child know the sound of /t/ but is unable to handle the *-tion* ending of words?

Is the child unable to grasp the concept of silent letters?

Is the child unaware of the final-e rule?

Is the child unable to utilize context to help figure out the meaning of new words?

Is the child overly prone to word-by-word reading?

INSTRUCTIONAL DEFICITS AND READING

Children should never be allowed to go beyond the third grade without being checked for the adequacy of reading instruction during the first three primary grades. There is no excuse for an otherwise-normal child being passed year-after-year and *remediation* commenced only after he/she gets to junior high school. They need *compensatory* reading instruction just as soon as they are discovered as being children who are the victims of educational inconsistencies or inadequacies.

We have coined the term, *compensatory reading*, to designate exactly what the name implies: specific reading-skills instruction, intensified to compensate for prior inadequate systematic reading instruction.

Compensatory Reading Techniques for Children with Systematic Instructional Deficits

1. Identify the negative environmental cause or causes of the deficit. Correct the negative cause or causes if possible. If not, remove the child (if possible) from the causes. Let us suppose that there is a personality conflict between child and teacher. Move the child from the negative environment.
2. With the help of the reading consultant (if any) test the child for skill deficits, using one of the several diagnostic reading tests or criterion-referenced tests.
3. Develop a profile of the child's strengths and weaknesses in reading skills.
4. Arrange a progressive sequence of skills to be learned.
5. Place the child in a small group that is scheduled to learn the first skill on the list. This group may be taught by you, or may be on-going in one of your colleague's classes. This requires total-school cooperation.
6. After a period of instruction, test to verify mastery of that skill.
7. Move the child to the next targeted skill.
8. Encourage the child to progress as rapidly as possible. This is what we call "continuous progress."
9. Reinforce the word-recognition skills with additional work in the language arts, especially spelling and writing (composition).
10. Inform the child of daily progress. Older and more responsible children can help keep their own records of progress.
11. Enchance the positive self-concept of every child.

Children who have systematic instructional deficits in reading skills are children who were not adequately taught to read in the first place. These deficits do not, by themselves, reflect a native inability to learn. They do, however, suggest that, if the causative factors are removed, and basic instruction commenced and carried forward on a continuum, the child will most likely learn as well as any other child just starting to learn to read in a more positive and supportive environment.

The techniques are the same. The groupings are small at first. The materials are those that are designed for nitty-gritty step-by-step skill development as described in detail in Chapters 4 and 5. Most compensatory reading can be carried out by the regular classroom teacher, provided, of course, that there is not a much-larger global cluster of socioeconomic-cultural-linguistic factors that cannot be bypassed.

HOW DO I ASSESS READING ACHIEVEMENT SO ALL MAY LEARN?

As noted in the introduction to this final unit of our text, assessment is essential to all reading instruction and is particularly vital for the discovery of reading deficiencies. Tests may be divided into two major categories: psychometric reading tests and edumetric reading tests.

PSYCHOMETRIC READING TESTS

Psychometric reading tests are "standardized" tests in that their results are evaluated on the basis of the performance of a large geographic and cultural sample. These tests give us a series of measures called grade and/or age norms, representing average scores obtained by the average child of a particular age on a specific test. Regardless of chronological age, a child who obtains the average test score of a particular age group is considered to be equivalent to the average child in that group (or grade). Psychometric reading tests provide assessment of a particular child's achievement related to that of thousands of other children of the same age. They are thus *relative* measures, comparing the performance of a child with the performance of his/her peers.

General Reading Ability Tests   General reading ability tests are psychometric tests designed to measure general reading ability and, frequently, reading rate. They usually consist of a vocabulary sampling and several contextual paragraphs. They are silent-reading tests and can be taken individually or in a group. Test scores are called "raw scores," and can be converted to grade-level equivalents, or "norms."

If we wish to know just where a child stands among all others in his/her grade who took the test, percentile equivalents should be used. A child who has a raw score equivalent to the 50th percentile is right in the middle of the group. Percentiles are essential if we wish to compare a test score with a child's I.Q. percentile. (We discussed I.Q. percentiles at the beginning of this chapter.)

Individualized testing should provide on-going assessment from the prereading stage through the entire elementary years. How can a school mount and handle a longitudinal program of testing and "management" in reading?

Specific Reading Ability Tests   Specific reading ability tests are designed to test reading ability in a particular academic area: literature, mathematics, science, social studies, and so on. They are usually similar to the general reading ability test except that they utilize vocabulary and reading matter specifically related to the particular academic subject. Because they assume a certain amount of subject-area expertise, specific reading ability tests are primarily for secondary school students.

Diagnostic Reading Tests   Diagnostic reading tests are standardized tests designed to ascertain reading habits and uncover specific reading deficienceis and particular types of errors. The test is administered individually by a reading expert trained in the discovery of habitual errors that retard efficient reading. Diagnostic tests are used to help ascertain whether a particular child needs outside remedial help or can remain in the regular classroom for reading instruction.

EDUMETRIC READING TESTS

Edumetric Tests   Edumetric tests are specifically designed to determine whether or not a child has mastered a particular skill. Although levels and norms may be taken into consideration as expectancy bases, these concepts are strictly secondary in edumetric testing.

Cloze Tests   The cloze test is based upon the principles of gestalt psychology and derives its name from the psychological concept of "closure." For example, the subject visualizes a complete square after contemplating a partially completed square, a five-pointed star after studying a partially completed one, and so on.

Applied to reading, the test is predicated upon the assumption that the ability to fill in blanks in reading material (ability to cloze) is a test of the reader's comprehension. The validity of the cloze test as a measure of comprehension seems fairly well established. It is not, however, of much help in identifying specific reading deficiencies.

Example of a Cloze Test*

The school house which _____ to be the center _____ our social life stood _____ the bare prairie and, _____ thousands of other similar _____ in the west, had _____ a leaf to shade _____ in summer nor a _____ to break the winds _____ of savage winter. "There's been _____ good deal of talk _____ setting out a wind _____," neighbor Button explained _____ us, "but nothing has as _____ been done."

It was _____ a square pine box _____ a glaring white on _____ outside and a desolate _____ within; at least drab _____ the original color, but _____ benches were mainly so _____ and hacked that original _____ were obscured. It had _____ doors on the eastern _____ and three windows on _____ side.

A long square stove, _____ wooden chair, and a _____ table in one corner _____ the use of the _____, completed the moveable furniture. _____ walls were roughly plastered, _____ the windows had no _____.

*From Hamlin Garland's autobiography: *Son of the Middle Border*, New York, The Macmillan Co., 1923, p. 95.

Informal Reading Inventory (IRI)   The informal reading inventory test (IRI) is a kind of informal diagnostic reading ability test administered by the classroom teacher. The test may be constructed with pages from a graded reader series arranged in a sequence of increasing difficulty. As the child reads the materials aloud, the teacher, who has his/her own copy of the materials, monitors the reading for accuracy and records misreadings and miscues. After the material is read, the teacher asks questions designed to test comprehension of literal facts, inferences, cause-and-effect, and so on. The child who can read and comprehend materials at a certain grade-level with relative ease and few errors is designated "informally" as reading at a specific grade level. The IRI is especially useful for assessing the reading level of new classroom entrants for whom previous records may not be available.

Pioneers in developing the IRI were Dr. Donald Durrell (1940) and Dr. Emmett Betts (1946). Both suggested that we should assign "levels" of ability, and proposed the *expectancy level, independent level, instructional level, and frustration level.*

1. *Expectancy level.* The highest grade-level materials that can be comprehanded satisfactorily by the child who *listens* to the passages being read is said to be the child's *expectancy* level; the optimum level that child may be able to reach. When the child is given materials that he/she must read aloud, three other levels are significant measures of comprehension.
2. *Independent level.* At the independent level, the child reads orally with practically no errors and is able to answer comprehension questions with 90% accuracy. This is the child's *comfortable* level of personalized reading without being pushed.
3. *Instructional level.* At this level the child reads orally with no more than 5% errors and achieves 75% accuracy on comprehension questions. In the words of Betts: "The child is challenged but not frustrated."
4. *Frustration level.* At this level the child reads orally with 10% or more errors and is unable to comprehend more than 50% of the material. Betts observed that at this level the child will exhibit several indications of frustration such as finger movements, head movements, tension, withdrawal, word-by-word pronunciation, substitutions, repetitions, and omissions. "This level is to be avoided."

Construction and administration of "homemade" informal reading inventory tests can be a rewarding experience for the classroom teacher. The process will help you become more aware of the range of reading abilities among the children, the types of errors made and the comprehension problems commonly encountered by the children, and the possible need for special vocabulary instruction. (For an excellent guide to construction and administration of informal reading inventory tests, see Johnson and Kress, *Informal Reading Inventories,* as cited in the bibliography at the end of this chapter.)

The "management" components of many basal reader series also have informal reading inventories that may be used to determine a child's "point of entry" into the reading program.

Criterion-Referenced Tests　The behavioral-objectives fad of the 1960s generated interest in criterion-referenced tests that are directly related to specific objectives. (They could, perhaps, more accurately be called objective-referenced tests.) The procedure for using criterion-referenced testing in reading is essentially as follows:

Determine the skills that need to be learned.

State each of these skills as a specific objective.

Administer a test specifically designed to determine if the child has mastered that skill. (One test for each separate objective.)

Separate the children who have mastered the skill from those who have not.

Teach the skill to those who have not learned it.

Retest these children after the instruction.

Allow children who have attained the objective to move on to a new learning skill.

Advantages and Disadvantages of Criterion-Referenced Testing The principle advantage of criterion-referenced testing is that it enables you to identify which essential skills and subskills the child has already mastered and those that remain to be attained. You do not have to rely solely on observation or on guesswork based upon the child's past educational experiences. Upon completion of testing, children with similar skill deficits can be grouped together for learning an unmastered skill. Later, each child can again be tested to assure that the objective has actually been attained before moving on to the next skill.

On the other hand, there is a danger that criterion-referenced testing (and teaching) can become rigidly programmed to the extent that certain important factors of learning to read are slighted or even completely disregarded—the relevance of reading materials, for example, or quality of teaching, or learning aptitude, or motivational factors. In addition, particular care must be taken that constant attention to the nitty-gritty of learning specific skills and subskills does not become merely a mechanical exercise and consequently boring and unproductive.

IDENTIFYING SPECIFIC READING SKILLS

A good deal of research has been done in recent years to attempt to identify specific skills needed in the learning-to-read process. Perhaps the most ambitious of such studies was that conducted in the late 1960s by the Wisconsin Research and Development Center for Cognitive Learning (University of Wisconsin). *The Wisconsin Design* delineated six general skill areas: (a) word attack, (b) comprehension, (c) study skills, (d) self-directed reading, (e) interpretive reading, and (f) creative reading. Specific skill tests were designed to encompass the following skills at various grade levels:

> *Level "A"* (Kindergarten): Rhyming words, rhyming phrases, shapes, letters; numerals, words and phrases, initial consonants.
>
> *Level "B"* (First Grade): Some sight vocabulary, beginning consonants, ending consonants, blends, short vowels, consonant digraphs, compound words, contractions, roots and endings, plurals, possessives.
>
> *Level "C"* (Second Grade): More sight vocabulary, consonant variants, more blends, long vowel sounds, vowels + *r*, a + l, a + w, diphthongs, "long" and "short" *oo*, more consonant digraphs, plurals, homonyms, synonyms-antonyms, multiple meanings.
>
> *Level "D"* (Third Grade): More sight vocabulary, trigraphs, silent letters, syllabication, accent, schwa, possessives.

Checksheets   No matter what kind of assessment for reading achievement is employed, good records are a must. Check sheets have had a long history of use by classroom teachers as a simple and reliable means for recording the child's progress in reading instruction and the skills and subskills the child needs to be taught. The particular check sheet "system" you choose to use may be as simple or as elaborate as instructional circumstances require and as time and effort permit.

Setting Up the Checksheet   The checksheet itself is a simple enough device. You may construct your own sheet by drawing graph lines on paper. A more convenient method is to purchase a pad of printed graph paper at a stationery or office-supply store. Select a pad having squares of a suitable size for the entries you wish to make. You can, of course, use two or more graph squares for entries too large to be contained in a single square. For example, one square on an ordinary graph may not be adequate for digraphs, and certainly would not be large enough to contain derivative endings such as *-less* or *-ist*.

Be sure your graph paper has enough lines to accommodate the names of all the children. It is good practice to use last names as well as first names. Aside from the fact that more than one child may have a particular given name, last names may be essential if your checklists are passed along to other teachers as part of the child's records.

Mastery Learning Checksheet   _____
(Grade)

_____   _____
(Reading Skill)   (School Year)

Names

Andy Andrews

Betty Barr

Corrine Corbs

Danny Danielson

Ellen Egberto

Fanny Farmer

Gus Gustafsson

Herb Hermann

Izzy Inmann

Jane Jolly

Karin Kuhlman

Lena Larsen

Manny Mangold

Nelly Nelson

Ozzy Oswald

Pauline Perils

Questor Quigley

Ruthene Ruthover

Sammy Sanderman

Tilly Tilman

Ulysses Ulmsted
Veronica Vorman
Willie Williams
Xavier Xeres
Yolanda Yorovitch
Zamantha Zacharius

Using the Checksheet What instructional elements should be entered on the checksheet? This, of course, depends on the particular skill or skills with which you are currently concerned. Let us say, for example, that you are covering the chief components of the phonics segment of word identification. Here are lists of phonics elements and vowel sounds represented by various graphemes for use with checksheets:

Vowel Sounds Represented by Various Graphemes
For Use on Checksheet for Mastery Learning

Initial	Initial	Vowels "short"	digraphs	"r-controlled"
Consonant	Consonant		ai (rain)	är (farm)
sounds	Sounds	ă	ou (out)	er (her) ûr
b	*Cont'*	ĕ	oa (coat)	ir (first) ûr
"soft" c	s	ĭ	ea (read)	ûr (hurt) ûr
d	t	ŏ	ea (head)	ear (early) ûr
f	v	ŭ	ou (young)	or (word) ûr
g	w		ie (field)	
		'long"		"y as vowel"
h	x	ā	ē̄e (beet)	ay (pay)
j (g)	y	ē	oo (book)	ey (they)
k (c)	z	ī	ŏo (moon)	oy (toy)
l		ō		
			Diphthongs	ey (honey)
m		ū	oi (oil)	y (berry)
n			oy (boy)	
p			ou (out)	
qu			ow (cow)	
r				

**Phonics Elements Represented by Various Graphemes
For Use on Checksheet for Mastery Learning**

Final-e	*Sounds of initial consonant digraphs and blends*	*double vowels*	*Inflected forms*
rule			
			plurals
a + e	bl	ǣ	-s
e + e	br	ŏo ōo	-es
i + e	cl		-en
		double consonants	
o + e	ch		*Tense*
u + e	cr	ff	-rd
	dr	ll	-ing
Sound of	fl	mm	-t
final	fr	nn	-d
consonants	gl	pp	*Derivations*
and blends	gr	rr	
-l	pl	ss	-er
-m	pr	tt	-est
-n	sh	zz	-ing
-t	sk	*schwa*	-most
-g	sl	ə ər	-ly
-ing		*other vowel*	-ment
-d		*sounds*	-al
-ck	sm	a	-or
-lk	sn	o	-ness
-nk	sp		-less
-st	st		-ous
-nd	sw		-able
-ch	*th* (the)		-ship
-ly	th (three)		-ant
-ny	tr		-age
-s (-zh-)	wr		-ist
	wh /hw/		

Which particular phonics elements are entered on the checksheets will depend, of course, on the grade level of the children. One checksheet can be used for a particular type of phonics element, or several types may be contained on a sheet, depending on the number of entries. For example, the initial consonant graphemes will undoubtedly fill one heading, thus:

b c d f g h j(g) k(c) l m n p qu r s t v w x y z

The short vowels and long vowels may be represented on a single sheet, thus:

$$\breve{a}\,\breve{e}\,\breve{i}\,\breve{o}\,\breve{u} \quad \bar{a}\,\bar{e}\,\bar{i}\,\bar{o}\,\bar{u} \quad \bar{e}\,\bar{e} \quad \breve{oo} \quad \bar{oo} \quad \text{schwa} \quad \vartheta\,\ddot{a}\,\hat{o}$$

(The double-vowel graphemes and the schwa are appropriate additions to that chart heading. You may also wish to add ä, as in *father* and ô as in *saw,* or *caught*).

Various classroom methods for determining reading progress and instructional needs have been detailed throughout this text. For phonics elements, for example, children may be systematically tested with sight words containing various phonics elements either orally in groups or in an individual conference. As previously noted, there are numerous other appropriate assessment techniques for phonics skills and all other elements of reading instruction.

Whatever procedure is used for assessment of learnings, from simple observation to formal criterion-referenced testing, your checksheet is more than a record of skills learned or not learned, more than simply a matter of checks, or circles, or x's recording progress. It is a blueprint for action.

Regardless of individual or special differences, no child should ever fail to learn to read simply because the child's instructional needs have been somehow overlooked. Your checksheet can help assure that this will not happen in your classroom. Use it creatively. It can be an important tool in helping you achieve your basic objective—teaching reading so that all may learn.

HOW DO I TEACH READING SO ALL MAY LEARN?—SOME FINAL THOUGHTS

"How do I teach reading so *all* may learn?" is a question inherent in the very process of being a "teacher"; for, sooner or later, we all must face up to two problems:

1. What is teaching?
2. What is learning?

If we are honest with ourselves, we will discover that there is no such thing as "teaching" . . . that we are merely *arranging* for learning to take place. When this truth is internalized, we then will realize that in our "teaching" of reading we must be *arranging* for children with special deficits and for children with special talents to learn to read to their greatest potentials.

We have herein presented observations and a point-of-view based upon many years as classroom teachers. We have many reasons to believe that the suggestions proposed here are not only workable but are viable. We also are fully aware of the fact that, when working with humans, there is no such thing as the ultimate, final word, that all conclusions must be open-ended, subject to adjustment as new research discovers new "truths."

We agree with Dr. Lawrence Kasdon who wrote, "We should never become smug about what we know concerning the causes of reading difficulties. In the inexorable advance of science, today's fact may become tomorrow's fiction." Regardless of new discoveries of new "truths" and the scuttling of old "facts," there is one thing that will remain: it is the reality of *individual differences.*

Those children with cultural and linguistic differences need to be understood. They frequently need individualized help to get them ready for learning to read in standard English format. They need special reading materials that reflect their own cultures, so they can identify with the characters in the stories and with the realities of the environments that they already know. Most of all, they need to be loved for the individuals they are.

The gifted and the slow learners need individual attention, each to assure that he/she will reach his/her reading potential. The potentials of the gifted are almost limitless; hence the need for very special help and a wealth of materials. The potentials of the slow may be circumscribed by any number of limiting variables operating singly or in combination; hence the need for individual attention to the etiology of their problems and individual one-to-one help in reading.

Children with psychological and emotional differences need their eroded self-images restored and their egos enhanced by supportive teachers and by rewarding reading materials. This, too, means individualized attention and individualized reading strategies.

Those with physical differences that do not call for special classes and/or special schools can benefit by special attention by teacher or aide in helping them compensate for their physical abnormalities. Extreme cases must not be left to languish in the regular classroom. They deserve the very best special help in clinics designed to aid such unfortunates.

Children with common deficiencies in reading due to educational neglect are children with specific needs. Compensatory reading instruction involves a determination of their special skills deficits and small-group or even individual instruction in those skills in which they are deficient.

In all cases of children with special needs in reading, we cannot mainstream them and then proceed with classroom "business-as-usual!" In the end, if we are to follow the proposals and the point-of-view proposed herein, we will come to the full understanding of the fact that

> *In every classroom there are children with special needs, because each child in some way or another is "special."*

We are sure that all this could have been said with less words; but, after many years of teaching and observation of others, we feel that it has been necessary to establish this strong case for *individual differences* as the top priority in teaching reading to *all* children. To mention the need for individual differences is one thing; to delineate the reasons why, and to suggest specific materials and strategies are, in the end, two of the main purposes of this book: *How Do I Teach Reading?*

BIBLIOGRAPHY

Abel, Midge B., "American Indian Life as Portrayed in Children's Literature," *Elementary English*, **50** (1973), 202–208.

Abrams, Jules C., "Learning Disabilities—A Complex Phenomenon," *Reading Teacher*, **23**:4 (1970), 299–303.

Abrams, Jules C., and Herman S. Belmont, "Different Approaches to the Remediation of Severe Reading Disability in Children," *Journal of Learning Disabilities*, **2**:3 (1969), 136–141.

Adams, Gerald R., and Allan S. Cohen, "Characteristics of Children and Teacher Expectancy: An Extension of the Child's Social and Family Life," *Journal of Educational Research*, **70**:2 (1976), 87–90.

Adams, Richard C. "Dyslexia: A Discussion of its Definition," *Journal of Learning Disabilities*, **2**:12 (1969), 616–633.

Adenika, T. Jean, and Gordon L. Berry, "Teacher's Attitudes Toward the Education of the Black Child," *Education*, **97**:2 (1976), 102–114.

Alexander, Clara Franklin, "Black English Dialect and the Classroom Teacher," *The Reading Teacher*, **33**:5 (1980), 571–577.

Allen, Virginia French, "Trends in the Teaching of Reading," an address delivered at the TESL Conference, East-West Center, University of Hawaii. January, 1973, and printed in the *TESL Reporter*, **6**:4 (1973), 1–2; 15–19.

Allen, Virginia G., "The Non-English Speaking Child in Your Classroom," *Reading Teacher*, **30**:5 (1977), 504–508.

Ames, Louise Bates, "A Low Intelligence Qoutient Often Not Recognized as the Chief Cause of Many Learning Difficulites," *Journal of Learning Disabilities*, **1**:12 (1968), 735–739.

Anderson, Irving H., Byron O. Hughes, and W. R. Dixon, "The Rate of Reading Development and Its Relationship to Age of Learning to Read, Sex, and Intelligence," *Journal of Educational Research*, **50** (1957), 481–494.

Aribi, John O. O., "Reading in Nigeria," *Reading Teacher*, **30**:5 (1977), 509–514. An enlightening account of how reading is taught in English and in the vernacular in Nigerian elementary schools.

Arnold, Richard D., "Reading Skills of Afro- and Mexican-American Students," in *Better Reading in Urban Schools*, J. Allen Figurel (Editor), Newark, DE: International Reading Association, 1972, 25–33.

Artley, A. Sterl, and Veralee B. Hardin, "A Current Dilemma: Reading Disability or Learning Disability?", *Reading Teacher*, **29**:4 (1976), 361–366.

Ashton-Warner, Sylvia, *Teacher*, New York: Simon and Schuster, 1963.

Association of American Indian Affairs, 432 Park Avenue South, New York City.

Aukerman, Robert C., *Approaches to Beginning Reading*, New York: Wiley, 1971.

Austin, David, Velma Clark, and Gladys Fitchett, *Reading Rights for Boys*. New York: Appleton-Century-Crofts, 1971.

Bailey, David S., "Deprivation and Achievement as Factors in Auditory Comprehension," In *Twentieth Yearbook*, Tallahasse: Florida State University, *National Reading Conference*, 1971, 341–347.

Baker, Augusta, *The Black Experience in Children's Books*, New York: Office of Children's Services, New York Public Library, 1971.

Ball, Howard G., "How Johnny Can't Learn," *Reading Horizons*, **16**:2 (1976), 87–96. This is an excellent presentation of some of the causes for Black Johnny not being able to learn.

Balow, I.H., "Sex Differences in First Grade Reading," *Elementary English*, **40** (1963), 303–306.

Banks, James A. (Editor), *Teaching Ethnic Studies: Concepts and Strategies*. Washington, D.C.: National Council for the Social Studies. 1973.

Baratz, Joan C., "Teaching Reading in an Urban School System," in *Teaching Black Children to Read*, Joan C. Baratz and Roger W. Shuy (Editors), Washington, D.C.: Center for Applied Linguistics, 1969, 92–116.

Baratz, Joan C., "Teaching Reading in an Urban Negro School System," in *Language and Poverty*, Frederick Williams (Editor), Chicago: Markham, 1970, 11–24.

Baratz, Joan C. and Roger W. Shuy (Editors), *Teaching Black Children to Read*. Washington, D.C.: Center for Applied Linguistics, 1969.

Barnitz, John G., "Black English and Other Dialects: Sociolinguistic Implications for Reading Instruction," *Reading Teacher*, **33**:7 (1980), 779–786.

Barbe, Walter B., and Joseph Renzulli, "Innovative Programs for the Gifted and Creative," in *Reading for the Gifted and Creative Student*, Paul Witty (Editor), Newark, DE: International Reading Association, 1971.

Bauer, Evelyn, "Teaching English to North American Indians," *Linguistic Reporter*, **10** (1968), 2.

Beezer, Bruce, "Bilingual Legislation and State Legislatures," *The Educational Forum*, **40**:4 (1976), 537–542.

Belmont, Ira, and Herbert G. Birch, "The Effect of Supplemental Intervention on

Children with Low-Reading-Readiness Scores," *Journal of Special Education*, 8:1 (1974), 81–89.

Bender, Loretta, "Use of the Visual Motor Gestalt Test in the Diagnosis of Learning Disabilities," *Journal of Special Education*, 4:1 (1970), 29–39.

Bentley, Robert H., and Samuel D. Crawford (Editors), *Black Language Reader*. Glenview, IL: Scott, Foresman and Co., 1973.

Benton, Arthur L., "Neuropsychological Aspects of Mental Retardation," *Journal of Special Education*, 4:1 (1970), p. 9.

Berkowitz, L., "Control of Aggression," in *Review of Child Development Research*, Vol. 3, Chicago: University Chicago Press 1974, 95–140.

Bertrand, Alvin L., "Social Backgrounds: Whites," in *Reading for the Disadvantaged: Problems of Linguistically Different Learners*, An IRA Publication, published by Harcourt, Brace, and World, Inc., 1970, p. 21–29.

Betts, Emmett A., *Foundations of Reading Instruction*, New York: American Book Co., 1946, 1950, 1954, 1957. Ch. 21 "Discovering Specific Reading Needs."

Bilingual Education Services, P. O. Box 669, Pasadena, California, 91030.

Bilingual Education Service Center, "The Bilingual Gifted Child," *Newsletter*, 2 (1975), p. 5.

Birch, H.G., and J.D. Gussow, *Disadvantaged Children, Health, and School Failure*, New York: Harcourt, Brace, and World, 1970.

Black, Frank S., and Robert R. Nargar, "Relating Pupil Mobility and Reading Achievement," *Reading Teacher*, 28:4 (1975), 370–374.

Blau, Theodore H., "Diagnosis of Disturbed Children," *American Psychologist*, 34:10 (1979), 969–972.

Bloomer, Richard H., "The Cloze Procedure as a Remedial Reading Exercise," *Journal of Developmental Reading*, 5 (1962), 173–181.

Bond, Guy L. and Miles A. Tinker, *Reading Difficulties: Their Diagnosis and Correction*. New York: Appleton-Century-Crofts, 1967.

Boothby, Paula R., "Creative and Critical Reading for the Gifted," *The Reading Teacher*, 33:6, (1980) 674–676.

Bormuth, John, "Comparable Cloze and Multiple-Choice Comprehension Test Scores," *Journal of Reading* 10 (1967), 291–299.

Bradford, Arthur, *Teaching English to Sepakers of English*, New York: Harcourt Brace Jovanovich, 1973, especially Chapter 6, "The Effects of Dialect Differences on Reading and Writing" and Chapter 3, "The Linguistics of Reading."

Brandes, Paul D., and Jeutonne Brewer, *Dialect Clash in America: Issues and Answers*, Metuchen, NJ: Scarecrow Press, 1977. This is one of the best surveys of the effects of six American dialects on school achievement and what can be done about it.

Brown, Laray, " 'Correctness' and Reading," *Reading Teacher* **28**:3 (1974), 277 – 278.

Brown, Lou, and others: "Using Behavior-Modification Principles to Teach Sight Vocabulary," *Teaching Exceptional Children*, **2**, 1970, 120 – 128.

Brown, Lou and Lucille Perlmutter, "Teaching Functional Reading to Trainable-Level Retarded Students," *Education and Training of the Mentally Retarded* **6** (1971), 74 – 84.

Brown, Lou and others, "Teaching Functional Reading to Young Trainable Students," *Journal of Special Education*, **6** (1972), 237 – 246.

Brown, Lou, Barbara Huppler, Laura Pierce, Bob York, and Ed Sontag, "Teaching Trainable-Level Students to Read Unconjugated Action Verbs," *Journal of Special Education*, **8**:1 (1974), 56.

Buktineka, Norman A., "Perceptual/Social Aspects of Learning to Read: A Transactional Process," *Peabody Journal of Education*, **54**:3 (1977), 154 – 161.

Burg, Leslie A., "Affective Teaching—Neglected Practice in Innercity Schools?" *Reading Teacher*, **28**:4 (1975), 360 – 363.

Burling, Robbins, *English in Black and White*, New York: Holt, Rinehart, and Winston, 1973.

Cagney, Margaret A., "Children's Ability to Understand Standard English and Black Dialect," *Reading Teacher*, **30**:6 (1977), 607 – 610.

Caldwell, Bettye M., "Aggression and Hostility in Young Children," *Young Children*, **32**:2 (1977), 4 – 13.

Camp, Bonnie W., Sara G. Zimet, William J. Van Doorninck, and Nancy W. Daheem, "Verbal Abilities in Young Aggressive Boys," *Journal of Educational Psychology*, **69**:2 (1977), 129 – 135.

Carver, Ronald P., "Reading Tests in 1970 versus 1980: Psychometric versus Edumetric," *Reading Teacher*, **26**:3 (1972), 299 – 302.

Carver, Ronald P., "Two Dimensions of Tests," *American Psychologist*, **(29)**:7 (1974), 512 – 518.

Cassidy, Jack and Carol Vukelich, "Do the Gifted Read Early?" *The Reading Teacher*, **33**:5 (1980), 578 – 582.

Center for Applied Linguistics, English as a Second Language Program, 1717 Massachusetts Avenue, N.W., Washington, DC, 20036.

Chang, Theresa S., "The Self-Concept of Children in Ethnic Groups: Black American and Korean American," *Elementary School Journal*, **76**:1 (1975), 52–58.

Chase, H.P., and H.P. Martin, "Undernutrition and Child Development," *New England Journal of Medicine*, 282 (1970), 933–939.

Cheyney, Arnold, *Teaching Children of Different Cultures in the Classroom*, 2nd edition, Columbus, OH: Merrill, 1976.

Ching, Doris C., *Reading and the Bilingual Child*, Reading Aids Series, Newark, DE: International Reading Association, 1976.

Chiu, Lian-Hwang, "Reading Preferences of Fourth-grade Children Related to Sex and Reading Ability," *Journal of Educational Research*, **66** (1973), 369–373.

Chomsky, Carol, "Reading, Writing, and Phonology," *Harvard Educational Review*, **40** (1970), 287–309.

Chomsky, Noam, "Phonology and Reading," in *Basic Studies in Reading*, Harry Levin and Joanna P. Williams (Editors), New York: Basic Books, 1970, 3–18.

Cicirelli, Victor G., "The Relation of Socio-Economic Status and Ethnicity to Primary Grade Children's Self-Concept," *Psychology in the Schools*, **14**:2 (1977), 213–215.

Clark, Carl A., and Herbert J. Walberg, "The Influence of Massive Rewards on Reading Achievement in Potential Urban School Dropouts," in *Readings in Learning and Human Abilities*, Richard E. Ripple (Editor), New York: Harper & Row, 1971, 216–220.

Clay, Marie M., "Early Childhood and Cultural Diversity in New Zealand," *Reading Teacher*, **29**:4 (1976), 333–342.

Clay, Marie M., "Language Skills: A Comparison of Maori, Samoan, and Pakeha Children Aged 5 to 7 Years," *New Zealand Journal of Educational Studies* (1970), 153–162.

Cohen, S. Allan, "Oral Language Deficits; or Why Henry Will Never Make It," *Reading World*, **16**:2 (1976), 138–140.

Commission for Mexican-American Affairs, 1514 Buena Vista, San Antonio, Texas, 78207.

Commissioner of Education, *Education of the Gifted and Talented*, Report to the Congress by the U. S. Commissioner of Education, 72-502-0, Washington, DC: U. S. Government Printing Office, 1972.

Cramer, Ronald L., "Dialectology—A Case for Language Experience," *Reading Teacher*, **25** (1971), 33–39.

Critchlow, Donald E. (Editor), *Reading and the Spanish-Speaking Child.* Laredo, TX: Texas State Council of the International Reading Association, Reading-Learning Center, Texas A. & M. University, 1976.

Critchlow, Donald F. (Editor), *Reading and the Spanish Speaking Child,* Laredo, Texas: Texas State Council of IRA, Reading-Learning Center, Texas A. & M. University, 1978.

Cronbach, Lee J., "Five Decades of Public Controversy Over Mental Testing," *American Psychologist,* **30** (1975), 1–14.

Cullinan, Bernice (Editor), *Black Dialects and Reading,* Urbana, IL: National Council of Teachers of English, 1974.

Cullinan, Bernice E., Angela M. Jaggar, and Dorothy Strickland, "Language Expansion for Black Children in the Primary Grades," *Young Children,* **29** (1974), 98–112.

Cunningham, Patricia M., "Teachers' Correction Responses to Black-Dialect Miscues," *Reading Research Quarterly,* **12**:4 (1976–1977), 637–653.

Dakin, Karen E. C., "A Longitudinal Study of Sex Differences in Reading Achievement in Grades Four Through Eight," unpublished M.A. Thesis, Rutgers University, 1970.

Das, J. P., "Cultural Deprivation and Cognitive Competence," in *International Review of Research in Mental Retardation,* Vol. 6, N. R. Ellis (Editor), New York: Academic Press, 1973.

Das, J. P., and Emma Pivato, "The Effect of Malnutrition on Cognitive Competence," paper presented at the annual meetings of the American Psychological Association, 1975.

DeCano, Pio, "Asian/Asian-American Perspective", in *The Right to Read in Every Culture* (pamphlet), Washington State University Right-to-Read Project, 1976.

DeStefano, Johanna S., "Social Variation in Language: Implications for Teaching Reading to Black Ghetto Children," in *Better Reading in Urban Schools,* J. Allen Figurel (Editor), Newark, DE: International Reading Association, 1972, 18–24.

Dissemination Center for Bilingual and Bicultural Education 6504 Tractor Lane, Austin, Texas 78721.

Dixon, Carol N., "Teaching Strategies for the Mexican American Child," *Reading Teacher,* **30**:2 (1976), 141–145.

Drummond, Robert J., Clayton A. Pinette, and R. Kent Smith, "Examining the Effects of Self-Concept and Work Values on Reading Achievement," *Reading World,* **16**:3 (1977), 206–212.

Dulay, H., and M. Burt, "Natural Sequences in Child Second Language Acquisition," *Language Learning,* **24** (1974), 37–53.

Dunlop, Kathleen H., "Mainstreaming: Valuing Diversity in Children," *Young Children,* **32**:4 (1977), 26–32.

Durkin, Dolores, "A Six-Year Study of Children Who Learned to Read in School at the Age of Four," *Reading Research Quarterly,* **10**:1 (1974–1975), 9–61.

Durrell, Donald D., *Improving Reading Instruction,* New York: World Book, 1940, 1956, Chapter 5.

Dwyer, Carol A., "Sex Differences in Reading: An Evaluation and a Critique of Current Theories," *Review of Educational Research,* **43** (1973), 455–467.

Eichenwald, H. F. and P. C. Fry, "Nutrition and Learning," *Science* 163 (1969), 644–648.

Elkind, David, "Ethnicity and Reading: Three Avoidable Dangers," in *Reading, Children's Books, and Our Pluralistic Society,* Harold Tanyzer and Jean Karl (Editors), Newark, DE: International Reading Association, 1972, 4–8.

Farmer, Cornelia R., and Sol L. Garfield, "The Relationship Between Ability to Read and the Meaning and Expression of Emotion," *Journal of Learning Disabilities,* **4** (1971), 558–562.

Fasold, Ralph W., and Walt Wolfram, "Some Linguistic Features of Negro Dialect," in *Teaching Standard English in the Inner City,* (Fasold and Shuy, Editors), Washington, DC: Center for Applied Linguistics, 1970, 41–86.

Feagin, Crawford, *The Verb Phrase in Alabama White English,* Washington, DC: Georgetown University Press, 1979.

Fearn, L. "Report on Three Pilot Studies into Initial Reading with Navajo Children," *Elementary English,* **48** (1971), 390–394.

Feitelson, Dina (Editor), *Mother Tongue or Second Language?* Newark, DE: International Reading Association, 1979. Includes papers presented at the 6th World Congress on Reading, Singapore, 1976.

Feldhusen, John F., John R. Thurston, and James J. Benning, "Aggressive Classroom Behavior and School Achievement" in *Journal of Special Education,* **4**:4 (1970), 431–439.

Finocchiaro, Mary, *English as a Second Language: From Theory to Practice,* New York: Regents Publishing Co., 1964.

Fischer, Maurice D., and Robert V. Turner, "The Effects of a Perceptual-Motor Training Program Upon the Academic Readiness of Culturally-

Disadvantaged Kindergarten Children," *Journal of Negro Education*, **41** (1972), 142–150.

Flynn, James R., Richard C. Gacka, and David A Sundean, "Are Classroom Teachers Prepared for Mainstreaming?" *Phi Delta Kappan*, **59**:8 (1978), 562.

Fry, Maurine, and Carole S. Johnson, "Oral Language Production and Reading Achievement Among Selected Students," *Journal of American Indian Education*, **13** (1973), 22–27.

Fuller, Reneé, *In Search of the I. Q. Correlation*, Stony Brook, NY: Ball-Stick-Bird Publications (P.O. Box 592), 1977. Reports experiments with patients with I. Q.s of 30 who were taught to read.

Gaarder, A. B., "Organization of the Bi-lingual School," *Journal of Social Issues*, **23** (1967), 110–120.

Galarza, Ernesto, *Mexican Americans in the Southwest*, Santa Barbara, CA: McNally and Loftin, 1970.

Gallagher, James A., *Teaching the Gifted Child*, 2nd edition, Boston: Allyn & Bacon, 1980.

Gantt, Walter N., Robert M. Wilson, and C. Mitchell Dayton, "An Initial Investigation of the Relationship Between Syntactical Divergency and the Listening Comprehension of Black Children," *Reading Research Quarterly*, **10**:2 (1974–1975), 193–211.

Gardner, R. C., and W. E. Lambert, *Attitude and Motivation in Second Language Learning*, Rowley, MA: Newberry House, 1972.

Garcia, Ricardo L., "Mexican Americans Learn Through Language Experience," *Reading Teacher*, **28**:3 (1974), 301–305. This article provides more than a dozen resources for teaching reading to Chicano children.

Gates, Arthur I., "Sex Differences in Reading Ability," *Elementary School Journal*, **61** (1961), 431–434.

Gay, Judy, and Ryan D. Tweney, "Development of Linguistic Comprehension and Production in Lower-Class Black Children," paper presented at the 83rd Annual Convention of the American Psychological Association, Chicago, September, 1975.

Gibson, Eleanor J., "The Ontogeny of Reading," *American Psychologist*, **25** (1970), 136–143.

Gibson, Eleanor J., and Harry Levin, *The Psychology of Reading*. Cambridge, MA: MIT Press, 1975. See especially the section entitled: "Do Variations in Dialect Affect Learning to Read?" 505–518.

Gillespie-Silver, Patricia, *Teaching Reading to Children With Special Needs*, Columbus, OH: Merrill, 1979.

Ginsburg, Herbert, *The Myth of the Deprived Child*, Englewood Cliffs, NJ: Prentice-Hall, 1972.

Godwin, Douglas C., "The Bilingual Teachers Aide: Classroom Asset," *Elementary School Journal*, **77**:4 (1977), 265–267.

Golub, Lester S., "Reading, Writing, and Black English," *Elementary School Journal*, **72** (1972), 195–202.

Goodman, Kenneth S., "Dialect Barriers to Reading Comprehension," *Elementary English*, **42** (1965), 853–860.

Goodman, Kenneth S., and Catherine Buck, "Dialect Barriers to Reading Comprehension Revisited," *Reading Teacher*, **27**:1 (1973), 6–12.

Gowan, John C., and E. Paul Torrence (Editors), *Educating the Ablest*, Itasca, IL: F. E. Peacock, 1971.

Guilford, J. P., "Potential for Creativity," *Gifted Child Quarterly*, **6** (1962).

Guilford, J. P., *The Nature of Human Intelligence*, New York: McGraw-Hill, 1967.

Gunderson, Doris V., "Sex Differences in Language and Reading," *Language Arts*, **53** (1976), 300–308.

Hackney, Ann, "Epilepsy: An Invisible Handicap," in *Trends in Education*, London: 1976, 27–33.

Hagin, Rosa A., Archie Silver, and Carol G. Corwin, "Scanning School Samples for Vulnerable Children," paper presented at the American Psychological Association annual meeting, New Orleans, Sept., 1974.

Hakuta, Kenji, and Herlinda Cancino, "Trends in Second-Language Research," *Harvard Educational Review*, **47**:3 (1977), 294–316.

Hale, Thomas M., "Some Guidelines Concerning the Role of the Regular Classroom Teachers and Administrators in Assisting the Non-English Speaking Students in Hawaii's Public Schools," Office of Instructional Services, Department of Education, Honolulu, Hawaii, August, 1973.

Hall, Vernon C., and Daniel B. Kaye, "Patterns of Early Cognition Development Among Boys in Four Sub-Cultural Groups," *Journal of Educational Psychology*, **69**:1 (1977), 66–87. Found more similarities than one would anticipate.

Hammon, S., "Sound Polluted Schools," *School Management*, **14**:1 (1970), 14–15.

Hare, Bruce R., "Black and White Children's Self-Esteem in Social Sciences: An Overview," *Journal of Negro Education*, **46**:2 (1977), 141–156.

Harper, Frederick D., "Developing a Curriculum of Self-Esteem for Black Youth," *Journal of Negro Education,* **46**:2 (1977), 133−140.

Harrington, Gordon M., "Minority Test Bias as a Psychometric Artifact: The Experimental Evidence," paper presented to the American Psychological Association, September 6, 1976.

Hatch, Evelyn, "Research on Reading A Second Language," *Journal of Reading Behavior,* **6** (1974), 53−61.

Heber, F. R., "Sociocultural Mental Retardation—A Longitudinal Study," in D. Forgays (Editor), *Primary Prevention of Psychopathology: Vol. 2 Environmental Influences.* Hanover, NY: University Press of New England, 1978.

Heitzman, Andrew J., "Effects of a Token Reinforcement System on the Reading Behavior of Black Migrant Primary School Pupils," *Journal of Educational Research,* **67** (1974), 299−302.

Henderson, Keith J., "Bilingualism: Where to Draw the Line," in *Inchworm, Inchworm: Persistent Problems in Reading Education* Constance M. McCullough (Editor), Newark, DE: International Reading Association, 1980, 44−50.

Hertzig, Margaret E., H. G. Birch, and S. A. Richardson, "Intellectual Levels of School Children Severely Malnourished During the First Two Years of Life," *Pediatrics,* **49** (1972), 814−824.

Hess, Karin M., "The Nonstandard Speakers in Our Schools: What Should Be Done?" *Elementary School Journal,* **74** (1974), 280−290.

Hill, Charles H., and Linda J. Gattis, "Teaching the Restless Ones," *Reading World,* **16**:1 (1976), 28−34.

Hollingworth, Leta S. *Children Above 180 I.Q.* Yonkers, New York: World Book Co., 1942. One of the first landmark books on the gifted. A "classic."

Hoover, Mary Rhodes, "Characteristics of Black Schools at Grade Level," *The Reading Teacher,* **31**:7 (1978), 757−762.

Hopkins, Thomas R., "American Indians and the English Language Arts," From *Linguistic-Cultural Differences and American Education,* special issue of *Florida FL Reporter,* **7**:1 (1969), 145−146.

Hunt, Barbara C., "Black Dialect and Third- and Fourth-Graders' Performance on the *Gray Oral Reading Test,*" *Reading Research Quarterly,* **10**:1 (1974−1975), 103−123.

Hunt, Barbara C., Lucy Serling, and Ethel Mae Theriault, "Teaching Reading in an Inner city School: A Program that Works," *Reading Teacher,* **27**:1 (1973), 25−28.

Jassoy, Mary E., "Migrant Children: We Can Teach Them," in *Reading Interaction,* Leonard Courtney (Editor), Newark, DE: International Reading Association, 1976, 67–74.

Jensen, Arthur R., "Cumulative Deficit in I.Q. of Blacks in the Rural South," *Developmental Psychology,* **13**:3 (1977), 184–191.

Johnson, Henry S., and William J. Hernandez (Editors), *Educating the Mexican-American,* Valley Forge, PA: Judson Press, 1970.

Journal of American Indian Education commencing with **1** (1961).

Johnson, Kenneth R., "Pedagogical Problems of Using Second Language Techniques for Teaching Standard English to Speakers of Non-Standard Negro Dialect," *Florida FL Reporter,* **7**:2 (1969), 78–80; 154.

Johnson, Kenneth R., "Should Black Children Learn Standard English?" *Viewpoints,* **47** (1971), 83–101.

Johnson, Kenneth R., "Teachers' Attitude Toward NonStandard Negro Dialect—Let's Change It," *Elementary English,* **48**:2 (1971), 176–184.

Johnson, Marjorie S., and Roy A. Kress. *Informal Reading Inventories,* Reading Aids Series, Newark, DE: International Reading Association, 1965.

Kachuck, Beatrice, "Dialect in the Language of Inner-City Children," *Elementary School Journal,* **76**:2 (1975), 104–112.

Kaplan, Robert B. "On the Conditions of Bilingualism," in *Essays on Teaching English as a Second Language and as a Second Dialect,* Robert P. Fox (Editor). Urbana, IL: National Council of Teachers of English, 1973.

Karlsen, Bjorn and Margaret Blocker, "Black Children and Final Consonant Blends," *Reading Teacher* **27** (1974), 462–463.

Karnes, Frances A., and Emily C. Collins, *Handbook of Instructional Resources and References for Teaching the Gifted,* Rockleigh, NJ: Longwood Division, Allyn & Bacon, 1980. This is the best resource currently available.

Kasdon, Lawrence M., "Causes of Reading Difficulties", in *Parents and Reading,* Carl B. Smith (Editor), Newark, DE: International Reading Association, 1971, 23–36.

Keith, Mary T., "Sustained Primary Program for Bilingual Children," in *Reading Goals for the Disadvantaged,* J. Allen Figurel (Editor), Newark, DE: International Reading Association, 1970, 262.

Kersey, Harry, and Rebecca Fadjo, "A Comparison of Seminole Reading Vocabulary and the Dolch Word Lists," *Journal of American Indian Education,* **11** (1971), 16–18.

Ketcham, Warren A., "Can Instruction for the Gifted be Improved?" *Innovator* **7**:1 (1975),, 4—7.

Ketcham, Warren A., and Mamdouth R. Daoud, "How Should the Gifted be Defined and Identified?" *Innovator* **8**:1 (1976), 8—10.

Kholset, Rolf, "Bilingual Education Programs in the United States: For Assimilation or Pluralism?", in *Language Education of Minority Children*, Bernard Spolsky (Editor). Rowley, MA: Newberry House, 1975.

Kingston, Albert J., and Wendell W. Weaver, "Feasability of Cloze Techniques for Teaching and Evaluating Culturally Disadvantaged Beginning Readers," *Journal of Social Psychology*, 82 (1970), 205—214.

Kirby, Clara L., "Using the Cloze Procedure as a Testing Technique," in *Reading Diagnosis and Evaluation*. IRA Proceedings 1968 Convention, **13**:4 (1970), 68—77. A comparative study of Cloze and three other tests used in grades one through six.

Klasen, Edith, *The Syndrome of Specific Dyslexia*, Baltimore: University Park Press, 1972. Highly technical data drawn from the card files of 1500 dyslexics at the Raskob Institute.

Knight, Lester N., *Language Arts for the Exceptional: The Gifted and the Linguistically-Different*. Itasca, IL: F. E. Peacock, 1974.

Kotch, J., "Protein-Calorie Malnutrition and Mental Retardation," *Social Sciences and Medicine*, **4** (1970), 629—644.

Labov, William et. al. *A Study of the Non-Standard English of Negro and Puerto Rican Speakers in New York City*. Final Report, Coop. Research Project #3288, USPE, Washington, DC, 1968.

Labov, William, *The Logic of Non-Standard English*, Monograph No. 22, 20th Roundtable Meeting on Languages and Linguistics, Washington, DC: Georgetown University Press, 1969, 1—22.

Labov, William, "Some Sources of Reading Problems for Negro Speakers of Non-Standard English", in *New Directions in Education*, Champaign, IL: National Council of Teachers of English, 1969, 140—167.

Labov, William, "Language Characteristics: Blacks", in *Reading for the Disadvantaged: Problems of Linguistically-Different Readers*, Thomas D. Horn (Editor), Newark, DE: International Reading Association, 1970, 139—140.

Labov, William, *Language in the Inner City: Studies in the Black Engish Vernacular*. Philadelphia: University of Pennsylvania Press, 1972.

Labuda, Michael, "Gifted and Creative Pupils: Reasons for Concern, in *Creative*

Reading for Gifted Learners: A Design for Excellence. Newark, DE: International Reading Association, 1974, 2–7.

Lado, Robert. "Evidence For an Expanded Role for Reading in Foreign Language Teaching," *Foreign Language Annals,* 5 (1972), 451–454.

Leviton, Harvey, "The Implications of the Relationship Between Self-Concept and Academic Achievement," *Child Study Journal* 5:1 (1975), 25–36.

Levy, Beatrice K., "Is the Oral Language of Inner-City Children Adequate for Beginning Reading Instruction?" *Research in the Teaching of English,* 7 (1973), 51–60.

Levy, Betty B., "Dialect Proficiency and Auditory Comprehension in Standard and Non-Standard English," paper presented to the annual convention, American Educational Research Association, Chicago, April, 1972.

Liu, Stella F., "An Investigation of Oral Reading Miscues Made by Nonstandard-Dialect-Speaking Black Children," *Reading Research Quarterly,* 9:2 (1975–1976), 193–197. The author concluded that the use of a text written in Black dialect would not be of value over materials written in standard English. Black dialect tends to have low status stigma, but should be accepted in the classroom while, at the same time, standard English is offered as an additional dialect.

Loban, Walter, "Teaching Children Who Speak Social-Class Dialects," *Elementary English,* **45** (1968), 592–5.

Lohnes, Paul R., and Marian M. Gray, "Intelligence and the Cooperative Reading Studies," *Reading Research Quarterly,* **7**:3 (1972), 466–476.

MacGinitie, Walter H., "Testing Reading Achievement in Urban Schools," *Reading Teacher,* **27**:1 (1973), 13–21.

MacMillan, Robert W., "A Study of the Effect of Socioeconomic Factors on the School Achievement of Spanish-Speaking School Beginners", unpublished Ph.D., dissertation, Austin: University of Texas, 1966.

MacMillan, Robert W., "Economic Backgrounds: Their Impact on Schoolchildren," in *Reading for the Disadvantaged: Problems of the Linguistically-Different Learners,* New York: Harcourt, Brace, and World, 1970, 49–73.

McDonald, Thomas F., and Earl Moody, "A Basic Communication Project for Migrant Children," *Reading Teacher,* **24**:1 (1970), 29–32.

McLaughlin, Barry, "Second Language Learning in Children," *Psychological Review,* 84:3 (1977), 438–459.

Marckwardt, Albert H., *The Place of Literature in the Teaching of English as a Second or Foreign Language,* Honolulu: East-West Center and University Press of Hawaii, 1978.

Materials en Marcha, ESEA Title VII Dissemination Center, 2950 National Avenue, San Diego, California 92113.

Mathis, Sharon Bell, "Who Speaks for a Culture?" in *Reading, Children's Books, and Our Pluralistic Society,* Newark, DE: International Reading Association, 1972, 31.

Mattila, Ruth H., "As I See Spanish-Speaking Students," *Reading Teacher,* **26**:6 (1973), 605–608.

Mead, Margaret, "The Gifted Child in American Culture Today," *Journal of Teacher Education,* **5** (1954). A landmark article on the gifted by a most "gifted" world-renouned sociologist.

Menyuk, Paula, *The Acquisition and Development of Language.* Englewood Cliffs, NJ: Prentice-Hall, 1971, Chaper 8.

Michal-Smith, Harold, Murry Morgenstern, and Etta Karp, "Dyslexia in Four Siblings", *Journal of Learning Disabilities* **3**:4 (1970), 185–192.

Mickelson, M.I., and C. G. Galloway, "Cumulative Language Deficit Among Indian Children," *Exceptional Children,* **36** (1969), 187–190.

Miller, D. D., and Gail Johnson, "What We've Learned About Teaching Reading to Navajo Indians," *Reading Teacher,* **27**:6 (1974), 550–554.

Miller, Mary S., "Who are the Kid's Heroes and Heroines?", *Ladies Home Journal,* **93**:8 (1976), 108–109.

Mishra, Shitala, and M. Hurt, Jr., "The Use of the Metropolitan Readiness Tests with Mexican-American Children," *California Journal of Educational Research,* **21** (1970), 182–187.

Money, John, "On Learning and Not Learning to Read," in *The Disabled Reader,* John Money and Gilbert Schiffman (Editors), Baltimore: Johns Hopkins Press, 1966, 21–40.

Modiano, Nancy, "National or Mother Language in Begining Reading: A Comparative Study," *Research in The Teaching of English,* 1968, 32–43.

Monaghan, E. Jennifer, "A History of the Syndrome of Dyslexia With Implications for its Treatment," in *Inchworm, Inchworm: Persistent Problems in Reading Education, Constance M. McMullough (Editor),* Newark, DE: International Reading Association, 1980, 87–101.

Monteith, Mary K., "Implications of the Ann Arbor Decision: Black English and the Reading Teacher," *Journal of Reading,* **23**:6 (1980), 556–559.

Morehead, Donald M., and Ann E., *Normal and Deficient Child Language,* Baltimore: University Park Press, 1976.

Natalicio, Diana S., "Reading and the Bilingual Child," in *Theory and Practice of*

Early Reading, Vol. 3. Lauren B. Resnick and Phyllis A. Weaver (Editors), Hillsdale, NJ: Erlbaum, 1979, 131–149.

National Assessment of Educational Progress, *Reading in America*, Denver: Education Commission of the States, Reading Report No. 06-R-01, 1976.

National Association for Bilingual Education, University of Texas, San Antonio, 78285.

New York State Education Department, *Reading Achievement Related to Educational and Environmental Conditions in 12 New York City Elementary Schools*, 1974.

Nichols, Patricia C., "A Sociolinguistic Perspective on Reading and Black Children," *Language Arts*, **54**:2 (1977), 150–157.

Nolen, Patricia S., "Reading Non-Standard Dialect Materials: a Study of Grades Two and Four," *Child Development*, **43** (1972), 1092–1097.

O'Brien, Carmen A., *Teaching the Language-Different Child to Read*. Columbus, OH: Merrill, 1973.

Ogden, Melita H., "The Fulfillment of Promise: 40-Year Follow-up of the Terman Gifted Group," *Genetic Psychology Monographs*, **77** (1968), 3–93.

Otto, Wayne and Eunice Askov, "Wisconsin Design For Reading Skill Development," in *The Quest for Competency in Teaching Reading*. Howard A. Klein (Editor), selected papers from the IRA Convention, Newark, DE: International Reading Association, 1972, 93–105.

Owens, T. R., and R. A. Gustafson, "A Comparison of Self-Esteem Levels of Mexican-American and Non-Mexican-American Children in Grades Three, Six, and Nine," paper presented to annual conference of the American Psychological Association, Washington, DC, September, 1971.

Pack, Alice E. (Editor), *TESL Reporter*. a quarterly publication of the Laie, Hawaii Campus of Brigham Young University.

Packer, Athol B., "Ashton-Warner's Key Vocabulary for the Disadvantaged," *Reading Teacher*, **23** (1970), 559–564.

Park, G. E., "Biological Changes Associated With Dyslexia," *Archives of Pediatrics*, (1955), 83.

Past, Kay Cude, Al Past, and Sheila B. Guzman, "A Bilingual Kindergarten Immersed in Print," *Reading Teacher*, **33**:8 (1980), 907–913.

Piestrup, Ann, *Black Dialect Interference and Accommodation of Reading Instruction in First Grade*. Berkley: University of California, Language Behavior Research Laboratory, 1973.

Pikulski, John, "A Critical Review: Informal Reading Inventories," *Reading Teacher,* **28**:2 (1974), 141–151.

Pilon, Barbara, and Rudine Sims, *Dialects and Reading: Implications for Change,* Urbana, IL: National Council of Teachers of English, 1975.

Powell, William, and Colin Dunkeld, "Validity of the I.R.I. Reading Levels," *Elementary English,* **48**:6 (1971), 637–642.

Preston, Ralph C., "Reading Achievement of German and American Children," *School and Society,* **90** (1962), 350–354.

Purkey, William W., *Self-Concept and School Achievement,* Englewood Cliffs, NJ: Prentice-Hall, 1978.

Quandt, Ivan, *Self-Concept and Reading,* Newark, DE: International Reading Association, 1972.

Reading Teacher, **29** (1976). See this entire issue on debate over the differences in reading abilities due to sex differences.

Reifel, Ben, "Cultural Factors in Social Adjustment," *Indian Education* **298** (1957), 42.

Rentel, Victor M., and John J. Kennedy, "Effects of Pattern Drill on the Phonology, Syntax, and Reading Achievement of Rural Appalachian Children," *American Educational Research Journal,* **9**:1 (1972), 87–100.

Rhodes, Odus O., "Some Implications for Teaching Reading to Speakers of Black Dialect," in *Understanding Prerequisites for Teaching the Disadvantaged Child,* J. Brown (Editor), Bloomington, IN: Indiana University Press, 1970.

Robeck, Mildred C., and John A. R. Wilson, *Psychology of Reading: Foundations of Instruction.* New York, Wiley, 1974, Chapter 10.

Robinson, Marion E., and Lindi B. Schwartz, Visuo-Motor Skills and Reading Ability: A Longitudinal Study," *Developmental Medicine and Child Neurology,* **15** (1973), 281–286.

Rosenthal, Robert, and Lenore Jacobson, "Teachers' Expectancies: Determinants of Pupils' I.Q. Gains," *Psychological Reports,* **19** (1966), 115–116; also their popularized *Pygmalion in the Classroom,* New York: Holt, Rinehart and Winston, 1968.

Rosner, Jerome, "Teaching Hard-to-Teach Children to Read: A Rationale for Compensatory Education," in *Theory and Practice of Early Reading,* Vol. 2, Lauren B. Resnick and Phyllis A. Weaver (Editors), Hillsdale, NJ: Erlbaum, 1979, 135–148.

Rubin, Rosalyn, "Sex Differences in Effects of Kindergarten Attendance on

Devleopment of School Readiness and Language Skills," *Elementary School Journal,* **72** (1972), 265–274.

Rubin, Rosalyn A., "Reading Ability and Assigned Materials: Accommodation for the Slow But Not the Accelerated," *Elementary School Journal,* **75**:6 (1975), 373–377.

Russell, Noma (Editor), *Navajo and Zuni: A Bibliography Of Selected Materials,* Gallup, New Mexico: Gallup-McKinley County Public Schools publication, 1975. This is a rare collection of materials relevant to these two Native American cultures.

Rystrom, Richard, "Dialect Training and Reading: A Further Look," *Reading Research Quarterly,* **5**:4 (1970), 581–599.

Samstead, H. H. et. al., "Nutritional Deficiencies in Disadvantaged Preschool Children," *American Journal of Diseases of Children,* **121** (1971), 455–463.

Samuels, S. Jay, and Patricia R. Dahl, "Ghetto Children Can Learn to Read—a Personal Report," *Reading Teacher,* **27**:1 (October, 1973), 22–24.

Saville, Muriel R., "Language and the Disadvantaged," in *Reading for the Disadvantaged,* Thomas D. Horn (Editor), New York: Harcourt-Brace Jovanovich, 1970, 117.

Schifani, John W., Robert M. Anderson, and Sara J. Odle (Editors), *Implementing Learning in the Least-Restrictive Environment: Handicapped Children in the Mainstream,* Baltimore: University Park Press, 1980.

Schneyer, Wesley J., "Use of the Cloze Procedure for Improving Reading Comprehension," *Reading Teacher,* **19** (1965), 174.

Searls, Evelyn F., *How to Use WISC Scores in Reading Diagnosis,* Newark, DE: International Reading Association, 1975.

Sears, Pauline S., and Ann H. Barbee, "Career and Life Satisfactions Among Terman's Gifted Women," in *The Gifted and the Creative: Fifty-Year Perspective,* J. Stanley, W. George, and C. Solano (Editors), Baltimore: Johns Hopkins University Press, 1977.

Sears, Robert R., "Sources of Life Satisfactions of the Terman Gifted Men," *American Psychologist,* **32**:2 (1977), 119–128.

Seitz, Victoria, *Social Class and Ethnic Group Differences in Learning to Read,* Newark, DE: International Reading Association, 1977.

Sewell, Trevor, and Roger A. Severson, "Intelligence and Achievement in First-Grade Black Children," *Journal of Consulting and Clinical Psychology,* **43** (1975), 112–114.

Sheridan, E. Marcia (Compiler), *Sex Differences and Reading,* Newark, DE:

International Reading Association, 1976. An annotated bibliography covering interest, attitude, achievement, cognitive differences, psychological differences, and sex-role socialization.

Shuy, Roger W., Walter A. Wolfram, and William K. Riley, *Linguistic Correlates of Social Stratification in Detroit Speech*, Cooperative Research Report, Project 6-1347, U. S. Office of Education, Washington, DC, 1967.

Simons, Herbert D., "Black Dialect Phonology and Word Recognition," *Journal of Educational Research*, **68** (1974), 67–70.

Simons, Herbert D., and Kenneth R. Johnson, "Black English Syntax and Reading Interference," *Research in the Teaching of English*, **8** (1974), 339–358.

Simons, Herbert D., "Black Dialect, Reading Interference, and Classroom Interaction," in *Theory and Practice of Early Reading*, Lauren B. Resnick and Phyllis A. Weaver (Editors), Hillsdale, NJ: Erlbaum, 1979.

Sinks, Naomi B., and Marvin Powell, "Sex and Intelligence as Factors in Achievement in Reading in Grades Four Through Eight," *Journal of Genetic Psychology*, **106** (1965), 67–79.

Smith, Helen K. (Editor), *Perception and Reading*, part 4, Vol 12. Annual Proceedings, International Reading Association, 1968.

Smith, Helen K. (Editor), *Meeting Individual Needs in Reading*, Newark, DE: International Reading Association, 1971.

Smith, Carl B., "The Effect of Environment on Learning to Read," in *Parents and Reading*, a joint publication of IRA and National Conference of Parents and Teachers. Newark, DE: International Reading Association, 1971, 10–22.

Somerville, Mary Ann, "Dialect and Reading: A Review of Alternative Solutions," *Review of Educational Research*, **45** (1975), 247–262.

Stanchfield, Jo., "Sex Factors in Learning to Read," *Illinois Reading Council Journal*, **3** (1975), 10–13.

Stanley, Julian C., "Identifying and Nurturing the Gifted Child," *Phi Delta Kappan*, **58**:3 (1976), 234–237.

Stauffer, Russell G., *The Language-Experience Approach to the Teaching of Reading*, New York: Harper and Row, 1970.

Stewart, William A., "Sociolinguistic Factors in the History of American Negro Dialects," *Florida FL Reporter*, **5**:2 (1967), 1–4.

Stewart, William A., "Language Teaching Problems in Appalachia," in *Language and the Language Arts*, Johanna S. DeStefano and Sharon E. Fox (Editors), Boston: Little, Brown, 1974.

Strickland, Dorothy S., "Expanding Language Power of Black Children: a

Literature Approach," in *Better Reading in Urban Schools,* J. Allen Figurel (Editor), Newark, DE: International Reading Association, 1972, 9–17.

Strickland, Dorothy S., "A Program for Linguistically-Different Black Children," *Research in the Teaching of English,* **7** (1973), 79–86.

Sullivan, Allen R., "The Influence of Social Processes on the Learning Abilities of Afro-American School Children: Some Educational Implications," *Journal of Negro Education,* **41** (1972), 127–136.

Swift, Marshall S., and George Spivak, "Theraputic Teaching: A Review of Teaching Methods for Behaviorally Troubled Children," *Journal of Special Education,* **8**:3 (1974), 259–289.

Tarnopol, Lester and Muriel Tarnopol, *Brain Function and Reading Disabilities,* Baltimore: University Park Press, 1977.

Taylor, Calvin, "The Highest Potentials of Man," *Gifted Child Quarterly,* **13** (1969).

Taylor, H. Gerry, Paul Satz, and Janette Friel, "Developmental Dyslexia in Relation to Other Childhood Reading Disorders: Significance and Clinical Utility," *Reading Research Quarterly,* **15**:1 (1979), 84–101.

Taylor, Wilson L. "Cloze Procedures: A New Tool For Measuring Readability," *Journalism Quarterly,* **30** (1953), 360–368.

Terman, Lewis M., and Melita H. Oden, *The Gifted Child Grows Up,* Stanford University Press, 1947. See follow-up studies by Oden and by Sears.

Teachers of English to Speakers of Other Languages, School of Languages and Linguistics, Washington, DC: Georgetown University, 20007.

Thompson, G. Brian, "Sex Differences in Reading Attainment," *Educational Research,* **18**:1 (1975), 16–23.

Thonis, Eleanor W., *Literacy for America's Spanish Speaking Children,* Newark, DE: International Reading Association, Reading Aids Series, 1976.

Thorndike, Robert L. (Editor), *Reading Comprehension Education in Fifteen Countries,* New York: Wiley, 1973. The one major significant find of this survey of some reading performances of children in several countries clearly indicated that home and family backgrounds were the dominant factors affecting good or poor reading achievement. Similarly, the *National Assessment of Educational Progress Report* 02-R-30 (April, 1974) singled out (a) level of parent's education; (b) type of community; (c) region; (d) race; and (e) sex as the factors most important in affecting differences in reading performance.

Tierney, Robert J., and Diane Lapp (Editors), *National Assessment of Educational Progress in Reading,* Newark, DE: International Reading Association, 1979. This is a committee report on the facts, concerns, and implications of the results of the 1970–71 and 1974–75 national assessments in reading of 9-, 13-, and 17-year-olds.

Toynbee, Arnold, "Is America Neglecting Her Creative Minority?", *Accent on Talent,* **2** (1968).

Tyler, Leona E., *Individual Differences: Abilities and Motivational Directions.* Englewood Cliffs, NJ: Prentice-Hall, 1974. This best-seller is now in paperback. It gives one of the very best accounts of what psychologists have learned about individual differences and how such human diversity may be valued and utilized.

United States Commission on Civil Rights, *A Better Chance to Learn: Bilingual Bicultural Education,* Clearing House Publication No. 51, Washington, DC, May, 1975.

U. S. Commissioner of Education, *Education of the Gifted,* "Report to the Congress, Washington, DC: U. S. Government Printing Office, March, 1972.

Vernon, Philip E., and Margaret C. Mitchell, "Social-Class Differences in Associative Learning," *Journal of Special Education,* **8**:4 (1974), 294–311.

Wagner, Robert E., "Nutrition, Metabolism, Brain Functioning, and Learning," *Academic Therapy,* **12**:3 (1977), 321–326.

Wagner, Rudolph, *Dyslexia in Young Children,* New York: Harper and Row, 1971.

Wagner, Rudolph F., "Bilingualism, Multiple Dyslexia, and Polyglot Aphasia," *Academic Therapy,* **12**:1 (Fall, 1976).

Walker, Hill M., *The Acting-Out Child: Coping With Classroom Disruption,* Boston: Allyn & Bacon, 1980.

Wallach, Michael A., and Lise Wallach, "Helping Disadvantaged Children Learn to Read by Teaching Them Phoneme Identification Skills," in *Theory and Practice of Early Reading,* Vol. 3, Lauren B. Resnick and Phyllis A. Weaver (Editors), Hillsdale, NJ: Erlbaum, 1979, 197–215.

Warner, Dolores, "Lingual Deviation, Visual Perception, and Reading Achievement," *Reading Horizons,* **9**:1 (1968), 7–18. "Intelligence appeared to be the variable most related to reading achievement within a comparison of the four ethnic groups. (40 Caucasian, 40 Mexican-American, 40 Oriental, and 40 Negroes) third and fourth graders.

Warren, N., "Malnutrition and Mental Development," *Psychological Bulletin,* **80** (1973), 324–328.

Washington, Kenneth R., "The Effects of Systematic Reinforcement and A Self-Awareness Program on the Self-Concept of Black Pre-School Children," *Child Study Journal,* **6**:4 (1976), 199–208.

Washington, Kenneth R., "An Analysis of the Attitudes of White Prospective Teachers Toward the Inner-City Schools," *Review of Educational Research,* **46**:1 (1977), 31—38.

Wassermann, Selma, "Aspen Mornings with Sylvia Ashton-Warner," *Childhood Education,* **48** (1972), 348—353.

Weaver, W. W., and Albert J. Kingston, "A Factor Analysis of Cloze Procedure and Measures of Reading and Language Ability," *Journal of Communication,* **13** (1963), 253.

Weintraub, Samuel (Editor), *Vision—Visual Discrimination* (A Reading Research Profile). Newark, DE: International Reading Association, 1973. This is an exhaustive bibliography of research reports published during the 1950s and early 1960s.

Wepman, Joseph, "Learning Disability," *Issues in the Classification of Children,* N. Dobbs (Editor), San Francisco: Josey-Bass, 1974, Chapter 11.

White, Pura Belpre, "Folkloric Tales: Cultural Heritage of the Puerto Rican Child," *New England Reading Association Journal,* **9**:3 (1973—1974), 24—25.

Williams, Jean H., "The Relationship of Self-Concept and Reading Achievement in First Grade Children," *Journal of Educational Research,* **66** (1973), 378—380.

Williams, Peggy E., "Auditory Discrimination Differences Versus Deficits," in *Help for the Reading Teacher: New Directions in Research,* W. D. Page (Editor), National Conference on Research in English, 1975, 91—99.

Wilkins, Wallace, "Self-Fulfilling Prophecy: Is There a Phonemenon to Explain?" *Psychological Bulletin,* **84**:1 (1977), 55—56. There is little empirical evidence that self-fulfilling prophesies exist. Refutes the Rosenthal notion.

Witty, Paul (Editor), *Reading for the Gifted and Creative Student,* Newark, DE: International Reading Association, 1971.

Wolf, Maryanne and Mark K. McQuillan (Editors), *Thought and Language/ Language and Reading,* Cambridge, MA: Harvard University Press, 1980.

Wolf, Robert L., and Barbara L. Tymitz, "Ethnography and Reading: Matching Inquiry Mode to Process," Guest editorial, *Reading Research Quarterly,* **13**:1 (1976—1977), 5—12.

Wolfram, Walt, *Black/White Speech Differences Revisited,* Washington, DC: Center for Applied Linguistics, 1969.

Wolfram, Walt, "Sociolinguistic Implications for Educational Sequencing," in *Teaching Standard English in the Inner City,* Fasold, Ralph W., and Roger W. Shuy (Editors), Washington, DC: Center for Applied Linguistics, 1970, 120—141.

Wolfram, Walt, "Sociolinguistic Alternatives in Teaching Reading to Non-standard Speakers," *Reading Research Quarterly,* **6**:1 (1970), 9–33. Wolfram suggested that materials in dialect might result in better reading achievement. Although several logical reasons were advanced, subsequent research does not support this notion.

Wooden, Sharon Lee, and Timothy J. Pettibone, "A Comparative Study of Three Beginning Reading Programs for the Spanish-Speaking Child," *Journal of Reading Behavior,* **5** (1973), 192–199.

Wright, Loyd S., "Conduct Problem or Learning Disability," *The Journal of Special Education,* **8**:4 (1974), 331–336.

Glossary*

Ad hoc In reading, the establishment of temporary groups for teaching a particular skill. Hence *ad hoc* "for the time being," "for a particular purpose."

Advance organizers Questions, special typeface, captions, previews, headings and subheadings, and so on that serve as guides to conceptualization of the content of the reading material.

Affective A term referring to the emotional responses stimulated by certain reading materials; an indication that the reading material "affects" the reader.

Affective learning Learning that affects an individual. In reading, the passage being read has a psychological and emotional impact on the reader. It stirs feelings.

Affixes Prefixes and suffixes added to base words.

Analytic phonics Using knowledge of phonics to determine the pronunciation of the word.

Ancillary A term applied to supportive, supplementary, and/or remedial materials that are "extras" and not part of the basic program.

Anglos Term used primarily in the Southwest to differentiate individuals of European ancestry from Chicanos, individuals of Spanish ancestry (chiefly Mexican-Americans).

Anticonvulsant drugs Drugs given to control convulsions or spasms that are visible signs of epileptic seizures.

Antonym A word that stands for exactly the opposite of the word with which it is matched or contrasted.

Applicative The use of reading skills and study skills by transferring them to new selections and new reading/study situations.

Articulation A term used in education to describe the close working or cooperation between two or more segments of the educational system.

Assessment The process of utilizing reading test scores to determine where in the program to place a child or which reading skills a particular child needs yet to learn, or whether or not certain reading skills have been mastered.

Assimilative The use of information, concepts, ideas, and so on from several reading sources to form a body of knowledge.

Note: The words and phrases in this glossary are defined in the manner in which they are used in this book.

Associative learning   Connecting the new with the old; the unknown to the known; stimulus-response (S-R), in which, for example, the sight of the letter *t* (stimulus) results in pronunciation /t/.

Attention span   The length of time a child can attend to a task. In this case, it might be listening to a story, taking part in a phonics lesson, or reading a selection.

Auditory acuity   Ability to differentiate sounds.

Auditory discrimination   The ability to distinguish spoken sounds, phonemes, words, and phrases from all possible spoken sounds, phonemes, words, and phrases.

Auditory memory   The ability to recall from one's memory those sounds (phonemes or words) previously associated with visual symbols or with spoken phonemes or words.

Avoidance   The conscious or subconscious motivation that results in an individual shunning a responsibility or task, usually for fear of failure.

Basal reader series   Those books and teachers' lesson plans containing reading materials of gradually increasing difficulty from the preprimers through first reader, second reader, on up through sixth-grade or eighth-grade. Fifteen publishers produce series of this type.

Basics   In reading, those skills necessary to serve as tools for efficient reading: phonics, syllabication, comprehension skills, experiential background, and so on.

Bibliotherapy   Use of books to help an individual see that others have had similar problems and have overcome them.

Bidialectical   Children who speak two dialects of English; for example, Black English and Mainstream English.

Bilingual   Individuals who speak two separate languages.

Blend (noun)   Two consonant letters which are to be pronounced with one breath sound: *-ng*; *pl*; *bl*; *br*.

Blend (verb)   The pronunciation of two consonants by merging the sound of the first into the sound of the second without losing the individuality of each: for example, /bl-/ and /br-/ are blends.

CAI   Computer-assisted instruction, in which the computer is programmed to accept test results and to print out directions for the next learning activity appropriate for each pupil's performance.

Categorizing   Separating items into groups according to common characteristics; for example: vegetables, fruits, flowering shrubs.

Characterization   The means by which an author portrays, for example, the lifestyles, habits, behavior, attitudes, and prejudices of the characters in the story.

Chicanos   Mexican-Americans.

Chronological age   Age of an individual stated in years and months.

Cloze tests   Tests of comprehension in which every fifth word or so is left out—to be filled in by the reader.

Clusters Several letters that appear together. Most frequently applied to groups of conconant letters: *spl-, schr-,* etc.

Cognitive Concept, knowing, understanding. To know.

Cognitive learning Learning that involves knowing. Learning that includes an element of understanding. In reading, the meaning of a word is included as well as ability to pronounce it.

Cognitive organizers Questions or outlines that serve as guides for pupils in their reading of a selection and in their understanding of the content.

Comparative measures All intelligence scores or reading scores provide estimates by which learners may be compared with each other. None of the testing, scores, or estimates are perfect or unchangeable, but only can be used to compare performance.

Compensatory Programs designed to provide experiences with the places and events of the mainstream culture that may be lacking in children from minority homes. Extra language training may also be compensatory.

Compounds Words devised by putting two words together; for example: *baseball, hairnet, clothesline.*

Configuration Shapes of words. Some words have similar shapes, and therefore are confused: *through, trough, thorough.*

Connotation The meaning that is implied as being additional to the basic meaning of a word.

Consistent invariants Those features of our language that remain constant and do not vary. In reading, for example, we know that pronouns refer to some previously stated person, place, or thing. This is a consistent feature of language.

Consonant A speech sound produced with some obstruction of the breath stream. Consonant phonemes are represented by consonant letters (graphemes).

Context The verbal setting in which words are found. The running flow of language that embellishes words with enriched meanings.

Contextual clozure Filling in the blanks to complete the sense of the passage.

Contiguity In reading, things that go together should be learned together. Phrases that go together, for example, are *in the garden, eating breakfast,* and should be learned as phrases.

Continuous progress A plan whereby children progress through the various steps in learning to read, moving from one step to the next (when one has been completed) without regard for grade levels. Each child moves upward at his/her own speed and ability.

Correspondences The relationshps of printer letters to the sounds they represent. Generally referred to as letter-sound relationships or grapheme-phoneme relationships.

Creative Reading in which the reader draws upon past experiences and extends activities beyond the reading by engaging in dramatics, art, poetry, etc.

Criterion A standard measure. On informal reading inventories, for example, an 80% achievement is an acceptable criterion.

Criterion-referenced tests Reading tests designed to assess mastery of specific skills. Mastery is frequently designated as demanding 80% accuracy on the comprehension questions, or on the skills being tested.

Critical In reading, a term applied to the process of reading (critical reading) in which the reader questions the material to determine propaganda, slanted writing, omissions of fact, etc.

Cue reduction When learning to associate spoken responses to visual cues, one must practice enough so the cues necessary are reduced to a minimum.

Cumulative records The folder and/or sheets of test scores, teacher evaluations, etc. that comprise the profile of each individual child from year to year as the child progresses through the elementary grades.

Decoding The process of using phonics symbols as keys to the sounds they represent. Using the phonics "code" (knowledge of phonics) to determine the pronunication of words. Frequently called "breaking the code."

Deductive "Reading between the lines" is sometimes necessary for the reader to determine what the writer really meant. Surface meaning may be stated, but the subtle meaning may be implied.

Deficit In reading, this usually refers to a lack of some necessary prerequisite, such as a hearing deficit, visual deficit, and, most frequently an experiential deficit, or environmental deficit.

Denotation The clear and precise meaning of a word.

Deprivation Lack of common environmental support. This may be nourishment (food, vitamins, sleep), experiences, education, etc.

Derivatives Words that have been modified by prefixes, suffixes and endings: *cross; crosses; crossed; crossing.*

Diacritical marks Marks used to indicate the pronunciation of a letter.

Diagnosis Testing and utilizing the results of tests to determine the level at which a child can read independently or with help or with difficulty; the reading skills each child lacks or needs to have strengthened; and the errors that need to be corrected.

Diagnostic-prescriptive teaching A routine consisting of these steps: test to determine what skills the pupil lacks; teach those skills; test again; reteach those still lacking; test again, hoping for mastery.

Dialect A particular substandard manner of speaking the mainstream or standard language.

Digraph Two letters together . . . especially two consonants in which each is "sounded" separately j)*st-*; *sp-*) or two vowels, only one of which is "sounded" (*ea; ie; oe*).

Diphthongs Two vowels that form a union in which each are pronounced; for example: *oi* (*boil*); *oy* (*boy*); *ou* (*out*).

Directionality The habit of eye movement along the direction of print. This habit has to be established by the child. In our language, the movement is from left-to-right.

Distinctive features Those letters or shapes of words that make it possible for the reader to identify the words quickly from all other possible choices.

Diversity Differences. In reading, there is diversity in the meaning of words. Words mean different things depending upon the context in which they are found.

Dolch list A list of 220 words that occur most frequently in the reading materials of children.

DRL A Directed Reading Lesson is conducted by the teacher by means of detailed lesson plans.

DRQ Directed Reading Questions serve as guides for 'what to look for" during the reading of a story or informational article.

Dyslexia The inability of an otherwise-normal individual to retain the association between visual symbols and the spoken sounds they represent.

Eclectic Choosing from two or more sources . . . using the best of each. In reading, using the best practices and materials from several approaches to learning to read.

Economy of perception Short cuts. In reading, one does not process letters in words individually, but as groups or as wholes. Certain features of a word make instant recognition possible without processing each part of the word.

Edumetric tests Tests providing measures of performance that may be related to the one child's objectives or abilities or limitations. The child's performance on the test is not compared with the performance of others nor with a national norm.

EEG Electorencephalogram: a graphic record of brain activity.

Etymology The origin and history of words. Study of word origins.

Expectancy level The reading level that a child may reasonably be expected to attain in the light of his/her intelligence, background, ability, age, or whatever measures are used.

Experiential factors One's environments (home, school, community, world) and one's exposure to the facets of those environments and the people, places, things, and forces therein.

Extrinsic Usually used with the concept of rewards that have little or nothing to do with accomplishing the task of learning. For example: bribes, gold stars, tokens, privileges.

Feedback As one reads, one is thinking about the meanings of what is being processed. One's past experience is supporting the sense of what is being read. Experience is "feeding back" responses that may be positive or negative.

Figurative Full of figures of speech; the use of words, not in their literal meaning, but suggestive of some dramatic image; for example: "the rolling fields of grain"; "the happy faces of daisies."

Flashcards Cards containing one word each or one letter or group of letters each, used by teachers of children who are beginning to read as drill practice for instant recognition of the letters and words.

Flocked letters Fuzzy or wooly-type of surface applied to alphabet letters, thus making it possible for children to trace over them and "feel" their shape. This is one method of employing one sensory modality.

Forward scanning   As one reads, the eyes are moving along ahead, picking up clues that embellish what is, in the meantime, being pronounced and processed by the brain.

Frustration level   That difficulty of reading in which the child needs help on or makes reading errors on more than 50% of the words of running text.

Generalizations   Conclusions based upon the reoccurence of a number of cases where the same factor seems to be operating; hence, phonics generalizations are "rules" that appear to hold true enough times to be used as guides in pronunciation.

Genres   Types of literature: poetry, short story, novel, haiku, historical novel, expository articles, drama, etc.

Gestalt   A psychological term from the German school of psychology. In reading, it refers to a configuration (shape) of a word, or to the whole meaning of a phrase.

Gestalt theory   The psychological concept that stresses organization and configuration in perception. Symbols and words have meanings largely dependent upon the background (content) in which they appear.

Gifted and talented   Those individuals at the top of the ability scale—usually in the upper 80% (having I.Qs of 120 or better and acquired abilities and skills (or potentials for such) that make them exceptional when compared with others of their peers.

Grade-level   The difficulty of the reading material which the average child in a particular grade can handle.

Graphemes   Written symbols (letters) used to represent speech sounds either singly or in combination, for example, *l, bl, -ng*.

Gross shapes   The total shape of a word. Several different words may have the same overall shape and, consequently, may be mistaken for each other.

Grouping   The placement of children together according to common characteristics. Children may be placed toether for instruction on the basis of age, reading ability, I.Q., etc.

Heightened attending   Paying close attention to the stimuli (letters, groups of letters, words, and context) when reading.

Heterogeneous grouping   Placing of individuals together in a class with little or no concern for their reading ability or intelligence.

High-frequency words   The frequently occurring words in our language. Years ago Dolch listed 220 such words.

High interest/low vocabulary   Reading materials especially "written down" to a low level of difficulty, but retaining high interest for older pupils.

Hi-lo materials   Reading materials of high interest but written in simplified style; hence high interest-low readability.

Homogeneous grouping   Placing of individuals together according to one or more measured characteristics: usually intelligence and, perhaps, reading ability, but chronological age of less importance.

Homographs   Words spelled identically but having different meanings; for example: *dear/dear; pound/pound*.

Homophones   Words identical in sound, but having different meanings and usually spelled differently; for example, *here/hear, him/hymn.*

Identification   The attachment of an individual to some hero or heroine figure and to model behavior after that person's behavior and to imitate the characteristics of the hero/heroine.

Ideographs   Designs intended to be in a similar shape as that of letters. The design is supposed to have a name that begins with the same sound as the sound represented by the letter it is similar to.

Independent level   The difficulty of reading materials that a pupil can read comfortably with little or no help from the teacher.

Individualized reading   A method of classroom organization in which children are free to select books; to read them at their own pace; to reject those they find are not to their liking; to have a teacher-pupil progress conference; etc.

Individualizing   Teaching one child exclusively by one teacher. This is usually done with children who have severe handicaps and/or learning disabilities.

Inductive   Reaching a general conclusion from a number of specific instances in which a common factor appears to be present.

Inferential   Making educated guesses based upon stated facts. The child makes inferences (guesses) as to what will happen next on the basis of the information given so far in the story.

Initial consonants   Consonant sounds and consonant letters at the beginning of words.

In loco parentis   In the place of the parents. Having jurisdiction and responsibility for children while in school. It frequently includes the time a child leaves home until he/she returns after school.

Instructional level   A measure of the difficulty of reading when a child makes errors or needs help on 35% or so of the words of a running text.

Intelligence   The complex of mental abilities (thinking, reasoning, problem-solving, utilizing past experience, etc.) that result in performance of certain tasks, adapting to the environment, functioning in normal social situations, and learning.

Internal structure of words   The parts of a word commonly called syllables, roots, prefixes, suffixes, and endings. These parts are used by the student to help him/her identify the word.

Internalize   To make a concept or idea a part of one's thoughts and feelings.

Interpretive   The manner in which a reader expresses an opinion concerning the feelings, motives, aspirations, etc. of the story characters. A subjective explanation by the reader.

Intrinsic   Usually referring to the self-satisfaction one receives from reading something that is rewarding to oneself.

Invariants   Those features of the English language that are always the same. For example, *m* is always /m/; *-ish* is always *ish* and never *sih*; *-tual* is never *taul* when used in an adjective; etc.

IPA   International Phonetic Alphabet. When first published at the "turn of the century," it identified 26 vowel sounds and 52 consonant sounds with diacritical marks.

IPI   Individually Prescribed Instruction. Each day the child is given a reading worksheet specially planned to provide exercises that will teach new skills and strengthen those that the last test indicated in need of strengthening.

IRI   Individual Reading Inventory. A group of paragraphs, each progressively more difficult. The pupil reads up to the level of frustration. The level below that is the instructional level.

Kinesthetic   In reading, referring to the use of large muscles in tracing the shapes of letters and words. This is one sensory modality.

Laissez faire   From the French "let act," or let alone. In the reading classroom, it denotes a method in which children are left alone to learn to read in whatever way they can.

Language-experience stories   Stories told by the children in their own words about their own experiences and written on large sheets of paper by the teacher.

Language patterns.   Recurring word-parts that are used as the "building blocks" of language. Included are the bases or phonograms upon which many different words are built:-*at, -and, -up,* etc.

Learning modalities   One's channels for receiving and processing information during reading: visual, visual and auditory (seeing the printed page and hearing a tape recording) visual and kinesthetic (tracing the letters in a word, etc.

Letter strings   Groups of letters that "go together." In reading, for example, *-ing, -gth, -able, str-, spl-.* These groupings are learned as wholes and are seen as such when reading.

Levels   Divisions of the contents of the books in the basal reader series into units or segments that can be mastered by pupils regardless of grade. When a certain "level" has been mastered, the child moves to the next level (at any time of the year).

Linguistics   The scientific study of language structure, language utterance, sounds of language (phonology), meanings (semantics), and language usage.

Literal   The exact meaning of a word. The exact restatement of facts in answer to a question such as "Who?", "When?", "Where?", etc.

Mainstreaming   A controversial plan to place handicapped children into the regular classroom for reading and the content area studies. This is a reaction against segregating them into special classes or special schools.

Management   The tests and the manner in which they are used to place children in reading groups and/or to assess their progress of deficits in reading.

Manuscript   A method of printing letters that appear close to the type face children first encounter in their Readers. Manuscript writing is "sans serif" and, therefore, is easily converted into cursive writing.

Mastery learning   A measure of each child's skills in reading. The ability to use the skills should be demonstrated with 80% accuracy to warrant the term "mastery."

Maturational readiness That state of being in which a child exhibits the ability to work with others in a group, to use language according to the norm, to see likenesses and differences, etc.

Meaning-bearing signals Groups of words, phrases, and/or sentences whose parts are all needed to convey the total meaning, "the whole being greater than the sum of its parts."

Medial A letter in the middle of a word. Usually used as "medial vowel"; for example, *e* is the medial vowel in *let*.

Medial vowels Vowel letters placed within a word.

Mediation When reading, an individual is "thinking." This takes place very rapidly between the stimuli being processed visually on the page and the audible or subvocal prununication of the words. It is the process of bringing meaning to the reading.

Mental age An individual's score on the intelligence test, expressed in years and months in relationship to the average age of children who obtain the same score on that same test.

Chronological age Age of an idividual stated in years and months.

Mind set Because of past experience, one anticipates certain outcomes from certain events; certain responses to certain stimuli. One's thoughts move ahead to probable conclusions.

Minimal differences The addition of one letter in place of another letter, the result being a completely different word. Example: *place/plate*; *some/same*; *cat/bat*; *can/ban*.

Miscues At one time these were throught to be errors. Now, these changes made by children when reading standard English and transforming the words and structure into their own dialects simultaneously are considered to be evidences of good comprehension and ability.

Modalities One's means for learning. The sensory channels for receiving information.

Mode A means or a way of responding to reading materials and questions on the materials. For example, questions that require brief factual answers are in the *literal* mode.

Modeling In reading, this term is usually used to describe the psychological characteristic of children who imitate the behavior os some significant hero or heroine.

Montessori A medical doctor in Italy at the turn of the century. She devised some objects and apparatus to aid children in learning to read.

Motivation The process and materials used to encourage pupils to want to read a certain selection for their own intrinsic pleasure and satisfaction.

Multifaceted stimuli A letter seldom stands alone as a stimulus; neither does a word. Stimuli in reading cluster together, with groups of letters and groupings of words in phrases providing several concurrent features that make for word recognition and meaning.

Newbery awards Established in honor of John Newbery, citing the most distinguished contribution (book) in American literature for children. An annual award (medal) is given.

Open classroom A management arrangement that provides a number of learning "stations" within a room and permits freedom of movement of children from one learning or "experience" activity to another.

Ordering Placing events in a certain sequence. Also refers to the sequence in which phonics elements or some other skills are placed for introduction in the learning-to-read program.

Paired associates In learning letter-sound relationships, children establish a good number of pairs: the letter *b* and the sound /b/; the letter *t* and the sound /t/; etc.

Percentiles Any of the 99 segments that divide an entire group. One hundred percent of a class may be divided into 99 percentiles; those at the top being in the 99th percentile, those in the middle being in the 50th percentile.

Perceptual discrimination Ability to differentiate visual symbols or auditory sounds, one from another. In reading, ability to "tell the difference" between letters *b* and *d* when heard or seen in print. Similarly, the ability to differentiate words.

Perceptual learning Learning about the world around us through our senses: sight, hearing, taste, smell, etc.

Performance objectives Statements of the skills that a particular reading lesson is designed to teach. Example: "The pupils will be able to distinguish between *m* and *p* and between sounds /m/ and /p/."

Petit mal A mild form of epilepsy.

Phonemes The most basic distinctive sounds in the language, usually beginning with the same letter, but sounding differently because of other letters in the group, or because of stress, intonation, etc. There are said to be 44 speech sounds in our language; only 26 letters.

Phonetic Speech sounds and the symbols used to represent them. A phonetic language is one in which one speech sound is represented regularly by one letter. English is only partially phonetic.

Phonetic analysis The process of inspecting words and attempting to determine their pronunciation by applying knowledge of phonics.

Phonics In reading, the association of phonemes (language sounds) to the letters and groups of letters that represent them.

Phonogram In reading, the term used for a root word, language pattern, to which prefixes and/or suffixes may be added; for example: *-eigh* is a phonogram to which letters may be added to form *sleigh, eight,* etc.

Pidgin Simplified form of English used in the Hawaiian Islands for communication with oriental field workers. Pidgin English is used as the "street language" by children in Hawaii.

Prefixes Letters or syllables added to the beginnings of base words, the effect being that the meaning is altered.

Psychological variables Those factors that are not constant; or those factors that are part of one's whole being and, together, account for the differences in individuals: intelligence, physical stamina, vitality, vision, past experiences, etc.

Psychometric tests Tests using norms based on the performance of thousands of children's scores. The tests, therefore, allow comparisons to be made with national norms (averages).

Readability The reading difficulty of a particular book or selection. Readability is influenced by length of sentences, number of multisyllable words, number of abstract concepts, number of technical words, etc.

Readiness for reading That point at which an individual exhibits the ability to perform the basic tasks necessary to learn to read: ability to attend to the task; ability to handle a book; ability to move from left to right along a line of print, etc.

Reading expectancy The grade level at which we might be justified in anticipating that an individual child should be able to read, given certain characteristics and conditions.

Reading readiness Activities designed to develop prereading competencies: ability to differentiate shapes, sounds, letters, words; a few whole words; experiences; left-to-right; etc.

Realia Those things in the environment that may be brought into the classroom to add reality to words that are unknown to children; for example: a gourd, a kumquat, a spatula.

Rebuses Pictures of objects and people. These pictures are used in beginning reading to stand in the place of words children do not yet know. The child can read the sentence, incorporating the name of the picture as the word or part of a word.

Redundancy The constant repetition of words and phrases in various settings in our environment, resulting in them being "learned by heart."

Reinforcement Drill on phonics elements or some other reading skill usually by some oral or written exercises in groups of learners or in workbooks or on duplicating master sheets. The drill is prescribed after the lesson has been taught.

Relational aspect Certain groups of letters are related to each other as wholes. For example, -ight is a grouping which is learned as a whole, and if misspelled, it "doesn't look right."

Relevance Reading that is of particular interest to the children for whom it is intended. Reading that is important to particular children in a specific environment at a particular time.

Restructuring In reading, meaning may be more apparent if a phrase is restructured (restated) in the pupil's own words. Headings may serve better if restated as questions which become the purpose for reading the selection.

Retroactive inhibition The process of "forgetting" that takes place when new material blocks out recall of previously learned material.

Reversals Young children frequently reverse letters within words and pronounce/saw/for *was*; /to/ instead of/not/; etc.

Role playing   Pretending to be a character in a story, or pretending to be some adult an an adult role during free play time.

Satisfiers   A term suggested by Thorndike to mean the intrinsic rewards or feelings of pleasure derived from a certain response.

Scanning   Searching through a selection to find a particular fact or answer to a particular question or problem.

Scope-and-sequence   A listing or reading skills and the levels at which each is introduced and repeated in the reading program.

SELF   The feeling of individual satisfaction from becoming what one wants to become. Achievement; actualization of one's wishes and dreams.

Self-actualization   The process of arriving at a satisfactory level of achievement of one's wishes, desires, and dreams.

Self-concept   One's vision of himself/herself as being a certain type of individual or of becoming such an individual. This feeling of self frequently is influenced by feedback from peers and society.

Self-monitoring   The mind is making a constant check on what is being read to indicate whether or not it "makes sense."

Sensory modalities   One's channels for receiving information: visual, auditory, kinesthetic. In reading, some pupils do better with visual materials, and some do better by tracing.

Sequencing   Placing events in the order in which they occurred. In reading, it also refers to the order in which certain skills (such as phonics) are introduced.

Service words   The 220 words recurring most frequently in children's stories and being of "most service" in their efforts to read. Most of those words have to be learned as whole words.

Set   The anticipation of what is probably to come.

Set for diversity   The expectation that seldom is there just one meaning to a word, and that meaning depends largely on context.

Sight words   Those words learned as whole words by children who are beginning to learn to read. They are most often learned "by rote," with little or no knowledge of the sounds that the letters within the words represent.

Significant others   Some hero or heroine figure whose attitudes, beliefs, behavior, dress, and/or lifestyles become the pattern for a child who emulates them.

Skimming   Glancing though a selection quickly to "get the gist" of it; to glean the main idea and a few details.

Social maturation   The ability of a child to work together with peers.

SQ3R   Robinson's "Survey-Question-Read-Review-Recite" technique of handling informational content reading materials.

SSR   Sustained Silent Reading. A term devised by Dr. Lyman Hunt.

Stereotype   An oversimplified description or concept of members of a group, in which they are all described as having the same characteristics . . . frequently a degrading or biased description or concept of them.

Stimulus   A letter, group of letters, a word, a group of words, a phrase, each of which acts as a visual cue to pronunciation and, perhaps, to meaning.

Stimulus substitution In reading, a simple stimulus word may conjure up a complex of ideas not contained in the original printed word. For example, the name *Barbara* invokes many mental pictures of people we have known by that name.

Strategies Methods used by the teacher.

Study skills Skimming, scanning, previewing, picking out main ideas, outlining, etc.

Suffixes Letters, syllables, etc. added on the ends of base words, the result being to alter their meanings.

Synthetic phonics Using a knowledge of phonics to construct a word. This system begins with teaching letter sounds and combining them into whole words.

Synonym A word that expresses the same or nearly same idea. A "substitute" word.

Systematic differences Differences that regularly recur and are so common (in speech, for example) that they become part of the (speech/communication) system. A dialect contains regular differences (ways of speaking the language.

Systems approach A circular routine involving these steps: test; teach whatever skills a pupil (or group of pupils) needs; retest to determine which skills have been mastered; reteach those still lacking; test again; set up remedial group if necessary.

Syntactic constructs Grammatical arrangements; sentence construction. In English, there are several ways to say the same thing; to express the same concept.

Tachistoscope A projector, equipped with a shutter, for the purpose of flashing words and phrases onto a screen in fractions of a second. The purpose is drill in fast recognition of words.

Tactile Sense of touch employed when children are given sandpaper or flocked letters to trace over with their fingers. This is one of the sensory modalities.

Talented Those individuals who have either the potential or the acquired abilities to perform in one or more areas of human activity far above the average performance of their peers.

Talk stories Folk tales and/or experiences (real or imaginary) told and retold to and by children in primitive cultures. Talk stories are frequently used as language-experience stories in beginning reading instruction.

Tradebooks Children's books purchased in a bookstore. Not textbooks.

Transfer of learning The use of previous learning to make new learning easy. The use of common elements in previously learned words to help in learning new words in which they are a part. For example: *farm, farmer, farming, farmed,* etc.

Rote learning Learning to pronounce words without learning the meaning.

Trigraph   Three letters, usually consonants; for example: *spl, str.*

USSR   Uninterrupted Sustained Silent Reading. A term devised by Dr. Lyman Hunt.

VAKT   Vusual-Auditory-Kinesthetic-Tactile.

Variables   Those features of our language that we cannot depend on by themselves to give us the key to pronunciation and/or meaning.

Variant   A word that has been changed by the addition of letters or syllables to change its tense, number, or person.

Verbal identification   The ability of a child to distinguish sounds of letters and words.

Visual discrimination   The ability to distinguish printed letters, groups of letters, words, and phrases from all other possible printed letters, groups of letters, words, and phrases.

Visual memory   The ability to recall from one's memory those visual symbols and images previously received through the visual sensory system.

Vowels   Phonemes made by the free flow of air from the voice mechanism.

Whole word approach   The method of teaching beginning reading in which whole words are learned before any phonics is learned to aid in identifying new, unknown words.

Word attack   Usually called word-attack skills, meaning those skills that enable a child to identify a word. These include a knowledge of phonics, syllabication, roots, affixes, context, etc.

Word analysis   The process of taking a word apart by means of phonic elements, syllables, root and affix, and then reassembling those elements in an attempt to pronounce and identify the word.

Word elements   Parts of words such as roots, prefixes, suffixes.

Word families   Language patterns; for example: the following bases *-an; -at; -and, -ing, -ough* are the common elements in the "families" of words that may be made from them.

Words in context   Words in phrases and/or sentences rather than in isolation.

Word recognition   The ability to identify a word by means of phonics, syllabication, division into root and affixes, and/or reference to its probable meaning in context.

Photo Credits

Chapter 1
Chapter Opener: Elizabeth Crews. Page 14: Reproduced through the Courtesy of Houghton Mifflin Company, *Getting Ready to Read* by Juanita Lewis, M. Lucile Harrison, William K. Durr and Paul McKee, copyright, 1976. Page 17 and 18: The New York Public Library Picture Collection. Page 20: Michal Heron. Page 25: Richard Balagur/Nancy Palmer.

Chapter 2
Chapter Opener: Will McIntyre/Photo Researchers. Page 57: Teri Leigh Stratford. Page 59: Jean-Claude LeJeune/Stock, Boston. Page 60: Terence Lennon. Page 64: Henry Barnard School of Rhode Island College. Photo by Roger Merolla. Page 67: Paul Fusco/Magnum.

Chapter 3
Chapter Opener: Ed Lettau/Photo Researchers. Page 94: Sybil Shelton/Peter Arnold. Page 109: Teri Leigh Stratford. Page 113: Paul Conklin/Monkmeyer. Page 118: Elizabeth Crews. Page 133: Teri Leigh Stratford.

Chapter 4
Chapter Opener: Michal Heron.

Chapter 5
Chapter Opener: Teri Leigh Stratford. Page 187: Lynn McLauren/Photo Researchers. Page 188: Reproduced through the courtesy of Mrs. Beth Swanson Groleau. Page 191 and 192: From *The New Phonics We Use Learning Games Kits* developed by Dr. Pose Lamb and Dr. Arthur W. Heilman. Reprinted by permission of Rand McNally and Company. Page 224: From *Rational Method of Reading*, Edward G. Ward, Boston: Silver Burdett and Company.

Chapter 6
Chapter Opener: Michal Heron. Page 264: General Research Division, The New York Public Library, Astor, Lenox, and Tilden Foundation. Page 270: Henry Barnard School of Rhode Island College. Photo by Roger Merolla.

Chapter 7
Chapter Opener: Inger McCabe/Rapho-Photo Researchers. Page 279: Wayne Atkinson. Page 285: Terence Lennon. Page 292: Lucille Dardiri.

Chapter 8
Chapter Opener: Mark Jones/Jeroboam. Page 335: Advertising flyer for *HBJ Bookmark Reading Program*, published in 1979 by Harcourt, Brace and Jovanovich, Inc. Page 346: Courtesy of Esther Bourziel, Elementary Coordinator, Freemont, Michigan Public Schools. Page 348: ©Dick Hanley/Photo Researchers. Page 354: Ken Karp. Page 357: Elizabeth Crews/ICON.

Chapter 9
Chapter Opener: Ken Karp. Page 368: Elizabeth Crews. Page 370: Richard Nesbett. Page 385: Ken Karp. Page 387: Terence Lennon.

Chapter 10
Chapter Opener: Terence Lennon. Page 403: Courtesy Ginn and Company. Pages 404–407: From Rand McNally *Young America, Basic Series*, copyright 1981. Reprinted by permission of Rand McNally and Company. Page 411: From *Take Flight*, Level G. Copyright 1975, 1966, The Charles E. Merrill Company. Used by permission. Page 414: Scope and Sequence Chart reproduced through the courtesy of J.B. Lippincott/Harper and Row, publishers of *Lippincott Basic Reading*, copyright, 1981. Page 415: Terence Lennon. Page 427: *The American Readers* basal series published by the American Book Company, 1980.

Chapter 11
Chapter Opener: B. Kliewe/Jeroboam. Page 464: Terry W. Bisbee. Page 466: Suzanne Szasz. Page 468: Reproduced through the courtesy of the American Optometrical Association. Page 472: Michal Heron. Page 475: Elizabeth Crews/ICON. Page 479: Terence Lennon. Page 486: Esther Bourziel, Elementary Coordinator, Freemont, Michigan Public Schools.

Index